THE CATECHISM EXPLAINED

AN EXHAUSTIVE EXPOSITION OF THE CHRISTIAN RELIGION,

WITH SPECIAL REFERENCE TO THE PRESENT STATE OF SOCIETY AND THE SPIRIT OF THE AGE.

A PRACTICAL MANUAL

FOR THE USE OF THE PREACHER, THE CATECHIST, THE TEACHER, AND THE FAMILY.

MADE ATTRACTIVE AND INTERESTING BY

ILLUSTRATIONS, COMPARISONS, AND QUOTATIONS

FROM THE

SCRIPTURES, THE FATHERS, AND OTHER WRITERS.

FROM THE ORIGINAL OF

REV. FRANCIS SPIRAGO,
Professor of Theology.

EDITED BY

REV. RICHARD F. CLARKE, S.J.

Nihil Obstat.

Thos. L. Kinkead,
Censor Librorum.

Imprimatur.

✝ MICHAEL AUGUSTINE,
Archbishop of New York.

New York, August 8, 1899.

PREFACE.

THIS Catechism is suited to the needs of the day, and may either be placed in the hands of the people, or employed as a manual for the use of Priests and Catechists. The small print is the part adapted for popular reading or for catechetical instruction. The author thinks it necessary to give the following explanation of the plan of the book.

1. This Catechism is divided into three parts : The first part treats of *faith*, the second of *morals*, the third of *the means of grace*. In the first part Our Lord appears in His character of Teacher ; in the second in His character of King ; and in the third in His character of High Priest. And since this Catechism proposes as its primary object to answer the question, for what purpose are we here upon earth, thereby emphasizing and giving prominence to man's high calling and destiny, it is especially suited to the present day, when the pursuit of material interests, self-indulgence and pleasure, engrosses the attention of so many. This Catechism is in fact nothing more nor less than an abstract of Our Lord's teaching, and may be called a guide book for the Christian on the road to heaven. First the goal of the traveller is indicated, and then the means whereby he is to reach his destination. In the first part we are told what is to be done by the use of the understanding : we must seek to attain to the knowledge of God by believing the truths He reveals ; in the second part we are told what is to be done by the aid of the will : we must submit our will to the will of God by keeping the commandments ; in the third part we are told what we must do in order to enlighten our understanding and strengthen our will, which have been respectively obscured and weakened by original sin : we must obtain the grace of the Holy Spirit through use of the appointed means of grace, for by the grace of the Holy

5

Spirit the understanding is enlightened and the will strengthened. Thus a close connection exists between the different parts of this Catechism. Each part is subdivided and arranged to form a whole, so that the connection between and the coherence of all the truths of religion are plainly apparent. This is a very important point. For the more clearly we perceive the manner in which the truths of religion are linked together, the easier will it be for us to apprehend each one singly. The Catechism is a marvellously connected system of revealed truth. If Catholics were thoroughly acquainted in their childhood with the fundamental truths of religion ; if they were taught to see how all the different parts of this divine edifice combine to form one beauteous structure, the darts of hell would have no power to injure them.

2. The large print in this Catechism is the scaffolding, or skeleton ; it contains all the essential truths of religion. The small print might, as a matter of fact, be omitted; but in that case there would be nothing calculated to touch the heart and kindle the flame of charity towards God and one's neighbor, and is not this the effect which every good hand-book of religion, every good sermon, every good catechetical instruction ought to produce ? We already possess in abundance catechisms and religious manuals which appeal only to the intellect ; books which do not aim at the warmth of expression and the fervent, persuasive eloquence which appeal to the heart, the force and vivifying power which affect the will through the influence of the Holy Spirit.

3. This Catechism aims at cultivating, to an equal extent, all the three powers of the soul : the understanding, the affections, and the will. It does not therefore content itself with mere definitions. The principal object proposed in it is not to teach men to philosophize about religion, but to make them good Christians who will delight in their faith. Consequently questions of scholastic theology, doctrines debated among divines, are either omitted altogether or merely receive a passing mention. The author has endeavored to divest religious teaching of the appearance of learning, and to present it in a popular and simple form. Technical terms, in which almost all religious manuals abound, even those intended for children, are carefully eliminated from his pages since, while useful and necessary for seminarians and theologians, they are out of place in a book intended for the laity. Popular manuals of religion ought to be couched in plain and

simple language, like that used by Our Lord and the apostles, easy of comprehension ; for what we need is something that will touch the heart and influence the will, not cram the mind with knowledge unattractive to the reader. The present book is, moreover, not an adaptation of catechisms already in use, but an original work, intended for practical purposes. Attention may also be called to the fact that the teaching of the Church is not presented in a dry, abstract form, but is rendered attractive and interesting by illustrations, comparisons, and quotations from well-known writers. Thus there is no danger that it will be thrown aside as unreadable. The extracts from the writings of the Fathers are not always given *verbatim,* the idea alone being in many cases borrowed, as a literal rendering of the language employed, beautiful and forcible as it is, might prove rather misleading than edifying to the young and unlearned. The same may be said of some passages taken from Holy Scripture. What is of paramount importance in a book of this nature is to make use of expressions that are clear and intelligible. The writings of the Fathers are quoted mainly to elucidate and illustrate, not to prove the truths that are enunciated.

4. In preparing this Catechism for publication, the author has kept in view his purpose of assisting the teacher. To this end he has made it his endeavor to arrange his matter according to a clear and methodical system ; to place his ideas in logical sequence, and to clothe them in simple language composed of short sentences. All the several branches of religious teaching—the Catechism, Bible history, the liturgy, controversy, ecclesiastical history—have been comprehended in one course of instruction, which has unquestionably the effect of enhancing the interest and appealing to the understanding as well as to the heart and the will. The old-fashioned form of embodying the instruction to be given in question and answer has not been followed. That form is not sufficient, and needs further elaboration. Faith comes by hearing, not by questioning only. A knowledge of all the truths of our holy religion is not so universal that they can be thoroughly learned by question and answer : they must be regularly taught by oral instruction. This form of teaching calls for the exercise of more thought ; question and answer, moreover, do nothing towards simplifying the truths to be imparted, or rendering them more intelligible to the learner.

5. The state of society and the spirit of the age have also been taken into consideration in the preparation of this book. The writer has endeavored in the first place to combat the self-seeking, pleasure-loving materialism of the day. This appears in the opening part and also in the fact that the moral law is enlarged upon at great length. It was not deemed sufficient merely to enumerate the several virtues and vices—virtue is depicted in all its beauty and excellence, vice in all its hideousness and malice—at the same time the remedies for the different vices are added. Furthermore, precepts of great importance, suited to the exigencies of the time, far from being passed over, are elaborately explained. Under the heading of the Third Commandment the obligation of work and the Christian view of labor are treated, in accordance with the directions of the Council of Trent. Under the Fourth Commandment our duty towards the Pope and the ruler of our country, the duty of Catholics in regard to elections is expounded. Under the Fifth Commandment the nature of human life and the sinfulness of injuring one's health for the sake of vanity or pleasure are shown. Under the Tenth Commandment, a plain statement is made of Socialistic and democratic principles ; and after this, the proper use to be made of money and the duty of almsgiving are set forth. Prominence is given to the works of mercy, which Our Lord declares to be essential to salvation, and which are an amplification of the Decalogue; while under the occasions of sin, the evils of the day, the exaggerated craving for excitement and pleasure, love of dress, the desire to be fashionable, besides society papers, objectionable plays, etc., are duly censured. Charity to God and one's neighbor, a virtue too rare in the present day, is treated at some length, and a considerable space is also devoted to the consideration of the Christian's attitude in regard to affliction and poverty, the duty of gratitude, the deceitful nature of earthly possessions and earthly enjoyments, and the necessity of self-conquest. Also in matters such as civil marriage, cremation, Catholic congresses, Passion plays, etc., it cannot be alleged that this Catechism is not fully up to date.

6. In its present form this Catechism is intended primarily for the use of Priests and Catechists ; it will save them much time in preparing their instructions, as they will find examples, comparisons, and explanations ready to hand. By abridging the small print it will also serve as a school-catechism. When instructing

beginners the Catechist must confine himself to the large print; it will be sufficient for children of moderate abilities to know and understand that thoroughly. It is, and ever will be, the basis upon which the whole structure of religious knowledge, raised by oral instruction, will rest. In after years what is wanted will not be so much an increase of theological knowledge, as a lucid explanation of the truths already learned, and further proofs are added for the sake of deepening religious conviction.

The small print may be considerably abridged for use in schools, but it must not be left out altogether, as it will serve to recall to the minds of the children the truths they have been taught. It contains also many useful suggestions for the Catechist on subjects of importance which must hold a place in his instructions. Moreover, parents who go through the Catechism with their children at home will be compelled to read the small print, and thus, with no effort on their part, they will obtain a more intimate knowledge of Christian doctrine.

It is most important in these days of unbelief that the school should be the means of reviving a Christian spirit in the family. Hence it is advisable that the Catechist should take the chief points and the plan of his instruction from a book, and it should not be left to each individual to propound what truths he pleases. Besides, it is desirable that the catechumens themselves should have the essential part of the instruction placed before them in black and white; for it is a known fact that what is not seen by the eye is not long retained by the memory. If the impression received, the feelings excited, the resolutions called forth are to be permanent, they must be re-awakened by reading the Catechism. Thus the Catechism becomes not merely a class-book, but a book of spiritual reading, to be taken up again and re-read in after years. Hence we see what a wide sphere of usefulness the books used in our schools may have. Ought a book whose influence is so extensive, which contains the most important of all teaching, present that teaching in a dry, uninteresting form, or give a scanty outline, the mere framework of the truths of religion?

In publishing an English translation of this manual of Christian truth, it is hoped that it may find as hearty a welcome among English-speaking nations as the original did in the author's own country. He ventures to hope that it may greatly promote the glory of God and the salvation of souls. In order to secure the blessing of God upon his labors, he dedicated the work to the Immaculate Mother of God ; and it cannot be doubted that the blessings of the Most High rests upon it, for although at the outset it encountered formidable obstacles, it has since had an unexpectedly widespread and rapid circulation.

CONTENTS.

11

Introduction.

I. FOR WHAT END ARE WE ON THIS EARTH ?

We are upon this earth in order that we may glorify God, and so win for ourselves eternal happiness............................ 73

II. HOW ARE WE TO ATTAIN TO ETERNAL HAPPINESS ?

We shall attain to eternal happiness by the following means:
1. We must strive to know God by means of faith in the truths He has revealed to us... 74
2. We must fulfil the will of God by keeping His commandments.... 74
3. We must, therefore, avail ourselves of the means of grace; of which the chief are holy Mass, the sacraments and prayers...... 75

III. CAN WE ATTAIN PERFECT HAPPINESS ON EARTH?

1. Earthly goods, such as riches, honor, pleasure, cannot by themselves make us happy; for they cannot satisfy our soul; they often only make life bitter, and invariably forsake us in death.. 75
2. Only the Gospel of Christ is capable of giving us a partial happiness on earth, for he who follows the teaching of Christ is certain to have peace in his soul.. 76
3. He who follows Christ will have to endure persecution; but these persecutions can do him no harm.............................. 76
4. Hence perfect happiness is impossible on earth; for no man can entirely avoid suffering.. 77

PART I.

Faith.

I. THE KNOWLEDGE OF GOD.

1. The happiness of the angels and saints consists in the knowledge of God.. 79

VII. ON THE ABSENCE AND LOSS OF FAITH.

VIII. ON THE DUTY OF CONFESSING OUR FAITH.

IX. THE SIGN OF THE CROSS.

X. THE APOSTLES' CREED.

6. THE LIFE OF CHRIST.

The Childhood of Christ.

The Public Life of Christ.

The Sufferings of Christ.

The Exaltation of Christ.

The Seven Gifts of the Holy Ghost and the Extraordinary Graces.

The Holy Ghost as Guide of the Church.

3. APPARITIONS OF THE HOLY GHOST.

NINTH ARTICLE OF THE CREED: THE CATHOLIC CHURCH.

1. THE CATHOLIC CHURCH AND ITS INSTITUTION.

2. The Head of the Church.

3. Bishops, Priests, the Faithful.

4. Foundation and Spread of the Church.

5. The Catholic Church is Indestructible and Infallible.

Indestructibility of the Church.

The Infallibility of the Church.

6. The Hierarchy of the Church.

7. Notes of the True Church.

8. The Catholic Church alone gives Salvation.

9. The Relations between Church and State.

PART II.

A. The Commandments.

I. WHAT COMMANDMENTS (OR LAWS) HAS GOD GIVEN US?

II. THE TWO COMMANDMENTS OF CHARITY.

III. THE PRECEPT OF THE LOVE OF GOD.

THE KINDS OF SIN.

THE COMPARATIVE MAGNITUDE OF SIN.

THE CONSEQUENCES OF SIN.

THE CONSEQUENCES OF VENIAL SIN.

IV. VICE.

C. Christian Perfection.

PART III.

The Means of Grace.

I. THE HOLY SACRIFICE OF THE MASS.

1. ON SACRIFICE IN GENERAL.

THE EFFECTS OF PENANCE.

THE WORTHY RECEPTION OF THE SACRAMENT OF PENANCE.

GENERAL CONFESSION.

Confession a Divine Institution.

The Advantages of Confession.

The Sin of Relapse.

Indulgences.

5. Extreme Unction.

Contents.   53

The Celebration of Matrimony.

The Duties of the Married.

Mixed Marriages.

The Unmarried State.

III. THE SACRAMENTALS.

IV. PRAYER.

1. The Nature of Prayer

2. The Utility and Necessity of Prayer.

3. How Ought we to Pray ?

4. When Ought we to Pray?

5. Where Ought we to Pray?

6. For What Ought we to Pray?

7. Meditation.

THE PRINCIPAL DEVOTIONAL EXERCISES.

Processions.

Christian Burial.

Pilgrimages.

The Way of the Cross.

DEVOTIONS.

I. Prayers and Precepts of the Church.

1. The Sign of the Cross.

In the name of the Father, and of the Son, and of the Holy Ghost. Amen.

2. The Lord's Prayer, or Our Father.

Our Father, Who art in heaven, hallowed be Thy name. Thy kingdom come. Thy will be done on earth as it is in heaven. Give us this day our daily bread. And forgive us our trespasses as we forgive those who trespass against us. And lead us not into temptation, but deliver us from evil. Amen.

3. The Angelical Salutation, or Hail Mary.

Hail Mary, full of grace, the Lord is with thee. Blessed art thou amongst women, and blessed is the fruit of thy womb, Jesus. Holy Mary, Mother of God, pray for us sinners, now and at the hour of our death. Amen.

4. The Apostles' Creed.

[1] I believe in God, the Father almighty, Creator of heaven and earth ; [2] and in Jesus Christ, His only Son, Our Lord : [3] Who was conceived by the Holy Ghost, born of the Virgin Mary, [4] suffered under Pontius Pilate, was crucified ; died, and was buried. [5] He descended into hell ; the third day He arose again from the dead ; [6] He ascended into heaven, sitteth at the right hand of God, the Father almighty ; [7] from thence He shall come to judge the living and the dead. [That is to say, those who are alive at the Last Day, and who, as a matter of course, must die

before the final judgment ; besides those who died previously ; or it may also mean the redeemed and the reprobate.] [8] I believe in the Holy Ghost ; [9] the holy Catholic Church, the communion of saints, [10] the forgiveness [remission] of sins, [11] the resurrection of the body, [12] and the life everlasting. Amen.

5. *The Two Precepts of Charity.* (Mark xii. 30, 31.)

(1). Thou shalt love the Lord thy God with thy whole heart, and with thy whole soul, and with thy whole mind, and with thy whole strength.

(2). Thou shalt love thy neighbor as thyself.

6. *The Ten Commandments of God.* (Exod. xx. 1–17.)

(1). Thou shalt have no strange gods before Me. [That is to say, thou shalt believe in the one true God alone, and not worship any other.]

(2). Thou shalt not take the name of the Lord thy God in vain. [That is, thou shalt not utter the name of God irreverently.]

(3). Thou shalt keep holy the Sabbath day. [Under the Christian Dispensation the Sunday.]

(4). Thou shalt honor thy father and thy mother, that thou mayst be long-lived upon the land which the Lord thy God will give thee.

(5). Thou shalt not kill.

(6). Thou shalt not commit adultery.

(7). Thou shalt not steal.

(8). Thou shalt not bear false witness against thy neighbor.

(9). Thou shalt not covet thy neighbor's wife.

(10). Thou shalt not covet thy neighbor's house, nor his servant, nor his ox, nor his ass, nor anything that is his.

7. *The Six Precepts of the Church.*

(These are an amplification of the Third Commandment of God.)

(1). To hear Mass on Sundays and holydays of obligation.

(2). To fast and abstain on the days appointed.

(3). To confess at least once a year.

(4). To receive the Holy Eucharist during the Easter time.

(5). To contribute to the support of our pastors.

(6). Not to marry persons who are not Catholics, or who are

related to us within the fourth degree of kindred, nor privately without witnesses, nor to solemnize marriage at forbidden times.

II. PRAYERS WHICH MAY BE USED DAILY AT DIFFERENT TIMES.

1. A Morning Prayer.

Thy goodness, O my God, and might,
Have brought me to this morning's light.
Keep and preserve me every hour,
From sorrow, sin, temptation's power.
Grant me Thy blessing, Lord, this day,
On all I think, or do, or say.

2. A Night Prayer.

When to rest I lay me down
God's protecting love I own ;
Hands and heart to Him I raise,
For His gifts I give Him praise.
The ill that I this day have done,
Forgive me, Lord, for Thy dear Son.
Thou, Who hast kept me through the day,
Watch o'er me through this night, I pray.

3. An Act of Good Intention. (Bl. Clement Hofbauer.)

Let my object ever be
To give glory, Lord, to Thee ;
If I work, or if I rest,
May God's holy name be blest.
Grant me grace my all to give
Unto Him by Whom I live ;
Jesus, for Thy help I plead :
Mary, for me intercede.

4. Grace before Meals.

Bless us, O Lord, and these Thy gifts, which we are about to receive from Thy bounty, through Jesus Christ Our Lord. Amen.

5. Grace after Meals.

We give Thee thanks, O Lord, for these and all Thy gifts, which of Thy bounty we have received, and may the souls of the faithful, through the mercy of God, rest in peace. Amen.

6. *Prayer for One's Parents.*

O my God, I commend my parents to Thee; protect them, and spare them long to me, and requite them for all the good that they have done to me.

III. PRAYERS TO BE SAID AT DIFFERENT TIMES WHEN THE CHURCH BELL IS HEARD.

1. *The Angelus.* (Morning, noon, and evening.)

V. The angel of the Lord declared unto Mary.

R. And she conceived of the Holy Ghost. Hail Mary, etc.

V. Behold the handmaid of the Lord:

R. Be it done unto me according to Thy word. Hail Mary, etc.

V. And the Word was made flesh.

R. And dwelt amongst us. Hail Mary, etc.

V. Pray for us, O holy Mother of God;

R. That we may be made worthy of the promises of Christ.

Let us Pray.

Pour forth, we beseech Thee, O Lord, Thy grace into our hearts; that we to whom the Incarnation of Christ Thy Son was made known by the message of an angel, may, by His Passion and cross, be brought to the glory of His resurrection; through the same Christ Our Lord. Amen.

(An indulgence of one hundred days may be gained each time that the Angelus is said kneeling (except on Saturday evening and on Sunday, when it is said standing), and a plenary indulgence. once a month, on the usual conditions. if it has been said daily for a whole month. Those who are reasonably prevented from saying the prayers kneeling, or who cannot hear the bell, are still able to gain the indulgence if the prayers are duly recited.)

2. *Prayer in Commemoration of Our Lord's Passion, to be said at three o'clock on Fridays.*

I bless Thee, O Thou Lord of heaven!
Whose life for sinful man was given.
Let not Thy cross and bitter pain
Have been for me borne all in vain.

*3. Prayer for the Souls in Purgatory, to be said when the Church
Bell is Tolled or after the Evening Angelus.*

Thy mercy, Lord, we humbly crave
For souls whom Thou didst die to save.
Suffering amidst the cleansing fire,
To see Thy face they yet aspire.
Grant them, O Lord, a swift release,
And bring them where all pain shall cease.

Eternal rest give unto all the faithful departed, O Lord, and
let perpetual light shine upon them. May they rest in peace.
Amen.

4. Prayers to be Said when the Bell is Rung at Mass.

When the priest, standing at the foot of the altar, begins the prayers of
the Mass, make the sign of the cross, direct your intention, and commence
your prayers. At the Gospel stand up and cross yourself on forehead, lips,
and breast.

5. Prayer at the Offertory.

Accept, O Lord, this sacrifice, which, in union with the priest,
I offer to Thy divine majesty, together with all I have and all I am.
Mercifully pardon my sins, and grant that I may find acceptance in
Thy sight.

6. At the Consecration.

Kneel down, bless yourself, clasp your hands, and fixing your eyes upon
the altar, say :

Flesh of Christ, hail, sweet oblation,
Sacrifice for our salvation ;
On the cross a victim slain.
Bread of angels, ever living,
Health and hope to mortals giving.

Remain upon your knees, motionless, until the bell rings again at the elevation of the chalice. Then bless yourself again, and say :

O fount of love, good Jesus, Lord,
Cleanse us, unclean, in Thy all-cleansing blood ;
Of which one single drop for sinners spilt,
Can free the entire world from all its guilt.

7. *At the Communion.*

When the bell rings, bless yourself, strike your breast, and say with the priest :

Lord, I am not worthy that Thou shouldst enter under my roof ; say but the word, and my soul shall be healed.

Bless yourself again here, and also when the priest gives the blessing. At the last Gospel do the same as when the first was read.

IV. DEVOTIONS FOR CONFESSION AND COMMUNION.

1. *The Form for Confession.*

Kneeling down in the confessional, make the sign of the cross when the priest gives you his blessing ; then say the first part of the *Confiteor*, and accuse yourself of the sins you have committed since your last confession, following the order of the Ten Commandments, the precepts of the Church, and the seven deadly sins. After having confessed all that you can remember, conclude with these or similar words :

For these and all the sins of my past life I am heartily sorry, because I have thereby offended my Father in heaven and deserved His chastisements. I purpose amendment for the future, and humbly ask pardon of God and absolution and penance of you, Father.

Listen attentively to the instructions the priest gives you, especially in regard to the penance he sets you. When he gives you absolution and his blessing, bless yourself; then go to the altar to give thanks to God for having granted you forgiveness of sin, and perform the penance enjoined on you.

2. *Acts of the Three Theological Virtues.*

(1). *An Act of Faith.* I believe that there is one God, and that in this one God there are three persons. That the Son of God was made man for us, that He died upon the cross, rose again from the dead and ascended into heaven. I believe that the Son of God will come again at the Last Day, and call all men to judgment. I believe this because Christ is the Son of God and therefore can neither deceive nor be deceived ; and because He has confirmed His teaching by many miracles. Moreover I believe whatever the Catholic Church by Christ's authority proposes to us to be believed ; I believe it because the Catholic Church is guided and defended against error by the Holy Spirit : and because even down to the present day God corroborates by miracles the truths which the Catholic Church teaches. O God, increase my faith.

(2). *An Act of Hope.* O my God, I hope that after death Thou wilt admit me to everlasting happiness, and that Thou wilt give me here such means as are essential to the attainment of that happiness. I trust that Thou wilt grant me for this end the grace of the Holy Spirit, such temporal good things as are necessary to me, pardon of sin, help in time of need, and a gracious answer to my petitions. I hope this, because Thou, Who art almighty and all-bountiful and ever-faithful to Thy promises, hast promised these things to me, and because Jesus Christ, my Lord and Saviour, has merited them for me by His cruel death upon the cross. O God, increase my hope.

(3). *An Act of Charity.* My God, I love Thee with my whole heart, and above all things, because Thou art supreme beauty and perfection, because Thou art my greatest benefactor and Thy love for me is infinite. I will, therefore, think of Thee in all my actions ; I will avoid even the slightest sins ; I will give thanks to Thee for all Thy benefits and for all Thou givest me to suffer, and I will love my neighbor because he is Thy child and made after Thy image. O God, increase my charity.

(As often as acts of the three theological virtues are made, either by the use of this formula, or in the words our own devotion may suggest, an indulgence of seven years and seven quarantines may be gained ; and for daily repetition of these acts a plenary indulgence once a month is granted, on the usual conditions. Also a plenary indulgence at the hour of death.)

3. An Act of Contrition.

O God of infinite majesty, I, a sinner, have offended against Thee. Thou art my heavenly Father; Thou hast given Thy Son for me, and hast lavished innumerable benefits upon me, and yet I have grieved Thee. Thou art a just God ; I know that Thou dost leave no sin unpunished, and yet I was so ungrateful as to offend Thee. I am exceedingly sorry for having sinned ; I will henceforth avoid sin and keep Thy commandments. Grant me Thy pardon, and receive me again as Thy child.

4. Renewal of Baptismal Vows.

I thank Thee, O my God, for having made me Thy child by holy Baptism. I desire this day to renew the covenant then made with Thee : I promise to renounce all the sinful pleasures of the world, to believe and to follow the teaching of the Gospel. I hope for Thy grace to enable me to do this, and after death to enter into eternal felicity.

DEVOTIONS TO THE HOLY GHOST.

1.   Prayer to the Holy Ghost.

To Thee, O Holy Ghost, we cry
Thou highest gift of God most
    high :
Enlighten us with light divine,
Keep far from us the foe
    malign.

Strengthen the weakness of our
    will,
Help us our duty to fulfil ;
Give solace to the troubled
    breast,
And after death, eternal rest.

2.   Hymn to the Holy Ghost.

Come, O Creator, Spirit blest !
And in our souls take up Thy
    rest ;
Come, with Thy grace and
    heavenly aid,
To fill the hearts that Thou
    hast made.

Kindle our senses from above,
And make our hearts o'erflow
    with love ;
With patience firm and virtue
    high,
The weakness of our flesh sup-
    ply.

Great Paraclete ! to Thee we
    cry
O highest gift of God most
    high !
O fount of life, O fire of love,
And sweet anointing from
    above !

Far from us drive the foe we
    dread,
And grant us Thy true peace
    instead ;
So shall we not, with Thee for
    guide,
Turn from the path of life aside.

Thou in Thy sevenfold gifts art
    known ;
The finger of God's hand we
    own ;
The promise of the Father Thou,
Who dost the tongue with
    power endow.

Oh, may Thy grace on us
    bestow
The Father and the Son to
    know,
And Thee through endless time
    confest,
Of both the eternal Spirit blest.

All glory while the ages run
Be to the Father and the Son
Who rose from death ; the same to Thee,
O Holy Ghost, eternally.   Amen.

(An indulgence of three hundred days may be gained each time this hymn
is said, and a plenary indulgence once a month.—Pius VI , 1796.)

VI. Special Prayers.

1. The Salve Regina.

Hail, holy Queen, Mother of mercy, our life, our sweetness and our hope ! To thee do we cry, poor banished children of Eve, to thee do we send up our sighs, mourning and weeping in this valley of tears. Turn then, most gracious advocate, thine eyes of mercy towards us, and after this, our exile, show unto us the blessed fruit of thy womb, Jesus. O clement, O loving, O sweet Virgin Mary !

V. Pray for us, O Holy Mother of God.

R. That we may be made worthy of the promises of Christ.

V. Make me worthy to praise thee, holy Virgin.

R. Give me strength against thine enemies.

V. Blessed be God in His saints.

R. Amen.

We fly to thy protection, O holy Mother of God ! Despise not our petitions in our necessities, and deliver us from all dangers, O ever glorious and blessed Virgin. Reconcile us with thy Son, commend us to thy Son, present us to thy Son !

2. The Memorare.

Remember, O most gracious Virgin Mary, that never was it known that any one who fled to thy protection, implored thy help and sought thy intercession, was left unaided. Inspired with this confidence, I fly unto thee, O Virgin of virgins, my Mother; to thee I come ; before thee I stand, sinful and sorrowful. O Mother of the Word Incarnate, despise not my petitions, but in thy mercy hear and answer me. Amen.

(An indulgence of three hundred days may be gained each time the *Memorare* is said ; and a plenary once a month, on the usual conditions, by those who repeat it daily.)

3. The Holy Rosary.

The Creed is repeated first, then one Our Father and three Hail Marys, followed by Glory be to the Father, etc. Fifteen decades are then said, each decade consisting of one Our Father and ten Hail Marys, and ending with a Glory be to the Father.

The Mysteries of the Rosary are :

The five Joyful Mysteries, which may be said chiefly from Advent to Lent, or on Mondays and Thursdays.

(1), The Annunciation, (2), The Visitation, (3), The Nativity of Our Lord, (4), The Presentation of Our Lord in the Temple, (5), The Finding of the Child Jesus in Jerusalem.

The five Sorrowful Mysteries, which may be said chiefly during Lent, or on Tuesdays and Fridays.

(1), The Prayer and Agony of Our Lord in the Garden, (2), The Scourging, (3), The Crowning with Thorns, (4), The Carrying of the Cross, (5), The Crucifixion.

The five Glorious Mysteries, which may be used chiefly from Easter until Advent, or on Wednesdays, Saturdays, and Sundays.

(1), The Resurrection of Our Lord, (2), The Ascension, (3), The Descent of the Holy Ghost on the Apostles, (4), The Assumption of the Blessed Virgin into Heaven, (5), The Coronation of the Blessed Virgin Mary.

Thus each chaplet of the Rosary consists of the Creed, six Our Fathers, six Glorys and fifty-three Hail Marys.

The beads must be blessed and the indulgences attached by a priest who has the powers. If this be duly done the faithful can gain an indulgence of one hundred days for every Creed, Our Father, and Hail Mary, each time the Rosary is recited.

4. *Prayer to St. Joseph.*

Glorious Joseph, kind father and friend,
Humbly to thee myself I commend ;
Keep me, watch over me, help and defend.
By virtue's path lead to the heavenly land,
And in my last hour be thou near at hand.

5. *Prayer to Our Guardian Angel.*

Holy angel, guardian mine,
Given me by love divine ;
Day and night watch over me,
From harm, from sin, let me be free.
By a pious life I fain
Would eternal joys attain.

GENERAL SURVEY.

PART I.

We are on earth for the purpose of giving glory to God, and thereby working out our eternal salvation. We are to attain our end by the following means.

We must strive to acquire the knowledge of God through faith in the truths which He has revealed.

Here we speak of the knowledge of God, of revelation, of faith, the motives of faith, the opposite of faith, the confession of faith; and finally of the sign of the cross.

An explanation is given of the twelve articles of the Apostles' Creed.

Art. 1. The existence of God, His being, His attributes, His triune nature, the creation of the world and divine providence, angels and men, original sin; the promise of a Redeemer, the expectation of a Redeemer.

Art. 2–7. Jesus is the Messias, the Son of God; Himself God and Our Lord. The Incarnation, the life of Christ.

Art. 8. The Holy Ghost and the doctrine of grace.

Art. 9. The Catholic Church, its institution, development, and divine maintenance. The supreme Head of the Church, the hierarchy, the notes of the Church. In the Church alone is salvation. Church and State. The communion of saints.

Art. 10. Forgiveness of sins.

Art. 11–12. Death, the particular judgment, heaven, hell, purgatory, the resurrection of the dead, the final judgment.

At the close of the Apostles' Creed mention is made of the good things which we hope for from God. The nature of Christian hope is considered, its advantages and what is opposed to it.

PART II.

We must keep the commandments of God. These are: The two precepts of charity.

The precept of charity towards God, which is set forth more fully in the first four commandments of the Decalogue.

In His character of sovereign King God requires from us: In the First Commandment worship and fidelity; in the Second, reverence; in the Third, service; in the Fourth, respect towards His representatives.

The precept of charity towards one's neighbor. By this we are forbidden to injure our neighbor. In the Fifth Commandment we are forbidden to injure his life; in the Sixth, his innocence; in the Seventh, his property; in the Eighth, his reputation; in the Ninth and Tenth, his household.

We are also commanded to help him in time of need by the performance of the works of mercy.

The commandments of the Church are an amplification of the Third Commandment of the Decalogue.

After the consideration of the love of God, the love of the world is spoken of.

After the consideration of the love of one's neighbor, the love of one's friends, of one's enemies, of one's self is enlarged upon; after the consideration of the First Commandment, the veneration of the saints, the oath born of religion and otherwise; under the Third Commandment of God, the obligation of labor; under the first commandment of the Church, the ecclesiastical year; under the Fourth Commandment of God, the Christian's duty towards the Pope and chief ruler, and the obligations resting on those who are in authority; under the Fifth Commandment of God, the treatment of animals; and under the works of mercy, the right use of money, the duty of gratitude, and the spirit of poverty.

The fulfilling of the commandments consists in the practice of good works and the exercise of virtue, as well as the abandonment of sin and vice; finally, in the avoidance of everything that might lead to sin, temptation to sin, and occasions of sin.

The most important virtues are those which are called the seven capital virtues, the opposites to which are the seven deadly sins.

In order to obey the commandments strictly we must make use of the means for attaining perfection. The general means are intended for all; the special means, the three evangelical counsels, are only for individuals.

By walking in this way we shall enjoy happiness even on earth.

The precepts which Christ gave us in the Sermon on the Mount, and which are called the eight beatitudes.

In order to believe revealed truth and to keep the commandments, we require the assistance of divine grace, and this we can obtain by the use of the means of grace.

PART III.

We must make use of the means of grace. These are: The holy sacrifice of the Mass, the sacraments, and prayer.

Before entering upon the subject of the sacrifice of the Mass, sacrifice in general and the sacrifice of the cross are considered. In treating of the holy sacrifice of the Mass the points explained are: The institution, the nature, the parts, and the ceremonies of the Mass; the relation of the Mass to the sacrifice of the cross, the benefits derived from the Mass, the manner of offering it, devotions during Mass, the obligation of hearing Mass, the time and place of celebrating Mass, the vestments and vessels used at Mass, the color of the vestments, the language used in the Mass, and the musical accompaniment of the Mass. The duty of hearing the word of God next follows; then the doctrine of the sacraments in general and of each individually. Under the Sacrament of the Altar the institution and nature of the sacrament are considered, likewise the reception of the sacraments and the fruits produced thereby, the preparation before receiving communion and the subsequent thanksgiving, and also spiritual communion. Under the Sacrament of Penance the points considered are: The institution, nature, and necessity of

penance; the office of the confessor, the effects of the Sacrament
of Penance. The worthy reception of the sacrament (in its
five parts), general confessions, the institution and excellence
of confession, the sin of relapse, and the doctrine of indulgences.
Under matrimony, the institution and nature of marriage are
treated of, the duties of married people, mixed marriages, and
the single state. Hereupon follows the teaching concerning
sacramentals.

In treating of prayer an explanation is given of the nature,
the use, the necessity, the time, the place, the object of prayer
and of contemplation. Furthermore explanations are given of
the most important prayers (the Lord's Prayer and prayer to
the Mother of God); the principal public services morning and
evening, processions, pilgrimages, the Way of the Cross, Exposition of the Blessed Sacrament, missions, Catholic congresses,
Passion plays, and religious associations. The latter include
third orders, confraternities, and charitable societies.

INTRODUCTION.

I. FOR WHAT END ARE WE ON THIS EARTH?

As the scholar goes to school in order that he may afterwards attain a certain position in life, so man is placed on this earth in order that he may attain to the lofty end of eternal happiness. As the servant serves his master and so earns his bread, so man has to serve God, and through his service attains happiness to some extent in this life, and in its fulness after death.

We are upon this earth in order that we may glorify God, and so win for ourselves eternal happiness.

The glory of God is the end of all creation. All creatures on the earth are created for this end, that they may manifest in themselves the divine perfections and God's dominion over His rational creatures, that is, over angels and men, and that He may be loved and praised by them. Even the material world, and creatures not possessed of reason—animals, trees, plants, stones, metals, etc., all praise God after their own fashion. "The Lord has made all things for Himself" (Prov. xvi. 4). Man is created for this end, that he should proclaim the majesty of God. He must do so whether he wills it or not. The construction of the body of man, the lofty powers of his soul, the rewards of the good, the punishment of the wicked, all proclaim the majesty of God, His omnipotence, wisdom, goodness, justice, etc. Even the reprobate will have to contribute to the glory of God (Prov. xvi. 4). In the end he will show how great is the holiness and justice of God. Man, from being possessed of reason and free will, is through these enabled in an especial way to give glory to God. This he does when he knows, loves, and honors God. Man is created chiefly for the life beyond the grave. In this life he is a stranger, a wanderer, and a pilgrim. "We have not here a lasting city, but we seek one that is to come" (Heb. xiii. 14). Heaven is our true country; here we are in exile.

Hence we are not upon earth only to collect earthly treasures, to attain earthly honors, to eat and to drink, or to enjoy earthly pleasures.

He who pursues ends like these behaves as foolishly as a servant who, instead of serving his master, devotes himself to some passing amusement. He stands idle in the market-place, instead of working in his master's vineyard. He is like a traveller who, attracted by the beauty of the scenery, does not pursue his journey, and so allows the

73

night to overtake him. We are not made for earth; we are made to look upward to heaven. The trees, the plants point upward to heaven, as if to remind us that it is our home.

For this reason Our Lord says: " One thing is necessary " (Luke x. 42), and again " Seek first the kingdom of God and His justice, and all other things shall be added unto you " (Matt. vi. 33.)

Unhappily, too many forget their last end, and fix their hearts on money, influence, honor, etc. They are like the kings of that heathen country who, although they reigned but for a year and after that had to go and live on a barren island, spent all their time in luxury and feasting, and did not lay up any provision for the future on the island whither they were bound. He who does not think on his last end is not a pilgrim, but a *tramp*, and falls into the hands of the devil as a tramp into the hands of the police. He is like a sailor who knows not whither he is sailing, and so wrecks his ship. Our Lord compares such to the servant who sleeps, instead of watching for his master's coming (Matt. xxiv. 42).

II. HOW ARE WE TO ATTAIN TO ETERNAL HAPPINESS?

Eternal happiness consists in union with God, through the exercise of the intellect contemplating God and the will loving Him. If we wish to attain it, we must begin to draw near to it in this life. We must seek to know and love God. But love of God consists in keeping His commandments (John xiv. 23). From this it follows that:

We shall attain to eternal happiness by the following means: 1. We must strive to know God by means of faith in the truths He has revealed to us.

Our Lord says: " This is eternal life, that they may know Thee, the only true God, and Jesus Christ, Whom Thou hast sent " (John xvii. 3). That is to say, the knowledge of God brings man to eternal happiness.

2. We must fulfil the will of God by keeping His commandments.

Our Lord says to the rich young man: " If thou wilt enter into life, keep the commandments " (Matt. xix. 17).

By means of our own strength we can neither believe nor keep the commandments; for this we need the grace of God.

Even Adam and Eve in a state of innocence needed the help of grace. He who travels to a distant country, besides his own exertions needs money for the journey. The farmer cannot cultivate his land without the aid of sunshine and of rain. Man, too, has a special weakness by reason of original sin. This makes grace the more indispensable. The blind man needs a guide, the sick man strengthening food. We are like a man who through weakness has fallen to the ground, and has no power, of himself, to rise. He must look around for one to aid him. So Our Lord tells us: " Without Me you can do nothing " (John xv. 5). As the sun is necessary to the earth, to enlighten and warm it, so is grace necessary to our soul.

We obtain the grace of God through the means of grace instituted by Jesus Christ.

3. We must therefore avail ourselves of the means of grace; of which the chief are holy Mass, the sacraments, and prayer.

The means of grace are a channel through which grace is conveyed to our soul. Faith is the road which leads to heaven, the commandments are like sign-posts by the way, the means of grace the money for the journey. " The way that leads to life is narrow and thorny; the way that leads to destruction is broad, and many are they who go in thereat " (Matt. vii. 13).

It is also true that he who desires happiness must have religion.

Religion consists in a knowledge of God and a life corresponding to the will of God. Religion is not a matter of feeling; it is a matter of the will and of action, and consists in following out the principles that God has laid down. Mere knowledge does not constitute religion, else the devil would have religion; the service of God is necessarily included in it. We do not call a man a baseball player or cricketer because he knows the rules and nature of the game; practice is also required.

It is also true that he who desires to be happy must strive to be like to God.

Man becomes like to God when all his thought and action resemble the divine thought and action. The commandments of God are a mirror, in which we recognize whether our actions are like or unlike those of God.

III. CAN WE ATTAIN PERFECT HAPPINESS ON EARTH?

1. Earthly goods, such as riches, honor, pleasure, cannot by themselves make us happy, for they cannot satisfy our soul; they often only make life bitter, and invariably forsake us in death.

Earthly goods deceive us; they are like soap-bubbles, which reflect all the colors of the rainbow but are really only drops of water. Earthly joys are like artificial fruit, beautiful to behold, but disappointing to the taste. Earthly pleasures are like drops of water: they do not quench the fire of the passions, but only make it burn more fiercely. Man can no more be happy without God than a fish can live out of the water. Hence St. Augustine says: " Unquiet is the heart of man until it rests in God." No sensible or material goods will nourish or satisfy the soul. Hence Our Lord says to the Samaritan woman: " He who drinks of this water will thirst again."

Riches will no more satisfy the soul than salt water will quench thirst. In the days of the early empire of Rome, when riches and sensual pleasures abounded, suicide was most widely prevalent. Earthly possessions are a continual source of anxiety; he who rests in them is tormented by them, like a man who reposes on thorns. As the fresh waters of the rivers are changed into the salt waters of the sea, so all earthly pleasures sooner or later turn to bitterness. Forbidden pleasures soon bring misery after them, like the forbidden fruit. They are like bait that has a hook concealed within it. Earthly goods all forsake us when we die: " We brought nothing into the world, and certainly we cannot carry anything out of it " (1 Tim. vi. 7). When the Pope is crowned, a handful of tow is kindled, and while it blazes up the choir sing: " Thus passes the glory of the world." As the spider spins a web out of its own bowels and in a moment the broom sweeps it all away, so man labors for long years to obtain some honor, or possession, or office. Some obstacle comes in the way, death or sickness visits him, and all the labor is gone for naught. As the glow-worm shines in the night, but in the light of day is but an ugly insect, so the delights of earth are brilliant during the night of life on earth, but under the light of the Day of Judgment will show themselves vain and worthless.

Earthly goods are given to us only that through them we may attain to eternal happiness.

Every creature on earth is intended as a step to bring us nearer to God. As in the workshop of the painter, brushes, colors, oils, are all destined to serve to the completion of the picture, so all things in the world are intended to contribute to our eternal happiness in heaven. Not to use earthly things for this end is to lose the hope of eternal happiness; but to make them our end and to be dependent on them no less deprives us of the end for which we were created. Earthly goods are like the surgeon's instruments; if they are ill-employed, they kill instead of curing. We must therefore use them only in so far as they help us towards the attainment of our last end. When they hinder us we must cut ourselves free from them. We must not serve them, they must serve us.

2. Only the Gospel of Christ is capable of giving us a partial happiness on earth, for he who follows the teaching of Christ is certain to have peace in his soul.

This is why Christ says to the Samaritan woman: " He that shall drink of the water that I shall give him, shall not thirst forever " (John iv. 13). And again: " He that cometh to Me, shall never hunger " (John vi. 35). The teaching of Christ can alone satisfy the heart of man. The reason of this is, that earthly sufferings do not render unhappy the man who follows Christ.

3. He who follows Christ will have to endure persecution; but these persecutions can do him no harm.

St. Paul tells us that " All who will live godly in Christ Jesus, shall suffer persecution " (2 Tim. iii. 12).

The whole life of the Christian is a carrying of the cross and a suffering of persecution. Christ Himself says: " The servant is not above his master " (Matt. x. 24). That is, the servant of Christ has no claim to a better lot than his Master Christ. We must expect the men of the world (that is, those who seek their happiness in this life) to regard us as erratic people and as fools, to condemn us and to hate us (1 Cor. iv. 3, 10; John xvii. 14; xv. 20). To be loved and praised by the world is to be the enemy of Christ. The principles of the world are in contradiction with those of Christ, and the world regards as a fool him whom Christ declares blessed (Matt. v. 3, 10).

Yet Christ tells us: " Every one that heareth My words and doeth them, shall be likened to a wise man, that built his house upon a rock " (Matt. vii. 24).

He who trusts in God builds on solid ground. The patriarch Joseph derived advantage, not harm, from being persecuted; the pious David was persecuted, first by Saul, and then by his own son Absalom. From his own experience he was able to say: " Many are the afflictions of the just; but out of them all the Lord will deliver them " (Ps. xxxiii. 20). All the saints of Christ have been persecuted, but God has turned to good the evil that their enemies thought to do them. " If God is with us, who can be against us? "

4. Hence perfect happiness is impossible on earth; for no man can entirely avoid suffering.

The end of the worldling is misery as we have seen, and the just man is persecuted. No one can escape sickness, suffering, death. The world is a valley of tears; it is a big hospital, containing as many sick men as there are human beings. The world is a place of banishment, where we are far from our true country. In the world good and ill fortune succeed each other like sunshine and storm. Prosperity is the sure forerunner of adversity. In life we are on a sea, now lifted up to heaven, now cast down to hell. Society is always sure to be full of all kinds of miseries, whatever efforts may be made to improve the condition of mankind. Vain indeed are the hopes of the modern school of social democrats who dream of gradually abolishing all evil and misery from the world.

PART I.—FAITH.

I. THE KNOWLEDGE OF GOD.

The knowledge of God consists in the knowledge of His perfections, His works, His will, and the means of grace instituted by Him. St. Paul bids us "increase in the knowledge of God" (Col. i. 10). *Now* we only know God through a glass in a dark manner; only in heaven shall we see Him face to face, and have a clear knowledge of His perfections (1 Cor. xiii. 12).

1. The happiness of the angels and the saints consists in the knowledge of God.

Our Lord tells us that "this is eternal life, that they may know Thee, the only true God, and Jesus Christ Whom Thou hast sent" (John xvii. 3). This is the food of which the archangel Raphael spoke, when he said to Tobias: "I use an invisible meat and drink, which cannot be seen by men" (Tob. xii. 19). In heaven the saints and angels have an immediate knowledge of God in the beatific vision. We on earth only know God through the medium of His works and of what He has revealed to us. Our knowledge, compared with that of the saints and angels, is like the knowledge of a country that one gets from maps and pictures as compared with the knowledge of one who has himself visited it.

2. The knowledge of God is all-important, for without it there cannot be any happiness on earth, or a well-ordered life.

The knowledge of God is the food of our soul. Without it the soul feels hungry; we become discontented. He who does not possess interior peace, cannot enjoy riches, health, or any of the goods of this life; they all become distasteful to him. Yet few think about this food of the soul; they busy themselves, as Our Lord says, with the "meat that perishes" (John vi. 27). Without the knowledge of God a man is like one who walks in the dark, and stumbles at every step; he has no end or aim in life, no consolation in misfortune, and no hope in death. He cannot have any solid or lasting happiness, or any true contentment. Without a knowledge of God a well-ordered life is impossible. Just as an untilled field produces no good fruit, so a man who has not the knowledge of God can produce no good works. Ignorance and forgetfulness of God are the causes of most of the sins that men commit. Rash and false oaths, neglect of the service of God and of the sacraments, the love of gold, the sinful indulgence of the passions, are all due to wilful ignorance and forgetfulness of God. Thus the prophet Osee exclaims " There is no knowledge of God in the land. Cursing and lying and killing and theft and adultery have overflowed" (Osee iv. 2, 3). And St. Ignatius of Loyola cries out, " O God, Thou joy of my soul, if only men knew Thee, they never would offend Thee," and experience shows that in the jails the greater part of the prisoners are those who knew nothing of God. When Frederick of Prussia at length recognized that the want of the knowledge of God was the cause of the increase in crime, he exclaimed, " Then I will have religion introduced into the country." This is why the learning and the understanding of the Catechism, which is nothing else than an abridgement of the Christian religion, is all-important. But a mere knowledge of the truths of religion is not sufficient; they must also be practised.

3. We arrive at a right knowledge of God through faith in the truths which God has revealed.

It is true that by means of reason and from the contemplation of the creatures that God has made man can arrive at a knowledge of God (Rom. i. 20). "The heavens show forth the glory of God" (Ps. xviii. 2). But our reason is so weak and prone to err, that without revelation it is very difficult for man to attain to a clear and correct knowledge of God. What strange and perverted views of the Deity we find among heathen nations (Cf. Wisd. ix. 16, 17). God therefore in His mercy comes to our aid with revelation. Through believing the truths that God has revealed, man attains to a clear and correct knowledge of God. Hence St. Anselm says, " The more I am nourished with the food of faith, the more my understanding is satisfied." Faith is a divine light that shines in our souls (2 Cor. iv. 6). It is like a watch tower, from which we can see that which cannot be seen from the plain below; we learn respecting God that which cannot be learned by mere reason from the world around. It is a glass through which we perceive all the divine perfections. It is a staff which supports our feeble reason, and enables it to know God better. There are two books from which we gain a knowledge of God; the book of Nature, and Holy Scripture, which is the book of revelation.

II. DIVINE REVELATION.

If any one stands in a room behind a gauze curtain he perceives all those who are passing in the street, and they see him not. But if he makes himself known by speaking, the passers-by are able to recognize him. Such is our relation to God; He sees us, but conceals Himself from our eyes. Yet He has in many ways made Himself known to men; to Abraham, to Moses in the burning bush, to the Israelites on Mount Sinai, etc.

1. God has in His mercy in the course of ages often revealed Himself to men (Heb. i. 1-2).

God has often communicated to men a knowledge of His perfections, His decrees, and His holy will. Such revelation is called supernatural, as opposed to the natural revelation of Himself that He makes through the external world.

2. God's revelation to man is generally made in the following way: He speaks to individuals and orders them to communicate to their fellow-men the revelation made to them.

Thus God spoke to Abraham, Noe, and Moses. He sent Noe to preach to sinful men before the Flood, He sent Moses to the Israelites when they were oppressed by Pharao. Sometimes God spoke to a number of men who were assembled together, as when He gave the law to the people on Mount Sinai, or when Our Lord was baptized by St. John and the Holy Spirit descended like a dove, a voice being heard from heaven: " This is My beloved Son, in Whom I am well pleas'ed." Sometimes God revealed Himself through angels, as for instance to Tobias through the archangel Raphael. When God spoke to men, He took the visible form of a man or of an angel, or He spoke from a cloud (as on Sinai), or from a burning' bush, as He did to Moses, or amid a bright light from heaven, as to St. Paul, or in the whispering of the wind, as He did to Elias, or by some interior illumination (Deut. ii. 6-8). Those to whom God revealed Himself, and who had to bear witness before others to the divine message, were called messengers from God, and often received from Him the power of working miracles and of prophecy, in proof of their divine mission. (Cf. the miracles of Moses before Pharao, of Elias, the apostles, etc.)

3. Those who were specially intrusted with the communication to men of the divine revelation were the following: the patriarchs, the prophets, Jesus Christ the Son of God (Heb. i. 1), and His apostles.

Revelation is to mankind in general what education is to individual men. Revelation corresponds to the needs of the successive stages of human development, to the infancy, childhood, and youth of mankind. The patriarchs, who had more of the nature of children, needed less in the way of precepts, and God dealt with them in more familiar fashion; the people of Israel, in whom, as in the season of youth, self-will and sensuality were strong, had to be trained by strict laws and constant correction; but when mankind had arrived at the period of manhood, then God sent His Son and introduced the law of love (1 Cor. xiii. 11; Gal. iii. 24). Of all those who declared to men the divine revelation, the Son of God was pre-eminently the true witness. He says of Himself, " For this I was born, and for this I came into the world, that I should bear testimony to the truth " (John xviii. 37). He was of all witnesses the best, because He alone had seen God (John i. 18). The apostles also had to declare to men the divine revelation. They had to bear witness of what they had seen, and above all of the resurrection of Jesus Christ (Acts x. 39). With the revelation given through Christ and His apostles, the revelation that was given for the instruction of all mankind was concluded.

4. Even since the death of Our Lord and His apostles God has often revealed Himself to men; yet these subsequent reve-

lations are no continuation of the earlier revelation on which our faith rests.

Instances of these subsequent revelations are the appearances of Our Lord to Blessed Margaret Mary, and of Our Lady at Lourdes. Such revelations must not be too lightly credited, as men are liable to be deceived; yet they must not be rejected without examination. Many of the saints have had such revelations, i.e., St. Francis of Assisi, to whom Our Lord appeared upon the cross, and St. Anthony of Padua, in whose arms the Child Jesus deigned to rest. These private revelations were more especially given to those who were striving after perfection, in order to encourage them to greater perfection still. Yet God sometimes revealed Himself to wicked men, i.e., to Baltassar in the handwriting on the wall (Dan. v. 5, *seq.*). Hence a private revelation given to any one is not necessarily a mark of holiness. These revelations, moreover, were no further continuation of the revelation intended for the instruction of the whole of mankind, which ended with the death of the last of the apostles; they are rather a confirmation of truths already revealed. Thus Our Lady, when she appeared at Lourdes, proclaimed herself the "Immaculate Conception," so confirming the dogma which Pius IX. had defined four years previously, and the countless miracles and cures that have taken place there have established the truth of the apparition. Yet it is always possible that the malice of the devil may introduce deceptions into private revelations. No one is therefore bound to give to them a firmer belief (even though they have in general been approved by the Church), than he would give to the assertions of an honest and trustworthy man.

5. Revelation was necessary because, in consequence of original sin, man without revelation has never had a correct knowledge of God and of His will; and also because it was necessary that man should be prepared for the coming of the Redeemer.

The three Wise Men would never have found Christ if He had not revealed Himself to them by means of a star; so mankind would have lived far off from God, and would never have attained to a true knowledge of Him, if He had not revealed Himself to them. As the eye needs light to see things of sense, so human reason, which is the eye of the soul, needs revelation to perceive things divine (St. Augustine). Original sin and the indulgence of the senses had so dimmed human reason that it could no longer recognize God in His works (Wisd. ix. 16). This is proved by the history of paganism. The heathen worshipped countless deities, idols, beasts, and wicked men, and his worship was often immoral and horrible, as in the human sacrifices offered by him. The gods were often the patrons of vice. The greatest men among the heathens approved practices forbidden by the natural law. Thus Cicero approved of suicide, Plato of the exposing to death those children who were weak or deformed. Their theories when good were at variance with their practice. Socrates denounced polytheism, but before his death told his disciples to sacrifice a cock to Æsculapius. Many of the best of the heathens recognized and lamented their ignorance of God. Besides, without a previous revelation the Saviour would have been neither known nor honored as He ought to have been known and honored; it was fitting that He should be announced beforehand, like a king coming to take possession of his kingdom. We ought indeed to be grateful to God that He has given us the light of revelation, just as a blind man is grateful to the physician who has restored his sight. Yet how many there are who wilfully shut their eyes to the light of revelation even now !

III. THE PREACHING OF THE GOSPEL.

1. The truths revealed by God to men were, by God's command, proclaimed to all nations of the earth by the Catholic Church, and especially by means of the living word, that is, by preaching.

The command to proclaim to all nations of the earth the truths revealed by God, was given to the apostles by Our Lord at the time of His ascension.

Our Lord, before ascending into heaven, spoke to His apostles as follows: " All power is given to Me in heaven and in earth; going, therefore, teach ye all nations: baptizing them in the name of the Father and of the Son, and of the Holy Ghost: . . . and behold I am with you all days, even to the end of the world " (Matt. xxviii. 18-20). For this reason the apostles and their successors have never allowed themselves to be prohibited by any earthly authority from preaching the Gospel (Cf. Acts v. 29). Nor has the Church ever been turned aside from fulfilling her mission of preaching the Gospel, by the opposition of the world. Even now in many countries the State seeks to make the Church dependent on her. It is in consequence of the command given by Our Lord to the apostles, that the Popes send missionaries to the heathens, and issue Papal briefs and rescripts to Christendom; that bishops send priests throughout their dioceses, and publish pastoral letters; that parish priests instruct their people by sermons and Catechism. While the Catholic Church spreads the Word of God by means of preaching, Mahometans spread their beliefs with fire and sword, and Protestants by means of the Bible.

It is an error to suppose that Holy Scripture is the only means intended by almighty God to communicate to the nations of the earth the truths of revelation.

It was the will of God to make use of preaching for the conversion of the world. Our Lord said to His apostles, " Go and teach all nations," not " Go and write to all nations." Out of the apostles only two wrote; all the rest preached. The apostles themselves were the books of the faithful (St. Augustine). St. Paul tells us that " Faith cometh by hearing " (Rom. x. 17), not from mere books. Teaching by word of mouth corresponds to human needs; every one prefers to be taught, rather than to have to hunt out the truth from books by study. If writings were the only means by which men could arrive at a knowledge of revealed truth the Christians of the first two centuries would have been at a terrible disadvantage; so too would those who cannot read, as well as the great mass of mankind in the present day, who have neither the knowledge nor the capacity to penetrate the meaning of the written Word. Yet it is the will of God that "All men should come to a knowledge of the truth" (1 Tim. ii. 4). Holy Scripture soon loses its value in the eyes of those who have not the assurance of the living Word that it is truly of divine origin. St. Augustine says: "I should not believe the Gospel unless the authority of the Church moved me to do so."

A truth which the Church puts before us as revealed by God is called a truth of faith, or a *dogma.*

Either a universal council (i.e., one consisting of the bishops of the whole world) acting under the authority of the Pope, or the Pope himself, has power to declare a truth to be revealed by God. Thus the Council of Nicæa declared the divinity of Our Lord to be an article of faith; and Pope Pius IX. the Immaculate Conception of the holy Mother of God (1854). Thereby no new doctrines were taught, but these truths were declared to have been truly revealed by God, and thenceforth they became dogmas of the faith. When a child advances in its knowledge of religious truth, it does not really change its belief; so the Church, the collected body of all the faithful, receives dogmas new to it, when, on the appearance of some new form of error, it sets forth, after careful examination, certain truths of religion in explicit form and imposes their acceptance on all the faithful. Before the definition of it by the Church it was only a "pious opinion," or one proximate to faith. Such is at the present time the belief in the assumption of the body of Our Lady into heaven.

2. The Catholic Church derives from Holy Scripture and from Tradition the truths that God has revealed.

Holy Scripture and Tradition are of equal authority, and claim from us equal respect. Holy Scripture is the written, Tradition the unwritten Word of God. St. Paul exhorts the faithful to hold fast the traditions they have received, whether it be by word of mouth or by writing (2 Thess. ii. 14).

IV. HOLY SCRIPTURE AND TRADITION.

1. Holy Scripture or the Bible consists of seventy-two books, which were written by men inspired by God, and under the guidance and influence of the Holy Ghost. These seventy-two books are recognized by the Church as "the Word of God."

The Holy Ghost inspired in a very special way the writers of Holy Scripture ; He moved them to write, and guided and enlightened them while they were writing (Cf. 2 Tim. iii. 16; Matt. xv. 3; Mark xii. 36). The Council of Trent and the Vatican Council have expressly declared that God is the Author (*auctor*) of Holy Scripture. St. Augustine says: "It is as if the Gospels were written down with Christ's own hand." "The writers of Holy Scripture," says St. Laurence Justinian, "were like a musical instrument on which the Holy Spirit played." Yet they were not mere passive instruments; each writer brings his own personal character with him into what he writes. They are like a number of painters, who all paint a building which they see in the clear daylight, quite correctly, but yet with a great many points of difference, according to their respective talent and skill. Hence it follows that there are no errors in Scripture. We must not look to the individual words, but to the general sense. We must not take offence at popular expressions which are not scientifically correct, as when the motion of the sun, sunrise, and sunset, are alluded to. Moreover, since the Bible contains the Word of God, we must treat it with great reverence. Thus the people always stand up when the Gospel is being read at Mass; oaths are taken on the book of the Gospels; in Mass the deacon approaches the book of the Gospels with incense and lights. The Council of Trent imposes special penalties on those who mock at Holy Scripture. The Jews had the greatest reverence for the Scriptures and the precepts therein contained.

The seventy-two books of Holy Scripture are divided into forty-five books of the Old Testament and twenty-seven of the New. They are moreover divided into doctrinal, historical, and prophetical books.

Old Testament. The historical books comprise (1), The five books of Moses, which contain the early history of man, the lives of the patriarchs, and the history of the Jewish people up to the time of their entrance into the Holy Land. (2), The books of Josue and Judges, which relate their conquest of Palestine and their struggles with surrounding nations. (3), The four books of Kings, which recount their history under their kings. (4), The book of Tobias, which gives an account of the life of Tobias and his son during the captivity. (5), The books of the Machabees, which relate the oppression of the Jews under Antiochus, etc. The doctrinal books comprise the story of Job, the Psalms of David, the Proverbs of Solomon, and the books of Ecclesiastes, Wisdom, and Ecclesiasticus. The prophetical books comprise the four greater prophets, Isaias, Jeremias, Ezechiel, and Daniel, and the twelve lesser prophets, Jonas, Habacuc, etc.

New Testament. The historical books are the four Gospels, and the Acts of the Apostles. The doctrinal books are the twenty-one Epistles, including fourteen of St. Paul's epistles. The prophetical book is the Apocalypse of St. John, which tells in obscure language the future destinies of the Church. Most of the books of the Old Testament were originally written in Hebrew, most of the New in Greek. The Latin translation of the Bible called the Vulgate is an amended version of the translation made by St. Jerome about A.D. 400. The Vulgate is declared by the Council of Trent to be an authentic rendering of the original.

The most important books of Holy Scripture are the four Gospels and the Acts of the Apostles. The four Evangelists relate the life and teaching of Our Lord; the Acts of the Apostles recount the labors of St. Peter and St. Paul.

The writers of the Four Gospels are called the four Evangelists. Two of them, St. Matthew and St. John, were apostles, St. Mark was a companion of St. Peter, and St. Luke of St. Paul on his apostolic journeys. St. Matthew's gospel was originally written in Hebrew, for the benefit of the Jews of Palestine. He shows how Jesus of Nazareth fulfilled the prophecies of the Old Testament, and proved Himself to be the true Messias. St. Mark wrote for the Christians of Rome and shows Christ to be the Son of God. St. Luke wrote for a distinguished citizen of Rome, named Theophilus, in order to instruct him in the life and doctrine of Christ. We owe to St. Luke many details about Our Lady, and many parables not given by the other Evangelists. St. John wrote his gospel in his old age, to prove against the heretics of the time that Jesus Christ is truly God. He quotes chiefly those sayings of Christ from which His divinity is most clearly proved. The Gospels were probably written in the order in which they stand: St. Matthew wrote about A.D. 40, St. Mark and St. Luke some twenty-five years later, St. John about A.D. 90. The four Gospels were collected into one volume in the second century.

It can be proved from internal evidence that the Gospels were written by disciples of Christ, and narrate what is true. We can also prove from the oldest copies, from translations, and from quotations, that no change has been made in them since they were first written. The Gospels are therefore genuine, worthy of belief, and incorrupt.

On reading the Gospels we recognize at once that they were the work of Jews. The writers introduce Hebrew expressions (Luke viii. 14; John xvii. 12). They wrote before the destruction of Jerusalem, as we gather from their intimate acquaintance with the city. If they had written in the second century, they could not have possessed this knowledge. Their style shows that they were unlettered men. The vividness of their descriptions proves them to have witnessed the scenes and events they describe. The testimony of the most ancient Christian writers, and the consent of the churches also prove the genuineness of the Gospels. The truthfulness of the Evangelists appears in their quiet and passionless manner of writing; they do not conceal their own faults, and narrate what they knew would expose them to persecution and danger of death; they all draw the selfsame picture of Christ, though writing in different places and to various readers; the apparent discrepancies disprove any sort of conspiracy among them or any copying from one another. Lastly, it would be impossible to invent such a lofty type of character as that of Jesus Christ. The Gospels have not been in any way altered in the course of time. The earliest copies and translations agree with our present Bibles, e.g., the Syrian translation (called the *Peshito*), which dates from the second century, and the Latin (called the *Itala*), which dates from A.D. 370, besides numerous copies of the original text dating from the fourth century onwards. During the first two centuries the Scriptures were read every Sunday in the various Christian churches and were most carefully guarded. We also find a mass of quotations in the early Christian writers, which prove their text to have been identical with our own. The Old

Testament has always been most jealously guarded by the Jews, who in their reverence for it counted the very letters. There is, moreover, no doubt that God watched over the integrity of Holy Scripture, and would no more have allowed the early centuries alone to profit by it, than He would have created the sun for the first generations of men only.

The reading of Holy Scripture is permitted to Catholics, and is very profitable to them; but the text used by them must have been authorized by the Pope, and must be provided with explanatory notes.

In Holy Scripture we learn to know God aright; we see His omnipotence (in creation and all the wonders narrated in the Bible), His wisdom (in guidance of individuals and of the whole human race), His goodness (in the Incarnation and the sufferings of Our Lord). We have in the saints, and above all in Jesus Christ, glorious examples of virtue to incite us to the like. " The Bible," says St. Ephrem, " is like a trumpet that inspires courage into soldiers. It is like a lighthouse, which guides us to a safe haven, as we sail over the perilous sea of life." It also warns us against sin, shows its awful consequences, as in the story of the Fall, of the Flood, of the cities of the plain, of Saul, Absalom, Judas, Herod, etc. It contains all that is profitable to man, and a great deal more than can be found elsewhere. It is like an overflowing well that can never be exhausted. There is always something new to be found in it. But he who desires to understand and profit by it, must have something of the spirit with which the minds of its writers were full; else he will never penetrate beneath the surface, or arrive at its true meaning.

The reason why we are not permitted to read any version of the Bible that we choose is (1), Because the unaltered text and true explanation of it are only to be found in the Catholic Church. (2), Because the greater part of it is very difficult to understand.

It is only to the Catholic Church, i.e., to the apostles and their successors, the bishops, that Our Lord has promised the gift of the Holy Spirit, and that the gates of hell shall not prevail against it. Hence the Holy Scripture, out of which the Catholic Church draws her teaching, cannot possibly be altered or corrupted. Heretics have on the other hand sometimes changed the meaning of particular passages in their own favor, or have omitted whole portions if they did not please them. Thus Luther rejected the epistle of St. James, because the apostle says that faith without works is dead. The difficulty of understanding Holy Scripture is a further reason for the Church's restrictions. How few there are who can honestly say that they thoroughly understand the epistles that are read at Mass—and these are chosen for their simple and practical character. St. Peter himself says (2 Pet. iii. 16) that in the epistles of St. Paul there are some things hard to be understood, and that the unstable would pervert these to their own destruction. St. Augustine says: " There are more things in the Bible which I cannot understand than those I can understand." The prophetical books are specially obscure. Hence the necessity of an authentic exposition of the Bible. Heretics often give half a dozen different meanings to the same passage. The Catholic Church is the authority that God has appointed to explain Holy Scripture; for to her the Holy Spirit has been given. The child brings the nut that has been given it to its mother to be cracked; so the Catholic comes to the Church for the explanation of the Bible. This is why only Bibles with explanatory notes are allowed to Catholics.

2. The truths of divine revelation, which have not been written down in the pages of Holy Scripture, but have been transmitted by word of mouth, are called Tradition.

The apostles received from Our Lord the command to preach, not to write. Their writings are concerned more with the doings than with the teaching of Christ, hence their instructions on points of doctrine are very incomplete. They themselves say that there is much that they have delivered to the faithful by word of mouth (2 John 12; 1 Cor. xi. 2; John xxi. 25). Accordingly we are referred to Tradition. It is by Tradition that we know that Our Lord instituted seven sacraments. It is by Tradition that we are taught that there is a purgatory, that Sunday is to be kept holy, and that infants are to be baptized. It is Tradition which teaches us what books belong to Holy Scripture, etc. Tradition comes down to us from the time of the apostles. Just as those who follow up the course of a stream gradually draw near to the fountain-head, and thus discover how far the water flows, so we can search out the historical sources of the teaching of the earlier centuries of the Church, and arrive at her true doctrine. Every doctrine that has always been believed in by the universal Church, comes down to us from the apostles. If therefore there is any doctrine of the Church that we do not find in Holy Scripture, we shall find it in the stream of Tradition, and shall be able to trace it up to the first ages of Christianity.

The chief sources of Tradition are the writings of the Fathers, the decrees of Councils, and the Creeds and prayers of the Church.

The Fathers of the Church were those who were distinguished in the early ages of the Church by their great learning and holiness. Such are St. Justin, the philosopher and zealous defender of the Christian religion (A.D. 166), St. Irenæus, Bishop of Lyons (A.D. 202), St. Cyprian, Bishop of Carthage, etc. Many of these were disciples of the apostles, and are termed apostolic Fathers, as St. Ignatius, Bishop of Antioch (A.D. 107). The Doctors of the Church were those who in later times were distinguished for their learned writings and their sanctity. There are four great Greek Doctors, Saints Athanasius, Basil, Gregory, and John Chrysostom; and four Latin, Saints Ambrose, Augustine, Jerome, and Pope Gregory, called Gregory the Great. In the Middle Ages there were four other great Doctors of the Church, St. Anselm, Archbishop of Canterbury, St. Bernard, Abbot of Clairvaux, St. Thomas Aquinas, and St. Bonaventure. Among the most distinguished Doctors of later times were St. Francis of

Sales, Bishop of Geneva, and St. Alphonsus Liguori. We shall speak hereafter of the decrees of Councils and of Creeds as the sources of Tradition. The prayers of the Church are to be found primarily in the Missal, but also in other books used in the administration of the sacraments and other rites of the Church. Thus we find in the Missal prayers for the dead, whence it follows that the Church teaches their efficacy.

V. THE CHRISTIAN FAITH.

1. Christian faith is the firm conviction, arrived at with the grace of God, that all that Jesus Christ taught on earth is true, as well as all that the Catholic Church teaches by the commission she has received from Him.

At the Last Supper Our Lord said " This is My body," " This is My blood." Although the apostles had the evidence of their senses that what lay before them was only bread and wine, yet they believed that the words of Christ were true. The holiness of the life of Christ, the numerous miracles that He worked, the predictions of His that were fulfilled, had convinced the apostles that He was the Son of God, and that therefore every word that He spoke was true. God promised Abraham many descendants, and then commanded him to slay his only son. Abraham obeyed, because he knew that God's word must come true (Heb. xi. 19; Rom. iv. 9). This was a splendid example of faith. St. Paul (Heb. xi. 1) calls faith " the evidence of things that do not appear."

Christian faith is at the same time a matter of the understanding and the will.

Before a man believes, he inquires whether what he is asked to believe was really revealed by God. This inquiry is a duty, for God exacts of us a reasonable service (Rom. xii. 1), and warns us that " he who is hasty to believe is light in heart" (Ecclus. xix. 4). But when once a man has arrived at the conviction that the truth which is in question was really revealed by God, then the will must at once submit to what God has laid down, even though the reason cannot fully grasp its meaning. If the will does not submit, faith is impossible. No man can believe unless he wills to believe.

2. Faith is concerned with many things which we cannot perceive with our senses and cannot grasp with our understanding.

Faith is a conviction respecting that which we see not (Heb. xi. 1). We believe in God, though we do not see Him; we believe in angels though we have never seen them. We believe in the resurrection of our bodies, though we do not understand how it can be. So, too, we believe in the mysteries of the Blessed Trinity, of the Incarnation, and of the Blessed Sacrament of the Altar. This is why faith is so pleasing to God. " Blessed are they," says Our Lord to St. Thomas, " who have not seen but have believed " (John xx. 29).

Faith never requires us to believe anything that is contradictory to human reason.

The mysteries of faith are above and beyond our reason, but are never opposed to reason. For God has given us our reason, and it is the same God Who has given us the teaching of Christ and of the Church. He who rejects any doctrine of the Church ultimately finds himself involved in a contradiction. Hence Bacon truly says: "A little philosophy takes a man away from religion, but a sound knowledge of philosophy brings him back to religion."

3. We act quite in accordance with reason when we believe, because we trust ourselves to God's truthfulness, and because we know for certain that the truths of faith are revealed to us by God.

A short-sighted man believes a man with longer sight when he tells him that a balloon is floating in the heavens. A blind man believes one with sound sight when he tells him that the map before him is a map of Europe. We believe in the existence of the cities of Constantinople, Pekin, and Buenos Ayres, though we may never have seen them. In so doing we act reasonably. But how far more reasonably do we act when we believe God! Man may be mistaken, or may be deceiving us, whereas God cannot err and cannot deceive us. It is the truthfulness of God on which we rely when we make an act of faith. We must, however, previously be certain that the doctrine or fact which we are asked to believe is one that has really been revealed by God. God bears witness to Himself as the Author of the truths of faith by many actions that He alone can perform, such as miracles and prophecies. The man of good will can always find a sufficient reason for believing, a man of bad will an excuse for not believing.

We believe the words of Christ, because He is the Son of God, and can neither deceive nor be deceived. Moreover He has established the truth of what He taught by the miracles that He worked.

It would be a blasphemy to suppose that Our Lord, Who is truth itself, could ever have, in one single instance, deceived us. Hence faith gives us a greater certainty than the evidence of our senses. Our senses can deceive us—God cannot deceive us. Christ Himself appeals to the miracles He wrought, when He says, "If any one will not believe Me, let him believe the works" (John x. 38).

We believe the teaching of the Church because Christ guides the Church to all truth through the Holy Spirit, and guards it against all error, and also because God, even up to the present day, has confirmed the truth of the teaching of the Catholic Church by miracles.

Our Lord before His ascension said to His apostles: "Behold I am with you all days even to the end of the world" (Matt. xxviii. 20). And at the Last Supper: "I will ask the Father, and He will give you another Paraclete, that He may remain with you forever, the Spirit of truth" (John xiv. 16). The Holy Spirit is therefore still in the midst of the Church, just as He was on the Day of Pentecost. God moreover still works miracles in the Catholic Church. Witness, e.g., the countless miracles of Lourdes, and those that take place at the well of St. Winifred in Wales; and also those that must precede every beatification. Witness again the numerous bodies of the saints that have remained incorrupt for long years after their death, as those of St. Francis Xavier, St. Teresa, St. Elizabeth of Portugal, St. John of the Cross, and many others. Witness again the head of the Venerable Oliver Plunkett in the Dominican Convent at Drogheda, which not only remains incorrupt, but emits a most delicious fragrance. Most of these bodies were buried in the earth for years, and were found incorrupt when their graves were opened. Witness again the miracle which takes place at Naples every year, when the blood of St. Januarius becomes liquid on being brought near the silver case in which the head of the saint is kept, and again solidifies as soon as it is removed. Faith gives us a more certain knowledge than that which we gain through our senses, or that which we arrive at by our reasoning powers. Our senses can mislead us, God cannot; e.g., a stick, part of which is in the water, looks bent; a sound that strikes against a flat building seems to come from the opposite quarter to that whence it really proceeds. Our intellect, too, can deceive us, weakened as it is by original sin. As we see better with a telescope than with the naked eye when the object is far away, so faith sees further and better than reason. We must not confuse faith with opinion. Faith is certain and sure, opinion is not.

4. The Christian faith comprises all the doctrines of the Catholic faith.

He who wilfully disbelieves a single doctrine of the Catholic Church has no true faith, for he who receives some of the words of Christ and rejects others, does not really believe that Jesus Christ is the Son of God and that He guides the Catholic Church.

A faith which does not comprise all the doctrines of the Catholic Church is no faith at all. It is like a house without a foundation. A man who believes all other Catholic doctrines, but rejects the infallibility of the Pope, has no true faith. What insolence it is on the part of men to treat God like a dishonest dealer, some of whose goods they accept, and others reject ! What utter folly to think that we know better than God ! As a bell in which there is one little crack is worthless, as one false note destroys a harmony, as a grain of sand in the eye prevents one from seeing, so the rejection of a single dogma makes faith impossible. He who wilfully rejects a single dogma sins against the whole body of doctrine of the Catholic Church. Hence no heretic, if he is so through his own fault, can make an act of faith, even in the existence of God or the divinity of Jesus Christ.

Although it is necessary to faith that all the teaching of the Catholic Church should be believed, yet it is not necessary to be acquainted with every one of her doctrines. But a Catholic must at the very least know that there is a God, and that God directs the life of men, rewards the good, and punishes the wicked; he must also know that there are three persons in God, and that the Second Person of the Blessed Trinity has become man, and has redeemed us on the cross.

St. Paul tells us that " He that cometh to God must believe that He is, and that He is the rewarder of them that seek Him " (Heb. xi. 6). This was the minimum required before the coming of Christ, and is now required of those who have never come within reach of the Gospel. In a country where the Gospel is preached the case is quite different, and no one can be admitted to the Sacraments of Baptism or Penance until he has been instructed in the above-mentioned truths.

He who has an opportunity of being instructed must also learn and understand the Apostles' Creed, the commandments of God and of the Church, and also he must have some knowledge of the doctrines of grace, of the sacraments, and of prayer, as set forth in some Catechism authorized by the bishops of the country where he lives.

5. **Faith is a gift of God, since the power to believe can only be attained through the grace of God.**

St. Paul tells us " By grace you are saved through faith, and that not of yourselves. It is the gift of God " (Eph. ii. 8). And Our Lord says, " No man can come to Me, unless it be given to him by My Father " (John vi. 66). God gives us the gift of faith in Baptism; hence Baptism is called " the sacrament of faith." Until the newly baptized child comes to the use of reason, he cannot use this power of believing, or make an act of faith. He is like a child who is asleep, who has the faculty of sight, but cannot use it until he opens his eyes. Then he can see the objects around him under the influence of the light. So the child who attains to reason is able to believe the truths of religion under the influence of the grace of God.

God bestows the knowledge of the truth and the gift of faith chiefly on those who (1), strive after it with earnestness and perseverance; (2), live a God-fearing life; (3), pray that they may find the truth.

An earnest desire after truth is a sure means of attaining to it, for Our Lord has said that " Those who hunger and thirst after justice shall have their fill" (Matt. v. 6). And again God says through the mouth of the prophet, " You shall find Me when you seek Me with your whole heart" (Jer. xxix. 13). The Roman philosopher Justinus was an instance of the fulfilment of this promise, for God rewarded his earnest desire for truth by causing him to fall in with an old man on the banks of the Tiber, who instructed him in the truths of the Christian faith. A life in accordance with the law of God will also obtain the grace of faith. " If any one shall do the will of God, he shall know of the doctrine " (John vii. 17). To such a one God will give an interior light, or will send some one to instruct him, as He did to Cornelius (Acts x. 30 *seq.*). So Cardinal Newman prayed for long years for the " kindly light " which at last brought him to the door of the Catholic Church and the same was the case with countless other converts from Protestantism. Sometimes God in His mercy gives the gift of faith even to the enemies of the Church, as He did to St. Paul, but it is for the most part to those who are in good faith in their errors.

When God bestows upon a man the gift of faith, He either employs one of the ordinary means of grace, such as preaching, or in some cases an extraordinary means, such as a miracle.

' The ordinary means are preaching, reading, and personal instruction. St. Augustine was converted by the preaching of St. Ambrose in the Cathedral of Milan, St. Ignatius of Loyola by reading the lives of the saints, the Ethiopian eunuch by his conversation with St. Philip. Extraordinary means are those of which we find many at the beginning of the Christian era; such as the star that the Magi followed, the light that shone upon St. Paul on his journey to Damascus and the voice that he heard from heaven; the great cross that the Emperor Constantine saw in the sky, with the words " *In hoc signo vinces;*" the vision of Our Lady that Ratisbonne saw in the Church of St. Andrea in Rome in the year 1842. So the heathen boy Theophilus was converted by the roses that fell at his feet in the month of January, after the martyrdom of his playmate Dorothea (A.D. 308).

Many men fail to attain to the Christian faith through pride, self-will, and an unwillingness to give up the indulgence of their passions.

It is the lack of good will that debars many from the faith. Our Lord is the true light that enlighteneth every man that comes into the world (John i. 9). It is the will of God that all men should come to the truth. Men too often shut their eyes to the light, because they are unwilling to change their evil life: " they love darkness rather than light, because their deeds are evil " (John iii. 19). Pride is also a fatal hindrance to faith. God loves to make use of simple means to bring men to the knowledge of the truth, and this the proud resent, just as Naaman resented Eliseus' advice to go and wash in the Jordan. So Christ was rejected and despised by the Jews, and especially by the Scribes and Pharisees, because He was born of poor parents and lived in a town that was held in contempt: " Can any good thing come out of Nazareth? " (John i. 46.) So the upper class at Rome were unwilling to receive the truth from a nation that was despised by them, and from men who were in general very deficient in culture or position. So, too, in the present day God allows His Church to be oppressed and persecuted and looked down upon. Hence there is no miracle at which the proud do not scoff. God hides the secrets of His providence from the proud, and more than this, He positively resists them (1 Pet. v. 5).

6. Faith is necessary to eternal salvation.

Faith is like the root of the tree, without which it cannot exist; it is the first step on the road to heaven; it is the key which opens

the treasure-house of all the virtues. How happy is the wanderer
when he lights on the road which will carry him to his journey's end;
how far happier is he who has been wandering in the search after
truth when he attains to a belief in the Catholic Church; he has
found the road to eternal life. The saints always set the greatest
store on the possession of the faith. " I thank God unceasingly," said
the good King Alphonsus of Castile, "not that I am a king,
but that I am a Catholic." Without faith there is no salvation.
Our Lord says "He that believeth not shall be condemned " (Mark
xvi. 16). St. Paul says that "Without faith it is impossible to
please God" (Heb. xi. 6). Faith is like a boat; as without a boat
you cannot cross the sea, so without faith you cannot arrive at the
port of eternal salvation. It is like the pillar of the cloud which led
the Israelites across the desert, or like the star that guided the Wise
Men to Christ. Without faith we can do no good works pleasing to
God, or which will merit for us a reward in heaven. Acts of kindness, etc., done from a natural motive earn a reward in this life, but
not in the next. They are like a building which has no foundation. Just as from the root placed in the ground arises the beautiful plant, with its leaves and flowers, so from the root of faith arises
good works. Faith in God gives rise to a love of Him, and confidence
in Him, and this enables us to labor and suffer for Him. Faith in
our eternal reward encourages us in our toilsome journey through
life. It gave Job his patience, Tobias his generosity to the poor, and
the martyrs their constancy. Faith provides us with the means of
resisting temptation; it is the lighthouse which enables the mariner
to avoid the hidden rocks and quicksands. It is the shield that
enables us to extinguish all the fiery darts of the wicked one (Eph.
vi. 16). On the amount of our faith depends the amount that we
possess of the other virtues, and the amount of grace that we receive
from God.

7. Faith alone is not sufficient for salvation.

It must be a living faith; that is, we must add to it good
works and must be ready to confess it openly.

A living faith is one which produces works pleasing to God.
Our Lord says "Not every one who saith to Me, Lord, Lord, shall
enter into the kingdom of heaven, but he that doth the will of My
Father Who is in heaven " (Matt. vii. 21). He who has done no works
of mercy will be condemned at the judgment (Matt. xxv. 41). Such a
one is like the devils, who believe and disobey (Jas. ii. 19). "As the
body without the spirit is dead, so faith without works is dead also "
(Jas. ii. 26). Faith without works is like a tree without fruit, or like
a lamp without oil. The foolish virgins had faith, but no works.
Good works, such as are necessary for salvation, can only be performed by one who is in possession of sanctifying grace, and loves
God in his heart. Hence St. Paul says, "If I should have all faith,
so that I could remove mountains and have not charity, I am nothing " (1 Cor. xiii. 2). We must also be ready to confess our faith.
"With the heart we believe unto justice; and with the mouth confession is made unto salvation " (Rom. x. 10). Man consists of
body and soul, and therefore must honor God, not only inwardly, but

also outwardly. Christ promises the kingdom of heaven only to those who confess Him before men (Matt. x. 32).

VI. THE MOTIVES OF FAITH.

1. The external motives which move us to believe are chiefly miracles and prophecy.

It is through these that we attain to a certain knowledge that this or that truth of faith is really from God.

The veracity of God is of course the ultimate motive of faith, for we make an act of faith in the truths revealed by God, because we know that God is true and cannot deceive or be deceived. But no reasonable man can make an act of faith in any truth, until he is quite sure that it is one of the truths revealed by God. For this reason the external evidences through which God establishes the fact that He has really spoken are for men a most important and necessary motive of faith. It was in great measure because the apostles had seen the countless miracles worked by Christ, and had seen the prophecies of the Jewish prophets fulfilled in Him, that they believed Him without doubting when He said, "This is My body, this is My blood." The miracle of the gift of tongues at Pentecost moved three thousand men to believe in Christianity; that of the healing of the lame man at the Beautiful Gate of the Temple moved two thousand more; the wonders wrought by the apostles induced the heathen to accept the Christian faith. How many were led to believe or confirmed in the faith by the fulfilment, in the year A.D. 70, of Our Lord's prophecy respecting the destruction of Jerusalem, and again by the failure of the attempts to rebuild the Temple in A.D. 361! Besides miracles and prophecy there are also other motives of faith, such as the constancy of the martyrs, the wonderful spread of Christianity, and its still more wonderful permanency in the face of all the persecution and opposition that the Church has had to endure, the four attributes of the Church, etc.

The greater number of miracles were performed in the early days of the Church, because they were the means God employed for the spread of Christianity.

God is like a gardener who waters his plants while they are still tender and small.

2. Miracles are such extraordinary works as cannot be performed by the mere powers of nature, but are brought about by the intervention of a higher power.

An extraordinary work is one that fills us with astonishment, because we have never seen or heard of anything like it and are unable to find any natural explanation of it: e.g., the telegraph and the phonograph were extraordinary wonders at the time of their first invention. But their unwonted character is not sufficient to constitute these things as miracles; a miracle must also surpass all the forces of nature. Thus the raising of the dead to life is not only an extraordinary fact, but it is one that no amount of skill or knowledge will enable a man to perform. Miracles are thus exceptions to the ordinary course of nature; they appear to transgress the laws of nature, but they do not really do so. The laws of nature still hold good, but they are suspended in their action by an intervening power.

There are true and false miracles.

The former are worked by the power of almighty God, the latter appear to surpass the powers of nature, but are really the effect of the employment of the powers of nature by evil spirits, who by reason of their greater knowledge and power are able to produce results that deceive and mislead us. Miracles are divided into miracles of the first class and miracles of the second class. The former are those which altogether surpass all the powers of nature, as the raising of the dead to life. Miracles of the second class are extraordinary actions which might have been performed by the powers of nature, but not in the same way or in the same space of time, as the healing of a sick man by a word, or the sudden acquisition of the knowledge of a foreign language.

3. Miracles are wrought by almighty God only for His own glory, and especially for the confirmation of true doctrine.

Sometimes it is to show that a man is a true messenger sent by God; sometimes to bear witness to the holiness of one who is dead, or to his virtue or justice. God never works a miracle in confirmation of false doctrine.

All important documents must bear the stamp or signature of the person sending them out, as a mark of their being genuine. God also has His stamp, by which He certifies that some doctrine is from Him, or that some messenger is sent by Him. This stamp consists in miracles. It is one that cannot be counterfeited. Our Lord Himself appeals to His miracles as a proof of His divine mission (Matt. xi. 4, 5; John x. 37). Elias did the same (3 Kings xviii.). Miracles still continue to be worked in the Catholic Church in proof of the truth of her teaching. God also works miracles in proof of the holiness of the dead, often at their graves, as at that of Eliseus (4 Kings xiii. 21), or for those who invoke them. Two miracles must be attested as having been worked by the intercession of a servant of God, before he is beatified, and others before he is canonized. Under the Jewish covenant the saints worked miracles chiefly during their life; under the Christian covenant they work the greater number after their death. God also works miracles to manifest His goodness and His justice, as when the water flowed in the desert to supply the thirsting Israelites, and when Ananias and Saphira were struck dead. God never works miracles in proof of false doctrine, though He sometimes permits wicked men to be deceived by the false miracles worked by the devil. Thus the devil sometimes heals the sick rapidly or suddenly through his superior knowledge of the powers of nature.

4. In working miracles God usually makes use of the intervention of man, sometimes even of wicked men.

Those whom God has created can only work miracles when God gives them the power. The saints always worked miracles in the name of God, or of Our Lord. Our Lord alone could work miracles in His own name. Bad men are sometimes employed by God as the instruments of the miracles by which He establishes the truth (Matt. vii. 22, 23). We must not be too ready to have recourse to the hypothesis of a miracle, if the fact supposed to be miraculous can be accounted for in any other way.

5. Prophesies are clear and definite predictions of future events that can be known to God alone.

Prophecy also includes a prediction of future events, which depend on the free will of man, for such events can only be foreseen by God Himself. The most thorough knowledge of material causes avails nothing. They are often just the opposite of what our previous knowledge would have led us to expect, e.g., the denial of Our Lord by St. Peter (Cf. Mark xiv. 31), which Our Lord predicted. Prophecies may be called miracles of the omniscience of God, as distinguished from the miracles of His omnipotence, for prophecy requires an acquaintance with the heart of man such as God alone possesses (Is. xli. 23). The oracles of the heathen correspond to the false miracles of which we have already spoken. They were mostly obscure and sometimes ambiguous, as when the oracle at Delphi told Crœsus that if he crossed the river Halys with his army he would destroy a mighty kingdom, but did not say whether that kingdom was to be his own or that of his enemies. Many predictions were given by the oracles and the heathen soothsayers which were not true prophecies, but were guesses made from a knowledge of the laws of nature and from the laws that regulate the general course of human development. The evil spirits, through their superior knowledge, were often able to foretell events that men could not foresee, such as the approach of a storm or pestilence, or the death of some individual.

6. God for the most part intrusts the prophesying of future events to His messengers, for the confirmation of the true faith or for the benefit of men.

Thus God intrusted the prophets of the Jewish covenant with the prophecy of a Redeemer to come, in order to confirm the belief in Him, to convince those to whom He came that He was the true Messias and those who have lived since His coming of the truth of the Christian religion. He sent Noe to prophesy the Flood, in order to lead men to do penance. Sometimes He revealed the future to wicked men, as when to Baltassar He foretold his coming destruction by the handwriting on the wall. Sometimes He employed wicked men as the instruments through which He foretold the future, as e.g., Balaam (Numb. xxiv. 1 *seq.*), and Caiphas, as being the high priest of the year (John xi. 49). But in general He only employed as instruments of prophecy His own faithful servants, revealing the future event either through a vision, or by an angel, or through some interior illumination. Thus the archangel Gabriel was sent to instruct Daniel during the Babylonian captivity respecting the time of the coming of the Messias. The prophecies of the Apocalypse were mostly put before St. John in the form of a vision. Such communications were given to the prophets only from time to time. None of them had a permanent knowledge of future events. Thus Samuel did not know who was to be the future king of Israel till David was actually presented to him (1 Kings xvi. 6-12).

The gift of prophecy is therefore, generally speaking, a proof that he who possesses it is a messenger from God.

The fulfilment of the prophecy is, of course, necessary before we recognize it as a proof that he who utters it is a messenger from God. It must not contradict any revealed doctrine, or be inconsistent with the holiness of God. It must be edifying and profitable to men (1 Cor. xiv. 3). It must be uttered with prudence and calmness, for it is a mark of false prophets to show no control of self.

VII. ON THE ABSENCE AND LOSS OF FAITH.

Faith is the road to heaven. Unhappily there are very many who are wanderers and strangers to the Christian faith.

1. Those who do not possess Christian faith are either: (1) heretics or (2) infidels.

1. Heretics are those who reject some one or more of the truths revealed by God.

Heretics are those who hold to some of the doctrines revealed by God, and reject others. Those who induce others to a false belief are called leaders of heresy, or arch-heretics. It is always pride that leads them away from the truth. Among these arch-heretics was Arius, a priest of Alexandria, who denied the divinity of Christ, and was condemned at the Council of Nicæa in A.D. 325; Macedonius, who denied the divinity of the Holy Ghost, and was condemned in the Council of Constantinople A.D. 381; Martin Luther, who assailed the divine institution of the Papacy and the right of the Church to teach; Henry VIII., King of England, who threw off the authority of the Pope and proclaimed himself the Head of the Church in England, because the Pope refused to declare invalid his valid marriage with Queen Catherine; Döllinger, who was a professor in the University of Munich, and was celebrated for his literary labors, but on the definition of the infallibility of the Pope refused to accept the dogma, and was excommunicated. He died in 1890 without being reconciled or giving any sign of repentance. Döllinger was the chief mover in the establishment of the sect of "Old Catholics." Most of the founders of heresy were either bishops or priests. They are like the coiners of false money who put into circulation worthless metal in the place of the pure gold of truth. Or like dishonest traders, who mix the pure wine of the Gospel with some injurious compound. They are murderers of souls, for they take men away from the road that leads to eternal life, and tempt them into that which leads to eternal death. It is of them that Our Lord says "Woe to them by whom scandals come," and again, "Beware of false prophets, who come to you in the clothing of sheep, but inwardly they are ravening wolves" (Matt. vii. 5). Their object is not to spread the faith in its purity, but to satisfy their own evil inclinations, their pride, their sensual desires, or their love of money. Their religious teaching is only a cloak for these. They look out for the weak side of human nature, as Satan does. Thus Luther tempted princes with the spoil of churches and monasteries, and priests with the bait of marriage. To the class of heretics belong also those schismatics who accept, or profess to accept, all Catholic doctrine, but will not acknowledge the supremacy of the Holy See. Thus the Greek Church is a schismatical Church, though its denial of Papal infallibility constitutes it, since the Vatican Council, heretical also. Heresy is one of the greatest of all sins, when it is not the result of invincible ignorance. St. Paul writes to the Galatians that if an angel from heaven preached to them any Gospel different from that they had received, he was to be anathema or accursed (Gal. i. 8). St. Jerome says that there is no one so far removed from God as a wilful heretic.

At the same time, he who lives in heresy through ignorance for which he is not himself to blame, is not a heretic in the sight of God.

Thus those who are brought up in Protestantism, and have no opportunity of obtaining a sufficient instruction in the Catholic religion, are not heretics in the sight of God, for in them there is no obstinate denial or doubt of the truth. They are no more heretics than the man who takes the property of another unwittingly is a thief.

2. Rationalists or unbelievers are those who will not believe anything unless they can either perceive it with their senses, or comprehend it with their understanding.

Thus St. Thomas was an unbeliever when he refused to believe in the resurrection of Jesus Christ, unless he should put his finger into the sacred wounds of Our Lord's hands and feet, and put his hand into His side (John xx. 24). There are many in the present day like St. Thomas; they will believe nothing except what they can see with their eyes, or grasp with their reason; all else, e.g., all the mysteries of the faith, they reject. "Unbelief," says St. John Chrysostom, "is like a sandy soil, that produces no fruit however much rain falls upon it." The unbeliever does God the same injustice that a subject would do to his king, if he refused to acknowledge his authority in spite of the clearest proofs of it.

Unbelief springs for the most part from a bad life.

The sun is clearly reflected in pure and clear water, but not in dirty water. So it is with men; a man of blameless life easily finds his way to the truth, but the sensual man does not perceive the things that are of the Spirit of God (1 Cor. ii. 14). A mirror that is dim reflects badly, or not at all. So the soul, which is a mirror on which the light falls from God, cannot receive the truths of faith if it is dimmed by vice.

2. Faith is for the most part lost either: (1), By indifference to the doctrines of faith; (2), By wilful doubt respecting the truths of faith; (3), By reading books or other literature that is hostile to the faith; (4), By frequenting the assemblies of those who are hostile to the faith; (5), By neglecting the practice of one's religion.

He who through culpable indifference does not trouble himself about the doctrines of faith, gradually loses the gift of faith. He is like the plant that is not watered, or the lamp that is not filled with oil. Such men know that they are very ignorant of their religion, and yet they take no pains to get instructed; they are engrossed with this world; they never pray or hear a sermon, and if they are parents, they take no pains to get their children properly instructed. Perhaps they fancy themselves men of enlightenment, and look with pitying contempt on those who are conscientious and earnest in the practice of their religion. The body must be nourished, else it will perish from hunger; the soul must be nourished, else it, too, will perish. Its nourishment is the teaching of Christ. He Himself says, in His conversation with the woman of Samaria, that the water that He would give her, i.e., His divine doctrine, should be to her a well of water, springing up unto life everlasting (John iv. 14). And in the synagogue of Capharnaum "I am the Bread of life; he that cometh to Me shall not hunger, and he that believeth on Me shall never thirst" (John vi. 35). This is why the careful instruction of children and of converts is so all-important. When converts fall away, the cause very often is that they have not been well instructed before their reception into the Church. The Catholic must not suppose that he is freed from the study of the doctrines of faith, because he has been duly instructed in his youth. The plant must be watered even when it is grown up; the soul of the adult needs to renew its acquaintance with the truths of faith by hearing sermons, reading pious books, etc., else it will soon lose the vigor of its faith. He who allows himself wilfully to doubt of any of the doctrines of the Church, commits a serious sin against faith, and is sure, little by little, to lose his faith altogether. That house is sure to fall of which the foundations are loosened. He who doubts any revealed truth seriously offends God. Sara doubted God's promise that she should bear a son in her old age and was reproved by God for her incredulity (Gen. xviii. 10 *seq.*). Zacharias doubted the announcement of the angel that John Baptist should be born to him, and as a punishment lost for a time the power of speech (Luke i. 18 *seq.*). Yet doubts that come into our mind involve no sin, if we do not wilfully consent to them. If doubts come into our mind we should not argue with them, but should make an act of faith and pray for more faith. Those however, who are outside the Church, and have not the faith, are bound, if they doubt, to search and inquire, until they have found the truth; with them doubt is no sin, so long as their search after truth is made in a spirit of humility, and with a sincere desire to arrive at truth. Faith is also destroyed by the reading of books hostile to the faith. In this way John Huss, who disseminated false doctrine over Bohemia, is said to have been corrupted by the works of the English heretic, Wyclif. It was the writings of Luther that chiefly contributed to the apostasy of Calvin and Zwingli. Julian the Apostate (A.D. 363) is said to have lost his faith by reading the writings of the heretic Libanius during his expedition to Nicomedia. In the present day the books against the faith are countless. Among the most mischievous are the works of Rousseau, Voltaire, Zola, Renan, Gibbon, Ingersoll, Huxley, etc. The Church, like a good mother, seeing how books dangerous to faith were on the increase, established in 1571 the Congregation of the Index, through which the Apostolic See forbids to Catholics a number of books, which are judged to be a source of danger to faith or morals. Any one who reads such books, prints them, or even has them in his possession without permission from his ecclesiastical superiors incurs the penalty of excommunication reserved to the Pope. The penalty, however, is not incurred by any one who reads such a book without knowing that it was forbidden. At one time all books had to be sanctioned by the bishop of the diocese, but this was afterwards limited to books touching on religion. By these means the Church sought to preserve the purity of Christian doctrine. Many, too, have lost their faith by habitually reading newspapers hostile to the faith. As the body cannot remain in health if it is fed with unwholesome food, so the mind becomes diseased and corrupt if a man feeds it with unwholesome and pernicious literature. The process may be a slow one, but it is like the solid rock which wears away little by little as the drops of water fall upon it. Bad reading is like unwholesome food, which ere long induces sickness and even death. Among the enemies of faith are the Freemasons. In Protestant countries they seem harmless enough, and many converts who have belonged to the Masonic order have borne witness that they have never encountered anything in it which was opposed either to throne or altar, but the real object aimed at by the leaders of Freemasonry is to destroy all authority that comes from God, and all revealed religion. Their secret oath of obedience, taken as it is without any reserve, is absolutely unlawful, and the symbolism of many of its lodges is grossly blasphemous and insulting to Christianity. The idea of Freemasonry is taken from the Masonic guilds of the Middle Ages, the members of which employed themselves in the construction of cathedrals and churches. It professes to have for its object the construction of a spiritual temple to humanity and enlightenment, but Freemasons are invariably the bitter foes of Christianity and of the Catholic Church. Every one joining them is *ipso facto excommunicate*, and the Pope alone can restore him to the membership of the Church, except at the hour of death, when any priest has power to do so.

3. All men who through their own fault die without Christian faith are, by the just judgment of God, sentenced to eternal perdition.

Unhappy indeed are those who have not faith; " they sit in darkness and in the shadow of death " (Luke i. 79). Our Lord says, " He who believeth not shall be condemned " (Mark xvi. 16), and again " He who believeth not is condemned already " (John iii. 18). Of

heretics St. Paul says that they are condemned by their own judgment (Tit. iii. 11). We ought to pray often for heretics and unbelievers, that God may in His mercy bring them to the true faith.

VIII. ON THE DUTY OF CONFESSING OUR FAITH.

**1. God requires of us that we should make outward profession
of our faith.**

Christ says, " So let your light shine before men, that they
may see your good works, and glorify your Father Who is in
heaven " (Matt. v. 16).

We are bound in our words and actions to let men know that we
are Christians and Catholics. It is by the open profession of our faith
that we help others (as we see from the above words of Our Lord), to
know God better and to honor Him more. We also thereby lead them
to imitate our good deeds; for men are like sheep, which though lazy
in themselves and unwilling to move, will follow where one of them
leads the way. The open profession of our faith also strengthens us
in all that is good, for " practice makes perfect." Unhappily men are
too often cowards. For fear of being laughed at by those around
them, or through the dread of suffering some injury in their business,
or some disadvantage in their worldly affairs or interests, they have
not the courage openly to profess their faith, or to defend their religion when it is attacked; they laugh at indecent or profane stories,
join in immodest conversation, or in talk against the Church, priests,
and religious, eat meat on Friday in order to escape the jests of
their companions, and miss Mass on Sunday without excuse. They
forget that those who laugh them out of doing what is right only
despise them in their hearts, and would respect and honor them if
they stood firm. They forget, too, that at the Day of Judgment the
tables will be turned, and that those who now mock at them will be
full of terror and of shame, and those who have been loyal to their
religion will be the objects of the envy and admiration of their persecutors, who will bitterly lament their folly and wickedness (Wisd. i.
1-5). Among the splendid instances of those who were faithful to
their religion and fearlessly made confession of their faith, were the
three young men who refused to adore the golden image set up by
Nabuchodonosor (Dan. ii.); the holy Tobias, who alone of all his kindred refused to go to the golden calves at Dan and Bethel, and
went up every year to the Temple in Jerusalem (Tob. i. 5, 6); Eleazar,
who preferred death to even appearing to eat swine's flesh (2 Mach.
vi. 18 *seq.*); St. Ignatius the martyr, St. Agnes, St. Lucy, St. Maurice and the Theban legion, and countless other Christian martyrs and
confessors. It is by way of an open profession of her faith that holy
Church has instituted processions like those of Corpus Christi, processions of Our Lady, etc.

We are only bound openly to confess our faith when our
omission to do so would bring religion into contempt, or do some
injury to our neighbor, or when we are in some way challenged
to declare and make profession of our religion.

We are not bound always and on all occasions to confess our faith, but only when the honor due to God, or the edification due to our neighbor requires it. If officious people question us about our faith, we are not bound to answer them; we can refuse to answer, or turn away. But if we are questioned by some one who possesses legitimate authority to do so, we are bound to confess our faith, even though it should cost us our lives, as Our Lord did when questioned before Caiphas, and as thousands of the early Christians did when called upon to sacrifice to the idols. In such cases the words of Our Lord apply, " Fear not them that kill the body, and are not able to kill the soul" (Matt. x. 28). To fear man more than God is to bring down on us His anger. We also should try and avoid all wrangling discussions and controversies about religion, which generally do harm and embitter men against the truth. Our faith is so holy a thing that it must be spoken of with great discretion and prudence.

2. Our Lord has promised eternal life to him who fearlessly makes profession of his faith.

For He has said " Every one that confesseth Me before men, him I will also confess before My Father Who is in heaven " (Matt. x. 32).

St. Peter made a bold profession of his faith before his fellow apostles, and Our Lord made him at once the head of the apostles, and the foundation of His Church (Matt. xvi. 18). The three young men in Babylon confessed their belief in the true God, and God delivered them from the fiery furnace, and caused them to be raised to high honor. Daniel confessed his faith by disobeying the king's edict and continuing his prayers in the sight of all men, and God saved him from the lions.

A great reward in heaven will be given to those who suffer persecution or death for the sake of their religion.

" Blessed are they," says Our Lord, " that suffer persecution for justice' sake; for theirs is the kingdom of heaven. Blessed are ye, when men shall revile you and persecute you, and shall say all manner of evil against you untruly, for My sake. Be glad and rejoice, for your reward is very great in heaven " (Matt. v. 11-13). Those who suffer great persecutions for the sake of their faith are called confessors; those who are put to death for their faith are called martyrs. A martyr goes straight to heaven at his death, without passing through purgatory. " We should be doing injustice to a martyr," says Pope Innocent III., " if we were to pray for him." A martyr possesses the love of God in the highest degree, since he despises life, the greatest of all earthly goods, for God's sake. Every martyr is a conqueror, and is therefore depicted with a palm in his hand, since the palm is the mark of victory. Yet no one is bound purposely to seek after persecution or a martyr's death. Any one who does so without an express inspiration from almighty God, is almost sure to yield to the persecutors. Nor is it forbidden to flee from persecution. " When they shall persecute you in one city," says Our Lord (Matt. x. 23), " flee into another." Our Lord Himself fled before persecution (John

xi. 53-54). So did the apostles and many of the saints, e.g., St.
Cyprian and St. Athanasius. Yet the pastors of souls must not fly
when the good of the faithful requires their presence. " The hireling fleeth, because he is a hireling," says Our Lord, " and careth not
for the sheep " (John x. 13). Yet they may fly if their presence is
not required, or if it seems likely to give rise to fresh persecutions.
The heretic who dies for his heresy is no true martyr, for St. Paul
tells us that if we give our body to be burned, and have not charity,
it profits us nothing (1 Cor. xiii. 3). John Huss, who was burned at
Prague in 1415, rather than give up his heresy, was no martyr, nor
were Cranmer, Ridley, nor Latimer, who were burned at Oxford in
the reign of Queen Mary. A man is a true martyr who receives a
grievous wound for the sake of the faith and afterwards dies from the
effects of it. So, too, are those who suffer imprisonment for life for
their faith, or who die in defence of some Christian virtue or some
law of the Church. Thus St. John Nepomucene, who was put to
death because he would not violate the seal of confession, and St.
John the Baptist, whose death was the result of his defence of the
law of purity, were true martyrs. The whole number of the martyrs
has been estimated at sixteen millions.

The man who denies his religion through fear or shame,
or apostatizes from the faith, is under sentence of eternal damnation, for Christ says, " He that shall deny Me before men,
him I will also deny before My Father Who is in heaven" (Matt.
x. 33), and again, " He that shall be ashamed of Me and of My
word, of him the Son of man shall be ashamed, when He cometh
in His majesty and that of His Father and the holy angels "
(Luke ix. 26).

He who denies the faith denies Christ Himself. In the times of
persecution there were many who denied their faith. Even now there
are some who, through fear of worldly loss or of being dismissed
from their employment, deny their religion. Others from the same
motives, though they do not explicitly deny that they are Catholics,
yet do so implicitly by attending and taking part in the services of a
false religion, or by being married in a Protestant church, or by a
merely civil marriage, or by taking Protestants for the godfathers or
godmothers of their children, or by allowing their children to be
brought up in a false religion. (But there is no sin in attending a
Protestant funeral or marriage out of courtesy, so long as no part is
taken in the service.) Others again, though they do not deny their
religion, are ashamed of it, because in many countries it is the
religion of the poor, or because Catholics are not allowed to believe
what they like. Those who deny or conceal their religion out of
human respect are only despised by non-Catholics. The Emperor
Constantius, father of Constantine the Great, once ordered all those
of his servants whom he knew were Christians to sacrifice to the
false gods. Those who obeyed he dismissed from his service, those
who refused he promoted to the places of those he sent away. He
who apostatizes from the faith is even worse than he who denies it
from worldly motives. Solomon, whom God had filled with divine

wisdom, in his old age was persuaded by his heathen wives to apostatize from the true religion and to worship their false gods. The Emperor Julian the Apostate fell away from the Christian religion and became a cruel persecutor. In the present day it too often happens that Catholics give up their faith through motives of worldly interest, or because they want to marry a Protestant, or sometimes because they quarrel with the priest. A vicious and sinful life often prepares the way for an apostasy. No good man, from the time of Our Lord till now, has ever fallen away from the Catholic faith. The tree must be rotten within before it is blown down by the wind; the wind does not scatter the grains of corn, but the empty husks. He who apostatizes crucifies the Son of God afresh. He commits a sin almost unpardonable; he ceases to belong to the Church, and can no longer call God his Father, for as St. Cyprian says, " He cannot have God for his Father who has not the Church as his Mother." The Catholic must therefore keep far away from all occasions which could endanger his faith, for " he who loses his goods loses much; he who loses his life loses more; but he who loses his faith loses all."

IX. THE SIGN OF THE CROSS.

The Catholic makes confession of his faith most especially by the sign of the holy cross.

By it he lets men know that he makes profession of belonging to the religion of the crucified Saviour. To Jews and Turks the cross is an object of hatred and contempt; Protestants, too, pay no honor to the holy cross, though there are indeed some of them who, in the present day, have learned the practice from the children of the Church. The sign of the cross is thus the peculiar property of Catholics all the world over. It is a custom so ancient that it is generally believed to have been introduced by the apostles. The sign of the cross is made by touching with the outstretched fingers of the right hand first the forehead, then the centre of the breast, then the left, and finally the right shoulder, saying meanwhile the words, " In the name of the Father [touch forehead], and of the Son [touch breast], and of the Holy Ghost [touch left shoulder], Amen [touch right shoulder]." There is also another way of making the sign of the cross, by making three crosses with the thumb of the right hand on the forehead, lips, and breast successively, repeating the above words, so that each of the three crosses is made simultaneously with the name of one of the three persons of the Blessed Trinity. In making the sign of the cross the left hand should be laid across the breast, and the sign should be made deliberately—not hurriedly, as is too often done

1. In making the sign of the cross we make profession of the most important of all the mysteries of our holy religion, *viz.*, the doctrine of the Blessed Trinity and of the Incarnation of Our Lord Jesus Christ.

By uniting all the three persons, Father, Son, and Holy

Ghost, under one name, we make profession of our belief in the unity of God.

The " name " of God indicates His authority and power, and that we act under His commission (Mark xvi. 17; Acts iii. 16, 17; iv. 10).

In making the sign of the cross, we make profession of our belief in the Blessed Trinity by the words " In the name of the Father, and of the Son and of the Holy Ghost."

In making the sign of the cross, by the very form of the cross which we make upon ourselves, we make profession that the Son of God died for us upon the cross.

Thus we see that in the sign of the cross we have a short summary of the whole Catholic faith. The Catholic Church holds the sign of the cross in great honor. It is repeated over and over again in holy Mass, in all the sacraments, in all blessings and consecrations; the cross is placed on our churches, over our altars, on banners, on sacred vestments, and over the graves of the departed. Churches are built in the form of a cross.

2. By means of the sign of the cross we obtain a blessing from God; and especially by it are we protected from the assaults of the devil and from all dangers both to body and to soul.

The sign of the cross is no empty ceremony, but it is of itself a blessing, and a prayer for a blessing from God. The sign of the cross chases away the devil and his temptations; as the dog fears the whip with which he has been beaten, so the evil one dreads the sign of the cross, for it reminds him of the holy cross by which he was vanquished on Calvary. There was once a stag which bore between its antlers a tablet on which were written in golden letters the words, " I belong to the emperor, hurt me not." No huntsman ventured to shoot this stag. So whenever we make the sign of the cross, we bear the inscription, " I belong to Jesus Christ," and this protects us from our enemy, the devil. In war no one ventures to injure those who wear on their arm a band of white to indicate that they are physicians, or nurses, or ministers of religion; so the devil does not dare attack those who are signed with the holy sign of the cross. " The sign of the cross," says St. John Damascene, " is a seal, at the sight of which the destroying angel passes on, and does us no harm." The brazen serpent fastened on a pole in the desert was an image of the cross of Christ (Numb. xxi.; John iii. 14), and protected all who looked upon it from being bitten by the fiery serpents; so the sign of the cross recalls to our minds the cross of Christ, and protects us from the snares of that old serpent, the devil. In the year 312, Constantine the Great, with his whole army, saw a cross of light in the sky, and upon it the words: " In this sign thou shalt conquer." These words are also true of the sign of the cross. " Even to remember the cross of Christ," says St. Augustine, " puts our hellish foe to flight, and give us strength to resist his temptations." Many of the saints used to make the sign of the cross whenever any evil thoughts assailed them. In the times of persecution the heathen gods often fell prostrate to the ground at the sign of the cross. On the occasion of the finding of the holy cross by St. Helena, a woman who was blind was restored to sight by merely touching it. The sign of the cross often frees men from bodily evils also. Many of the holy martyrs, on making the sign of the cross, felt no more pain in their torments. St. John the Divine once had a cup with a poisoned draught put into his hand to drink. He made the sign of the cross over it, and then drank it without receiving any harm from it. Something similar happened also to St. Benedict. In the Old Testament we find an allusion to the sign of the cross in the letter *Thau*, mentioned by the prophet Ezechiel. God sent destruction upon the inhabitants of Jerusalem on account of the abominations committed there; but an angel was previously commanded to mark the sign *Thau* upon the foreheads of all those who mourned and lamented on account of the sins of the city (Ezech. ix. 4-6).

We should often make the sign of the cross, especially when we rise in the morning and when we retire to rest, before and after our prayers, before and after our meals, whenever we are tempted to sin, and when we have any important duty to perform.

We should make the sign of the cross in the morning in order to obtain the blessing of God on the day; in the evening to ask for His protection during the night; before all important undertakings, that they may turn out well; before our prayers, in order that we may not be distracted in saying them, etc. The early Christians made continual use of the sign of the cross. Tertullian (A.D. 240) says, " At the beginning and during the performance of all that we do, when we go in and out of the house, when we dress ourselves, when we lie down to rest, in fact in everything, we mark ourselves on the forehead with the sign of the cross." The sign of the cross should also be made during holy Mass; at the beginning, at the absolution which the priest gives at the foot of the altar, at the Gospel, at the Consecration, and at the priest's blessing at the end of Mass. St. Edith, the daughter of the King of England, often made the sign of the cross with her thumb upon her forehead; thirteen years after her death her thumb remained quite incorrupt. Each time we make the sign of the cross with contrite hearts, we gain an indulgence of fifty days (Pius IX., July 28, 1863).

When we make the sign of the cross, we should, if possible, make it with holy water.

Holy water has a special power to defend us against all attacks of the devil: When we make the sign of the cross with holy water, we gain each time an indulgence of one hundred days (Pius IX., March 23, 1876). Holy water is placed at the doors of our churches, and should be placed at the door of our rooms. We must never be ashamed of the sign of the cross, lest Christ be ashamed of us. The devil rejoices when he sees any one neglect to make the sign of the cross, for he knows that the cross is his destruction and a sign of victory over his temptations.

X. THE APOSTLES' CREED.

Besides the Apostles' Creed, which is repeated at Baptism, there is also the Nicene Creed (composed at the Council of Nicæa, 325), and enlarged at the Council of Constantinople. Also the Creed of Pope Pius IV., which contains the teaching of the Council of Trent, and was published by the authority of Pope Pius IV. in 1564. Some additions have been made to it by the Vatican Council (1870). The Nicene Creed is repeated on certain days by the priest in holy Mass, and the Creed of Pope Pius IV. has to be repeated by a convert when he is received into the Church, and also by parish priests when they enter on their benefices.

1. The Apostles' Creed contains in brief all that a Catholic must know and believe.

In its few words are contained all the mysteries of the faith. It is like the body of a child which contains the limbs of a full-grown man, or like a seed that contains the tree with all its branches. It is called in Latin the *symbolum*, or distinguishing mark, because in early days the recital of it was the mark by which a man was recognized as a Christian. No one was admitted to be present at holy Mass unless he knew it by heart. It could not be divulged to any unbaptized person. It is called the *symbolum*, as being the watchword of the Christian warfare.

The Apostles' Creed is so called because it originated with the apostles.

The holy apostles, before they separated from one another, established a certain and fixed rule of their teaching, so that it might be the same in all the different countries where they preached. Yet it is only the outlines of the Apostles' Creed that date from the apostles themselves. Between their time and the year 600 a number of new clauses were added, in order to meet various heresies. Thus the words " Creator of heaven and earth " were added to meet the Manichean doctrine that the world was created by the principle of evil; the word Catholic was added to distinguish the Church from the sects around her, etc. The influence of St. Peter in drawing up the Creed appears from the fact that the principles which are developed in his speeches as recorded in the Acts of the Apostles, are those which are found in the Creed. It was required before Baptism as an evidence of fitness for the reception of that sacrament.

2. The Apostles' Creed may be divided into three several parts.

The first part treats of God the Father and of creation.

The second part treats of God the Son and of our redemption.

The third part treats of God the Holy Ghost and of our sanctification.

3. The Apostles' Creed may also be divided into twelve articles.

An article is a member belonging to the whole, as a limb belongs to the whole body. The articles of the Creed are so called because of their inseparable connection with one another. As you cannot take away one of the links of a chain without the chain being broken, so you cannot take away one of the articles of the Creed without faith being destroyed. There are various images in the Old Testament of the twelve articles of the Creed, e.g., the twelve precious stones on the breastplate of the high priest (Exod. xxviii. 17-21), and the twelve loaves of proposition (Lev. xxiv. 6). The articles of the Creed which we should wear on our breast, i.e., should believe and confess, should be like the stones in the high priest's breastplate: shining and spreading light around.

The number of the articles of the Creed is the same as that of the apostles of Our Lord, and is intended to remind us that they contain the doctrine taught by the twelve apostles.

Every Christian should know the Creed by heart. It should be repeated every day at our prayers, by way of renewing and strengthening our faith, and of confirming the covenant we entered on with God at our Baptism. It is the shield of faith, by the repetition of which we can extinguish all the fiery darts of the most wicked one (Eph. vi. 16).

FIRST ARTICLE OF THE CREED: "I BELIEVE IN GOD, THE FATHER ALMIGHTY."

1. THE EXISTENCE OF A SUPREME BEING.

1. We can infer from the created world around us that there exists a supreme Being.

We cannot see the souls of men, but we can infer their existence by a process of reasoning; so it is with the existence of God.

The heavens and the earth could not have come into existence of themselves; nor could the heavenly bodies move through space by their own power.

We infer, when we see footprints in the snow, that some one has passed that way; so we infer from the things around us that there exists a supreme Being. The planets could no more have come into existence of themselves than a town could be built of itself. The astronomer Kirchner had a friend who doubted the existence of God. He had a globe made and placed in his study. His friend came to see him one day and asked where the globe came from. Kirchner answered that it made itself. When his friend laughed at such an answer, Kirchner replied, "It would be much easier for a little globe like that to make itself than the great one on which we live." A light cannot kindle itself, and after it is kindled it will go out in a few hours. But the heavens are lighted by the glorious light of the sun, which has burned for many thousands of years without losing any of its brightness. Look at the millions of the stars. Who made them all, and caused them to illumine the night? The Psalmist truly says "The heavens declare the glory of God, and the firmament shows forth the work of His hands" (Ps. xviii. 2). The great astronomer Newton used always to uncover and bow his head when the name of God was mentioned. We may also infer the existence of God from the creatures on the earth. Thus Job says "Ask now the beasts and they shall teach thee; and the birds of the air, and they shall tell thee. Speak to the earth and it shall answer thee; and the fishes of the sea shall tell. Who is ignorant that the hand of the Lord hath made all these things?" (Job xii. 7-9.) If any one were to find a beautiful marble statue on a desert island, he would say without any hesitation that men had been there. If one were to say that the wind and rain had torn it from the mountain side, and given it its form, we should count him as a fool. A greater fool is he who asserts that this wondrous world had no Creator.

The wonderful arrangement and order of the world also leads us to infer that it has been framed by an Architect of surpassing skill.

If a ship sails on its way and arrives safely at its destination, we conclude that it had a clever pilot. To say that the stars of the heaven of themselves direct their course, is as foolish as it would be to say that a ship had started from New York, sailed round the world, and returned safely without any one to guide it. Cicero said long ago, "When we contemplate the heavens, we arrive at the conviction that they are all guided by a Being of surpassing skill." In all that is upon the earth we see traces of design and of a most wise Designer —in the construction of the bodies of animals, and of the bodies of men, in the succession of the seasons, in trees and plants. The adaptation of means to ends in the human eye, the ear, and the various parts of the body, all imply an adapting intelligence, just as the adaptation of a watch to indicate the time, or the building of a house to shelter us, implies an intelligent constructor. As it would be impossible that the letters of the alphabet should be grouped together by mere chance in the order of the "Iliad," so it is impossible that the arrangements of the universe could have come about by chance, and without the knowledge and direction of a mighty intelligence.

All the nations of the earth have an inner conviction of the existence of a supreme Being.

Among all nations, even the most degraded, we find invariably the worship of some kind of deity. We find towns without walls, without a ruler, without laws, without coin, but never without some sort of temple, without prayer, without sacrifice. Now, universal consent is a mark of truth. The belief in God is an inner conviction, which may be said to be inborn, inasmuch as every one can arrive at it with the greatest ease.

Only the fool says in his heart: there is no God (Ps. xiii. 1).

Those who say that there is no God in spite of the glories of creation which they see around them, are those of whom Our Lord says that "seeing they perceive not, and hearing they do not understand" (Mark iv. 12). Such men are called atheists or infidels. They are invariably men who either are eaten up with pride or live vicious lives, or both. "He who denies the existence of God," says St. Augustine, "has some reason for wishing that God did not exist." Atheists, for the most part, use language which is at variance with their real convictions. Many of them are the first to cry to God for help when they are in some imminent danger. Their bold talk means very little. They are like boys who whistle in the dark to show that they are not afraid. God will take atheists at their word one day and will show Himself no loving God for them. So He took at their word those of the Israelites who doubted His power to give them victory over their enemies and possession of the Promised Land. They died before they entered it (Numb. xiv. 28-32).

2. The existence of God is also proved from revelation.

God has at sundry times and in divers manners spoken to men (Heb. i. 1), and has given them a knowledge of Himself. To Moses He appeared in the burning bush, and called Himself the God of Abraham, Isaac, and Jacob; to distinguish Himself from the false gods, He gives to Himself the name of "the self-existent One," or "I am Who am" (Exod. iii. 14). So in giving the law on Sinai He says, "I am the Lord your God. Thou shalt have none other gods beside Me" (Deut. v. 6, 7). God also worked miracles at various times in proof of His existence, e.g., by sending down fire from heaven to consume the sacrifice of Elias on Carmel (3 Kings xviii. 24, *seq.*), by saving Daniel from the lions at Babylon, and the three young men from the fiery furnace.

2. THE DIVINE ESSENCE.

What God is in His divine nature or essence is known to us partly from created things, but more clearly from His revelation of Himself.

St. Paul tells us that, " The invisible things of God from the creation of the world are clearly seen, being understood by the things that are made " (Rom. i. 20). Creation is a sort of mirror that reflects the divine perfections; thus from the beauty of things created we can infer the greater beauty of Him Who created them (Wisd. xiii. 1). So again from the order that prevails in the visible world we can conclude that He Who made it is a Being of surpassing wisdom, and from its vastness we learn the power of Him Who upholds and supports it. Yet the knowledge thus obtained is always imperfect and obscure. From a beautiful picture we do not learn much about the character of the painter. In creatures we see God only as through a glass and in a dark manner (1 Cor. xiii. 12). The heathens, before the coming of Christ, were sunk in the grossest vices, and this darkened their intellect and rendered them still less able to arrive at a knowledge of God from His works (Wisd. ix. 16). In order to enlighten this ignorance God revealed Himself to men, speaking to them by the mouth of the patriarchs and prophets, and above all by the mouth of His Son, Jesus Christ (Heb. i. 1, 2). It was Christ Who gave to men the clearest manifestation of the nature of God; all the rest spoke somewhat obscurely, for none of them had seen God face to face.

Even since God's revelation of Himself, man is not capable of a thorough or complete knowledge of the nature of God; the reason of this is that God is infinite, and man is only finite.

Just as we cannot inclose a boundless ocean in a little vessel, so we cannot take in the infinite majesty of God with our finite understanding. "Behold, God is great, exceeding our knowledge" (Job xxxviii. 26). "The things that are of God no man knoweth, but the Spirit of God" (1 Cor. ii. 11). We can neither express in words nor conceive in thought what God really is. When the sage Simonides was asked by Hiero, King of Syracuse, what God is, he took first one, then two days to consider the question; then he requested four days more; then eight; and finally said to the king that the longer he thought about the matter, the more obscure did it become to him. It is easier to say what God is not than what He is. He who attempts to fathom the majesty of God becomes profane. It is told of Icarus in the old mythology, that he fastened wings to his sides with wax, and attempted to fly up to heaven; but when he came too near the sun, it melted the wax and he fell into the sea and perished. So it is with those who seek to fathom the nature of God; He casts them down into the sea of doubt and unbelief. He who gazes upon the sun becomes dazzled; so is it with those who seek to penetrate into the nature of God. Even the angels veil their faces before God (Ezech. i. 23). The most perfect of them cannot comprehend His majesty. They are like a man who looks upon the sea from some high point; he sees the sea, but he does not see the whole of it. How can we expect to reach heights which even the angels cannot attain to ?

We can only give an imperfect and incomplete explanation of the nature of God, viz.:

1. God is a self-existent Being, infinite in His perfections, glory, and beatitude, the Creator and Ruler of the whole world.

When Moses asked almighty God His name, on the occasion of His appearing in the burning bush, God answered, " I am Who am " (Exod. iii. 14) i.e., " I exist of Myself, I derive My being from Myself." All other beings derive their existence from God, and therefore in comparison of Him are as nothing. Hence David says, " My substance is as nothing before Thee " (Ps. xxxviii. 6). God also possesses the highest perfection. We see how some beings upon the earth are more perfect than others. Some things have only existence without life, as stones and metals; others have life, but without sensation, as trees and plants; others have sensation and movement as well, as birds and beasts; man has a spiritual life, with intellect and free will. Above man there are countless numbers of pure spirits, each with a special perfection of its own, and each increasing in virtue as it ascends towards the throne of God. But they can never arrive at infinite perfection, since the most perfect among them can always attain to some higher excellence. Hence we must believe in a Being of infinite perfection, from Whom all other beings derive their virtues, Who possesses in Himself, and Who is infinitely exalted beyond, all existing or possible perfections that can be found in all other beings than Himself. Nothing greater than God can either exist or even be thought of. God is also infinite in glory and beauty. For if on the earth there exist so many beautiful things, how far greater must be the beauty and glory of God, since it is He Who gave them all their beauty. He could not have given it unless He already possessed it. He is like the boundless ocean, and the beauty of all created things is like a series of drops taken from the ocean. God is also infinite in His supreme happiness or beatitude. He lives in endless and infinite joy; no creature can interfere with the perfection of His happiness. None can either increase or diminish it (1 Tim. vi. 15). As the sun needs no light from other bodies, because it is itself the light, so God needs nothing from others, because He is Himself in possession of all good. We can only give Him what we have already received from Him. God is the Creator of the whole world, of heaven, earth, and sea. He is also the King and Lord of all, and has made all things outside of Himself subject to certain fixed laws. The earth is subject to fixed laws. It goes round the sun in three hundred and sixty-five and a quarter days, and revolves on its own axis in twenty-four hours. All the heavenly bodies move according to fixed laws, so that we can foretell eclipses of the sun and moon, etc.; there are laws which regulate all the material things on the face of the earth. Plants, trees, and animals have their growth and development governed by stated laws. The actions of reasonable beings are also governed by laws, which, however, by reason of their free will, they are able to disobey. The penalties for transgression are laid down by almighty God. God is the King of kings, the eternal King (Tob. xiii. 6). The majesty of the greatest of earthly kings is but a feeble and faint reflection of the majesty of God. Hence we are bound to obey Him, because He is our King and He will have all subject to Him, either willingly in this life, or against their will to their eternal misery.

2. We cannot see God, because He is a spirit, i.e., a being without body, immortal, possessed of intellect and free will.

Our Lord says: " God is a spirit, and they that adore Him must adore Him in spirit and in truth " (John iv. 24). It is because God is a spirit that the Jews were strictly forbidden to make any image of Him (Exod. xx. 4). God cannot be seen by man; there is a veil between us and God. We cannot see the stars during the day, but only when darkness comes on. So we cannot see God during the day of our life on earth, but only when the darkness of death comes over us. In this life God is a hidden God (Is. xlv. 15). He inhabits the inaccessible light (1 Tim. vi. 16).

Yet God has often assumed visible forms.

Thus He appeared to Abraham as a traveller, at the baptism of

Our Lord under the form of a dove, and in the shape of tongues of fire at Pentecost. But the external form under which God appeared was not God Himself. In the same way we often read of the eyes, ears, etc., of God; but this is only to impress upon us the fact that God sees us, hears us, etc.

3. There is one God, and one only.

The most perfect being in the world must be only one. The tallest tree in the wood is but one. To say that there are more Gods than one is like saying that there can be more than one soul in a human body, or more than one captain on a ship. Even the pagan Greeks and Romans honored one god as supreme among the rest. The plurality of gods probably arose from the plurality of the forces of nature (such as thunder, lightning, fire, etc.), which filled the beholders with fear, and caused them to adore these forces as gods. Or it may have arisen from the deification of heroes, or from the power of the evil spirits which, having attracted notice, caused them to be worshipped as gods.

3. THE DIVINE ATTRIBUTES.

We ascribe to God various attributes, because the unity of the divine perfection is reflected in different ways in creatures.

The sun is sometimes red, sometimes yellow, or a palish white. It is the mists around the earth that cause the variety in it as it is seen by us. The attributes of God are therefore various manifestations of God's one and indivisible perfection or essence. In God they are all one and the same; His goodness is the same as His justice, His wisdom as His power, and His power as His eternity, etc. The divine attributes are also identical with God Himself; God is wisdom, power, eternity, etc. God is a Being of the most perfect and absolute simplicity; there is no sort of multiplicity or obscurity in Him. There is no sort of division between His attributes; it is from our understanding that the distinction between them arises. In created things it is quite different; they possess attributes which are really distinct from each other.

The attributes of God may be divided into those which belong to God's essence, those that belong to His understanding, and those that belong to His will.

The attributes of the divine essence are omnipresence, eternity, immutability; those that belong to His understanding are omniscience, perfect wisdom, etc.; those that belong to His will are omnipotence, goodness, holiness, justice, truth, and faithfulness.

1. God is eternal, i.e., always was, is, and ever will be.

God's words to Moses "I am Who am" (Exod. iii. 14), express His eternity. There never was a time when God did not exist; He never began to exist. He existed before the world, as a builder must exist before the house that he builds, and the watchmaker before the watch that he fashions. God can never cease to live, as men do. Hence He is called the living God (Matt. xvi. 16) and immortal (1 Tim. i. 17). He existed before all time, and He will exist to all eternity. With Him there is no past or future; all is present with Him. The whole history of the world is and has ever been in His sight; there is for Him no succession of events; for Him there is no time. "One day is with the Lord as a thousand years, and a thousand years as one day" (2 Pet. iii. 8). Millions of ages are as nothing compared with eternity. If a bird were to carry away from the ocean one drop of water every thousand years, the time would come when the ocean would be dry; but that immense period of time, which seems to us inexhaustible, is less than the shortest moment compared with the eternity of God's existence. "Dost thou desire eternal joy," says St. Augustine, "thou must be faithful to Him Who is the Eternal."

2. God is omnipresent, i.e., He is in every place.

After Jacob had seen, in the open country, the ladder reaching up to heaven, he exclaimed, "God is in this place, and I knew it not" (Gen. xxviii. 16). The same words are true of every place. God is not only present everywhere with His power, but He Himself fills and penetrates all space. "Do not I fill heaven and earth, saith the Lord?" (Jer. xxiii. 24.)

1. God is everywhere present, because all created things exist in God.

All creatures exist in God, as thought exists in our minds. As mind is of more extent than thought, so God is of more extent than the world and all it contains. As mind penetrates thought, so God penetrates the world. "In Him we live, and move, and exist" (Acts xvii. 28). God is at the same time quite distinct from creatures and from the whole world.

2. God is not circumscribed by any place, nor by the whole of creation, because He has no limits, either actual or possible.

In his prayer at the dedication of the Temple Solomon said: "If heaven and the heaven of heavens cannot contain Thee, how much less this house that I have built" (3 Kings viii. 27). The infinite cannot be contained in measurable space. Only bodies are contained in space. Spirits indeed are not contained in space, but they cannot be in more than one place at the same time. "God is everywhere," says St. Bernard, "and yet nowhere. He is near us and yet is far away. All creation is in Him, and yet it is as if He were not in it."

3. Yet God is of more extent than space, and therefore can be in every place at the same time.

Though God is of more extent than all space, and His presence extends from earth to heaven and far beyond, He is not scattered over the universe, partly on earth and partly in heaven, but He is wholly everywhere and wholly in each separate place; wholly in heaven and wholly on earth. He fills heaven and earth. So the soul of man fills his entire body, but yet it is wholly in every separate portion of His body.

4. God is present in a special manner in heaven, in the Blessed Sacrament, and in the souls of the just.

God is present in heaven to the gaze of the angels and saints. He is present as the God-man in the Blessed Sacrament; He is present in the souls of men through the Holy Ghost Who is given to them. A king is present in his whole palace, but is specially present in the chamber where he sits on his throne, and gives audiences to his subjects.

5. There is no place where God is not.

"The eyes of the Lord in every place behold the good and the evil" (Prov. xv. 3). We sometimes see in churches a large eye painted over the altar, to remind us that God is present everywhere. "No one can hide himself from God" (Jer. xxiii. 23, 24). Hence no one can escape from God (Ps. cxxxviii. 7, 8). Jonas made the attempt, but with very poor success. Hence learn to avoid every sin. See with what unspeakable shame a man is filled, if he is detected by one of his fellow-men in a despicable action. Yet we are not ashamed to practise the most disgraceful vices in the presence of God (St. Augustine).

6. We ought therefore continually to bear in mind that God is always present with us.

Think, wherever you are, that God is near you. As there is no moment of time when we are not enjoying some benefit from the hand of God, so there ought to be no moment of time when we have not God in our thoughts. "He who always has God in his thoughts," says St. Ephrem, "will become like an angel on the earth."

The continual remembrance of the presence of God is very profitable to us. It has great power to deter us from sin, and to keep us in the grace of God; it incites us to good works and makes us intrepid in His service.

The remembrance of the presence of God gives strength in time of temptation and holds us back from sin. Look at Joseph in Egypt. A soldier fights more bravely in the presence of his king. The remembrance of the presence of God is also the best means of remaining in the grace of God. It is like Ariadne's clew, by means of which we, like Theseus, can find the way through the labyrinth of our life on earth, and remain unscathed by the Minotaur of hell. The remembrance of the presence of God increases our zeal in God's service and leads us on to the practice of all the virtues; it makes us more careful in the performance of all our duties. The nearer the water is to the spring the purer it is; the nearer one is to the fire the greater the warmth; the closer we keep to God, the greater our perfection. When the tree is closely united to the root, it brings forth plenteous fruit. The Christian brings forth good fruit to eternal life if he is closely united to God. The thought of God also renders us fearless,

When the Empress Eudoxia threatened St. John Chrysostom with banishment, he answered " You will not frighten me, unless you are able to send me to some place where God is not." David says to God: " Though I walk in the midst of the shadow of death, I will fear no evil, for Thou art with me " (Ps. xxii. 4). If a timid man has a companion with him, his fear disappears; so we shall not fear if God, the all-powerful God, is with us.

3. God is immutable, i.e., He ever remains the same.

God never changes; He never becomes better or worse; He never breaks His word (Numb. xxiii. 19). Creation made no change in God; from all eternity He had decreed the creation of the universe. God changes His works, but not His eternal decrees. By the Incarnation humanity was changed, but the Godhead underwent no change, just as the sun is in no way changed when it hides itself behind a cloud. Our thoughts are not changed when they clothe themselves in words; so the divinity was not changed when it clothed itself in the nature of man. God does not change when He punishes the sinner. When the heart of man is in friendship with God, God shows Himself to him as a God of infinite love and mercy; when the heart is estranged from Him, the sinner sees in the unchangeable God an angry and avenging judge. When the eye is sound, the light is pleasant to it; but if it is diseased, light causes it pain: it is not the light that is changed, but the eye that looks upon it. When an angry man looks in the glass he sees a different reflection from that which he saw when he was cheerful and in good-humor; it is not the glass that has changed, but the man. When the sun shines through colored glass, its rays take the color of the glass; the sun does not change, but the light is changed by the medium through which it passes. So when God rewards, it is not God Who changes, but man, who performs different and better actions, thereby meriting the grace of God. When in Scripture we read that God repented of having made man, that God is angry with the wicked, the phrases used are accommodated to our imperfect comprehension.

4. God is omniscient, i.e., He knows all things, the past, the present, and the future, and also our inmost thoughts (Jer. xvii. 10).

God knew that Adam and Eve had eaten of the forbidden fruit. Our Lord foreknew St. Peter's denial, the destruction of Jerusalem, etc. He knew the thoughts of Simon the Pharisee, and that he was angry at Our Lord showing such kindness to Magdalen the sinner. God sees as in a glass all men, and their every action (Ps. xxxii. 13). " He that planted the ear shall He not hear ? He that made the eye shall He not see ? " (Ps. xciii. 9.) God also foresees evil, but man is not thereby constrained to do evil. It is just as if we see from a distance a man who is committing some crime. God sees the deed because the man does it; the man does not do it because God sees it. When some past action is present to our thoughts, it did not happen because it is in our thoughts; so when God foresees some future action, it does not happen because God has foreseen it, but He has foreseen it because the man is going to commit it—the man is not compelled to commit because God has foreseen it. When God foresees that some man will be lost forever, God's foreknowledge is not the cause of the man's damnation. The physician foresees the approaching death of his patient, but his knowledge is not the cause of the man's death. The learned Franciscan Duns Scotus, once heard a farmer uttering terrible curses and begged him not to damn his soul so thoughtlessly. The farmer answered: "God knows everything. He knows whether I shall go to heaven or to hell. If He knows that I shall go to heaven, why to heaven I shall go; if He knows that I shall go to hell, I shall go to hell. What, then, does it matter what I do or say?" The priest answered, "In that case why plough your fields? God knows whether they will bear a good crop or not. If He knows that they will bear a good harvest, the harvest will be good, whether you plough the land or not. If He knows that they will be unfruitful, why unfruitful they will be. Why then should you waste your time in ploughing?" Then the farmer understood that it is not the omniscience of God, but the free action of man, that determines both our temporal and our eternal happiness or misery.

God also knows what would have happened under certain given circumstances; this is the reason why He sends us trials, in order to prevent greater evils that otherwise would have happened to us.

Thus Our Lord knew that the inhabitants of Tyre and Sidon would have done penance if such wonders had been worked among them as He worked in Corozain and Bethsaida. God foresees that some of the just will be led astray by the seductions of the world, and sometimes in His mercy takes them at an early age to Himself. He foresees that some will be ruined by riches or by prosperity, and therefore brings them to poverty and to earthly misfortune. This ought to make us bear our troubles with patience. The trials of the just are an opportunity offered them to advance in virtue.

God, Who knows all things, will one day bring all hidden things to light.

Our Lord says, "There is nothing hidden that shall not be made manifest; or secret that shall not be known and come abroad" (Luke viii. 17). God will, in the Last Day, disclose and make known our whole life. As the morning sun shows all things in their true light, so Christ, the Sun of justice, will at the Day of Judgment reveal all our actions in their true light. All prayers, alms, fasts, penances, that are done according to His will, will be made manifest to the whole world. Nothing is so small as to escape notice at the Last Day.

We should think on God's omniscience, especially when we are tempted, that we may pass through our temptations unscathed.

A little boy who was in a strange house saw there a basket full of beautiful apples. As he could see no one in the room, he was much tempted to help himself to some. But the thought came to him of God's omniscience. "No," he said, "I must not take them, for God sees me." At that moment a man who was hidden from him by a curtain, called out to him, "You may take as many apples as you like." What a blessing it was for him that he had not taken them without permission. If we know that some one is watching us we are very careful what we do; if we remember that God sees us, we shall be still more careful. Job took refuge in God's knowledge of his innocence, when he was mocked at by his friends; so did Susanna when falsely accused (Job xvi. 16; Dan. xiii. 42).

⁀ **5. God is supremely wise, i.e., He knows how to direct everything for the best in order to carry out His designs.**

The design at which God aims is nothing else than His own glory, and the good of His creatures. If the farmer wishes for a good harvest, he ploughs his field, manures it, sows good seed, etc. Such a farmer is a wise man, because he chooses the means best qualified to attain his end. God acts in an exactly similar way. He prepared the world for the coming of the Redeemer by the call of Abraham, the sending of the prophets, etc. The wisdom of God shows itself in the life of individuals, e.g., of Joseph in Egypt, of Moses, of St. Paul, and also in the history of nations and kingdoms. (Cf. Rom. xi. 33).

1. The wisdom of God shows itself especially in the way in which He brings good out of evil.

The life of the patriarch Joseph is an excellent example of this. God's ways are not as our ways, or His thoughts as our thoughts. Man proposes and God disposes. A man inexperienced in war would be puzzled by the orders issued by the general, and would not be able to understand how they all could tend to insure victory. We shall understand God's ways in heaven, but we cannot understand them here. A child saw how the thorns tore away little pieces from the fleece of a sheep and wanted to remove the thorns. Presently the child saw how the singing-birds collected the bits of wool to make their nests, and no longer wished to remove the thorns. Many men are like this child.

2. The wisdom of God is also displayed in this, that God makes use of the most unlikely means for His own honor.

St. Paul says: "The weak things of this world God has chosen to confound the strong" (1 Cor. i. 27). God chose the small and despised land of Palestine as the cradle of Christianity; He chose a poor maiden to be the Mother of God, and a poor carpenter to be His foster-father. He chose poor, ignorant fishermen to preach the Gospel and spread it over all the earth. He often uses the most improbable means in helping His friends. St. Felix of Nola, when flying from his persecutors, took refuge in a hole in a rock. A spider came and spun its web at the mouth of the cave, and his pursuers, on seeing this, concluded that he could not be inside. A poor woman was summoned to pay some money which had already been paid by her husband, who was dead. She searched everywhere for the receipt, but in vain. The very morning when she had to appear before the court a cockchafer flew in at the window, and behind a press. One of the children wanted to get it, so the mother moved the press a little to reach it, and from behind the press the long-sought receipt fell to the ground. This was God's answer to the poor widow's prayers. It is God's law that all works done for God should meet with difficulties and hindrances. "A work that begins with brilliant promise," St. Philip Neri used to say, "has not God for its author and protector."

3. Lastly the wisdom of God shows itself in directing the course of the world to carry out His purposes.

All things in the world have a mutual relation to one another. If a man removes or displaces a single wheel in a watch, the watch stops; so if anything were altered in the arrangement of the world, all things would be confused; e.g., without the birds the insects would soon destroy all vegetation. So the animals that serve us for food increase rapidly, while the beasts of prey breed but slowly. Nothing in the world is useless; the alternations of sunshine and rain, summer and winter, day and night, all serve some useful end. How useful is the uneven distribution of wealth, of the talents of men, etc.! The smallest insect has its usefulness in the world; the butterfly, going from flower to flower, carries with it the fertilizing pollen. Even the destructive agencies in the world, storms, earthquakes, and floods, serve God's purposes, and are intended by Him to help men to save their souls. How wonderful, too, is the orderly course of the heavenly bodies! The movement of the earth around the sun, and of the moon around the earth, serve to make this world a pleasant habitation for man. The beautiful arrangement of the universe compels us to recognize the wisdom and prudence of Him Who has created it. "How great are Thy works, O Lord! Thou hast made all things in wisdom; the earth is filled with Thy riches" (Ps. ciii. 24).

6. God is almighty, i.e., God can do all that He wills, and that by a mere act of His will.

God can do things which appear to men impossible, e.g., the preservation of the three young men in the midst of the fiery furnace of Babylon. A thousand similar wonders occurred in the time of the persecutions of the Christians. Our Lord says "With God nothing is impossible" (Matt. xix. 26). Yet God cannot do that which is in contradiction with His own perfections. He cannot lie, and He cannot deceive. God could always have done more wonderful works than He has done. He could have created a more beautiful world than this and more creatures than He has actually made. When any of the creatures that God has made desires to do anything, he can only make use of the things that God has made, and in accordance with the laws that God has established. But God is bound by no laws save those of His own infinite goodness and truth. He has only to will a thing and what He wills happens at once. "He spoke, and the heavens were created; He commanded, and they were created" (Ps. cxlviii. 5).

The omnipotence of God shows itself especially in the creation of the world, in the miracles wrought by Our Lord, and in those miracles which before and after Our Lord's time God has worked for the confirmation of the true religion.

The earth is 24,899 miles in circumference; the sun is far larger, for its diameter is one hundred times greater than that of the earth. Some of the heavenly bodies are far greater; some of them if they occupied the place of the sun and were to begin to rise at 6 A.M., would not have completely risen above the horizon by 6 P.M. Our earth is over ninety-one million miles distant from the sun. A body travelling from the earth to the sun at the ordinary rate of a cannon-ball, would take twenty-five years to reach the sun. The planet Neptune, according to the latest information, is 2,794,000,000 miles distant from the sun. A cannon-ball would take eight hundred years to travel thence to the sun. There are stars outside our planetary system which are a million times further from us. Light which travels at the rate of 24,000 miles a second would take many millions of years to reach these stars. Around our sun there move eight larger and two hundred and eighty smaller planets. The nearest (Mercury) is thirty-six million miles distant from the sun, and the most distant (Neptune) over two billion miles. There are also in the heavens thirty million fixed stars, all of them real suns and mostly larger than our sun, and around these move many other heavenly bodies. All these God has created out of nothing. How infinite, then, is the power of God ! Think also of the miracles wrought by Christ, the raising of Lazarus, the stilling of the tempest, etc., the healing of the lame man at the Beautiful Gate of the Temple, the wonders that are now being worked at Lourdes, etc. " Who shall declare the powers of the Lord, or set forth all His praises ? " (Ps. cv. 2.)

Since God is almighty, we can hope for help from Him in our greatest needs.

God has a thousand different ways of helping us. He can send an angel to help us, as He did to St. Peter in prison; or work a miracle, as He did to feed the multitude in the desert; as a rule He makes use of the most unlikely means, and thereby shows the greatness of His power. He freed Bethulia from the Assyrians by means of a woman. He saved the Israelites from their enemies by making a path through the sea. It is easy for the Lord to save by many or by few.

7. God is supremely good, i.e., He loves His creatures far more than a father loves his children.

God loves His creatures and loads them with benefits. He is love itself (1 John iv. 8).

The spring cannot but send forth water and the sun light. The goodness of God differs from that of His creatures as the sun differs from the light shed upon a wall. His creatures are good, because God sheds His goodness upon them. Hence Our Lord says: " None is good but One, that is God " (Mark x. 18).

1. The love of God extends to all the creatures that He has made (Wisd. xi. 25).

As the sun lights up the boundless firmament, so God extends His goodness to all creatures. Not one of them is excluded from it. "Not one of them is forgotten by God" (Luke xii. 6).

2. But God has an especial love for mankind. He imparts countless benefits to them and sent His Son on earth to redeem them.

What wonderful bodies God has given us ! He has bestowed upon us our senses, and the gift of speech. How many gifts He has conferred upon our souls ! He has given us understanding, free will, and memory. For our bodies He gives us food, drink, clothing, health, etc. How well He has provided for our necessities on this earth: light, warmth, the air, the plants, the trees, and their various fruits. How many powers He has implanted in nature, for us to use for our own benefit: coal, salt, stone, marble, precious stones, etc. He has, in fact, made man the lord of the whole world. He loves us far more than we love ourselves. His love for us is far greater than that of the fondest mother for her child. The love of all creatures for God is not nearly as great as the love of God for each one of us. But above all, God has shown His love for us in this—that He gave His only-begotten Son for us (John iii. 16). Abraham could not show his love for God in any more perfect way than this, that he gave to God that which was dearest to him, *viz.,* his only son. God did just the same; He gave us His dearest and best possession, His only-begotten Son. Our Lord says of Himself: "Greater love no man has than this, that a man lay down his life for his friends" (John xv. 13). He underwent His sacred Passion and death in order to prove the excess of His love for us. His attitude on the cross proclaims it. His head bowed, to give us the kiss of peace, His arms extended to embrace us, His Heart opened to admit us therein. In the Blessed Sacrament His love keeps Him in the midst of us, and seeks the closest union with us in holy communion. Finally He promised to grant all the prayers that we offer in His name (John xiv. 14).

3. Among men God shows the greatest love to the just.

"A perfect soul," says St. Alphonsus, "is dearer to God than a thousand imperfect ones." "To them that love God all things work together for good" (Rom. viii. 28). "O how great is the multitude of Thy sweetness, O Lord, which Thou hast hidden for them that fear Thee" (Ps. xxx. 20). God rewards the good works of the just far beyond what they deserve. He repays them a hundredfold, even in this present life (Matt. xix. 29). He loves the just in spite of their sins and imperfections, just as a mother loves her child tenderly in spite of its many defects.

4. God manifests His love even to sinners.

God continues to confer graces and benefits upon sinners until the last moment of their life (Matt. v. 44). He sends them troubles to bring them to repentance. He finds some good in all, and He also

loves them for what He hopes they may become. The love of God
is like the powerful magnet that draws iron to itself. Sometimes
there is an obstacle in the way, so that the piece of iron cannot reach
the magnet, but the magnet continues to draw it all the same. So
God continues to draw sinners, even though they do not come near to
Him. God hates only the devil and the lost. Even in hell He shows
His goodness by not punishing the lost as much as they deserve.
It is because of God's love for men that hell will be so intolerable.
The lost will say, "If God had not loved us so much, we should not be
so miserable now." Since God loves us so dearly we should love Him
dearly in return (1 John iv. 19). We should not be afraid of Him,
but should draw near to Him with childlike confidence. Since
God is so good to us we must also be good to our fellow-men. God
has given us a command to love Him, to love our neighbors, to love
our enemies, and also to perform works of mercy. God also wishes us
to be kind and merciful to the brute creation.

8. God is very patient, i.e., He leaves the sinner time for repentance and a change of life.

Men are wont to punish quickly; not so God. He endures long the
rebellion of the wicked. It is not the will of God that a sinner
should die, but that he should be converted from his wicked ways, and
live (Ezech. xviii. 23). God often gives men long warning of coming
judgments. He gave those who lived in the days of Noe a warning
of one hundred and twenty years; to the Ninivites of forty days; to
the Jews a warning of forty years before the destruction of Jerusalem. A storm does not break at once; we are forewarned by the
gathering clouds and the darkness; so God warns us of coming punishment. He does not at once cut down the barren tree (Luke xiii.
8, 9). God's manner of action is opposite to that of man. Man
constructs slowly, and destroys quickly. God constructed the universe in six days, but He took seven days for the destruction of the
little town of Jericho. Even man prefers to build up, rather than
to destroy; much more so God.

God is so patient with us because He has compassion on our
weakness, and because He desires to make conversion easy to the
sinner.

God deals with us as a mother deals with a peevish infant; she
presses it closer to her breast and coaxes it to be good. "Knowest
thou not," says St. Paul, "that the goodness of God leadeth thee to
penance?" (Rom. ii. 4.) God deals with us patiently for our
sakes, not being willing that any should perish, but that all should
come to penance (2 Pet. iii. 9). With many sinners God's patience
has not been lost, e.g., St. Mary Magdalen, St. Augustine, St. Mary
of Egypt, etc., but with others it effects nothing. The same sunlight
hardens mud and softens wax. If God were not patient with us, no
one could be saved, for we are all sinners who have been unfaithful
to Him. But though God is so patient, it is dangerous to put off
conversion. For the longer God delays His vengeance, the more
terrible it is when it comes upon the sinner. It is just like an arrow
from the bow; the more the bow is drawn back, the greater the force

with which the arrow flies. Compare the awful end of Antiochus Epiphanes (2 Mach. ix. 5 *seq.*). We must not think, because God is so patient, that He has forgotten our sins. " Say not, I have sinned, and what harm hath befallen me ? The Most High is a patient rewarder " (Ecclus. v. 4).

9. God is full of mercy and compassion, i.e., He very readily forgives our sins when we are sincerely sorry for them.

Our Lord gives a beautiful object-lesson of the mercy of God in the story of the prodigal son. See how quickly God forgave the sin of David (2 Kings xii. 13). It is a property of God to have mercy and to spare. His mercy is infinite; like the sea, it has no bounds. God requires of us that we should forgive seventy times seven; how immeasurably merciful therefore must God be !

The mercy of God especially shows itself in the way in which He seeks out the sinner, seeking to win him both by benefits and by the sufferings He inflicts; and also in the love with which He receives again and again the greatest sinner, after his conversion showing him a greater good will than before.

God is like the good shepherd who goes after the lost sheep until he finds it (Luke xv. 4). God sent the prophet Nathan to David; He Himself sought out the Samaritan woman (John iv.). Often He sends troubles that through them the prodigal son may be brought to his senses. He is like a fisherman who tries every sort of device to entice fishes into his net. God is always ready to pardon even the greatest sinner; for He says, " If your sins be as scarlet, they shall be made white as snow; and if they be red like crimson, they shall be white as wool " (Is. i. 18). In fact, the greater the sinner the more lovingly does God receive him if he is willing to amend. Hence David says to God, " Be merciful to my sin, for it is great " (Ps. xxiv. 11). God is like a fisherman, who is more glad to catch big fish than small ones. No one is lost because he has committed great sins, but many are lost because they have committed one sin of which they will not repent. Even Judas would have received forgiveness if he had asked for it. God sometimes forgives the sinner in the last moment of life. He received the good thief on the cross. Yet this is no reason for putting off repentance till the last. " God justified one man at the last moment that none might despair; but only one, that none might presume," says St. Augustine. A deathbed repentance is generally a very doubtful business; the dying sinner forsakes his sins rather because he cannot help it, than because from his heart he detests them; he is like the mariner who throws his goods into the sea simply from fear of death, not because he wishes to get rid of them. Witness how rarely a conversion made in peril of death proves lasting if the sick man recovers. " It is absurd," says St. Bernardin of Sienna, " that a man who would not fight when he was well and strong, should be moved to the combat when he is sick and weak." God also receives the repentant sinner most lovingly. See how Christ received with tender compassion Magdalen, the woman taken in adultery, and the thief on the cross (Luke vii. 47;

John viii. 11; Luke xxiii. 43). How kindly the father of the prodigal son received him ! God receives the sinner far more kindly than that. " Before he knocks at the door, it is opened to him; before he falls on his knees before Thee, Thou stretchest out Thy hand to him " (St. Ephrem). Our Lord says that there is more joy in heaven over one sinner doing penance, than over ninety-nine just men, who need not penance (Luke xv. 7). The reason of this is that the sinner who does penance generally serves God more zealously and faithfully. God bestows upon the sinner after his conversion greater benefits than He did before he went astray. The father of the prodigal son killed the fatted calf, and made a great feast, with music and dancing. Sometimes the benefits God bestows on the converted sinner are external, more often they are inner consolations and graces. Witness St. Paul, raised to the third heaven (2 Cor. xii. 2). The Good Shepherd has more joy over the return of the one wandering sheep, than over the ninety-nine that never went astray.

10. God is infinitely holy, i.e., He loves good and hates all evil.

God's holiness is nothing else than a love of His own infinite perfections. He is free from the faintest stain, and therefore desires that all should be like to Himself. How pure is the blue heaven on which there is no cloud! How pure is the white snow on which no spot is to be found ! Yet God is infinitely purer. Even angels are not pure in His sight (Job iv. 18). The purity of the angels as compared with that of God is like the light of a lamp compared with the light of the sun. " All our justice is like a soiled rag before Thee, O God ! " (Is. lxiv. 6.) He says to us: " Be ye holy, because I am holy " (Lev. xi. 44). With this object He implants in our breast the natural law (conscience); with this object He gave the law on Mount Sinai; with this object He attached evil consequences to evil deeds. And to cleanse the just from the impurities that cling to them, He purifies them by suffering (John xv. 2). He also cleanses them by the fire of purgatory, since nothing unclean can enter heaven. Why is it that the saints and angels in heaven are represented as dressed in white garments ? Why is it that at Baptism a white robe is given to the newly baptized ? Be pure and holy, and then you will be a child of God.

11. God is infinitely just, i.e., He rewards all good and punishes all evil deeds.

God's justice is identical with His goodness. He punishes men to make them better, and to make them happy.

1. God punishes and rewards men partly on earth, but chiefly after death.

Good actions bring men respect, sometimes riches, health, and a peaceful conscience. Bad actions bring just the opposite. Abraham, Noe, the patriarch Joseph, were rewarded in this life. Absalom, the sons of Heli, and Antiochus Epiphanes were punished in this life. But it is in the next life, and especially after the resurrection, that body and soul alike will receive their full reward. If all sins were punished in this life men would not believe in the Judgment Day.

If none were punished here they would not believe in God's retributive justice (St. Augustine).

2. God rewards the least good action, and punishes the smallest sin.

Christ tells us that even a cup of cold water given in His name will have its reward. A mere look or gesture will meet with its due reward. Christ tells us that we shall give account for every idle word (Matt. xii. 36).

3. God punishes men for the most part in kind, i.e., in the same way in which they have sinned.

"By what things a man sinneth," says the Wise Man, "by the same he also is tormented." Absalom prided himself on his long hair and it caused his death. The rich glutton sinned with his palate and it was his tongue and palate that were tormented in the fire of hell. Antiochus tormented the seven Machabean brethren by tearing and maiming their flesh, and his own flesh was eaten by worms (2 Mach. ix. 6). Aman wished to hang Mardochai, and prepared a gallows for him, and on the same gallows he was himself hanged. The women of Bethlehem would not shelter the Mother of God and the divine Son, and their children perished at the revengeful and cruel hand of Herod. Napoleon I. imprisoned the Holy Father, and in his turn was imprisoned first in Elba, and then in St. Helena. In these and many similar events, the Christian sees the finger of God.

4. In rewarding and punishing, God has regard to the circumstances of the individual, and especially to the intention with which he acts, and to the talents that he possesses.

Men judge from the outward appearance of any action, God judges from the heart (1 Kings xvi. 7). The poor widow who threw in only two mites into the treasury of the Temple, had more merit before God than many of the rich men who gave large gifts (Luke xxi. 4). The servant who knows his lord's will and does it not, will receive more stripes than the servant who did not know the will of his lord (Luke xii. 47, 48). The more knowledge any one has of God, the more severely will God punish him for his sins.

5. God is no respecter of persons.

Many who are first in this world will be last in the world to come. The story of the rich glutton and poor Lazarus is an instance of this. Many who have their names in the mouths of men, and in the records of their country, will not have their names written in the book of life.

Because God is a God of perfect justice we have good reason to fear Him.

Christ exhorts us to fear God, Who is able to cast both body and soul into hell (Matt. x. 28). On account of one single sin, that of our first parents, millions of men have to suffer pain and death; and countless numbers will be forever miserable. Thence we gather how God hates sin. The same conclusion follows from the fact that Our Lord had to die an agonizing death to atone for sin. Who, then, can fail to fear God ? But our fear of God must be a filial, not a servile fear, i.e., we must fear not so much the punishment of sin, as the offence against God. A filial fear is the result of a great love of God. Yet we must try and avoid, from fear of punishment, those sins from which the love of God is not sufficient to deter us.

The fear of God is of great advantage to us; it keeps us back from sin, leads us on to perfection, and insures for us peace and happiness both in time and in eternity.

The fear of God keeps us back from sin. It was the fear of God that held back the aged Eleazar from eating swine's flesh (2 Mach. vi. 26). He who fears God knows no other fear. As the wind drives away the clouds, so the fear of God drives away fleshly lusts, and enables us to escape the snares of the devil. He who fears God casts aside all attachment to things of earth, as the mariner in danger throws overboard the wares that otherwise would sink his ship. As the needle pierces the stuff and makes way for the thread, so the fear of God prepares the way for the love of God and for every virtue. "The fear of God," says the Psalmist, " is the beginning of wisdom " (Ps. cx. 10). The fear of man is full of bitterness and makes a man a slave; the fear of God is full of sweetness, and makes him a free man. The fear of God brings with it honor and glory; it is crowned with joy and gladness, it gladdens the heart, and gives strength and happiness and long life. " Blessed is the man that feareth the Lord " (Ps. cxi. 1). The more we fear God now, the less we shall fear His judgments at the Last Day.

The fear of God is a special grace given by God to those who love Him.

The fear of God is a special gift of the Holy Ghost. God says of His people, " I will give My fear in their hearts, that they may not revolt from Me." Hence our prayer should be, " Pierce Thou my flesh with Thy fear " (Ps. cxviii. 120).

12. God is a God of perfect truth, i.e., all that He reveals to man is true.

God cannot err for He is omniscient; He cannot deceive for He is all-holy. " God is not as a man that He should lie, nor the son of man, that He should be changed " (Numb. xxiii. 19). Hence we must believe all that God has revealed, even though our feeble understanding cannot comprehend it—e.g., the mysteries of the Christian religion, the Blessed Trinity, the Incarnation, the Blessed Sacrament of the Altar.

13. God is faithful, i.e., He keeps His promises and carries out His threats.

See how exactly God carried out His threat of death to our first parents, and His subsequent promise of a Redeemer. See again how exactly Our Lord's prediction of the destruction of Jerusalem was fulfilled; and how the prophecy of Daniel, that the Temple would never again be rebuilt (Dan. ix. 27) was accomplished; for when Julian the Apostate made an attempt to rebuild it, an earthquake destroyed the foundations, and flames issuing from the ground compelled the builders to fly. Promises and threats are necessary to move our feeble wills. Our Lord used the fear of punishment as an incentive to virtue. Ordinary men are more influenced by fear than by any higher motive. With them the fear of hell is a stronger motive for virtuous living than the hope of heaven. God threatens us out of mercy. The man who cries " Beware " does not want to strike. So God threatens punishment that He may not have to punish.

Hence all that Our Lord and the prophets have foretold either has already happened, or will happen in the future.

The time will therefore never come when the Catholic Church will be destroyed, or when the Papacy will cease to exist (Matt. xvi. 18). The Jews will all be converted before the end of the world (Osee iii. 5). Awful signs in the heaven and earth will precede the final judgment (Matt. xxiv. 29). If we trust our fellow-men they give us their promise on paper; how much more should we trust Christ, since He has left us whole books, i.e., the Scriptures, filled with His promises!

4. *THE BLESSED TRINITY.*

At the baptism of Jesus Christ all the three persons of the Blessed Trinity manifested themselves; the Father by a voice from heaven, the Son through His baptism, and the Holy Ghost in the form of a dove (Matt. iii. 16).

1. The Blessed Trinity is one God in three persons.

The three persons are called Father, Son, and Holy Ghost.

The number three is often found both in nature and in religion. There are three persons in the Holy Family; three parts in the sacraments (intention, matter, and form); Our Lord hung for three hours on the cross, and remained three days in the grave. He taught on earth for three years, and has the triple office of Prophet, Priest, and King. So in time there are past, present, and future; three kingdoms in creation, the material, the vegetable, and the animal worlds. The number four is also of frequent occurrence; there are four gospels, four cardinal virtues, four seasons of the year, four thousand years from the Fall to the Incarnation, etc. The number seven is also common; there are seven days of the week, seven sacraments, seven works of mercy, seven gifts of the Holy Ghost, seven sacred orders ending in the priesthood, etc. Three is sometimes called the number of God, four the number of the world, by reason of the four continents, and seven represents the combination of the two.

2. We cannot, with our feeble understanding, grasp the doctrine of the Blessed Trinity, and it is therefore called a mystery.

We are unable to comprehend that there are three persons in God, yet only one God. He who gazes at the sun is dazzled by it;

if he continues to gaze at it he loses his sight. So is it with the Blessed Trinity; he who inquires into it is dazzled. He who refuses to believe in it because he does not understand it, is like a blind man, who will not believe in the existence of the sun because he cannot see it. How many things there are in nature that we cannot understand! We cannot understand the growth of plants, trees, and animals; we cannot understand the nature of electricity and magnetism. We cannot understand how the color red is formed by the vibration of the ether at the rate of one hundred and thirty millions of vibrations in a second, or violet by double that number. To count the vibrations of the ether that take place in one second in the forming of the color violet, we should have to go on counting for more than ten thousand years without ceasing either day or night. Much less can we understand what belongs to God. Jeremias says, "Great art Thou, O Lord, in counsel, and incomprehensible in thought" (Jer. xxxii. 19). "No one understands what Thou art, O God, except Thou Thyself." We can, however, understand something of the nature of the Blessed Trinity by comparing it with certain facts of nature which in some way correspond to and illustrate it. The flames of three candles placed together form but one flame; the white light can be divided into red, yellow, and blue rays, which, however, together form but one light. The orb of the sun, its light, and its heat, are three different things, which are at the same time really one. The soul of man contains memory, understanding, and will, which are but different manifestations of the same spiritual substance. Yet all these are but imperfect analogies, and cannot carry us very far in attempting to understand something of the incomprehensible mystery of the Blessed Trinity. Unbelievers sometimes say: "How is it possible that three can be one, and one three?" They show that they do not know what the teaching of the Church really is. "They blaspheme those things that they know not" (Jude 10). The Church does not say there are three persons and one person, but there are three persons, and one nature or essence.

3. The nature, the attributes, and the works of the three persons of the Blessed Trinity are common to all of them.

There are therefore not three gods, but one God.

The Father is therefore different from the Son, because He is a different person; but He has not a different being, because He has the same nature.

For this reason each of the three persons is, in exactly the same sense, omniscient, omnipotent, eternal, and absolutely perfect, as are the other two.

When Our Lord spoke of His return to the Father, He said, "My Father is greater than I" (John xiv, 28). Here He was speaking of Himself as man; else He could not have spoken of His return to the Father.

Hence the creation of the world, the redemption and the sanctification of men is wrought by all the three divine persons together.

Yet we are accustomed to say: "The Father made the world, the Son redeemed it, and the Holy Ghost sanctifies it."

4. The three divine persons are divided only in their origin.

In a tree the trunk comes forth from the root, and from both comes the fruit. Such is the relation between the three divine persons.

God the Father has no origin and proceeds from no other person; God the Son proceeds from the Father; God the Holy Ghost proceeds both from the Father and from the Son.

In order to mark the order of procession, we name the Father first, the Son second, and the Holy Ghost third. But there is no succession in time; the Son proceeds from the Father from all eternity, and so does the Holy Ghost from the Father and the Son. The Son is begotten of the Father before all creation. The Father produced, by an act of divine knowledge, the Son as an image like to Himself in all things, just as we, when we think, produce an intellectual image in our minds. We may illustrate this by the relation existing between fire and light. Light proceeds from fire, but is contemporaneous with it. If there were an eternal fire, there would also be an eternal light. The Son is the brightness of God's glory (Heb. i. 3), the unspotted image of His majesty (Wisd. vii. 26). Just as one torch is kindled from another, without the first losing any of its light, so the Son is begotten of the Father, without taking anything away from Him. The Son is called the Word of the Father (John i. 1). Just as the word formed in our minds (the thought) is made manifest by the external or spoken word, so the Word of God, dwelling in the bosom of the Father, was made manifest to the world when the Word was made flesh and dwelt among us (John i. 14). As the Son has His origin in the knowledge of God, so the Holy Ghost has His origin in the love of God. The Holy Ghost is none other than the mutual love of the Father and the Son. He is the Spirit of love, who engenders in our hearts the love of God and of each other. The word spirit is well chosen, because by it we express the attractiveness and the force of love. The Holy Ghost proceeds from the Father and the Son, as warmth proceeds from the sun and its light.

On account of the difference in their origin we appropriate to the Father the works of omnipotence, to the Son the works of wisdom, and to the Holy Ghost the works of love.

These various works have a certain correspondence with the attributes of the persons, that are connected with their origin. The Father begets the Son; for this reason there is appropriated to Him the bringing of perishable things also, out of nothing, i.e., of creation. He is therefore called the almighty Father. He is also called the God of compassion, because He is ever ready to receive the sinner who comes back to Him in a true spirit of penance. The Son is the eternal wisdom of the Father. To Him therefore is appropriated the beautiful arrangement of the world. As the artist, through the working of his reflective mind designs the plan of his work, so the Father, through His Son, produced order in the world. To the Son, too, is ascribed the restoration of order, as for this end He took upon Himself the nature of man. To the Holy Ghost, as the mutual love of the Father and the Son, are ascribed all the benefits of God to man; especially the bestowal upon him of his natural life in creation (the Spirit of God moved upon the face of the waters), and of his spiritual life by his sanctification through grace. To Him, as the finger of God's right hand, are ascribed all miracles, and above all the work of the Incarnation, as being of all miracles the greatest. The love of God has ever occupied itself with men, but the Incarnation of the Son of God by the operation of the Holy Ghost surpassed all other benefits wrought by Him. It brought mercy to sinners, truth to the erring, life to those who were dead, and hope and faith to the whole world.

5. We are taught the mystery of the Blessed Trinity by Christ Himself, but it was partly known in the time of the Old Testament.

We know, from the fact of creation, the infinite power, wisdom, and goodness of God, but it does not reveal to us the mystery of the Blessed Trinity. Nor is there any proof of this doctrine to be found in nature, though we may find certain analogies to it, some of which we have given. But the mystery itself can only be made known to us by revelation. " The Father no man knoweth but the Son, and he to whom the Son shall reveal Him " (Matt. xi. 27). Our Lord revealed this mystery to His Church when He said to His apostles before His ascension, " Go and teach all nations, baptizing them in the name of the Father, and of the Son, and of the Holy Ghost " (Matt. xxviii. 19). In the time of the Old Testament the Jewish priests, when they blessed the people, had to repeat the name of God three times (Numb. vi. 23). Isaias tells us that the seraphim in heaven cry, " Holy, holy, holy, Lord God of hosts " (Is. vi. 3). Before the creation, God said, " Let us make man " (Gen. i. 26). David says, " The Lord said to My Lord, sit on My right hand." But before the Incarnation the mystery of the Blessed Trinity was veiled in a cloud which was only dispelled under the New Law. " The Church," says St. Hilary, " knows this mystery. The Synagogue believed it not. Philosophy understood it not."

6. The belief in the Blessed Trinity is expressed in the Apostles' Creed, in Baptism, and in the other sacraments, in all consecrations and blessings, and in the feast of the Most Holy Trinity.

The mystery of the Blessed Trinity is the foundation of our religion. Without a knowledge of this truth we cannot understand our redemption by the Son of God. We ought frequently to make an act of faith in this mystery, especially by the repetition of the *Gloria Patri*. We should repeat it whenever we receive any benefit from God, and also when He sends us any cross or trial.

5. HISTORY OF CREATION.

We are instructed by the writer of the book of Genesis in the story of creation.

The account given of the creation in the book of Genesis is not a fable, but is founded on truth. The sacred writer was enlightened by the Holy Ghost, and his words are a part of the Word of God. Perhaps God gave him a vision of the course of creation. The story is in exact agreement with the conclusions of natural philosophy. All investigations into the crust of the earth show that organic life was developed in the order set forth in Genesis.

1. In the beginning God created the spiritual and material universe.

"In the beginning"—i.e., in the beginning of time, when there was nothing else existing except God. Time began with the world, so that before the creation there was no time. Holy Scripture does not tell us when the world was created. The world may have existed for millions of years before the creation of man. The fact that it takes millions of years for the light of some of the heavenly bodies to reach the earth, seems to show this to have been the case. "Created," i.e., made out of nothing. How God produced the materials out of which the world was made we know not. Instead of the spiritual and the material world, St. Paul says, "things visible and invisible" (Col. i. 16). The words of Genesis are, "In the beginning God created the heaven and the earth." The heaven does not mean the star-bespangled sky, the creation of which is narrated subsequently (Gen. i. 6-8; 14-19). It means the abode of the angels and the saints. The material world is called the earth, because the earth is for men the most important part of the material world. The first words of the Bible, "God created heaven," are intended to remind man of his last end and future destiny.

The spiritual world consists of the angels, and the heaven where they dwell.

The angels are called the "Morning-stars" (Job xxxviii. 7), because they were created before this material world, and in the morning of the universe. Hell was not created at the beginning of the universe (Matt. xxv. 34), but at a later period, after the fall of the rebel angels (Matt. xxv. 41).

The material world includes all things which are found in the visible universe.

Men are a union of spirit and body, and were created later.

2. The material world was at first without form, without inhabitants, and without light.

God first created the material elements out of which the world was formed. Natural philosophy tells us that the world existed first of all in the form of a vast mass of vapor, and that this vast mass gradually was condensed, under the influence of an intense heat, into the material universe. This is perfectly in accordance with the account of the creation given in Genesis.

3. God gave to the material universe its present form in the course of six days.

The days are probably long periods of time, consisting of many thousands of years; for the seventh day, the day of rest, lasts until the end of the world. Moreover four of the days were already elapsed before the sun was formed, and therefore they cannot have been days as we now understand the word. The word day is chosen because the week of creation was to be a sort of pattern of our present week.

On the first day God made the light.

We read in Genesis that God said, " Let there be light," and there was light. The expression, "Let there be," denotes that something came into existence which did not exist before. This was the luminous matter which is now gathered in the sun; it is not dependent on the sun, but the sun on it. The gaseous matter was at first unformed, i.e., it had no forces. God imparted to it the law of gravitation, by means of which the various particles of matter were set in motion and drawn together, and thus were condensed gradually into a solid mass. By this process warmth, and at last fire, were developed. On the first day fire, the main source of light, was produced by the movement given to the gaseous particles, and the existing vapor was condensed into masses endowed with fire and light.

On the second day God made the firmament.

The words of Genesis are, " God said, Let there be a firmament made amidst the waters, and let it divide the waters from the waters. And God called the firmament heaven " (Gen. i. 6, 8). On this day there was a separation, arrangement, and establishment of the created masses, which were divided into parts according to their constitution and magnitude, parted from one another, and arranged in the places that God had destined for them. This planting of the various worlds in their places in space constituted the " firmament," which God called " heaven," in which the sun and moon and stars pursue the course that was allotted to each. This firmament is the material heaven, as opposed to the spiritual heaven which is identical with the celestial paradise. The earth on which we live was one of the condensed masses which took its place among the other heavenly bodies. God at the same time divided off the planets that move around the sun, which forms the centre of their system from the fixed stars (v. 7).

On the third day God made the dry land and the plants.

Here the sacred writer concerns himself more especially with our earth. The earth, which was originally a fiery ball of gas, gradually lost its heat, as it cooled down in the midst of space. The great masses of mist divided themselves off into the sea and land. The solid elements were drawn together, and formed the crust of the earth, through which the water forced itself from within. Thus were made the various oceans or seas, and by this upheaval the surface of the earth as it exists at present was gradually formed, with its continents, and islands, its mountains and valleys. Under the influence of the warmth of the earth the moist surface was now ready for the development of organic life. This did not arise out of nothing, like the original primary matter; it was already implanted in the earth by almighty God, and was evolved therefrom as soon as circumstances favorable to its development presented themselves. No organic life can arise from mere inorganic matter. No possible combination of mere inorganic materials can ever produce any kind of organic life. The original germs out of which life arose were already existing in the vapor-cloud out of which the earth was formed, but were not able to develop themselves under the conditions of extreme heat and cold. They remained as undeveloped germs until the more moderate temperature enabled them to produce plants and trees under the influence of warmth and moisture.

On the fourth day God made the sun, moon, and stars.

On the fourth day of creation, the earth, which had been involved in darkness by the thick mist that surrounded it as long as it had not fully cooled down, began to have a clearer atmosphere, and only a few clouds floated over its surface, instead of the dense vapor that had encircled it. The shining bodies in the heaven became visible; the sun began to exercise an influence upon the earth, and produced the alternations of day and night, and the various seasons of the year. The sun had previously a feeble power of radiation, but during this fourth period it assumed its present form. We do not know whether there exist living beings on any of the stars; if there are such, they must be of a very different nature from our own. We know that in the moon there is no atmosphere, no fire, no water, no sound, no rain, no wind, no vegetation, and a long night of three hundred and fifty hours.

On the fifth day God made the fishes and the birds.

On the sixth day God made the animals and, last of all, man.

The animals were next made in order to proclaim the power of their Creator by their number, variety, greatness, strength, and cleverness, and also to serve man, to nourish him, clothe him, and labor for his benefit. Man was produced the last of all the animals, and surpasses them all in dignity, and in the possession of reason and free will. Man is the crown of God's creation. God prepared the world for his reception, that he might enter and take possession of it as a king takes possession of his kingdom. The world would not have been complete without man; all else was made for his sake. In all the rest of the work of creation God simply said " Let it be," but before He created man He is represented as taking counsel with Himself. This is to show the importance and the dignity of man.

4. On the seventh day God rested from all His work that He had done.

God's rest consists in this, that on the seventh day He brought nothing more into existence. It was the working out, without any further creative action on the part of God, of the order that He had established. The fact that God rested does not mean that He ceased from working (John v. 17). God must continue to work in the world, else it would cease to exist. As God rested after His work, so we shall one day rest in Him when our work is done.

From the story of creation we learn that God made the world after a fixed plan.

God in creation proceeded from the lower to the higher. He first made all things that were necessary for what was afterwards to come into life, e.g., He made first the plants and then the animals that needed them for food. In the first three days He separated the various parts of the world from each other; in the three following days He developed and adorned creation. The three first days correspond to the three last; for on the first He made light, on the fourth luminous bodies; on the second He separated water and air from each other, on the fifth He filled the water with fishes and the air with birds; on the third He made the dry land and on the sixth He filled it with animals.

From the account of creation we also learn that the world is not eternal.

The heathen thought that the world sprung from the accidental concurrence of a number of eternal atoms. But the present wonderful order could not possibly have arisen by chance, and the atoms are all dependent on one another, and therefore could not be eternal. The atoms, too, could never have put themselves in motion. Others thought that the materials of the world were eternal, and that God simply arranged them. Others imagined that the world was developed out of the divine essence (the Pantheists). But this would make the world indivisible and unchangeable, and we know that this is not so. God indeed is everywhere, but the world is not God; it is something different from Him, and separated from His being.

From What, and for what End has God Created the World?

1. God made the world out of nothing, simply because it pleased Him to make it.

Man can only make anything out of pre-existing materials. God made the materials. Men have to employ implements, they have to labor, and require a certain time to produce their work. God spoke, and the world was made. He did not need even to speak; all that was needed was that He should will what He desired done.

All that God created was very good.

God Himself commended His own works (Gen. i. 31). The world was very good, because it in no way diverged from the divine idea but was in perfect accordance with it. God praised His own works, because no one else could praise them sufficiently. We also should praise God in His works, as the three young men did in the fiery furnace at Babylon. Evil is evil, because creatures make a bad use of their free will. Nothing that exists can be bad in itself, but everything must at least be in some way good.

2. God was moved to make the world by His great goodness.

His object was to make His reasonable creatures happy.

As a good father shows pictures to his children, to please them and make them love him, so God has manifested His works to His reasonable creatures, to make them happy and earn their love. God made all earthly things for our good; some for the support of men (plants and animals), some for their instruction, some for their enjoyment, some for their trial, as sickness, suffering, etc. "All things that I see upon the earth," says St. Augustine, "proclaim that Thou hast made them from love of me, and call upon me to love Thee." God did not need the world. He made it for our sakes.

3. The end of creation is necessarily to proclaim to men the glory of God.

In every work we have to distinguish between the end of the maker of the work, i.e., that which moved the artificer to make the work, and the end of the work itself, i.e., that for which the work is destined. In a clock, e.g., the end of the maker of the clock is his own profit; the end of the clock is to indicate the time. In the world the motive of the Artificer is God's great goodness; the end of the work is God's glory and the happiness of His reasonable creatures. The motive of the countless number and variety of living and lifeless beings and the innumerable number of the stars, is that angels and men may know and admire the majesty of God. The end and object of the existence of angels and men are that they may know-ingly behold and praise God (Is. vi. 3). St. Augustine says, "Thou hast made us for Thyself, O God, and how unquiet is our heart so long as it finds not its rest in Thee!" Even the devils are compelled to contribute, in spite of themselves, to the glory of God; for by their punishment they show how holy and just God is, and God employs them also for the perfection of His elect through resistance to their temptations. Even the lost in hell manifest the justice and holiness of God and His hatred of sin. "God has made all things for Himself; the wicked also for the evil day" (Prov. xvi. 4). Yet God did not make the world with a view to any increase in His glory; for God is infinitely happy in Himself, and has no need of anything or any one outside of Himself.

Since we are made for the glory of God, we should in all our works have the intention of honoring God.

St. Paul instructs us that, "whether we eat or drink, or whatever we do, we should do all to the glory of God" (1 Cor. x. 31). Nothing is easier than to give glory to God, since we can direct our most minute actions to this end. When we wake in the morning, and oftentimes during the day we should renew this intention.

6. *DIVINE PROVIDENCE.*

We call by the name of divine providence God's preservation and government of the world.

1. God maintains the world, i.e., He preserves all creatures in existence as long as He wills.

A ball hanging from a piece of string falls to the ground as soon as the string is cut. So the whole world would sink into nothing if God were to withdraw from it His supporting power for a single instant. In order that creatures may continue to exist, He provides all that is needed for their sustenance: wheat, vegetables, the various fruits of the earth, etc. As soon as God wills it, they die. " When Thou shalt take away their breath, they shall die, and return again to the dust" (Ps. ciii. 29). If the sun were to cease to cast its rays upon the earth, all light would disappear from the world; so if God cease to support us in existence, our life at once fails us. When Our Lord says, "Heaven and earth shall pass away," He does not mean that they will be annihilated, but that they will be changed into a better. St. Peter says, "We look for a new heaven and a new earth, wherein dwelleth justice" (2 Pet. iii. 13).

2. God governs the world, i.e., He conducts all things in the world, so that they contribute to His glory and to our advantage.

What the engine is to the train, and the pilot to the vessel, God is to the world. He guides the stars according to fixed laws, so that the firmament proclaims His glory. He guides all nations (Dan. iv. 32). We see His guiding hand in the lives of the patriarchs, in the history of the Jews, in that of the Christian Church. Yet we cannot understand God's arrangements at the first glance; often we cannot understand them at all, and never shall till we get to heaven. Yet in our own lives we can trace again and again the good providence of God. But as to the world generally we are forced to exclaim, "How incomprehensible are God's judgments, and how unsearchable His ways!" (Rom. xi. 33.)

There is no one on the earth for whom God does not care, and provide for his welfare.

A mother would sooner forget her child than God would forget us (Is. xlix. 15). God cares even for the irrational creatures; for the beasts and birds and plants (Matt. vi. 25-30).

God has a special care for those who are in humble circumstances, and are despised by the world.

God has made small as well as great, and cares equally for them (Wisd. vi. 8). God loves to declare His glory by means of the little (1 Cor. i. 27). He chose poor shepherds to receive the first news of the birth of Christ; He chose poor fishermen for His apostles; a poor maiden for His Mother; it is to the humble that He gives His grace (Jas. iv. 6). "He raises the needy from the earth, and takes the poor from the dunghill, that He may place him among princes" (Ps. cxii. 7, 8).

Nothing happens to us all through our lives without the will or the permission of God.

Hence the patriarch Joseph says to his brethren, "Not by your counsel was I sent hither, but by the will of God" (Gen. xlv. 8). Our Lord says that the very hairs of our head are all numbered, i.e., the providence of God descends to the smallest details of our life. Hence there is nothing that happens by chance. There are indeed many things, the causes of which we are ignorant of, but all have some cause, and God guides all. There are many things in the world that God does not will, and of which He is not the cause, e.g., murder, theft, and every crime. But God permits them, i.e., He does not prevent them. This is a consequence of His having given to man free will. Moreover, God knows how to bring good out of evil, and all evil He employs for His good purposes.

Even the evil that God permits is for our good.

God, in His love for us, has in all that happens to us the intention to make us happy. He turns to our good all temporal misfortunes, the temptations of the devil, the sins of other men. "To those who love God all things work together for good" (Rom. viii. 28). We see this in the history of the patriarch Joseph; his imprisonment was the means of bringing him to high honor, and of saving Egypt from the horrors of famine. The captivity of the Jews was the means of spreading the knowledge of the true God among heathen nations (Tob. xiii. 4). The persecution of the early Christians in Palestine and in Rome was the means of making known the Gospel in the countries to which they fled or were banished; so, too, was the expulsion of the religious Orders from Italy, France, and Germany in modern times. So again the persecution of the Irish has done much to Christianize America and England. "The unbelief of St. Thomas," says St. Augustine, "has been more useful to us than the belief of the other apostles." The sin of Peter made him humble and forbearing towards others. The fury of the Jews against Our Lord was the instrument of the redemption of mankind. "How inscrutable are God's judgments and how unsearchable His ways!" (Rom. xi. 33.) The very means employed by wicked men against the saints were the means of bringing them glory and honor.

3. For this reason a pious Christian should resign himself entirely to the will of God.

Christ teaches us to pray: "Thy will be done on earth, as it is in heaven." St. Peter exhorts us to cast all our care upon God, for He cares for us (1 Pet. v. 7). Holy David says: "Though an army should stand in battle against me, my heart will not fear" (Ps. xxvi. 3). We must not allow ourselves to be troubled about the arrangements of God's providence, which we cannot alter, but must resign ourselves to the will of God, e.g., in sickness, loss of money, the death of those dear to us, persecution, war, etc. Above all we must resign ourselves to the will of God in the hour of our death. "He who dies resigned to the will of God," says St. Alphonsus, "leaves in the minds of others the knowledge that he has saved his soul." In order to gain the friendship of men we adapt ourselves to their humors and fancies; but we take too little trouble to win the friendship of God by adapting ourselves to His holy will.

The man who cheerfully resigns himself to the will of God obtains true peace of mind, attains great perfection, and will be blessed by God.

The soul resigned to the will of God is like the needle pointing to the North. The soul that submits itself to all God's arrangements has already begun to live the life of heaven upon earth. If trouble comes, its peace is not disturbed; every trial is extinguished, like a spark that falls into the sea; it loves sufferings, because it knows that they come from God's hand. A man resigned to God's will has his cross carried for him. He who renounces his own will in order to carry out the holy will of God, soon attains to perfection. Thus the resigning of our will to God's is the most perfect offering we can make Him. The man who is resigned is like a ship in the hands of the pilot; he is sure to arrive safely into port. A farmer whose fields bore better crops than those of others was asked the reason for it. He answered that he always got the weather that he wanted. When asked to explain himself, he replied, "I am always content with the weather that God sends. This pleases God and so He blesses my crops."

Our Lord in the Garden of Gethsemani is a beautiful example of submission to the will of God.

Christ's prayer was "Father, not My will, but Thine be done." He was obedient to His heavenly Father even to death, the death of the cross (Phil. ii. 8). The holy angels find their happiness in the fulfilment of the will of God. St. Mary Magdalen of Pazzi said, "I would bear with joy the heaviest troubles, so soon as I knew that they were the will of God." So also said all the saints.

How are the Misfortunes of the Good and the Prosperity of the Wicked to be Reconciled with the Providence of God?

The answer is that these are only apparent, not real. Seneca says that the prosperity of those who are clad in purple is often like the splendor of the actor, who is dressed up in royal purple. The sinner after a time loses all enjoyment from his sins.

1. No sinner has true happiness, and no servant of God true misery. For true happiness is impossible without inner peace and contentment; and this is possessed by the true servant of God, but not by the sinner.

The world, i.e., riches, honors, sensual pleasures, eating, drinking, etc., can never give us true peace (John xiv. 27). This can only be attained by following the teaching of Christ. True peace and happiness are the fruits of the Holy Spirit. The wicked have no peace; they are like the raging sea, which cannot rest (Is. lvii. 20). Peace and happiness do not come of riches, or of a high position, or of bodily strength, or of intellectual vigor; still less do they come from the wearing of fine clothes, or from the enjoyment of rich feasts, but from peace of soul and a good conscience. The beggar at the gate of the rich Dives was a happier man, even in this world, than Dives himself.

2. Moreover the good fortune of the sinner is for the most part only transitory.

The prosperity of the wicked is like the cedar of Lebanon, which in a few hours is cut down and is no more seen. It is a building built on sand: the storms and winds soon lay it low. How quickly Napoleon the Great fell from the height to which his vaulting ambition had raised him at the cost of so many lives !

3. The real recompense of man only begins after death.

Hence Our Lord says, " Many that are first shall be last, and the last first " (Matt. xix. 30). Many rich and distinguished men will be far below those who have been beggars at their door. God has provided for His friends in the next life an enjoyment and happiness far surpassing any enjoyments on this earth. This is the explanation of the apparent injustice of the present life. Our Lord says to His disciples, " Amen, Amen, I say to you, that you shall lament and weep, and the world shall rejoice; and you shall be made sorrowful, but your sorrow shall be turned into joy " (John xvi. 20).

4. Sinners are rewarded on this earth for the little good that they have done. The just on the other hand are for the most part punished in this life for the evil they have done.

Our Lord says, " Woe to you that are rich; for you have your consolation," i.e., your reward for the good you have done is given you in this world (Luke vi. 24).

How is Sin to be Reconciled with the Providence of God?

1. It is not God Who is responsible for sin and its consequences, but man's wrong use of his free will.

God created man free, and therefore does not hinder even those free actions which are evil. There are also many reasons why He should not hinder evil. If there were no evil in the world, man would have no opportunity of doing what is good; he would not have the choice between good and evil, and would not be able to earn the reward of good accomplished. Compare the parable of the cockle among the wheat. " God," says St. Augustine, " would never have permitted evil if He had not intended to bring some greater good out of it."

2. God in His wisdom employs even sin for a good end.

The patriarch Joseph very truly said to his brethren, " You thought evil against me, but God turned it into good " (Gen. l. 20). God turned to good even the treachery of Judas; it contributed to the work of man's redemption. The bee makes honey out of poisonous plants; the potter makes beautiful vessels out of dirty earth. God does something similar to this.

3. Besides, it does not become us to pry into the secret designs of God; we poor miserable creatures must adore His wisdom and submit ourselves humbly to what He ordains.

What is true of sin, is true of all the suffering that is the consequence of sin.

7. THE CHRISTIAN UNDER SUFFERING.

Man can suffer in body or soul or both. The apostles, when they were scourged (Acts v. 41), suffered in body; Judas, when he threw down the pieces of silver in the Temple, suffered in his soul. Holy Job suffered in both. Suffering is either merited or unmerited. The sufferings of the prodigal son were merited, those of the patriarch Joseph were unmerited. Yet all sufferings are merited by original sin.

1. No one can attain to eternal salvation without suffering.

" No one is crowned unless he strive lawfully " (2 Tim. ii. 5).

Even Christ had to enter into His glory through suffering (Luke xxiv. 26). Our Lord says " He that taketh not up his cross and followeth after Me, is not worthy of Me " (Matt. x. 38). The road to heaven is a rough one. In order to make the flax that grows in the earth into pure white linen, it must be rubbed, stretched, and thoroughly cleansed, and woven. The corn has to be threshed and winnowed; the pure gold has to pass through fire. Not to suffer is a sign that no future happiness is in store for you. Suffering and holiness are inseparably bound up together. There is no good work that does not meet with obstacles, no virtue that does not have to fight and struggle.

For this reason God leaves no just man without suffering.

God treats us as a physician treats his patients; those of whose recovery he despairs he leaves alone; but to those whom he hopes to cure, he administers bitter medicines. As milk is the food of children, so are contradictions the food of God's elect. To His chosen God gives a sword on earth to pierce their heart, and a crown in heaven to adorn their heads. Yet God mingles with the bitterness of suffering the sweets of consolation. We see this throughout the history of Our Lady, which consists of alternate joys and sorrows. So, too, we celebrate the seven joys and sorrows of St. Joseph.

2. All suffering comes from God, and is a sign of His love and favor.

We find in the lives of the saints that the more good works they undertook for God, the more did suffering assail them, as in the case of Tobias, and of holy Job. Sufferings seem to be the reward of good works performed. They are a precious gift, which will avail us to all eternity. To suffer something for God is in itself a great privilege and honor. It is a better gift than that of performing miracles and raising the dead. Parents often punish their children to cure them of their faults. If they see the same faults in the children of others, they do not trouble themselves about them, because they do not care for them. So it is with God; the children whom He loves He often corrects. Hence Raphael said to Tobias, "Because thou wast pleasing to God, it was necessary that temptation should prove thee" (Tob. xii. 13). St. Paul says, "Whom the Lord loveth He chastiseth; and scourgeth every son whom He receiveth" (Heb. xii. 6). "Gold and silver are tried in the fire, and acceptable men in the furnace of tribulation" (Ecclus. ii. 5). The greater a saint, the greater were in most cases his sufferings. Our Lady was the Queen of martyrs. The apostles had to suffer much, especially St. Peter and St. Paul (Cf. 2 Cor. xi. 23, *seq.*). To be free from suffering is a bad sign. St. Augustine says: "There is no greater misfortune than the good fortune of sinners. He who does not suffer now will have to suffer hereafter."

Yet God never sends us any suffering that is beyond our powers of endurance.

St. Paul says "God is faithful; Who will not permit you to suffer above that which you are able" (1 Cor. x. 13). The peasant knows how much his beast of burden can carry, and does not load him beyond his strength. Will God, the all-wise, the all-merciful, lay more on us than we can bear? The potter does not leave his vessels too long in the fire lest they should crack. He who plays on an instrument is careful not to tighten the strings too much, lest they should break; nor too little, for then they would produce no sound. The physician apportions his remedies to the power of his patient; so the heavenly Physician sends us sufferings in proportion to our power of bearing them. There are some people who make sufferings for themselves, because they find fault with what gives no cause for complaint. Even in real sufferings much complaining is a sign of faint-heartedness and makes us more sensible to suffering.

3. God sends suffering to the sinner to bring him back into the right way and to save him from eternal death.

How many have been converted by means of sufferings, e.g., Manasses in the prison at Babylon (2 Paral. xxxiii. 12, 13), Jonas, the prodigal son, even the wicked Achab (3 Kings xxi. 27). God is like a surgeon, who cuts away the diseased flesh that it may not cause death. Sufferings also bring about a disgust for earthly things and make the sinful pleasures of the world bitter; they destroy our dependence on earthly things, and take away the desire for the enjoyments and the pleasures of this valley of tears, and turn our thoughts to heaven. Sufferings again impress upon us our own helplessness, compel us to have recourse to God in prayer. They teach us a knowledge of ourselves and of our own sinfulness. As the trees, after the winter, flower and bring forth fruit, so does man after suffering bring forth works pleasing to God. " Sufferings," says St. Teresa, " though very hard to bear, are the surest way to God."

God frequently sends bodily sickness to the sinner for the healing of the sickness of his soul.

How many there are who have been converted to God through the means of bodily sickness, e.g., St. Francis of Assisi and St. Ignatius of Loyola. The Wise Man says, " A grievous sickness makes the soul sober " (Ecclus. xxxi. 2). In sickness God knocks at the door of the heart and asks for admission. " I am always glad," said St. Ignatius, " when I see a sinner fall ill, for sickness brings back to God." How foolish it is then to regard sickness as a mark of God's anger, when it is really a mark of His compassion.

4. God sends suffering to the just man to try him whether he loves God most or creatures.

Job, who had always lived a God-fearing life, lost all his property, his children, and his health, and was derided by his wife and his friends. Tobias had buried the dead at the peril of his life and given most liberal alms. God took away his sight, and left him poor and unable to earn anything for himself. Thus God tries His friends. As the storm tests the tree, whether it is firmly rooted, so suffering tests the just, whether they are firmly established in their love of God. As the wind separates the chaff from the wheat, so trouble marks off the sinner from the just. Sweet herbs smell the sweetest when they are bruised; so the just are most pleasing to God in the time of tribulation. God often takes away from us what we love best, and that which is injurious or dangerous, just as a father takes from his little child a razor or sharp knife.

At the same time the sufferings of the just man are a great advantage to him; they serve him as a penance for his sins; they cleanse him from all imperfections; increase his zeal in the practice of good, in the love of God, and in the love of prayer; they also increase his merit in heaven, and often, too, his happiness in this world.

By sufferings the punishment due for sin is cancelled. Hence St. Augustine prayed, " In this life, O Lord, burn, scorch, and wound me, only spare me in the life to come." " Think yourself happy," said St. Francis Xavier, " if you can exchange the agonizing pains of purgatory for sufferings in this world." Sufferings also purify the soul from its imperfections. Gold is tried in the fire; so the soul is purged by suffering. " Every branch that bears fruit God purges, that it may bring forth more fruit " (John xv. 2). A sharp file cleanses iron from rust. As soap cleanses the body, so suffering cleanses the soul. Suffering also increases our strength, just as the blows of the hammer make the iron stronger and harder. Toil strengthens the body; suffering strengthens the soul. The vessels that the potter places in the fire come out hard and strong. Suffering also adds to our love of God. As the ark of Noe was raised nearer to heaven by the floods that overspread the earth, so we are brought nearer to heaven and to God by the floods of suffering. As the gold leaf is spread out by the blows of the hammer, so our love of God is extended by suffering. Sufferings detach us from the love of earthly things, and destroy our love of this world. Hence St. Augustine prayed, "Make all things bitter to me, that so Thou alone mayest appear sweet to my soul." Sufferings also increase our gratitude to God, for the loss of health and other gifts of God makes us value what we have lost. Sufferings also make us humble. The just must be tried by evil, that so they may not grow proud of their virtues. Sufferings also increase the earnestness of our prayers. They compel us to pray. We see this in the case of the apostles in the storm-tossed boat. The prayers of David under persecution have become the prayers of the Church. Long peace makes us careless and slack. The ox that is not stirred by the goad becomes lazy. Sufferings are often the means of bringing us to prosperity even in this world. Witness Job, the patriarch Joseph, and Tobias. "The Lord maketh poor and maketh rich; He humbleth and He exalteth" (1 Kings ii. 7). "You shall be sorrowful," says Our Lord, "but your sorrow shall be turned into joy" (John xvi. 20). Lastly, sufferings increase our eternal happiness. Our present momentary and light tribulation worketh for us above measure exceedingly an eternal weight of glory (2 Cor. iv. 17). The just are ripened for heaven by suffering, as ears of corn are ripened by the heat of the sun. Jewels are rendered more beautiful by being ground and polished. "When God sends us some great trouble," says St. Ignatius, "it is a sign that He designs great things for us, and desires to raise us to great holiness." Nay, the more we suffer in this life, the greater will be our reward in the life to come. "To those who love God all things work together for good" (Rom. viii. 28). Give yourself up, then, to God's guidance, for He allows nothing to happen you which will not be for your advantage, though you may see it not. What pruning is to the fruit-tree, suffering is to men.

5. Sufferings then are no real evil, but are benefits from the hand of God.

They are the means of bringing us both to temporal and eternal happiness.

God, Who loves us tenderly, has no other object in sending us sufferings but to make us happy. What we count as an evil is the bitterness of the medicine that is necessary for the health of our soul. There is really no evil in the world except sin. Sufferings can never really make us unhappy; men can be happy in spite of all kinds of sufferings. We see this in Job, in Tobias, in Our Lady. St. Paul says, "I am filled with comfort; I exceedingly abound with joy in all our tribulation" (2 Cor. vii. 4).

6. For this reason we should be patient under suffering, and should resign ourselves to the will of God.

Nay, more, we should rejoice in suffering, and thank God for it.

We should say with Job, " As it hath pleased the Lord, so it is done; blessed be the name of the Lord " (Job i. 21), or with Our Lord in the Garden of Olives, " Not My will, but Thine be done." We should behave as a sensible man behaves when he is sick; he willingly obeys the injunctions of the physician. God has lightened our sufferings for us, not only by His own example, but also by the promise of an eternal reward. See how the apostles rejoiced in their scourging (Acts v. 41). The Christian under suffering should rejoice as a workman rejoices who labors much, and looks forward to good pay, or as a tradesman, who amid the toilsome monotony of his business, thinks of the delightful holiday that is not far off. We must grasp sufferings as men grasp stinging nettles if they do not wish to be stung, firmly and boldly, not lightly and timorously; then they will do us no harm. In suffering we should repeat again and again the *Gloria Patri.* Men too often grumble and grow impatient under their sufferings. If a man asks the return of something he has lent us, we give it back with thanks; but if God does so, we grumble and are discontented. This want of patience increases our sufferings, besides offending God. The impatient are like oxen, who kick against the goad and only wound themselves the more. Yet it is no sin to be sorrowful and troubled under suffering; for Our Lord in the Garden of Olives was sorrowful even unto death. We must never despond in evil days, for after sorrow and suffering come joy and gladness.

By patience under suffering we quickly attain to a high degree of perfection, and lay up for ourselves a great store of merit.

When we resign ourselves patiently to the will of God amid contradictions, we are like a ship carried on by a strong breeze, and sail rapidly to the haven of eternal rest. " Blessed is the man that endureth temptation; for when he has been proved, he will receive a crown of life which God hath promised to them that love Him " (Jas. i. 12).

From our willingness to suffer can be ascertained how far we have advanced in perfection.

The courage of a soldier displays itself, not in peace, but in war. The sinner murmurs under suffering; the beginner is troubled, but is sorry for his impatience; the man more advanced in virtue is frightened, but takes courage and praises God; the perfect man does not wait for suffering, but goes boldly to meet it. The perfect do not ask God that they may be free from temptation or from suffering. They desire it, and value it as highly as men of the world value riches and gold and precious stones. Hence the prayer of St. Teresa was either to suffer or to die. " He who is able," says St. Francis of Sales, " to thank God equally for chastisement and for prosperity, has arrived at the summit of Christian perfection, and will find his happiness in God."

8. THE ANGELS.

1. The angels are pure spirits.

They can, however, take a visible form.

The angels are pure spirits without bodies, whereas men have both body and spirit. Yet the angels can take to themselves a bodily form, as did St. Raphael (Tob. v. 18), when he undertook to accompany the young Tobias on his journey. At the sepulchre of Our Lord, after the resurrection, the angels appeared in the form of young men, and the same was the case after Our Lord's ascension (Mark xvi. 5; Acts i. 10).

The nature of the angels is nobler than that of man; they have greater knowledge and greater power.

The angels excel all other beings that Our Lord has created. Our Lord says that not even the angels know when the Day of Judgment will come (Matt. xxiv. 36), thereby indicating that their knowledge is greater than that of men. So also is their power. An angel destroyed all the first-born of Egypt. Another angel caused the death of one hundred and eighty-five thousand soldiers of the King of Assyria, who had blasphemed God (Is. xxxvii. 36). An angel protected the three young men in the furnace at Babylon (Dan. iii. 49).

God created the angels for His own glory and service, as well as for their own happiness.

Among all the creatures that God has made, the angels resemble Him the most, and therefore the divine perfections shine forth the most brightly in them. They also glorify God by ceaselessly singing hymns of praise to Him in heaven. The angels also serve God. The word angel signifies messenger. "Are they not all ministering spirits," says St. Paul, "sent forth to minister to them that shall receive the inheritance of salvation?" (Heb. i. 14.) Even the bad angels promote the glory of God, for God turns their attacks on us to His glory and our profit. Goethe rightly describes Satan as "a power that always wills evil, and effects good."

The number of the angels is immeasurably great.

Daniel, in describing the throne of God says: "Thousands of thousands ministered to Him; and ten thousand times a hundred thousand stood before Him" (Dan. vii. 10). Holy Scripture calls them the heavenly host. In the Garden of Olives Our Lord said that if He were to ask the Father, He would presently send Him twelve legions of angels (Matt. xxvi. 53). The number of the angels is greater than that of all men who ever have lived or ever will live. "The number of the angels," says St. Dionysius the Areopagite, "is greater than that of the stars in heaven, or of the grains of sand on the seashore."

The angels are not all equal; there are nine choirs or ranks among them.

The rank of the angels is determined by the amount of the gifts that God has given them, and according to the office assigned them. Nearest to the throne of God are the seraphim, who burn more than the rest with the love of God; next to them are the cherubim, who are distinguished by the vastness of their knowledge. We also read in Scripture of thrones, dominations, principalities, powers, and also of three archangels, St. Michael, St. Gabriel, and St. Raphael. There is also a corresponding division among the fallen angels.

2. All the angels whom God created were, at the beginning, in the grace of God and well pleasing to Him. But many of the angels sinned through pride, and were cast down by God into hell forever (2 Pet. ii. 4).

When God created the angels, He created them all in His grace. But none can be crowned without a struggle (2 Tim. ii. 5), and God subjected the angels to trial, that so, according to the universal law of the universe, they might earn their reward of eternal happiness. In this trial a large number of the angels fell. They desired to be equal to God, and refused to submit their will to His (Cf. Is. xiv. 12-14). They did not abide in the truth (John viii. 44). Hence arose a great war in heaven. Michael and his angels fought with the dragon, and the dragon and his angels fought, and prevailed not, neither was their place found any more in heaven. The dragon was cast out and all his angels with him (Apoc. xii. 8, 9). They were all cast down to hell; not that they were confined to any local hell, for they are allowed to wander about the earth tempting men, but they carry their hell with them wherever they go, inasmuch as they everywhere suffer the torments of hell. Their leader was Satan, or Lucifer, for this was his name before he fell, and he is said to have been the highest of all the angels. The number of the fallen angels is less than that of those who remained faithful. The fall of the angels was the more terrible, because they had previously enjoyed such a high estate. The higher the place from which we fall, the worse the fall. At the Last Day the evil angels will be judged, and their wickedness and its punishment will be made known to the whole world (Jude 6; 2 Pet. ii. 4). To deny the existence of the evil angels is a grievous sin against faith.

3. The evil angels are our enemies; they envy us, seek to lead us to sin, and can, with God's permission, injure us in our bodies, or in our worldly goods.

The evil spirits are our enemies. With all their spite they can do nothing against God; so they vent their fury against men, who bear the image of God. Many theologians have asserted that the places of the angels who fell will be filled in heaven by men. " The knowledge that a creature of earth will occupy his place in heaven," says St. Thomas, " causes the devil more pain than the flames of hell." It was the devil who led our first parents to sin, and also Judas (John xiii. 27). The devil can also, so far as God permits, injure the bodies and the goods of men, as in the case of Job and the possessed in Our Lord's time. The devil's great object is to effect the ruin of the Church, which he knows is to be the means of destroying his power on earth (Matt. xvi. 18; Luke xxii. 31). He also knows that he and his angels will one day be judged by the saints (1 Cor. vi. 3). Many believe that as God assigns to each child at its birth a guardian angel, so the devil assigns to each a special devil to tempt it. Hence we must imitate the Jews when rebuilding the Temple (2 Esdr. iv. 17). We must work with one hand and with the other defend ourselves against the foe.

Yet the devil cannot do real harm to any one who keeps the commandments of God and avoids all sin.

The dog that is tied up cannot do any harm to those who keep out of range of his chain. The devil is like this dog. He can work on our memory and our imagination, but he has no power over our will or our understanding. He can persuade us, but he cannot compel us to evil. We must therefore energetically and promptly repel all bad thoughts that the devil puts into our heads. "Resist the devil," says St. James (iv. 7), "and he will fly from you." Our Lord dispatched the devil very promptly when He said "Begone, Satan!" It is a great thing to treat the devil and his temptations with great contempt, and also to turn our thoughts to other things, and not allow ourselves to be disturbed or troubled by his suggestions. He who allows himself to dwell on evil thoughts draws near to the dog who is chained, and is almost sure to be bitten by him. If the devil were allowed to use his full power against us we could not resist him, for when he fell he did not lose any of his natural powers, though he lost eternal happiness.

God gives the devil special power over some men:

1. God often allows men who are striving after high perfection, whom He especially favors, to be tried by the devil for long years in some extraordinary way, in order to cleanse them from their imperfections, and thoroughly humble them.

God allows His elect to be constantly besieged by the devil for years, and to endure temptations of extraordinary violence. Sometimes the devil appears to them in visible form; sometimes he assails their ears with hideous sounds; sometimes he is permitted to strike them and to throw them on the ground. God protects their life, but allows the devil to torment them with bodily pain and with sickness. They suffer the most terrible temptations against faith and against purity. The evil one has no power over their souls, but sometimes God allows him power over their bodies, so that they do and say the most extraordinary things in spite of themselves, in order that so they may be humbled in the eyes of men. Sometimes they even pour forth blasphemous words, and have no power to prevent themselves from doing so. These assaults of the devil are called obsession. Holy Job was assailed by the devil; and so was Our Lord in the desert; so were St. Anthony, St. Teresa, St. Mary Magdalen of Pazzi, the Curé d'Ars, and many other saints. These holy persons knew that God would never allow them to be tempted beyond their powers of resistance, and that God permitted these temptations for their greater sanctification. They were perfectly resigned to the will of God, and at length drove away the devil by their fearless resistance to his assaults. Thus when the devil threatened the life of St. Catharine of Sienna, she answered, " Do what you can; what is pleasing to God is pleasing to me." St. Mary Magdalen of Pazzi said to him, " You do not seem to know that you are preparing for me a glorious victory." St. Anthony in the desert defied him, saying, " How feeble you are ! I suppose that is why you are bringing such a crowd of devils to tempt me." When those who are tempted meet the devil with the courage of a lion, he has no more power against them than a startled hare, but when they fear him, then he comes on with all the force and boldness of a lion. He can always be driven away by the means of grace provided by the Church; by the sign of the cross, by invoking the name of Jesus and Mary, by holy water, by earnest prayer, by the use of relics, etc. The more violent the assaults of the devil, the greater will be the protection afforded by almighty God to His servants; often during times of trial they have revelations from God, or saints and angels appear to them to console and strengthen them. Those who deny the reality of these occurrences, of which we so often read in the lives of the saints, show very little acquaintance with the spiritual life. Yet it is the spirit of the Church to receive all accounts of these preternatural and supernatural occurrences with great caution, as there is always a danger of illusion or deceit. Nor need ordinary mortals fear such special attacks of the evil one; they are reserved for the special friends and favorites of God.

2. It also sometimes happens that God allows men of vicious lives, or those who sin against faith, to be punished or led astray by evil spirits.

God sometimes permits that the bodies of men who have given themselves over to the indulgence of their passions be possessed by evil spirits, as a town is occupied by a general who has conquered it. This state is called possession. In the time of Our Lord there were many thus possessed, and who in consequence were dumb (Matt. ix. 32), blind (Matt. xii. 22), and exceeding fierce (Matt. viii. 28). God permitted that then there should be many such, that He might show the power of the Son of God and the feebleness of the devils in His presence, and that He might drive them forth from those whom they tormented. Yet it does not follow that all who were possessed were necessarily so through their own fault. Some children were possessed from their birth (Mark ix. 20). Sometimes God allowed even holy men to be possessed for a time; but more often it was a punishment for grievous sin, and especially for a deliberate friendship with the devil, as was the case with the witch of Endor (1 Kings xxviii. 7 *seq.*; Cf. Acts xvi. 16). Such cases are not unfrequent now in pagan countries. God also permits the evil spirits to mislead those who practise spiritualism, which consists in the invoking of the spirits of the dead in order to discover things secret, or that are taking place at a distance. The devils personate the spirits invoked, and by their superior knowledge are able to reveal many things, by which they delude those who deal with them into thinking that they are really conversing with some departed relative or friend. On these occasions the spirits will sometimes take a material form. Spiritualism leads to the loss of faith or of morals, or at least to the ruin of the peace of mind of the person practising it. Very often it is mixed up with a great deal of imposture.

4. The angels who remained faithful to God behold the face of God continually and sing His praises.

Our Lord says of our guardian angels, "I say to you, that their angels always behold the face of My Father Who is in heaven." The angels at Our Lord's birth sang the praises of God. Their songs of praise are different, just as their knowledge and their love of God are different. The angels are sometimes represented as children, because they are immortal and therefore ever young; sometimes with wings to express the swiftness with which they pass from place to place, and their promptness in carrying out the will of God; sometimes with lilies in their hands to show their perfect spotlessness; sometimes with harps to signify that the praise of God is their constant employment; sometimes without any body, but only a head and wings, to show that they are intellectual beings. The holy angels also possess exceeding beauty and splendor. If an angel were to appear in the firmament of heaven in his full glory, the sun would disappear before his brightness, just as the stars now disappear before the brightness of the sun. When St. John saw an angel in all his glory, he thought he must be God Himself, and fell at his feet to adore him (Apoc. xxii. 8). In appearing to men the holy angels hide their glory. The angels will be our companions in heaven. This is why they take so great an interest in us while we are on earth, and rejoice over the sinner doing penance. They often intervene to help us in our spiritual and temporal needs, if we do not, by our resistance to grace, put obstacles in their way.

5. The holy angels are also called guardian angels, because they watch over us (Heb. i. 14).

Jacob saw a ladder reaching up to heaven, and the angels ascending and descending (Gen. xxviii. 12). This was to signify that they come down on earth to protect us, and ascend back to heaven to sing praise to God. The guardian angels watch over us, as a shepherd over his flock. They count it as their happiness that they are appointed to watch over the servants of God, and promote the welfare of souls, and no wonder, when we remember that the King and Lord of all things came "not to minister, but to be ministered unto." The service they render us causes them no trouble or anxiety, but rather joy and happiness, for their one desire is that the will of God should be done, and they rejoice in contributing to this. The general opinion of theologians is that every one has a special guardian angel, who watches over him all through his life. The dignity of the angels given to us depends on the dignity of the persons to whom they are assigned. Ordinary Christians have one of the lower orders of angels; priests, bishops, kings, etc., have nobler spirits to guard them. Cities, countries, parishes, religious houses, have each their guardian angel.

Our guardian angels help us in the following ways:

1. They put good thoughts into our minds, and move our will to what is good.

The angels who appeared to the shepherds at Bethlehem, and who were seen at the tomb of Christ, and after His ascension, made themselves visible and spoke to men; but generally they influence us without being seen or heard by us. They move us to some step that is conducive to the welfare of our souls or bodies, and often save us from some impending danger by a secret impulse, without which we should have incurred death or misfortune.

2. They offer our prayers and our good works to God.

Thus St. Raphael offered the prayers of Tobias (Tob. xii. 12). The angel in the Apocalypse offers the prayers of the saints in a golden censer (Apoc. viii. 3). This is not because God Himself does not hear our prayers, but the angels mingle their prayers with ours, and so make them more acceptable to God. "In all the benefits we receive from God," says St. Thomas, "our guardian angel takes part, because he helps in obtaining them for us."

3. They protect us in danger.

Thus St. Peter was delivered from prison by an angel (Acts xii. 7 *seq.*), Daniel was kept safe in the den of lions, and the three young men in the fiery furnace (Dan. vi. 22; iii. 49). We read stories sometimes of children being run over, or falling from a height, and escaping unhurt. We can scarcely doubt that this was owing to the intervention of their guardian angels. God has commissioned the angels thus to help us. "He hath given His angels charge over thee, to keep thee in all thy ways. In their hands they shall bear thee up, lest thou dash thy foot against a stone" (Ps. xc. 11). But the chief office of our guardian angel is to preserve us from the snares of the devil; the holy angels have powers over the evil spirits, who fly away at their approach (Cf. Tob. viii. 3). We must therefore commit ourselves to the care of our guardian angels in all times of danger, and before undertaking a journey, or any new enterprise, and we should wish our friends when they start on a journey, the good wish of Tobias when his son was leaving his home, "May the angel of God accompany you !"

4. They often reveal to men the will of God.

Instances in point are the sacrifice of Abraham, the message of the angel to Zacharias and to Our Lady. The appearance of an angel sometimes causes fear at first, but it soon changes to consolation and joy. It is just the opposite with the appearances of the evil angels; they give consolation to begin with, but this soon changes to confusion and fear.

If we desire the protection of the holy angels, we must try and imitate them by a holy life; we must also honor them, and often invoke their aid.

Experience teaches us that innocent children enjoy a wonderful protection from the angels. Innocence attracts them, and sin drives them away, as smoke drives away bees. We cannot expect our guardian angels to take care of us when we are doing what we know is displeasing to God. We must also beg for the aid of our guardian angel; we must congratulate him on his faithfulness to God; we must salute him when we go out and when we come in; we must thank him for all his benefits. We must say with Tobias, "What can be worthy of his benefits, and what can we give him sufficient for these things?" (Tob. xii. 3.) The Church honors our guardian angels on the second of October; in some places on the first Sunday in September.

9. MAN.

The Creation of Man.

The account of the creation of man is found in the beginning of the book of Genesis. Nothing is said about the time when man was created, but the general belief fixes the date at 4000 B.C. The four weeks of Advent seem to indicate that the Church adopts this view.

1. God made the body of man out of the dust of the earth, and breathed into him a living soul.

The soul of man is a spiritual substance. The materialist who denies the existence of the soul because it cannot be perceived by his senses, might as well deny the existence of human reason because he cannot see it. The soul is endowed with the two faculties of reason and free will. Some have supposed that there are in man two souls, on account of the different inclinations which strive for mastery in him, and the struggle that takes place between the leaning towards sensual enjoyment and the reason that condemns it. But this struggle only proves that the soul has different tendencies, in virtue of our nature being partly material and partly spiritual. The relations between the body and the soul of man are as follows: the body is the dwelling-place of the soul. As the nutshell to the kernel, as the dress to the man, as the hut to the hermit, such is the body to the soul. The body is also the instrument of the soul, whereby it may attain to eternal happiness. What his tools are to the carpenter, his brush to the painter, the organ to the organist, such the body is to the soul. The soul is the guide of the body, as the driver of his steed, or the captain of his ship. Too often the soul allows the evil desires of the body to lead it astray, to the ruin of both. The body is a good servant but a bad master. The soul also is the life of the body; as soon as the two are parted, the body soon returns to the dust from which it was formed. The souls of men are essentially different from those of the lower animals; and have different faculties and capabilities. The souls of animals are incapable of striving after perfection, or of searching into the causes of things; hence they can have no knowledge of their end; they are led by instinct, not by reason. They have no craving after a higher happiness and are quite satisfied with the enjoyment of sense; they have no spiritual nature, but are essentially dependent on matter.

It is an error to think that the bodies of men are developed out of those of the lower animals.

Many think that men are sprung from the lower animals by a process of gradual development. This is the theory advanced by the English naturalist, Darwin, who believed that the first man was a highly developed kind of monkey. There is an essential difference between the shape of the body of a man and an ape, and between the form of their skulls. The brain of man is far larger and heavier than that of an ape. Man has the gift of speech, the ape has not. Man has the power of forming abstract ideas, the ape has not. Man has a long period of growth, and a gradual development of his faculties; the ape shoots up very quickly to its full development. The ape only lives about thirty years; man can attain to the age of eighty or even one hundred years. Man is capable of the highest cultivation; the ape is not. No bones have ever yet been found which bridge over the impassable gulf that separates men from apes. There is no difference between the bones of men in the present day and those of men who lived thousands of years ago. Tradition and language bear witness to an early period when men enjoyed a higher cultivation, from which they afterwards fell away through sin and vice. The apes which bear the greatest resemblance to man in bodily form are stupid and without intelligence, and seem to have been created in order that we may see what man would have been if God had not breathed into him an immortal soul, and made him like to Himself. To those who trace the origin of men from apes may be applied the words of Holy Scripture, " Man when he was in honor did not understand; he hath been compared to senseless beasts, and made like to them" (Ps. xlviii. 21).

2. The first human beings that God created were Adam and Eve.

Eve was made from a rib of Adam while he slept, and from Adam and Eve all the millions who now cover the face of the earth were descended. Hence all are members of one and the same family. The differences of color and of the shape of the skull are the result of differences of climate, food, and way of living. We find that animals gradually change their shape and color under a different climate. All men have certain common bodily characteristics, and also the mental faculties of will, memory, and understanding. The oldest legends of all existing peoples tell of a primeval happiness from which man fell, of a deluge over all the inhabited portion of the earth, etc., and so bear witness to a common origin.

Yet all men derive only their bodies from Adam; for the soul of every man is created by God.

It is not man, but God, Who communicates to each of us his soul when he comes into existence. " The Lord formeth the spirit of man in him" (Zach. xii. 1). Just as the Holy Spirit in Baptism or in the Sacrament of Penance descends into the soul of man, and gives it spiritual life, so God gives natural life to the body of man when formed, and places the soul in it. So He did with the bodies of Adam and Eve at their creation. God creates each soul and at the same moment places it in the body which He has prepared for it. It is therefore an error to suppose, as Tertullian did, that the soul of the child is sprung from the soul of its parent, as one flame is engendered from another. Some have foolishly asserted that all men have one and the same soul, others that God created the souls of all men when He first created the world. This was the doctrine of Plato and Origen, and is entirely false.

10. THE SOUL OF MAN.

1. The soul of man is made in the image of God, since it is a spirit like to God.

Before the creation of man God said, " Let us make man to our own image and likeness and let him have dominion over the beasts and the whole earth " (Gen i. 26). Man is made in the image of God; his likeness to God is to be found in his soul, which possesses reason and free will, and thence has the power of knowing what is beautiful and good, and of loving it. He, moreover, through these two faculties has dominion over the visible world, as God has dominion over the whole universe. In the words spoken before the creation of man, God joined together the likeness of Himself and dominion over the earth. Man attains to a perfect likeness to God only when he is in the grace of God, for in this case he is made a " partaker of the divine nature " (2 Pet. i. 4). The just man is truly the lord of the whole earth and of all creatures upon it, whereas the sinner is the slave of creatures. Man, through his likeness to God, has not only the power of knowing the true and the beautiful and the good, but he has also the power of knowing, loving, and enjoying God in His divine majesty. Just as a globe has a feeble resemblance to the earth, so the soul of man has a feeble resemblance to God. The soul is also an image of the Blessed Trinity, in virtue of its three powers, memory, understanding, and will. In its memory it resembles the Father, in its understanding the Son, and in its will the Holy Ghost. As these three powers are united in one soul, so the three persons of the Blessed Trinity are united in one and the same nature. Notice the words used at the creation: " Let *us* make man," thereby indicating the plurality of persons in the Blessed Trinity. It is its likeness to the Blessed Trinity that gives to every single soul its priceless value; it is this which explains the Incarnation. The soul of man is worth more than all the stars of heaven. The body of man is not made in the image of God, for God is a pure spirit, but yet the likeness to God stamps itself in some way on the body, as being the instrument of the soul, both in its upright bearing, and in the dominion it exerts over the irrational animals (Cf. Ps. viii. 5, 6). " What is man that Thou art mindful of him ? Thou hast crowned him with glory and honor, and hast given him dominion over the works of Thy hands."

2. The soul of man is immortal, i.e., it can never cease to exist.

The soul can never cease to exist, but it becomes spiritually dead when it loses the grace of God by mortal sin. It cannot lose consciousness, but it can lose God. A branch that falls from the tree continues to exist, but is nevertheless dead. Sinners are thus dead, even while they live; the just on the other hand live even after they are dead.

That the soul of man is immortal we know from the words of Jesus Christ.

Our Lord says, " Fear not them who can kill the body, but cannot kill the soul " (Matt. x. 28), and to the good thief on the cross He says, " To-day thou shalt be with Me in paradise " (Luke xxiii. 43). He teaches the same truth in the story of the rich man and Lazarus (Luke xvi. 19). " God is the God of Abraham and Isaac and Jacob; and is not the God of the dead but of the living " (Matt. xxii. 32).

We learn the same truth from the numberless appearances of the dead to the living.

At Our Lord's transfiguration Moses appeared, who had been long dead (Matt. xvii. 3). At the time of Our Lord's crucifixion many who were dead appeared in Jerusalem (Matt. xxvii. 53). The prophet Jeremias and the priest Onias appeared to Judas Maccabeus before his victory over Nicanor (2 Mach. xv. 11 *seq.*). Our Lady has constantly appeared to saints and to others, and so have many of the saints as well as those who are suffering in purgatory; sometimes to console and encourage the living, sometimes to warn them, and in the case of the holy souls, to ask for prayers. The lost rarely (and some think never) appear to men, unless it may be in some rare cases to warn the living. It is unlawful to invoke the appearance of the dead, and those who do so are tricked by the devil, who takes the form of the person invoked, or indicates their supposed presence by sounds, raps, etc. All true appearances of the dead are wrought by the instrumentality of the angels. We must be very cautious in accepting such appearances as real, but yet we ought not to reject them altogether. Many reject all such appearances, because they know that, if they acknowledged them to be true, they would have to change their way of living, and this they are not willing to do.

We can also prove from reason that the soul is immortal.

Man has a longing after a perfect and lasting happiness. This longing is common to all men, and is implanted in them by their Creator. Such happiness can never be attained in this world—and therefore if man possessed the desire for it, without any hope of its being satisfied, he would be more unfortunate than the brutes who have no such desire, and God, in implanting it in his breast would be, not good, but cruel. If man had no immortal soul, the wicked who do evil all their lives long would go unpunished, and the just, who by self-sacrifice have robbed themselves of the enjoyments of life, would go unrewarded. This would be an injustice impossible to a God of perfect justice. We are also conscious of an individual unity in each one of us, which is independent of our body, which perseveres in spite of all bodily changes, and continues from childhood to old age. It is present during sleep as well as during waking hours, and is active when all our bodily senses are wrapped in repose and inactivity. St. Augustine tells a story of Gennadius, a physician of Carthage, who would not believe in the immortality of the soul. One night he had a dream, in which he saw standing before him a beautiful young man, clothed in white, who said to him: " Dost thou see me ? " He answered, " Yes, I see you." The young man rejoined, " Dost thou see me with thine eyes ? " " No," answered Gennadius, " for they are closed in sleep." " With what, then, dost thou see me ? " " I know not." The young man continued: " Dost thou hear me ? " " Yes." " With thine ears ? " " No, for these too are wrapped in sleep." " With what then dost thou hear me ? " " I know not." " Are you speaking to me ? " was the next question. " Yes." " With thy mouth ? " " No." " With what then ? " " I know not." Then the young man said: " See now, thou sleepest—and yet thou seest, hearest, and speakest. The hour will come when thou wilt sleep in death, and yet thou wilt see and hear and speak and feel." Gennadius woke, and knew that God had sent an angel to teach him the immortality of the soul. No particle of matter is ever lost. Matter takes different forms, but the same amount of matter remains throughout. If matter never perishes, is it possible that the soul, which belongs to a far higher order, is destined to perish ?

All nations of the earth believe in the immortality of the soul.

When Jacob heard of the death of his son Joseph, he expressed a wish to go and join him in the nether world (Gen. xxxvii. 35). The Jews were forbidden to call up the dead or hold intercourse with them (Deut. xviii. 11). The Greeks and Romans believed in Tartarus and Elysium. The Egyptians believed that the soul wandered about for three thousand years before finding rest. In other nations the offerings for the dead, and the cultus of the departed spirits or Manes, testify to the same belief. There are only a few, and those men who are in mortal sin, who declare that they think that death is the end of our existence. Most of those who put an end to their lives do so, not with the idea that after death they will cease to be, but because they imagine life is intolerable—not realizing the consequences of their act.

11. *THE SUPERNATURAL ENDOWMENTS OF MAN.*

Our first parents before the Fall had a happiness almost equal to that of the angels when first created. Hence the Psalmist says of man, " Thou hast made him a little lower than the angels; Thou hast crowned him with glory and honor " (Ps. viii. 6). Heathen nations have legends of the happiness of the first man; they termed it the golden age. Hesiod says that men lived then like gods, in perfect happiness.

1. Our first parents were created in the grace of God, and therefore possessed singular perfections of soul and body.

" Adam was created," says the Council of Trent, " in justice and holiness; he was a partaker of the divine nature." This justice and holiness he did not have of himself, but God gave it to him; just as the eye does not possess light from within, but absorbs it from without.

The special privileges granted to the soul of man at his first creation were as follows: An enlightened understanding, a will free from all weakness, and the possession of sanctifying grace. Through means of these he was the child of God, the heir of heaven, and well-pleasing in the sight of God.

"God filled them with wisdom and the knowledge of understanding," says the Wise Man (Ecclus. xvii. 5, 6). He gave Adam an insight into the inner nature of things, so that he was able to give appropriate names to all the animals. He also knew by inspiration the indissolubility of marriage. The will of man was weakened by no sensual desires. Adam and Eve were naked, but felt no shame, because in them there was no rebellion of the flesh against the spirit, no struggle necessary to avoid sin. They also had the Holy Spirit dwelling within them, and His sanctifying grace; they were like to God, full of love for Him, and children of God; and because children, also heirs of God and joint-heirs with Christ.

The special perfections of their bodies were that they were immortal, and free from all liability to sickness and disease; they were in paradise, and had dominion over all the creatures around them.

God created man immortal (Wisd. ii. 23). Death only came in as the punishment of disobedience (Gen. ii. 17). The death threatened was bodily as well as spiritual death, for the punishment of their sin was " Dust thou art, and unto dust thou shalt return " (Gen. iii. 19). Man had indeed to work in paradise, but this work was part of his happiness, and caused him no fatigue. He had no sickness, for sickness is the forerunner of death. Paradise was a lovely garden, full of noble trees and lovely flowers, and the fairest fruits; many beautiful animals were there, who were perfectly obedient to his behests. There was also a river in paradise divided into four branches. In the midst of the garden was the tree of the knowledge of good and evil, and close by it the tree of life, the fruits of which were a protection against disease and death. Paradise is said to have been situated between the Tigris and the Euphrates. Man had also a complete dominion over all the wild beasts. Not that their nature was then different from now, but the grace and dignity of man rendered them submissive to his will, and made them fear and obey him (Ecclus. xvii. 4). Something of this power still remains to man; it is said that no wild beast can look a man steadily in the face. We see the same thing in the natural order now, in the wild beast tamers; and in the supernatural in the power that many of the saints possessed over the wild beasts, e.g., St. Francis of Assisi, and many of the martyrs before whose feet the fiercest of the animals in the Roman amphitheatre lay down in prostrate homage. This was due to their great purity and freedom from sin.

2. These special perfections of our first parents we call supernatural gifts, because they are something altogether beyond, and were added to, human nature.

Thus a rich man out of compassion provides a poor orphan with food, clothing, lodging, instruction in a trade. These would correspond to the natural gifts given by God to man. But the rich man in his bounty goes further; he adopts the orphan, clothes him as if he were his own son, gives him a room in his own house, and the education of a gentleman. These would correspond in some way to the supernatural gifts given by God to man. The first of natural gifts bestow upon the orphan a sort of likeness to the giver, but the second impart to him a far closer likeness. So the supernatural gifts of God to man impart to him a far closer likeness to God than the natural. Or to take another illustration; a painter can trace the portrait of a man with a few strokes in black and white. But if he takes his brush and colors the drawing, if he paints the eyes blue, the cheeks red, the hair brown, etc., the likeness becomes more beautiful and corresponds more closely to the original. So it is with the natural and the supernatural gifts of God. When God at man's creation said, "Let us make man in our image and likeness," the image refers to the natural, the likeness to the supernatural gifts of God.

12. ORIGINAL SIN.

The story of the Fall of man is a true story, not a mere fable. This is the general opinion of theologians.

1. God imposed on man in paradise a precept; He forbade him to eat the fruit of one of the trees which stood in the midst of the Garden of Eden.

The fruit of the tree of good and evil was not bad in itself, for God did not place anything that was evil in paradise; it was only bad and injurious to man because it was forbidden.

By obedience to this precept God intended that Adam and Eve should merit eternal happiness.

It was the intention of God to bestow upon our first parents eternal happiness—an inheritance that was to be theirs as children of God. But as a happiness that is earned is a greater happiness, and one of greater value than if it were bestowed without any action deserving of it, God in His goodness decreed that man should earn it as a reward of obedience. If man had not transgressed the command of God, he would have passed without pain and without death from the earthly into the celestial paradise. The posterity of Adam would have come into existence, like him, in a state of original justice. They would have died as Adam died if they had sinned like him, but the sin would not have passed on to their children, for Adam alone was the appointed head and representative of the human race.

2. Man allowed himself to be led astray by the devil, and transgressed the precept of his Creator.

The devil was envious of the happiness of our first parents. "By the envy of the devil death came into the world" (Wisd. ii. 24). "The devil was a murderer from the beginning" (John viii. 4). He deceived Eve by a lie. Hence Our Lord calls him the father of lies (John viii. 4). He took a visible form because a mere internal suggestion would have had no power to influence the mind of our first parents in their state of original justice. He took the form of a serpent, because God would allow him to take no other and the serpent was a fit emblem of his cunning and poisonous wickedness. St. Augustine tells us that Adam and Eve had already admitted· the beginnings of evil by thinking little of God and allowing themselves to be distracted by visible and palpable things. This was the occasion of the temptation. Their great happiness had made them unwary, and Eve foolishly lingered near the tree of the knowledge of good and evil, and listened to the serpent, instead of turning away at once. The common tradition among the Fathers is that Adam was created on a Friday and fell on the following Friday, at the same hour at which Our Lord on Good Friday died upon the cross.

3. The transgression of the precept of God had disastrous consequences; man lost sanctifying grace, and all his supernatural gifts, and also suffered injuries both in soul and body.

The disobedience of our first parents received this severe punishment, because the law given them was one that it was easy for them to obey, and because they had such a high degree of knowledge. The sin they committed ·was a mortal sin, else it would not have been necessary for God Himself to die upon the cross in order to expiate it. From the cost of the remedy we may judge of the deadly nature of the wound. Just as the man who fell among the thieves on the road to Jericho was robbed of his goods, and also sorely wounded, so man was robbed by Satan of his supernatural gifts, and was sorely wounded in his natural gifts. In other words, the supernatural likeness to God was lost, and his whole nature, body and soul alike, was disfigured and weakened.

Original sin injured the soul of man in the following ways: His understanding was darkened, his will weakened and made prone to evil; he lost supernatural grace and thus became displeasing to God, and could no more enter into the kingdom of heaven.

His understanding was darkened, i.e., he had not the same knowledge of the nature of God, of the will of God, the end of life, etc. His will was weakened. for by sin the harmony between his spiritual and his sensible faculties was destroyed, so that the inclinations of his senses no longer submitted without revolt to the dominion of his reason. The flesh rebelled against the spirit in punishment for man's rebellion against God. Hence St. Paul says, " I see another law in my members, fighting against the law of my mind " (Rom. vii. 23). " The flesh lusteth against the spirit " (Gal. v. 17). Henceforward man's nature was drawn towards the things of sense, as iron is drawn by the power of the magnet. Many other evil tendencies also arose in him. Doubt in the goodness of God, in His truth and justice; vanity and pride, etc. Eve, who had fancied that she was going to become like to God, condemned herself and her posterity to a foolish curiosity, to a love of dress, and ill-timed loquacity. Man has not lost the freedom of his will by original sin, else he would not have that consciousness of being able to exercise choice, or that feeling of remorse when he had yielded. Our first parents also lost sanctifying grace, the justice and holiness in which they were created, and the friendship of God which accompanied it. He who dies still burdened with original sin cannot see the face of God in heaven, but he does not suffer the pains of hell unless he has committed grievous sin himself. Children who die unbaptized are excluded from heaven, but it does not follow that their existence is one of pain or misery.

Original sin did injury to the body of man in the following ways: He became subject to sickness and death; he was shut out from paradise and had to labor and to suffer. Woman became subject to man; the forces of nature and the lower animals had power to injure man; lastly the devil had permission from God to tempt him to sin, and to injure him in his temporal possessions.

Man was condemned to die in consequence of original sin. God said to Adam " In the sweat of thy brow thou shalt eat bread, until thou return to the earth from which thou wast taken; for dust thou art and to dust thou shalt return " (Gen. iii. 19). Of these words the Church reminds us on Ash Wednesday, when the priest places the ashes on the heads of the faithful. Death is the worst consequence of original sin. But the death of the body is but the sensible image of the terrible and eternal death of the soul, from which man can only be delivered through the redemption of Christ and by penance. The exclusion from the earthly paradise also had its meaning, and was meant to remind man how sin excludes him from the celestial paradise of heaven. Man had also to labor hard. God said to Adam: " Cursed is the earth in thy work. With labor and toil thou shalt eat the fruit thereof all the days of thy life " (Gen iii. 17). Because of this curse the Church makes use of various blessings on material things. Woman had to be subject to her husband, because she had led him into disobedience, and had to bear children in sorrow because she had involved them in sorrow through her disobedience The lower animals also received power to injure man. He had revolted against God, his Master; so it was only just that they should rebel against him. The devil has also a great influence over man, in accordance with the saying of Holy Scripture: " By whom a man is overcome, of the same also he is made the slave " (2 Pet. ii. 19). He can tempt them more easily and lead them to mortal sin; he can also injure them in their worldly goods (Cf. Job). He is the prince of this world, and has the empire of death (Heb. ii. 14). A heavy yoke lies upon the shoulders of the children of Adam from the day of their birth to the day of their death (Ecclus. xl. 1). The punishments that God sent upon man were a valuable medicine to counteract the effects of sin. Sickness, death, the necessity of labor, and the subjection of men one to another were intended to check pride and sensuality. Man was driven out of paradise lest he should eat of the tree of life, and so live forever in this valley of tears. His banishment was also an effective means of leading him to penance.

4. The sin of our first parents with all its evil consequences has passed on to their descendants.

Not merely the consequences of sin, but the sin itself, has in some sense passed on from Adam to his descendants, so that it is true of all of them that they have sinned in Adam. If it were not so, God could not with justice have visited that sin upon them. We are all by nature children of wrath (Eph. ii. 3). But we partake in the sin of Adam, as the members of the body partake in the sin which the soul commits through their agency, by putting them in motion to perform the sinful act. Suppose a king bestows an estate upon one of his servants, on the condition that the servant remain faithful to him. He is unfaithful, and thereby loses the estate—not he only, but also his whole posterity. So it is with original sin. We must also remember that original sin and all its consequences are not anything positive, but are the absence of that which would otherwise be present. It is the absence of the supernatural grace of God; of original justice, with all the privileges and perfections that it carries with it. When we say that we have sinned in Adam, this does not mean that we have imitated Adam's sin by some positive act of our own. All children have sinned in Adam, even though absolutely free from any personal act of sin.

The sin that we inherit from Adam is called original sin.

We are already tainted with sin before we draw our first breath, or see the light of day. We are conceived in sin (Ps. l. 7). Even the children of Christians are born in sin. Not only the seed of the wild olive, but also of the cultivated olive comes up as a wild plant. So is it with the children of Christian as well as of heathen parents.

Only Jesus Christ and His holy Mother were free from original sin.

All mankind save Christ and our blessed Lady were conceived in sin. St. John the Baptist (Luke i. 15) and probably the prophet Jeremias (Jer. i. 5), were born without sin, having been cleansed from sin in their mothers' womb, but they were not conceived without sin. Some believe that St. Joseph was also born free from sin. All other men were cleansed from sin in baptism. The history of man is unintelligible to those who do not believe in the doctrine of original sin. Oh, how great is the misery that original sin has brought into the world ! Yet how few there are who are conscious of their misery ! Men are like children born in slavery, who laugh, and play, and enjoy themselves, as if they were free. It is only the saints, who know the emptiness of the joys of earth, who lament over the misery of sin.

SECOND TO SEVENTH ARTICLE OF THE CREED :
JESUS CHRIST.

1. *THE REDEMPTION.*

Our Lord Jesus Christ, Our Redeemer, has freed us from the evil consequences of sin.

Man after the Fall was unable to regain for himself his former holiness and justice, and all the goods that were bound up with these. A man whose body is dead cannot raise himself again to bodily life; so one who is spiritually dead cannot raise himself again to spiritual life. Man after the Fall became like a sick man who cannot move hand or foot, or arise from the bed on which he is lying. What the Good Samaritan was to the man who had fallen among thieves, Our Lord is to the man who has been wounded by the craft of the devil and robbed of his spiritual and supernatural gifts. Jesus Christ is also called Our Saviour or Our Redeemer, because He saved us from hell and brought us back at the cost of His own precious blood.

Christ freed us from the spiritual consequences of sin in the following manner: He enlightened our understanding by His teaching, inclined our will to good by His precepts and promises, and by His sacrifice of Himself upon the cross won for us the means of grace by which we once more attain to sanctification and become the children of God and heirs of the kingdom of heaven.

Christ took upon Himself a threefold office, that of Prophet or Teacher, Priest, and King. This threefold office he ascribes to Himself under various titles. He calls Himself the Light of the world (John xii. 46), because He enlightens the darkness of our understanding by His doctrine. As a light makes distant objects clear and visible, so Christ makes clear to us the most distant objects, God and His perfections, the world to come, heaven and hell, time and eternity. Before Pilate He calls Himself the King Whose kingdom is not of this world (John xviii. 36). He also calls Himself the Good Shepherd, Who gives His life for His sheep (John x. 11). He also often compares Himself to a guide or leader (John xiv. 6; Matt. x. 38). We are wanderers in this world; we have here no abiding dwelling-place, but seek one that is to come. The road is rough, steep, and surrounded with precipices, and we in our ignorance are in constant danger of wandering from the way. Christ undertakes to be our Guide. He says, "I am the way, the truth, and the life" (John xiv. 6), and He promises that if we take Him for our Guide, and follow in His sacred footsteps, we shall never go wrong. St. Paul calls Christ our great High Priest (Heb. ii. 17), Who needs not, like other priests, first to offer sacrifices for his own sins, and then for the people. By His obedience He atoned for Adam's disobedience (Rom. v. 19), for He was obedient to death, even to the death of the cross (Phil. ii. 8). Christ opened heaven again to us by earning for us the means of grace. By which, and especially by the sacraments and holy Mass, we can obtain sanctifying grace and be made children of God. In opening heaven to us, Christ tore away the veil which shut us out from the holy of holies (Matt. xxvii. 51), i.e., from heaven, and by His blood gave us a sure hope of entering in (Heb. x. 19). The cross is thus the key of heaven for us.

Christ freed us also from the consequences of sin as it affected our bodies; He has died instead of us, and has thus earned for us the resurrection of our bodies; He has by His teaching and His example taught us what we must do in order to be happy in this world, to overcome the world, and so to attain to the celestial paradise; lastly He has given us the means by which we may vanquish and drive far from us the enemy of our souls.

By His own resurrection Christ insured for us the resurrection of our bodies. " By man came death, and by man came also the resurrection from the dead " (1 Cor. xv. 21). By following the teaching of Christ, we shall secure true peace on earth (Cf. John iv. 13), and by practising the virtues that He taught us, especially humility, chastity, and liberality, we shall overcome the devil and the world. By the sacramentals we drive away from us the evil one. Christ has broken the power of the devil (Apoc. xii. 10, 11), but the final victory over him will be at the end of the world (1 Cor. xv. 24, 25; Cf. Luke x. 18). By the death of Christ we have won back almost all that was lost by original sin, though some of its consequences still remain, such as sickness, death, and evil tendencies. Yet we have won more by the death of Christ than we lost by sin. Where sin abounded, grace did the more abound (Rom. v. 20). Hence the Church exclaims in the Office for Holy Saturday: " O happy fault, which obtained for us so great a Redeemer ! "

2. THE PROMISE OF THE REDEEMER.

God forgave fallen man, though He had not forgiven the angels. Man's sin was not so grievous; he had less light and knowledge, and moreover was tempted by them. Besides, he at once to some extent confessed and lamented his sin. Lastly God would not, for the guilt of one, thrust down into eternal banishment from Himself the whole race of men.

1. Immediately after the Fall God promised man a Redeemer.

For He said to the serpent, " I will put enmity between thee and the woman, between thy seed and her seed; she shall crush thy head " (Gen. iii. 15).

The seed of the woman here referred to is Our Lord Jesus Christ, and the woman is in all probability the Blessed Virgin Mary. There is to be a complete enmity between Our Lord and His holy Mother on one side, and the devil and his friends on the other. These words of almighty God are a promise that the power of the devil should be destroyed, and that the whole race of men, who through original sin had fallen under the power of the devil, in that he had great influence over them in persuading them to sin, should be freed from their subjection to him. These words are called the Protevangelium or first Gospel, inasmuch as they are the first promise of a Redeemer to come. Yet He was not to come at once. Man had to learn by experience and by suffering the evil of sin, and by seeing the effects of God's anger against it, e.g., in the Flood, the destruction of the cities of the plain, in the destruction of the Tower of Babel, etc.

2. Two thousand years later God promised to Abraham that the Redeemer should be one of his descendants.

Abraham lived in Ur in Chaldea, and later in Haran in Mesopotamia. He preserved amid the idolatry around him the worship of the true God. God commanded him to leave his father's house, and journey forth into a land which was to be shown him. In reward for his prompt obedience God promised him that in him all the families of the earth should be blessed (Gen. xii. 2, 3). He directed his steps towards the fertile land of Palestine, and promised him a numerous posterity. Abraham is called the father of the faithful (Rom. iv. 11). God repeated the same promise when the three angels visited Abraham (Gen. xviii. 18), and again when Abraham, in obedience to God's command, offered up his only son Isaac (Gen. xxii. 17).

The same promise that God had made to Abraham He repeated to Isaac and to Jacob, and one thousand years later to King David.

God appeared to Isaac when he was about to fly into Egypt on account of the famine in Palestine (Gen. xxvi. 2 *seq.*), and to Jacob when he was flying from his brother Esau, and saw the ladder reaching to heaven (Gen. xxviii. 12), and repeated to each the same promise. To King David the prophet Nathan announced, by God's command, that He would raise up to him a son whose throne should be established forever (2 Kings vii. 13). The men who belonged to the family from which Christ was to be born were termed patriarchs. All the patriarchs reached a good old age. God had ordained this in order that they might hand down the knowledge of Him to their posterity.

3. At a later time God sent the prophets, and through their mouth foretold many things about the coming, the birth, the person, the sufferings, the death, and the final triumph and glory of the Redeemer.

The prophets were men enlightened by God (men of God), who spoke to the people of Israel in God's name and with His authority. Their chief task was to keep the people from sin, and to reprove them when they had sinned, and also to prepare the mind of men for the advent of the Redeemer. They were from different classes in society;

Isaias was of royal blood, Amos was a herdsman, Eliseus was called from the plough to the prophetical office. God gave them the power of working miracles, of foretelling His judgments, and also of prophesying respecting the Messias. Most of them lived a life of penance; they were held in great veneration by the people, but were persecuted and in many cases suffered a violent death (Matt. xxiii. 30). There were in all about seventy prophets. Moses was one of the greatest of the prophets (Deut. xxxiv. 10), and Isaias was greater still, on account of his clear prophesies respecting the Messias. The last of the prophets was Malachias, who prophesied about B.C. 450. Sixteen of the prophets left writing behind them. Four of these are called the greater prophets (Isaias, Jeremias, Ezechiel, Daniel); twelve the lesser prophets, on account of the smaller amount of their writings.

4. Of the advent of the Messias the prophets have given the following account:

1. The Messias was to be born in Bethlehem.

Micheas says: "Thou Bethlehem Ephrata, art a little one among the thousands of Juda; out of thee shall come forth unto me He Who is to be the Ruler in Israel; and His going forth is from the beginning unto the days of eternity" (Mich. v. 2). Hence the three kings were informed that Christ would be born in Bethlehem (Matt. ii. 5).

2. The Messias was to come at a time when the Temple was still standing.

When the Jews after their return from captivity began to rebuild the Temple, the old men who had seen the former Temple began to weep. They saw from the character of the foundations that the new Temple would not be as large, nor as beautiful as the old one. The prophet Aggeus comforted them by telling them that in this new Temple "the Desired of all nations should come, and fill it with glory" (Agg. ii. 8-10). But this second Temple was destroyed by Titus seventy years after Christ, and was never rebuilt.

3. The Messias was to come when the Jews no longer were an independent kingdom.

Jacob, in blessing his sons before his death, said to Juda: "The sceptre shall not be taken away from Juda, till He come that is to be sent, and to Him shall be the expectation of the nations" (Gen. xlix. 10). From this time the tribe of Juda was the leading tribe (Numb. ii. 3-9). King David was of the tribe of Juda, and so were his successors up to the captivity in Babylon. Zorobabel, who brought the Jews back from captivity, was of the same tribe. When the Jews regained their liberty, they were under the rule of the Maccabees, who also belonged to Juda. It was not till the year 39 B.C. that the Jewish monarchs were deprived of their sovereignty, and Herod the Great, a foreigner and a pagan, was raised to the throne by the authority of the Romans. In the time of Herod a Redeemer was looked for all over Judea. Herod was alarmed at the inquiry of the Magi for the new-born King (Matt. ii. 3); the Jewish people thought that St. John the Baptist was the Messias (Luke iii. 15); the Samaritan woman to whom Our Lord talked at Jacob's well was looking forward to the advent of the Messias (John iv. 25). The chief priest conjured Jesus to tell them whether He was the Messias (Matt. xxvi. 63). As many as sixty impostors about this time gave out that they were the Christ, and deceived many. Even among the heathen there was, at the time of Christ, an expectation of a deliverer, who would banish crime and restore peace to the world (Cf. Virg., Ecl. 9).

4. The prophet Daniel (605–530) foretold that from the rebuilding of Jerusalem (453), until the public appearance of the Messias, there would be sixty-nine weeks of years, and until the death of the Messias sixty-nine and a half weeks of years.

This prediction was revealed to him by the archangel Gabriel, as he was one day offering the evening oblation, and was praying for the deliverance of his people out of captivity. Cyrus, in the year 536, gave the Jewish people leave to return to Palestine and to rebuild their city. In the year 453 the King Artaxerxes gave his cup-bearer Nehemias full powers to fortify Jerusalem; this had not been allowed by Cyrus, on account of which the Jews had been exposed to the constant attacks of their enemies. Now if we add to 453 sixty-nine weeks of years (483 years) we have the date of the commencement of Christ's public ministry or if we add sixty-nine and one half weeks of years (486½ years) we have the date of the crucifixion (A.D. 33½).

5. The Messias was to be born of a virgin of the House of David.

As a sign God gave to King Achaz the following prophecy: "Behold a virgin shall conceive, and bear a son, and His name shall be called Emmanuel [God with us]" (Is. vii. 14). And of the tribe of which the Messias is to be born the prophet Jeremias says, "Behold the days come, saith the Lord, that I will raise up to David a just branch, and a king shall reign and shall be wise, and shall execute judgment and justice on the earth" (Jer. xxiii. 5), and His name shall be "the Lord our just One."

6. The Messias was to be preceded by a precursor or forerunner, who was to preach in the desert, and to live an angelic life.

Isaias says of this forerunner, that he was to be "the voice of one crying in the desert: Prepare ye the way of the Lord, make straight in the desert a path for our God" (Is. xl. 3). And God says through the mouth of Malachias " Behold, I send My angel, and he shall prepare My way before My face. And presently the Lord, Whom you seek, shall come to His Temple " (Mal. iii. 1). This precursor was St. John the Baptist.

7. With the Messias a new star was to appear.

The prophet Balaam announced to the King of Moab, when the Israelites were approaching: " I shall see Him, but not now; I shall behold Him, but not near; a star shall come out of Jacob, and a sceptre shall rise up from Israel " (Numb. xxiv. 17).

8. The Messias was to be adored by kings from distant lands, and they were to bring Him gifts (Ps. lxxi. 10).

9. At the time of the birth of the Messias many children were to be put to death.

We read in the prophet Jeremias, "A voice was heard on high, of lamentation and mourning and weeping; of Rachel weeping for her children, and refusing to be comforted, because they are not " (Jer. xxxi. 15). Rachel here represents the Jewish people. She died in Bethlehem and was buried there (Gen. xxv. 19).

10. The Messias was to fly to Egypt, and to return again from thence (Osee xi. 11).

5. Of the person of the Messias the following prophecies had been uttered:

1. The Messias was to be the Son of God (Ps. ii. 7).

Through the prophet Nathan God promises David the Redeemer, and says: "He will call Me Father and I will call Him Son " (2 Kings vii. 14). In a psalm God addresses the Messias: "Thou art My Son; this day have I begotten Thee " (Ps. ii. 7).

2. He shall be at the same time both God and man.

Isaias says, "A Child is born to us, and a Son is given to us; and His name shall be called Wonderful, Counsellor, God, the Mighty, the Father of the world to come, the Prince of peace " (Is. ix. 6).

3. He was to be a great worker of miracles.

"God Himself shall come and save you. Then shall the eyes of the blind be opened and the ears of the deaf shall be unstopped. Then shall the lame man leap as the hart, and the tongue of the dumb shall be unstopped " (Is. xxxv. 5-7).

4. He was to be a priest like to Melchisedech.

"The Lord hath sworn and He will not repent: Thou art a priest forever after the order of Melchisedech " (Ps. cix. 4). Christ offered bread and wine at the Last Supper, and offers it daily in holy Mass through the hands of the priests who are His representatives.

5. He was to be a prophet or teacher of the people.

To Moses God had said, "I will raise up unto them a prophet, out of the midst of thy brethren, like to thee " (Deut. xviii. 18). Hence the Jews named the Messias, "the Prophet Who was to come into the world " (John vi. 14). As prophet the Messias was to teach and to prophesy. He was also to be the teacher of the nations (Is. xlix. 1-6).

6. He was to be King of a new kingdom (Jer. xxiii. 5),

which was never to be destroyed, and was to embrace all other kingdoms (Dan. ii. 44).

This kingdom is the Catholic Church, or the Church of the whole world. Before Pilate Christ proclaimed Himself a king, and said, "My kingdom is not of this world," i.e., His kingdom was to be a spiritual one (John xviii. 36).

6. Of the sufferings of the Messias the prophets spoke as follows:

1. The Messias was to enter into Jerusalem riding on an ass (Zach. ix. 9).

2. He was to be sold for thirty pieces of silver. " And I took the thirty pieces of silver, and I cast them into the house of the Lord " (Zach. xi. 12, 13).

The words of Zacharias were exactly fulfilled; Judas threw down the money in the Temple, and with it was bought a field belonging to a potter, as a burying-place for strangers (Matt. xxvii. 5-7).

3. He was to be betrayed by one who ate at the same table with Him (Ps. xl. 10).

Judas went out from the Last Supper to betray his Master (John xiii. 30).

4. His disciples were to forsake Him at the time of His Passion (Zach. xiii. 7).

5. He was to be mocked (Ps. xxi. 7), beaten, spit upon (Is. l. 6), scourged (Ps. lxxii. 14), crowned with thorns (Cant. iii. 11), and given gall and vinegar to drink (Ps. lxviii. 22).

The chief priests and Scribes at the crucifixion mocked Our Lord, and said among themselves, "He saved others; Himself He cannot save" (Mark xv. 31; Cf. v. 29). In the house of Annas a servant gave Him a blow (John xviii. 22). In the house of Caiphas, when He declared Himself the Son of God, the servants spit upon His face, and gave Him blows; Pilate had Him scourged (John xix. 1), and handed Him over to the soldiers, who crowned Him with thorns, put upon Him a purple robe (in mockery of the imperial purple), struck Him on the head with a reed, and derided Him (Mark xv. 15-19). On Golgotha they gave Him to drink wine mixed with gall, which, when He had tasted it, He would not drink (Matt. xxvii. 34).

6. For His garments lots were to be cast (Ps. xxi. 19).

The soldiers divided His garments into four parts, and gave to each soldier a part. His coat they would not divide, for it was without seam, woven from the top throughout. They therefore cast lots for it (John xix. 23).

7. His hands and feet were to be pierced with nails (Ps. xxi. 17).

Our Lord was really fastened by nails to the cross; for He showed to St. Thomas the wounds in His hands and feet, and told him to place his finger in them (John xx. 27). The usual practice was to tie condemned criminals to the cross with ropes.

8. He was to die between two evil-doers.

The prophet Isaias says: " They shall give the ungodly for His burial, and the rich for His death " (Is. liii. 9). He died between two highway robbers, who were crucified at the same time with Him (Luke xxiii. 33).

9. He was to be patient as a lamb in His sufferings (Is. liii. 7), and was to pray for His enemies (Is. liii. 12).

10. He was to die willingly and for our sins (Is. liii. 4–7).

7. Of the glory of the Messias the prophets made the following predictions:

1. He was to make His grave with the rich (Is. liii. 9), and it was to be glorious (Is. xi. 10).

2. His body was not to undergo corruption (Ps. xv. 10).

3. He was to return to heaven (Ps. lxvii. 34), and was to sit on the right hand of God (Ps. cix. 1).

4. His doctrine was to spread from Jerusalem and from Mount Sion over the whole world (Joel ii. 28; Is. ii. 3).

The hall of the Last Supper, where the apostles received the Holy Ghost, was situated on Mount Sion.

5. The heathen nations of the whole earth were to be received into His kingdom, and to adore Him (Ps. xxi. 28, 29).

6. The Jewish people, who had put the Messias to death, were to be severely punished, and scattered over the face of the earth (Deut. xxviii. 64).

The city of Jerusalem was to be destroyed as well as the Temple; the Jewish sacrifices and the Jewish priesthood were to cease, and the Temple was never to be rebuilt (Dan. ix. 26, 27; Osee iii. 4).

7. In every place throughout the world, a " clean oblation " (holy Mass) was to be offered to Him (Mal. i. 11).

8. He will one day judge all men (Ps. cix. 6). Before the Day of Judgment Elias will be again sent on the earth (Mal. iv. 5).

8. The Messias was announced through many types.

The twilight announces the approach of the sun; so the lives of the patriarchs announced and foreshadowed the coming of Christ. Almost all the ceremonies of the tabernacle foreshadowed the ceremonies of the religion of Christ (Col. ii. 16, 17). The relation of the whole of the Old Testament to the New is that of the shadow to the substance (Heb. x. 1), of the image to the object that it represents. The ancient covenant was the veil which concealed the new. The persons and things which thus represent in the Old Testament the persons and things of the New, are called types.

The types of the Messias were as follows: Abel, Noe, Melchisedech, Isaac, Jacob, Joseph, Moses, David, Jonas, the archangel Raphael, the paschal lamb, the offering on the Day of Atonement, the brazen serpent, and the manna.

Abel was the first of just men; Christ the first of the saints; Abel was a shepherd and offered to God an acceptable offering; he was gentle as a lamb, but he was hated by his brother and murdered by him. Noe was the only just man among all those around him; Christ alone was without sin. Noe amid his course of preaching built the ark; so Christ the Church. Noe saved the human race from temporal death; so Christ from eternal death. Noe's sacrifice on his quitting the ark was the beginning of a new covenant; so Christ's on leaving the world. Melchisedech, i.e., king of justice, was King of Salem, i.e., King of peace; Christ was both King and Priest; He offered to God bread and wine. Isaac was the only-begotten and well-beloved son of his father. He himself carried the wood on which he was to be sacrificed, and offered himself willingly; he was restored to his father, and from him sprang a countless offspring. Jacob was persecuted by his brother, but afterwards was reconciled to him. Though the son of a rich father he wandered in a strange land and there won his bride by long service; so Christ the Church. He had twelve sons, of whom one was the beloved son; so Christ had twelve disciples, of whom St. John was the beloved disciple. Joseph, the well-beloved son of his father, was hated by his brethren, and sold by them for a few pieces of silver; after great humiliation he was raised to the highest honor, and by his counsel saved the whole people from death. Heralds proclaimed that all should bow the knee before him and he was reconciled to his brethren. Moses when a little child, escaped the cruel command of the king, spent his youth in Egypt, fasted forty days before the publication of the ancient law, freed the Israelites from slavery, and brought them to the Promised Land, worked miracles in proof of his divine mission, interceded for the people to God (Exod. xxxii. 11; Numb. xiv. 13); appeared on Mount Sinai with a shining countenance (as Christ on Thabor), and was the mediator of the ancient covenant. David was born in Bethlehem, spent his youth in a humble state, vanquished the giant Goliath, the enemy of the people of the Lord; was King of Israel, had much to suffer, and triumphed over all his enemies. Jonas was three days and three nights in the belly of the whale (Matt. xii. 40), and preached penance to the Ninivites. The archangel Gabriel came down from heaven to conduct safely on his journey one of the children of men; delivered Tobias from blindness, and Sara from the devil. The paschal lamb was slain just before the departure of the Israelites from Egypt, and therefore on the Friday preceding the paschal Sabbath; it was offered to God and afterwards eaten; it was to be without spot, and in the prime of its age; not a bone of it was to be broken (John xix. 36); its blood sprinkled on the posts of the door preserved from temporal death, as the blood of Christ from spiritual death. It was eaten on the eve of the departure of the Israelites to the Promised Land; so Our Lord is given as Viaticum on our departure for heaven. The emissary goat on the day of expiation was presented by the high priest before the Lord, and the priest then laid his hands upon its head, in order thereby to signify that the sins of all the people were transferred to it, and it was then driven out to die in the desert (Lev. xvi. 10). So Christ had the sins of the whole world laid upon Him, and passed from heaven into the desert of this sinful world to die for us. The brazen serpent in the desert was set up on a piece of wood, and all who looked upon it were healed of the bite of the fiery serpents (Numb. xxi. 6-9). So Christ was raised up on the wood of the cross, and all who look to Him with faith and hope are saved from the deadly effects of sin. Hence Our Lord says: " As Moses lifted up the serpent in the desert, so must the Son of man be lifted up, that whoever believeth in Him may not perish, but may have life everlasting " (John iii. 14, 15). Lastly the manna is a type of Christ in the Blessed Sacrament of the Altar; it was white and small, came down from heaven every day, was to be consumed in the early morning, was given only during the journey through the desert, and contained in itself all sweetness. In all these things it resembles the Blessed Sacrament. Our Lord says that there is this difference between the manna and the Blessed Sacrament of the Altar: that Moses did not give the Israelites bread from heaven, but that the Blessed Sacrament is the bread that came down from heaven, and giveth life to the world (John vi. 32, 33).

3. PREPARATION OF MANKIND FOR THE REDEEMER.

1. God chose for Himself a special nation, and prepared it for the coming of a Redeemer; this chosen people was the seed of Abraham, usually called by the name of Israelites, or Jews.

Cf. the call of Abraham (Gen. xii.); the Jews to be a priestly nation (Exod. xix. 6). No rejection of the other nations is implied in this election of the Jews, for every renewal of the promise of a Redeemer recalled a blessing that all the nations were to share (Gen. xii. 3; xxvi. 4; xxviii. 14).

The ways by which God prepared His chosen people for the Redeemer's advent were: the infliction of heavy trials, the imposition of severe laws, the performance for them of miracles, and the giving of a series of prophecies.

The sensuality of the chosen people had to be combated by many trials, such as Pharao's edict against the children, hunger and thirst in the desert, the fiery serpents, the attacks of their enemies, and their long exile. This same sensuality and insensibility required that the law should be promulgated with the awe-inspiring accompaniments of thunder and lightning. Idolatry was another sin to which the chosen people were prone, as we see in the incident of the golden calf (Exod. xxxii. 1), so miracles were called in to strengthen their faith and trust in God, such as those performed in Egypt, in the passage of the Red Sea and the Jordan, the manna in the desert, the water drawn from the dry rock, and the falling down of the walls of Jericho, etc. The prophesies tended in the same direction, as well as to maintain the desire of the coming Redeemer.

Of the history of the Jewish people the following facts are known to us:

1. The descendants of Abraham first dwelt in Palestine, and went later to Egypt, where they remained for the space of four hundred years, and were cruelly oppressed.

About the year 2000 B.C., God called Abraham and bade him settle in Palestine; here he had a son, Isaac, who was the father of Esau and Jacob; Jacob secured Esau's birthright and had to fly in consequence. Jacob (also called Israel) had twelve sons, of whom cne was Joseph, who being sold into Egypt became the ruler of the land under the king, invited his relatives, some sixty-six in number, to join him, giving them the fertile district of Goshen, lying eastwards of the Nile delta, to dwell in (about 1900 B.C.). Here the Jews increased greatly in numbers and had much to endure later from the Egyptian kings.

2. Under the leadership of Moses, the Israelites left Egypt and wandered in the desert for forty years.

Some 2,000,000 people crossed the Red Sea (about 1500 B.C.) into the Arabian desert, where they were fed with manna and received the Ten Commandments. Moses died on Mount Nebo.

3. Under Josue they entered the Promised Land, but had to fight under their Judges for over three hundred years, against their enemies (1450–1100 B.C.).

Josue, the successor of Moses, divided the land among the twelve tribes. The Judges were men raised by God for times of special need, such, for instance, as Gedeon, Jephte, Samson and Samuel.

4. The Israelites were then ruled over by kings, Saul, David, and Solomon being especially famous (1100–975 B.C.).

Saul was unhappy in his career and died a suicide. David, his successor (1055-1015), was distinguished for his piety; he composed many of the Psalms and received from God the promise that the Redeemer should be of his family. On two occasions he fell into grievous sin and was visited with severe chastisements. His son and successor Solomon built the Temple of Jerusalem (1012), and was known far and wide for his wisdom and splendor.

5. After Solomon's death the kingdom was divided into two parts, forming the kingdom of Israel in the north (975–722) and Juda in the south (975–588).

Solomon's son, Roboam, alienated the ten northern tribes by his taxations, and only the two southern tribes, Juda and Benjamin, remained to form the kingdom of Juda.

6. Both kingdoms fell away from the true God, and were in consequence destroyed, and their inhabitants led away into captivity.

Israel had nineteen kings, who led the people into idolatry in spite of the efforts of the prophets. At last, Salmanasar, in 722, destroyed the kingdom and carried the people away into the Assyrian captivity; the fall of the Assyrian power brought the exiles under the dominion of the Babylonians and in 538 under that of the Persian king Cyrus. The kingdom of Juda had twenty kings, and held out longer, but was finally reduced by Nabuchodonosor; the people were led away into captivity (606 and 599) and Jerusalem and the Temple destroyed.

7. After the return from the captivity (536) the Jews lived in peace until they came, in 203, under the power of Antiochus, King of Syria.

From the year 606 the inhabitants of Juda and Israel dwelt under the same ruler, and came to be known indifferently as Jews. Cyrus, who obtained possession of the Babylonian kingdom in 538, gave permission two years later to the Jews to return and rebuild their Temple; some 42,000 Jews availed themselves of this concession to return under Zorobabel to Jerusalem, where they raised a new Temple after twenty years of work; in the year 453 Artaxerxes allowed them to build walls; they still remained for about two hundred years under Persian dominion and were well treated. Alexander the Great and his successors then had the mastery, till the time of Antiochus Epiphanes IV., who began a religious persecution, putting the Machabean brothers and Eleazar to death, and placing idols in the Temple.

8. The Jews regained their freedom after a bloody war, and were again ruled for one hundred years by Jewish kings, from 140 to 39 B.C.

Machabeus and his five sons helped the Jews to shake off the Syrian yoke. Simon, one of the Machabees, reigned as high priest and king in 140, and was succeeded by his descendants till the advent of Pompey in 64, who reduced the Jewish king to the subjection of Rome.

9. In 38 B.C., a Gentile, Herod, became King of Judea.

As Judea was always a focus of rebellion, the Jewish king was deposed and replaced by Herod, the first of the kings who was not a Jew. He it was who massacred the children at Bethlehem. At his death he was succeeded by his son Herod Antipas, who put John the Baptist to death and treated Our Lord as a fool. His successor was his uncle Herod Agrippa the Great, who beheaded St. James the Elder, and cast St. Peter into prison. He usurped the name of God and died a miserable death, eaten by worms, in 44 A.D. In 70 A.D. Jerusalem was destroyed by Titus, and the Jews scattered among the nations.

2. The other nations of the earth were prepared for the coming of the Redeemer by contact with the chosen people, or by the influence of exceptionally gifted men, or by other extraordinary methods.

The ordinary intercourse of trade, as well as the enforced exile, afforded means of contact with the heathen, and that this was not unfruitful we learn from Tobias. " Give glory to the Lord, ye children of Israel . . . because He hath therefore scattered you among the Gentiles, who know not Him, that you may declare His wonderful works and make them know that there is no other almighty God besides Him " (Tob. xiii. 3, 4). Such men as Socrates, in Greece, had their mission in decrying the cult of idols, and exhibiting in their persons the virtues of courage, gentleness, and moderation; we might enumerate also Job in Arabia, Joseph in Egypt, Jonas in Ninive, Daniel in Babylon and others. The virtues of such men, their courage in confessing the true God, and the miracles by which their profession was verified, as, for instance, the cases of the children in the furnace of Nabuchodonosor and Daniel in the lions' den, furnished abundant motives to the heathen for discerning the true God; and that this was the case is corroborated by the numbers of proselytes. Besides all these, other methods were not left untried; e.g., the miraculous star which led the three Magi to Bethlehem (Matt. ii. 2), the angel's message to Cornelius the centurion (Acts x. 3), the mysterious handwriting on the wall of the palace where Baltassar was profaning the sacred vessels (Dan. v. 2), the dream of Nabuchodonosor (Dan. ii.), the prophecy of Balaam's ass, etc.

3. Before the arrival of the Redeemer God permitted that mankind should experience the deepest misery, in order to rouse it to a longing for a Redeemer.

The greatest dissension reigned among the Jews; three different sects claimed precedence : the Sadducees, the moneyed class, denied eternal life; the Pharisees adhered rigidly to the written law; the Essenes withdrew entirely from the world and led a life of strict penance. Among the heathen there was a general ignorance of any religious life, together with monstrous immorality. The gods, according to Hesiod, were too numerous to be counted and were indifferently idols, or men of abominable lives, or even animals, whose worship was signalized by scenes of debauchery and human sacrifices; heathens were not wanting who recognized the sad state of affairs; Horace, for instance, in one of his odes bewails the civil wars, and prays the virgin-born Son to come and reign among His people. Long before him Socrates had expressed the wish that some mediator should come from heaven to teach man his duty to God. Jacob (Gen. xlix. 10) and the prophets (Agg. ii. 8) only echoed the popular feeling when they called the Redeemer " the expectation of the nations." As in nations, so is God's action to be seen in individuals, and the struggles of a St. Paul and a St. Augustine served to make them more open to the action of the Holy Ghost and more zealous in their conversion to God.

4. *THE LIFE AND TIMES OF THE REDEEMER.*

1. The Redeemer lived some nineteen hundred years ago and remained thirty-three years on the earth.

In the early Christian times the date was reckoned by the consuls of the year.

From the time of the great Christian persecution under Diocletian, the Christians began to reckon their years from the accession of that tyrant (the era of the martyrs). Dionysius Exiguus, in 525, was the first to reckon from the Annunciation of Our Lady, i.e., the conception of Christ. Charlemagne introduced the custom of dating from the birth of Christ. There is an error, however, of four years, so that Christ was actually born four years before the year 1 of the Christian era.

The time preceding Christ is known as that of the Old Testament or the Old Law, that following as the New Testament or New Law (Heb. ix. 15–17).

The word testament is appropriate as expressing the will of God, recalling the legacy of the Promised Land to the Jews, and to Christians, the one sealed with the blood of animals, the other with the blood of Christ.

2. The work of the Redeemer was confined for the most part to Palestine.

Palestine is the ancient Chanaan, known later as Judea or the "land of promise" or the "holy land," made holy by the presence of Christ. Its small extent (it was only about half the size of Switzerland) had many counterbalancing advantages; its central position adapted it for the spreading of the true religion, its fertility in the midst of the surrounding desert made it independent of other nations, and secured its inhabitants from undesirable intercourse with the heathen. The population in the time of Our Lord was about 5,000,-000, of whom 1,000,000 lived at Jerusalem. At the present day the whole population is only half a million, and in Jerusalem hardly 25,000.

Palestine is situated on the Mediterranean, and includes both banks of the Jordan.

The boundaries of Palestine are: Phœnicia on the north, the desert on the east, Arabia on the south, and the Mediterranean on the west. The Jordan, a river varying from eighty to one hundred and fifty feet in width, the scene of the passage of the Jews and the baptism of Our Lord, flows in a turbid, yellow current, and passes through the little lake of Merom and the lake of Genesareth, the scene of so many of Christ's labors, and finally into the Dead Sea, the site of Sodom and Gomorrha. On its way it receives the brooks Karith and Cedron.

The divisions of Palestine are: in the south, Judea; in the

centre, Samaria; in the north, Galilee, and in the east, beyond the Jordan, Peræa, Ituræa, and the district of Trachonitis.

The inhabitants of Judea were the firmest adherents of the true faith; those of Samaria had given themselves up to the worship of idols, and the Galileans, especially in the north, were in part pagans, despised by the Jews as well on that account as for their uncouth dialect.

The most important city of Palestine was Jerusalem, where the Temple stood.

Jerusalem (i.e., City of Peace), is situate on four hills, of which the highest is Sion, lying westward of the hill of Acre, with the pool of Siloe lying south; to the north is Mount Moriah, on which the Temple stood, and further still to the north is the hill of Bezetha and the modern town. Westward of Moriah is Golgotha or Calvary. These hills lie between two valleys, of which the westward is called Hinnom (or hell, because there the Jews used to sacrifice their children to Moloch), and the eastern, the valley of Josaphat (or judgment of God, on account of the tradition that God would judge the world there). To the east of the valley of Josaphat is the Mount of Olives and the Garden of Gethsemani. Jerusalem was in existence at the time of Melchisedech, who reigned there about 2000 B.C.; it became, under David (about 1000 B.C.), the residence of the Jewish kings; about four hundred years later (in 588 B.C.) it was destroyed by Nabuchodonosor, restored again about fifty years later (536 B.C.), and again destroyed by the Romans under Titus in the year 70 A.D. The Temple in Our Lord's time was a magnificent and imposing building (Cf. Mark xiii. 1) of white stone: it had an outer court, the court of the Gentiles, and an inner, the court of the priests, containing the altar of burnt offerings. Within this court again was the Temple proper, a building of about thirty metres in length, ten in breadth, and fifteen in height, with a flat roof of cedar. The Temple proper consisted of the vestibule, the holy place, and the holy of holies; the walls of the two last places were covered with solid plates of gold and the two chambers were separated by a veil, the veil of the Temple. In the holy of holies, between two great golden cherubim, lay the ark of the covenant containing the tables of the law, Aaron's staff, and the manna; and here in a cloud rested the majesty of God, the Shechinah. The Temple was built by Solomon about 1000 B.C., was destroyed by Nabuchodonosor in 588 B.C., and in 516 was rebuilt by Zorobabel on the return from the Babylonian exile (though the ark was no longer there), and was restored again by Herod in the time of Christ. In the year 64 A.D., the restoration was complete, till the Romans came in 70 A.D., and destroyed the building. Julian the Apostate endeavored to rebuild it in 361, but an earthquake cast down the works, and fire coming from the earth drove away the workmen. The Temple will never be rebuilt till the end of the world (Dan. ix. 27).

Besides Jerusalem the towns of Bethlehem and Nazareth deserve mention.

Places of interest in Judea: South of Jerusalem lies Bethlehem, the birthplace of Christ; further south still is Hebron, where dwelt Abraham, Isaac, and Jacob, and the parents of St. John the Baptist; east of Jerusalem is Bethany, the village where Lazarus dwelt, and the desert of Quarantania, where Our Lord went through His forty days' fast. Northeast of Jerusalem is Jericho, the city of palms, the abode of Zacheus, the penitent tax-gatherer; north of Jerusalem is Emmaus, where Our Lord appeared to His two disciples after the resurrection; on the seacoast is Joppe, famous in the annals of the crusades, where Peter restored Tabitha to life and was summoned to receive the Gentile centurion, Cornelius; further to the south and extending along the coast is the district which was formerly the land of the Philistines, with its towns of Gaza and Ascalon; westward of the Dead Sea is the desert of Inda, otherwise called the desert of St. John. Places of interest in Samaria: The capital Samaria is situated near the centre of the district; south of it is Jacob's well, near Sicham, where Our Lord spoke with the Samaritan woman; eastward is Garizim, where the Samaritans had a temple dedicated to the service of idols; in the south is Siloe, where from the time of Josue, the tables of the law were kept for over three hundred and fifty years; along the coast of the Mediterranean stretches the fertile plain of Sharon; by the sea is situated Cæsarea, the residence of the governors. In the northwest, close by the sea and on the boundary, is Mount Carmel, rising some thousand feet, its fertility, beauty, and numerous caves making it peculiarly adapted to the wants of the hermits who dwelt there; it was the scene of the sacrifice of Elias and of the priests of Baal. Places of interest in Galilee: Nazareth, or the city of flowers, the residence of the Mother of God at the time of the Annunciation, and of Christ till His thirtieth year. South of it is Mount Thabor, where the transfiguration took place, and Naim, where Christ restored the young man to life. East of Nazareth is Cana, where Christ performed His first miracle at the wedding-feast. On the lake of Genesareth are situated: Capharnaum, "Christ's own city," in which He dwelt and where He worked so many miracles, e.g., the cure of the centurion's son, and the raising of the daughter of Jairus; here, too, He promised the institution of the Blessed Sacrament and called the apostle Matthew; to the south is Bethsaida, whence came the apostles Andrew and Philip; then comes Magdala, the dwelling-place of the sinner Magdalen; Tiberias is also a town on this lake. In the north of Galilee is Cæsarea Philippi, where Peter received the power of the keys. Quite beyond the boundaries of Galilee, in Phœnicia, on the coast, are the two cities of Tyre and Sidon, more than once visited by Christ. On the borders of Galilee is the range of the Lebanon, ascending to 10,000 meters, and covered with perpetual snow; not more than three hundred cedars remain of its once famous forest; to the east is Hermon, rising about 9500 metres; and still further east is Damascus, in the neighborhood of which St. Paul was converted. Places of interest in Peræa: Close by the Dead Sea, and eastward of the mouth of the Jordan, near to Bethabara is the place where St. John baptized; here he pointed out Christ and called Him the Lamb of God; further to the east is Mount Nebo, on which Moses died; south of the lake of Genesareth is Pella, the refuge of the Christians during the siege of Jerusalem in the year 70 A.D.

5. *JESUS OF NAZARETH IS THE REDEEMER OR CHRIST.*

The Jews called the coming Redeemer the Messias (in Hebrew), or the Christ (in Greek), i.e., the Anointed One. The "anointed of the Lord" was the usual epithet among the Jews for prophets, high priests, and kings, because they were anointed in sign of their mission on their appointment to office, and this anointing symbolized the light and strength of the Holy Ghost, and reminded them of the duty of clemency. The coming Messias was to be prophet, priest, and king, all in one, and the greatest of them all, hence it was usual to call Him simply, "the anointed of the Lord." This unction of the Messias was not a physical, exterior act, but the interior dwelling of the Holy Spirit (Ps. xliv. 8; Acts x. 38).

1. Jesus of Nazareth is the Redeemer, because all the prophecies have their fulfilment in Him.

Jesus often appealed to this circumstance (John v. 39; Luke xviii. 31), especially in His conversation with the two disciples on the way to Emmaus (Luke xxiv. 26). St. Matthew points out in his gospel how the prophecies are fulfilled in Christ. Many Jews have been converted on comparing the life of Christ with the prophecies.

2. Jesus of Nazareth is the Messias, because the kingdom founded by Him on earth has been enduring.

The success of many of those who claimed to be the Messias has ever been merely temporary; but Jesus of Nazareth has had His followers in every age. Had His kingdom, the Church, been the work of men, it would have been destroyed long ago. That it has survived, in spite, too, of so much persecution, is a proof that it is God's work, and that its founder must be the heaven-sent Messias (Cf. the words of Gamaliel, Acts v. 38).

3. Jesus Himself claimed the name of Redeemer.

On the occasion of His conversation with the Samaritan woman, and in presence of the high priest Caiphas.

The Samaritan woman said to Christ at the well: "I know that the Messias cometh Who is called Christ," and Christ replied: "I am He Who am speaking with thee" (John iv. 25, 26). The high priest Caiphas said to Christ: "I adjure Thee by the living God that Thou tell us if Thou be Christ the Son of God," and Christ answered: "Thou hast said it" (Matt. xxvi. 64). On another occasion St. Peter was commended for calling Him "the Christ, the Son of the living God" (Matt. xvi. 16).

4. The angels announced Him as the Redeemer.

When they appeared to the shepherds near Bethlehem, and in St. Joseph's vision.

An angel stood by the shepherds and said: " Fear not, for behold I bring you good tidings of great joy that shall be to all the people; for this day is born to you a Saviour, Who is Christ the Lord " (Luke ii. 10). When St. Joseph was thinking of dismissing our blessed Lady, an angel appeared to him in sleep and announced the birth of Christ: " Thou shalt call His name Jesus, for He shall save His people from their sins " (Matt. i. 21). Since Jesus of Nazareth is the Christ or Messias, He is called Jesus Christ, and this is the name He Himself uses in John xvii. 3.

6. THE LIFE OF CHRIST.

The Childhood of Christ.

The birth of Christ was announced by the archangel Gabriel to the Blessed Virgin Mary at Nazareth (Luke i. 28).

This event is commemorated by the feast of the Annunciation, which is kept on the twenty-fifth of March, by the Angelus, and in the first words of the Hail Mary. After the angel's salutation Our Lady set out to visit her cousin, St. Elizabeth, who greeted her with the words contained in the second part of the Hail Mary, and Our Lady replied in the solemn words of the *Magnificat* (Luke i.). The visitation is kept on the second of July, immediately after the octave of the nativity of St. John Baptist. St. Joseph also was warned of the birth of Christ by an angel (Matt. i. 18-25), when debating on the advisability of putting away Our Lady.

1. Christ was born of the Blessed Virgin Mary in a stable at Bethlehem.

Mary and Joseph had to repair to their native place of Bethlehem to be enrolled in the census which was being held by command of the Emperor Augustus. They were obliged to seek refuge in a stable, because there was no room for them in Bethlehem (Luke ii. 7). As in the conception, so in the birth of Christ, was exception made to the ordinary course of nature. Mary was free from the penalties described in Gen. iii. 16, because, as St. Bernard says, she alone had conceived without carnal pleasure. St. Augustine exclaims: " Behold He Who rules the world lies in a manger. He Who feeds the angels is suckled by His Mother. Strength becomes weak, that weakness may be made strong;" and again, " A great Physician came down from heaven to heal a great disease on earth; He healed in a way hitherto unheard of, for He took our ills on Himself." " Being rich He became poor, that through His poverty we might be made rich " (2 Cor. viii. 9). Every circumstance attending the birth of Christ has a deep meaning. Christ was born at Bethlehem (the house of bread) because, as St. Jerome says, He is the living bread. He is born far away from His home in Nazareth because He descended from heaven, His true home, and is a stranger among men. He is born amid the shepherds and their flocks, because He is to be the " Good Shepherd " (John x. 11) of a great flock. He is born in a stable, because the earth in comparison of heaven is but a stable,

He is born not in a house, but in a stable, that all might have confidence and approach Him, says St. Peter Chrysologus. He is born in obscurity, because He is the " hidden God " (Is. xlv. 15), Whom we cannot see in this life, and Who loves good deeds done in secret. He is laid in a manger, where cattle feed, because He was to be the food of man; and He is laid on the wood to recall to us that He came down from heaven to die on the cross. So too He dwells in our tabernacles. He is born at midnight, because the greater portion of mankind was buried in darkness, and knew nothing of the true God. He is born in the winter season, and at night (notice that the nights in Palestine are particularly cold), because the hearts of men were cold, unwarmed yet with the fire of charity. Christ drops from heaven in the night time like the dew (Cf. Is. xlv. 8), to refresh the hearts of men. At the time of His birth the temple of Janus in Rome was closed, and there was peace over all the earth, because Christ was the Prince of peace (Is. ix. 6); and the God of peace (1 Cor. xiv. 33), i.e., Our Lord, came as a little child that man might approach Him with more confidence; had He come as a great king, men would have shrunk away, while as a child He invited, not awe, but sympathy. Christ comes in poverty and renunciation to teach us that the road to heaven is the way of suffering and self-conquest, not of pleasure and self-indulgence. Besides this He would show that He is the Friend of the poor to whom He is appointed to preach the Gospel (Luke iv. 18). A light appeared to the shepherds to remind us that the Light of the world is come (John viii. 12), Who is to shine in the midst of the darkness (John i. 5). The hymn of the angels is the keynote of His mission, to glorify God (John xiii. 32), and to give peace to men (John xiv. 27), especially peace with God, reconciling man to God by His death on the cross, peace with self, the true peace which comes from the knowledge and practice of the Gospel, and peace with the neighbor by the virtues of brotherly love, love of one's enemy, and meekness. He announced His birth by the voice of an angel to the shepherds, and not to the proud Pharisees and Scribes, because He would hide His mysteries from the wise and prudent and reveal them to the little ones (Matt. xi. 25); because He gives His graces to the humble and resists the proud (1 Pet. v. 5). Such, too, is the disposition of God's providence in all time; to the proud, whatever their learning, the teachings of Christ are a sealed book, while the lowly and humble receive God's light. The first to receive the call to the crib were the Jews in the person of the shepherds, and after them the Gentiles, in the persons of the three kings; all to signify that Christ would first call into His Church the Jews (Matt. xv. 24), and afterwards the Gentiles by means of His apostles. The wonderful star in the East was to announce that Christ "the wonderful " (Is. ix. 6) had come down from heaven. The census of the people at the time of His birth reminds us of the great enrolment which will take place at His second coming. " Christ begins to teach us in His birth even before uttering a word." " The deeds of the Lord are commands; if He does anything in silence, He means that we should imitate Him," is the comment of St. Gregory the Great.

In the liturgy of the Church we celebrate Our Lord's birth on the twenty-fifth of December (Christmas Day). On that day every priest has the privilege of saying three Masses, which recall the threefold birth of Christ: the eternal birth from God the Father, the birth in time from the womb of Mary, and His spiritual birth in our hearts. A crib is generally erected in most churches, a practice originated by St. Francis of Assisi. In many households there is kept up the custom of the Christmas-tree, a reminder of the fatal tree of paradise, and also of the tree of the cross. The Christmas-boxes recall to our minds the gifts of God the Father to mankind on this day. Immediately following Christmas are the feasts of St. Stephen, St. John, and the Holy Innocents, as though the Church would say: " If you would follow Christ, you must become a martyr like St. Stephen, if not to the shedding of blood, at least to the denial of self and the bearing of suffering. You must love God and your neighbor like St. John, and do works of mercy; and finally you must be like a child with God."

The new-born Child is adored first by the shepherds and then by the Magi.

The shepherds were told by an angel of the birth of the Saviour (Luke ii. 9); the three kings were led to Him by a star (Matt. ii. 9). This star was something exceptional, for it had a proper motion of its own in the heavens; according to St. John Chrysostom, it may have been an angel, under the appearance of a star. Catherine Emmerich, in her revelations, says that this star had various aspects; at times it appeared as a child carrying a cross, or a woman with a child; again as a chalice with grapes and wheat ornamenting it, as a church, or forming the word Judea, etc. St. Irenæus remarks that the presents indicated their esteem of Him to Whom the three kings offered them. Gold, the symbol of homage, is offered to Him as King; incense, the symbol of prayer, because He is God; and myrrh, the symbol of mortification, because as Our Redeemer, He was to suffer. The Magi returned to their homes by another way, " to show us," says St. Gregory the Great, " that if we wish to reach our true home in paradise we must forsake the path in which we have hitherto walked, and tread in the way of penance, obedience, and self-denial." The shepherds represented the Jews and the poor; the three kings the Gentiles and the rich. The relics of the three kings were taken from the East to Cologne in 1162 by Barbarossa, and now repose in the Cathedral there. The feast of the three kings is held on the sixth of January. In many countries there still exists the custom of blessing on this day the water of the three kings, and the blessing of chalk and salt is not unusual. The initials of the names of the three kings are sometimes marked on the doors of houses to claim their patronage. This feast is called also the Epiphany, because in former times the birth of Christ, or appearance of Christ to mankind, was celebrated on this day. Hence in the Greek Church the season of Advent is prolonged till the Epiphany. This day is also celebrated as the one on which Christ was baptized in the Jordan, and performed His first miracle at Cana.

When the Child was eight days old He was circumcised, and received the name Jesus (Luke ii. 21).

Jesus (in Hebrew Joshua or Josue) means Saviour. This name is, as St. Paul says, above all names (Phil. ii. 9), for it was chosen by God Himself and revealed to the Virgin Mary (Matt. i. 21). Moreover the holy name has great virtue; its invocation brings help in temptation and affliction; the powers of hell shrink from it (Mark xvi. 17). The name usually given by the prophets was Emmanuel, i.e., "God with us" (Is. vii. 14). The feast of the Circumcision on the first of January is also New Year's Day. The Church would thus teach us to begin everything in the name of Jesus. Innocent XII., in 1691, was the first to order the practice of beginning the New Year on the first of January; previously it had been Christmas Day. It is a pious custom in many places to have a solemn thanksgiving service and to sing the *Te Deum* on the last day of the year, in thanksgiving for past favors.

When the Child was forty days old, He was presented in the Temple (Luke ii. 39).

Mary complied with the law of Moses (Lev. xii.), though, being free from sin, she needed no purification. The feast of the Purification is called also Candlemas; on that day candles are blessed, and carried in procession in memory of these words of holy Simeon calling Our Lord the "light for the revelation of the Gentiles" (Luke ii. 32).

2. Christ spent the first years of His childhood in Egypt, and after that lived at Nazareth till He was thirty.

An angel told Joseph to fly because Herod was seeking to kill the Child (Matt. ii. 13). After the escape of Our Lord Herod put to death all the children in Bethlehem under two years of age. This was a judgment on the people of Bethlehem for their refusal of hospitality to the Holy Family; the little children themselves gained by their death the joys of heaven. In Egypt there is still to be seen the dwelling-place of the Holy Family in a suburb of Cairo, the ancient Heliopolis. The land so sanctified by the presence of Our Lord became later the abode of thousands of monks, who led lives like to those of the angels; men such as, for instance, St. Anthony and St. Paul of Thebes; here St. Pachomius founded the first monastery, on an island of the Nile. After His return from Egypt Christ went to live in Nazareth, a place of little esteem among the Jews, therefore useful in teaching us the lesson of humility; and for thirty years He stayed there that we might learn from Him the lesson of detachment from the world.

When Christ was twelve years old He went up to the Temple in Jerusalem.

It was on this occasion that He made the doctors of the law marvel at His wisdom (Luke ii. 47).

When Christ was grown up John the Baptist began to preach His coming in the desert.

We have the following facts about John the Baptist. The archangel Gabriel announced his approaching birth to Zachary at the hour of sacrifice in the Temple; and when the latter was incredulous he was struck dumb (Luke i.), regaining his speech at the birth of St. John and using it to proclaim the noble canticle of the *Benedictus* (Luke i. 68-79). St. John spent his life in the desert in penance and preparation for his office as forerunner of the Redeemer. When Christ had reached His twenty-eighth year (Luke iii. 1), the Baptist came from his solitude, and preached to the Jews who flocked to him on the banks of the Jordan, the doctrine of penance and baptism (Matt. iii.). It was he who pointed out Christ: "Behold the Lamb of God Who taketh away the sins of the world" (John i. 29). His courageous rebuke to Herod caused him to be cast into prison (Matt. xiv. 4), and later to be beheaded (Matt. xiv. 10). He, like Elias, is the forerunner and the type of hermit life.

The Public Life of Christ.

1. When Christ was thirty years old, He was baptized by John in the Jordan (Matt. iii. 13), and fasted forty days in the desert, where He was tempted by the devil (Matt. iv.).

All apostolic men have sought retirement before entering on their mission, e.g., Moses, John the Baptist, and the apostles before the coming of the Holy Spirit. By His fasting and His victory over the devil Christ would satisfy for Adam's self-indulgence and defeat in the garden of paradise. The number forty has a special significance; it rained forty days on earth at the Flood, Moses and Elias fasted forty days, the Ninivites had forty days in which to repent, Christ dwelt on earth forty days after His resurrection, the Jews wandered forty years in the desert. The forty days of Lent are intended to commemorate the fasting of Christ; they begin with Ash-Wednesday and continue till Easter. During this time those who are of age should take only one full meal a day, and all Christians should avoid boisterous amusements and meditate on the sufferings of Christ. Thus sermons are preached on the sufferings of Christ; on Passion Sunday the images in the church are veiled and the priest says Mass in purple vestments. The three days before Ash Wednesday are called Shrovetide, and in order to divert the faithful from vicious pleasures it is usual in some places to have Exposition of the Blessed Sacrament.

2. Christ taught for about three and a half years, gathered some seventy-two disciples, and from these chose twelve apostles.

His first miracle was at the wedding-feast of Cana, to teach mankind that the heaven to which He would lead us is a wedding-feast (Matt. xxii. 2). He often addressed large crowds, counting four or five thousand, as in the case of the miraculous multiplication of loaves; thus Zacheus had to climb a tree in order to see Him among the crowd. The constant companions of Christ were the apostles and disciples, who heard His words and saw His deeds and published them later to the world. The bishops of the Church are prefigured in the apostles, and the priests in the seventy-two disciples. The teaching of Christ is rightly called *Evangelium*, "good tidings," or by our

English name Gospel, i.e., God's spell or narrative. Christ is the Master among teachers. He taught as one having power, so that the people marvelled at His doctrine (Mark i. 22; Matt. vii. 29).

Christ taught so that all might understand Him without difficulty; He used plain, homely words, and illustrated His teaching with signs and parables and by references to natural objects.

Christ's teaching is likened to the treasure buried in a field (Matt. xiii. 44). The language of apostolic men has always been simple, their object not so much to please as to be understood and to be useful. The signs which Christ made use of were breathing on the apostles when He gave them the Holy Spirit, lifting up His hands (Luke xxiv. 50) when He gave them power to teach and baptize, spitting on the earth and making clay, with which He touched the eyes of the man born blind (John ix. 6), and sending him to wash in the pool of Siloe. All this signified that the living doctrine which is imparted to man, the creature of earth, from the mouth of God, is to clear his spiritual sight, and even after that the washing of baptism is still necessary. The parables used were, for example, the prodigal son, the Good Samaritan, Dives and Lazarus, the wise and foolish virgins, the good shepherd, the lost sheep, the lost groat, the fig tree, the laborers in the vineyard, etc., and the seven figures of the kingdom of heaven, such as the pearl of great price, the buried treasure, the seine, the grain of mustard-seed, the cockle and wheat, the sower, the leaven. The objects in nature on which He drew for illustration were, among others, the shepherd with his sheep, the lilies of the field, the crops, the vineyards, etc. It is only reasonable that nature and religion should have many resemblances, coming as they do from the same God.

The poor were the especial objects of Christ's mission.

His own words to the disciples of John were: "The poor have the Gospel preached to them" (Matt. xi. 5). And in the synagogue at Nazareth He applied to Himself as the Messias (Luke iv. 18), the words of the prophet: "to preach the Gospel to the poor He hath sent Me."

The leading idea in the teaching of Christ was: "Seek the kingdom of God."

His own words in the Sermon on the Mount were: "Seek first the kingdom of God" (Matt. vi. 33). The Evangelists sum up His teaching in the words: "Do penance and believe the Gospel, for the kingdom of heaven is nigh" (Matt. iv. 17; Mark i. 15).

Christ taught a new rule of faith, gave new commandments, and established a new system of means of grace.

For example He taught the mystery of the Blessed Trinity, His own divinity, the Last Judgment; He gave the two precepts of love, and extended the Ten Commandments (forbidding rash anger and harsh words). He instituted the Mass and the seven sacraments and taught us the Our Father.

3. Christ proved His divine mission and the truth of His doctrine by many miracles, by His knowledge of all things, and by the holiness of His life.

Christ Himself appealed to His miracles: "Though you will not believe Me, believe the works" (John x. 38). Nicodemus was convinced of the divine mission of Christ by His miracles: "No man can do these signs which Thou dost, unless God be with Him" (John iii. 2). Christ of His own power worked miracles; others in the name of God or of Christ. Christ knew all things—the most hidden sins of men, those of the Samaritan woman, those of the Pharisees who dragged before Him the woman taken in adultery; He knew of Judas' plot against Himself, of Peter's coming denial, and related many incidents of His Passion just as they afterwards happened. We see in Christ the highest holiness; never were seen before or since, such patience, gentleness, love, etc. How could such a one say anything but the truth ?

The Scribes and Pharisees hated and persecuted Him because He failed to realize their carnal views of the Messias, and because He publicly rebuked their sins; after the raising of Lazarus they resolved to seek His death.

They tried to stone Him in the Temple (John x. 31), and at Nazareth to cast Him over the cliff; they calumniated Him, calling Him an agent of the devil (Matt. xii. 24), a leader of revolt, a Sabbathbreaker; they tried to catch Him in His speech, as in the case of Cæsar's coin. The Jews thought that the Messias was to be an earthly being, who would free them from the Roman yoke, and raise them above the nations of the earth. Instead of which He came in poverty and lowliness and taught self-denial, mercy, etc. Besides He accused the Pharisees of hypocrisy, calling them whitened sepulchres (Matt. xxiii. 27), and children of the devil (John viii. 44).

The Sufferings of Christ.

1. On the Sunday preceding the feast of Easter Christ made a solemn entry into Jerusalem and taught in the Temple during the days following.

The Church celebrates this solemn entry by the blessing of palms and the procession on Palm Sunday. In the course of the High Mass the history of the Passion as related by St. Matthew is read by the celebrant and sung by the choir. During the blessing of the palms the priest prays that God may preserve from sin and danger those who receive these palms and keep them in their houses. The week following Palm Sunday is called Holy Week.

2. On Holy Thursday evening Christ ate the Pasch with His disciples, instituted the Blessed Sacrament, and then went out to the Mount of Olives, where He suffered His agony and bloody sweat.

Before the institution of the Blessed Sacrament He washed the

feet of His apostles to teach us humility. His conduct in the
Garden of Gethsemani was a lesson of humble prayer, conformity to
God's will, and patience under suffering. In the words of St. Ambrose: "The Lord took my griefs on Him that He might share His
joys with me." In many places it is the custom to ring a bell at eight
o'clock in the evening to recall the agony in the garden. The following ceremonies are in more general use: The Pope washes the
feet of twelve priests—a practice kept up since the time of Gregory the Great. The bishops and governors in many places wash the
feet of twelve old men. During the *Gloria* in the High Mass all the
bells are rung, and the priests and laity go to communion to commemorate the institution of the Blessed Sacrament. The procession
of the Blessed Sacrament to the altar of repose is to recall Our
Lord's journey to the Mount of Olives. The stripping of the altars
and the silence of the bells are signs of the Church's sympathy with
her Saviour. The blessing of the oils which takes place in the Cathedral churches, which is of ancient institution, suggests that Christ
may have instituted some of the sacraments at the Last Supper. .

Christ was seized by the soldiers in the garden, led before the
high priest, and condemned to death.

On the Wednesday, Thursday, and Friday of Holy Week, *Tenebræ*
is celebrated in the evening. On a triangular frame in front of the
altar there are placed fourteen candles of unbleached wax, and at the
upper angle one of white wax; the white candle represents Our Lord
and the unbleached candles His apostles and disciples. At each of
the antiphones which recur at intervals during the recital of the
psalms, a candle is extinguished to represent the flight of the disciples
after the capture of Our Lord. At the end of the service the white
candle is hidden for a time behind the altar, a noise is made, and the
candle replaced on the stand; all signifying the death and resurrection of Our Lord with the accompanying convulsions of nature.

From the court of the high priest Christ was led by the Jews
before Pontius Pilate, to receive the ratification of the death-
sentence.

The Jews had no power to put any one to death, so they were
obliged to have recourse to the Roman governor (John xviii. 31).
Pilate could see no reason for condemning Christ, and made several
attempts to set Him at liberty; he sent Him to Herod and offered
to give up Barabbas in exchange; to enlist the sympathy of the Jews,
he caused Our Lord to be scourged and crowned with thorns and in
that state to be presented to the crowd, but they clamored only the
more for the blood of Jesus, and threatened to accuse Pilate to the
emperor.   .

Pilate, alarmed by the threats of the Jews, condemned Our
Lord to the death of the cross.

The devotion of the Stations of the Cross commemorates all these
details of the Passion. The distance to Calvary was some thirteen
hundred paces.

3. On Good Friday at noon, Christ was nailed to the cross on the hill of Calvary, just outside Jerusalem, and died on the cross about three o'clock.

Cicero is our authority that crucifixion was at that time the most shameful and terrible of deaths, to which none but the greatest criminals were subjected. Hence the doctrine of the Crucified was a scandal to the Jews and folly to the heathen (1 Cor. i. 23). Yet to-day the cross is the badge of honor, worn in the crowns of kings, and on the breasts of men proud of the decoration. In the words of St. Athanasius sin was repaired on the tree where sin was committed; and where death began there life arose, as the Church sings in the preface of the Mass. Christ was not beheaded, nor His body dismembered; so are we taught that His mystical body, the Church, should remain ever undivided. Christ bent His head to kiss us, spread His arms to embrace us, and opened His Heart to love us (St. Augustine). The Heart of Jesus was opened that its wounds might reveal to us the hidden wounds of His love for us (St. Bernard). It was not the soldiers, but His love for us, which nailed Christ to the cross (St. Augustine).

During these three hours the sun was darkened over the earth, though an eclipse was impossible at the time of the full moon.

As St. John Chrysostom says, the sun hid his rays that he might not behold the sufferings of his Maker. This darkening of the sun is mentioned by heathen writers.

At the death of Christ the earth opened, the rocks split, the veil of the Temple was rent, and many of the dead arose and appeared in Jerusalem.

All creation was in sympathy with Christ, excepting man, for whom Christ was suffering (St. Jerome). These marvels caused many to acknowledge the Godhead of Christ, as in the case of the centurion, who exclaimed: "Indeed, this was the Son of God!" (Matt. xxvii. 54.) One may still see on Calvary a rent in the rock between the site of Our Lord's cross and that of the thief on His left.

Christ spoke on the cross the seven last words.

These words were: (1). "Father, forgive them." (2). "To-day thou shalt be with Me in paradise." (3). "Behold thy Mother." (4). "My God, My God, why hast Thou forsaken Me!" (5). "I thirst." (6). "It is consummated." (7). "Father, into Thy hands I commend My spirit." The great cry which Christ gave before His death was a sign that He gave up His life of His own free will, and that He had strength enough to go on living. The cross, as St. Augustine says, is no longer the instrument of Christ suffering, but the pulpit of Christ preaching; from it He teaches the lessons of love of our enemies, gentleness, patience, obedience, God's mercy, goodness, justice and power, the immortality of the soul, the Last Judgment and the resurrection. In many churches it is the custom to toll the bells at three o'clock on Fridays in memory of Christ's death; and since Christ crucified His flesh for our sins on that day the Church has forbidden the eating of flesh meat. On Friday of Holy Week the Church is in mourning: the altars are stripped, the lights put out, and the bells silenced, and the sacred ministers in their black vestments lie prostrate at the foot of the altar. The celebrant prays for all conditions of men, even for heathens and Jews, since Christ died on this day for all men. The crucifix is unveiled. Then the celebrant lays it on the ground and kisses the feet of the image, and the people come up in turn to offer the same homage. On Good Friday there is no Mass, properly so called, but the ceremonies are gone through with a Host consecrated for the purpose on the preceding day. An altar of repose (or sepulchre) is chosen in the church where the Host is kept in the interval.

In the evening Our Lord's body was taken down from the cross and laid in the grave which belonged to Joseph of Arimathea.

4. During Easter Saturday, that is, on the greatest feast day of the Jews, Our Lord remained in the sepulchre.

On Holy Saturday fire is struck from a flint, and blessed outside the church doors, and from this fire the triple candle, the paschal candle, and the sanctuary lamp are lit. Each branch of the triple candle is lit separately, one at the door, another in the middle of the church, and the third in front of the high altar, to represent the gradual development of the knowledge of the Blessed Trinity. The paschal candle is also blessed on this day, and the five grains of incense imbedded in it remind us of the wounds of Christ. The baptismal font is also blessed, a relic of the times when the catechumens used to be solemnly baptized, and solemn High Mass follows.

The Exaltation of Christ.

Christ humbled Himself, "becoming obedient unto death, even the death of the cross. For which cause God also hath exalted Him" (Phil. ii. 8, 9). As St. John Chrysostom warns us: "The exaltation of Christ referred only to His humanity. As God He possessed all earthly happiness and needed no further exaltation." And St. Cyprian confirms him when he says that it was not the Almighty but the humanity of the Almighty which was exalted.

1. Immediately after the death of Christ His soul went down in triumph into the place where the souls of those justified under the Old Law were detained (Fourth Council of Lateran).

This place is called limbo, and is quite distinct from purgatory, though the two places had this feature in common, that in neither place is there the vision of God: for while there is pain to be suffered in purgatory, there was none in limbo; nor was limbo the same as hell, where the pains are eternal; on the contrary the souls in limbo had some consolation (Luke xvi. 25), though entrance to heaven was deferred (Heb. ix. 8); hence they longed for the coming of the Saviour to open to them the gates of heaven. Limbo is called in Scripture the "bosom of Abraham" (Luke xvi. 22); the "prison" (1 Pet. iii. 19). Our Lord called the place "paradise" (Luke xxiii. 43), because by His arrival the prison-house would be turned into paradise. After the death of Christ limbo ceased to exist. There were in that place among others, Adam and Eve, Abel, Noe, Abraham, Isaac, Jacob, Joseph, David, Isaias, Daniel, Job, Tobias, the foster-father of Christ, and many others, including those of Noe's contemporaries who had done penance and repented at the Flood (1 Pet. iii. 20).

Christ went down into limbo to announce to the souls detained there the news of the redemption, and to set them free.

Christ went down to announce to the souls in limbo that He had accomplished the redemption (1 Pet. iii. 19). St. Epiphanius tells us that the soul of Christ, united with the Godhead, went down into limbo, and St. Irenæus says that the Lord spent three days there. According to St. Ignatius of Antioch, Our Lord returned with a large company of souls. "He went," says St. Cyprian, "like a great king who delivers his subjects from a prison where they have been kept in durance." Christ revealed Himself also to the souls in hell, and they were compelled to bow the knee to Him (Phil. ii. 10).

2. On Easter Sunday before sunrise Christ rose glorious from the tomb by His own almighty power.

Christ often foretold that He would rise again on "the third day" (Luke xviii. 33); He compared Himself to Jonas (Matt. xii. 40); on the occasion of His driving the money-sellers out of the Temple, He said of His own body: "Destroy this temple and in three days I will raise it up" (John ii. 19); He claimed the power of laying down His life and taking it up again (John x. 18). When it is said in Holy Scripture that the Father raised Him (Rom. vi. 4; viii. 11), it is meant that as Christ is one with the Father all that Christ does the Father does also. The resurrection is a most undoubted fact. The Jews asserted that the disciples had stolen the body of Christ (Matt. xxviii. 13). Such an act was far beyond their power. The great stone that covered the sepulchre could not have been moved without waking some, at least, of the guards; "besides," as St. Augustine says, "these could not be accepted as witnesses if they were asleep;" and it is a remarkable circumstance that the soldiers were not punished for their breach of duty. Many free-thinkers urge that Christ was dead only in appearance, and after an interval recovered from His swoon and left the grave. The pain and loss of blood following on the scourging and crowning with thorns would have been enough to cause death, and the wound in the side alone, so great that St. Thomas could thrust in his hand, would have been fatal. Even when Christ was going to the place of execution, He was too weak to carry His cross; how could He, after thirty-six hours in the tomb, remove the long wrappings of His grave-clothes, roll away the stone, and make His way out on feet yet fresh from the wounds of the nails? The death of Christ was officially verified and reported to Pilate (Mark xv. 45), and His bones were not broken by the soldiers because they saw that He was dead (John xix. 33). The blood and water which flowed from the side of Christ after the piercing with the lance, were a sign of death (John xix. 34). His holy Mother and His friends would never have placed Him in the tomb unless He had been dead. All the Evangelists agree in testifying to the death of Christ.

The risen Lord bore in His body the five wounds, and it had the properties of agility, subtility, clarity and impassibility.

Christ retained the five wounds, for He ordered the unbelieving apostle to place his finger in the wounds of the nails, and his hand in the wound of the side (John xx. 27). Our Lord would keep the marks of the wounds in heaven to show us that He would not forget us, bearing in His hands, as St. Bernard says, the writ of our redemption written in His own blood; and St. Ambrose adds, that Our Lord bore these wounds to be a perpetual reminder to His heavenly Father of the price of our redemption, to renew the sacrifice of the cross forever in heaven (Heb. viii. 1-6).

Christ rose again to prove to us that He is God, and that we, too, are to rise again.

Christ is the first-fruits of them that sleep (1 Cor. xv. 20), and as Christ, our Head arose, so shall we all rise again (St. Irenæus). He called first His own body to life; later He will call the members of His mystical body to share its life (St. Athanasius). The hope of the resurrection was Job's consolation in his trouble (Job xix. 25). Throughout Christendom Easter is celebrated as the feast of the resurrection. In the Old Testament the Paschal Sabbath was kept in remembrance of the delivery from the Egyptian yoke. Among Christians, in accordance with a decision of the Council of Nicæa, 325 A.D., the feast is celebrated on the first Sunday after the full moon which comes next after the spring equinox. In consequence Easter may fall anywhere between the twenty-second of March and the twenty-fifth of April. The heathen wakes to a new spiritual life in the waters of baptism; hence the blessing of the font on Holy Saturday; and all those who perform their Easter duties have a spiritual resurrection from the dead (Rom. vi. 4). In the words of St. Ambrose, if we are to rise from the grave of the flesh we must first rise from the grave of our sins. The Paschal candle, which is blessed on Holy Saturday is, on account of its five incense grains, which represent the five wounds, a figure of Our Lord; and it is lighted at all services till Ascension Thursday. The Easter eggs are a type of the resurrection: just as the young bird breaks from the shell, so will mankind arise again from the earth. The season itself is typical of the new life in the reawakening of nature.

The risen Lord remained forty days on earth, and appeared frequently during this time to His disciples.

St. Ambrose tells us that Christ appeared first to His holy Mother. St. Peter was the first of the apostles to see the risen Lord (Luke xxiv. 34). Early in the morning of Easter Sunday Christ appeared to Mary Magdalen by the sepulchre (Mark xvi. 9; John xx. 15), and then to the holy women as they were leaving the grave (Matt. xxviii. 9); in the evening He appeared to the two disciples who were going to Emmaus (Luke xxiv.), and immediately after to the assembled disciples in the cenacle. He ate fish and honey in their presence, and afterwards gave them the power of forgiving sins (John xx.). On the following Sunday He appeared again in the same house and reproved Thomas for his want of faith (John xx.). He again appeared to seven of the disciples on the lake of Genesareth and gave St. Peter authority over the apostles and the faithful, telling him at the same time what death he should die (John xxi.). A more solemn occasion was the appearance to five hundred disciples on a mountain in Galilee, when He gave them the command to go forth into the world, teaching and baptizing (Matt. xxviii. 16). He spent there forty days in speaking to the disciples of the kingdom of God (Acts i. 3). The last appearance was on the occasion of His ascent into heaven. He appeared not in the night, but in the full light of day, not once only but repeatedly, not in some one place but in many places; nor were they instantaneous apparitions, but He remained some time, and spoke with His apostles. The resurrection was a point on which the apostles testified in person. They gave no credit to the women who came from the grave with their account of the angel (Luke xxiv. 11). They doubted the evidence of their own senses when Christ Himself appeared to them; then it was that He showed them His wounds, and allowed them to touch Him, and ate in their presence (Luke xxiv. 42). Thomas refused to believe the ten apostles (John xx. 25), and this unbelief of St. Thomas is a greater help to our faith, to use the words of St. Gregory the Great, than the belief of all the rest. There was nothing of which the apostles had a stronger conviction than of the reality of the resurrection, and this they preached on the feast of Pentecost, before the Council, in the Temple, etc.

3. Forty days after His resurrection Our Lord ascended into heaven from the Mount of Olives, and now sits at the right hand of God the Father.

Before ascending Christ raised His hands and blessed His apostles, enjoining on them to preach the Gospel to all nations, and promising to be with them all days, till the end of the world (Matt. xxviii. 18; Luke xxiv. 50). After the ascent two angels appeared and consoled the apostles (Acts i. 10). St. Jerome tells us that the impress of Christ's sacred feet used to be shown to pilgrims; there remains now only the trace of the left foot, that of the right having been removed by the Turks. It is remarkable that from the direction of this footprint Our Lord must have been facing Europe as He mounted into heaven, just as He faced it during the crucifixion. Christ made His ascent from the Mount of Olives, where He began His Passion, to show us that the road to heaven must be through suffering. He ascended into heaven by His own power, not like Elias borne on a chariot (4 Kings ii. 11), or like Habacuc carried by an angel (Dan. xiv. 36). His escort into heaven was formed of the souls released from limbo (Eph. iv. 8). The Fathers are of one mind in teaching that Christ has never descended in the flesh from heaven since then, except during holy Mass. Forty days after Easter the feast of Ascension Thursday is kept, preceded by the three Rogation days with their processions, symbolic of the going out of Christ with His apostles to the Mount of Olives.

Christ ascended into heaven in order, as man, to enter into His kingdom (Eph. iv. 10), to send down the Holy Spirit (John xvi. 7), to intercede for us with the Father (John xiv. 16), to prepare a place for us there (John xiv. 2).

Christ is the mediator between God and man (1 Tim. ii. 5), and our advocate with the Father (1 John ii. 1). " If," says St. Bernard, " you fear to go to God the Father, turn to Jesus Christ, Who has been given to us as a mediator. What can such a Father refuse to such a Son?" Christ is often likened to the sun, which sheds its light and warmth the higher it rises in the heavens.

Christ sits on the right hand of God, that is, as man He has power over all creatures.

To sit on the right hand was a mark of special honor (3 Kings ii. 19); hence the expression " Christ sits on the right hand of God " is equivalent to: " Christ is next in honor to God." He is therefore above all the angels (Eph. i. 21). God the Father has no body; so that when we speak of the right hand of God, we mean, as St. John Damascene tells us, the glory of His Godhead, of which Christ took possession in the flesh. The expression, " sits," is significant of His royal and judicial powers. The words of Christ Himself were: " All power is given to Me in heaven and on earth " (Matt. xxviii. 18). Hence all creatures owe Him divine homage (Phil. ii. 9-11).

4. On the tenth day after His ascending into heaven Christ sent down the Holy Ghost on the apostles.

The Holy Ghost descended on a Sunday, about nine o'clock in the morning (Acts ii. 15). The signs accompanying His descent were symbolical of His action; the rush of wind represented the strengthening of the will, the fire the illumination of the understanding, the tongues the gift of tongues to the apostles and the teaching of the Gospel to all nations. Pentecost is the day of foundation of the Church, because it began on that day by the baptism of three thousand new members. Pentecost is celebrated fifty days after Easter— Pentecost meaning fifty. In the Old Law this day was celebrated fifty days after the Exodus, in memory of the promulgation of the commandments on Mount Sinai. On Mount Sion as on Mount Sinai was God's will declared amid lightning and thunder, and in both cases fifty days after the release in one instance from bodily, in the other from spiritual slavery. It is the custom to bless the font in memory of the three thousand who were baptized on this day. The Saturday preceding was always observed as a fast day, that like the apostles we might prepare for the coming of the Holy Spirit. The Sunday following Whitsunday is Trinity Sunday, and on the Thursday following is kept the feast of Corpus Christi.

At the end of the world Christ will come again to judge all men.

7. *THE PERSON OF THE REDEEMER.*

Jesus Christ, Our Redeemer, is the Son of God made man; hence He is God Himself.

The Incarnation of the Son of God.

The heathen had very early conceived the idea that God had descended from heaven and mixed with men; the Greek mythology is full of it. Now God has actually come down to earth (John iii. 13) at the moment of the Annunciation (Luke i. 26-38).

1. The second divine person became man in the womb of the Blessed Virgin Mary by the action of the Holy Ghost at the moment of the Annunciation.

Louis of Granada writes: " Just as the sun must be wrapped in clouds if we are to gaze upon it with eyes undimmed, so God wrapped Himself in flesh as in a cloud, so that the eyes of our soul might bear to look upon Him." Human thought must be clothed in words to reach our ears; so God clothed Himself in human nature to reach the souls of men. " The Word [i.e., the Son of God] was made flesh [i.e., became man] and dwelt amongst us " (John i. 14). The Incarnation took place in the instant when Our Lady uttered the words: " Be it done unto me according to thy word " (Luke i. 38). They err who think that the human nature was first formed and afterwards united to the divine person, just as the Valentinians were wrong in asserting that Christ brought His human body from heaven. Christ received His body from the Virgin Mary. He was made from a woman (Gal. iv. 4), and was of the seed of David (Rom. i. 3). The Son of man came down from heaven, it is true (John iii. 13), in regard of the divine person, but not in regard of His human nature; we must not, however, imagine that the divine essence came down from heaven and united itself to the human nature; this would mean that all three persons of the Blessed Trinity has assumed our human nature. Such a thing is impossible, for such a union would require a change in the divine essence, which is incapable of change. Only one of the divine persons, the Son of God, assumed our human nature. God (i.e., a divine person) not the Godhead (i.e., the divine essence) became man. There is, however, an intimate union between the nature of God and the nature of man in the person of the Son; and it is certain that all the divine persons had their share in the work of the Incarnation, for in the work which God does outside Himself all three persons of the Trinity have their share.

The Incarnation is in a peculiar manner the work of the three divine persons.

The three divine persons formed a human soul and a human body and united to them the Second Person of the Trinity. As St. Augustine puts it: " In the guitar the sound seems to come from the strings alone, yet three elements are wanted, the human hand, the skill of the player and then the string." Or as St. Fulgentius explains it: " Body and soul are necessary for a man to profit by his food, yet the body alone receives the nourishment." So the three persons of the Trinity co-operated in the Incarnation, but the Second Person only was united to the flesh. The Incarnation is ascribed in a special manner to the Holy Ghost, because it is the greatest work of God's love. The Church teaches that the works of love are ascribed to the Holy Ghost, Who is the love of the Father and the Son. According to the Fathers there is no doubt that either God the Father or the Holy Ghost might have become man; but it was meet that He Who is the Son of God from all eternity should become the Son of man; that He Who is the perfect image of God should restore to mankind that supernatural image which had been lost by sin.

2. The Father of Jesus is therefore God the Father in heaven; Joseph, the spouse of Mary, is only the foster-father of Jesus.

St. Gregory the Great tells us that Christ is the Son of God, not only because He is the Second Person of the Blessed Trinity, but also because God formed His sacred humanity. In the first promise of the Redeemer as we read it in the Protevangelium Christ is called, not the seed of man, but the seed of the woman (Gen. iii. 15), and in the genealogy of Christ recorded by St. Matthew, no mention is made of His descent from Joseph, but only from Mary (Matt. i. 16). Yet Christ was commonly thought to be the Son of Joseph (Luke iii. 23). Mary was espoused to St. Joseph that no accusation might be made against her by the world, and that she might have in him a protector. About St. Joseph we have the following facts: He was a carpenter (Matt. xiii. 55); he was a just man (Matt. i. 19). St. Jerome tells us he was perfect in every virtue, and St. Thomas Aquinas gives as the reason for his holiness that he was so close to the fount of holiness, just as the spring is clearer as we approach its source. St. Francis of Sales tells us that St. Joseph was conspicuous for his purity, and therein surpassed all the saints and even the angels. To him was granted the honor which kings and prophets sighed for in vain; he might take his Lord into his arms, kiss Him, speak with Him, clothe Him, protect Him (St. Bernard). He was called father by Him Whose Father was in heaven (St. Basil). Many saints assert that St. Joseph has a very high place in heaven as the spouse of the Blessed Virgin, and that he will be called upon by men in the last days of the world and give signs of his great power. St. Joseph is the patron of the Church (Pius IX., Dec. 8, 1870); i.e., his prayers for the Church have great efficacy at the throne of God. He is also the patron of a happy death, dying as he did himself in the arms of Jesus and Mary. He is also invoked for temporal wants, since his care on this earth was the support of the Holy Family. St. Thomas Aquinas says that St. Joseph received power from God to help in all necessities; and St. Teresa declared that no prayer of hers to St. Joseph in temporal or spiritual need was ever left unanswered. The Catholic Church has always honored St. Joseph in a special manner, after Our Lady and above the other saints.

3. The Incarnation of the Son of God is a mystery which we cannot understand, but only admire and honor.

The conception and Incarnation are as little understood by us as the flowering of the rod of Aaron (Numb. xvii.). " Shut thy eyes, O Reason," says St. Bernard, " for under the veil of faith thou canst see the sheen of this mystery, just as the eye of the body can bear the light of the sun when shaded by a cloud." " I know that the Son of God became man, but how I do not know " (St. John Chrysostom). The following are illustrations which have been used to convey the idea of the union of the Godhead and the human nature in Christ: The divinity and the humanity are united in Christ as body and soul are united in man (Athanasian Creed). If spirit and matter, so essentially distinct, are united in man, all the less matter of surprise is it that the divinity and humanity, which after all have their points of resemblance, are found united in Christ. " Speech is a sort of incarnation," says St. Augustine. " At first the word is conceived as a mere thought, something purely spiritual. If that thought is to be conveyed to another, it is put in words; yet, though it appeals to the senses, it is none the less produced from the soul. So the Word of God has appeared to many and ceases not to remain with the Father." Other illustrations to show the action of the Holy Ghost in Christ's conception: St. Isidore tells us that Christ was formed from Mary just as Eve was formed from Adam. The Incarnation resembles in some respects the creation, when everything was produced by God's almighty power without co-operation of man.

The mystery of the Incarnation is commemorated by the ringing of the Angelus bell.

The words of the Angelus recall in the most lively way the scene of the Annunciation. At the words in the *Credo* of the Mass: " He took flesh in the womb of the Blessed Virgin Mary by the Holy Ghost" the celebrant always kneels, also at the words in the Last Gospel: " And the Word was made flesh." On Christmas Day and the Annunciation (the twenty-fifth of March), the sacred ministers at High Mass kneel on the altar steps and bow their heads at the "Et incarnatus est " of the *Credo*. The angels also venerate the mystery of the Incarnation.

4. The Incarnation of the Son of God was necessary to give perfect satisfaction to the injured majesty of God.

God might have chosen some other means for redeeming man. He might, by special exercise of His goodness, have been content with an imperfect satisfaction, or have remitted the guilt without demanding any satisfaction at all. St. Augustine on this subject writes: " There are some foolish people who think that God could not have redeemed mankind otherwise than by Himself taking flesh, and suffering at the hands of sinners. He might have followed quite another plan." As we shall see in treating of the death of Christ God wished to have perfect satisfaction, to display His justice as well as His mercy. Perfect satisfaction could be given only by a God-man. The greatness of an injury is measured by the dignity of the person who suffers; hence the offence given to God is infinitely great. No finite being, not even the most perfect angel, could atone for an offence against God, only God Himself. " So that," to use the words of St. Anselm, " to redeem man it was necessary that God should become man." As God only He could not suffer; as man only He could not redeem; hence the Godhead assumed a human nature (St. Proclus). If a valuable portrait be damaged beyond recognition it cannot be restored unless the sitter present himself to the artist; thus God had to come down on earth to restore His likeness in man (St. Athanasius).

The God-man could satisfy perfectly the injured majesty of God by appearing on earth in a state of lowliness.

Had He appeared in His majesty men would never have dared to crucify Him (1 Cor. ii. 8). Like Codrus, the Athenian king, He secured victory to His own by dying for them. The oracle had promised the Athenians victory if their king died by the hands of the enemy, and Codrus, disguising his royal dress, marched into the enemy's camp and was by them put to death. The prophets had foretold that mankind should be saved by the death of its King, and Christ, taking on the form of a slave, was put to death. The evil spirits fled when they saw Whom they had killed. "If," as Louis of Granada says, "a king would prove his courage in battle, he must put away all symbols of his rank, to proclaim them only when he is victor;" and this is what Our Lord did. He will come again with great power and majesty (Matt. xxvi. 64). St. Thomas says that we cannot affirm with certainty that God would have become man had man not sinned; it certainly would not have been beyond His power.

5. The Second Person always remained God though He became man, and by the Incarnation He lost none of His dignity.

When we assert that the Son of God came down on earth, we do not mean that He left heaven. So a star may become visible to us without leaving the firmament. As St. Ambrose says, the divinity of Christ is not destroyed, but only hidden by His human nature, just as the sun is not put out, but veiled only by the clouds. And as the thought, because spoken, does not cease to be a product of the soul, so the Word of God did not cease to be with the Father (St. Augustine). As a word, though spoken only for the benefit of one person may be heard by all the bystanders, so the divine Word was not limited by the body which He assumed, but still fills heaven and earth. Moreover God lost none of His dignity by the Incarnation. The sunlight which plays over filth is not defiled; still less is the Godhead defiled by taking flesh from the pure womb of Mary (St. Odilo). If a prince put on a slave's dress and in it picked a precious ring from the gutter to place it on his finger, there is no loss of dignity; so, too, the Son of God was not degraded by taking on Himself the form of a slave, and coming down on earth to save souls and gain them to Him (Tert.). When the Apostle says that Jesus Christ debased Himself by taking the form of a servant (Phil. ii. 7), he does not mean that God lost anything, but only that He assumed a nature lower than His own, and gave us thereby an example of humility. "He humbled Himself" (Phil. ii. 8).

6. By the Incarnation of the Son of God all the members of the human race have acquired a special dignity.

The human nature of the Son of God is like the yeast which leavens the whole mass (Matt. xiii. 33). Christ is the vine, and we are the branches (John xv.). The angels even fall short of us in this respect, for though they are exempt from sickness and death they cannot claim God for their Brother; were they capable of envy, they would envy us that honor. As St. Ambrose says: "The Almighty took the form of a slave that the slave might become a king." "The Son of God became the Son of man that the children of men might become children of God" (St. Athanasius). "Oh, what a wondrous redemption is that where man is, as it were, put on a par with God !" (St. Hilary.)

What Truths follow from the Mystery of the Redemption?

1. Christ is true God and true man; hence we call Him the God-man.

Every being gets its nature whence it has its origin; thus a child gets its human nature by being born of man. Christ, therefore, having His origin from God the Father, derives from Him His divine nature, and by being born of Mary, derives from her His human nature. He claimed both divine and human attributes. He said, for example, "The Father is greater than I" (John xiv. 28), and yet on another occasion: "The Father and I are one" (John x. 30). As God He calls Mary "woman," as on the occasion of the wedding-feast at Cana, and as man He calls her "Mother." He called Himself at times "Son of God" and again "Son of man."

Christ, as man, is like to us in all things except sin (Council of Chalcedon).

Christ became like to His brethren (Heb. ii. 17); He was made in the likeness of man and in habit formed as a man (Phil. ii. 7). Christ had a human body, with all its consequent needs of eating and drinking and sleeping, as well as of suffering and dying; and He had a real body, not a fictitious one, as the Docetæ taught. Christ had a human soul, and so a human intellect, and a human will (for He prayed in the garden: "Father, not My will, but Thine be done" (Luke xxii. 42). At His death Christ gave His soul into the hands of His heavenly Father (Luke xxiii. 46). St. Paul (1 Cor. xv. 47) calls Christ the "heavenly" man, in opposition to the "earthly" man, Adam; his meaning being that Christ's body was heavenly in the sense that it was formed supernaturally in the womb of a virgin by the action of the Holy Spirit and that it displayed on earth some of the properties of glorified bodies, as on Mount Thabor and the walking on the waters.

2. In Christ there are two natures, human and divine, which despite their intimate union are quite distinct.

The nature or essence is the total of the powers belonging to a being. The person is the possessor of this nature; or perhaps more strictly, that which is common to all men is the nature and that which constitutes man an independent individual is the person. Thus the nature may embrace many individuals, but not so the person. Just as iron and gold may be welded into one solid mass, and still remain with all their individual properties distinct, so are the two natures united in Christ. Nor is the human nature changed into the divine nature, as the water was changed into wine at Cana; nor again is the human nature, as Eutyches thought, absorbed into the Godhead as a drop of honey might be lost in the expanse of the ocean; nor have the two natures combined to form a third, as hydrogen and oxygen combine to form water.

Hence Christ has a twofold knowledge, human and divine.

As God He knew all things, even the thoughts of men; and He also knew all things as man on account of the hypostatic union; the reason why He denied all knowledge of the day and hour of the Last Judgment was because He was not intrusted with His knowledge to communicate it to man (Mark xiii. 32).

Hence also Christ has a twofold will, human and divine, the human being subject to the divine (Third Council Constant.).

We learn from the prayer in the garden that Christ had a human will: "Not My will but Thine be done" (Luke xxii. 42), subject however to the divine will: "I seek not My own will but the will of Him that sent Me" (John v. 30). So a patient may shrink from the pain of an operation, and yet submit himself to the hands of the surgeon.

Thus Christ has a twofold activity, human and divine (Third Council Constantinople, A.D. 680).

To His divine activity belong the miracles and prophesies, to the human principle of action the operations of sleeping, eating, drinking and suffering. The three persons of the Blessed Trinity have only one nature and so one principle of action.

3. In Christ there is only one person, and that person is divine.

Ænobius compares this with the two eyes forming only one image, or the two ears conveying one sound. In the words of the Athanasian Creed: "As the rational soul and the flesh is one man, so God and man is one Christ." The human nature in Christ, though completed by a divine and not a human personality, is for that very reason more perfect; just as in man the body is more perfect on account of being informed by a human soul, than in the lower animals. Moreover as in man the body is an instrument by which the soul acts, so in Christ the human nature is the instrument by which the divine person acts; nor is Christ's body a lifeless tool, like a pen in the hand of a writer, but it is full of life and has its own special activity. The humanity of Christ is, it must be remembered, not an instrument of God's action in the same way as were the prophets or the apostles, etc. Its union and action are far more intimate, just as the eye and the hand of the workman are more concerned in his work than the tools. We must avoid the error of Nestorius, condemned at the Council of Ephesus, in which he taught that in Christ the Godhead dwelt in a distinct person (i.e., that the God Christ dwelt in the man Christ) as in a temple.

Since in Christ the divine and human natures are inseparably united by His divine personality, the following propositions are true:

1. Christ is, as man, the true Son of God.

St. Paul's words on the subject are: " He spared not His own Son, but delivered Him up for us all " (Rom. viii. 32).

2. Mary, the Mother of Christ, is really Mother of God.

St. Elizabeth called her the Mother of God (Luke i. 43). Nestorius' heresy that Mary should be called only the Mother of Christ, was condemned at the Council of Ephesus in A.D. 431. " If," as St. Cyril says, " Our Lord Jesus Christ is God, how can it be that the holy Virgin who bore Him is not Mother of God? " Though the mother does not give the soul to her offspring, she is none the less called the mother; so Mary is called the Mother of God, though she did not give to Christ His divine nature.

3. Christ, as man, could neither sin nor err.

Christ did no sin either in word or in deed (1 Pet. ii. 22) ; or, in the words of St. Gregory the Great: " As light permits no darkness in its neighborhood, so the Son of God admitted no sin in His human nature." Christ had from His birth all wisdom and knowledge (Col. ii. 3). The words " Christ grew in wisdom and grace " (Luke ii. 52), mean that with the passage of time He ever showed more of the wisdom and grace of God in His speech and conduct. There must have been in His person something majestic (Ps. xliv. 3) ; St. Jerome says that the glory and majesty of the Godhead was reflected on His face, and gave it a beauty which attracted and subjected all those who had the happiness of gazing upon Him.

4. All Christ's human actions have an infinite value.

What Christ did as man was a human action, and also a divine action, inasmuch as He was God. St. John Damascene says: " Just as iron raised to a glow burns not because burning is a property of the iron itself, but because it has acquired the property from the fire, so the human actions of Christ were divine, not of their own nature, but on account of the intimate union with the Godh ad." The very least prayer or suffering of Christ might thus have redeemed all men.

5. Christ's humanity is worthy of adoration.

This adoration is directed, not to the human nature, but to the divine person. Thus a child kissing the hand of its parent is paying homage to the parent, not to the hand. As St. Thomas says: " We pay honor to the king and the purple which he wears; so in Christ we adore the humanity along with the Godhead, since they are inseparable." St. John Damascene points out that we do not adore mere flesh, but the flesh as united to the divinity. Thus the Church adores the five wounds, the Sacred Heart, the precious blood, etc.

6. Human attributes may be predicated of Christ as God,

and divine attributes of Christ as man (the so-called communication of characters or idioms).

Hence St. Peter's reproach: " The Author of life you have killed " (Acts iii. 15), and St. Paul's words: " If they had known it they would never have crucified the Lord of glory " (1 Cor. ii. 8), as well as St. John's " Therein do we know the love of God, that He laid down His life for us." Since the second divine person and the man Christ Jesus are one and the same person, whatever is said of Christ as God may also be said of Him as man (e.g., this man is omniscient or almighty), and what we say of Christ as man may be said of the second divine person (e.g., God suffered for us, died for us, etc.). When a man is both good and rich, we may say without error: " This rich man is good," or " This good man is rich," because we are talking of the person who is rich and good. We may do the same in regard of the divine person Who is at the same time God and man, and in consequence has the attributes proper to God and man. So we might say " This sufferer is God," " This dying man is almighty." But we *cannot* say " The Godhead suffered or died," because the word " Godhead " means the divine nature, and it never suffered. Hence St. John Damascene wrote: " Though the Godhead was in a suffering form, the Godhead did not suffer. The sun is not hurt, though the tree on which it shines is felled."

Jesus Christ is the Son of God.

Christ called Himself the only-begotten Son of God (John iii. 16), and this because He and He alone is the Second Person of the Trinity, begotten of the Father. In addition He is far removed above the angels and mankind, who are likewise called the children of God. For to these latter God has not communicated His own nature (Phil. ii. 6) and has adopted them only by a special grace (Gal. iv. 5).

1. **Jesus Christ solemnly declared before the high priest that He was the Son of God (Matt. xxvi. 64).**

And He called Himself the Son of God also on the occasion of His healing of the man born blind (John ix. 37).

2. **God the Father called Jesus Christ His Son on the occasion of His baptism in the Jordan and of the transfiguration on Mount Thabor (Matt. iii. 17; xvii. 5).**

3. The archangel Gabriel called Jesus Christ the " Son of the Most High " when he announced His birth to Mary (Luke i. 32).

4. St. Peter also publicly addressed Jesus Christ as " Son of the living God," and was commended by Christ for this confession (Matt. xvi. 16).

5. Even the devils cried out: " What have we to do with Thee, Jesus, Son of God? Art Thou come hither to torment us before the time? " (Matt. viii. 29.)

Jesus Christ is God Himself.

It had already been foretold: " God Himself will come and will save you " (Is. xxxv. 4), and Isaias said that the Child Who was to be born for the redemption of men was God Himself (Is. ix. 6). The heretic Arius denied Christ's Godhead; his heresy was condemned at the Council of Nicæa in A.D. 325, and it was expressly defined that Jesus Christ was of the same nature as God and therefore Himself God. Our whole position rests on this doctrine, hence its great importance. When the rich disciple addressed Christ as " good master," Our Lord answered at once, " Why dost thou call Me good ? None is good but God alone " (Luke xviii. 19); He would thereby teach us that we must before all things recognize Him as God.

1. That Jesus Christ is God we learn from His own words and from those of His apostles.

When ascending into heaven He said: " All power is given to Me in heaven and on earth " (Matt. xxviii. 18); and again: " I and the Father are one " (John x. 30). These last words were treated by the Jews as blasphemy, and they threatened to stone Our Lord for them (John x. 33). Christ claimed in a special manner attributes and works such as belong to God alone. He proclaimed His eternity when He said: " Glorify Thou Me, O Father, with Thyself with the glory which I had before the world was, with Thee " (John xvii. 5). And again: " Before Abraham was, I am " (John viii. 58). He claimed the power of forgiving sins as in the case of Magdalen (Luke vii. 48), and the man sick of the palsy (Matt. ix. 2). He laid claim to awaken the dead (John v. 28), to judge the world (Matt. xxv. 31), to be the Author of life (John xi. 25). On another occasion He said: " If any man keep My word, he shall not see death forever " (John viii. 51). The apostles believed and solemnly proclaimed that Christ was God, St. Thomas for instance, in the words: " My Lord and my God ! " In St. Paul's epistles we read: " In Christ dwelleth all the fulness of the Godhead corporally " (Col. ii. 9), and " In Him were created all things . . . and He is before all, and by Him all things consist " (Col. i. 16, 17).

2. That Jesus Christ is God we conclude from His miracles and prophecies.

The numerous miracles which Christ wrought in His own name testify to His almighty power.

The miracles may be divided into five classes. (1). Those performed on inanimate substances, such as the changing of the water into wine, the calming of the storm, etc. (2). The healing of the sick, the blind, and the lame (Matt. xi. 3-5). (3). The raising of the dead to life, for example, in the case of the daughter of Jairus, of the son of the widow of Naim, of Lazarus. (4). The expelling of devils from possessed persons. (5). The miracles on His own person, as the transfiguration and the ascension. Moreover Christ proved that He had power over all creation as no other had. Others did miracles in the name of God, as, for example, when St. Peter and St. John cured the man at the gate of the Temple. Christ did not appeal in God's name. He said simply: "Young man, I say to thee, arise!" (Luke vii. 14.) "I will. Be thou made clean" (Matt. viii. 3); "Peace, be still." Benedict XIV. is careful to tell us that if Christ prayed to the Father it was to dispel the notion that His miracles were from the devil. The miracles attributed to the founders of false religions are often very absurd and childish; that Buddha rode on a sunbeam, that Mohammed caused the moon to pass through his sleeve, that Apollonius of Tyana raised a storm in a barrel, etc. So different from the majesty displayed by Christ!

The prophecies of Christ with respect to His own fate, the treachery of Judas, and the denial of St. Peter, the death of St. John and St. Peter, the destruction of Jerusalem, the fate of the Jews, and the career of the Church, all show His omniscience.

Christ foretold that He would be put to death in Jerusalem (Luke xiii. 32), that He would be scourged and crucified, and would rise again after three days (Matt. xx. 17-19). At the Last Supper He foretold the treachery of Judas (John xiii. 26), and that Peter would deny Him thrice before the cock would crow (Matt. xxvi. 34). After His resurrection He prophesied to Peter his death on the cross, and to John that he should die a natural death (John xxi. 18-22). After His triumphal entry into Jerusalem (Luke xix. 41, 44), and during His discourse on the Last Judgment on the Mount of Olives (Matt. xxiv.) He foretold how Jerusalem should be surrounded by her enemies and destroyed. He also knew that the Jews should be scattered among the nations (Luke xxi. 24), that His Church should spread rapidly among the nations of the earth (John x. 16; Matt. xiii. 31) in spite of the persecution of His apostles (John xvi. 2).

3. That Jesus Christ is God we conclude from the elevation of His teaching and His character.

The teaching of Christ surpasses that of the wisest who have ever lived on earth, and is far removed from the teaching of all other religions.

Christ's doctrine answers all the needs of the human heart, and is adapted to all, whatever be their station, age, sex, or nation; the greatest philosophers, even men like St. Augustine, found in it the peace they longed for. Christ's doctrine is a perfect revelation of the highest end of man and of the creation, besides inculcating the loftiest virtues: such as love of one's neighbor, humility, gentleness, patience, love of one's enemies, poverty, which up to the time of Christ had been quite unknown. Kant confesses that reason would not, even at the present day, have discovered the universal moral law unless Christianity had taught it. Christ's teaching, besides being lofty, was so simple, and announced with such clearness, that the people marvelled to hear Him (Matt. vii. 28). Even Strauss does not hesitate to declare that to surpass the teaching of Jesus is an impossible task for all time. There is absolutely nothing in the Christian religion that is opposed to sound reason, or can lower the true dignity of man. Of how many of the other forms of religion can that be said? Mohammedanism teaches fatalism and is propagated by the sword. Even the Talmud contains a large mixture of very imperfect doctrine.

Christ was free from all sin, and was so conspicuous for virtue that for all time He must remain the model for all men.

The traitor Judas confessed that he had shed "innocent blood" (Matt. xxxvii. 4); Pilate could find no cause in Christ (John xviii. 38); Christ Himself challenged the Jews: "Which of you shall convince Me of sin?" and none of them dared reply (John viii. 46). He was quite free from all prejudices and narrow-mindedness, which are the result of surroundings and nationality. We see this in His relations to the Samaritans and Romans, more especially in the beautiful parable of the Good Samaritan (Matt. x. 30-37). The following virtues were most conspicuous: His love of His neighbor: "He went about doing good" (Acts x. 38) and laid down His life for others; His humility, which was seen in His associating with the most despised among the people; His gentleness in His forbearance with His enemies and even with the disciple who betrayed Him; His patience in suffering the greatest tortures; His clemency in His conduct towards sinners; His love of His enemies in His praying for them on the cross; His love of prayer in spending whole nights praying to the Father. His whole character is one of the wonders of history. His greatest enemies even felt awe in His presence; no one, for instance, dared resist Him when He drove the buyers and sellers out of the Temple (Matt. xxi. 12). When the Pharisees wished to stone Him for claiming to be God, He went through their midst and they made way for Him (John x. 39). The soldiers in the garden fell to the ground at a word from His lips (John xviii. 6).

4. That Jesus Christ is God we conclude from the rapid spread of His teaching and from the miracles which accompanied this teaching throughout the world.

His teaching was propagated in spite of the greatest obstacles, and by the simplest of means.

The obstacles among the heathen were: The laws condemning to death or banishment those who professed a new religion. Calumnies the grossest were uttered against the Christians, accusing them of being godless, of cannibalism, attributing to them various misfortunes such as wars, pestilence, and famine. All this led to a persecution extending over some three hundred years; up to the edict of Constantine the Great there are reckoned about ten persecutions. The doctrines of the Christians afforded another series of obstacles; the reverence paid to One Who had suffered the death of the cross was accounted a folly, added to which this doctrine was introduced by Jews, a sect held in the lowest esteem by the Romans. No less repulsive to the sensual and pleasure-loving heathen were the restraint and self-denial inculcated by the Christian religion. The means employed for converting the world were twelve poor fishermen, unequipped with eloquence to persuade, or with the countenance of the great ones of the earth to support their mission. They did indeed

work miracles, but, as St. Augustine says, the spread of Christianity
without miracles would have been the greatest miracle of any. On
Pentecost five thousand were baptized; two thousand more after the
miracle at the gate of the Temple, and in the year A.D. 100 Christianity had extended over the whole Roman world. Pliny, the Governor of
Bithynia, reported to the Emperor Trajan that the heathen temples
were left empty because all were becoming Christians in the towns
and villages. St. Justinus, the philosopher, wrote in A.D. 150:
"There is not a nation where prayers are not offered to the heavenly
Father in the name of the Crucified."

The effect of Christ's teaching was that idolatry with its
horrible abuses disappeared, and that the whole life of man was
reformed and ennobled.

The sacrifice of human victims was abolished, and the bloody
spectacles of the gladiatorial shows. All kinds of charitable institutions arose for the blind, the poor, the sick, etc., owing their existence
to the teaching of Christian mercy. Polygamy died out, and woman
regained her dignity. Order was established in the family life by
the Christian doctrine of the indissolubility of the marriage tie.
Slavery was gradually abolished, for every man saw in his neighbor
the image of God. The cruel laws against malefactors became milder,
and wars became less frequent. Trade, science, and art were
cultivated more, and labor acquired a new dignity. Even Julian the
Apostate counselled the heathen to imitate the Christians in the generosity and purity of their lives. A religion which produces so much
good must be from God. It is sometimes urged that Christ's teaching has been the cause of many religious wars and schisms. The
answer to this objection is that it is not Christ's teaching but man's
perversity in not following that teaching, or wresting it to his own
destruction, which causes so much evil.

Jesus Christ is Our Lord.

Christ's words at the Last Supper were: "You call Me Master
and Lord, and you say well, for so I am " (John xiii. 13).

**We call Christ " Our Lord " because He is our Creator, Re-
deemer, Lawgiver, Teacher, and Judge.**

Christ is our Creator: "In Him were all things created in heaven
and on earth, visible and invisible " (Col. i. 16), and by His Son God
made the world (Heb. i. 2). St. John calls Christ the Word, and
says: "Without Him was made nothing that was made " (John i. 3).
Christ is our Redeemer. By Him we are set free from the slavery of
the devil (1 Pet. i. 18). Hence the Apostle says: "Know ye not that
. . . ye are not your own, for you are bought with a great price " (1
Cor. vi. 19). He is also our Lawgiver, for He developed the teaching
of the Ten Commandments, and gave the two precepts of love. He
called Himself the "Lord of the Sabbath " (Luke vi. 5). Christ is
our Teacher, because He taught men to be like to God, and in John
xiii. 13, He calls Himself our Master. Christ is also our Judge, for
He will come again in glory to summon all mankind before His judg-

ment-seat and separate the sheep from the goats (Matt. xxv. 31, 32). Then will the just as well as the wicked address Him, saying: " Lord, when did we see Thee hungry or thirsty, or a stranger, or naked, or sick, or in prison? " (Matt. xxv. 37, 44.) " He is the blessed and only mighty, the King of kings and Lord of lords . . . to Whom be honor and empire everlasting. Amen " (1 Tim. vi. 15, 16).

EIGHTH ARTICLE OF THE CREED : THE HOLY GHOST.

1. THE GRACE OF THE HOLY GHOST IS NECESSARY TO US.

1. The Holy Ghost is the Third Person of the Blessed Trinity, and is therefore God Himself.

Hence He is eternal, omnipresent, omniscient, almighty.

" The Holy Ghost," says Tertullian, " is God of God, as light is of light." St. Cyril of Alexandria compares the Holy Ghost in His likeness to the Father and the Son, to the vapor arising from water, which is like in its nature to the water producing it. St. Isidore, commenting on these words of Christ: " I drive out devils through the finger of God," says that as the finger is of the same nature as the body, so the Holy Ghost is of the nature of God. St. Athanasius writes that the Holy Ghost is called the finger of God, because it is only through Him that the Father and the Son enter into communication with man. Through Him it was that the tables of stone were written. In the second General Council of Constantinople in A.D. 381, it was defined that the Holy Ghost is eternal, omnipresent, etc., in opposition to the heresy of Macedonius. The Holy Ghost proceeds from the Father and the Son. The Greeks, who denied this article of faith and fell away from the Church in A.D. 867 and A.D. 1053 fell under the Turkish yoke in the year 1453 A.D., and strangely enough on the feast of Pentecost.

2. The Holy Ghost dispenses the graces which Christ merited by the sacrifice of the cross.

The Holy Ghost produces nothing in addition to what Christ gained for us. He only increases and perfects that work of Christ; just as the sun when shining on a field does not sow new seed, but develops that which is already sown. A grace is a favor granted to a person who has no claim to the favor. If a sovereign grants a reprieve to a criminal under sentence of death, that reprieve is a grace. So, too, God acts with regard to man, granting Him numberless favors without any merit on the part of man (Rom. iii. 24). These favors or graces may be temporal, such as health, riches, station; or spiritual, such as forgiveness of our sins. It is with the latter class of favors that we are dealing now, and it was to secure these for us that Christ consented to die on the cross.

3. Hence the assistance of the Holy Ghost is absolutely necessary for salvation.

No mere natural act of a man can gain for him eternal salvation. The following illustration may help us. A little boy longs to reach some fruit on a tree; he stretches out his arms to the utmost, but the fruit is still out of reach; the child's father then lifts him up, so that he can pluck the fruit for himself. Thus man cannot attain salvation by his own efforts till the Holy Ghost gives him the super-natural strength. Just as the eye cannot discern distant objects without a telescope, and the arm cannot lift heavy weights without a lever, so the natural powers of man require supernatural help in order that salvation may be obtained. Hence the words of Christ: "Unless a man be born again of water and the Holy Ghost, he cannot enter into the kingdom of God" (John iii. 5).

Without the help of the Holy Ghost we cannot do the least work deserving of salvation.

We can do nothing without God's help. "Our sufficiency is from God" (2 Cor. iii. 5). As St. Thomas Aquinas says, we are, since the Fall, like a sick man who cannot leave his bed without help. The following may serve as illustrations. A man cannot work without light; thus too he cannot do any good work without the light of the Holy Ghost. The body is helpless unless animated by the soul; in like manner man can do no good unless the Holy Spirit, Who is the life of the soul, come to his aid (St. Fulgentius). Our souls bring forth no fruit unless they are watered by the rain of the grace of the Holy Spirit (St. Hilary). As grace can do nothing without the co-operation of the will, so neither can the will achieve any result without grace. Compare the action of earth: it can produce no fruits without rain, and the rain cannot produce without the earth (St. John Chrysostom). As ink is required for the pen, so the grace of the Holy Ghost is necessary to inscribe the virtues in our souls (St. Thomas Aquinas). Every good work is the effect of two co-ordinate principles: the Holy Ghost and our own free will (1 Cor. xv. 10); we may compare the action of the schoolmaster who guides a boy's hand while he writes. Thus we can never ascribe the merit of our good works to ourselves. The earth does not bring forth flowers, but rather the sun by means of the earth. As we ascribe the activity of the body to the soul, so we should ascribe our good works to the grace of God. We might put down our good works to our own account with as much truth as a soldier might claim the victory without reference to his commander.

With the help of the Holy Ghost we can carry out the most difficult works.

St. Paul says: "I can do all in Him Who strengtheneth me" (Phil. iv. 13).

2. ACTION OF THE HOLY GHOST.

The graces conferred by the Holy Ghost are as follows:
1. He gives to all men actual graces.
2. He gives to some men sanctifying grace.

3. He usually gives the seven special gifts, and occasionally quite extraordinary graces.

4. He sustains and guides the Catholic Church.

Actual Grace.

1. The Holy Ghost influences our lives by enlightening the mind and strengthening the will. Such passing influence of the Holy Spirit is called " actual grace."

Before Pentecost the apostles were still ignorant; "slow of heart," as Our Lord expressed it (Luke xxiv. 25); the Holy Ghost in descending upon them enlightened their understanding and strengthened their will; the fear which had caused them to keep in concealment was now changed into undaunted courage. The fiery tongues symbolized the enlightenment of their minds, the whirlwind the strength which they received. The Holy Ghost is like the sun, giving light and warmth. When the sun begins to shine, the stars which were visible before begin to wane, and we see nothing in the firmament but the sun. When the Holy Ghost enlightens our souls we despise all earthly objects which formerly attracted our love, such as eating, drinking, playing, etc., and all our thoughts are turned towards God. Moreover the light of the sun reveals to us the true form of objects, the stones which we have gathered, the various roads before us. The light of the Holy Ghost shows us the true value of earthly things, our own sins, and the true goal of life. When the sun comes the ice begins to melt and the plants to blossom. So, too, the Holy Ghost warms our hearts, stirring them with the love of God and of our neighbor, and helps us to do actions deserving of heaven. The Holy Ghost is therefore a light, descending from the Father of light (Jas. i. 17); as St. Augustine says: "Actual grace is a light which enlightens and moves the sinner."

There are many and various channels through which the Holy Ghost makes His influence act; for instance, sermons, the reading of good books, illness and death, the good example of others, religious pictures, the advice of superiors and friends, etc.

The people were moved by the Holy Ghost at Pentecost when they heard the preaching of the apostles; so too St. Anthony the Hermit (356), on hearing a sermon on the rich young man; St. Ignatius of Loyola (1556), by the reading of the lives of the saints; St. Francis of Assisi (1226) during an illness; St. Francis Borgia (1572) on seeing the dead body of the Queen Isabella; St. Norbert (1134) on seeing a death by lightning, etc., etc. In all these cases there was a sudden interior change, which the Holy Ghost took occasion of to speak to their hearts. All of them might have said with St. Cyprian: "When the Holy Ghost came into my heart, He changed me into another man." Often God sends us suffering, before the Holy Ghost speaks to us. Just as wax must be subjected to the flame and the stamp before receiving an impression, so the heart of man must be softened by suffering in order to receive the impress of the Holy Spirit. Before paper can be used for writing, it must be prepared and finished; in a similar manner man must be purified from his evil desires before he is fit for the working of the Holy Ghost in his soul.

2. The action of the Holy Spirit sometimes makes itself perceptible to the senses.

For example, the appearance of the dove and the voice from heaven at the baptism of Christ. the fiery tongues and the rushing as of wind on Pentecost. We might reflect also how Christ instituted the Sacraments with forms appealing to the senses.

3. The Holy Ghost does not force us, but leaves us in perfect possession of our free will.

The Holy Ghost is, as it were, a guide Whom men may follow or not as they list. He is the light proceeding from God, to which man can, if he will, close his eyes; as St. Augustine says: " To obey the voice of God or not is left to a man's free will." God does not act upon us as if we were inanimate objects without intellect or free will. Man's freedom is very sacred to God, nor will He deprive him of it even when he uses it to his own perdition. In the words of St. Gertrude: " As God would not allow our great enemy to deprive us of our freedom, so neither would He take it from us Himself."

Man can co-operate with actual grace or reject it (Ps. xciv. 8).

Saul of Tarsus co-operated with grace, the rich young man (Luke xviii. 18-25) rejected it. The people who on Pentecost reviled the apostles rejected grace (Acts ii. 13), as also those who mocked at St. Paul when he spoke to them on the Areopagus of the Gospel and the resurrection of the dead (Acts xvii. 32). Herod, too, when he heard of the birth of Christ from the Magi, failed to co-operate with grace. St. Francis de Sales draws an illustration from marriage: When a man wishes to marry he offers his hand to some suitable person, and that person may accept or reject the offer; thus God acts. He offers us His grace and we may accept it or reject it. Whoever constantly resists actual grace, and dies in that resistance is guilty of grave sin against the Holy Ghost, a sin which cannot be forgiven. Such a man resembles the devil, who is ever resisting the truth.

Whoever co-operates with actual grace acquires greater graces; but he who resists loses other graces and must answer at the judgment for his obstinacy.

The first grace. if responded to. brings with it a string of other graces. The servant who employed well his five talents received five talents more (Matt. xxv. 28). Hence the words of Christ: He that hath, to him shall be given and he shall abound (Matt. xxv. 29). The punishment which fell on the city of Jerusalem in A.D. 70 is a terrible example of the rejection of grace, because it did not know the time of its visitation (Luke xix. 44). To him who rejects grace apply those words of Christ: " The unprofitable servant cast ye out into the exterior darkness. There shall be weeping and gnashing of teeth " (Matt. xxv. 30). It is an insult to a great lord to refuse his gifts, all the more if he be the Lord of heaven and earth and God Himself. He who rejects graces has as little chance of getting to heaven as the traveller of reaching his destination who should neglect to enter the train while it is in the station. The moment of actual grace is like the crisis of a sickness, when a little carelessness may cause death. Many people give a poor reception to the Holy Ghost when He comes to them on the occasion of a death, the reception of the sacraments, or the celebration of great feasts, by giving way to worldly distractions and following their inclinations. They should then seek solitude and time for recollection and prayer, or purify their souls from sin by confession. Thus acted St. Ignatius of Loyola when after his conversion he retired into the cave at Manresa; thus too St. Mary of Egypt who retired into the desert. "Sailors put out to sea," says Louis of Granada, "as soon as they see that a favorable wind is blowing; with like promptitude ought we to act when we feel the influence of the Holy Spirit." If we delay God will withdraw His graces, just as in the case of the Israelites. Those who failed to rise in the early morning to gather the manna found it had melted away after sunrise. "The greater the graces we receive," says St. Gregory the Great, "the greater is our responsibility." Christ's own words are: "Unto whomsoever much is given, of him much shall be required" (Luke xii. 48).

4. The Holy Ghost acts on every man, on the sinner as well as on the just; and more on Catholics than on non-Catholics and unbelievers.

God is the Good Shepherd (John x.), Who seeks the lost sheep till He finds it (Luke xv.). Christ, the Light of the world, enlightens every man that comes into the world (John i. 9). God's will is that all men be saved, and come to the knowledge of the truth (1 Tim. ii. 4). Besides all this God has a very special love for the souls of men. "My delight is to be with the children of men" (Prov. viii. 31).

The Holy Ghost was even from the beginning of the world active in promoting the salvation of mankind, but on Pentecost He came into the world in a much more efficacious manner.

While the Jews were in exile in Babylon, the Holy Ghost was working in the heathen by the many miracles which were wrought to demonstrate God's power: as in the incident of the three children in the furnace and Daniel in the lion's den. He was working not only in the patriarchs and prophets, but even in heathens like Socrates (who taught the existence of one God, and for that reason was condemned to death in 399 B.C.). Just as the sunrise is preceded by the dawn, so the sun of justice, Christ, is preceded by the dawn of the Holy Ghost.

The Holy Ghost does not distribute His gifts equally to all men; the members of the Catholic Church receive the richest share.

One servant five talents, another two, and another one talent (Matt. xxv. 15). The Jews received more than the heathen; the blessed Mother of God more than all other men. The towns of Corozain and Bethsaida received more graces than Tyre and Sidon, Capharnaum more than Sodom (Matt. xi. 21, 23). There are ordinary graces which are given to all men without distinction, and there are special graces which God grants only to a few souls, and that with a view to some special work. Many graces may be obtained, especially by the prayers of others and by co-operation with the first grace. St. Augustine received many more graces than other men in consequence of the prayers of St. Monica; so, too, St. Paul through the dying prayer of St. Stephen. The holy apostles obeyed the first call of Our Lord, and thus obtained many other graces.

The action of the Holy Ghost on the souls of men is not constant, but occasional.

Hence the exhortation of St. Paul: "Now is the acceptable time; behold now is the day of salvation" (2 Cor. vi. 2). Compare the parable of the vineyard where the workmen received only one summons (Matt. xx.). Times of special grace are the seasons of Lent or when a mission is being given, or the jubilee year. These times of grace are like the market-days when things are easier to obtain; with this difference, that no money is required. "Come buy wine and milk, without money, and without any price" (Is. lv. 1).

5. Actual graces are obtained by the performance of good works, especially by prayer, fasting, and almsdeeds; and more especially by the use of the means of grace provided by the Church, by hearing of holy Mass, worthy reception of the sacraments, and attendance at sermons.

God's grace cannot be merited by our own good works alone, otherwise it would not be grace (Rom. xi. 6), yet these good works are necessary, for, as St. Augustine says: "God, Who created us without our co-operation will not save us without our co-operation." Not according to the works which we have done but out of His mercy has God saved us (Tit. iii. 5). The Holy Ghost gives to each one as He wills (1 Cor. xii. 11), with regard, however, to the preparation and co-operation of each individual (Council of Trent. 6, 7). Hence it is that a man receives more actual grace as he is richer in good works. In particular we know that prayer to the Holy Ghost is very efficacious, for the Father in heaven gives the Holy Spirit to those who ask Him. Prayer to the Mother of God is also very efficacious: for she is "full of grace," and "the dispenser of all God's gifts." "Let no one," says St. Alphonsus, "consider this last title extravagant, for the greatest saints have so spoken of her, and the saints, as we know, were inspired by the Holy Ghost, the Spirit of truth." Prayer to the Blessed Sacrament also confers many graces. So, too, retirement from the world, or the solitude in which God speaks to the heart (Osee ii. 14), and the mortification of the senses are excellent means of drawing down grace; a good example is found in the conduct of the apostles during the time preceding Pentecost.

Sanctifying Grace.

1. When the sinner co-operates with actual grace, the Holy Ghost enters his soul and confers on it a brightness and beauty which claim the friendship of God. This indwelling beauty of the soul is due to the presence of the Holy Spirit and is called " sanctifying grace."

Iron placed in a fire becomes heated, and glows like the fire itself; so the Holy Spirit, entering into a soul and dwelling there (1 Cor. vi. 19), gives it a new nature, a light and glory which we call " sanctifying grace." That God is drawn to men by their co-operation with His grace appears from God's own words: " Turn ye to Me. . . . .and I will turn to you " (Zach. i. 3). Sanctifying grace is like a new garment, so it is represented by the wedding-garment and the parable of the supper (Matt. xxii.), and of the prodigal son (Luke xv.). " The soul acquires a great beauty by the presence of the Holy Spirit," says St. John Chrysostom. " He who enters into the state of grace, is like a man bowed down with infirmities and age, who, by a miracle, has been transformed into a beautiful youth dressed in purple and carrying a sceptre." " If," says Blosius, " the beauty of a soul in the state of grace could be seen, mankind would be transported with wonder and delight." Just as a palace must be beautifully furnished when the king comes to dwell in it, so the soul of man must be made into a beautiful temple by the Holy Ghost before God can dwell in it. After the resurrection the appearance of the body will be determined by that of the soul. " Let us therefore," says St. John Chrysostom, " give all our care to the soul; for this is the true interest of our bodies, which otherwise will perish with the soul." Sanctifying grace is not merely a gift of God (Council of Trent, 6, 11), but God gives us of His Spirit (1 John iv. 13). The Holy Ghost penetrates us through and through like fire; He is not in us merely like a ray of sunshine in a room. In consequence of this supernatural beauty the soul is enriched with the friendship of God. St. Mary Magdalene of Pazzi says that if a man in the state of sanctifying grace knew how pleasing his soul is to God he would die of excess of joy. We are, in consequence of sanctifying grace, no longer the servants of God but His friends (John xv. 15). The expression " friendship " implies of itself a certain likeness; and this elevation from the state of sin to that of friendship with God is called "justification" (Council of Trent, 6, 4), or regeneration (John iii. 5; Tit. iii. 4-7), or the putting off of the old man and the putting on of the new (Eph. iv. 22). Examples: As soon as David, Paul, and the prodigal son repented, they received the Holy Ghost and the gift of sanctifying grace; otherwise they would never have accomplished their great sacrifice. David and Saul spent many days in fasting and prayer, and the prodigal son faced the humiliation of returning to his father's roof. It is quite certain that whoever has perfect contrition receives the Holy Spirit even before confessing. Thus the patriarchs and prophets had sanctifying grace in consequence of their penitential spirit, and their belief in a Saviour. We know, too, that the Holy Spirit resides in some men even before Baptism, as in the case of the

centurion Cornelius, and the people assembled in his house (Acts **x.**
44).

**2. Usually, however, the Holy Spirit makes His entry on the
reception of the Sacraments of Baptism or Penance.**

The sinner under the action of the Holy Ghost begins to believe
in God, to fear Him, to hope in Him, and love Him; then to bewail
his sins, and finally decides to seek the means of grace in the Sacraments of Baptism or Penance. Then only is his conversion perfect.
And actual experience goes to prove that Baptism or a general confession is in most sinners the beginning of a new life. Even in children their baptism is the beginning of a new spiritual life.

**3. When the Holy Spirit enters into us, He brings with Him
a new spiritual life.**

God is the God of life, and His presence diffuses life. His presence in our souls is like the presence of the soul in our bodies. Our
souls have a natural life of their own, and by means of the intellect
and the will learn to appreciate the true, the beautiful, and the good.
But this natural life, compared with the life imparted by God, is like
the statue compared to its living original. This divine life is acquired
by the soul when the Holy Spirit takes possession of the soul with
His grace, and it enables the soul to know, love, and enjoy God; this
is the supernatural life. Just as Elias (3 Kings xvii.) and Eliseus (4
Kings iv.) restored the dead children to life by measuring their
bodies over that of the child, mouth to mouth, hand to hand, member
to member, so does the Holy Ghost breathe the divine life into us,
giving us to see with His sight, to work with His power; and thus
our soul is born to a new life (1 Pet. i. 3, 4). Grace is, in the words
of Our Saviour, "a fountain of water springing into life everlasting" (John iv. 14). "A heavenly seed is sown in us," says St. Peter
Chrysologus, "destined to spring up to everlasting life. We are of a
heavenly family, and Our Father is throned in heaven. See to what
heights grace has raised thee!" While our bodies decay from day to
day, our souls become daily more full of the strength of youth by virtue of grace (2 Cor. iv. 16). Even in our bodies God's grace lays the
germ of everlasting life: "And if the spirit of Him that raised up
Jesus from the dead, dwell in you; He that raised up Jesus Christ
from the dead shall quicken also your mortal bodies, because of His
spirit that dwelleth in you" (Rom. viii. 11).

The following are some of the effects of the Holy Spirit
when He acts upon us by His grace:

1. He purifies us from all mortal sin.

As metals are purified by fire from their dross, so are our souls
cleansed of their sins when penetrated by the fire of the Holy Spirit.
Sanctifying grace and mortal sin are incompatible. The Holy Spirit
dwells in all who are free from mortal sin, and the evil spirit in
those who are guilty of mortal sin. Although the grace of God brings
a cure to the soul of man, it does not cure the body; in his flesh is left
the remains of sin, or concupiscence. Thus in great saints even,
there remains the inclination to evil against which must be waged a

lifelong struggle. Hence the words of St. Paul: " I know that there dwelleth not in me, that is to say, in my flesh, that which is good " (Rom. vii. 18). " Concupiscence," says St. Augustine, " may be lessened in this life but not destroyed." It remains with us as an object lesson of the deadly effects of sin, and to give occasion, by our resistance to it, of gaining merit in heaven.

2. He unites us to God and makes us into temples of God.

He who has the Holy Spirit is united with Christ, like the branches with the vine (John xv. 5). In the words of St. Gregory Nazianzen, our nature is united with God by the virtue of the Holy Ghost, like a drop of water poured into a measure of wine; it acquires the color, the taste, and the smell of the wine. The Holy Spirit makes us sharers of the divine nature (2 Pet. i. 4). " By the action of the Holy Spirit," says St. Thomas Aquinas, " we are transformed into gods "; and St. Maximus: " The Godhead is conferred on us with grace," and " As iron glows when heated in the fire, so is man changed by the Holy Spirit into the Godhead " (St. Basil; St. Thomas Aquinas). Hence men are often called gods (John x. 34; Ps. lxxxi. 6). Lucifer and the first man wished to be as God, but independently of Him. God wills that we should strive to be as He is, but in union with Him. The presence of the Holy Ghost makes us temples of God. " The Holy Spirit," says St. Augustine, " dwells primarily in the soul, and gives it its true life; and since the soul is in the body, the Holy Ghost dwells therefore in our bodies." St. Paul insists on this point: " Know you not that you are the temple of God, and the Spirit of God dwelleth in you ? " (1 Cor. iii. 16); " You are the temple of the living God " (2 Cor. vi. 16). In the Our Father we say " Our Father, Who art in heaven "; " the heaven," says St. Augustine, " is the just man on earth, because God dwells in him." Christ Himself said that the Father and He would take up their abode with the man who loves Christ (John xiv. 23).

3. He illumines the mind, and makes the divine and moral precepts possible.

He strengthens our faculties of the intellect and will, just as a ray of sunlight passing through a crystal turns it into a mass of light. More especially does He give the light of faith (2 Cor. iv. 6), and kindle the fire of divine love (Rom. v. 5). In short He gives the three theological virtues (Council of Trent, 6, 7). He also makes us able and willing to co-operate with the inspirations of the Holy Spirit; that is, He gives us the seven gifts of the Holy Ghost. Just as iron softens in the fire, so the soul of man under the influence of the Holy Spirit is inclined to good works; this we see exemplified in St. Paul, for hardly had the Holy Ghost acted upon him when he asks: " Lord, what wilt Thou that I do ? " (Acts ix. 6.) Through this inclination of the will towards what is good, the moral virtues are present as possibilities; practice is all that is required to make them facts. Thus the whole spiritual life is changed, and we see how far apart is the inner life of a saint and that of a worldling. The latter thinks only of his own satisfaction in eating, drinking, the pursuit of ambition and pleasure; in short, he loves the world. The man in whom the Holy Spirit dwells, directs his thoughts for the m st part to God and tries to please Him; that is, he loves God. He can say with St. Paul, " I live, now not I; but Christ liveth in me" (Gal. ii. 20). Such a man despises the things of this world, and whatever be his sufferings he enjoys peace from within and unspeakable consolation; for the Holy Ghost is the Comforter (John xiv. 26).

4. He gives us true peace.

Through Him man acquires the peace which surpasses all understanding (Phil. iv. 7). The man who has the light of the Holy Ghost in him is like a traveller performing his journey in sunshine and fair weather; quite otherwise is the case of him from whom that light is cut off by the clouds of sin; he is like the unwilling traveller, forced to make his way through wind and storm.

5. He becomes our Teacher and Guide.

He instructs us in the teachings of the Catholic Church. The unction which we have received from Him teacheth us of all things (1 John ii. 27). Whoever has not the Holy Ghost may indeed study the truths of the Christian religion, but their significance escapes him; it is an unfruitful knowledge. Just as a book cannot be read in the dark without the help of a light, so the Word of God is unintelligible without light from the Holy Ghost. Though it is quite true that whatever the Holy Ghost imparts to us is free from error, yet we require to be certain that what we have received is indeed imparted by the Holy Spirit. Hence, no matter what a man's lights may be, he must keep fast hold of the teaching of the Church; and whoever fails to do this has not the Holy Spirit in him (1 John iv. 6). The Holy Ghost is our Guide, " leading us," says Louis of Granada, " as a father who leads his child by the hand over a difficult path." Those who are in the grace of God are led in a special manner. Such can say: " No longer do I live, but Christ lives in me." It is in this manner that the just have the kingdom of God within them (Luke xvii. 21).

6. He inspires us to do good works and makes them meritorious for the kingdom of heaven.

Just as the Holy Spirit brooded over the waters of the deep, and created plants, animals, and men, so too does He hover over the souls of men, bringing forth fruits that are to last forever. As the flower expands when touched by the sun, so is the heart of the most hardened sinner expanded by the grace of the Holy Spirit, and breathes out the perfume of virtue and piety. The Holy Ghost is ever active, like fire, and always inciting to good works. As the wind keeps the windmill ever in motion, so the Holy Spirit is ever moving the heart of man. And He makes our actions meritorious. As the soul raises our ordinary and merely animal operations to the level of rational and intellectual acts, so the Holy Ghost elevates the acts of our soul to a supernatural and divine plane. The Holy Ghost is, as it were, the gardener of our souls. A gardener grafts a good branch on to an uncultivated stock, which then brings forth sweet fruit, in place of its former sour and poor fruit; so the Holy Ghost engrafts upon us a branch from Christ, the tree of life, and we bear no longer our merely natural fruit, but supernatural. When we are in the state of grace, we are the branches united with the vine, Jesus Christ (John xv. 4). Good works done in the state of mortal sin obtain for us only actual graces to help towards our conversion.

7. He makes us children of God and heirs of heaven.

When the Holy Ghost enters our souls it is with us as with Christ at His baptism, when the Holy Spirit descended upon Him; God the Father receives us as His well-beloved children, and the heavens are opened to us; we have no longer the spirit of slavery, but the spirit of adoption of sons whereby we cry " Abba, Father " (Rom. viii. 15). All who are led by the Spirit of God are the sons of God (Rom. viii. 14). If we are sons of God, we are also heirs: heirs indeed of God, joint heirs with Christ (Rom. viii. 17), for children have a claim to their heritage from their parents. " We know if our earthly house of this habitation be dissolved that we have a building of God, a house not made with hands, eternal in heaven " (2 Cor. v. 1). The Holy Spirit will remain with us forever (John xiv. 16). " To be numbered among the sons of God," says St. Cyprian, " is the highest nobility." Such is man's privilege when in the state of grace, but like the uncut diamond, all the glory of his soul is not yet visible. Well might David cry out: " Be glad in the Lord, and rejoice, ye just " (Ps. xxxi. 11). He who has the Holy Spirit has the greatest of kingdoms, the kingdom of God in himself (Luke xvii. 21). Alas ! that so many men should neglect this, their privilege, and give themselves up to the lusts of their flesh, the food of worms.

4. Sanctifying grace is secured and increased by doing good works and using the means of grace offered by the Church; it is lost by a single mortal sin.

Sanctifying grace can always be increased in the soul: " He that is just let him be justified still; and he that is holy, let him be sanctified still " (Apoc. xxii. 11). By good works the sanctifying grace which we have received may be confirmed and increased in us (Council of Trent, 6, 26). Thus, for example, St. Stephen was a man " full of the Holy Spirit " (Acts vi. 5). Stones and weeds prevent the sun from reaching the earth and giving it increase; so do our sins hinder the Holy Ghost from acting on our souls; hence they must be removed by the sacraments of confession and communion; and as the soil must be prepared, so must our souls be nourished with the teaching of Christ in order to receive the action of the Holy Ghost. This was the case even with the apostles. One mortal sin is enough to rob us of sanctifying grace, for it is by mortal sin only that the soul is separated entirely from God. " God never deserts him who has once been sanctified by His grace, unless He Himself be first deserted." Hence the warning of the Apostle: " Extinguish not the Spirit " (1 Thess. v. 19). In the instant of committing mortal sin, storm clouds arise between God, the Sun of justice, and our souls, the brightness of which is at once extinguished. With the departure of the Holy Ghost are united the darkening of the understanding and the weakening of the will. " When the sun goes down," says Louis of Granada, " the eye is darkened and can no longer make out objects. So when the light of the Holy Ghost is taken from the soul, it is filled with darkness, and loses the knowledge of the truth." Whoever has lost sanctifying grace can recover it by means of the Sacrament of Penance, but not without an earnest effort; for the wicked spirit has entered into such a man and has taken with him seven more spirits more wicked than himself (Matt. xii. 45). It is impossible for those who were once illuminated and are fallen away to be renewed again to penance (Heb. vi. 4-6).

5. He who has not sanctifying grace is spiritually dead and will suffer eternal ruin.

St. Augustine says that as the body without the soul is dead, so the soul without the grace of the Holy Spirit is dead for heaven. He who has not the Holy Ghost sits "in darkness and in the shadow of death" (Luke i. 79); he cannot understand the things of the Spirit, for they are to him foolishness (1 Cor. ii. 14). He who has not on the wedding-garment, that is, sanctifying grace, is cast into outer darkness (Matt. xxii. 12). And as the branch which is not united to the vine withers and is cast into the fire, so is he cast off who does not remain united to Christ by His grace (John xv. 6). If any man have not the spirit of Christ, he is not of Christ (Rom. viii. 9).

6. No one knows for certain whether he have sanctifying grace or will receive it at the hour of death.

Man knows not whether he is worthy of love or hatred (Eccles. ix. 1). Even St. Paul says of himself: "I am not conscious to myself of anything, yet am I not hereby justified" (1 Cor. iv. 4). Solomon even became an idolater before his death; and St. Bernard warns us: "Even if a man have the light of grace and the love of God, let him remember that he is still under the open sky and not in the house, and that a breeze may put out this holy light forever." "We carry our treasure in earthen vessels" (2 Cor. iv. 7), and in the words of Theophylact, "Our hearts are like earthen vessels, easily broken and prone to spill the water in them; so may the Holy Spirit be lost by one sin." No wonder St. Paul warns us: "Work out your salvation in fear and trembling" (Phil. ii. 12). We may indeed have confidence that we are in the grace of God, but without a special revelation we cannot have absolute certainty (Council of Trent, 6, 6). It may be surmised from the good works which a man does that he is in the grace of God, for an evil tree cannot bring forth good fruit (Matt. vii. 18).

The Seven Gifts of the Holy Ghost and the Extraordinary Graces.

1. The Holy Ghost gives to all who have sanctifying grace the seven gifts of the Holy Spirit, that is, seven virtues of the soul, by which it easily responds to His light and inspirations.

The light of the sun is split up into seven distinct colors, and the seven-branched candlestick in the Temple was a type of the seven gifts. These seven gifts embrace the four cardinal virtues. They remove entirely the barriers which divide us from God, especially by subjecting our concupiscence to the dictates of reason (St. Thomas Aquinas). The seven gifts give us a definite movement towards God; they perfect the powers of our souls, so that the Holy Ghost can easily move them. Just as teaching in the elementary school prepares the scholar for higher forms of instruction, so the seven gifts prepare the soul for the higher influence of the Holy Ghost. The three theological virtues are higher than the seven gifts, because the latter only give us a movement towards God, while the former unite us intimately with Him. These gifts are lost by mortal sin, but are increased as one advances in perfection. Confirmation also increases these gifts.

The seven gifts of the Holy Spirit are : Wisdom, understanding, knowledge, counsel, fortitude, piety, and the fear of God.

The first four enlighten the understanding, the others strengthen the will. These gifts are enumerated by Isaias as belonging to the Redeemer of mankind (Is. xi. 2).

1. The gift of wisdom enables us to recognize the emptiness of earthly things, and to regard God as the highest good.

St. Paul counts all that the world loves and admires for loss (Phil. iii. 8). Solomon, after tasting of the joys of this world calls them "vanities" (Eccles. i. 2). St. Ignatius of Loyola used often to exclaim: " Oh! how poor are the things of earth when I look at the heavens." Compare, too, the prayer of St. Francis of Assisi, "My God and my all."

2. The gift of understanding enables us to distinguish Catholic teaching from all other doctrine, and to rest in it.

Blessed Clement Hofbauer, the apostle of Vienna (A.D. 1820), though he began his studies very late in life, and had only just enough knowledge of theology to be ordained, was often consulted by the dignitaries of the Church on the accuracy of the doctrine taught in the books passing through the press. A very short examination enabled him to detect at once what was unsound. St. Catharine of Alexandria (A.D. 307), reduced some fifty pagan doctors to silence, and made them into Christians. Our Lord's own promise was: " I will give you a mouth and wisdom which all your adversaries shall not be able to resist and gainsay " (Luke xxi. 15).

3. The gift of knowledge enables us to obtain a clear grasp of the teaching of the Catholic Church without special study.

The Curé of Ars had done but little study, yet his sermons were so remarkable that even bishops were eager to hear them, and marvelled at his knowledge. St. Thomas Aquinas used to say that he learned more at the foot of the altar than out of books; and St. Ignatius of Loyola declared that he had learned more in the cave at Manresa than all the doctors in the world could teach him. How did the old man Simeon know that the child in the Temple was the Messias (Luke ii. 34)? Were not the apostles, after the coming of the Holy Ghost, "endowed with power from on high" (Luke xxiv. 49)? Was not St. Paul rapt into paradise to hear words such as no man had heard (2 Cor. xii. 4)?

4. The gift of counsel enables us to know under difficult circumstances what the will of God is.

We might recall the answer made by Christ to the question whether tribute should be paid to Cæsar (Matt. xxii. 21), and the judgment of Solomon (3 Kings iii.). Our Lord, when warning the apostles of the persecutions awaiting them, had said, "Be not solicitous how you shall answer or what you shall say; for the Holy Ghost shall teach you in the same hour what you must say" (Luke xii. 11, 12).

5. The gift of fortitude enables us to bear courageously whatever is necessary in carrying out God's will.

St. John Nepomucene (1393) chose rather to be imprisoned, tortured with hot irons, and finally cast into the Moldau, rather than betray the secret of the confessional. Job was patient in spite of the loss of his property, his children, and his health, and in spite of the mockery of his wife and friends. Abraham was ready to sacrifice his only son. The gift of fortitude is especially prominent in the holy martyrs, and most of all in Our Lady, the Queen of martyrs. "She herself," says St. Alphonsus, "would have nailed her Son to the cross had such been God's will; for she possessed the gift of fortitude in a higher degree than Abraham."

6. The gift of piety enables us to make continual efforts to honor God more and more in our hearts, and to carry out His will more perfectly.

St. Teresa took a vow always to choose what was most perfect, and St. Alphonsus never to waste time. St. Aloysius would spend hours in presence of the Blessed Sacrament, till his confessor had to command him to shorten his devotions. Many of the saints used to melt into tears during their prayer or in meditating on heavenly subjects.

7. The gift of the fear of God enables us to fear giving offence to God more than all the evils in the world.

Such was the gift, for instance, of the three children in the furnace, and of all the martyrs. It enables us to overcome the fear of man and human respect.

2. The Holy Ghost gives to many graces of a rarer kind; for instance, the gift of tongues, of miracles, of prophecy, of discernment of spirits, of visions, of ecstasies, etc.

The apostles received on the feast of Pentecost the gift of tongues, and we find it recorded also in the life of St. Francis Xavier, as having been possessed by him. The prophets of the Old Law foretold future events. St. Peter knew the thoughts of Ananias. St.

Catharine of Sienna after communion used to be raised in the air and rapt out of her senses. St. Francis of Assisi received the stigmata, or impression on his body of the sacred wounds of Our Lord. Instances of all these gifts occur again and again in the lives of the saints, and are, after all, only the fulfilment of the promise of Our Lord in Mark xvi. 17, 18. These graces are conferred by the Holy Ghost on whom He will (1 Cor. xii. 11). Louis of Granada beautifully expresses it: " As the sun shines on the flowers, and brings out their various perfumes, so does the light of the Holy Spirit fall on pious souls, according to their peculiarities, and develops in them His graces and gifts."

These extraordinary graces are conferred by the Holy Ghost generally for the benefit of others and in aid of His Church.

The time of the apostles was conspicuous for extraordinary gifts (1 Cor. xii.-xiv.). " God is like a gardener," says St. Gregory the Great, " who waters the flowers only while they are young." Extraordinary graces ought to be used with due discretion for the benefit of others (1 Cor. xiv. 12). In the words of St. Irenæus, " A merchant does not leave his money idle in his chests, but he makes the best use he can of it in business; so God's will is that His graces should not be left unemployed, but that men should make good use of them." These extraordinary gifts of themselves do not make men better. They are indeed great graces, available for great good, and are the free gift of God, like riches, health, etc. Hence the words of St. Teresa: " Not for all the goods and joys of this world would I give up a single one of the graces given me; I esteemed them always as a singular gift of God and a very great treasure." It is the right use of these gifts, and not the gifts themselves, which make them of service to man. St. Fulgentius writes: " One may have the gift of miracles, and yet lose his soul. Miracles give no certainty of one's salvation." Nor are these extraordinary graces a sign of holiness in the possessor of them; Our Lord's own words convey this in Matthew vii. 22. Yet there is no saint of the Church who has not had these gifts. Benedict XIV. says: " They are, as a rule, given not to sinners but to the just. When they are found in union with heroic virtue in a man, they are a strong proof of his sanctity." These gifts are usually accompanied by great sufferings, such as desolation of spirit, struggles with the devil, sickness, persecutions, etc.

3. **The gifts of the Holy Spirit were conspicuous in a special degree in Jesus Christ (Acts x. 38), His holy Mother, the apostles, the patriarchs and prophets of the Old Law, and all the saints of the Catholic Church.**

The Holy Ghost as Guide of the Church.

The Holy Ghost maintains and guides the Catholic Church.

As the soul is to the body, so is the Holy Ghost to the Catholic Church, and, like the soul, His action is invisible. He is the Architect of the Church; His action produced the Incarnation (Luke i. 35); He exercised His powers through the humanity of Christ (Luke

iv. 18; Acts x. 38); He perfects the Church founded by the Redeemer (Eph. ii. 20-22).

1. The Holy Spirit secures the Catholic Church from destruction (Matt. xvi. 18), and preserves it from error (John xiv. 16).

2. The Holy Ghost supports the rulers of the Church in the duties of their office (Acts xx. 28), and especially the Vicar of Christ, the Pope.

The Holy Ghost gives to them what they shall say (Matt. x. 19). He speaks through them as on Pentecost He spoke through the apostles (Matt. x. 20). In the words of St. Basil: "As the pen writes what the writer wishes, so the preacher of the Gospel speaks nothing of his own but what the Holy Spirit gives to him."

3. The Holy Ghost raises up in times of danger for the Church able champions of her cause.

For example St. Athanasius (A.D. 373) in the time of the Arians; the holy Pope Gregory VII. (A.D. 1085) when the Church was in general disorder; St. Dominic (A.D. 1221) at the time of the Albigenses; St. Catharine of Sienna (A.D. 1380), at the time of the great Papal schism; St. Ignatius of Loyola (A.D. 1556) at the time of Luther.

4. The Holy Ghost is the cause that there are so many saints in the Church in all ages.

Almost every year new saints are canonized in Rome.

3. APPARITIONS OF THE HOLY GHOST.

The Holy Ghost has appeared under the form of a dove, of fire, and of tongues, to signify His office in the Church.

"The Holy Ghost," says St. Gregory the Great, "appeared in the form of a dove and of fire, because His work is done gently and zealously, and whoever is wanting in gentleness and zeal is not under His influence. He appeared in the form of tongues, because He gives to man the gift of speech, by which he may inflame others to the love of God." The Holy Ghost appeared under the form of fire, because He consumes the dross of our sins, drives the darkness of ignorance out of our souls, melts the icy coldness of our hearts, and inflames us with love of God and of our neighbor, and because He hardens and strengthens the heart of man whom He has made from the clay of the earth. "Our God is a consuming fire" (Heb. xii. 29).

NINTH ARTICLE OF THE CREED : THE CATHOLIC CHURCH.

1. *THE CATHOLIC CHURCH AND ITS INSTITUTION.*

1. The Catholic Church is a visible institution, founded by Christ, in which men are trained for heaven.

The Church may be compared with a school; the latter prepares its pupils to become good citizens of the State, the former trains up citizens of heaven. And just as a school has its head master, its staff of teachers, its pupils, along with its regulations for discipline, and appliances of education, so is the Church provided. It has a visible head, the visible ceremony of Baptism by which members are received, and a visible formula of belief. Hence Christ compares the Church with visible objects, with a city placed on a mountain, with a light on a candlestick; it is also called a body (Eph. i. 22), the house of God (1 Tim. iii. 15), a holy city (Apoc. xxi. 10). Wherever Catholic priests and Catholics are to be found, there is the Catholic Church. Two classes of people maintain that the Church is not visible: heretics, who have been cut off from it yet would gladly belong to the Church, and free thinkers, who wish to shirk the obligation of obeying a visible Church. The expression " Catholic Church " does not imply a mere building of stone or wood, though the comparison is frequently made in the Scriptures (Eph. ii. 21), the Church having a living corner-stone, Christ (Ps. cxvii. 22) Who binds the faithful into one divine family, and the foundation-stones of the apostles (Apoc. xxi. 14), the faithful being the stones of the edifice (1 Pet. ii. 5). Nor by " Catholic Church " do we mean " Catholic religion; " the Church is to the religion as the body to the soul.

The Catholic Church is often called the " kingdom of heaven," " kingdom of God," " community of the faithful."

John the Baptist and Christ Himself announced that the kingdom of heaven was at hand (Matt. iii. 2; iv. 17). The parables on the kingdom of heaven bring out the various features of the Church. The gradation of offices in the Church—(Pope, cardinals, bishops, priests, ordinary Christians), is very suggestive of a kingdom, in which the aim is to lead men to heaven. " The Church is the people of God scattered through the world," says St. Augustine; or in the words of St. Thomas Aquinas, the community of the faithful. Our Lord compares it with a fold where He wishes to keep all His sheep.

The Church is very properly called the " Mother of Christians," because she gives to men the true life of the soul, and because she trains her members as a mother brings up her children.

The Church confers in Baptism the gift of sanctifying grace, the true life of the soul, for this grace gives a claim to heaven. As the father who goes away on a journey leaves all his power in the hands of the mother, so Christ, in leaving this earth, gave His Church full power (John xx. 21). "We should love God as Our Father," says St. Augustine, "and the Church as our Mother." "If we love our native land so dearly," says Leo XIII., "because we were born and bred there, and are ready even to die for it, how much deeper should be our love for the Church, which has given us the life which has no end."

2. The Church prepares man for heaven by carrying out the threefold office which Christ conferred upon her; the office of teacher, of priest, and of shepherd.

The Church teaches the doctrine of Christ, ministers the means of grace appointed by Christ, and is a guide and shepherd to the faithful. The teaching is carried on by sermons; the means of grace consist in the holy sacrifice of the Mass, the sacraments, blessings, and the holding of special devotions; the guidance consists in the laying down of certain precepts, e.g., the commandments of the Church, and the prohibition of what is sinful or dangerous, e.g., the reading of bad books.

This triple office was first exercised by Christ, and then passed on to the apostles and their successors.

Christ used to preach, as we see in the sermon on the mount. He dispensed the means of grace, forgiving Magdalen her sins, giving His body and blood to the apostles at the Last Supper, blessing the little children. Christ was the Guide of men. He gave commandments, sent the apostles on missions, instructed them, and reproved the tyranny of the Pharisees, etc. He gave the apostles commission (1), to teach all nations (Matt. xxviii. 19), and also (2), to exercise the power of the priesthood, to offer sacrifice (Luke xxii. 19), and to forgive sins (John xx. 23); (3), in addition the apostles received the office of pastor, and with it the power of reproving and correcting (Matt. xviii. 17), and of binding and loosing, i.e., of making and revoking laws. The words of Christ included the successors of the apostles as well as the apostles themselves: "I am with you all days, even to the consummation of the world" (Matt. xxviii. 20).

3. The Lord and King of the Church is Christ.

The prophets had foretold (Ps. ii.), that the Messias should be a great king, whose kingdom should last forever and embrace all other kingdoms. The archangel Gabriel told Mary that the Redeemer should be a king and His kingdom should be eternal (Luke i. 33). Christ calls Himself a king to Pilate, but denies that His kingdom is of this world (John xviii. 36). Christ directs the Church through the Holy Ghost; hence He is called the Head of the Church (Eph. i. 23), of which Christians form the body, each one being a member of the body (1 Cor. xii. 27). He is also called the invisible Head, because He no longer mixes personally with man on earth. On account of His love for the Church, He is called her Bridegroom, and she is called His Bride (Apoc. xxi. 9). Christ compared Himself to a bridegroom on several occasions (Matt. xxii.). Like Jacob, who served seven years for Rachel, Christ would serve many years for His Church (Phil. ii. 7), and even gave His life for it (Eph. v. 25).

4. The Catholic Church consists of a teaching and a hearing body. To the former belong the Pope, bishops, and priests; to the latter the faithful.

The word "Pope" comes from the Latin *papa*, i.e., father; "bishop" is from the Greek *episcopos*, i.e., overseer; priest is from the Greek word *presbyter*, meaning "the elder." In Latin, priest is *sacerdos*.

2. THE HEAD OF THE CHURCH.

The mainstay of the Church is the Pope. He is the rock on which the Church rests (Matt. xvi. 18); and his office secures the maintenance of unity. St. John Chrysostom says that the Church would fail if it were not for its Head, who is the centre of its unity, as a ship would be wrecked if deprived of its pilot; and St. Cyprian adds that the enemies of the Church direct their attacks against its Head, in the hope that deprived of his guidance it may be shipwrecked. Among the Popes are counted no less than forty martyrs.

1. Christ conferred on St. Peter the primacy over the apostles and the faithful by the command: "Feed My lambs, feed My sheep;" by giving over to him "the keys of the kingdom of heaven," and by special marks of distinction.

After His resurrection Christ appeared to the apostles on the lake of Genesareth, and after the triple question to Peter "Lovest thou Me?" gave him the solemn precept: "Feed My lambs; [i.e., the faithful], . . . feed My sheep [i.e., the apostles]" (John xxi. 15). This office had been promised to St. Peter before the resurrection, on the occasion of his confession at Cæsarea Philippi: "Thou art Peter, and upon this rock I will build My Church and the gates of hell shall not prevail against it. And I will give to thee the keys of the kingdom of heaven. And whatsoever thou shalt bind upon earth, it shall be bound in heaven, and whatsoever thou shalt loose upon earth it shall be loosed also in heaven" (Matt. xvi. 18, 19). The special marks of distinction conferred on St. Peter were the following: Christ gave him a new name, Peter; He chose him to be with Him on the most solemn occasions, as on Mount Thabor and in the Garden of Olives; He appeared to St. Peter after His resurrection before showing Himself to any of the other apostles (Luke xxiv. 34; 1 Cor. xv. 5, etc.).

St. Peter always acted as chief of the apostles and was so acknowledged by them.

He spoke in the name of the other apostles on Pentecost; he received into the Church its first Jewish and Gentile members; he performed the first miracle; it was he who moved for the choice of a new apostle; he defended the apostles before the Jewish tribunal; his opinion prevailed at the council of the apostles. The apostles recognized his pre-eminence, for the Evangelists in giving the list of the apostles always place St. Peter first (Matt. x. 2; Mark i. 36; Acts ii. 14); and St. Paul, after his conversion, regarded it as his duty to present himself to St. Peter (Gal. i. 18; ii. 2).

2. St. Peter was Bishop of Rome for some twenty-five years and died Bishop of Rome; and the dignity and power of St. Peter descended to the succeeding Bishops of Rome.

There is a great amount of evidence for the presence of St. Peter in Rome from the year 44 to 69. St. Peter writes about the year 65: "The Church that is in Babylon . . . saluteth you; and so doth my son Mark" (1 Pet. v. 13). Babylon was the name given by the early Christians to Rome, on account of its greatness and immorality. St. Clement of Rome writes about the year 100: "Peter and Paul were with an enormous number of the Christians martyred in Rome." Tertullian, a priest of Carthage, about the year 200, congratulates the Church of Rome, because St. Peter died there, crucified like his Lord, and St. Paul died like another John the Baptist. In addition the grave of St. Peter was long ago discovered; his body lay in a catacomb under Nero's circus; the third Pope erected a small chapel over it, to be replaced by a beautiful edifice built by Constantine (324); when this fell into disrepair, the present building of St. Peter's was erected, in 1629.

The Bishops of Rome have always exercised supreme power in the Church, and that power has always been acknowledged.

When dissensions arose in the Church of Corinth about the year 100, the matter was referred not to the apostle St. John at Ephesus, but to the Bishop of Rome, St. Clement. About the year 190 the Pope Victor commanded the people of Asia Minor to conform to the Roman usage in the celebration of Easter, and those who demurred were threatened with excommunication, whereupon they yielded. About the year 250 Pope Stephen forbade the Bishops of North Africa to rebaptize those who returned to the bosom of the Church, and excommunicated those who resisted. The Bishops of Rome had the first place in all general councils. When heresy broke out the Bishop of Rome always inquired into it; and to him other bishops appealed when unjustly oppressed; thus when St. Athanasius was deposed by the emperor, the Pope reinstated him. From the earliest times the titles "high priest" and "bishop of bishops" have been given to the Bishop of Rome. When, at the Council of Chalcedon, the letter of Pope Leo was read to the assembled bishops, they cried out with one voice: "Peter has spoken by Leo; let him be anathema who believes otherwise." The Vatican Council declares that it is the will of Christ that till the end of the world there be successors to St. Peter.

3. The Bishop of Rome is called Pope, or Holy Father.

He is also called, on account of his great dignity, the "holy Father," "His Holiness," "Vicar of Christ," "Father of Christendom."

On account of the opening words of Christ's speech to St. Peter

" Blessed art thou," etc. (Matt. xvi. 17) the Pope is addressed as *Beatissime Pater.* The office is called the See of Peter, the Holy See, or the Apostolic See. The chair of St. Peter is still to be seen in Rome.

The Pope is also called from his see the Pope of Rome, and the Church under him the Roman Catholic Church.

Pope Leo XIII. was born at Carpineto, in Italy, on March 2, 1810, ordained priest December 31, 1837, Archbishop of Perugia, 1846, and Pope February 20, 1878. To his energy we owe the abolition of slavery in Brazil, the campaign against it in Africa by the European nations, the repeal of many laws against the Church in Germany, the prevention of war between Germany and Spain, the founding of over one hundred bishoprics, especially among the heathen, etc. By his encyclicals he has denounced the Freemasons, recommended in a special manner the Third Order of St. Francis, and the devotion of the Rosary, displayed his zeal for the working classes, and exerted himself to produce reunion of the various Christian communities with the Catholic Church, etc. He is the two hundred and fifty-ninth Pope.

The Pope has precedence of honor over all other bishops, and also of jurisdiction over the whole Church (Vatican Council, 4, 3).

" The Pope," says St. Bernard, " is the high priest, the prince among bishops." The following are some of his prerogatives: He assumes a new name on his election, as St. Peter received a new name from Our Lord, to signify that he is wholly devoted to his new office. From the tenth century onwards it has been the custom to choose the name from those of previous Popes, St. Peter's alone being excepted out of reverence. He is privileged to wear the tiara, or mitre with the triple crown, expressive of the triple office of teacher, priest, and pastor; he has also a crosier ending in a cross, and a soutane of white silk. His foot is kissed in memory of those words of St. Paul: " How beautiful are the feet of them that preach the gospel of peace, of them that bring glad tidings of good things " (Rom. x. 15). He has the highest power in the Church as " teacher of all Christians " (Vatican Council) and " chief-shepherd of the shepherds and their flocks." He has the most complete jurisdiction in deciding questions of faith and morals, and in arranging the discipline of the universal Church. This power extends over every single church, and every single bishop and pastor. He may elect and depose bishops, call together councils, make and unmake laws, send out missionaries, confer privileges and dispensations, and reserve sins to his own tribunal. For the same reason he may personally teach and guide any of the bishops or their flocks. He is the supreme judge of all the faithful; to him remains the final appeal. The Pope may choose seventy cardinals to act as his counsellors; they may have the right of choosing a new Pope after the see has been vacant for twelve days. Their dress is a scarlet hat and mantle, to remind them of their duty of loyalty to the Pope at the cost even of their blood. They form the various committees or congregations, e.g., the Congregation of Rites, of Indulgences, etc.

The Pope is quite independent of every temporal sovereignty and of every spiritual power.

For many years the Popes were temporal sovereigns, and ruled as such the States of the Church. The growth of the latter came about in the following manner: In the first centuries many estates were bestowed on the Popes as a free gift. From the time of Constantine the Great, the emperors lived away from Rome, and thus the Papacy began to exercise a certain authority over the city and central Italy. In 754 A.D., Pepin, the Frankish king, gave over to the Pope the territory he had won by the sword in the neighborhood of Rome, and also some towns on the eastern coast of Italy. This grant was confirmed by Pepin's son, Charlemagne, in 774. The Popes lost and regained these possessions some seventy-seven times. In 1859 all the territory except Rome was torn from the Pope, and in 1870 Rome itself, so that now all the Pope possesses is the Vatican. This temporal sovereignty was of great advantage to the Church; it secured the Pope's independence in the exercise of his authority, it gave him a status among the powers of the earth, and supplied him with funds for carrying on the business connected with the Church, besides insuring liberty in the choice of a Pope. At present he is helped by the alms of the faithful, called Peter's pence. Though deprived of his possessions the Pope is still recognized as a sovereign, even in Italy; and he has acted as arbitrator between nations. Many will remember his decision in 1885 in the disputed claims of Spain and Germany to the Caroline Islands. He also issues medals, confers orders, has the gold and white standard, adopted in allusion to the words of St. Peter: " Silver and gold I have none" (Acts iii. 6), and has ambassadors (legates and Nuncios) at various courts, etc. The Pope is supreme on earth, not being subject even to a general council (Eugenius IV., Sept. 4, 1439; Vatican Council, 4, 3). Any who appeal from the Pope to a general council are liable to excommunication (Pius IX., October 12, 1869).

3. BISHOPS, PRIESTS, THE FAITHFUL.

1. The bishops are the successors of the apostles.

This is the express teaching of the Vatican Council. The bishops differ only from the apostles in having a limited jurisdiction, while the mission of the apostles was to the whole world; moreover the apostles were personally infallible in their teaching, and having an extraordinary mission they had extraordinary gifts, such as infallibility, the gift of tongues, and miracles.

The bishops have the following powers: They guide that portion of the Church assigned to them by the Pope, and assist him in the government of the universal Church.

From apostolic times bishops were appointed to single sees, e.g., Titus to Crete (Tit. i. 5). These divisions of the Church are called sees or dioceses; some of them are very large. Paris, for example, contains more than 3,000,000 souls. The duties of a bishop are to educate candidates for the priesthood, to create and confer offices in the Church, to gave faculties to confessors, to see to the religious education of his flock, to revise books written on religious subjects, to settle the days of fasting, etc. In addition he confers the Sacraments of Confirmation and Orders, reserves certain sins to his own jurisdiction, consecrates churches, chalices, the holy oils, etc. Each bishop has also the right of voting in general councils.

The bishops are not merely assistants to the Pope, but they are actually guides of the Church.

They are the shepherds of their respective flocks (Vatican Council, 4, 3) and are appointed by the Holy Ghost to rule the Church of God (Acts xx. 28). They are also called " princes of the Church," and since they have ordinary or immediate jurisdiction they are often called " Ordinaries." They are assisted by a number of canons, who make up the body called the chapter; one of these canons becomes vicar capitular if the see becomes vacant, and governs the diocese till a new bishop be elected. The bishop himself usually appoints the chapter, in rare instances the Pope or the archbishop. Many bishops have an assistant in the form of a coadjutor-bishop or a vicar-general. " The dignity of a bishop," says St. Ambrose, " is higher than that of a king." The privileges of the order are as follows: The right to wear a mitre, the sign of his leadership, and to carry a crosier, which is curved at the end in sign of his limited jurisdiction. He also wears a ring, symbolical of his union with the diocese, and a pectoral cross. The faithful kiss his hand, and he is addressed by the Pope as brother, because as bishop he has the same rank as the Pope.

The bishops are subject to the Pope and owe him obedience.

The Pope gives their jurisdiction to the bishops; and no bishop may exercise his office before being recognized and confirmed by the Pope. He is obliged also to go to Rome (*ad limina apostolorum*) to report on the state of his diocese. An appeal may always be made from a bishop to the Pope. Bishops, such as the Greek or Anglican, who decline submission to the Pope, are neither members of the Church, nor have they jurisdiction, even where they have valid orders.

Archbishops or metropolitans are bishops who have powers over other bishops.

Some have the privilege of wearing the pallium, a white strip of wool on the shoulders symbolical of gentleness and humility. The Primate is a still higher dignitary, and is the bishop of the whole nation. Above him in rank is the Patriarch or Exarch, who in former times was set over the metropolitans. The Bishops of Antioch, Alexandria, and Rome were patriarchs, because these sees were founded by St. Peter. In our days the titles patriarch and Primate signify nothing more than a precedence of dignity; they are not of divine institution. There are also others of the clergy who are termed prelates; some of them enjoy most or all of the powers of bishops, and are called vicars apostolic. There are others whose title is merely honorary.

2. The priests are the assistants of the bishops.

They receive their Orders from the bishop, and so are his spiritual sons; and their business is to carry out the commands of the bishop; even when called in to assist at councils, they do not vote as judges but only as counsellors, nor have they powers to excommunicate.

The priests have only a portion of the episcopal power, and their office may be exercised only with sanction from the bishop.

This sanction is called the canonical mission (*missio canonica*). The dress of the priest is a soutane, or black garment reaching to the feet.

Parish priests are those to whom the bishop has confided permanently the charge of a district.

The district is called a parish. Dean is the title given to parish priests of larger districts. In the assignment of a parish the bishop usually shows some consideration for the wishes of the patron or patrons, i.e., the person or persons who have been and are conspicuous benefactors in the district. The parish priest is the representative of the bishop, and no one may, without his leave, exercise spiritual functions in the parish, such as preaching, baptizing, giving extreme unction, marrying, and burying.

Parish priests who are appointed by the bishop over the priests of a large district are called rural deans.

They make a visitation of the parishes and act as intermediaries with the bishop.

Parish priests of larger districts have assistants, or curates.

3. A Catholic is one who has been baptized and professes himself to be a member of the Catholic Church.

The Church is a community into which admittance is gained by Baptism. Thus the three thousand baptized on the first Pentecost became members of the Church (Acts ii. 41). Moreover a man must make external profession of being a member of the Church, so that any one who breaks away, for instance, by heresy, no longer belongs to the Church in spite of his baptism, though he is not thereby freed from his obligations to the Church. Neither heathens, Jews, heretics, nor schismatics are members of the Church (Council of Florence), though children baptized validly in other communions really belong to it. "For," as St. Augustine says, "Baptism is the privilege of the true Church, and so the benefits which flow from Baptism are necessarily fruits which belong only to the true Church. Children baptized in other communions cease to be members of the Church only when, after reaching the age of reason, they make formal profession of heresy, as, for example, by receiving communion in a non-Catholic church." The Christians were at first known by the name of Nazareans, from Nazareth, or Galileans, from Galilee; it was first in

Antioch that the name Christian came to be in use (Acts xi. 26), and the name Christians is appropriate. We are followers of Christ, willing to be conformed to the image of Christ (Rom. viii. 29). "We receive our name," says St. John Chrysostom, "not from an earthly ruler, nor from an angel, nor from an archangel, nor from a seraphim, but from the King of all the earth."

A true Catholic is not only one who has been baptized and belongs to the Church, but who also makes serious efforts to secure his eternal salvation; who believes the teaching of the Church, keeps the commandments of God, and of the Church, who receives the sacraments, and prays to God in the manner prescribed by Christ.

He is not a true Christian who is ignorant of his faith. Such a one might as well call himself a doctor though knowing nothing of medicine. "Nor is he a true Christian," says St. Justin, "who does not live as Christ taught him to live." Our Lord said to the Jews: "If you be the children of Abraham do the works of Abraham" (John viii. 39), and He might say to the Christians "If you be Christians do the works of Christ." "If you want to be a Christian," says St. Gregory Nazianzen, "you must live the life of Christ;" and St. Augustine: "A true Christian is the man who is gentle, good, and merciful to all, and shares his bread with the poor." Christ Himself said that His disciples should be known by their love one for another (John xiii. 35). A Christian who neglects the sacraments is like a soldier who has no weapons; what a responsibility he incurs ! Louis of Granada says, "A field which is well tended is expected to yield a richer harvest; so more good works are expected from a Christian than from a heathen, because the Christian has greater graces."

Every Catholic has rights and duties. He has an especial claim to the means of grace supplied by the Church, and he is obliged to obey his ecclesiastical superiors in spiritual matters, and to make provision for their support as well as for that of God's service.

A good Catholic ought also to hear the word of God, receive the necessary sacraments, take part in divine service, and he has a right to Christian burial, etc. The Church forces nobody to enter its pale, but whoever becomes a member of his own free will, and remains so, must be subject to the laws of the Church. Under certain circumstances those who disobey the laws of the Church are excommunicated or shut out from the Church. They lose their claim to the spiritual goods of the Church; they may not join in the divine service, nor receive the sacraments, nor an office in the Church, nor Christian burial. Some offences involve excommunication *ipso facto;* for instance, apostasy, duelling, freemasonry (Pius IX., October 12, 1869). In other cases the excommunication must be formally pronounced, and that, too, after warning and trial, as in the case of the Old Catholic bishops Reinkens and Döllinger. St. Ambrose forbade the Emperor Theodosius to enter the Church after the latter had, by his orders, caused the slaughter of some seven thousand people in Thessalonica; and it was only after doing severe penance that he was admitted. We know, too, that St. Paul cut off from the Church a vicious Corinthian (1 Cor. v. 13). The State exercises a similar power in banishing criminals.

4. FOUNDATION AND SPREAD OF THE CHURCH.

Christ compared the Church to a grain of mustard-seed, which is the smallest of seeds, but grows into a tree in which the birds of the air build their nests (Matt. xiii. 31, 32).

1. Christ laid the foundation of the Church when, in the course of His teaching, He gathered a number of disciples, and chose twelve of these to preside over the rest and one to be Head of all.

2. The Church first began its life on Pentecost, when some three thousand people were baptized.

Pentecost is the birthday of the Church. After the miracle at the gate of the Temple some two thousand more were baptized.

3. Soon after the descent of the Holy Ghost the apostles began to preach the Gospel throughout the world, in accordance with the commands of Christ (Mark xvi. 15), and founded Christian communities in many places.

St. Paul, after his conversion in 34 A.D., labored more abundantly than all the apostles (1 Cor. xv. 10); he traversed Asia Minor, the greater part of Southern Europe, and many islands of the Mediterranean. After him St. Peter labored most. After escaping by a miracle from his prison in Jerusalem, he founded his see at Rome where, in company with St. Paul, he suffered martyrdom. St. John, the beloved disciple, lived at Ephesus with our blessed Lady, and governed the Church in Asia Minor. His brother, St. James the Greater, travelled as far as Spain, and was beheaded in Jerusalem in 44 A.D. His body rests at Compostella. St. James the Less governed the Church at Jerusalem, and was cast down from a pinnacle of the Temple in A.D. 63. St. Andrew preached to the people living along the lower Danube, and died on a cross in Achaia. St. Thomas and St. Bartholomew made their way to the Euphrates and Tigris, and as far as India. St. Simon evangelized Egypt and North Africa.

The apostles established their communities after the following plan: having converted and baptized a number of men in a place, they chose assistants, to whom they imparted a greater or less portion of their own powers; and before leaving the place they made choice of a successor, and gave him full powers (Acts xiv. 22).

Those who received only a small portion of the apostolic power were called deacons, and priests those who had ampler faculties. The representatives of the apostles were called bishops. Christ gave the apostles power to choose successors when He gave to them the self-same power which He had received from the Father (John xx. 21); and it was His wish that they should choose successors, for He told the apostles that their mission should continue to the end of the world (Matt. xxviii. 20).

Among all the Christian communities that of Rome took the highest rank, because it was presided over by St. Peter, the chief of the apostles, and because to the Head of that community as successor of St. Peter the primacy of St. Peter was transferred.

St. Ignatius, Bishop of Antioch (107 A.D.) in a letter to the Christians of Rome, begs them not to set him free and calls the Roman community the "chief community of the holy band of the faithful;" and St. Irenæus, Bishop of Lyons (202 A.D.), says "All the faithful over the whole world must conform to the Roman Church on account of its principality."

All Christian communities which have been formed in the course of time professed the same faith, and acknowledged the same means of grace and the same Head. Hence they formed one large community—the Catholic Church.

4. When the great persecutions broke out, the Church spread more rapidly over the earth.

During the first three centuries there were ten persecutions, the severest being under Nero and Diocletian (284-385 A.D.), the latter monster condemning some 2,000,000 Christians. They were martyred in various ways; they were beheaded like St. Paul, crucified like St. Peter, stoned like St. Stephen, thrown to the lions like St. Ignatius of Antioch, roasted on gridirons like St. Lawrence, drowned like St. Florian, flayed like St. Bartholomew, cast over cliffs or from high places like St. James, burned at the scaffold like St. Polycarp, buried alive like St. Chrysanthus, etc. The very means adopted to exterminate the Christian religion helped to propagate it. The speeches of the Christians before their judges often converted the hearers. The joy with which they faced death, their superhuman patience, and their love of their enemies, were powerful influences on the heathen. Added to this were the miracles which often happened during the martyrdoms, as for instance in the case of St. Polycarp and St. John at the Lateran Gate. In the words of St. Rupert, the martyrs are like the seed which is buried in the earth, and sprouts and brings forth much fruit; or of St. Leo the Great, if the storm scatters the seed this benefit results that instead of one, some fifty other trees grow up. "The blood of the martyrs," says Tertullian, "is the seed of Christians." The life of the Christians was then a model, and they abounded in saints. At the risk of their life they prayed to God in the catacombs. Two years of probation were demanded of the catechumens before reception.

When the Roman emperor, Constantine the Great, had permitted his subjects to become Christians and later made the

Christian religion the State religion (324 A.D.), the Church indeed flourished externally, but fervor and religious discipline soon began to suffer.

Constantine was led to this step by the appearance of the luminous cross in the heavens (312 A.D.), and still more by his holy mother St. Helena. The following were some of his ordinances: Sundays and feast days were to be observed with solemnity; the temples of the heathen were to be handed over to the bishops; the gladiatorial combats and the crucifixion of criminals were forbidden, and many churches were built. By the miraculous draught of fishes related in the fifth chapter of St. Luke and the two boats almost sunk with the weight of fish, was prefigured the future of the Church, which should suffer schism with the increase of its members, while Christians should sink down to earthly things. The heresy of Arius (318 A.D.) began its deadly work in the time of Constantine, and had a great following. At this time also ceased the test of the catechumens, so that it was easier to become a member of the Church. St. Augustine had reason to say: "If the Church is harassed by external foes, there are many in her bosom who by their unruly life make sad the hearts of the faithful."

5. In the Middle Ages nearly all the heathen nations began to enter the Church.

In Austria about 450 A.D., the monk Severinus preached the Gospel for thirty years along the banks of the Danube. St. Gregory the Great, in 600 A.D., sent St. Augustine at the head of a number of missioners to convert England; eighty years later the country was Christian and had twenty-six sees. Germany owes most to St. Boniface, who preached the Gospel there for about forty years (755 A.D.). The Greek monks Saints Cyril and Methodius worked among the Slavs, mainly of Bohemia and Moravia, with great success. The Hungarians were converted by their holy king Stephen (1038 A.D.) "the apostolic king." Christianity was gradually introduced into Iceland, Denmark, Sweden, Norway, Russia and Poland after 1000 A.D.

The Church was hard pressed by Islam during the Middle Ages.

Islamism or Mohammedanism was founded by Mohammed, a native of Mecca, who gave himself out to be a prophet of the one true God, promised sensual joy after death, allowed plurality of wives, imposed a pilgrimage to Mecca, taught fatalism, and after propagating his doctrines by fire and sword, was poisoned in 632 A.D., by a Jewess. The Koran is the sacred book of the Mohammedans. They keep the Friday with great solemnity, and pray five times a day turned towards Mecca. Mohammed's successors were the caliphs, who undertook wars of conquest on a large scale, everywhere rooting out the Christian religion. They overran a great part of Asia, North Africa, Spain and the islands of the Mediterranean. Charles Martel, in a series of victories (732-738 A.D.), arrested their advance into France, and ever since their failure in 1638 before Vienna, their progress in the West was arrested.

In addition the Church lost many adherents in the Middle Ages by the Greek schism.

The causes of the schism were as follows: The emperors of the East kept trying to make the patriarchs of Constantinople independent of Rome, while these were often for their heresies put under ban by the councils. In time it came about that the ambitious Photius, backed up by the emperor, held a council of the Eastern bishops, and broke away from Rome (867 A.D.). The succeeding emperor re-established the old relations with Rome. Two hundred years later, however, the patriarch Michael Cerularius renewed the contest (1054 A.D.), and the schism effected by him lasts till the present day. They call themselves the Orthodox Greeks, while we call them the Schismatic Greeks, in opposition to the United Greeks or Uniates, who preserved their allegiance to Rome.

6. In later times many nations of the newly discovered countries were converted.

The Spaniards and Portuguese led the van of missionary enterprise. One of the most famous of these missionaries is St. Francis Xavier, the apostle of the Indies, who used to call the little children together with a bell, as he made his way through the cities of India, the islands of Molucca, and Japan, to teach them the truths of religion (1552 A.D.); he had the gift of tongues, and baptized some two million heathens. After his death great work was done in China by the Jesuits, especially Ricci and Schall. Another great missionary is St. Peter Claver (1654 A.D.) whose work was mostly among the negroes in South America. Cardinal Lavigerie in our own time has done much in Africa, especially in resisting the slave trade, and founding a congregation for the conversion of the natives. The College of Propaganda was founded at Rome in 1662 for the training of young men from all nations for a missionary career. At present some 15,000 priests, 5,000 lay brothers and 50,000 nuns are at work in the foreign missions; the missionaries belong for the most part to the Orders of Jesuits, Franciscans, Capuchins, Benedictines, and Lazarists. The organizations for the support of the missions are the Propagation of the Faith and the Holy Childhood. It is a sacred obligation to help in such work, and the efforts of non-Catholics in this direction may well put us to shame.

In later times the Church has lost many members by the Lutheran and Anglican heresies.

Martin Luther, an Augustinian monk of Erfurt, and later teacher in the high school at Wittenburg, took offence because he thought that he was not sufficiently held in esteem at Rome. When Pope Leo X., anxious to complete the building of St. Peter's, gave indulgences to those who should subscribe to the work, and sent out preachers to promulgate these indulgences, Luther came forward with his ninety-five propositions on indulgences, and nailed them to the door of the church at Wittenburg. These propositions at first condemned only the abuses of indulgences in the Church, but later went on to combat the teaching of the Church on the subject (1517).

Refusing to withdraw them at the command of the Pope he was excommunicated (1520), and also outlawed by the emperor for not answering the summons requiring him to appear before the council at Worms. He sought protection from the Elector of Saxony. His heresy soon spread over Germany and led to many religious wars. The name Protestant was assumed by the Lutherans at Spires in 1529, on account of their protest against Catholic doctrine. The Peace of Augsburg secured to the Protestants the same rights as Catholics (1555). The Council of Trent set forth the points in dispute between Catholics and Protestants (1545-1563). Luther died in 1546. His chief errors are contained in the following propositions: (1). There is no supreme teaching power in the Church. (2). The temporal sovereign has supreme power in matters ecclesiastical. (3). There are no priests. (4). All that is to be believed is in the Scripture. (5). Each one may interpret the Holy Scriptures as he likes. (6). Faith alone saves, good works are superfluous. (7). This last follows from the fact that man lost his free will by original sin. (8). There are no saints, no Christian sacrifice, no sacrament of confession, no purgatory. The Jesuits, founded by St. Ignatius of Loyola (1540), won many back again to the fold of the Church. Zwingli and Calvin in Switzerland, and Henry VIII. in England, about the same time helped in Luther's deadly work. The errors of the Anglican Church were drawn up later in the form of Thirty-nine Articles, which are quite Lutheran in tone.

7. At present the Catholic Church numbers about 260,000,000 members.

These are under the direction of about 1200 bishops, counting about 15 patriarchs, 200 archbishops and 20 prelates with dioceses. There are some 350,000 Catholic priests in the whole world. The inhabitants of Italy, Spain, France, Austria, Belgium, and Ireland are nearly all Catholics. In Switzerland about half are Catholics; in Germany over a third of the population, and in Russia 11,000,000. In Europe about three-quarters of the entire population are Catholic. In America there are 80,000,000 Catholics, of whom there are 10,000,-000 in the United States, forming one-seventh of the entire population, while Mexico, south and central America, with the exception of Brazil, are almost entirely Catholic. The adjacent islands are mainly Catholic. In Asia there are only 10,000,000 Catholics, in Africa 3,000,000, in Australia 1,000,000. The Protestants, comprising the various sects of Lutherans, Calvinists, Anglicans, etc., number 150,-000,000; they inhabit England, North and Central Germany, the Netherlands, Denmark, Sweden, Norway, parts of Switzerland and Hungary, and the United States of America. The Oriental Greeks or Schismatic Greeks number about 100,000,000. They occupy for the most part the Balkan peninsula and Russia. Besides these there are some 10,000,000 of various other Christian sects, hence a total of 520,000,000 Christians. Since the inhabitants of the earth amount to about 1,500,000,000 only a little over one-third of the human race is Christian. The Mohammedans number 170,000,000; they inhabit Arabia, Western Asia, the northern half of Africa, and part of Turkey. In addition there are 8,000,000 Jews; they are for the greater part in Russia and Austria. Finally there are still 800,000,000 heathens, dwelling for the most part in Southern Africa, India, China and Japan.

5. THE CATHOLIC CHURCH IS INDESTRUCTIBLE AND INFALLIBLE.

Indestructibility of the Church.

The Catholic Church is indestructible; i.e., it will remain till the end of the world, for Christ said: " The gates of hell shall not prevail against it " (Matt. xvi. 18).

Hence there will always be Popes, bishops, and faithful, and God's revealed truths will ever be found in the Catholic Church. The archangel Gabriel had announced to Mary: " Of His kingdom there shall be no end " (Luke i. 33). " The Church," says St. Ambrose, " is like the moon; it may wane, but never be destroyed; it may be darkened, but it can never disappear." " The bark of the Church," says St. Anselm, " may be swept by the waves, but it can never sink because Christ is there."

1. Of all the persecutors of the Church none have succeeded against it, and some have come to a fearful end.

Judas' end is the type of those of his imitators. Herod, the murderer of the infants of Bethlehem, died in unspeakable tortures; so, too, Herod the murderer of St. James was devoured by worms. Pilate was banished by the emperor to Vienne, in France, and there he took his own life. During the siege of Jerusalem 1,000,000 Jews died of hunger or sickness, or in battle, the city itself was reduced to ashes and some hundred thousand Jews carried off into captivity. The tyrant Nero was deposed, and in his flight from Rome was stabbed by a slave. Diocletian came to a shameful end. Before his death his family were sent into exile, his statues were destroyed, and his body attacked with a loathsome disease. Julian the Apostate was struck down on the field of battle by a lance; his last words were: " Galilean, Thou hast conquered." The case of Napoleon is instructive. He kept Pius VII. a prisoner for five years, he himself was a prisoner for seven years; in the castle at Fontainebleau he forced the Pope 'to give up the States of the Church, promising a yearly income of 2,000,000 francs; in the same place he was himself forced to sign his abdication, and received a promise of a yearly income of the same amount. Four days after giving the order to unite the States of the Church with France he lost the battles of Aspern and Erlingen. He answered the excommunication launched against him, saying that the words of an old man would not make the arms drop from the hands of his soldiers. This actually happened in his Russian campaign from the intense cold: and on the same day on which Napoleon died at St. Helena, Pius VII. was celebrating his own feast day at Rome. No wonder the French have a saying: " Whoever eats of the Pope dies." The same fate is shared by the founders of heresies, and the enemies of religion. Arius burst asunder during a triumphal procession; Voltaire died in despair. These facts and many more of the same kind illustrate the words of Holy Writ: "It is a fearful thing to fall into the hands of the living God" (Heb. x. 31).

2. When the Church is in the greatest need, Christ ever comes to its help, either by miracles or by raising up saintly men.

The appearance of the cross in the heavens, for instance, seen by Constantine and his army, brought the Christian persecution to an end. "The Church," says St. Jerome, "is like Peter's bark. When the storm is at its height the Lord wakes from His sleep and commands peace."

3. "It is peculiar to the Church," says St. Hilary, "to flourish most when persecuted."

"Persecutions," says St. Augustine, "serve to bring forth saints." To the Church as well as to Eve were the words spoken: "In sorrow shalt thou bring forth children" (Gen. iii. 16). The members of the Church increase under persecution. The Church is a field, fruitful only when torn up by the plough, or it is a vine, stronger and richer for being pruned. "As fire is spread by the wind, so is the Church increased by persecution," says St. Rupert. Persecution purifies the Church; even if millions fall away, it is not a loss but a cleansing. The time of persecution is usually a period of miracles, attesting the divine origin of the Church, as in the Babylonish captivity they attested the truth of the religion of the Jews. How often have Christians come unhurt out of boiling liquid, like St. Cecilia, or remained unharmed in the midst of the flames, like St. Polycarp, or been thrown to the beasts and received their homage like St. Venantius ? Facts like these force the enemies of the Church to exclaim: "Mighty indeed is the God of the Christians." The Church comes triumphant out of every persecution. Easter always follows Good Friday. But a few years ago the bishops in Germany were cast into prison, the religious Orders driven out, the administration of the sacraments in part forbidden; at the present day the number of Catholic members in the Reichstag is over a hundred, the Catholic journals have increased to four or five hundred, yearly congresses take place, and all kinds of unions for Catholic objects are formed, while the Catholics themselves are stauncher and more self-sacrificing. "The more battles the Church has to fight, the more her powers are developed; and the more she is oppressed the higher she rises," are the words of Pius VII. Such a privilege belongs to no institution save the Church, and by that she may be recognized as the offspring of God, the Bride of Christ.

The Infallibility of the Church.

God has planted in our hearts a longing for truth which must be satisfied. Our first parents had no difficulties to face in the search for truth. "In the state of innocence," says St. Thomas, "it was impossible for man to mistake false for true." Ever since the Fall, to err is human. God, however, sent an infallible Teacher, His only-begotten Son, that man might again find the truth; hence the words of Christ to Pilate: "For this came I into the world that I should give testimony of the truth" (John xviii. 37). Christ was to be a light to our understandings, darkened as they were by sin (John iii. 19). As Christ was not to remain always on earth, He appointed another infallible teacher, His Church, and provided it with the necessary gifts, especially with the assistance of the Holy Spirit.

Christ conferred on His apostles and their successors the teaching office, and promised them His divine assistance.

Thus He said at His ascension into heaven: "Going, teach ye all nations . . . and behold I am with you all days, even to the consummation of the world" (Matt. xxviii. 19, 20); and at the Last Supper: "I will ask the Father and He shall give you another Paraclete that He may abide with you forever, the Spirit of truth" (John xiv. 16, 17). To St. Peter He said: "The gates of hell shall not prevail against the Church" (Matt. xvi. 18). Since Christ is the Son of God, His words must be true. If the Church, in the carrying out of her teaching office, could lead man into error, Christ would not have kept His word. Hence St. Paul calls the Church "the pillar and ground of the truth" (1 Tim. iii. 15), and the measures decided upon by the apostles in the Council of Jerusalem were introduced with the words: "For it hath seemed good to the Holy Ghost and to us" (Acts xv. 28). It is no recent belief that the Church is infallible. Long ago Origen writes, "As in the heavens there are two great sources of light, the sun, and the moon which borrows its light from the sun, so there are two sources of our interior light—Christ and the Church. Christ, the Light of the world, shares His light with the Church, and she enlightens all the earth." In the words of St. Irenæus: "Where the Church is, there is also the Spirit of God."

1. The Catholic Church is infallible in her teaching; i.e., the Holy Spirit assists the Church in such a manner that she cannot err in the preserving and announcing of revealed doctrine.

Just as our reason prevents us from making statements which are contrary to certain fundamental truths, so the Holy Ghost exerts His influence to prevent the Church giving any decision contrary to the truths taught by Christ. The infallibility of the Church is not in any way like that of God with God, for she attributes it not to herself but to God's special providence over her.

2. The Church delivers her infallible decisions through general councils and through the Pope.

In every kingdom some court is established for the settlement of doubtful cases; it is evident that the all-wise God must have instituted some such tribunal in His kingdom; and this tribunal is the general assembly of the bishops, for at His ascent into heaven He gave them the power to teach, and promised them immunity from error (Matt. xxviii. 18-20). Hence the expression of St. Cyprian: "The Church is in the bishops." Now since the bishops cannot always assemble together on account of their duties towards their particular dioceses, some other tribunal must exist with power to

give infallible decisions. This tribunal is the Pope speaking
ex cathedra. The priests have not this infallibility secured to them,
though their services are indispensable to the bishops in the carrying
out of the teaching office. Priests when present in the assemblies
of bishops are so as counsellors, but without any deciding vote in
the questions under consideration. So soon as the Church defines a
question of doctrine, every one is bound before God to submit under
pain of excommunication.

A general council is the assembly of the bishops of the world
presided over by the Pope.

The apostles in the year 51 held the first Council of Jerusalem,
and announced their decisions as coming from God. Of the first four
general councils St. Gregory the Great asserted that he held them in
equal honor with the four gospels. Since the Council at Jerusalem
there have been twenty general councils assembled. The first of
these was held at Nicæa, in the year 325, to repel the Arian heresy.
The following are specially worthy of note: the Third Council at
Ephesus in 425, where Mary was declared to be the Mother of God;
the Seventh General Council, or Second of Nicæa in 787, where the
veneration of images was declared lawful; the Twelfth General
Council or Fourth Lateran in 1215, which imposed the obligation of
the Easter communion; the Nineteenth General Council at Trent
(1545-1563), occasioned by Luther's heresies; the Twentieth General
Council in the Vatican (1870), where the infallibility of the Pope
was defined as an article of faith. The presence of all the bishops
is not required for a general council, but the greater number of them
must be there; nor is a unanimous vote in any way necessary to
secure a definition; a majority of votes approaching more or less to
unanimity is quite sufficient. Thus in the Vatican Council five hundred and thirty-three bishops voted for the definition of Papal infallibility; two voted against, and fifty-two were absent from the
meeting. Nor is it necessary that the Pope should preside in person;
he may act through his legates as in the first, third, and fourth general councils. All that is necessary is that the Pope should approve
of the decrees of the council. Others besides bishops have a vote,
such as the cardinals, generals of religious Orders, and all who have
episcopal authority, as in the case of many prelates and abbots;
suffragans have also a vote when they are summoned, as happened in
1870. The general council only settles questions after mature consideration, relying generally on the teaching of the Catholic Church
in the early ages. Besides general councils there are national councils, or assemblies of the bishops of a nation or kingdom under their
primate, and also provincial councils or meetings of the bishops and
dignitaries of a district under the archbishop; and finally diocesan
synods, or assemblies of the clergy under their bishop. Such assemblies have no claim to infallibility.

The general consent of the bishops all over the world confirmed by the Pope is also infallible; this may happen when the
Pope asks their opinion on a question of doctrine or morals.

A case of the kind happened in 1854. The Pope sent round to

the various bishops of the world to ascertain the feeling of Christians at large as regarded the Immaculate Conception of Our Lady. As nearly all the replies approved of the doctrine, it was solemnly defined as of faith. This consensus of the bishops, though living apart at the time, was infallible, because the Holy Spirit is not confined by limitations of place. Nor was this solemn declaration necessary; it was quite sufficient that all the bishops should teach in the same sense in regard of any given subject to make that teaching infallible; were it otherwise the Church would be capable of teaching heresy, or of falling away from the truth. Hence the Vatican Council declared that not only must that be accepted which has been solemnly defined by the Church, but also whatever is proposed by the lawful and general teaching authority (Vatican Council, 3, 3).

The Pope makes an infallible definition when, as teacher and guide of the Church, he proposes to the universal Church a doctrine of faith or morals. These decrees are called doctrinal.

The Vatican Council in 1870 decreed that all doctrinal decisions of the Pope were infallible. This is the logical consequence of the words of Christ to St. Peter: "Thou art Peter, and upon this rock I will build My Church" (Matt. xvi. 18). If the foundation of the Church were to fail, it would not be a rock but a quicksand. Moreover St. Peter was appointed shepherd of the apostles and the faithful in these words of Our Lord: "Feed My lambs, feed My sheep" (John xxi. 15, 17), and he received power to confirm his brethren in the faith (Luke xxii. 32). If then the Pope were to teach error, Our Lord's promise would have come to naught. Decisions in matters of doctrine were held in the greatest reverence from the earliest times. When the Roman See condemned in 417 the errors of Pelagius St. Augustine cried out: "Rome has spoken; the cause is at an end." And St. Cyprian says: "No heretics can gain admittance to the Church." Even general councils call the Bishop of Rome "the father and teacher of all Christians" (Council of Florence, 1439), and the Roman Church "the Mother and Teacher of the faithful" (Council of Lateran, iv., 1215); of course the Church understood here is the teaching, the "hearing" Church having no claim to teach. The Pope must be infallible for this reason, too, that "he has full power to govern the whole Church" (Council of Florence); for with this power is necessarily linked authority to teach. The supreme teaching office of the Church involves infallibility in accordance with the divine promise of the assistance of the Holy Ghost. In consequence of this the decisions of the Pope are infallible of themselves, quite independently of the consent of the bishops (Council of Vatican, iv. 4). Were it otherwise the rock (or successor of St. Peter) would derive its strength and solidity from the building raised upon it (the Church). It would, however, be quite wrong to assert that the Pope is infallible in all things; for he is a man and can make mistakes as other men in writing, speaking, etc. He can also commit sin as other men, and unhappily some of the Popes led very scandalous lives. When the Pope gives a decision on a doctrinal matter, it is Christ Who keeps him from error by the agency of the Holy Ghost; moreover the bishops are always consulted before any such decision is given. Addresses to pilgrims, letters to kings and princes, the brief of suppression of the Society of Jesus in 1773, are not infallible pronouncements. Doctrinal decisions are usually accompanied by sentence of excommunication against those who refuse to submit to them; hence such decisions are binding for all Catholics. Although the Pope is infallible in his solemn decisions, general councils are not for that reason superfluous; for they confer a greater external solemnity on the Pope's decrees, and the teaching of the Church can be more thoroughly examined in these assemblies. Hence these general councils may, under certain circumstances, be necessary as well as useful. Even the apostles held a general council at Jerusalem, though each single apostle was infallible in his office as teacher.

3. **The Church pronounces infallible judgments in the following cases: On doctrines of faith and morals and their meaning and interpretation, on the Holy Scripture and Tradition and their interpretation.**

If, for instance, the Church declares that the punishments of hell are eternal, the declaration is infallible, for it is made on a doctrine of faith; or again if it declare that the observation of Sunday is a command of God, the declaration turns on teaching with regard to morals and is therefore infallible. Christ made a special promise to His apostles that the Holy Ghost should teach them all truth (John xvi. 13); in other words that the Holy Ghost would teach them all truth bearing on religion; and that religion included morality as well as belief may be gathered from the words of Christ just before His ascent into heaven: "Going therefore teach ye all nations . . . teaching them to observe all things whatsoever I have commanded you" (Matt. xxviii. 19, 20), and with regard to this last order He promised them the assistance of the Holy Ghost, and consequently, infallibility. Since the Church derives her doctrine from two sources, Holy Scripture and Tradition, it must be infallible in its interpretation of both.

Moreover, it is certain that the Church is infallible when it declares that any given opinion on faith or morals is contrary to revealed teaching, as also in the canonization of saints.

It is the common opinion of theologians that the Church is infallible in judging whether a proposition is opposed to revealed teaching. If, for example, the Church were to condemn the assertion that man is the offspring of a pair of apes as contrary to revelation, it would be acting quite within the limits of its infallibility, and on a subject most intimately connected with revealed doctrine. If the Church can see truth it must also be able to recognize error. From the earliest times the Church has condemned error, whether taught by writing or by word of mouth. At the Council of Nicæa (325), the errors of Arius were condemned by the bishops. Up to the present day the Pope has continually condemned books which have attacked faith or morals; and this could not have been unless God had conferred such powers. Any mistake in either beatifying or canonizing seems well-nigh impossible even on natural grounds, on account of the strict examination insisted on. By the act of canonization, the veneration of a saint, and so to a certain extent the acknowledgment of the Church's belief in him, is imposed on the faithful, and he is then officially recognized in the Church's offices, as in the Mass and Breviary; hence if any one not a saint were declared holy, the whole Church would approve an error. Such a supposition is impossible. Pope Benedict XIV. declares his own experience in these cases of the assistance of the Holy Spirit in removing insuperable difficulties which beset a process, or, on the other hand, in breaking it off entirely. Finally the Church in its decisions whether of beatification or canonization is dealing with things which have the closest connection with doctrine of faith or morals.

6. THE HIERARCHY OF THE CHURCH.

1. The ministers of the Church fall into three classes of distinct dignity and power: bishops, priests, and deacons (Council of Trent, 23 c. 4. Can. 6).

These were foreshadowed in the high priest, the priests, and the Levites of the Temple, as well as in Our Lord, the apostles, and disciples. To the apostles Our Lord said: " As the Father hath sent Me, so I send you" (John xx. 21); to the disciples merely: " Go, behold I send you" (Luke x. 3). The apostles were sent to all the nations of the earth (Matt. xxviii. 20); the disciples only to those places where the Lord was Himself to go (Luke x. 1). The bishops are now the successors of the apostles (Council of Trent, xxiii. 4); hence the bishops are of higher rank than priests because they belong to a higher order of the clergy and have higher orders; besides that they have greater powers, being the only real pastors of the flock, and in virtue of their jurisdiction deciding how far any one else may share in their government of those committed to their charge. " The bishop alone can give orders," says St. Jerome, and according to St. Cyprian he is the only ordinary minister of Confirmation. The Council of Trent assigned to bishops many other privileges beyond those enjoyed by the other ministers of the Church. In addition they have a judicial vote in councils. Priests rank higher than deacons, having higher orders and greater powers; they can offer the holy sacrifice, and forgive sins, while deacons can only baptize, preach, and give communion.

2. This hierarchy was in force in the time of the apostles.

We see in the Scriptures Timothy appointed with powers to judge priests (1 Tim. v. 19), to ordain them (1 Tim. v. 22), and to appoint them to various cities (Tit. i. 5). St. Ignatius of Antioch (107 A.D.) names the three orders: " Let all obey the bishops as Jesus obeyed the Father; let them obey the priests as the apostles, and honor the deacons as being the messengers of God." Similar expressions occur in Clement of Rome (100 A.D.), and Clement of Alexandria (217 A.D.). There was, however, a certain vagueness in the use of terms in the time of the apostles; priests were called " elders " or " overseers." The former title owed its origin to the Jewish converts, the latter to the heathen. In every community there were several priests (1 Tim. iv. 14), of whom one was the superior or " high priest," known in later times as the bishop. He was often called priest merely because he was in reality a priest; even the apostles Peter and John called themselves priests (1 Pet. v. 1; 2 John i. 1).

3. The episcopal and priestly office was instituted by Christ Himself; the diaconate by the apostles.

The deacons were appointed by the apostles to distribute alms, and were consecrated to this duty by the laying on of hands, accompanied with prayer (Acts vi. 6); they also had spiritual functions as preaching (as in the case of St. Stephen) and baptizing (as in the case of St. Philip). In the early ages there were also deaconesses— widows who tended the sick and taught young girls. They were no part of the hierarchy, since it was a fixed principle in the Church that no woman should preach (1 Cor. xiv. 34), because she is subject to man and was first led astray in paradise (1 Tim. ii. 12, etc.).

4. Besides these three classes there are other degrees varying in their powers: for example, Pope, cardinals, archbishops.

The distribution of authority is the basis of this classification: all, without exception, owe obedience to the Pope; the bishop rules all the clergy of his diocese; the clergy are in authority over those committed to their charge (1 Pet. v. 5; Heb. xiii. 17). The Church has its differences of rank like an army (Council of Trent, xxiii. 24); without these grades it would be a society without organization.

7. *NOTES OF THE TRUE CHURCH.*

" When," says St. Cyprian, " the devil saw that the worship of idols was abolished, and the heathen temples emptied, he bethought him of a new poison, and led men into error under cover of the Christian religion, the poison of false doctrine and pride, through which more than two hundred churches have started up in opposition to the true Church founded by Christ." Now God has ordained that men should come to knowledge of the truth; i.e., of the true Church as distinguished from all others by certain marks.

1. The true Church is that one which is most persecuted by the world, and which has received God's seal in the form of miracles.

Christ often spoke to His disciples of these persecutions: " The servant is not greater than his Master. If they have persecuted Me they will also persecute you " (John xv. 20). " They will deliver you up in councils, and they will scourge you in their synagogues . . . you shall be hated by all men for My name's sake " (Matt. x. 17-22). " Yea, the hour cometh that whosoever killeth you, will think that he doth a service to God " (John xvi. 2). " Because you are not of the world, but I have chosen you out of the world, therefore the world hateth you " (John xv. 19). Never in the history of the Catholic Church has it been free from persecution. Whatever be the differences between the sects they unite against the Church. The apostles, especially St. Paul, were objects of hate to the Jews (Acts

xiii. 50; xvii. 8), and St. John (166 A.D.) testifies that their hatred of the Christians had not died out in his day. The present day is not wanting in examples in the sufferings inflicted on religious communities, in the interference of the secular governments in things spiritual, in the opposition made to processions and meetings and other devout practices. Can any Church be the true Church which does not oppose the spirit of the world ? Then too it is only in the Catholic Church that we have miracles: those, for instance, of the apostles, all the saints worked both in their lifetime and after death, either at their graves or by the application of their relics. We know that God would work miracles only in confirmation of the truth.

2. The true Church is that one in which the successor of St. Peter is to be found.

The Church rests on a rock and that rock is Peter: " Thou art Peter and upon this rock I will build My Church" (Matt. xxviii. 20). " Where Peter is, there is the Church," says St. Ambrose.

3. The true Church is known by the following four marks: she is One, Holy, Catholic, Apostolic.

The Catholic Church alone has these marks:

1. The true Church is One. She has at all times and in all places the same doctrine, the same means of grace, and only one Head.

Truth can only be one; hence the teaching of the Church cannot change. Christ wished His Church to be one; for that He prayed at the Last Supper (John xvii. 20); " There shall be one fold and one shepherd" (John x. 16); He appointed one Head for the whole Church (John xxi. 17). The Catholic Church is One: her Catechisms the world over teach precisely the same doctrine. Everywhere the holy sacrifice is offered, and the sacraments given in the same way; the same ceremonies and feasts are observed all over the world. All Catholics acknowledge the Pope as Head of the Church. If there were antipopes it is none the less true that some one was the true Pope; the existence of many pretenders to a throne does not exclude the claim of the true king. Nor can heresy destroy this unity, for the heretic who refuses to submit is no longer a member of the Church. None need accuse the Church of want of progress because it holds fast by its old established doctrines; there is no true progress in giving up the truth and adopting error. The truth cannot change; hence Bossuet might well say: " Protestantism, thou art changeable, therefore thou canst not be the truth ! "

2. The true Church is Holy, i.e., it has the means and the endeavor to lead all men to holiness.

Christ founded the Church for the very purpose of making men holy. The Catholic Church is holy. All its teaching is lofty and pure; the great principle underlying its commands are self-denial and the love of one's neighbor; all its sacraments, and especially penance and the Holy Eucharist are great aids to the sanctification of mankind, and the complete following out of the evangelical counsels can lead a man to the highest point of perfection; moreover the Catholic Church has a host of saints, whose holiness is attested by miracles. The misdeeds of some members, or abuses occurring within the Church are due not to the Church, but to the perversity of men. Even among the apostles there was a traitor, and Christ compared some members of the Church to weeds and worthless fish. Can any Church be holy which adopts Luther's teaching that faith alone is sufficient for salvation, and good works unnecessary ? or Calvin's doctrine that some men are predestined by God to hell fire ? or any Church which, on its own confession, owns that none of its members have been saints and their sanctity confirmed by miracle ?

3. The true Church is universal or Catholic, i.e., she is empowered to receive men into her bosom in all places and all times.

Christ died for all men, and on ascending into heaven gave His apostles the mission to teach all the nations of the earth till the end of time (Matt. xxviii. 20). Hence His Church was meant to be for all nations, and this is confirmed by the miracle of tongues on the first Pentecost. The Catholic Church is universal; her teaching applies to all people, the polished Greek, the victorious Roman, the rude barbarian as well as to the outcast slave. At present the Catholic Church is spread over the whole world. "Heretics are everywhere," said St. Augustine, "but no particular heresy is everywhere." The Church has about 260,000,000 members, hence it is more widespread than any other religion, and is continually sending missionaries to the heathen. Can, then, any Church which depends entirely on the government, as, for instance, the Russian Church, or the Anglican, which is wholly national in England, be the true Church ? or can one which has no real success among the heathen have a claim to truth ?

4. The true Church is Apostolic; i.e., she comes down from the time of the apostles, her teaching is always what it was in the time of the apostles, and her ministers are legitimate successors of the apostles.

The Church is built on the foundation of the apostles of which Christ is the corner-stone (Eph. ii. 20). "That is the true Church," says St. Jerome, "which was founded by the apostles and endures unto the present day." The Catholic Church is Apostolic; it has lasted nineteen hundred years, Luther himself confessed that it was the oldest. The teaching of the oldest of the Fathers agrees perfectly with our Catechism, and our services are substantially the same as those of the first ages.

The consideration of these notes and marks has, in the course of ages, led many of the noblest of men into the bosom of the Catholic Church.

It is remarkable that men of the greatest learning and virtue have, even in the face of great sacrifices, entered the Catholic Church, while those who have deserted it have generally shown by their lives what they really were. We have reason to rejoice in our religion that it offers us such special consolation in trouble and at the hour of death. Thus Melancthon wrote to his Catholic mother: " The Protestant faith is the best one to live in, but the Catholic is the best to die in," and again: " The new religion makes the best show, the Catholic gives most security."

8. THE CATHOLIC CHURCH ALONE GIVES SALVATION.

In other words: " Outside the Catholic Church there is no salvation."

1. The Catholic Church alone gives salvation; i.e., the Catholic Church alone possesses those means which lead to salvation, viz., the doctrine of Christ, the means of salvation appointed by Christ, and the teachers and guides of the Church established by Christ.

The Church cannot teach that truth and error lead equally well to salvation; she makes no declaration as to who is saved, but states only what is necessary for salvation. The judgment of particular individuals is left to the God Who searches hearts (Ps. vii. 10). Her doctrine is not a declaration of intolerance to the individual, but of intolerance of error, such an intolerance as God Himself expressed when He forbade false gods to appear before Him (1 Cor. v.). So far is the Church from hating those outside her pale that in her public prayers on Good Friday she begs God's mercy for them. The persecutions of the Middle Ages formed no part of the work of the Church, which desired not the death, but the conversion of the sinner; it was the civil power which used force to repress heretics, because as a rule they disturbed the public peace and morality. The Church is the way to salvation; it differs in this respect from the synagogue; the latter merely pointed out the way of salvation in the distant future, while the Church claims itself to be the true way. The Catholic Church is distinct from the heretical churches which have corrupted Christ's doctrine and have rejected the means of grace, especially Mass and penance. Their way is a roundabout way, or the wrong way. " The further one goes out of the right path," says St. Augustine, " the further he is from the goal of his journey."

2. Hence every man is bound to become a member of the Catholic Church.

Some will say that a man ought not to change his religion; they might just as well argue that a man may keep an inheritance which his father obtained unjustly. Others say: " One faith is as good as another, and all lead equally well to heaven." This is to profess indifferentism. It is certain that one religion only can be the true one, i.e., the one revealed by God; and reason alone would tell us that the truth is what we should aim at. It is absurd to suppose that God is unconcerned whether man adore Him or sticks and stones, or whether Christ be regarded as His Son or as a blasphemer. Why should Christ, and after Him the apostles, preach the Gospel amid so much persecution, if it were of no moment what a man believed ? Why were the apostles so vehement in denouncing those who perverted the teaching of Christ (Gal. i. 8; 2 John i. 10) ? Why should God have converted Saul, and sent an angel to Cornelius ? The apostles gave the reason: "There is no other name under heaven given to men whereby we must be saved" (Acts iv. 12). And Christ said: "I am the way, the truth and the life. No man cometh to the Father but by Me" (John xiv. 6). Hence it is that so many eminent people enter the Church, despite the sacrifices entailed. Queen Christina, the only daughter of Gustavus Adolphus of Sweden, the arch-enemy of the Catholics, studied the Catholic teaching and was persuaded of its truth; and as the laws of the land forbade her to practise her faith, she resigned her crown and spent the rest of her days in Rome. So, too, in the beginning of the century Count Stolberg resigned his post on his conversion. In England during the last few decades very many most distinguished men have entered the Church, especially Cardinals Newman and Manning. Even from Judaism there have been remarkable conversions, as, e.g., those of Ratisbonne and Liebermann.

3. Whoever through his own fault remains outside the Church will not be saved.

A man who, knowing the Catholic Church to be the true one, leaves it, say, to make a good marriage, or to push on his business, or for some such unworthy motive, will not be saved; so, too, of the man who from a cowardly fear of the reproaches or the disesteem of others, does not enter the Church. The same is true of the man who having solid doubts as to whether his Church is the true one, takes no pains to find out the truth. Such as these love the darkness better than the light (John iii. 19). "He cannot have God for a Father, who has not the Church for a Mother," says St. Cyprian. "He who has not Christ for a Head," are the words of St. Augustine, "cannot be saved; and he who does not belong to the body of Christ, i.e., to the Church of Christ, has not Christ for his Head." "He who breaks away from the Church separates himself from Christ" (Council of Lateran, iv.).

If, however, a man, through no fault of his own, remains outside the Church, he may be saved if he lead a God-fearing life; for such a one is to all intents and purposes a member of the Catholic Church.

The majority of men who have been brought up in heresy think that they belong to the true Church; their error is not due to hatred of God. A man who leads a good life and has the love of God in his heart, really belongs to the Church, and such a one is saved, not by his heresy, but by belonging to the Church. St. Peter said: "In every nation he that feareth God and worketh justice is acceptable to Him" (Acts x. 35). "The Catholic Church," says St. Gregory the Great, "embraces all the just from Abel to the last of the elect at the end of the world." All who lived up to their lights were Christians, though they might have been looked upon as godless, as, e.g., Socrates among the Greeks, Abraham and Elias among the Jews. They do not belong to the body of the Church, that is, they are not externally in union with the Church, but they are of the soul of the Church, i.e., they have the sentiments which the members of the Church should have.

Thus the Catholic Church has members both visible and invisible.

The visible members are those who have been received into the Church by Baptism. The following are not members: The unbaptized (heathens, Jews, Mohammedans), formal heretics (Protestants), and schismatics (the Greeks), those who are excommunicated. The invisible members are those who without any fault of their own are outside the Church leading God-fearing lives.

The visible members of the Church are called living or dead members, according as they are in the state of sanctifying grace or not.

It is an error to think that those who have fallen into grave sin are no longer members of the Church. The Church is like a field, in which grow both wheat and cockle (Matt. xiii. 24), or like a net which contains fish both good and bad (Matt. xiii. 47). It is not enough to belong to the Church; a man should also live up to his belief, otherwise · is membership will help only to his greater condemnation.

9. THE RELATIONS BETWEEN CHURCH AND STATE.

The State might be defined as an institution having for its end the promotion of the temporal well-being of its members. Church and State have similar ends in view, but the Church looks mainly to the eternal welfare of its members. Both have their power from God, the Church holding hers from Christ, while the State receives its powers, not from an assembly of men, but from God (Leo XIII.). There are various points of difference between Church and State: the Church is one, while States are many; the State includes one or more nations, the Church embraces all the nations of the earth; States grow up and pass away, the Church remains forever. The Church recognizes every form of existing government, for there is nothing in the various forms that contradicts Catholic teaching (Leo XIII.). Hence Leo XIII. has frequently enjoined on the French monarchists to recognize and support the existing republic. Christ Himself taught that what was Cæsar's should be given to Cæsar (Matt. xxii. 21).

1. The Church is, in its own department, absolutely independent of the State, for Christ left the teaching and government of His Church to the apostles and their successors, not to any temporal sovereign.

Hence the State has no claim to dictate to Christians what they are to believe and reject, nor to instruct priests what they are to preach, nor how and when they are to give the sacraments, say Mass, etc. Such interference has always been resented by the Church:

thus Hosius, at the Council of Nicæa, addressed the Roman emperor when the latter was meddling in matters of faith: " Here you have no right to dictate to us; it is rather your duty to follow our commands." The State, too, is in its own affairs independent of the Church. " The power of the State as well as that of the Church is circumscribed by limits within which it can work uncontrolled " (Leo XIII.). There are many points however where these limits touch; hence a mutual agreement is necessary on both sides. If contrary orders were given in the same matter strife would arise, and the subject would not know where his duty lay (Leo XIII.). Between the two powers there should be some such union as there is between the body and soul in man (Leo XIII.). Agreements between State and Church are of frequent occurrence in history: they are called Concordats. These are often conspicuous proofs of the tender love of the Church in pushing her mildness and toleration as far as is consistent with her duty (Leo XIII.).

2. The Church is an essential factor in promoting the welfare of the State, for she teaches obedience to authority, prevents many crimes, incites men to noble endeavor, and unites together various nations.

Plutarch speaks of religion forming a better protection for a city than its walls. The Church teaches that the civil authority has its power from God (Rom. xiii. 1), and that even wicked rulers are to be obeyed (1 Pet. ii. 18). How many sinners have been rescued by the Church and changed into saints and benefactors of mankind ! How many have been restrained from crime by the teaching of the Church, or God's judgments! How much unjustly acquired property has been restored, and how many enemies reconciled ! More than this, the Church teaches that salvation depends on works of mercy, and makes it a point of duty for her members to assist their suffering brethren. How many institutions for orphans, for the sick and blind and deaf-mutes, etc., owe their foundation to the servants of the Church! Indeed, the needy are the Church's first care. Moreover the Church binds the nations together in the bonds of brotherhood, both by a common profession of faith and by the precept of charity. Hence it is that as far as possible the priests of the Church should keep aloof from all strife between nations.

In consequence of this all good rulers and statesmen have supported the Church to the best of their power.

Such was the policy of Constantine the Great, of Charlemagne, of St. Stephen, King of Hungary, and St. Wenceslaus, King of Bohemia. Rulers who reject the Church saw at the branch which supports them; the people see in them no longer the representatives of God but merely the elected of the people removable at the people's will.

The States which have persecuted the Church have always sooner or later experienced the evil results of so doing.

Our Lord's words are very apt here: " Every kingdom divided against itself shall be brought to desolation " (Luke xi. 17). Religion is to the State what the soul is to the body. "The nation and the kingdom that will not serve Thee shall perish" (Is. lx. 12). "The surest sign of ruin in a State," writes Machiavelli, "is when religion is neglected." The fall of the great Roman empire and the horrors of the French revolution may be traced to the same cause. Even Napoleon confessed that no nation could be governed without religion. The absence of religion means the introduction of crime: "There is no knowledge of God in the land. Cursing, and lying, and killing, and theft, and adultery have overflowed" (Osee iv. 1, 2). Our prisons are filled with people who for the most part neglect religion.

3. The Church was, from the earliest times, the patron of true education and culture.

It is to the interest of the Church to promote culture. Ignorance and immorality are usually close companions. The world is a book displaying the wisdom of God; the more we know of this book, the more we shall know of God, and the more will our love for Him be increased. Hence it is the duty of the Church to encourage scientific research (Leo XIII.). It was Christianity which tamed the wild nations of Europe, civilizing them and making them the rulers of other peoples (Leo XIII.). "Had the Church been established with the view of ministering to the temporal wants of man, it could not have conferred greater benefits than it has done," is the judgment of St. Augustine on the work of the Church.

It was the Church which first charged itself with the education of the young and founded the first schools.

The schools of the monastery, cathedral and parish in the time of Charlemagne owed their origin to the Church. Most of the universities owe their existence to the Pope. Whole Orders of Religious, such as the Benedictines, Jesuits, Christian Brothers and others devote themselves to the education of youth. The success of the Jesuits was acknowledged even by their enemies, and in spite of their suppression in 1773 Frederick of Prussia, and Catherine of Russia, neither of them Catholics, retained them to instruct the youth of their kingdoms.

It was the Church which rescued the great works of antiquity from destruction.

The monks of the Middle Ages transcribed the works of the heathen philosophers and historians, thus preserving them to posterity. The great libraries of the monasteries, as well as the museums and libraries of the Popes, preserved many treasures. We might remark, too, that the Benedictines have produced sixteen thousand authors and the Jesuits, in their comparatively short existence, twelve thousand.

It was the Church which, from early times, raised the noblest buildings.

Such a structure, for instance, as St. Peter's in Rome, which was one hundred and ten years in building, or the Cathedral at Cologne, begun in 1249 and finished in 1880. Not to mention the glorious structures to be seen all over the Continent, in Germany, France, Spain, Italy. England is filled with magnificent buildings like Westminster, Lincoln, York, Durham, etc. A large proportion of the finest edifices in the United States are Catholic churches.

It was the Church which from the earliest times gave the greatest encouragement to the fine arts.

We owe Plain Chant or Gregorian to St. Ambrose, Bishop of Milan (397 A.D.) and St. Gregory the Great (604 A.D.), and its developments to many other artists. It was the Popes who encouraged men like Palestrina (1594). Twice in its history the Church resisted the Iconoclast (or image-breaking) movement, at Nicæa in 787, and at Trent in 1563. Artists of world-wide fame, such as Leonardo da Vinci (1519), Raphael (1520), Michael Angelo (1564), Correggio (1564), Canova (1822), etc., owed much of their success to the support of the Popes. It was the cloister which produced some of the finest artists and their works.

It was the Church which made whole tracts of land fertile and habitable.

The work of the Benedictines and Cistercians in the way of clearing and draining land and developing agriculture was especially conspicuous in the German forests. The same work is carried on in savage countries now by the Trappists and other religious Orders.

It is to priests and monks that we owe some of the greatest discoveries.

The Deacon Flavio Gioja discovered the magnet and compass in 1300; Veit, a monk of Arezzo, discovered the scale, the rules of music and harmony; the Dominican Spina the use of spectacles; the Franciscan Berthold Schwarz gunpowder (1300); the Jesuit Kircher exhibited the first burning glass (1646); Copernicus, a canon of Frauenberg discovered his famous system (1507); the Jesuit Cavaliere the components of white light (1647); the Spanish Benedictine Pontius invented a method of teaching deaf-mutes (1570); the Jesuit Lana a way of teaching the blind to read (1687); and the Jesuit Secchi (1878) made many discoveries with regard to sun-spots. Only lately the Dominican Calandoni invented a type-setter to replace the compositor. The enemies of the Church are always crying her down as opposed to progress, enlightenment and freedom.

10. THE COMMUNION OF SAINTS.

The members of the Church may be divided into three classes: those who are still on the earth, "having not here a lasting city, but seeking the one that is to come" (Heb. xiii. 14); those who have reached their goal in heaven, the saints; and those who are expiating their sins in purgatory. All are "fellow citizens with the saints and domestics of God," working together for the same object of union with God. The members of this great community are called "saints" because all are sanctified by Baptism (1 Cor. vi. 11), and are called to a holy life (1 Thess. iv. 3). Those in heaven have already attained to perfect holiness. Yet St. Paul calls the Christians still on earth "saints" (Eph. i. 1).

1. The communion of saints is the union and intercourse of Catholics on earth, of the souls in purgatory, and of the saints in heaven.

The Church on earth is called the Church Militant, because of its ceaseless struggle with its three enemies, the world, the flesh, and the devil. The souls in purgatory form the Church Suffering, because they are still expiating their sins in the cleansing fire. The blessed in heaven are called the Church Triumphant, because they have already secured their victory. These three divisions are one Church by the common bond of Baptism.

2. Catholics on earth, the souls in purgatory, and the blessed in heaven are united with Christ, just as are the members of a body with the head· (Rom. xii. 4).

The Holy Spirit works in all the members (1 Cor. xii. 13). "The soul," says St. Augustine, "animates all the organs of the body, and causes the eye to see, the ear to hear, etc;" just so does the Holy Spirit work in the members of Christ's body; and as the Holy Spirit proceeds from Christ, Christ is the head of the Christian body (Col. i. 18). He is the vine carrying strength and nourishment to the branches (John xv. 5). Each member of the body has its own special functions, so each member of the Church has his own gifts (1 Cor. xii. 6-10, 28). Each member of the body works for the whole body; so every member of the Church works for the common good. All the members of the body share the pain or pleasure felt by one, and the same is true of the mutual sympathy of the communion of saints: "If one member suffer anything, all the members suffer with it; or, if one member glory, all the members rejoice with it" (1 Cor. xii. 26). Thus the saints in heaven are not indifferent to our condition. Catholics who have fallen into mortal sin are still members of this great body, though dead members; but they cease to be members if they are excommunicated.

3. All the members of the communion of saints have a share in the spiritual goods of the Catholic Church, and can help one another by their prayers and other good works. The saints alone in heaven have no need of help.

In a similar manner all the people of a country have a share in the institutions supported by the country, such as hospitals, asylums, law courts, etc. So also, in the family circle, all the members have a claim to share in the common goods, such as riches or honors. Thus all the Masses, the means of grace, the prayers of the Church, and all the good works done by individuals, are for the benefit of all its members. In the Our Father we pray for others as well as for ourselves; holy Mass is offered for the dead as well as the living, and the same is true of the Office recited by the priest. Hence it is that one may have more hope of converting the greatest sinner who still belongs to the Church than a Freemason who outwardly leads a good life, yet who is cut off from it; and a Catholic may look forward to a quicker release from purgatory than others. St. Francis Xavier constantly cheered himself with the thought that the Church was praying for him, and supporting him with her good works. Moreover, all the members of the Church can give mutual help. There is the same sympathy as in the human body, where a sound member comes to the help of one that is weaker, and the possession of good lungs, a sound heart, or healthy stomach, may help the body to recover from what might otherwise have been a fatal illness. The eye does not act for itself alone; it guides the hands and feet. Sodom would have been saved had ten just men been found within its walls.

1. All Catholics can help each other by prayer and good works.

St. Peter was freed from prison by the prayers of the Christians. "The prayer of St. Stephen," says St. Augustine, "procured the conversion of St. Paul." The tears and prayers of St. Monica converted her son. Even in the Old Testament God promised that He would be merciful to the prayers of the priest (Lev. iv. 20). St. James bids us: "Pray one for another, that you may be saved" (Jas. v. 16), and St. Paul: "I beseech you . . . help me in your prayers for me to God" (Rom. xv. 30). Christ revealed to Marie Lataste that as Esther saved her people by her intercession with Assuerus, so the prayers of a single soul may save a whole nation from the avenging hand of God. Prayer is a work of mercy, and brings down a blessing on the one who prays and the one who is prayed for. Fasting and almsgiving are also means of help. As a man's debts may be paid off by his neighbor, so the debt of sin may in some measure be paid off by the good works of others; and thus it was in the early Church that penances were often remitted or shortened at the intercession of the martyrs.

2. We can also help the holy souls in purgatory by prayers and other good works; they in turn can help us by their prayers, especially when they reach heaven.

The Jews even believed that help could be given to the souls of the departed; for we read (2 Mach. xii.) how Judas Machabeus caused sacrifices to be offered for those who had fallen in battle, and sent money to the Temple for that purpose. The passing-bell and the knell are signals to pray for the dying and the dead. In the *Memento* after the Consecration at Mass a special petition is made for the departed. "Prayer," says St. Augustine, "is the key by which we open the gates of heaven to the suffering souls." The prayers of the living, especially holy Mass, almsdeeds, and other works of piety are of great efficacy in lessening the sufferings of the holy souls (Council of Lyons, 1274). The souls in purgatory can also help us. Many saints held that we can call the holy souls to our help (Bellarmine; St. Alphonsus). St. Catherine of Bologna (1463), used often to call upon the holy souls when the saints seemed to fail in helping her, and she never asked them in vain.

3. The saints in heaven can help us by their prayers before

the throne of God (Apoc. viii. 4), especially if we call upon them for help.

The saints must know much of what happens on earth, for their happiness consists in the complete satisfaction of all their desires. The devil knows all our weaknesses, as we know from the way in which he tempts us. The prophets of the Old Testament sometimes foretold future events, and knew the most hidden things; is it likely that the saints are less favored than they? They rejoice when a sinner is converted (Luke xv. 7). "What can escape those," says St. Thomas Aquinas, "who see Him Who sees all things?" And the Church teaches us that when we call upon the saints for their prayers, they join their prayers to ours. Their intercession has great efficacy, for the "continual prayer of a just man even on the earth availeth much" (Jas. v. 16). What power Abraham had when pleading for Sodom! (Gen. xviii.) "If," says St. Jerome, "the saints had such power when in the flesh, what can they not obtain for us now that they have secured their victory?" St. John Chrysostom compares their intercession to the pleading of old soldiers who display their wounds. This power has often been demonstrated by miracles.

Our dead relatives and friends, who are in heaven, are always pleading for us at the throne of God, and often save us from danger.

"Charity never dies" (1 Cor. xiii. 8), and the ties which bind us to those we love remain unbroken by death. Even in hell the wretched Dives showed he had some affection still for his relatives on earth (Luke xvi. 27). The prophet Jeremias, and the holy high priest Onias, prayed in limbo for the Jewish nation (2 Mach. xv. 14); and Christ promised His apostles that He would pray for them (John xiv. 16; 1 John ii. 1). St. Augustine, after the death of his mother St. Monica, and St. Wenceslaus after the death of his grandmother St. Ludmilla rapidly advanced to greater heights of sanctity. So too the saints help the souls in purgatory. "Our Lady alone rescues daily some souls from purgatory by her prayers." On the anniversary of the Assumption of Our Lady thousands of souls are delivered from their prison (St. Peter Damian; St. Alphonsus). On Saturdays, the day specially dedicated to Our Lady, she rescues many poor souls from purgatory (John XXII., Sabbatine Bull). Nor are the holy angels indifferent to their future companions; one of the Church's prayers speaks of St. Michael leading souls into heaven. Our angel guardian, and the angels whom we have specially honored on earth, will take up our cause in purgatory.

TENTH ARTICLE OF THE CREED : THE FORGIVENESS OF SINS.

(See the chapter on Sin, page 449.)

ELEVENTH AND TWELFTH ARTICLES OF THE CREED: THE LAST THINGS.

1. DEATH.

Every day some eighty-eight thousand men die; that is, one death per second.

1. At death the soul is separated from the body, and enters the world of spirits; the body decays, and falls into dust.

St. Paul speaks of death as a dissolution (2 Tim. iv. 6), and St. Peter calls the body a tabernacle of the soul (2 Pet. i. 14). The body is, as it were, a shell through which the soul breaks to enter in its new life. "The soul is freed from its prison at death," is the expression of St. Augustine. The body, deprived of the soul, is no longer alive, because it has no longer the principle of life. At death the spirit returns to the God Who gave it (Eccles. xii. 7). "Death," says St. John Chrysostom, "is a journey into eternity." Hence it is wrong to believe with the ancient Egyptians that the soul is joined to other forms, whether human or animal; and those too are mistaken who think that the soul enters into a sort of sleep till the day of judgment. After death the body returns to the dust from which it came (Gen. iii. 19); exception was made, however, in the case of the bodies of Christ and of His blessed Mother; and the bodies of some of the saints have been preserved free from corruption to the present day. At the last day our bodies will all rise again. Death is represented symbolically as a skeleton carrying a scythe, with which he cuts short our lives as the reaper mows the grass of the field (Ps. cii. 15); he is also represented carrying a key to open to us the gates of everlasting life.

2. All men must die, because death is the consequence of original sin.

Our first parents lost by their sin the gift of immortality, and as a consequence we all have to die. "By one man sin entered into the world and by sin death; and so death passed upon all men, in whom all have sinned" (Rom. v. 12). Death is the punishment of man's ambition to be as God. Henoch (Gen. v. 24) and Elias (4 Kings ii. 11) alone were removed from earth without dying, and they are to return before the Last Day, and then die; St. Thomas teaches that even those who survive till the Day of Judgment shall die. Christ alone was not under the law of death because He was free from all sin; His death for us was a purely voluntary act. "Life," says St. John Chrysostom, "is a play in which for a short time one man represents a judge, another a general, and so on; after the play no further account is made of the dignity which each one had." We are all like so many chess-men, who at the beginning of the game have our fixed places on the board, but at the end are all tumbled into a box. The rich man cannot take his riches along with him (Job xxvii. 15). After death many who have been the first on earth shall be last, and the last first (Matt. xix. 30). Our days upon earth are but a shadow (Job viii. 9); our years shall be considered as a spider's web (Ps. lxxxix. 9); life is a vapor which appeareth for a little while, and afterwards shall vanish away (Jas. iv. 15). The hour of our death is unknown to us. We shall die when we expect it not (Matt. xxiv. 44); death will come like a thief (Matt. xxiv. 43). To use the expression of St. Ephrem, death is like the pounce of the hawk, or the spring of the wolf. St. Gregory of Nyssa compares life to a torch, which a slight puff of wind may put out. To some of the saints the hour of their death has been revealed, but from most men it is hidden. We see in this arrangement the action of God's wisdom and goodness. Since we do not know the hour of our death, we should always be ready to die: " Wherefore be you also ready, because at what hour you know not the Son of man will come " (Matt. xxiv. 44). The parable of the ten virgins (Matt. xxv.) is another warning on this subject. " Death is a great lord," says St. Ephrem, " waiting on no one and demanding that all wait upon him." As a man lives, so he dies. Those who put off reforming their lives are like those students who begin to study when the examination is already upon them.

3. Death is terrible only to the sinner, in no wise to the just.

To the sensual and self-seeking only is death fearful, for it means the end of their enjoyment and the beginning of woe. " The death of the just man," says St. Vincent Ferrer, " is like the pruning of a tree preparing it to bear nobler fruit in the future; while the death of the sinner is the uprooting of the tree before it is cast into the fire." " For the just man there is no death but a passing into everlasting life." The saints rejoiced in death, desiring like St. Paul to be dissolved and to be with Christ (Phil. i. 23). St. John Chrysostom compares the desire of the saints for death with that of a traveller for the end of his journey, or a farmer for his harvest; in another place he speaks of death as of a change from a tumbledown cottage to a beautiful mansion. " O how sweet it is to die, if one's life has been a good one ! " exclaims St. Augustine. It is not the kind of death, but the state of the soul that is important: " As the tree falls so shall it lie," says Holy Writ (Eccles. xi. 3); so it is with man: as his will was directed on earth, so shall it be directed after death. Happy the man whose will has been always fixed on God; in other words who has in his heart the love of God and sanctifying grace; he will see God. Unhappily, many are bent solely on things of the earth, those, for instance, who love the world and are not in the state of grace; they remain separated from God forever.

4. In order to secure a happy death, we should in our daily prayer ask God to grant us a happy death, and of our own accord detach ourselves now from earthly goods and pleasures.

He dies a happy death who is reconciled with God, and has put his worldly affairs in order. We ought often to pray that God may give us the grace to receive the last sacraments before dying. It is also a duty to make a will in good time; to do this is to behave like a prudent captain who heaves his cargo overboard to avoid shipwreck. A sudden death is not a thing to be desired, for we cannot

then put into order our spiritual or temporal affairs; hence we pray in
the Litanies: "From a sudden and unprovided death deliver us, O
Lord." The Church often recalls the thought of death, on All Souls,
Ash Wednesday, by the passing-bell, etc. The thought of death is
useful for keeping us out of sin: "In all thy works remember thy
last end, and thou shalt never sin" (Ecclus. vii. 40). Whoever thinks
seriously of death will take as little pleasure in the things of the
world as the condemned criminal in a good meal; he is another
Damocles, with the sword hanging over him by a hair. Every day's
sunset is a reminder from God of death, and sleep is an image of it.
We ought to detach ourselves even now from earthly goods and
pleasures. After death our eyes will no longer see, nor our ears
hear, nor our tongues speak; and we should prepare for that state
by our voluntary restraint now. We should crush the curiosity of
the eyes and the ears, our unruly speech and inordinate enjoyment
of good, following the counsel of St. Basil: "Let us die that we may
live." The good works which the Church imposes on us, such as
prayer, fasting, and almsdeeds, are nothing but a loosening of the
heart from earthly ties. Only those who have this detachment shall
see God after death: "Blessed are the clean of heart for they shall
see God" (Matt. v. 8).

2. *THE PARTICULAR JUDGMENT.*

1. Immediately after death follows the particular judgment.

"As soon as the soul leaves the body," says St. Augustine, "it is
judged." We learn from the parable of Dives and Lazarus that both
were judged immediately after death. St. Paul tells us: "It is appointed unto man once to die, and after this the judgment" (Heb.
ix. 27). In the hour of death God will say to us: "Give an account
of thy stewardship" (Luke xvi. 2). After judgment comes the
sentence. If God has ordained that the workman should not be
kept waiting for his wage, it is not likely that He will delay to reward
him who has labored faithfully. "Death is the reward of merit, the
crown of the harvest" (St. Ambrose).

Christ will sit as Judge in the particular judgment. He will
examine our whole lives, and will deal with us as we have dealt
with our fellow-men.

Christ will be our Judge: "For neither doth the Father judge
any man, but hath given all judgment to the Son" (John v. 22). He
promised His apostles at the Last Supper to return after His ascension and take them to Himself (John xiv. 3). Evidently this meant
at their death; of St. John too He said: "So I will have him remain
till I come" (John xxi. 22). The apostles rejoiced at the thought of
seeing Christ again (1 John iii. 2); so long as they were in the flesh
they were in some sense far from Christ (2 Cor. v. 6). We are not
to imagine that the soul is led before Christ in heaven. He enlightens the departed soul in such a manner that it is quite convinced
that its Saviour has passed a true judgment upon it. "As lightning
cometh out of the east and appeareth even into the west, so shall

also the coming of the Son of man be " (Matt. xxiv. 27); that is, as Blessed Clement Hofbauer puts it, at our death, when Christ comes to us, our whole life will be revealed to us with the rapidity and clearness of lightning. A man's works shall be revealed at his death (Ecclus. xi. 29). All those who have been near to death say that in that moment all sorts of things long forgotten and occurring in childhood are presented to the mind. At death, too, our most secret deeds are brought to light: "For there is not anything secret that shall not be made manifest, nor hidden that shall not be known and come abroad" (Luke viii. 17). We must give an account even of every idle word that we have spoken (Matt. xii. 36). St. Basil compares the soul to an artist who has produced a number of pictures; at the hour of death the veil is removed from these, and they cover him with glory, or if they prove to be wretched work, condemn him to disgrace. As the sun reveals to us the floating particles in the air, so when the Sun of justice shines into our souls we shall see there even our slightest faults. " On the Day of Judgment," says Louis of Granada, " God will wear the same aspect to us as we have shown in our lifetime to our neighbor." God is, as it were, a mirror, reflecting most perfectly the image of him who looks into it. " With what measure you mete, it shall be measured to you again " (Matt. vii. 2).

2. After the particular judgment the souls of men go into hell, or heaven, or purgatory.

We see from the parable of Dives and Lazarus that the sentence of the judge is carried out at once (Luke xvi.). The Church has defined that those who have not sinned after Baptism, and those who having sinned after Baptism, have expiated those sins on earth or in purgatory, are received at once into heaven; while those who die in mortal sin descend at once to hell (Council of Lyons, ii., 1274). St. Gregory the Great and St. Justin taught the same in their time. Those are in error who believe, as in the Greek schismatic Church, that the souls of the just have merely a foretaste of their blessedness after death, and have complete happiness only when they are joined to their bodies, and that the wicked experience full damnation only after the resurrection. They are very few who enter heaven at once, for: " Nothing defiled can enter heaven " (Apoc. xxi. 27). According to Bellarmine it is seldom even that a just man escapes purgatory. All have it in their power to be saved, but not all use their graces. After the particular judgment there is to be a general judgment; in the former the soul receives its punishment or reward for the evil or good it has done; in the latter the body shares in the dispensation as the instrument of the soul.

3. HEAVEN.

Heaven is an abode of everlasting joy.

Christ gave His apostles on Mount Thabor some foretaste of the joys of heaven (Matt. xvii.). The heavens opened at the baptism of Christ (Matt. iii. 16). St. Stephen saw the heavens open (Acts vii. 55). St. Paul was rapt into the third heaven (2 Cor. xii. 2).

Heaven is both a place and a state. Many divines teach that it is
somewhere beyond the stars; though this view is not of faith, yet
it has some foundation, for Christ came down from heaven, and
ascended again to heaven. Heaven is also a state of the soul; it
consists in the vision of the Godhead (Matt. xviii. 10), and in the
peace and joy of the Holy Spirit (Rom. xiv. 17); so the angels and
saints do not leave heaven when they come to our assistance. Christ
is the King of heaven. He called Himself King before Pilate,
though He maintained that His kingdom was not of this world (John
xviii. 36); He was acknowledged as King by the penitent thief:
"Lord, remember me when Thou comest into Thy kingdom" (Luke
xxiii. 42); in heaven the angels worship Christ (Heb. i. 6). Heaven
is our true home; on this earth we are but strangers (2 Cor. v. 6).

The joys of heaven are unspeakably great: the blessed are
free from even the slightest pain; they enjoy the vision of God
and the friendship of all the inhabitants of heaven.

Of the joys of heaven St. Paul writes: "Eye hath not seen, nor
ear heard, neither hath it entered into the heart of man, what things
God hath prepared for them that love Him" (1 Cor. ii. 9). "This
happiness may be felt, but not described," says St. Augustine. And
David addresses God: "They shall be inebriated with the plenty of
Thy house, and Thou shalt make them drink of the torrent of Thy
pleasure" (Ps. xxxv. 9). "The present life," says St. Gregory the
Great, "in comparison of everlasting bliss, is more like death than
life." We shall enjoy there the same delights as God Himself (Matt.
xxv. 21), for we shall be made partakers of the divine nature (2 Pet.
i. 4) and like to God (1 John iii. 2). We shall be transformed in
heaven like the iron in the fire. In heaven there are many mansions
(John xiv. 2); the kingdom of heaven is like to a banquet (Matt.
viii. 11; Luke xiv. 16), in which Our Lord Himself waits upon the
guests (Luke xii. 37). In heaven there is no bodily, only a spiritual
food (Tob. xii. 19); there is a great light (1 Tim. vi. 16); there are
heard the songs of the angels (Ps. lxxxiii. 5). The saints are robed
in white (Apoc. vii. 14); they are crowned by their Lord (Wisd. v.
17); they have perfect freedom, and are set over all God's works
(Matt. xxiv. 47). "If, O my God, Thou dost give us such beautiful things here in our prison, what wilt Thou do in Thy palace!"
exclaims St. Augustine. Lastly the joys of heaven are not sensual
(Matt. xxii. 30). The blessed are free from all suffering. "It is
easier," says St. Augustine, "to name the evils from which the
blessed are free than to count up their joys." They shall neither
hunger nor thirst (Apoc. vii. 16); death shall be no more, nor mourning, nor sorrow (Apoc. xxi. 4); and night will no more be (Apoc.
xxii. 5). The blessed see always the face of God (Matt. xviii. 10);
they see God as He is (1 John iii. 2), and face to face (1 Cor. xiii.
12); nor do they see God as it were in an image, but He is as present
to the understanding as a visible object to the eye which sees it.
The blessed enjoy this vision not by any power of their own, but by
a special divine operation, called the light of glory, and in consequence of this they become like to God (1 John iii. 2). This vision
of God is the source of untold happiness. "The blessed," says St.
Bonaventure, "rejoice more over God's blessedness than over their

own." "If the contemplation of creation is so sweet," says St. Charles Borromeo, "how much more so must be the contemplation of the Creator!" With the knowledge of God is necessarily linked the love of God, and increase of one means increase of the other. Hence this great joy banishes all sadness. The blessed in heaven also love one another; they are as one (John xvii. 21). "The love of the elect in paradise," says Blessed Suso, "is so great that souls removed at an infinite distance from one another love with a greater affection than that which exists between parent and child." "It is love alone," says St. Augustine, "which separates the children of the eternal kingdom from the children of perdition. What happiness to meet again our relations and friends after so long and painful a separation!"

The joys of heaven last forever.

Christ says: "The just will enter into everlasting life." The Holy Spirit will be united with them forever (John xiv. 16). This joy no man can take from them (John xvi. 22). No one can snatch them from the hand of the Father (John x. 29). Great kings and princes support their dependents even when these are no longer capable of rendering service; surely God, Who is the King of kings, will not be less generous. His reward is eternal, the only one worthy of Him. Were it not so, the joy of heaven would be incomplete from the fear of its coming to an end.

1. The happiness of the blessed varies according to their merits.

The master in the gospel of St. Luke (xix. 16, etc.), gave to the servant who had used his ten talents to gain other ten talents the command of ten cities, and to the one who had successfully used his five talents the command of five cities. Thus God acts, and in so doing acts with the greatest justice. St. Paul says: "He who soweth sparingly shall also reap sparingly, and he who soweth in blessings shall also reap of blessings" (2 Cor. ix. 6). The just see in heaven the triune God, yet some see Him more perfectly than others according to their merits (Council of Florence). "One is the glory of the sun [Christ], another the glory of the moon [Mary], and another the glory of the stars [the saints]" (1 Cor. xv. 41). The knowledge and love of God are greater in one saint and less in another; and the same is true of the joy of heaven. Men are intended to take the place of the fallen angels, and of these there are some from all the nine choirs of angels. The degree of glory in heaven depends on the amount of sanctifying grace which a man has at his death (Eccles. xi. 3); in other words the degree of glory is greater in proportion as a man has at his death more of the Holy Spirit, or more of the love of God in his heart. The degree of glory in the blessed cannot be increased nor diminished throughout eternity; yet there are accidental delights, as for instance when special honor is paid to a saint. Our Lord revealed that there is a particular joy in heaven when a sinner is converted (Luke xv. 7). The canonization, beatification, the feast day of a saint on earth, the prayers, the holy sacrifice, and other good works which the faithful perform on earth in honor of a saint are a special source of joy to that saint. St. Gertrude saw on such occasions the saints clothed in more resplendent raiment, and surrounded by a glorious escort; they seemed also to be raised to a state of greater bliss. Yet among the blessed there is no envy. They are all children of one Father and have received their portion from Him (Matt. xx). To use the homely illustration of St. Francis de Sales: two children receive from their father a piece of cloth to make a garment; the smaller child will not envy his brother the bigger garment, but will be quite satisfied with the one that fits him. So it is in heaven, and more than this, each one rejoices over the happiness of the other as though it were in some measure his own.

2. Only those souls enter heaven which are free from all sin, and from the penalty due to sin.

According to the Council of Florence, the souls only of those who after Baptism have not sinned, or who, if they have sinned, have done perfect penance on earth or in purgatory, can enter heaven. "Nothing defiled can enter heaven" (Apoc. xxi. 27). Moreover none could enter heaven before the death of Christ; they had to remain in limbo.

3. Heaven is won by suffering and self-denial.

St. Paul writes: "By many tribulations must we enter the kingdom of God" (Acts xiv. 21), and Christ's words are: "He that loveth his life shall lose it, and he that hateth his life in this world keepeth it unto life eternal" (John xii. 25), i.e., he who goes after all the joys and pleasures of this world will be damned, and he who despises them will be saved. There is no blessedness without self-denial. The kingdom of heaven is like a treasure or a costly pearl; whoever will possess it must give his all for it (Matt. xiii. 44-46), i.e., he must give up all inordinate attachment to the things of this world. "The kingdom of heaven suffers violence" (Matt. xi. 12). "Narrow is the gate and straight is the way that leadeth to life" (Matt. vii. 14). He wins the prize in the race who runs swiftly and steadily, and refrains from all things (1 Cor. ix. 25). He who would be among the blessed must be a martyr at least in intention. The greater efforts we make to secure salvation, the greater will be our joy.

4. For the just heaven begins already on earth.

"While we seek life eternal we already enjoy it," says St. Augustine. The just have the true peace (John xiv. 28); they have the peace of God which surpasses all understanding (Phil. iv. 7); hence they are joyful even when fasting (Matt. vi. 17), and in the midst of sufferings (Matt. v. 12). The just possess the Holy Ghost, hence they are, even while still on earth united with God (1 John iv. 16). Christ ever dwells in their hearts (Eph. iii. 17); they have within them the kingdom of God (Luke xvii. 21). "Think of the reward and thou wilt suffer with joy," says St. Augustine. The sufferings of this world are not to be compared with the glory which shall be manifested unto us (Rom. viii. 18). "If we think of the joys of heaven, the things of this world will appear worthless" (St. Gregory the Great). "He who stands on a hill-top," says St. John Chrysostom, "either does not see objects in the valley, or they appear to him very small."

4. HELL.

1. Hell is the abode of everlasting torment.

The unhappy rich man of the Gospel prayed Abraham to send one from the dead to his brothers "that they might not come to this place of torments" (Luke xvi. 28). In His discourse on the general judgment Christ speaks of hell as "everlasting punishment" (Matt. xxv. 46). Hell is both a place and a state. As a place it is situated beneath the earth. Hence the expression in the Creed "Descended into hell"; and we call hell an abyss. In the exorcisms we find the expression: "God has cast you from the heights of heaven into the bowels of the earth." Hell is sharply defined from heaven; between them yawns a chasm (Luke xvi. 26). The lost are separated from the saints (Matt. xxiv. 51). With good reason St. John Chrysostom exhorts us not to inquire so much where hell is as how to avoid it. Hell is a state, and moreover the continuation of that same state in which the sinner is found at death. "Thus," says St. John Damascene, "the pains of hell are due not so much to God as to man himself." Since hell is also a state, it is quite clear that the evil spirits may be near to us (1 Pet. v. 8), and even dwell in sinners (Matt. xii. 45). Even the pagans believed in a hell; hence the story of Tantalus, condemned to suffer perpetual hunger and thirst, and unable to satisfy either, because the water which he tried to drink or the fruit which he attempted to eat withdrew from his lips; the Danaids, condemned to draw water in sieves, and Sisyphus, forced ever to push a great rock to the top of a hill only to see it roll down again, furnish other examples of this belief.

The torments of hell are terrible; for the damned never see God, they are in the company of evil spirits and in fire, they endure great anguish of mind, and after the resurrection will have to suffer in their bodies.

St. Paul says: "It is a fearful thing to fall into the hands of the living God" (Heb. x. 31). St. John of the Cross teaches us that as a hundredfold is promised for every sacrifice that is made, so for every unlawful pleasure indulged in, a hundredfold penalty must be paid. St. John Chrysostom applies the words of St. Paul on heaven to describe hell: "Neither eye hath seen nor ear heard, nor hath it entered the heart of man to conceive what God has prepared for them that love Him *not*" (1 Cor. ii. 9). Christ calls hell an "unquenchable fire" (Mark ix. 44), because the sensation of burning is the greatest pain which man can conceive on earth. In other places He speaks of the "outer darkness" (Matt. xxii. 13) because the damned never see God, the source of eternal light. It is the place where there is "weeping and gnashing of teeth" (Matt. viii. 12), where the "worm never dies" (Mark ix. 43), and conscience never ceases to reproach the damned. Christ also speaks of the lost as "bound hand and foot," to show that they have no freedom and are in a place of banishment. From the words used by Christ to the damned: "Depart from Me, into everlasting fire" (Matt. xxv. 41), we learn that they have a double pain; they are banished from the vision of God (pain of loss), and condemned to suffer torment (pain of sense). The pain of loss is the greatest of the sufferings of hell. The greater the value of what is lost, the greater is the pain of the loss. "The damned have lost what is of infinite worth, hence their pain is infinite," says St. Alphonsus. How keenly does he suffer who is cut off from the sight of the beauty of creation by blindness; yet how much greater is his suffering who is deprived of the sight of the infinite beauty of God (St. John Damascene). The possession of God, the highest good, is the end of every rational being. This is evident from the way in which man in this life strives after the greatest happiness. This longing increases after death, for then the things of earth no longer distract the mind, nor can they give any more satisfaction. What an awful fate if this longing can never throughout eternity be satisfied! In the words of St. Augustine: "It is right that he who rejects God should be rejected of God." The sorrow of Esau in the loss of his father's blessing is but a type of the sorrow of the damned for the loss of the vision of God. The saints have trembled at the mere thought of this loss. The damned have no communication with the blessed. They may see them as the rich man saw Lazarus: "They see them not to their joy, but to their sorrow," says St. Vincent Ferrer, "they see them as a hungry man may look on a plenteous table which he may not touch." Besides this the damned have much to suffer from evil spirits; and it is meet that those who sided with and subjected themselves to the evil spirits on earth should be of their company after death. We are warned in the book of Job and in the case of the possessed persons in the Gospel, how cruel the devil is when he has a little power. What an awful experience it must be for the damned in hell, where the devil has full power! The damned in hell cause one another great suffering; for they hate one another. In that region of hatred of God there is no love of God. Hence the numbers in hell only increase its torments. Moreover fire will torture the lost souls. "They shall be sunk in fire like fish in the sea," says St. Alphonsus. And we learn from the teaching of Christ (Luke xvi. 24) and the holy Fathers that this fire is a real fire. Even on earth God punished by fire the sins of Sodom and Gomorrha (Gen. xix. 24; 4 Kings i. 14). "If," says Bellarmine, "the soul can be united to the body so as to suffer in company with it, so can the soul be reached by this avenging fire." Is it so much beyond almighty power that God could not call into being all those sensations in the soul, which the latter had while in the body? It is probable also that the fire of hell is not like fire as we know it on earth. Our fire destroys; that of hell does not consume but rather preserves, as salt preserves meat (Mark ix. 48); our fire gives light, while in hell there is darkness (Matt. xxii. 13). Our fire warms, while the fire of hell is accompanied by an insupportable cold, and moreover it is much more painful; "Our fire," says St. Vincent Ferrer, "is cold in comparison with that of hell." The soul suffers also from continual remorse of conscience. The lost are given up to despair; they recognize what fools they were to reject God's grace so often, and to prefer a passing pleasure to eternal happiness. How unhappy they are in losing forever that God Who loved them so much! And their shame is ever present, for their sins are revealed to all, and those whom they despised and laughed to scorn on earth are now in honor.

"They will be tortured with envy," says St. Anthony, "for they will envy the blessed their glory." Our experience on earth teaches us that mental suffering is often greater than bodily pain; suicides confirm this. After the resurrection the lost will have to suffer also in the body: "They shall come forth to the resurrection of judgment" (John v. 29). All their senses will receive punishment; the sight by darkness, the hearing by the wailing and cursing of the other lost souls (Matt. viii. 12), the taste by hunger (Luke vi. 25) and thirst (Luke xvi. 24), the smell by the unbearable stench, and the sense of touch by the torture of heat and cold. Other pains may be added; for instance, we read of wicked men whose bodies were devoured by worms (Acts xii. 23).

The tortures of the damned are eternal.

Satan with his followers is cast into a pool of fire and brimstone, where he will be tormented day and night forever (Apoc. xx. 10). In hell there is no redemption, for the day of grace is gone (John iii. 36). Life in hell is the "everlasting death" or "second death" (Apoc. xxi. 8), for a life without joy and full of torture is rather death than life. "O Death!" says Innocent III., "how sweet wouldst thou be to those to whom thou wert so bitter!" Christ tells us that the pains of hell are eternal; He calls the fire of hell an everlasting fire (Matt. xxv. 41), the torment of hell eternal (Matt. xxv. 46). So too teaches the Church in the Council of Trent. The error attributed to Origen (254 A.D.) that the punishment of hell came to an end was condemned by the Church (Council of Constantinople, ii., 553). "Eternal woe is due to him who destroys in himself eternal good," says St. Augustine. Our judges on earth inflict lifelong punishment on criminals, and even a sentence of death.

The torments of the damned are not all alike, but vary according to the sin.

"The punishments in hell are not all alike" (Council of Florence). According to St. Thomas they are as various as the sins committed on earth; they depend on the nature, number, and gravity of the sin. Those who have lived in pleasure shall be punished by a corresponding amount of suffering and torment (Apoc. xviii. 7). The inhabitants of Sodom and Gomorrha will have a lighter judgment than that city which rejected the apostles (Matt. x. 15).

2. The souls of those who die in mortal sin go to hell.

By grave sin a man cuts himself off from God; and in that state is like a branch broken off from Christ the vine, which withers and is cast into the fire (John xv. 6). The souls of those who die in mortal sin go at once into hell (Council of Lyons, ii.). In particular the following go to hell: the enemies of Christ (Ps. cix. 1), all those who refuse to believe in the Gospel (John iii. 18), the impure, thieves, covetous. railers (1 Cor. vi. 10), all who have neglected the talents given to them by God (Matt. xxv. 30); many who were among the first on earth (Matt. xix. 30). Those, too, who die with only original sin on their souls (unbaptized children) go to hell; (i.e., are excluded from the vision of God), but are not visited with the sufferings of those who have committed actual sin (Council of Lyons, ii.). A single mortal sin, done however secretly, is enough to send a man to eternal perdition.

Sinners begin their hell even on earth.

The wicked are like the raging sea which can never rest (Is. lvii. 20). Every sinner sits in "darkness and in the shadow of death" (Luke i. 79). To him the lessons of religion are folly (1 Cor. ii. 14). It is in the hour of death that the worldling will awake to his misery; at present he feels it not, because he is distracted by a thousand things. Think often about hell; the thought will keep us from sin. "Often go down to hell during thy lifetime, that thou mayst not have to go after death" (St. Bernard). "He who despises hell or forgets it," says St. John Chrysostom, "will not escape it."

5. PURGATORY.

1. Purgatory is a place where the souls of those must suffer for a time, who, though dying without grave sin on their souls, have not done complete penance for their offences against God.

Judas Machabeus was convinced that the souls of those who had died in battle with idols on them had to be punished, and for that reason ordered sacrifices to be offered for them in Jerusalem (2 Mach. xii. 43). "The stains which the soul has received during its sojourn in the body must be removed by the purging fire," says St. Gregory of Nyssa; and St. Gregory Nazianzen tells us that in the future life there is a baptism of fire, a hard and weary baptism, to destroy what is earthly in man. As to the situation of purgatory, most of the saints seem to think it is beneath the earth; hence the prayer of the Church: *A porta inferi*, etc. ("From the gates of hell deliver him, O Lord!") and the *De Profundis* ("Out of the depths I have cried to Thee, O Lord"). Some also believe that many souls, for a time at least, suffer their purgatory in those places on earth where their sins were committed, and that they are often present at the prayers which are offered for them. It is certain also that the holy souls have appeared to many saints, e.g., to St. Teresa, St. Bridget, St. Philip Neri. As to the state of the holy souls, the saints are of opinion that they suffer in all resignation to God's will. St. Catherine of Genoa tells us that God fills them with His love, so that their greatest pains become tolerable. Moreover the knowledge that they will finally attain the vision of God and that they are secure of their eternal salvation, gives them great consolation. "Besides," as St. Frances of Rome tells us, "they are comforted by the prayers of the faithful on earth, and the blessed in heaven, and by the visits of holy angels." "The consciousness that they are making atonement to God and suffering for Him makes them courageous as martyrs" (St. Catherine of Genoa).

The holy souls suffer in purgatory to expiate either their venial sins, or those mortal sins, which, though absolved, have not been completely atoned for.

Venial sins are visited with temporal punishment, as in the case of Zachary who doubted the angel, or Moses. Mortal sins also, though repented of and put away, are often visited with temporal punishment, as in the case of Adam and David. The Council of Trent (6, 30), teaches that whoever does not satisfy completely for his sins on earth, must do so in purgatory. So on earth a man may be punished by a fine; if he does not pay it he must go to prison. Hence we should not be satisfied with the penance given us by our confessor; we should add something of our own. Much may be done by patient enduring of sickness or willing acceptance of death. Not even the least sins should be neglected; they must all be atoned for.

The sufferings in purgatory include exclusion from the vision of God and other great pains.

Hence the prayer: "Grant rest to the souls of the faithful departed, and let perpetual light shine upon them." When we burn candles by the coffins or on the graves of the dead, we pray that the poor souls may be admitted to the sight of God. Apart from the duration, there is no distinction between the torments of hell and those of purgatory (St. Thomas). "The same fire," says St. Augustine, "burns the lost and the saved." Hence we see why the Church, in the Requiem Mass, prays God to deliver the souls from the pains of hell (Benedict XIV.). St. Augustine tells us that the pains of purgatory are greater than the sufferings of all the martyrs; and St. Thomas teaches that the least pain in purgatory is greater than the greatest on earth. "All the tortures that one can conceive of in this world are," says St. Cyril of Alexandria, "refreshing, compared with the least pain of purgatory."

The greatness and duration of the sufferings in purgatory vary according to the gravity of the sins.

St. Augustine tells us that those are longer in the purging fire who have been more attached to the goods of this world; that those who have grown old in sin take longer to pass through the cleansing stream. The foundation Masses going on for centuries, lead us to suppose that some souls have to suffer through many generations of men; were this impossible the Church would have abolished such Masses. Catherine Emmerich, in her revelations, says that Our Lord descends into purgatory every Good Friday, and frees one or more souls of those who had been witnesses of His Passion. Even where the punishment has lasted only an hour, we are told by St. Bridget, that it appears intolerably long. Those who wear the scapular are assured of a considerable shortening of their sufferings. Several saints hold the view that some souls suffer no pain but are merely excluded from the vision of God. According to St. Mathilda the sufferings in purgatory are in intimate relation to the past sins. St. Bridget saw souls suffering most in those things in which they had sinned most; and St. Margaret of Cortona saw some who could not be released till the evil done by them on earth had been made good.

2. That there is a purgatory we learn from the teaching of Christ, and especially from the practice and doctrine of the Church.

Moreover, it is a remarkable fact that nearly all the nations
of the earth believe in a purging fire. In addition we know
from sound reason that there must be a purgatory.

Christ's words are: " He that shall speak against the Holy Ghost,
it shall not be forgiven him, neither in this world nor in the world
to come" (Matt. xii. 32); He compares purgatory to a prison:
" Amen, I say to thee, thou shalt not go out from thence till thou
repay the last farthing" (Matt. v. 26). And St. Paul adds that
many shall be saved, yet so as by fire (1 Cor. iii. 15). The practice
of the Church in the following points reminds us of purgatory: the
prayer for the dead said in every Mass (the *Memento* after the
Consecration); the Masses for the dead, in particular those on All
Souls' Day, on the day of death and burial, and on anniversaries;
the passing-bell (which calls upon us to pray for the departed), and
the solemnities on All Souls' Day, which were first introduced in
998 by the abbot Odilo of Cluny, and later extended by the Popes to
the universal Church. St. John Chrysostom reminds us that
" the practices of Christians are not meant for mere show, but
that they are ordained by the Holy Spirit." The bishops of the
Church at Florence (1439), and Trent (1445-1463) expressly defined
that there is a purgatory. The idea of purgatory is common among
the nations. The Egyptians believed in the transmigration of souls
into animals. Among the Greeks we have the story of Prometheus,
condemned to be bound to a rock and his liver gnawed by a
vulture, because he stole fire from heaven. The Jews had the same
belief, for they offered sacrifice for the dead, as we saw in the case
of Judas Machabeus. The early Christians were accustomed to pray
for the dead during the holy sacrifice. St. Augustine relates that
his mother St. Monica, on her death-bed, said to him and his brother:
" Bury me where you will; only, I pray you, think of me always at
God's altar." St. John Chrysostom declares that the Christians from
the very beginning prayed during Mass for the dead by order of the
apostles. St. Cyril of Jerusalem writes: "It is of great service to
pray for the dead when the holy sacrifice is being offered." Hence
the oldest Mass-books contain prayers for the dead. Reason also
teaches that there must be a purgatory. We know, for instance,
that nothing defiled can enter heaven (Apoc. xxi. 27); yet there is
many a man not so wicked as to be lost forever; and if he can enter
neither heaven nor hell there must be a third place where he can be
purified.

**3. The faithful on earth can help the holy souls in purgatory
by good works; in particular by prayer, fasting, alms-deeds, by
offering or being present at Mass, by receiving the sacraments
and gaining indulgences.**

The holy souls cannot help themselves, since they can no longer
do good works to satisfy for their sins. After death "the night
cometh when no man can work" (John ix. 4). Hence they must pay
off their debt by enduring the pains which God has laid upon them.
Yet we on earth can help to diminish their pains by Masses, by
prayer and almsgiving, and other works of piety (Council of Lyons,
ii., 1274); the holy sacrifice is of all things the most helpful to

them (Council of Trent, 25), and according to St. Bonaventure the offering of holy communion is of very great assistance. " Not by weeping," says St. John Chrysostom, " but by prayer and almsgiving are the dead relieved." No pompous funeral nor profusion of wreaths are of any avail without good works; it is far more to the purpose to give to the poor the money which is spent on idle show.' As to the prayers, God does not regard so much their length as their fervor. Christ once said to St. Gertrude: " A single word from the heart has far more power to free a soul than the recital of many prayers and psalms without devotion; the hands are cleaned better by a little water and much rubbing than by merely pouring a large quantity of water over them." We are not to conclude from this that in ordinary cases a short prayer, an Our Father, for instance, will at once set free a soul. " For," says Maldonatus, " God would be very cruel if He kept a soul, for which He had shed His own blood, in such terrible suffering for the sake of an Our Father which had been omitted." The Church uses holy water in the burial service because it has great efficacy for the holy souls. But the greatest help which we can give is the Heroic Act, that is, the resignation in their behalf of all the satisfaction made to God by our good works. Those who make this act gain, every time they approach the Holy Table, a plenary indulgence applicable to the holy souls; and priests, who make the Heroic Act, have, every day they say Mass, the personal privilege of a privileged altar (Pius IX., Sept. 10, 1852).

The relatives of the departed are bound to help them.

To them apply the words of Holy Writ: " Have pity on me, at least you my friends, because the hand of the Lord hath touched me " (Job xix. 21). God sometimes reveals the unhappy state of the dead to their relatives. In the year 202 St. Perpetua saw in a dream her young brother imprisoned in a dark place, all covered with dirt, and parched with thirst. She began to offer up fervent prayer for him, and soon after he appeared again to her but this time beautiful and happy (Meh. vi., 413). When St. Elizabeth of Thuringia received news of the death of her mother Gertrude, Queen of Hungary, she began to pray and scourge herself with disciplines, and soon she had the satisfaction of seeing her mother in a vision, and of knowing that she was delivered from purgatory. Yet we should not rely too much on the good works which our relatives may do for us after death; for the proverb comes often only too true: " Out of sight, out of mind;" and besides, after all, the works done for us after death can avail us only to a limited extent. " One Mass devoutly heard during life," says St. Anselm, " is of more value than a great sum left for the celebration of a hundred Masses after death." " God," says St. Bonaventure, " values more a little voluntary penance done in this life than a severe and involuntary satisfaction in the next."

Prayer for the dead is of great benefit to ourselves, for it is a work of mercy.

It might be objected that by doing too much for the holy souls, a man neglects himself. But this is not true. Prayer confers a blessing on him who is prayed for, and on him who prays. He who has pity on the holy souls will find in God a merciful Judge: " Blessed are the

merciful, for they shall obtain mercy" (Matt. v. 7); Christ accepts
every deed of mercy as a favor done to Himself (Cf. Matt. xxv. 40);
the departed also display their gratitude when they get to heaven.
Says Marie Lataste: "Thou canst do nothing more acceptable to God
or profitable to thyself than to pray for the holy souls; for they will
be mindful of your favors in heaven, and will pray unceasingly for
you . . . that you may become holier in life and be freed from purgatory soon after death." "It is a holy and wholesome thought to
pray for the dead, that they may be loosed from sins" (2 Mach. xii.
46).

6. THE RESURRECTION OF THE BODY.

The Jews had some sort of belief that the bodies of the dead
would rise again. Job consoled himself in the midst of his sufferings by the thought of the resurrection (Job xix. 25); so too the
brothers Machabees (2 Mach. vii. 11); and Martha said to Jesus:
"I know that my brother will rise again in the resurrection at the
Last Day" (John xi. 24).

**Christ on the Last Day will raise the bodies of all men from
the dead, and unite them to the soul forever.**

1. He often declared that He would raise the bodies of all
men from the grave, and proved His power by miracles; this
resurrection will be heralded by many signs in nature.

We proclaim in the Apostles' Creed that Christ will come to judge
the living and the dead; that is, He will call to life the bodies of those
who are already dead, while for those who survive till that day such
a change will take place in their bodies that in a moment they will die
and awake again to a new life (1 Thess. iv. 16); those will arise who
are in the grace of God as well as those who are in mortal sin (John
v. 28; Matt. xxv. 31); and this resurrection will take place in a moment (1 Cor. xv. 52). Christ announced that He would raise the
dead to life again: "The hour cometh wherein all that are in the
graves shall hear the voice of the Son of God. And they that have
done good things shall come forth unto the resurrection of life; but
they that have done evil unto the resurrection of judgment" (John v.
28, 29); on another occasion: "He that eateth My flesh and drinketh
My blood hath everlasting life, and I will raise him up in the Last
Day" (John vi. 55). Our Lord often compared death to sleep, e.g.,
when He said that the daughter of Jairus (Matt. ix. 24) and Lazarus
(John xi. 11) were sleeping. In face of the fact of the resurrection
death may well be called a sleep (1 Thess. iv. 13). The following
miracles were performed by Christ in proof of His power to raise the
dead; the raising of the daughter of Jairus in her own house, that of
the son of the widow of Naim before the gates of the city, and that of
Lazarus from the grave itself. We might add His own glorious
resurrection and that of His Virgin Mother. In very truth Christ
might say of Himself: "I am the resurrection and the life" (John
xi. 25). Many natural phenomena show that the idea of the resurrection is in harmony with the rest of nature; for instance, our own
periods of rest and activity, the reawakening of spring after the

winter sleep; the change in many insects of the larva into the pupa, and of the pupa again into the butterfly; the coming forth of the bird from the egg, the sprouting of the seed buried in the earth, and so on.

2. God will awake our bodies to life again to prove His justice, and to honor Our Redeemer.

If the soul only were rewarded, there would be a want of completeness; " for," as Tertullian says, " there are many good works, such as fasting, chastity, martyrdom, which can be carried out in their perfection only in the body; hence it is right that the latter should share in the reward of the soul." God's justice demands that the body should take part in the triumph. Again, Tertullian reminds us that Our Saviour redeemed mankind body and soul. Had the body been unredeemed the devil would have secured a triumph by destroying it. Such a thought is unworthy. " By a man came death, and by a man the resurrection of the dead " (1 Cor. xv. 21).

3. As to the state of our bodies after the resurrection, we have the following facts: (1). After the resurrection we shall have the same bodies as we now have. (2). The bodies of the just will be glorious and those of the wicked hideous. (3). All the risen bodies will be without defect and immortal.

We shall have the same bodies after the resurrection: " For this corruptible must put on incorruption, and this mortal must put on immortality " (1 Cor. xv. 53). This we learn also from the Athanasian Creed. Even Job knew it to be true: " I shall be clothed again with my skin, and in my flesh I shall see my God " (Job xix. 26) : and one of the Machabean brothers, in the midst of his torments addressed the tyrant thus as his limbs were being torn away: " These I have from heaven but for the laws of God I now despise them; because I hope to receive them again from Him " (2 Mach. vii. 11). While St. Perpetua and her fellow martyrs were being exposed to the vulgar gaze of the heathens, she addressed them thus: " Look well and mark now our faces, that you may know them again in the Day of Judgment; " and her words converted many of the bystanders. For this reason we rise in our bodies " that every one may receive the proper things of the body, according as he hath done whether it be good or evil " (2 Cor. v. 10). It is not beyond God's power to rejoin the scattered elements of our bodies; if He could make that which had no existence, He can replace that which already has had an existence. St. Thomas teaches us that just as our bodies remain the same bodies over periods of ten or twenty years, in which time the component elements have been renewed again and again, so the bodies of the risen will be the same, even supposing they are not composed of the same identical elements as before. It is the thought of the resurrection that makes Christians careful in the burial of the dead, and in their veneration of the relics of the saints. Our risen bodies will not be all alike. " We shall all rise again; but we shall not all be changed " (1 Cor. xv. 51). The bodies of the just will resemble the glorified body of Christ (Phil. iii. 21), and will have the following properties: they will be impassible (Apoc. xxi. 4), shining like the sun (Matt. xiii. 43), swift as thought, and capable of penetrating

matter. The word spiritual is sometimes used to describe the
risen body, because the latter will be quite subject to the spirit and
freed from earthly concupiscence (Luke xx. 35). The beauty of the
body will be in proportion to that of the soul (Rom. viii. 11; 1 Cor. xv.
41). The most wretched cripple, if he has lived a good life, will have
a beautiful body; while one who has had every personal charm and
lived a bad life, will rise again to be an object of aversion. The
bodies of sinners will have to suffer, and will be bound hand and foot
(Matt. xxii. 13). The risen bodies will be without any defect. The
martyrs will recover their limbs, and their wounds, visible like
Christ's, will be glorious and resplendent. The risen bodies will also
have no trace of old age, sickness, or mutilation. The wicked will
have their bodies also complete, but for punishment; for the more
perfect the body is the more it can suffer. All the bodies of the risen
will be immortal (1 Cor. xv. 42). Just as in paradise the fruit of the
tree of life gave immortality to the body, so now the Blessed Sacrament in communion, for it is a pledge of the resurrection and of immortality (John vi. 55). The bodies of the damned are also immortal, but for their torment.

4. Belief in the resurrection is a great help to us; it con-
soles us in our sufferings, and comforts our relatives and friends
when we come to die.

Job cheered himself with this reflection (Job xix. 25); and it was
belief in the resurrection which gave the early Christians such courage and calm in the great persecutions. Christians who believe in
the resurrection ought not to mourn for their dead like the heathen
who have no hope (1 Thess. iv. 12). St. Cyprian, Bishop of Carthage
(258 A.D.), used to caution his flock against such excessive grief, lest
the heathen should come to think that the Christians had no firm
belief in the life to come. Hence he considered it unbecoming to
wear mourning for those who were rejoicing before the throne of
God. Those only should be mourned for who died in mortal sin.

7. *THE GENERAL JUDGMENT.*

1. **Immediately after the resurrection the general judgment
will take place.**

For Christ has often said that after the resurrection all mankind will be assembled before Him to be judged.

The return of Christ as Judge was announced to the apostles by
the angels on the occasion of Our Lord's ascent into heaven (Acts
i. 11). Christ Himself spoke about the judgment in the following
terms: (1). The form of a cross is to appear in the heavens announcing the coming of Christ: and the sight of it will fill the wicked with
confusion (Matt. xxiv. 30). (2). Christ will come in great power
and majesty (Matt. xvi. 27; Luke xxi. 27). Hence we cannot conclude that the divine essence will be manifested to all at the judgment, for this no man could see without being rapt in heavenly joy.
According to St. Thomas, the lost will have some sort of perception
of God's majesty and essence. Possibly they will see it as manifested

through the veil of the sacred humanity of Christ at the Judgment.
(3). The holy angels will accompany Our Saviour (Matt. xxv. 31).
They helped to the salvation of mankind and now they will receive
their meed of honor. (4). All the nations of the earth will be assembled before Christ seated on His throne (Matt. xxv. 32). (5). He will
separate the sheep and the goats; the blessed will be placed on His
right hand, and the lost on His left (Matt. xxv. 33). When the
prophets speak of the judgment being held in the valley of Josaphat
(Joel iii. 2), they do not mean that the nations will be gathered into
that particular valley lying between Jerusalem and Mount Olivet;
they mean simply that mankind will be assembled in the vale of the
"judgment of God" (Josaphat in Hebrew means the judgment of
God), i.e., in some place appointed by God for this judgment. We
speak of the general judgment because angels as well as men will be
judged (Jude 6), and of the Last Judgment because it will be held
on the Last Day.

2. The general judgment will take place in order that God's
wisdom and justice may be made manifest to all creatures.
Christ will be Judge in order that the honor of which He was
robbed may be restored to Him before all creation.

On this day God will reveal to men with what wisdom He disposed the career of mankind and of each individual, so that all might
attain their end and be happy even on earth. It will then be seen
how various kinds of evil, the sufferings and even the sins of men
have been turned by God to their advantage. Much which the world
now esteems foolishness will then be seen to have been wisdom. This
judgment will also demonstrate God's justice; He will then bring
forward what could not have been brought forward at the particular
judgment. The deeds, words, writings, of many men have produced
their results often only after their death; what blessings, for instance,
apostles and missionaries have conferred on whole nations, and what
harm has been done by heretics, not only to their contemporaries, but
to those coming after them. Christ will be Judge, this office demanding wisdom in an especial degree, and Christ is the eternal wisdom. Moreover He will be Judge because the honor due to Him
was refused by so many and by all irreligious and godless men ever
since. He was condemned as a malefactor by Pilate and, as the Apostle says, "Christ crucified was to the Jews a stumbling block, and to
the Gentiles foolishness" (1 Cor. i. 23). Then will His enemies call
upon the mountains to fall upon them, and the hills to hide them
(Luke xxiii. 30); hence Christ's words: "For neither doth the Father
judge any man, but hath given all judgment to the Son. That all
men may honor the Son as they honor the Father" (John v. 22).
When Christ was on earth He repudiated all judicial power: "I
judge not any man" (John viii. 15). Christ is Judge at the Last
Day because He became man: "The Father hath given Him power
to do judgment because He is the Son of man" (John v. 27). God's
mercy, too, has ordained that the Judge of mankind should be a man.
No wonder St. Thomas of Villanova exclaimed in ecstasy, "Happy
am I to have my Saviour for my Judge."

3. Christ will conduct the judgment in the following man-

ner: He will reveal all, even the most hidden things, will exact
an account from all men of the works of mercy they have or
ought to have performed, and by a final sentence separate forever
the good from the bad.

The general judgment is thus a solemn repetition of the particular judgment; and it might also be called a repetition of the world's
history, for each event will be represented to the eyes of the assembled multitude: "And the books were opened . . . and the dead
were judged by those things which were written in the books according to their works" (Apoc. xx. 12). The Lord "will bring to light
the hidden things of darkness" (1 Cor. iv. 5). He "will search Jerusalem with lamps" (Sophon. i. 12). It is to the general judgment
that these words of Our Lord apply: "There is not anything secret
that shall not be made manifest, nor hidden that shall not be
known and come abroad" (Luke viii. 17). When the sun rises the
snows melt and leave bare all that lies beneath them; so shall it be
when the Sun of justice mounts the heavens. All sins will be revealed, and the revelation will be worse than hell to the sinner,
while to the just there will be glory because they did penance. "The
white robe of sanctifying grace," as St. Gertrude tells us, "will hide
the sin, and instead of the stains which were removed by penance
there will be ornaments of gold." All good works will then be revealed
(Eccles. xii. 14), and the secrets of men's hearts shall be known
(1 Cor. iv. 5). The martyrs will receive honor for the contempt
which they endured, and sinners will exclaim as they look on the
just: "These are they whom we had some time in derision and for a
parable of reproach. We fools, esteemed their life madness and their
end without honor. Behold how they are numbered among the children of God and their lot is among the saints" (Wisd. v. 3-5).
Works of mercy will be required of every man (Matt. xxv. 34-36);
the Gospel explains to us why the saints and all pious Christians are
so eager in the performance of works of mercy. When people asked
St. Elizabeth why she was so zealous in good works, she used to
answer: "I am preparing for the Day of Judgment." There will be
no question then of riches or social position, for God is no respecter
of persons (Rom. ii. 11); on the contrary: "to whomsoever much is
given, of him much shall be required" (Luke xii. 48). The judgment will end with the sentence of the Judge, which will divide forever the good from the bad (Matt. xxv. 46). This separation was
foreshadowed in the parable of the cockle: "Gather up first the cockle
and bind it in bundles to burn, but the wheat gather ye into My
barn" (Matt. xiii. 30). Many friends and relatives will be separated
forever on that day (Matt. xxiv. 40); many who were rich and powerful will be lost, and their dependents, or those who sued as beggars
to them, will be saved. "Then, too," says St. Augustine, "creation
will take on a new and glorious form, to correspond to the glorified
bodies of the elect." "We look for new heavens and a new earth
according to His promises, in which justice dwelleth" (2 Pet. iii.
13). The existing universe will be destroyed by fire, and this fire
will purge those who have yet to do penance for sin; and since there
will be no purgatory after the Day of Judgment the want of duration
will be made up by the intensity of the pain; as for the just, they,

like the three children in the furnace, will remain untouched by the flames. The thought of the judgment is a wholesome one. St. Methodius had a picture executed for the King of the Bulgarians, representing the dividing of the good from the bad at the Last Day; the king could never expel the image from his mind, and in consequence became a Christian and promoted Christianity with great zeal in his kingdom. In the Acts we read (Acts xxiv. 25) how Felix trembled when St. Paul spoke of the judgment to come; yet Felix does not seem to have acted up to grace, for he broke off the discourse and gave up St. Paul to the Jews.

2. The Day of Judgment is unknown to us, though certain signs have been revealed which are to herald its approach.

Christ said: " Of that day and hour no one knoweth; no not the angels of heaven, but the Father alone " (Matt. xxiv. 36). The knowledge of it would be of as little use as the knowledge of the hour of our death. St. Augustine recommends us to do now as we should do if to-morrow were to be the Last Day: then we shall have no occasion to dread the coming of the Judge. Christ gave some signs of the approach of the Last Day (Matt. xxiv. 3, etc.), so that Christians might remain steadfast and courageous. The signs are:

1. The Gospel shall be preached to the whole world (Matt. xxiv. 14).

Some two-thirds of the world are still pagans.

2. The greater part of mankind will be without faith (Luke xviii. 8; 2 Thess. ii. 3) and immersed in things of earth (Luke xvii. 26, etc.).

Mankind will be much as they were in the days of Noe (Matt. xxiv. 38).

3. Antichrist will appear.

Antichrist is a man who will give himself out to be Christ, and by the help of the devil will perform many wonders (2 Thess. ii. 9). He will be a terror by the persecution which he will raise (Apoc. xx. 3-9). It is probable that he will choose for his kingdom Jerusalem and those places where Christ lived. Our Lord will kill him on the Last Day (2 Thess. ii. 8). Types and forerunners of Antichrist have existed from time to time (1 John ii. 18), " for the mystery of iniquity already worketh " (2 Thess. ii. 7).

4. Henoch and Elias will return and preach penance.

" Behold I will send you Elias the prophet before the coming of the great and dreadful day of the Lord. And he shall turn the hearts of the fathers to the children and the hearts of the children to their fathers " (Mal. iv. 5) ; i.e., he will bring round the Jews to the sentiments of their forefathers, the patriarchs: Christ also foretold that Elias should come and restore all things (Matt. xvii. 11). Of Henoch we know that " Henoch pleased God and was translated into paradise that he may give repentance to the nations " (Ecclus. xliv. 16). Henoch and Elias will preach for three years and a half, and recover many souls from Antichrist, who in the end will kill them, and their bodies will be left unburied. After three days and a half God will raise them to life again (Apoc. xi. 3-11).

5. The Jews will be converted.

The conversion of the Jews was foretold by Osee: " The children of Israel shall sit many days without king, and without prince, and without sacrifice, and without altar, and without ephod, and without theraphim. And after this the children of Israel shall return and shall seek the Lord their God and David their king; and they shall fear the Lord and His goodness in the last days " (Osee iii. 4-5); blindness was to be the lot of Israel until the fulness of the Gentiles should come in (Rom. xi. 25). Elias is to restore the tribes of Jacob (Ecclus. xlviii. 10).

6. Dreadful signs will appear in the heavens and great tribulations will come upon mankind.

" The sun shall be darkened and the moon shall not give her light, and the stars shall fall from heaven and the powers of the heavens shall be moved " (Matt. xxiv. 29); war, pestilence, and famine shall come as at the time of the siege of Jerusalem (Matt. xxiv. 7, etc.). Men shall wither with fear and from expectation of the things that will come upon the earth (Luke xxi. 25).

CHRISTIAN HOPE.

1. THE ESSENCE OF CHRISTIAN HOPE.

Christian hope is the confident expectation of all those things which Christ promised us with regard to the fulfilment of God's will.

" Hope," says St. Paulinus, " gives us a foretaste of the promised joys of paradise." " How great is the multitude of Thy sweetness, O Lord . . . which Thou hast wrought for them that hope in Thee " (Ps. xxx. 20). Such hope may be called *holy,* because directed to God and supernatural things; by this is fulfilled the precept of the Apostle: " Seek the things that are above" (Col. iii. 1).

1. As the reward of carrying out God's will, Christ has promised us eternal happiness, and the means required for attaining it; in particular God's grace, temporal goods for the sustaining of life, forgiveness of sins, help in our necessities, and the answering of our prayers.

Christ promised us eternal happiness (1 John ii. 25); " In the house of My Father are many mansions. If not I would have told you that I go to prepare a place for you " (John xiv. 2); He has further promised to raise our bodies again after death (John v. 28). The desire for perfect happiness is planted deep in our nature. Christ also promised His grace, i.e., the help of the Holy Spirit, for His will is that all men be saved (1 Tim. ii. 4). Grace is absolutely necessary for salvation: actual grace for our conversion, sanctifying grace for entrance into heaven. Temporal goods are promised: " Be not solicitous for your life what you shall eat, nor for your body what you shall put on. . . . For your Father knoweth that you have need of all these things," and we are taught that since the Father feeds the birds of the air, and clothes the weeds of the field, much more will be His care for us (Matt. vi. 25-32). The experience of the saints in this matter is a great consolation and lesson to us; over and over again they have been in difficulties for the means of subsistence, yet help always came. Forgiveness of sin is assured to us if we wish to amend: " There shall be joy in heaven upon one sinner that doth penance, more than over ninety-nine just who need not penance " (Luke xv. 7). The parable of the prodigal son and of the lost sheep reveal to us how readily God will forgive the sinner: " So long as we are on the earth it is never too late to repent," says St. Cyprian. The penitent thief on the cross found salvation. " God wills not the death of the sinner, but that he be converted and live " (Ezech. xviii. 32). We are certain of help in our necessities. When the apostles were filled with fear at the storm on the lake, Christ's reproach to them was: " Why do you fear, O ye of little faith? " (Matt. viii. 26). God is called the " helper in tribulations " (Ps. xlv. 2). It is true He seems at times to delay answering our prayers, as in the marriage-feast at Cana, when He said: " My hour is not yet come " (John ii. 4); yet the longer we have to wait, the more wonderful is His answer, and we might reflect on the calming of the storm on the lake, on the release of St. Peter from prison, on the fate of Aman, the persecutor of the Jews (Esther vii.). " When our necessity is greatest," says St. Ambrose, " God's help is nearest." Christ promised that our petitions shall always be heard: " If you shall ask Me anything in My name, that will I do " (John xiv. 14). " Amen, Amen, I say to you; if you ask the Father anything in My name, He will give it you " (John xvi. 23).

Christ taught us in the Our Father to ask our heavenly Father for all these things.

The second petition is a prayer for salvation, the third for grace, the fourth for temporal necessities, the fifth for forgiveness of sins, the sixth and seventh for help in our needs.

2. Christian hope is based on faith, for we hope for the fulfilment of God's promises because we believe that God is infinitely true, infinitely powerful, and infinitely good, and that Christ has merited all for us.

" We are firmly convinced," says St. Clement of Rome, " that He Who forbade deceit cannot Himself deceive." Hence the words of St. Paul: " Let us hold fast the confession of our hope without wavering, for He is faithful that hath promised " (Heb. x. 23). Moreover, we are convinced that God, to Whom nothing is impossible (Luke i. 37), is able to carry out His promises (Rom. iv. 18); that God, Who is love itself (1 John iv. 8), is more ready to give than we are to receive (St. Jerome); that Christ, by His death on the cross, has merited for us salvation and all things necessary for its attainment. Thus St. Augustine, " I could never hope for pardon or heaven when I think of my great sins, but I venture to hope that through the merits of Christ I may be saved by means of penance and keeping of the commandments."

3. He only who carries out God's will can hope for the good things promised by Christ.

" Not every one that saith to Me, Lord, Lord. shall enter into the kingdom of heaven, but he that doth the will of My Father Who is in heaven " (Matt. vii. 21).

Hence the sinner can hope in God only when he really repents and is willing to reform his life.

" Hope without virtue is presumption," says St. Bernard. If the wicked do penance for their sins and do judgment and justice, God will no more remember their sins (Ezech. xviii. 21). Manasses, King of Israel, led his people into idolatry and put the prophets to death. For this he was given over to his enemies and led in chains to Babylon. There he repented and promised amendment. God then set him free, and gave him back his kingdom, and Manasses destroyed the temples of the idols and did much good (2 Paralip. xxxiii.).

The just man may hope that God will provide for all his needs; yet he must exert himself to gain those things which he hopes for from God.

Christ's words are: " Seek first the kingdom of God and His justice, and all other things shall be added unto you " (Matt. vi. 33). We are God's servants. As St. John of the Cross says: " It is our affair to serve the Lord; it is His to provide for us." No one who has been faithful to God's commands has ever been abandoned by Him (Ecclus. ii. 12). " We are unjust to God if we do not place great confidence in Him," says St. Augustine. " Cast all your care upon the Lord, for He hath care of you " (1 Pet. v. 7). We must not, however, desist from exerting ourselves; we must use those gifts which God has given to us; for God will give us only what we cannot obtain by our own exertions. In the words of St. Charles Borromeo: " We must hope for the best and do our best." " To expect help and to do nothing," says St. Francis of Sales, " is to tempt God." We ought to employ the natural means at our disposal; St. Paul, for example, though he had the gift of healing sickness, recommended Timothy to take a little wine for the sake of his health (1 Tim. v. 23). And all this is true of any kind of necessity: " Help yourself and God will help you."

4. A wholesome fear of falling into sin must always accompany Christian hope.

God's will is that we should work out our salvation in fear and trembling (Phil. ii. 12). No one has complete assurance that he belongs to the number of the elect, or that he will persevere in virtue till death (Council of Trent, 6, Can. 15, 16). Many an old and rotten ship has reached harbor, while many a great and noble vessel has sunk in the sea. Men, illumined of God, like Solomon, have fallen into godless ways before their death, and many a great sinner, like St. Augustine or St. Mary Magdalen, has become a very great saint.

" He that thinketh himself to stand take heed lest he fall" (1 Cor. x. 12). "We carry our treasure in frail and earthen vessels" (2 Cor. iv. 7). "Mistrust of ourselves," says St. Augustine, "should help us to hope." Hope and fear are companions; where they reign, the heavenly crown is easily secured (St. John Chrysostom). Hope makes us strong and fear makes us prudent. Hope is like the breeze to a ship, driving it in to the harbor; fear is like the ballast, steadying it and preventing shipwreck. Fear, so far from diminishing hope, increases it. "Trust in God and distrust of ourselves," says St. Francis of Sales, "are like the two arms of a balance; as one rises the other goes down; the more we distrust ourselves, the more we confide in God, and *vice versa.*"

5. Christian hope is necessary for salvation.

A man who has no hope will not do good works, nor avoid sin; while he who has hope is secure of his salvation, just as a man is certain of a plant when he has the seed; "for we are saved by hope" (Rom. viii. 24). "Belief in God's truth, His almighty power, and His love for us, is a triple cord," says St. Bernard, "which is let down into our prison from heaven; to this we must cling so that it may raise us to the vision of His glory." "The house of God (i.e., holiness which leads to salvation)," says St. Augustine, "is founded on faith, built up on hope, and finished in love." In heaven there is no more hope, for we shall then possess all that we hoped for.

6. Christian hope is a gift of God, and we can attain to this hope only by sanctifying grace.

In this respect we may speak of hope almost in the same words in which we spoke of faith. It is the Spirit of God which awakens in us a longing for heavenly things, and fills us with confidence in God. As sanctifying grace increases, this power of hoping increases; hence the saints hoped most at the approach of death. Hope, like a river, becomes wider as it approaches the sea.

2. THE ADVANTAGE OF CHRISTIAN HOPE.

1. He who hopes in God enjoys the special protection of God.

Examples may be seen in the three children in the furnace, in Joseph in the Egyptian prison, in our blessed Lady when St. Joseph had thoughts of putting her away. Modern history has also its examples, as when Vienna was besieged by the Turks in 1683. Two hundred and fifty thousand Turks were investing the city, which was defended by a garrison of sixteen thousand Christians. Again and again were the enemy repulsed, though the ramparts had been undermined and blown up. Yet as the case of the Christians became more desperate, so increased their trust in God; and at the last extremity there appeared Sobieski's force, an army of some ninety thousand men. The battle lasted but a day, and the Turks were put to complete rout. God protects those who hope in Him (Dan. xiii. 60). "A Christian whose hope is in God may be oppressed, but he cannot be overcome," says St. Cyprian. "Such a one," adds St. Francis of Sales, "is like a general backed by a strong reserve." "They that trust in the Lord shall be as Mount Sion" (Ps. cxxiv. 1). If a man

puts his entire confidence in God, God takes him under His special
protection, and he may be certain that no harm will come to him
(St. Vincent of Paul). The greater our confidence in God, the more
certainly will He protect us and come to our help in all dangers (St.
Francis of Sales). No one hath hoped in the Lord and been confounded (Ecclus. ii. 11). " We will not have you as the heathens that
have no hope " (1 Thess. iv. 12).

**2. He who hopes in God can obtain everything from Him; for
Christ said that such a one might move mountains (Mark xi. 23).**

St. Gregory Thaumaturgus did literally move a mountain. Such
was the confidence of Moses when he divided the Red Sea with his
staff, and of Elias when he prayed for rain. "Hope is an arrow
which pierces the Heart of Christ, and opens the founts of His
mercy to the soul that hopes in Him." " A man gets just as much as
he hopes for " (St. John of the Cross).

**3. He who hopes in God is strengthened by God, so that he is
not afraid of man, and is patient and courageous in suffering, and
more especially in face of death.**

We have examples in David before Goliath and Leo before Attila.
St. Martin was once attacked by robbers who threatened his life;
when they asked why he did not fear, he made reply: "I am a Christian and under God's protection. I have no need to fear; on the contrary, it is you who ought to be afraid." The man whose trust is in
God troubles himself little about the favors of the great or the sayings of his fellow-men; such was St. Paul's attitude (1 Cor. iv. 3).
He who puts his trust in God will be patient in suffering, for he
knows "that the sufferings of this time are not worthy to be compared with the glory to come that shall be revealed in us " (Rom. viii.
18). Job was patient in the midst of his sufferings because he looked
forward to the resurrection (Job xix. 25). How can he be unhappy
who looks to the unspeakable reward of heaven? St. Paul calls to us
amid his sufferings: "I exceedingly abound with joy in all our tribulations" (2 Cor. vii. 4). "To die is gain . . . having a desire to
be dissolved and to be with Christ" (Phil. i. 21-23); and again, " As
to the rest, there is laid up for me a crown of justice, which the Lord,
the just Judge, will render to me in that day" (2 Tim. iv. 8). So joyful was the death of St. Andrew (62 A.D.), that when he saw the cross
on which he was to die, he exclaimed: " Hail, blessed cross, sanctified
by the death of my God; with transports of joy I come to you: how
long have I sought you, how long have I desired you ! " St. Ignatius (107 A.D.), Bishop of Antioch, rejoiced when he heard his condemnation from the mouth of the Emperor Trajan: and when the
Christians in Rome were planning to set him free, he prayed them
not to deprive him of his martyr's crown: "I fear neither the beasts
nor the rending of my limbs, if only I can win Christ: " and so we
find innumerable instances in the lives of the saints. Hope is the
anchor of the soul (Heb. vi. 19). Like the eagle soaring into the
light of the sun, it rises above the cares and sorrows of earth.

**4. He who hopes in God is impelled to the performance of good
works and of heroic acts.**

This is the secret of the zeal of missionaries in the land of the heathen. The hope of the Christian is something more solid than that of the husbandman, or the warrior, or the artist. "He hopes for that which Truth itself has promised," says St. Paulinus. Our hope is as certain as though it were already an accomplished fact (St. Augustine).

3. THE OBJECT OF CHRISTIAN HOPE.

The Christian may not hope for more or less than what God has promised.

1. The Christian may not rely on his own powers, on his fellow-men, nor on earthly things more than upon God; otherwise he is sure to fail, because outside of God nothing is to be relied upon.

The hope of him who relies only on earthly means is not a heavenly nor a Christian hope, but merely human hope. St. Peter boasted of his strength, and yet he denied his Lord. Goliath trusted in his might, and he came to nought. St. Francis Borgia gave all his service to his patron, the Empress Isabella; she died and then he recognized the folly of it. It is better to trust in the Lord than to trust to men (Ps. cxvii. 8). To build on the favor of men is to raise one's house on sand or snow. Those who put their trust in men will perish like the priests of Baal on Mount Carmel (3 Kings xviii.). He who relies on his own strength and not upon God has only himself for protector; God will not protect him because he does not hope in His protection (St. Augustine).

2. The Christian may not despair; i.e., he may not give up hoping that God will forgive his sins, or help him in adversity.

Cain despaired when he said: "My sin is too great to be forgiven" (Gen. iv. 13). Saul despaired by throwing himself on his sword when hard pressed in battle by the Philistines (1 Kings xxxi.).

The Christian may not despair, because God's mercy is infinite, and God's help is nearest when the need is greatest.

"Before sinning fear God's justice," says St. Gregory the Great; "after sinning trust in His mercy." Who would doubt of being able to pay off his paltry debts if he were placed before a kingly treasure and told to help himself ? Much less should we doubt of God's mercy. "As a spark is to the ocean, so is the wickedness of man compared to the mercy of God," says St. John Chrysostom. The greater a sinner is, the dearer is he to God in his repentance, for more glory is given to God when the sins that He forgives are very great.

Despair often ends in suicide and everlasting death.

Judas is an example of this. Despair is a sin against the Holy Ghost, and as such is never forgiven. "Hope," says St. Isidore, "opens heaven's gates, while despair closes them." St. Augustine says that he who despairs of God's mercy, dishonors God as though he did not believe in His existence; and St. Jerome adds that the sin of Judas in despairing of God's mercy was greater than his sin of betraying Christ. He who sins kills his soul, but he who despairs is already in hell.

3. The Christian must never presume on his trust in God's mercy, i.e., he may not continue sinning with the idea that God's mercy can never condemn him to hell.

Confidence in God and fear of God must ever be equally present in us. It is wrong that there should be only fear of God without trust in Him, for this is despair. It is also wrong that there should be no fear at all; if a man thinks his salvation already secure he sins by presumption. "Despise not God's mercy," says St. Bernard, "if you would escape His justice." Christ says: "Unless you shall do penance, you shall all likewise perish" (Luke xiii. 3). No man may safely say to himself, "I can always do penance for this sin," or, "I will reform before my death."

4. The Christian may never tempt God; i.e., he must never expose himself rashly to danger in the hope that God will save him.

He only can hope for help who does what God requires of him. He who is indifferent to God's will, and acts with thoughtless rashness, is deserted by God. Hence: "He that loveth danger shall perish in it" (Ecclus. iii. 27). The devil urged Our Lord to tempt God by throwing Himself from the pinnacle of the Temple (Matt. iv. 6). So a man who should refuse to call in a doctor or to take medicines in a dangerous sickness, on the plea that God would come to his help, would be tempting God. Those who in the first ages of Christianity exposed themselves without reasonable cause to martyrdom were not accounted martyrs even when they died for the faith.

Part II

A. THE COMMANDMENTS.

I. WHAT COMMANDMENTS (OR LAWS) HAS GOD GIVEN US?

As God gave fixed laws to the heavenly bodies (Ps. cxlviii. 6), so He also gave commandments, or laws, unto men.

. God has given us commandments in order to make us happy in time and in eternity.

God never commands anything except for the greater good of those to whom He gives the command. He only imposes laws on us out of kindness, that He may have occasion to reward us. A heathen sage says: " Without laws the human race would be no better than wild beasts of prey, the stronger devouring and destroying the weaker."

1. God has imprinted the natural law on the heart of every man; this forms the fundamental rule of human actions.

A young child who has done something wrong—lied, perhaps, or committed a theft, feels uncomfortable, frightened, or ashamed; though it may never have heard of the Ten Commandments, it is conscious that it has done amiss. It is the same with the heathen who knows nothing about God's commandments. Hence we may conclude that there is a *law of nature* in every human heart, a law not written upon it, but inborn in it; an intuitive knowledge of right and wrong. St. Paul declares that the Gentiles do by nature those things that are of the law (what the Ten Commandments enjoin), and consequently they will be judged by God according to the natural law (Rom. ii. 14-16). The characters wherein this law is inscribed upon our hearts may be obscured but not obliterated; the Roman Catechism tells us no man can be unconscious of this law, divinely imprinted upon his understanding. This natural law teaches us the most important rules of morality. e.g., that homage is due to almighty God; that no man must wilfully injure himself; that we must not do to others what we would not have others do to us: furthermore from this moral code certain inferences directly follow; these are the Ten Commandments of God (the observance of the Sabbath excepted). Thus the natural law does not consist of a series of truths founded on reason, but is a definite expression of the will of God, which it is binding upon us to obey, and of which in individual cases we are made acquainted by means of reason. This consciousness of God's will is conscience. Hence it is erroneous to say reason is itself the law.

2. In addition to this natural law, God gave to man solemn precepts, more especially the Ten Commandments and the two precepts of charity. These are known as the revealed law.

To the *revealed law* appertain: (1). The pre-Mosaic law, given by God to Noe and Abraham; e.g., He forbade the former to eat flesh with blood (Gen. ix. 4), upon the latter He imposed the law of circumcision (Gen. xvii. 11). (2). The Mosaic law, which was given to the Jews through Moses. To this belong: The Decalogue; the regulations of divine worship, the civil law of the Jews. The Ten Commandments were not annulled by Christ (Matt. v. 17), but fulfilled, as the outline of a picture is not effaced, but filled in by the painter. The regulations of public worship (relating to the sacrifices, the Temple, etc.), were abolished at the death of Christ, because the ceremonial observances of the Old Testament were merely typical of the Redeemer. The civil law (regulating the social relations of the Jews) was exclusively suited to the Hebrew people. (3). The Christian law, comprising the two precepts of charity. This chiefly requires the practice of works of mercy, and interior spiritual worship (John iv. 24), whereas the Jewish law ordained the performance of exterior acts and ceremonies. The Mosaic law was written on tables of stone, but the commandments of charity are written within our hearts by the Holy Spirit (Heb. viii. 10); that is to say, the Holy Ghost enlightens the understanding that we may perceive them, and influences the will that we may follow them. The former laws were imperfect (Heb. vii. 19); the Christian law is perfect, for obedience to it brings man nearer to his ultimate goal, eternal felicity. The Old Law was given, on account of its imperfection, through the medium of an angel; the New Law was proclaimed by the Son of God Himself.

The revealed law is nothing more than a repetition, an exposition, and an amplification of the natural law.

Because the mind of man being darkened by sin, was no longer capable of discerning between good and evil, the natural law was explained and completed for him by God. Let us thank God for thus making His will plain to our understanding.

3. Finally, God gives us commandments through His representatives upon earth, through the ecclesiastical and secular authorities. These laws are called ecclesiastical and civil laws.

The Church lays her behests upon us in Christ's name: " He that heareth you heareth Me; and he that despiseth you, despiseth Me" (Luke x. 16). The secular authorities also derive their power from God, as St. Paul tells us (Rom. xiii. 1). The ecclesiastical and civil laws are distinguished from the divine laws (natural and revealed) in that the former govern our exterior actions and words alone, while the latter regulate our thoughts and desires as well.

The laws God gives us by His representatives are, however, only binding upon us provided they are not at variance with the revealed law.

That is no law which is opposed to the law of God. Wherefore if we are commanded to do anything that God forbids, " we ought to obey God rather than men " (Acts v. 29). Witness the conduct of the three children and of the seven Machabees.

4. From the knowledge of the law comes conscience; the consciousness, that is, whether an act is permitted or prohibited by the law.

Our understanding indicates to us, in individual cases in which we are called upon to act, how to shape our conduct in conformity to the known law. Thus by our understanding we attain to the knowledge of the law and of our duty. This knowledge is called conscience. Conscience is therefore a practical act of the intellect; it also impels our will powerfully towards what is good. Hence it is often called the voice of God within us.

Conscience makes itself heard in the following manner: Before an action it speaks either in encouragement or in warning; after the action it fills us either with peace or with disquiet, according as the action is good or evil.

Conscience filled Cain and Judas with unrest. Our conscience is either good or bad. A good conscience makes us bright and cheerful, it sweetens the bitterness of life; it brings rest and contentment. A bad conscience makes us morose and ill at ease; it is a worm, engendered by the corruption of sin, and this worm never dies (Mark ix. 43). A bad conscience embitters all the joys of life; the man who has a bad conscience is like a condemned criminal, who, whatever the enjoyments offered him in his last hours, takes no real pleasure in anything.

A man's conscience may be either tender or deadened.

A tender conscience shrinks from the least sin; a deadened conscience scarcely heeds great sins. The conscience of the saints was tender; they feared to offend God in the slightest degree; the conscience of men of the world is deadened; it glosses over sins that are unquestionably mortal. Yet such men will sometimes attach great importance to trifles; they strain out gnats and swallow camels (Matt. xxiii. 24). Thus the Jews who crucified Our Lord would not go into the court of Pilate lest they should be defiled (John xviii. 28). A man who has a tender conscience is called conscientious, while one whose conscience is blunted is said to be without conscience.

A man's conscience may be either lax (unscrupulous) or timid (over-scrupulous).

He whose conscience is lax persuades himself that the greatest sins are permissible: once in a way does not count, he will say, to err

is human; in consequence of his dissolute life he no longer heeds the
reproaches of conscience; in fact he scarcely hears them. But an
over-scrupulous conscience, on the other hand, makes a man see sin
where there is no sin. Like a timid horse that shies at a tree or a
stone, thus exposing his rider to the risk of falling, so a scrupulous
person imagines there is danger where there is none, and is liable to
fall into disobedience and other sins. Over-scrupulosity does not
arise from any misapprehension, but from an ill-regulated mind,
which has the effect of obscuring the reason. St. Francis of Sales
says that it has its source in pride. The over-scrupulous are timid;
thus they can never attain a high degree of perfection. They ought
not to dwell upon their doubts, for these are like glue or pitch. The
more they are touched, the more they adhere to one. St. Alphonsus
bids us contemn our scruples, and do that from which they would deter
us. The scrupulous should mistrust their own judgment and view
of things; they must in fact renounce them altogether if they are to
get rid of their timidity. " He who would do great things for God,"
says St. Ignatius, " must beware of being too cautious; had the
apostles been so they would never have undertaken the evangelization
of the world."

A man commits a sin if he acts against the dictates of his
conscience.

Conscience is nothing more than the law, applied to particular
cases. In acting against our conscience therefore, we disobey the
law even if we are under a mistake. For instance, if a man eats meat
on a Thursday, thinking it to be a Friday, he commits a sin.

**5. God's commandments do not deprive men in any way of true
freedom.**

They rather serve to make him independent of creatures. It is
the sinner who falls under the yoke of an ignominious servitude.
"Where the Spirit of the Lord is, there is liberty" (2 Cor. iii. 17).
Besides, liberty does not consist in the right to do whatever we will,
but whatever is permitted. The word is much abused in the present
day; many consider it to mean license, and they call the restraint
which the laws impose on their evil work tyranny and despotism.
Others think it signifies liberty for themselves and servitude for
others. Hence we often find so-called *liberals* the most intolerant of
mankind.

II. THE TWO COMMANDMENTS OF CHARITY.

**1. The most important commandments are the two command-
ments of charity, that is to say, the love of God and the love of
one's neighbor, for all the other commandments are comprised in
them.**

When Christ was once asked by one of the Scribes which was the
first of all the commandments, He answered: " Thou shalt love the
Lord thy God with thy whole heart (i.e., with the will) and with
thy whole soul (i.e., with the understanding) and with thy whole
mind (i.e., with the affections) and with thy whole strength (i.e., in

all thy actions. This is the first commandment. And the second is like unto it: Thou shalt love thy neighbor as thyself" (Mark xii. 30, 31). The same precepts were given to the Jews (Deut. vi. 5; Lev. xix. 18). These two commandments contain all the others, because they influence and direct all the powers of the soul of man; the understanding, the affections, the will, and all his actions besides. Thus he who fulfils these two commandments of charity keeps all the commandments; were they everywhere observed no other law would be necessary in the State or in the family. Hence Christ says: "On these two commandments dependeth the whole law and the prophets" (Matt. xxii. 40). The other commandments do but inculcate in detail what the commandments of charity enjoin.

In the command to love God the first four of the commandments of God are comprised; the other commandments of God and the obligation to perform works of mercy are comprehended in the second.

The first four commandments contain our duty to God. As our supreme Ruler He requires of us in the First Commandment worship and fidelity; in the Second, respect; in the Third, service; in the Fourth, respect towards His representatives upon earth. The other six enjoin on us our duty to our neighbor, forbidding us to injure him as regards his life in the Fifth; his purity in the Sixth; his property in the Seventh; his honor in the Eighth; his family in the Ninth and Tenth. The precept of Our Lord enjoining on us the performing of works of mercy (Matt. xxv. 31 *seq.*) is an amplification of the second commandment of charity, for it requires us to help our neighbor in his need. That the last six commandments of the Decalogue are a connected whole we gather from Our Lord's answer to the rich young man (Matt. xix. 18). St. Paul also classes them together (Rom. xiii. 9).

2. Without the love of God and of our neighbor no man can be saved.

St. John says: "He that loveth not, abideth in death" (1 John iii. 14). St. Augustine says that as we require two feet to walk, so we must have the love of God and of our neighbor if we would reach heaven, and enter into the presence of God. As the bird cannot fly without two wings, so must we be borne aloft upon these two pinions if we would soar up to heaven. The blessed in heaven love God and one another; we must do the same here on earth if we are to join their blissful company. "What is man, O God," asks St. Augustine, "that Thou dost command him to love Thee, and threaten him with terrible chastisements if he fails to do so?"

, 3. The capacity for loving God and our neighbor is bestowed upon us simultaneously with sanctifying grace.

Of ourselves we are incapable of loving God above all things. Ever since the blight of original sin fell upon us, it is with our heart as with the date-palm, which transplanted to a colder clime does indeed bear fruit, but cannot produce the ripe and delicious dates of the land where it is indigenous. So our hearts would fain love

God, but the power is lacking to them; they can only attain to
true charity when informed by divine grace. "To will is present
with me, but how to accomplish that which is good I know not"
(Rom. vii. 18). Not until the Holy Spirit takes possession of us by
Baptism or penance is the love of God shed abroad in our heart. The
love of our neighbor is implanted within us at the same time as the
love of God; they are but one, the only difference is in the object
towards which they are directed. The love of God and of our neighbor may be compared to two streams, issuing from one and the self-
same source. St. Augustine says that Christ gave the Holy Spirit to
the apostles twice (when He breathed upon them and on the Day of
Pentecost) because with the Holy Spirit a twofold charity is imparted to us

4. The love of God is inseparably united to tue love of our
neighbor.

As the plant is contained within the seed, so the love of our neighbor is comprised in the love of God. The two precepts are so constituted that the one cannot be observed without the other. This is
why Holy Scripture speaks of *one* commandment of charity. "If
any man say, I love God, and hateth his brother, he is a liar" (1
John iv. 20). Our love of our neighbor is therefore the best test of
our love of God. He who cherishes ill-will towards his fellow-man,
who hates him, envies him, injures him in any way, or who grudges
alms to the needy, is destitute of the love of God. The greater our
love of God, the greater will be our love of our neighbor.

III. THE PRECEPT OF THE LOVE OF GOD.

Man is so constituted by nature that he takes delight in what he
recognizes as good and beautiful. This delight, and the desire to attain it, is called love. Thus we see love to be an act of the understanding, the affections, and the will.

**1. We ought to love God (1), because Christ commands this;
(2), because He is in Himself essentially the highest beauty and
sovereign perfection; (3), because He loves us and continually
bestows benefits upon us.**

Christ commands us to love God, for He says: "Thou shalt love
the Lord thy God with thy whole heart, with thy whole soul, with thy
whole mind, and with thy whole strength" (Mark xii. 30). God
is the most beautiful of all beings, for if earthly beings are so beautiful, how much greater must be the beauty of God, Who is the
Creator of all these things! (Wisd. xiii. 3.) For one cannot give to
another what one has not got one's self, consequently God must possess in Himself all the perfections in their highest degree which we
admire in His creatures. God has manifested His love towards us
chiefly in this, that He sent His only-begotten Son to earth for our
salvation. Christ Himself says: "God so loved the world as to give
His only-begotten Son" (John iii. 16). He did not send Him to
live on earth in regal state, but as a lowly servant; not to live and die
as an ordinary man, but to live a life of privation and persecution,

and to die the death of the cross. God gave His well-beloved Son. The fewer children parents have, the more fondly do they generally love them, and they dote upon an only child. How intense must have been the love of God for His only-begotten Son, yet He gave Him for our redemption! "Thou didst deliver up the Son, O Lord," exclaims St. Augustine, "to save the servant!" Thus St. John admonishes us: "Let us love God, because God first hath loved us" (1 John iv. 19). Moreover God continually bestows benefits upon us; all in which we take pleasure comes from Him. Life, health, our daily bread, the clothes we wear, the roof that shelters us, all are His gifts. "Every best gift and every perfect gift is from above, coming down from the Father of lights" (Jas. i. 17). "What hast thou, O man, that thou hast not received?" (1 Cor. iv. 17.) The uninterrupted possession of these blessings has unfortunately the effect of making us think light of them. It were well for us therefore to contemplate the lot of those who are deprived of them, e.g., the blind, the sick, the destitute; we should then see how favored we are in comparison with these afflicted ones, and our love of God would become greater. Children love those to whom they owe their being, and so in a certain measure do the brute beasts. He, therefore, who does not love his Creator is worse than the brutes. The very fact that we owe our existence to God lays us under the obligation of loving Him above all things.

2. Our love of God is chiefly manifested by thinking of Him constantly, by avoiding whatever might separate us from Him, by laboring to promote His glory, and willingly accepting all that comes from His hand.

It is an error to imagine that the love of God is merely affective, a certain delight or joy we experience in God. It is rather an act of the understanding and of the will. Man recognizes God to be the supreme Good, and esteems Him above all creatures. This esteem causes him to strive to attain to the possession of this sovereign Good, by avoiding sin and leading a godly life. The love of God shows itself more in *deeds* than in *feelings*. The love of God is called a holy or supernatural love. It is to be distinguished from purely natural affection, such as that of a parent for his child, as well as from sensual affection, which chiefly regards the body.

1. He who loves God thinks of Him continually, delights in speaking of Him, and of hearing others talk of Him.

Love consists in striving after something, in order to be united to it. Hence it comes that one's thoughts dwell incessantly with the object of our affections. "Where thy treasure is, there is thy heart also" (Matt. vi. 21). He who truly loves God performs all his actions with the good intention of giving Him glory. So the course of a ship may be directed towards different points of the compass, yet the magnetic needle always points to the North. He who loves God utters ejaculatory prayers amid all his occupations, such as these: "Jesus, my God, I love Thee above all things"; "All to the greater glory of God": "My God and my all." "The time," says St. Bernard, "in which we do not think of God, is time lost." He who loves God delights in talking of divine things. "Out of the abundance of the heart the mouth speaketh " (Matt. xii. 34). He also loves to hear others speak of God: " He that is of God, heareth the words of God " (John viii. 47).

2. He who loves God avoids sin, and does not allow his heart to cling to the possessions and joys of earth.

He who loves God flies from sin because sin' separates him from God. Our Lord says: " If any man love Me, he will keep My word " (John xiv. 23). He who loves God is afraid of offending Him, rather than of His chastisements; for where love is, there is no chastisement to be dreaded. " Perfect charity casteth out fear " (1 John iv. 18). One who is inflamed with the love of God lays aside all desire for earthly possessions and enjoyments; the love of God and the love of the world cannot co-exist in the human heart.

3. He who loves God rejoices to labor for the glory of God.

The love of God excites in us the desire that He should be better known and loved by men, and thereby glorified. Zeal is the outcome of love: " Where there is no zeal there is no love," says St. Augustine. One who loves God is grieved, nay, indignant, when God is offended; Moses in his anger threw the stone tables of the law to the ground when he saw the people worshipping the golden calf. On the other hand those who love God rejoice when He is honored; they spare no exertion to bring wanderers back to Him. Consider what hardships the apostles and missioners endured in evangelizing heathen lands; or what St. Monica did for her erring son, Augustine. The love of God is the motive which actuates the angels in their care of us; and which makes us pray: " Hallowed be Thy name."

4. He who loves God gives God thanks for the benefits He confers, and bears willingly the sufferings He lays upon him.

If we really love God, all that comes from His hand will be welcome, whether it be pleasant or painful. If we receive favors from Him, we must do as Noe did when he came out of the Ark (Gen. viii. 20); as the three young men in the furnace of Babylon (Dan. iii. 51 *seq.*); or the leper Our Lord healed (Luke xvii. 16), and not be forgetful of our Benefactor, by omitting night prayers, or grace before meals. One should be thankful for the smallest gifts, for ingratitude betokens an unfeeling heart. Moreover the sufferings God sends should also be cheerfully accepted. Witness Job and St. Paul, who abounded with joy in all tribulation (2 Cor. vii. 4). The apostles and martyrs met death with gladness; St. Teresa said: " To suffer or to die." The heart that loves God loves the cross also; the greater our desire to suffer and be humbled for the sake of God, the greater is our love for Him; so say the saints.

5. He who loves God loves his neighbor also.

Every one that loves the Creator, loves the creatures that He has made. He loves his neighbor because he sees Our Lord in his person; this Christ Himself tells us (Matt. xxv. 40). He does not love the just only, he loves the sinner as well; for while we hate sin, because it is hateful in God's sight, we should love the sinner. We should only hate the evil spirits and the reprobate, whom God hates with an eternal hatred.

3. We must love God with all our faculties, and above all things else in the whole world.

We must love God with a special, a superexcellent love. Christ does not merely command us to love God, but to love Him with all our heart and mind and soul and strength. " The true measure of our love to God," says St. Francis of Sales, " is to love Him without measure."

We love God with all our strength if we refer all to Him; all our thoughts, words, and deeds.

Our first thought on rising in the morning should be of God, and of Him we should think in all we do during the day. All that is beautiful in creation should remind us of the glory of the Creator. To him who loves God all nature speaks in a voice inaudible to the world at large, but intelligible to his ear.

We love God more than anything else in the world, if we are ready to give up everything unhesitatingly, if such be His will.

God is, in fact, our final end; creatures are only means to the attainment of this end. Hence it is incumbent upon us to sacrifice them all in order to possess Him. We must be prepared to give up our bodily life, like the three Babylonian youths; we must be prepared to leave our relatives, as Abraham did; nay more, a father must even sacrifice his only son, as Abraham sacrificed Isaac, if God require this of him. God may be compared to the pearl of great price, to buy which a man must sell all that he hath (Matt. xiii. 46). God tries the just man to see if he loves Him more than this passing world: yet He often contents Himself with our good will, and does not take from us the beloved object, if we are ready to give it up to Him. He who is unduly cast down by afflictions does not love God above all; nor he who omits any good work from motives of human respect, for he esteems the favor of men more than the favor of God.

One may love creatures, but only for God's sake.

We may only take pleasure in creatures in so far as they are conducive to the service of the Most High. The Creator ought to be loved in His creatures, not the creatures in themselves. God calls Himself a jealous God (Exod. xx. 5), because He cannot tolerate our loving anything which interferes with our love for Him. He must reign supreme in our hearts, or hold no place in them at all (St. Francis of Sales). Because the patriarch Jacob was too fond of his youngest son. Joseph, He took him from him for a time, and He did the same with Benjamin. So He acts towards us now. Christ says · " He that loveth father or mother more than Me, is not worthy of Me " (Matt. x. 37). St. Augustine says: " He loves God too little who loves anything besides God; unless indeed he loves it out of love to God."

4. The love of God is of great advantage to us: Through it we are united to God here on earth, our minds are enlightened, our will is strengthened; we obtain pardon of sin, peace of soul, manifold proofs of God's favor, and after death celestial joys.

As avarice is the root of all evil, so the holy love of God is the root of all that is good. It is compared to oil, or to fire, for like these it rises upward, it gives light and warmth; it softens and purifies. He who loves God is the dwelling-place of the Holy Spirit; thus he is united to God. Through love God becomes present in our hearts as He is in heaven; for Christ says: "If any man love Me, My Father will love him, and we will come to him and make our abode with him" (John xiv. 23). Love of God and sanctifying grace cannot be dissevered; where one is, there is the other. He who loves God enjoys heaven upon earth. "Hence," says St. Francis of Sales, "we should not be too anxious to discover whether we are pleasing to God, but rather whether God is pleasing to us." The man who loves God obtains through the indwelling of the Holy Ghost enlightenment of the mind, strengthening of the will, pardon of sin, and true peace of soul. Our soul is like a mirror, which reflects the object towards which it is turned. If therefore we direct it towards God, the light of His divinity will shine into our soul, which will have a clear perception, that is, of divine things. "In the love of God is honorable wisdom" (Ecclus. i. 14). St. Francis of Sales calls love the compendium of theology; by it many unlearned men, monks and hermits, have attained proficiency in the divine science. As red-hot iron is easily shaped by the hammer of the blacksmith, so the soul which is inflamed by divine love is shaped by the influence of the Holy Spirit. Nothing gives courage and strength more than love does. The love of her offspring makes the timid hen so brave that she will fly at a man in their defence. And what will not a mother endure for the sake of her child ? "Charity beareth all things, endureth all things" (1 Cor. xiii. 7). What we love to do is no trouble to us, for love makes labor light. If then natural affection is so potent, what cannot the love of God do ? It enables us to accomplish the greatest undertakings. Through the love of God we obtain pardon of sin. Christ said of the Magdalen: "Many sins are forgiven her, because she hath loved much" (Luke vii. 47). "Charity covereth a multitude of sins" (1 Pet. iv. 8). Nothing clears a field of thistles and thorns as quickly as fire, and no less quickly does a spark of divine charity cleanse the heart from all sin. The Holy Ghost Who takes up His dwelling in the heart that loves God, brings peace to that heart. He is essentially the Comforter. Whosoever loves God feels within him the divine presence, and this affords him greater satisfaction than all the pleasures of the world. Without charity there is no true peace. He who loves God enjoys true peace, because his will is in entire conformity to the will of God. Charity procures for us many proofs of God's favor. Many of the saints received revelations from God. Christ says: "He that loveth Me shall be loved of My Father, and I will manifest Myself to him" (John xiv. 21). To others Christ Himself appeared, or His blessed Mother, or the angels. Of this many instances occur in both the New and the Old Testament. Or they obtained speedy answers to prayer, marvellous enlightenment in divine things, interior consolations such as the world cannot give. To His friends, i.e., those who love Him, God communicates His mysteries, to increase in them charity and sanctifying grace. Christ says: "I have called you friends, because all things whatsoever I have heard of My Father I have made known unto you" (John xv. 15). St. Paul tells us: "To them that love God all things work together for good" (Rom. viii. 28). Even trials and afflictions work for good to him who loves God, as was the case with Joseph, Jacob, and Tobias. Through the love of God we attain the joys of heaven. St. Paul says: "Eye hath not seen, nor ear heard, neither hath it entered into the heart of man, what things God hath prepared for them that love Him" (1 Cor. ii. 9). This is because he is rich in good works who is inflamed with divine charity, for love stimulates us to action. Hence the Apostle says: "The charity of Christ presses us" (2 Cor. v. 14). To behold God, as we shall in heaven, and to love Him is one and the same thing. We needs must love the highest when we see it. "He who knows by experience," says St. Alphonsus, "how sweet and delightful it is to love God, loses all taste for earthly things."

5. The merit of our good works and the degree of our future felicity is in proportion to the magnitude of our love for God.

"The greater is our love of God," says St. Francis of Sales, "the more meritorious are our actions. God does not regard the greatness of the work, but the love wherewith it is performed." The two mites of the poor widow had more value in the sight of God than the large contributions of the rich. St. Paul tells us that all gifts, however wonderful, all good works and austerities are utterly worthless without charity. Good works without the love of God are like lamps without oil. As food is tasteless and insipid without a condiment, so, if charity is lacking, our works are without savor before God. Moreover the measure of our eternal felicity depends upon the degree of charity we possess at our death. "He who has loved most shall receive the greatest glory," says St. Francis of Sales. An earthly father often bequeaths the largest legacy to the child who has shown the most affection for him. Even on earth he who loves God best is the recipient of the greatest graces. To such a one many sins are forgiven. When Mary Magdalen fell at Our Lord's feet in Simon's house, He said of her: "Many sins are forgiven her, because she hath loved much" (Luke vii. 47). A greater love of God brings with it a greater knowledge of God: like a fire which, the larger it is, the more radiance it emits. If we love God we are rich, richer far than those who own unbounded wealth, but who do not love Him; they are poor whoever they may be, or whatever they may possess.

The love of God may be increased in the soul by meditation upon the perfections of God and the benefits He confers on us; by practising detachment from earthly things and by frequently making acts of the love of God.

Just as a fire is kept up and increased in size by heaping on fuel, so the love of God within us is fed by meditation on the truths of religion. Meditation on Our Lord's Passion is specially calculated to increase in us the love of God. Even in the realms of celestial glory the Redeemer's death will form the strongest incentive to the blessed spirits to love God. Detachment from earthly things also contributes to augment our love. For as a stone gravitates towards the centre of the earth as soon as the obstacles in its way are removed, so our soul mounts upward with accelerated motion to God, the centre of our being and its final aim, if we free ourselves from the bonds that hold us captive upon earth. It is also useful to make frequent acts of the love of God. As in everything practice makes perfect, so by awakening within ourselves the love of God, we shall attain to a high degree of love. St. Francis of Assisi would repeat for whole days and nights the words: "My God and my all!" It is all the more important to make acts of love because the command to love God imposes it upon us as an obligation. St. Alphonsus declares that he who for a whole month neglects this practice can scarcely be exempt from mortal sin. Our love should be without limit or measure, as is God Himself.

The love of God is lost by mortal sin.

As water extinguishes fire, so the love of God is quenched in our hearts by mortal sin. He who has thus lost the love of God has turned his mind away from God, and directed it wholly to creatures. Except sin, nothing has power to deprive us of the love of God. Thus St. Paul exclaims: "I am sure that neither death nor life, nor angels nor principalities, nor powers, nor things present, nor things to come, nor any other creature, shall be able to separate us from the love of God" (Rom. viii. 38).

IV. THE LOVE OF THE WORLD IS OPPOSED TO THE LOVE OF GOD.

However cruel or depraved a man may be, his heart clings to some person or thing, his nature impels him to love some object. If he does not love God above all, he needs must love a creature above all.

1. The love of the world consists in loving, above all, money, or the gratification of one's appetite, or earthly honors or anything else in the world, instead of giving the first place to God.

The love of creatures is not in itself sinful, only when the creature is more loved than the Creator. All who love creatures more than God are idolaters, because they give to creatures the honor due to God. One loves money, like Judas; another eating and drinking, like Dives; and many others whose god is their belly; a third sacrifices all to ambition, like Absalom; others have an inordinate love of amusements, gambling and the like. All these resemble the Jews who danced round the golden calf at the foot of Mount Sinai. The maxim of the man of the world is: "Let us eat and drink, for to-morrow we die." The love of the world is worse than high treason; it makes a man a traitor to the King of kings.

2. Through love of the world we incur the loss of sanctifying grace, and eternal felicity.

The lover of the world does not possess sanctifying grace. As the dove does not rest upon anything that is unclean or corrupt, so the Holy Spirit does not dwell in the soul of the carnally-minded and evil (St. Ambrose). The Holy of holies cannot dwell in the soul that is stained with sin. "If thy heart be full of vinegar, how can it be filled with honey? It must first be emptied, and undergo a toilsome process of cleansing," says St. Augustine. He who is destitute of the presence of the Holy Spirit, that is, of sanctifying grace (the wedding-garment), shall be cast into exterior darkness (Matt. xxii. 12). Hence Christ threatens the votary of the world with eternal damnation: "He that loveth his life (who endeavors to get out of it all possible enjoyment) shall lose it" (John xii. 25). Again, "Woe to you that are filled, for you shall hunger. Woe to you that now laugh, for you shall mourn and weep" (Luke vi. 25). No more than a ship lying fast at anchor can sail into harbor, can a man who loves the world reach the haven of eternal felicity. "Which dost thou prefer?" asks St. Augustine, "to love the world and go to perdition, or to love Christ and enter into life everlasting?" He is a fool who for the sake of this passing world plays away eternal life.

3. The love of the world blinds the soul of man, and leads him away from God.

The love of the world blinds the soul of man. When earthly things intervene between God and the soul, the soul becomes dark, just as does the moon when the earth is between it and the sun. As Tobias the elder was blinded by the dung of a swallow, so earthly cares destroy the sight of the soul. Hence worldlings cannot comprehend the teaching of the Gospel; it is foolishness to them (1 Cor. ii. 14). As the sun's rays cannot penetrate muddy water, so the lover of the world cannot be enlightened by the Holy Spirit. The earth is like a limed twig; the bird that rests upon it cannot soar upwards. The cares of this world stifle the word of God in the heart of man. as thorns choke the sprouting seed. The votaries of the world resemble the men in the Gospel who were invited to the heavenly banquet, but who did not go because of their wife, their farm, their oxen (Luke xiv. 16).

4. The love of the world destroys interior peace, and makes men fear death greatly.

The worldling is a stranger to interior peace. It has been well said: A man must choose between indulgence of the senses and tranquillity of soul. The two are not compatible. One might as well try to fill a vessel that has holes in it, as to satisfy the heart that only strives after the pleasures of time and sense. And since the votaries of the world can never attain interior peace, they want a constant change of amusement, as one who cannot sleep turns restlessly from side to side in the hope of finding rest. Christ alone can give us true content. He said to His apostles: "Peace I leave with you, My peace I give unto you; not as the world giveth do I give unto you" (John xiv. 27). St. Augustine exclaims: "Our heart has no rest until it rest in Thee, O Lord!" The lover of the world fears death so much, because he will be parted from his idol, and because death will put an end to the happiness he makes it his object to attain. He has, besides, an inward presentiment of what will follow after death. On account of this all who love the world are filled with apprehension and even despair in the hour of death. The prisoner fears nothing so much as the summons to appear before the judge; and the sinner, though he is never free from alarm, dreads the moment above all when his soul will leave the body and enter the presence of her divine Judge (St. John Chrysostom). The fish that is caught on the hook scarcely feels pain until it is drawn out of the water; so those who are entangled in the meshes of the world first feel real anguish when their last hour comes. Think, O worldling, if the joys which the devil offers you are thus mixed with bitterness, what will the torments be which he prepares for you hereafter?

5. The love of the world gives rise to hatred of God and of His servants.

A man who loves the world cannot possibly have the love of God within him. Just as a ring which encircles one finger cannot at the same time encircle another, so the human heart cannot love God if love binds it to some earthly object. St. John says: "If any man love the world, the charity of the Father is not in him" (1 John ii. 15). We cannot look with the same eye both at heaven and earth at the same time. The lover of the world even goes so far as to hate God and divine things. Thus Christ says: "No man can serve two masters; for either he will hate the one and love the other, or he will sustain the one and despise the other" (Matt. vi. 24). What are we to conclude if we hear any one rail at priests and at religion? The lover of the world is therefore the enemy of God. "If thou wouldst not be the enemy of God," says St. Augustine, "be an enemy of the world."

6. The love of the world ceases at death.

There are many things which thou canst only love for a time; then love comes to an end; for either thou wilt be taken from the object of thy affections or it from thee. Hence we should not love that which we may lose, or from which we may be parted; we should only love those things that are eternal (St. Augustine). Wherefore let not thy heart cleave to earthly things. The true servant of God clings no more to his possessions than to his clothes, which he puts on and off at will; whereas the indifferent Christian makes them a part of his very being, like the skin of an animal (St. Francis of Sales). The true Christian should resemble the eagle, which inhabits the heights, only descending to earth in search of food. Or he should be like a tree, whose roots alone are in the ground, while it spreads its branches towards heaven. The soul of man is immortal, and it should only strive after what is immortal. "Seek those things that are above" (Col. iii. 1). "Therefore choose Him for thy friend," says Thomas à Kempis, "Who, when all others forsake thee, will not abandon thee."

V. THE COMMANDMENT OF CHARITY TOWARDS OUR NEIGHBOR.

Every human being is our neighbor, without distinction of religion, of race, of age, of sex, or of occupation.

In the parable of the Good Samaritan Christ teaches us that those who are strangers to us and even our enemies, are to be regarded as our neighbor. In the present day some people are so foolish as to consider none but their fellow-countrymen as their neighbors. In Christ there is neither Jew nor Greek, but all are one (Gal. iii. 28).

1. We ought to love our neighbor because this is Christ's command; furthermore because he is a child of God, made after His image, and also because we are all descended from the same parents and we are all called to attain eternal felicity.

Christ's precept is this: "Thou shalt love thy neighbor as thyself" (Mark xii. 31). He who loves the father will assuredly love his children (1 John v. 1). Now God is our common father, for He created us (Matt. ii. 10), we are all His children, and for that reason we ought to love one another. Those who are the offspring of one and the same parent are blood-relations; consequently since we all received our being from the self-same God, we stand in the relation of brethren one to another, and on this account ought to love one another. A man who loves his father shows respect for his portrait. Now, our fellow-man is an image of God; he was made to His image (Gen. i. 27); consequently we ought to love him. As the moon derives its light from the sun, so the love of our neighbor flows from the love of God. We are, moreover, all children of Adam, and thus members of one great family, and should love one another as such. Finally, we are called to the attainment of everlasting felicity; we shall all live together, we shall behold the face of God and sing His praises together. St. John says in the Apocalypse: "I saw a great multitude which no man could number, of all nations and tribes and peoples and tongues, standing before the throne and in sight of the Lamb" (Apoc. vii. 9). Now we find that on earth persons who follow the same calling, such as priests, teachers, etc., always hold together. So we, who share the same vocation to heaven with our fellow-men, ought to be united to them in the bond of charity.

2. The love of our neighbor shows itself in desiring the good of our neighbor from our heart; in abstaining from injuring him, and in doing him good.

The love of our neighbor does not consist merely in affectionate sentiments, in benevolent wishes; these would profit him little. St. James says: "If a brother or sister be naked, and want daily food; and one of you say to them: Go in peace, be ye warmed and filled, yet give them not these things that are necessary for the body, what shall it profit?" (Jas. ii. 15, 16). The love of our neighbor must be practical, it must display itself in doing good. "Let us not love in word or in tongue, but in deed and in truth" (1 John iii. 18).

The desire for our neighbor's good consists in this, that we rejoice with him in his prosperity, and grieve with him when he is in adversity.

St. Paul exhorts us to "rejoice with them that rejoice, and weep with them that weep" (Rom. xii. 15). Consider how Elizabeth rejoiced on hearing that Mary was the Mother of God (Luke i. 42); how the friends of Zacharias congratulated him when they witnessed the recovery of his speech at the birth of the Baptist (Luke i. 64). Consider how desirous Abraham was to have no strife between himself and Lot, how willingly he gave up to him the best tract of country. Consider how Moses desired the good of the Hebrews: " O that all the people might prophesy, and that the Lord would give them His spirit ! " (Numb. xi. 29.) The congratulations exchanged on birthdays, festivals, and other occasions, the greetings usual in society are signs of good will. The Redeemer greeted His apostles with, the words: " Peace be with you; " the archangel Gabriel saluted Mary. In some Catholic countries the custom still lingers of using the words: " Praised be Jesus Christ " as a greeting. Banish mutual good will and you take the sun out of the heavens; you make social intercourse impossible (St. Gregory the Great). " See," says St. Augustine, " how the different members of the body participate in each other's misfortune. If a thorn runs into the foot the eyes look for it, the tongue asks about it, the back bends towards it, the hand endeavors to extract it. We should conduct ourselves in like manner towards our neighbor." It is wrong, then, to rejoice when calamities befall our neighbor and to grieve over his good fortune. Malice and envy are the sentiments of the devil and the surest sign that a man is lacking in love for his neighbor.

We ought not to injure our neighbor; either as regards his life, his innocence, his property, his honor, or his household.

All this God has forbidden in the six last commandments of the Decalogue. He who violates one of them to any serious extent, shows himself to have no love of his neighbor.

We ought to do good to our neighbor, especially when he is in need.

Christ, our future Judge, requires from us works of mercy, for He makes our eternal salvation depend on having performed them (Matt. xxv. 35). In a building one stone supports another, otherwise the structure would fall to pieces; so in the spiritual building, the Church, one member must help and sustain another. Charity is a chain that links us to our neighbor, and makes us treat him with kindness.

3. We are commanded to love our neighbor as ourselves, but we are by no means obliged to love him better than ourselves.

Our Lord says: " Whatsoever you would that men should do to you, do you also to them " (Matt. vii. 12). Holy Tobias says: " See that thou never do to another what thou wouldst hate to have done to thee " (Tob. iv. 16). Put yourself in your neighbor's place and you will certainly treat him differently. Charity to one's neighbor has its limits, however. No one is bound to deprive himself of what is necessary, to relieve his neighbor's wants. In such cases to render assistance is heroic charity. " Greater love than this no man hath, that a man lay down his life for his friend " (John xv. 13). This Our Saviour did; and hundreds of missioners continually expose themselves to the risk of death to save souls. All the saints have incurred personal dangers for the sake of aiding others.

4. **All that we do to our neighbor, whether it be good or evil, we do to Christ Himself; for He has said: "What you did to one of these My least brethren, ye did it to Me" (Matt. xxv. 40).**

To Saul, when he was on the way to Damascus, Our Lord said: "Why persecutest thou Me?" (Acts ix. 4.) Yet we know that it was only the Christians that he was persecuting. When St. Martin had given half his cloak to a half-naked beggar at the gate of Amiens, Christ appeared to him in a dream wearing the half-cloak and accompanied by angels. "Martin," He said, "clothed Me to-day with this cloak." Thus God protects our neighbor; we cannot injure him without first injuring God.

5. Eternal happiness will be the unfailing reward of those who fulfil closely the precept of charity to their neighbor.

St. John the Evangelist exhorted the Christians continually with the words: "Little children, love one another." When asked why he always said the same, he replied: "If you love one another, you fulfil the whole law." St. Paul says the same (Rom. xiii. 8; Gal. v. 14). Our Lord promises eternal life to those who observe that portion of the Ten Commandments which has reference to one's neighbor; to those in fact, who perform works of mercy (Matt. xix. 21). Why does He do this? Because a man who never injures his neighbor, or who gives alms, cannot possibly be a bad man. We do not find the vicious and irreligious, who do not believe in a future recompense, giving alms. He who performs acts of charity possesses other virtues besides that of liberality to the poor. Beneficence is never unaccompanied by other virtues; it cannot exist without them any more than the heart can exist without the other organs of the body. Hence St. John Chrysostom says almsgiving may be called the mainspring of virtue.

6. The love of one's neighbor is the distinctive mark of the true Christian.

Our Lord says: "By this shall all men know that you are My disciples, if you have love one for another" (John xiii. 35). Christ loved us while we were yet unworthy of His love; and if we love and do good to those from whom we have never received any benefit, our love is like that of Christ, and we are really His disciples, easily to be distinguished from the mass of mankind, who usually only love their friends and benefactors. Our Lord calls this a new commandment (John xiii. 34), because the precept of charity to one's neighbor was not understood earlier in the sense He gives to it. Well indeed were it for the world if charity prevailed everywhere! No laws would be needed, no courts of justice, no punishments. Then no man would wrong his neighbor; the very name of murders, brawls, rebellion, robbery and the like, would be unknown. There would be no destitution, for every one would have the necessaries of life (St. John Chrysostom).

VI. LACK OF CHARITY TO ONE'S NEIGHBOR.

1. He who does not desire the good of his neighbor, but is envious of him, does not possess the love of his neighbor.

1. We call a man envious who merely through ill-will is vexed at the prosperity of another, or rejoices when misfortune overtakes him.

The envious man cannot bear to see the good fortune of another, and consequently he seeks by word and work to do him harm. He is like a certain kind of snake, which is said to gnaw away the root of trees which bear sweet-smelling blossoms, because it cannot endure the perfume; like the moth, that frets away the purple robe, or like rust that corrodes iron. The envious man who rejoices at the misfortune of his neighbor is like the raven that gloats over corrupt and stinking carrion. But our vexation or pleasure may arise from the love of God or of our neighbor, in which case it is not blameworthy; e.g., if a man is grieved because one who is an enemy to the Church is raised to a position of influence, or because great prosperity attends a sinner who will employ his good fortune to sin the more. Satan envied our first parents in paradise; Cain envied his brother Abel, because his offering was acceptable to God (Gen. iv. 5); the sons of Jacob were envious of Joseph because he was their father's favorite (Gen. xxxvii. 8); King Saul envied David on account of his having slain the giant and being honored by the people (1 Kings xviii. 8). Many a man grudges another a post more lucrative than his own. The height of envy is to grudge another the gifts of divine grace, and progress in virtue. This is one of the sins against the Holy Ghost. The high priests were jealous of Christ when they saw that He worked many miracles; they therefore determined to compass His death (John xi. 47). The devils feel this kind of envy; they are furious when they see the elect advancing towards perfection and at once assail them with persecutions.

2. No sin renders man so much like the devil as envy, for envy is peculiarly the devil's sin.

The envious man is an imitator of the devil, for by the envy of the devil death came into the world (Wisd. ii. 24). Just as Christ says: "By this shall all men know that you are My disciples if you have love one for another" (John xiii. 35), so on the other hand the devil can say: "By this shall all men know that you are my followers, if you envy one another as I have envied you" (St. Vincent Ferrer). The jealous man wishes to see nothing but misery around him. There is more malice in this sin than in any other. For all other sins and vices there is some pretext which a man may plead in his excuse; the excuse for intemperance is hunger; for revenge, the wrong one has received; for theft, extreme poverty, etc., but for envy no plea can be alleged. It is worse than open war. There is always a cause for war, but none for envy; besides when the war is over all animosity is at an end, but with envy it is unending (St. John Chrysostom). Moreover envy is the only evil quality which charity cannot overcome. One who is an enemy to you, or enraged against you, may be appeased by kindness, but the envious never. Among all sins, envy is the only one which affords no gratification to those who indulge it; the intemperate, the avaricious, the choleric, seem to gain something by yielding to their passions, but envy is sterile. It may be compared to the moth, which fluttering about the lamp, singes its own wings, but does not extinguish the flame or even cause it to burn less brightly.

3. Envy is most hurtful to a man; it robs him of inward content and bodily health; it leads to many cruel actions and finally to eternal perdition.

As the worm gnaws away the wood to which it owes its origin, so envy eats out the heart to which it gains admission; it harasses the mind, destroys peace of conscience, banishes gladness from the soul and fills it with despondency and sadness. When once it is firmly rooted within the soul, its presence becomes apparent outwardly; the pallid cheek, the hollow eyes, testify to the suffering it occasions. Thus we are told that Cain's countenance fell (Gen. iv. 5). When envy fixes its malevolent talons in the heart, and tears at a man's entrails, his food becomes distasteful to him, his drink no longer refreshes him (St. Cyprian). Envy shortens a man's days (Ecclus. xxx. 26). The envious man is his own executioner. As rust corrodes iron, so envy eats into the soul that harbors it. It brings its own punishment, for it frets away and destroys the individual who cherishes it. Envy leads to many acts of cruelty. Through envy the earth was first stained with a brother's blood, and through envy the Jews delivered Christ up to death. Envy causes us to murmur against the arrangements of divine providence. The laborers who had worked all day long in the vineyard murmured against the master of the house through envy, when those who had worked only one hour also received a penny (Matt. xx. 11). The envious man hates to see the benefits God bestows on others. Envy excludes from heaven; it is a sure pledge of eternal damnation. Through envy the angels fell from heaven, and man was driven out of paradise. If we are bound even to love our enemies, how great will be our punishment if we pursue with our envy those who could never have wronged us! (St. John Chrysostom.)

4. The best means of overcoming feelings of envy is to do all the good we possibly can to our fellow-men.

In order to thrust the monster of envy out of the heart, no sword, no breastplate, no helmet is needed, only the panoply of love. Do all the good you can to the person whom you envy; at least pray for him, that his happiness may be increased. Thus you will banish the demon from your heart; you will thereby deserve a twofold crown: the one for your victory over envy, the other for the charitable deed you have performed (St. John Chrysostom). Consider also how short-lived is all here below. In a little while we must leave all. It will not then matter what have been your possessions, what high offices you have filled; your future happiness will entirely depend upon your good works. If you will be great hereafter humble yourself now; love to be unknown and despised, for he that humbleth himself shall be exalted (Luke xiv. 11).

2. He does not love his neighbor who injures him, whether in regard to his life, his innocence, his property, his honor, or his household.

3. Nor does he love his neighbor, who performs no works of mercy.

" If thou dost not give thy neighbor, who is in want, sufficient to support life," says St. John Chrysostom, " thou dost not love him." To give alms is a strict duty for those who have the means of giving them. St. Ambrose severely censures the miserly rich men of his day. " The walls of your dwellings are hung with splendid tapestries, while you take the clothes off the poor man's back. A beggar at your door asks for the most trifling alms; you do not so much as vouchsafe him a glance as you pass by, debating within your mind what kind of marble will look best for the pavement of your palaces. A starving mendicant asks for a crust of bread in vain, while your horses are champing their golden bits. How terrible are the judgments, O rich man, which you prepare for yourself, who might give assistance to so many who are in want. The diamond you wear on your finger would alone suffice to feed a multitude." St. John Chrysostom speaks in like manner to the wealthy who are hardhearted. " What makes thy miserliness most reprehensible is that neither poverty nor hunger compels thee to it. Thy wife, thy house, the very dogs beside thy hearth glitter with gold, whereas the man made after God's image, redeemed by the blood of Christ, is left to perish through thy inhumanity. How many streams of fire will be the portion of such a soul!"

VII. LOVE OF ONE'S FRIENDS.

1. We call those men friends whose principles are the same as ours, and who cherish mutual good will, mutually support one another, and hold confidential intercourse one with another.

Those whose principles are the same soon become friends. We like what is like. Friends cherish more kindly feelings towards one another than they do towards the world at large. They are one heart and one soul. St. Jerome compares friendship to a mirror, which presents a faithful image of the object before it. If one who stands before a mirror laughs, or moves his head, the image in the mirror does the same. His very wishes and dislikes seem to be shared by the image in the mirror. So it is with friendship. Trifling differences do not dissever it, they rather clench it more firmly. The smith sprinkles water upon the fire to fan the flame, and a town that has been re-conquered is garrisoned more strongly than one which has never been lost to the crown. Friends support one another. Pythias and Damon were intimate friends. One of them was sentenced to death by Dionysius the tyrant. He asked permission to go home to set his affairs in order, his friend meanwhile acting as a hostage for him, prepared to die in his stead, did he not reappear at the appointed time. The hour for the execution struck, but the condemned man was not there. Yet his friend persisted that he would come, and so he did. The tyrant admired their mutual devotion and pardoned the one under sentence of death. David, the son of an ordinary citizen of Bethlehem, and Jonathan, the king's son, made each other's acquaintance in the camp, and finding in each other kindred souls, they formed a close friendship. When Jonathan heard that David's life was sought after, he could not eat for anxiety on his behalf, and when he had to part from him, he wept bitterly (1 Kings xx. 24; xviii. 1). Friends hold confidential intercourse with one another, they conceal nothing one from the other. When the door of a room is opened, you see all that is in it. So friends disclose to one another their inmost soul, and reveal the secrets of their heart. Christ communicated many mysteries to His disciples. Friends are consequently candid and open-hearted to one another; they tell one another of their failings. Thus Christ warned His apostles of their faults; for instance, He exhorted them to cultivate a more childlike spirit (Matt. xviii. 3). St. Gregory the Great used to say: " I only count those as my friends who have the generosity to point out my faults to me."

2. Those only are true friends whose friendship is based upon principles of religion.

Friendship, like a building, must rest upon a solid foundation; and only when this foundation is the fear of God and the love of God, will the structure of friendship stand firm. If it is based on wrong or selfish motives, it is founded upon sand. One who is the enemy of God cannot be a true friend to his neighbor; he only loves his friend aright who loves God in him (St. Augustine). When seen in the bed of the ocean, coral appears to be a bush of greenish hue, without any special beauty, but when taken out of the water it becomes bright, red and hard. So friendship acquires its brilliancy. its beauty, its solidity, when it is elevated into the atmosphere of divine love (St. Francis of Sales).

3. Those are false friends whose friendship rests on principles that are reprehensible; they ruin one another body and soul, and forsake one another in the time of adversity.

False friendships are those which are formed merely for the sake of pleasure or gain, or some bad purpose; or between men who need one another's assistance in perpetrating some dark deed. Thus Judas made an agreement with the high priests against Our Lord; and Pilate and Herod were made friends on the occasion of His condemnation. False friends are only steadfast as long as they need each other (Ecclus. vi. 7 *seq.*). When Judas in desperation took the money back to the chief priests with self-accusations, they spoke as if they knew nothing about him: " What is that to us? Look thou to it " (Matt. xxvii. 4). False friends act like the swallows; as long as it is warm here, they stay happily in this country with us; but as soon as they feel the inclement winter approaching, they take flight to a sunnier clime. Or they may be compared to bees, which fly away from a flower when they have sucked all the honey out of its cup (Segneri). They are like a reed, which breaks when one leans on it.

The Romans used to say: " As long as thou art happy thou wilt have many friends, but as soon as adversity overtakes thee thou wilt find thyself alone." Misfortune is the test of true friendship.

4. It is not wrong to have friends, and to love them more than other men; for Christ had friends whom He loved with a special predilection.

Our Lord loved all men, but He loved His disciples best; He called them His friends, His children, and treated them with familiarity and confidence. Among His disciples John was His special favorite; next to him He loved Peter and James; these three were with Him on the most memorable occasions of His life on earth, on Thabor and on Olivet. We are told also that Jesus loved Lazarus and his two sisters (John xi. 5). We know that God shows special predilection for, and confers most graces on those who are most like Him, and who love Him most; we therefore are warranted in doing the same, in loving and trusting those most in whom we find similarity of tastes and affection for ourselves. The need of friendship is implanted by the Creator in every human breast.

5. It is a great happiness for us to have true friends, for they add greatly to the enjoyment of life, and preserve us from dangers of soul and body.

Blessed is he that findeth a true friend (Ecclus. xxv. 12). A friend makes our life much pleasanter; his sympathy increases our happiness and makes our afflictions easier to bear. St. Augustine says there is no more salutary balm for our wounds than the consolations of a friend. Just as a stick is not broken as readily if it is bound up with others, so we are not as soon cast down by calamity, if faithful friends are at hand to succor us. A true friend is like another guardian angel; no defence is so efficacious as that which he affords us. " Nothing can be compared to a faithful friend; no weight of gold and silver is equal to his fidelity. They that fear the Lord shall find him " (Ecclus. vi. 15). Alexander the Great, on being asked where his treasures were, pointed to his friends and said: " Those are my treasures." True friendship does not cease at our death, for charity never falleth away (1 Cor. xiii. 8). Those who have been real friends on earth will see and love one another in heaven; Christ promises His apostles that they shall be with Him hereafter (John xvii. 24). False friends will curse one another after death, for having been a cause of sin and unhappiness to one another.

6. One must not be rash in forming friendships, nor must one do wrong to please a friend.

David complains: " The man in whom I trusted, who eat my bread, hath greatly supplanted me " (Ps. xl. 10). Holy Scripture also warns us to try a friend before taking him, and not to trust him too readily (Ecclus. vi. 7). Do not judge of him as much by his words as by his deeds. And if he asks you to do evil for his sake, answer him as the Greek answered the friend who wanted him to swear falsely in his interest: " I am only thy friend in so far as I do not lose the friendship of God." The friendship of God is indeed worth more than any human friendship.

VIII. THE COMMANDMENT TO LOVE OUR ENEMY.

We call him our enemy who hates us and seeks to do us harm.

Saul, for instance, was an enemy of the Christians. Those alone can be said to have the love of their neighbor who love their enemies too. A big fire is not extinguished but increased by the wind; so the love of one's neighbor, if it be real, is not destroyed, but deepened, by affronts and offences on the part of others. If we only love those who love us, we cannot look for any great reward (Matt. v. 46). We love our friends for our own sake, but we love our enemies for God's sake.

1. We ought to love our enemies because Christ commands it; He says: " Love your enemies, do good to them that hate you; pray for them that persecute and calumniate you " (Matt. v. 44).

Christ has given us the most striking example of the love of our enemies, for on the cross He prayed for His enemies, and in the Garden of Olives He healed the servant whose ear Peter had cut off. Our heavenly Father Himself sets us an example, for He makes His sun to rise upon the good and bad, and raineth upon the just and the unjust. He who loves his enemy therefore is like to God; he is a true child of his Father in heaven (Matt. v. 45).

Another reason why we ought to love our enemy is because he also is made after God's image, and is an instrument in His hand.

Our enemy is made after God's likeness. The king's effigy stamped upon the coin, is equally deserving of respect whether the coin be of copper or gold; so we are bound to love and honor the image of God, whether the man who bears it be vicious or virtuous. It is not the sin we love, but the sinner. Man is God's work, sin is man's work; " therefore," says St. Augustine, " love what God has made, not what man has done." We ought also to love our enemy because God uses him as His instrument. Evil men, unwittingly to themselves, are instruments in God's hands. As the physician employs the leech to draw the bad blood from the veins of the sick man, and effect his cure, so God employs our enemies to remove our imperfections (St. Gregory the Great). The evil shape the good, as file and hammer shape iron: they are to them as the plough to the fallow ground (St. John Chrysostom). They are, moreover, of service to us, by acquainting us with our faults and giving us an opportunity of practising virtue. Enemies are like bees; they sting, but they produce honey. When calumny assails you, console yourself with the thought that it is not the worst fruits that the wasps devour. Finally remember that no enemy can really injure one who loves God; for God makes all hostile designs work good to His own people (Rom. viii. 28). This is exemplified in Joseph's life. The truth will teach you to bear up against persecution.

2. The love of our enemy is shown in this: That we do not revenge ourselves on him, that we return good for evil, that we pray for him and forgive him willingly.

We ought not to revenge ourselves on our enemy. David gives us a beautiful example, for he twice had the opportunity of putting his persecutor King Saul, to death, and on neither occasion did he do him any harm. Our Lord, when He was reviled, did not revile again (1 Pet. ii. 23). Once when Christ was not received in a Samaritan village because He was a Jew, the apostles were so desirous of revenge that they wanted to call down fire from heaven. But Our Lord rebuked them, saying: "You know not of what spirit you are" (Luke ix. 55). Vengeance belongs to God, not to us (Rom. xii. 19). We ought to suffer wrong rather than take revenge; we are told, to him that striketh thee on the one cheek offer the other (Luke vi. 29). Be not overcome by evil, but overcome evil by good (Rom. xii. 21). Avenge yourself, as the saints did, by returning benefits for the evil done you; such vengeance is divine. St. Stephen prayed for his murderers; he was more grieved for the harm they did to themselves than for the injury they did to him. When the Apostle James, Bishop of Jerusalem, was thrown from the pinnacle of the Temple, he raised himself on his fractured knees to pray for his murderers. We should also be ready to forgive our enemies. King David forgave Semei, when he threw stones at him and cursed him (2 Kings xvi. 10). To do good to one's enemy is a proof of great magnanimity.

3. He who does not revenge himself on his enemy, or who even confers benefits upon him, puts his foe to shame and pacifies him, and will be rewarded by God; whereas he who hates his enemy and revenges himself on him commits a sin.

David by sparing Saul on two several occasions mollified and touched him to such a degree that he shed tears (1 Kings xxiv. 17). Blessed Clement Hofbauer being abused by a woman in the streets of Vienna, went up to her, picked up a handkerchief she had dropped, and spoke kindly to her. She was covered with confusion, and hastily withdrew. Just as the bore-worm, soft as it is, works its way through the hardest wood, so a conciliatory spirit overcomes the bitterest enemy and coarsest calumniator. By conferring benefits on your enemy, you will heap coals of fire upon his head (Rom. xii. 20), that is to say, he can no more resist your kindness than he could burning coals. Thus we are taught to be gentle and peaceable. He who does not revenge himself will be rewarded by God. David bore Semei's curses patiently, saying, "Perhaps the Lord will look upon my affliction, and may render me good for the cursing of this day" (2 Kings xvi. 12). Shortly after he won a signal victory. It is difficult to you to pray for your enemy; but the greater your self-conquest, the greater will be your recompense (St. Augustine). To revenge one's self is a sin; he who does this is like the bee, which revenges itself by stinging, but in doing so, dies. Besides, it is a foolish thing to revenge one's self; it is like the dog who bites the stick with which he is beaten, for we forget that our enemy is but an instrument in God's hand.

4. He who forgives his enemy will obtain forgiveness of his sins from God; but he who will not forgive his enemy God will not forgive.

To forgive one's enemy is a work of mercy and the greatest of all almsgiving (St. Augustine). If we forgive others, we can ask pardon for ourselves, as is expressed in the fifth petition of the Lord's Prayer. God shows mercy to him who willingly forgives his brother. He who does not forgive his brother brings down on himself no blessing when he repeats the Our Father. Christ says: "If you will not forgive men, neither will your heavenly Father forgive you your offences" (Matt. vi. 15). Remember the parable of the unmerciful servant (Matt. xviii. 23). We are not merely to forgive seven times, but seventy times seven times (v. 22).

IX. THE LOVE OF ONE'S SELF.

Among all classes of men each one is his own nearest neighbor. Consequently every man ought to love himself.

We ought to love ourselves because God wills it; furthermore because we are made after God's image, redeemed by the blood of Christ, and called to eternal felicity in heaven.

It is God's will that we should love ourselves, for Our Lord says: "Thou shalt love thy neighbor as thyself." In these words He declares the love of ourselves to be the rule and measure of our love of our neighbor. "Learn first to love God," says St. Augustine, "then to love thyself; then thy neighbor as thyself." God has not given us a special command to love ourselves, because every man does this in virtue of the natural law, and it is contained in the commandment to love one's neighbor. We ought besides to love ourselves because we are made after God's image. If we are to respect God's image in our neighbor, nay more, in our enemy, we must respect it in ourselves. Since, then, we love ourselves for the sake of God, it stands to reason that the right love of one's self increases in the same proportion as we advance in the love of God. We must also remember that we are bought with a great price. "You were not redeemed with corruptible things as gold or silver, but with the precious blood of Christ" (1 Pet. i. 18). We also have a high calling, we are destined for eternal felicity. St. Gregory the Great thus beautifully expresses it: "Recognize thy dignity, O Christian! Thou art made a participator in the divine nature, a member of Christ's body! Remember that thou hast been wrested from the powers of darkness, and destined to share in the glory of the kingdom of heaven!" Consider also that the Son of God was made man for us and became our Brother, that thus we have been made the children of God (1 John iii. 1); that the Holy Ghost dwells in us (1 Cor. vi. 19); that the angels minister to us (Heb. i. 14). These are all motives impelling us to love ourselves. Wherefore as the love of one's self is in reality only the love of one's neighbor applied to one's self personally, to love one's self is equivalent to esteeming one's self at one's true value (a matter of reason) desiring one's own good (a matter of the affections)—not injuring, but doing good to one's self (in will and in action). This is the right self-love, in contradistinction to the false love which manifests itself in arrogance, conceit, discourtesy, license, etc.

The true love of one's self shows itself herein, that we strive to attain that which will procure our real happiness; first and foremost our eternal felicity, and then such earthly things as are conducive to the attainment of eternal felicity.

The true lover of himself acts according to Christ's admonition: "Seek ye first the kingdom of God and His justice, and all these things shall be added unto you" (Matt. vi. 33). He will provide for his health, his clothing, etc., but without undue solicitude.

He is wanting in love of himself who only strives after earthly possessions and heeds not his eternal happiness; likewise he who despises the things that are helpful to the attainment of eternal happiness.

A great number of mankind regard self, not God, as their final end; and earthly riches not as means towards attaining eternal happiness, but as means for the gratification of the senses. Therefore they take delight in earthly things: honors, riches, dignities, etc., and are not willing to give them up for God's sake. Such love of one's self is a spurious love; it is selfishness, self-seeking. He who prefers what is temporal to what is eternal is his own enemy; for he will only enjoy a certain measure of happiness for a short period, then he will be unhappy forevermore. "They that commit sin and iniquity, are enemies to their own soul" (Tob. xii. 10). How many resemble the miser in the Gospel, who said to himself: "Thou hast much goods laid up for many years, take thy rest, eat, drink, make good cheer"; to whom God said: "Thou fool, this night do they require thy soul of thee, and whose shall those things be which thou hast provided?" (Luke xii. 19, 20.) "What doth it profit a man if he gain the whole world and suffer the loss of his own soul?" (Matt. xvi. 26.) "Learn," says St. Augustine, "to love thyself by not loving thyself." On the other hand those do wrong who despise those earthly things which promote their spiritual good, for by so doing they show contempt for their eternal salvation. What must one think of a man who does not provide for his own maintenance, who rashly endangers his life or even puts an end to it by his own act?

X. THE TEN COMMANDMENTS OF GOD.

1. The Ten Commandments were given by God to the Jews on Mount Sinai.

The proclamation of the commandments took place on the fiftieth day after the exit of the Israelites from Egypt. When giving them, God prefaced them with the solemn announcement: "I am the Lord thy God, etc." (Exod. xx. 2), acting as a monarch, who places his name and titles at the head of the decree he issues, to inspire his subjects with respect. The Ten Commandments were written by God on two tables of stone, to indicate that they were only an amplification of the two commandments of charity. They are called the commandments of God, because He is their Author; they are also known as the Decalogue, i.e., ten words. We must here remark that the Catholic Church, acting under the guidance of the Holy Spirit, has slightly altered the Decalogue in a Christian sense. The Jewish Decalogue, given on Mount Sinai, consists of these precepts: (1). The command to worship no God but the true God. (2). The prohibition against the worship of images. (3). The prohibition against taking God's name in vain. (4). The command to keep holy the Sabbath. (5). The command to honor one's parents. (6). The prohibition against murder. (7). Adultery. (8). Theft. (9). False witness. (10). Coveting other men's goods (Exod. xx. 1-17). The Catholic Church has joined the Second Commandment, forbidding the worship of images, to the first, and divided the tenth into two separate commands, in order that the Christian wife may be duly respected (*vide* Ninth Commandment). The command to keep holy the Sabbath is changed into the precept to sanctify Sundays and holy-days. The idea of the Jews that upon each table five laws were inscribed is probably correct, since the first five commandments of the Jewish Decalogue contained their duty towards God and His representatives, and the latter five their duty towards their neighbor. Moreover, Our Lord, when answering the rich young man, began with the precept against murder, and St. Paul classed together the last five commands of the Jewish Decalogue (which correspond to the last six of the Christian).

2. We Christians are bound to observe the Ten Commandments of God, both because God has imprinted them upon the human heart, and because Christ laid them upon us anew in a more full and perfect form.

The Ten Commandments are binding on us who are Christians; they were imprinted on the heart of every man. It was only because the divine light in man had been obscured by evil ways and corrupt manners that the law was given upon Sinai. Thus what man would no longer read in his own heart, was inscribed on tables of stone. Christ reiterated the Ten Commandments when speaking to the rich youth (Matt. xix. 18), and in the sermon on the mount He amplified several of them, e.g., the Second, by declaring unnecessary oaths to be sinful; or the Fifth and Eighth, when He proscribed hatred and calumny, and even enjoined the love of our enemies; the Sixth by condemning the indulgence of evil desires (Matt. v.).

3. The Ten Commandments of God are arranged in order.

The first three comprise our duty to God as our supreme Ruler.

In the First Commandment He requires from us worship and fidelity; in the Second, reverence; in the Third, service.

The Fourth contains our duty towards those who are God's representatives upon earth, and who are at the same time of all men our greatest benefactors.

The remaining six commandments contain our duties to ourselves and to our fellow-men. The Fifth is for the protection of life, the Sixth of purity, the Seventh of property, the Eighth of honor, the Ninth and Tenth of the domestic life of one's neighbor.

4. He who keeps all these commandments receives a great reward from God on earth, and after death he may look forward to eternal felicity as his portion.

God has ordained that what is to us the means of attaining everlasting happiness should also promote our welfare on earth. Godliness has the promise of the life that now is, and of that which is to come (1 Tim. iv. 8). He who observes God's commandments obtains interior content, health, honor, riches, and a more intimate knowledge of God. David says to God: "Much peace have they that love Thy law, and to them there is no stumbling-block" (Ps. cxviii. 165). "By Thy commandments I have had understanding" (v. 104). He who keeps God's commandments triumphs over sufferings and persecutions. His house is built upon a rock, and the force of the elements is impotent to overthrow it (Matt. vii. 25). Only by the bridge of obedience can we enter into heaven; it is a bridge with ten arches (St. Vincent Ferrer). If our reward on earth is but trifling, our reward in heaven will be all the greater; it will be a recompense surpassing all our hopes and expectations, without limit and without end. He fulfils his promise who gives more and better than was expected of him (St. Jerome).

5. Temporal and eternal chastisements await the man who grievously violates a single one of these commandments.

He who trangresses the commandments will have both temporal and eternal punishment. The temporal punishments of sin are in general, discontent, sickness, the loss of honor or of property, hunger and other miseries. He who does not keep God's commandments will have no help from God in the time of affliction. Our Lord says the house of such a one is built on the sand, and will be destroyed (Matt. vii. 27). The lightnings and smoke on Mount Sinai are typical of the fire which will be the penalty of those who transgress God's law. "Whosoever shall keep the whole law but offend in one point. is become guilty of all" (Jas. ii. 10). The reason of this is because all the commandments form one whole; they are so closely bound up together, that one cannot be maintained without the others. He who violates one commandment transgresses the law of charity, on which all the commandments depend (St. Augustine). In this they are like a stringed instrument; one broken string will ruin the melody. Or like the human body; if one member be diseased, it is enough to cause death. If the whole city is guarded and one part left unwatched the enemy will effect an entrance. The lost in hell kept a great many of the commandments; they are damned because they did not keep all.

6. It is not a difficult matter to keep these commandments as long as God helps us with His grace; hence Christ says to

His followers: " My yoke is easy and My burden is light " (Matt. xi. 30). ·

St. John says to the Christians: " His commandments are not heavy " (1 John v. 3). The burden is heavy in itself, out God assists us with His grace to bear it if we ask Him. St. Augustine says: " When God lays a command upon thee, He requires thee to do all thou canst, and in what thou canst not do to implore His help, and He will enable thee to do it." " I can do all things in Christ that strengtheneth me " (Phil. iv. 13). Moreover the example of the saints who went before us serves to encourage us.

THE FIRST COMMANDMENT OF GOD.

On Sinai God said: " Thou shalt not have strange gods before Me " (Exod. xx. 2-7). That is to say, " Thou shalt worship the true God only; thou shalt worship no false gods." In the First Commandment interior and exterior worship is required of us. To this commandment Our Lord referred when He said to Satan: " It is written the Lord thy God shalt thou adore, and Him only shalt thou serve " (Matt. iv. 10).

In the First Commandment God enjoins upon us to worship Him, and forbids idolatry and every false form of worship.

1. THE ADORATION OR WORSHIP OF GOD.

We are accustomed to show respect to any one who is superior to ourselves in any point, in power, in experience, in knowledge, etc. We also reverence kings, aged men, men eminent for learning or science, and the like. The greater a man's superiority to ourselves, the greater is our esteem, our reverence for him. Now as God is infinitely superior to us, we owe Him the utmost respect, worship and veneration of which we are capable. This highest worship we call adoration.

We ought to adore God because He is infinitely exalted above us, and because we are entirely dependent upon Him as our Creator.

Let us meditate a while upon the infinite sublimity of God. Consider first His *omnipotence;* this is displayed in the beauty of the star-spangled firmament. " The heavens show forth the glory of God " (Ps. xviii. 2). Consider also the *eternity* of God. " One day with the Lord is as a thousand years " (2 Pet. iii. 8). Think of the *wisdom* of God, the arrangements of Whose providence are so wonderful in creation, and Who can turn even what is evil to good. " O the depth of the riches of the wisdom and of the knowledge of God! How incomprehensible are His judgments! " (Rom. xi. 33.) Think of His *fatherly care* even for the most insignificant of His creatures. At the time of Our Lord's birth, He showed grace to poor shepherds and heathens; He chose for His Mother a lowly Virgin, unlearned fishermen for His apostles, to the poor He had the Gospel preached, etc. " Who is as the Lord our God, Who dwelleth on high, and looketh down on the low things?" (Ps. cxii. 5.) How infinite is the distance between God and man! We love God, because we know Him; we adore Him because we cannot comprehend Him (St. Gregory of Nazianzen). We are entirely dependent upon God; we belong wholly and solely to Him. The members of our body, the powers of our soul are His gift; to Him we owe our being, and by Him we have been redeemed. Since He has given us all that we have, it is just that we should serve Him and worship Him alone. The consideration of the divine benefits bestowed upon us teaches us to adore Him. We must, moreover, consider that we cannot exist without God's continual help. If He deprives us of food, we cannot live; if He takes away our life, we die; if He takes from us the light of the Holy Spirit, we become spiritually blind; if He were to permit the devil to have too much power over us, we should fall into mortal sin. What is true of man, is true of all other creatures; they also are entirely dependent upon their Creator. " Thou art worthy, O Lord our God, to receive glory and honor and power; because Thou hast created all things " (Apoc. iv. 11). " Come, let us adore and fall down before the Lord that made us. For He is the Lord our God; we are the people of His pasture and the sheep of His hand " (Ps. xciv. 7).

1. The adoration we pay to God consists in this: That we acknowledge both in our hearts and by our actions that He is Our Lord and we are His creatures and His servants.

To worship God is to acknowledge our own misery and His greatness. He who worships God says with David " My substance is as nothing before Thee!" (Ps. xxxviii. 6.) Our adoration of God manifests itself first by interior reverence, then by external signs. We call those persons pious who worship God in truth.

2. We worship God interiorly by acts of faith, hope, and charity.

By faith we give our assent to all the utterances of the most high and the true God, we adore God as the perfect truth. By hope we expect all good things from the almighty and most bountiful God, we adore Him as the source of all good. By charity we occupy ourselves exclusively with God, we adore Him as our final end. St. Augustine says that the worship of God necessarily commences with a correct knowledge of God, for it is impossible to know Him without venerating Him. And who that knows the omnipotence of God and His beneficence towards mankind, can do otherwise than place his hopes in Him? Who that is conscious of the many benefits God lavishes upon him, can fail to love Him? " Is it possible," asks St. Thomas of Villanova. " for a creature to know God without loving Him ?" Reverence for God, the worship of God, are inseparable from the love of God, for we adore what we love. " Love and adoration are as closely connected as fire and flame " (St. Francis of Sales). Thus the worship of God consists of these three things: faith, hope, and charity; by acts of these virtues we are to manifest our reverence for Him. Exterior worship is nothing more or less than the expression of faith, hope, and charity.

3. We adore God exteriorly by vocal prayer, sacrifice, genu-flections, prostrations, folding of hands, striking the breast, etc.

Sacrifice is the surrender or destruction of some visible gift of God, in order thereby to honor Him as our sovereign Lord. By sacrifice we attest our belief that God is the Author of all being, the supreme Lord of all, to Whom accordingly we owe allegiance. The oblation of visible objects is a sign of the interior, spiritual sacrifice, whereby the soul surrenders herself to God as her final and blissful end. By kneeling down or prostrating one's self, as Christ did in the Garden of Olives, we acknowledge our own insignificance before God; clasping the hands signifies that we are fettered, i.e., helpless; striking the heart, like the publican in the Temple, that we are deserving of chastisement.

1. We ought to pay God exterior worship, because we are bound to render Him the homage of our bodies, and because it serves to increase our interior devotion; furthermore, external worship answers to a need inherent in our human nature.

Body and soul are both God's work, consequently both are under the obligation of manifesting their subjection to Him. An omniscient God does not indeed need outward signs of reverence, because He sees the intention of the worshipper, yet these outward tokens are useful to us, because they inflame the interior affections and augment the fervor of interior worship. And since these external ceremonies during prayer are only means to an end (that of intensifying interior devotion) they can be dispensed with if they prove a hindrance to interior worship. For instance, if one is greatly fatigued, one may sit to say one's prayers. Nay more, one may pray while walking about or standing, if one finds that thus one can pray more devoutly. Do not weary yourself with protracted kneeling, or it will occasion distraction. It is enough if the posture of the soul before God is one of lowly adoration. Man is so constituted that he must needs give outward expression to his inward feelings. When a house is on fire within, the flames burst out externally; so when a man adores God in spirit, he manifests his devotion by outward signs; otherwise he would belie the impulse of his nature, were he to suppress all demonstration of the adoration he pays in thought and heart.

2. We ought never to render external adoration to God without having awakened within us the corresponding sentiments of devotion.

He who kneels down, clasps his hands, strikes his breast, without thinking of what he is doing, is little better than a hypocrite. How many people go through the usual ceremonies in the house of God merely from habit, without thinking of what they are doing ! We must not act in this like acquaintances who, meeting casually, repeat a formula of greeting without meaning a word of what they say. The ceremonies we observe when we worship God ought faithfully to express the feelings of our heart. Christ said to the Samaritan woman that God must be adored in spirit and in truth (John iv.

24), that is, exterior worship ought to be the expression of our spiritual worship, and correspond faithfully to the feelings of our heart. Those individuals who make a greater demonstration of devotion than their interior sentiments warrant, are like people who dress above their station, and give themselves out for richer than they really are. Vicious people sometimes make an outward profession of piety, by which they seek to conceal their evil life. In this they resemble those who seek to disguise some unpleasant odor by the use of a powerful perfume, or those who having a bad complexion by nature, employ cosmetics to give it a fictitious beauty and attractive brilliancy. The ancient Egyptians used to embalm dead bodies to preserve them from decomposition. So Satan imbues those who are spiritually dead with the aroma of a spurious piety, that their moral corruption may not be apparent. Persons who make a pretence of piety may be detected by their ostentatious display of devotion and their utter lack of charity. They court observation of their religious practices, accompany their prayers with extravagant gestures, affect a downcast mien, take a prominent part in all Catholic confraternities, and count it a crime not to go to confession on particular days. Meanwhile they do not scruple to conceal a grievous sin in the tribunal of penance, they live in enmity, they slander their neighbor, give no alms and indulge envy. Thus these would-be saints betray their real character as surely as a man betrays his nationality the moment he opens his lips. Piety that is simply external does not last, because it is not the outcome of interior devotion. " Planets and comets," says St. Francis of Sales, " are both luminous, heavenly bodies, and closely resemble each other, but the comets soon disappear, whereas the planets shine on to all time." So it is with real and unreal devotion. Those who make a pretence of piety render religion contemptible, and deter many right-minded persons from devotional practices, for no one likes to be classed with hypocrites.

3. We ought to avoid all exaggeration in devotion, and never omit the duties of our state in life.

We ought to avoid every kind of exaggeration in the worship of God. True piety does not consist in a gloomy demeanor, downcast looks, a melancholy manner. True piety is cheerful. The soul that rejoices in the possession of God, that is rich in virtue, produces a pleasant impression on others. It is also a mistake to load one's self with a great variety of religious practices. We should aim at simplicity in our devotions. A short prayer, repeated a hundred times over, is often worth more than a hundred different formulas. The duties of our station ought never to be neglected for the sake of prayer, for nothing is more pleasing to God than their right fulfilment. " He who performs the duties of his calling," says St. Francis of Sales, " with diligent care for the love of God, is truly pious and a man after God's heart." That piety which is incompatible with the duties of our station is false piety. True piety adapts itself to the duties of every state and calling, as a fluid takes the form of the vessel into which it is poured.

4. We must pay supreme worship to God only, for He alone is the sovereign Lord of heaven and of earth.

Our Lord said to the devil, when he tempted Him: " It is written, the Lord thy God shalt thou adore, and Him only shalt thou serve " (Matt. iv. 10). If I am in the presence of a personage of distinction, it would be showing contempt for him were I to turn away from him, and devote my attention to some one greatly his inferior; so it would not be right to allow any object but God to engross our mind and thoughts. It is however no sin to reverence creatures in whom the perfections of God are reflected. We do not worship them with supreme worship; we only honor and venerate them for God's sake. Thus it is permissible to venerate the saints.

2. IDOLATRY OR THE WORSHIP OF FALSE GODS.

Every human creature feels himself to be dependent upon one supreme Being, and therefore is conscious of an inward impulse to adore that supreme Being. He who does not adore the true God will adore a creature. This is idolatry. He who does not worship God in the manner which He has revealed and which the Church prescribes, will ere long come to worship Him after a debased and foolish fashion. This is the false worship of God.

1. Idolatry is the worship of a creature which is regarded as a deity; e.g., the sun, fire, animals, images, etc.

Idolatry is frequently met with in the history of the Jews: witness the worship of the golden calf (Exod. xxxii.), or the adoration of the statue Nabuchodonosor set up (Dan. iii.). Remember the soldiers who fought under Judas Machabeus, and who fell in battle because they had idols concealed under their coats. Judas had prayers and sacrifices offered for the men who were thus punished. In the time of persecution some of the early Christians were guilty of idolatry, because from fear of the torture awaiting them, they offered incense upon the altars of the pagan gods. And at the French revolution the people of France fell into the sin of idolatry when a woman, personating the Goddess of Reason, was adored in the house of God.

To this day the heathen worship idols.

The heathen changed the glory of the Creator into the glory of creatures (Rom. i. 23). In Asia, where the heavenly bodies shine with greater brilliance than in northern lands, the people looked upon the sun, the moon, the circle of stars as gods, and also fire, the source of light, the wind and the great waters (Wisd. xiii. 2). The Egyptians mostly worshipped animals which were either useful or hurtful, such as the cat, the hawk, the crocodile, and especially Apis, a black bull with a white scar on its forehead and other peculiar marks, which was kept in their temple. The Romans and Greeks again worshipped statues and images of the pagan gods. And as the heathen had fallen away from the true God, as a punishment He permitted them, through the practice of idolatry, to degrade themselves by the most hideous vices (Rom. i. 28). They represented their divinities as vicious themselves, and the patrons of vice in others; by indulging in the vice of which any particular god was the protector, they thought to do him honor. This worship of false gods was nothing less than the service of devils (1 Cor. x. 20), for the devil was the animating spirit of idolatry; he dwelt in the idols and oftentimes spoke through them. David says: "The gods of the Gentiles are devils" (Ps. xcv. 5). How thankful we ought to be to almighty God for the blessings of the Gospel. It is to show our gratitude for this benefit that we stand while the Gospel is read during Mass. Three-quarters of the human race are still plunged in pagan darkness, that is to say about eight hundred millions are heathens. They are to be found principally in Africa, India, China and Japan. Every year the Holy Father sends out more missioners to the heathen. Catholics ought to support these missioners by their prayers and their alms. The Association for the Propagation of the Faith, and of the Holy Childhood of Jesus, have been instituted for this object.

2. Another form of idolatry is when a human being gives up his whole self to a creature.

It would be absurd to call a man an idolater because he offers to a false god a few grains of incense which he ought to offer to the true God, and not to apply the same term to one who devotes his whole life to the world instead of to God. The avaricious are pre-eminently idolaters (Eph. v. 5), for they consecrate their every thought, their every exertion, they sacrifice their health, their life to Mammon, to the pursuit of this world's goods. "Covetousness is the service of idols" (Col. iii. 5).

All who are engrossed in material interests are guilty of idolatry, especially the avaricious, the proud, the intemperate, the unchaste.

Whatever a man desires and adores, that is his god. The god of the avaricious is gold (Osee viii. 4); the god of the proud is honor, the god of the glutton is his belly (Phil. iii. 19); the god of the unchaste his own lusts (1 Cor. vi. 15). The greed of gain, the pride of life, sensual pleasures, are worshipped by the worldling. Parents are also guilty of idolatry, if they cherish an inordinate affection for their children (Wisd. xiv. 15).

3. The service of idols is high treason against the majesty of God, and the most heinous of sins.

St. Thomas Aquinas declares the worship of idols to be the greatest of all sins. Among the Jews it was punishable by death (Exod. xxii. 20). On one occasion no less than twenty-three thousand Jews were put to death by God's command for this transgression (Exod. xxxii. 28). He who worships idols incurs the curse of God (Deut. xxvii. 15). Think of the lamentable condition of the heathen; some of them have become so degraded through idolatry that they have sunk into the vice of cannibalism. The Apostle says idolaters, adulterers, the covetous, drunkards, and others, shall not possess the kingdom of God (1 Cor. vi. 10).

3. FOOLISH OR PERVERTED WORSHIP.

1. Superstition, fortune-telling, spiritualism, and magic, are foolish and irrational forms of worship.

1. Superstition consists in ascribing to created things powers which they do not possess, either by nature or in virtue of the prayers of the Church.

Superstition is of pagan origin. Among the Romans the will of the gods was divined by the Haruspices from the entrails of animals. The Greeks consulted the oracle of Delphi: a priestess was seated upon a tripod above a fissure in the earth whence a stupefying vapor arose, and to her incoherent utterances when in a state of unconsciousness through this exhalation, a mystic meaning was attached. Many popular and local customs that linger among us in the present day are relics of heathen times. These superstitions are generally found among people who do not care for religion; superstition and unbelief go hand in hand. Children born on a Sunday are said to be fortune's favorites; Friday is considered an unlucky day for the commencement of an enterprise, or for starting on a journey; to sit down thirteen to table is regarded as a fatal omen. Some people wear charms, such as four-leaved clover, about them to ensure good fortune. What folly this is! These we call natural superstitions, because they refer to natural objects. On the other hand, those people are not to be called superstitious who make use of, or carry on their person things that the Church has consecrated or blessed, and which consequently are endued with supernatural efficacy. To wear a cross which has been blessed, or a rosary, or a relic, to take holy water, hoping thereby to be preserved by God from evil, is not superstitious. But if a greater efficacy than they possess is ascribed to these things, for instance, if it is thought that the fact of lighting a blessed candle during a storm will avert the thunderbolt, that the mere wearing of, or recital of certain prayers will preserve from drowning or death by fire, then we have an instance of superstition. This kind of superstition is called religious, because it has reference to sacred objects.

2. Fortune-telling or soothsaying is the attempt to discover hidden or future events by means of things that are not in themselves calculated to reveal them.

The heathens of old made use of astrology for this purpose: from the course or conjunction of the planets they forecast the destiny of individuals. Even nowadays many people regard the appearance of a comet as presaging war or famine. The Roman augurs predicted what was about to happen by watching the flight of birds, listening to the cries they uttered, or observing the manner in which the sacred fowls devoured their food. What a strange delusion! In the present day, however, Christians sometimes use cards as a means of divination; if the public papers are to be believed, there are in Paris eight hundred women who tell fortunes by cards, and they are invited to the houses of the great to exercise their art. There are also many who believe in the portents of dreams, or in palmistry, or who think to foretell the future by the combinations of numbers and figures, and the like contemptible devices. They attach superstitious meaning to the howling of a dog at night, which is said to predict the death of its owner; the hour at which a watch happens to stop, etc. Those who play lottery connect certain numbers with certain events, either real or the phantoms of dreams. On the occasion of an earthquake in Rome in 1895, a million of francs was put into the lottery on the number eleven, this being the date of the earthquake, other tickets for large sums being taken for the hour and minute at which it occurred. All these numbers were drawn blanks. And that in this nineteenth century, the age of enlightenment ! On the other hand, the forecasts of meteorologists, or the prediction of what weather may be expected from the observation of natural phenomena, is of course perfectly legitimate.

3. Spiritualism is the invocation of spirits in view of learning what is hidden from human ken.

Spiritualists offer themselves to act as instruments or mediums to the spirits, their design being that some unknown spirit (that is a devil) should communicate with mankind by means of their hand or voice, or by some other manifestation, such as rapping. St. Thomas Aquinas says it is sinful to seek instruction from the devil, since the Holy Scriptures, the Word of God, are placed within our reach. " Let there not be found any one that consulteth spirits, for the Lord abhorreth all these things " (Deut. xviii. 11). Spiritualists are often excused on the plea that they are Christians, and call upon the name of God; but for that very reason they are to be condemned, because they profane God's holy name, and while professing to be Christians, they act as do the heathen.

4. Magic or sorcery is the invocation of spirits in order to produce miraculous effects.

It is an undeniable fact that among the heathen there were individuals who worked wonders by the devil's aid. There were magicians in Egypt in the time of Moses, who by their enchantments imitated his miracles (Exod. vii. 11). In the days of the apostles a magician named Simon lived in Samaria and deluded many by his sorceries (Acts viii. 10). We are also told that Antichrist will perform many lying wonders with the assistance of the evil one (2 Thess. ii. 9). The name of magician is not to be given to jugglers, who by skill and sleight of hand perform astonishing feats.

2. This perverted form of worship is a grievous sin.

God says: " The soul that shall go aside after magicians and soothsayers I will destroy out of the midst of its people " (Lev. xx. 6). David says: " Thou hast hated them that regard vanities to no purpose " (Ps. xxx. 7). He who trusts to vain things or to evil spirits, ascribes more power to them than to God; he tacitly denies the divine attributes of sanctity, omnipotence, wisdom, etc. " How canst thou hope for grace from God," asks St. John Chrysostom, " if thou dost abandon Him and have recourse to the evil enemy ? " This sin brings down severe chastisements from God. Ochozias, one of the kings of Israel, sent to inquire of Beelzebub, the god of Accaron, whether he should recover of his sickness. The prophet Elias met the messengers, and said to them: " Go and return to the king that sent you, and say to him: Thus saith the Lord, Is it because there was no God in Israel that thou sendeth to Beelzebub? Therefore thou shalt not come down from thy bed but thou shalt surely die " (4 Kings i.). Ochozias expired shortly after. Superstitious people have no peace; they are timid and apprehensive; every trifle alarms them; they are dismayed and afraid to act when they perceive what they consider as portents. Other sins follow in the train of this perversion of the reverence due to God; such as abuse of holy things, for instance, relics and images; or injustice and want of charity towards one's neighbor. Superstitious people are easily misled by their omens into rash judgments and hasty condemnations of others; or they refuse to do them a service lest it should bring ill-luck, etc.

Sins Against the First Commandment.

The First Commandment of God is transgressed:

1. By neglecting prayer.

The heathen had their household gods; they were to be seen in the halls of palaces as well as above the threshold of the lowliest dwellings. Yet Catholics, who worship the true God, too often deny Him the daily homage due to Him. The followers of Mohammed never omit, when the muezzin calls to prayer, to kneel down and perform their orisons, even in public places, while Christians, who hold the true faith, do not scruple to dispense with prayer almost entirely. Unhappy is the household where family prayer is an unknown thing !

2. By opposing religion, either by speaking against the faith, or by the publication or dissemination of books and periodicals hostile to the faith, or by joining associations of an anti-Christian character.

3. By worshipping idols or being engrossed in material interests.

4. By superstitions.

5. By telling fortunes or having one's fortune told.

6. By invoking spirits, either for the purpose of searching out what is hidden, or of doing what cannot be done in the ordinary course of nature.

4. THE VENERATION OF SAINTS.

We call those saints who died in the grace of God, and who are already in heaven, more especially those whom the Church has canonized.

Canonization does not admit any one into heaven; it is only a solemn declaration on the part of the Pope that the man or woman in question has led a holy life (this having been proved by the examination of his or her life), and that (as the miracles proved to have been wrought by the individual testify) he or she is already in heaven, and is therefore to be venerated by the Church. Canonization is preceded by beatification; by this latter the individual is proposed for the veneration of a portion of the faithful only, whereas by canonization he is declared worthy to receive the cultus of the whole Church. The scrutiny to which the life and miracles are subjected is extremely rigorous; they are laid before a special congregation composed of cardinals, priests, physicians, scientists, who are appointed to examine them by the Supreme Pontiff himself. This examination does not take place as a rule until fifty years after the death of the servant of God. On account of the great number of the saints, their different degree of glory, and the fact that their life was more in heaven than on earth, they are compared to the stars; or again to precious stones, rarely found upon earth and valuable in God's sight; to the cypress, whose wood never decays, because they were not contaminated by the corruption of serious sin ; to the majestic cedars of Lebanon, by reason of the height of perfection they attained; to the fragrant lily, because by their good works they shed a sweet odor around them; to an anvil, unbroken by the blows of the hammer, for they stood steadfast beneath the strokes of misfortune. They are also said to be the pillars of the Church, for they sustain her by their prayers, and like the towers that crown a city, they add to her outward majesty and dignity.

The Church ordains that those saints alone whom she has canonized should be publicly venerated by the faithful.

The Church knows that the veneration of the saints is good and useful for us. Consequently she omits no opportunity of inciting us to it; at Baptism the name of a saint is given to the child who is made one of the members of the Church, and the same is done at Confirmation. Every day in the year some one or more saints are commemorated; statues and pictures of saints are placed in the churches, their names are mentioned in the Mass and invoked in litanies and public prayers.

1. We honor the saints because they are the friends of God, princes of the heavenly court, and benefactors to ourselves; also because we obtain great graces from God through venerating them.

We venerate the saints because they are the friends and servants of God. He who reverences the emperor will not fail to honor his servants, the ministers, or viceroy, etc., for the reverence paid to them is indirectly paid to the emperor himself. For this reason we venerate the friends and servants of God. Every man of good feeling likes his friends to be respected, and feels it to be a slight to himself if they are treated with contempt; how much more is this so with God. He desires that those who loved Him above all things on earth should receive special honor. While the saints lived here below, they fled from honors; nay, more, they were despised, calumniated, persecuted by evil men. Therefore God now wills that their innocence and virtue should be made clear, and they should be venerated by all

Christendom. God Himself gives honor to the saints; He works miracles through their intercession, and oftentimes inflicts condign punishment on those who show them disrespect. Christ Himself says: " If any man minister to Me, him will My Father honor " (John xii. 26). We venerate the saints on account of their exalted rank in heaven. If we show so much honor to kings by whom God rules the world, how much the more is it incumbent upon us to honor the celestial spirits whom God makes His instruments for the government of the Church, and of whole races of men, and also for the salvation of mankind; and whose dignity therefore far exceeds that of earthly princes. Most of the saints moreover have a claim on us for the services they have rendered to mankind; heathen countries have been evangelized by them (witness St. Boniface, the apostle of Germany); others have maintained and defended the faith, as St. Ignatius of Loyola by forming the Society of Jesus; or again they have enriched the Church by their writings, as did St. Augustine. Many a time the saints have prevailed upon God on behalf of their fellow-men. He would have spared Sodom for the sake of ten just men (Gen. xviii. 32); for Joseph's sake He blessed the house of Putiphar (Gen. xxxix. 5); for the sake of the elect the days of judgment shall be shortened (Matt. xxiv. 22). After their death the saints offer supplications before the throne of God for their kinsfolk and their people. The prophet Jeremias did not cease after death to pray for the Jewish people and for all the holy city (2 Mach. xv. 14). The saints in heaven and Christians upon earth are all members of one body. When one member suffers, all the members suffer with it, and they mutually succor one another. Thus the saints help us by their prayers. How much honor is paid to men who have deserved well of their contemporaries; their services are lauded and magnified, statues are erected to their memory, institutions, towns, streets are named after them; ought we not then to venerate our best benefactors? If the man who rescues me from drowning has a claim on my gratitude, how much more those who have spent their strength in endeavoring to save me from eternal perdition! Furthermore, the Council of Trent tells us that the veneration of the saints is of practical utility to ourselves; through them we obtain favors from God, besides a speedy answer to our prayers. Our petitions are much more favorably received by an earthly monarch if they are presented by one of his courtiers; so it is with God, and the more intercessors we have the better for us. What God might not grant to a single saint, He will not deny to several, just as an abbot cannot refuse to grant a request preferred by the whole of his community. Wherefore, as beggars go from house to house asking an alms, let us go through the streets of the heavenly city, appealing to the apostles, the martyrs, the virgins, and the confessors, imploring them to intercede on our behalf.

2. We venerate the saints if we entreat their intercession with God, if we celebrate their feasts, reverence their images and their relics; if we bear their name, claim their protection in matters of importance, and praise them in word and song. The best manner in which to venerate them is to imitate their virtues.

One day we are to be the companions of the saints in heaven, and this prospect unites us to them in a mutual love. Both they and we belong to the same great family whose father is God. This is the meaning of the communion of saints. Hence they espouse our cause, when we invoke their aid and their intercession with God. The fact of invoking them testifies to the esteem in which we hold them, and the value we attach to their prayers. We celebrate the feasts of the saints. In the earliest ages of the Church the day whereon the martyrs suffered was carefully noted down, to be commemorated annually. In the world great events are celebrated by a jubilee; why should not the same be done in the Church? The anniversaries of the saints are not holydays of obligation, excepting the feast of St. Peter and St. Paul in England, and the festival of All Saints here. And as we like to preserve in memory of the departed, little objects that have belonged to them, whether they be our own relatives and friends, or men of great renown, so the relics of the saints and their images are to be held in veneration. The names of heroes and great men are given to public institutions or buildings, so we receive the name of some saint or great servant of God at our Baptism and Confirmation, or on entering a religious Order, taking him or her for our patron. We also dedicate churches, towns, and countries to some saint, placing them under his protection. Heroes and illustrious men of past times often furnish a theme to the orator and the poet; so panegyrics are pronounced, and hymns sung in honor of the saints. But the most important thing is to imitate the saints. "To venerate the saints without following in their steps," says St. Augustine, "is merely offering them the incense of empty flattery." To read the lives of the saints is also a means of honoring them, for we read the record of their deeds in order to take them for patterns in our own actions.

3. The veneration we pay to the saints does not in the least detract from the honor due to God, for we only reverence the saints for God's sake, and by no means do we reverence them in the way that we reverence God, but only because they are the servants of God.

The veneration of the saints does not detract from the honor due to God. Who would think of saying that it showed want of respect to the emperor to honor his mother, his children, his friends, and faithful servants? On the contrary, it would rather evince our respect for him (St. Jerome). By venerating the saints of God we no more detract from the honor due to Him than we do by charity towards our neighbor, and we know that the love of God increases with the love of one's neighbor. We honor the saints because in them the divine image is reflected. We reverence a portrait of the king as being a faithful representation of the monarch to whom we owe allegiance; so we reverence the saints because we see the image of God in them. We love them as we love our fellow-men; they are made after God's image, and are His children. We also venerate the saints because they were instruments employed by God to perform new and signal deeds. We do not honor them for what they were in and by themselves; their works do not redound to their own glory, so much as to the glory of God, Who worked by their agency. Thus the credit of a beautiful picture does not belong to the brush, or a clever book to the pen, or an eloquent discourse to the lips that merely repeated it. God alone is wonderful in His saints. The Blessed Mother of God did not say: " I have done great things; " but, " He that is mighty hath done great things to me " (Luke i. 49). And as by venerating the saints we honor God, so by despising the saints we dishonor God. Our Lord declared that to despise His apostles was tantamount to despising Himself (Luke x. 16), and that He regarded every act of unkindness towards one's neighbor as an act of unkindness to Himself (Matt. xxv. 40). And since God loves the saints in heaven far more than men on earth, He must be deeply affronted by disrespect shown to them. An additional reason why veneration of the saints in no wise diminishes our reverence for God, is because we do not honor them as we honor God. We adore God, but we do not adore the saints, so we do not pay to them the *supreme* homage that we pay to God, for we know that the distance between Him and them is infinite. However superior the saints are to us, they are only creatures like ourselves. The esteem and veneration in which we hold them is the same in kind as that in which we hold the servants of God on earth, only it is greater in degree, because the saints have already passed as victors into the Church Triumphant. The saints do not desire the adoration of men. When Tobias and his family prostrated themselves before the angel, he said : " Bless ye God, sing praises to Him " (Tob. xii. 18). When St. John the Divine fell down before the feet of the angel, he said to him : " See thou do it not, adore God " (Apoc. xix. 10). And if we kneel beside the tomb or before the image of a saint, we no more adore him than a servant adores his master if he goes on his knees to ask a favor of him. If the holy sacrifice is offered in honor of a saint, if churches and altars are dedicated to him, it is only in the hope that he will unite his prayers to the sacrifices we offer, the prayers we say at his shrine; and we praise God, Who led the saint in so marvellous a way to the attainment of sanctity. Thus veneration of the saints is not idolatry, nor does it betray want of confidence in Christ, our great Mediator. It rather betokens mistrust of ourselves, a humble spirit. Conscious of our own unworthiness to present our petitions to Christ, we have recourse to a mediator whose prayers will have greater weight with Him than our own.

4. It is advisable under different circumstances of life to invoke certain saints.

Experience has proved how much is gained by invoking the saints in times of special need. We invoke St. Joseph as the patron of a happy death, because he expired in the arms of Jesus and Mary; also in seasons of temporal distress, for on him the Child Jesus was dependent for His maintenance. For diseases of the throat St. Blase is to be invoked, who miraculously cured a boy thus afflicted; for diseases of the eye we call on St. Ottilia for aid, because she, when blind, recovered her sight at her Baptism. Those who suffer through calumny find a protector in St. John Nepomucene, who was a martyr to the seal of confession; and when anything is lost, we have recourse to St. Anthony, through whose prayers the thief who had stolen from him a valuable manuscript, had no peace until he restored it.

It appears that God has given to individual saints special powers to help us in special needs. Many wonderful answers to prayer lead to the belief that the saints take particular interest in persons whose circumstances are the same as theirs were on earth, and whose calling or state of life is the same as was their own, as well as for the place where they lived and labored.

5. THE VENERATION OF THE MOTHER OF GOD.

Many are the types of our blessed Lady to be found in the Old Testament; e.g., Eve, the mother of all mankind; Noe's ark, wherein the human race was preserved from extinction; the Ark of the Covenant containing the manna; Judith who slew Holofernes, the archenemy of her people; Esther, who was exempted from the universal law (as Mary was from original sin), and by her mediation rescued her people from death; the mother of the Machabees, who witnessed the death of her seven sons, and whose heart, like Mary's, was pierced with seven swords, etc. The Gospels gave little information respecting the life of Our Lady; more concerning it may be learned from the revelations of the saints.

Mary, the Mother of Jesus Christ, is usually called the Mother of God or the Most Blessed Virgin.

Elizabeth was the first to call Mary Mother of God (Luke i. 43). The Council of Ephesus, in 431, confirmed this title, *Dei Genitrix,* and condemned the contrary doctrine asserted by the heretic Nestorius. Mary gave birth to Him Who is God and man in one person. A child does not receive its soul from its mother, but from God, yet she of whom it is born is called its mother; in like manner Mary is justly termed the "Mother of God," although Christ did not derive from her His divine nature. Mary is also rightly called "the Blessed Virgin." The words she spoke to the angel announced her determination to preserve her virginity inviolate (Luke i. 34). Many ages before the prophet Isaias foretold that a virgin should conceive and bear a Son (Is. vii. 14). In her conception, in child-bearing, and after the birth of Jesus, Mary remained a virgin. As the bush burned with fire and was not consumed, so Mary's virginity was not impaired by the birth of Christ; as Our Lord appeared in the midst of the apostles although the doors of the room where they were assembled were shut, so He came into the world, and her chastity remained intact. So the sun shines through glass without in any wise changing it. Mary is the window of heaven, through which the true Light came into the world. Those who are spoken of in the Gospels as the *brethren of Christ* (Matt. xiii. 55) are His blood relations; it was customary among the Jews to term near relatives brethren. Abraham called his nephew Lot by this name (Gen. xiii. 8). "Had Mary had other children who could have taken care of her, Our Lord upon the cross would not have commended her," as St. John Chrysostom remarks, "to the beloved disciple." Christ was called the "first-born," to indicate the fact that He was, according to Jewish law, sanctified to the Lord (Exod. xiii. 2). Christ was, in fact, the first-born among many brethren (Rom. viii. 29), that is, all Christian people, who are besides the children of Mary. Mary was espoused to Joseph by God's command, in order that she might not be stoned after the birth of Christ, and also in order to provide a guardian for her and the divine Child. The name Mary is a Hebrew word, meaning lady, or mistress.

We pay greater honor to Mary, the Mother of Christ, than to any other saint.

Even in her lifetime, Mary had great honor paid to her; at the Annunciation the angel addressed her as "full of grace," and "blessed among women" (Luke i. 28). It is a great honor if an angel appears to mortal men and affords them an opportunity of showing him reverence; yet at the Annunciation it was not man who reverenced the angel, but the angel who reverenced man. "Hence," St. Thomas Aquinas says, "we conclude that Mary excels the angels in dignity." How respectfully Elizabeth treated Mary; she called her blessed, and gave her the title of Mother of her Lord (Luke i. 42, 43). Mary herself foresaw that she would be praised by posterity, for she said: "From henceforth all generations shall call me blessed" (Luke i. 48). The Church invites us to honor the Mother of God with special devotion. The Hail Mary is almost invariably added to the Our Father; three times a day the Angelus bell reminds us of the mystery of the Incarnation, and bids us invoke the name of Mary; many festivals have been instituted in her honor, the Litany of Loretto is recited at the public services of the Church; the month of May, the fairest month in the year, is dedicated to her, and during October the Rosary is daily recited. Moreover, numerous churches are erected in all lands in honor of the Mother of God, not a few of these being renowned places of pilgrimage, where signal graces and favors are obtained; and the most glorious titles are given to her, such as: Channel of grace, Mother of mercy, Refuge of sinners, Help of Christians, Queen of heaven, etc. Yet the veneration we pay to Mary is distinct from the adoration due to God. Exalted honor is due to Mary, but the Father, the Son, and the Holy Ghost alone, do we adore.

1. We hold Mary in such great veneration because she is the Mother of God and our Mother.

Whoever truly loves God must assuredly honor the Mother of God, and honor her, too, far above all the saints, the friends of God. The honor paid to the Queen-Mother is reflected upon the King, her Son. One may judge of the measure in which a man loves God by his devotion to Mary. In fact, the greater the saint, the more intensely does he love Mary. She is actually our Mother, for Our Lord gave her to us upon the cross when He said to St. John: "Behold thy Mother" (John xix. 27), John representing on Calvary all the followers of Christ. Mary is the second Eve, the Mother of all mankind; as the disobedience of Eve brought misery upon the human race, so the obedience of Mary restores it to a state of grace. Through one woman death came into the world, through another, life. And since Mary is our Mother, our salvation is more a matter of concern to her than to any of the saints. After Christ no one cares for us as she does. St. Bernard declares that the love of all the mothers in the world does not equal the love Mary bears to each one of her children. And the reason she cares so much for us is because of her love for God, and consequently her charity towards her neighbor exceeds that of any other saint. As the glory of the moon surpasses that of the stars, so the love of Mary for us exceeds that of the angels; it is a boundless ocean of love. Mary knows all our circumstances; this even the angels do (Luke xv. 7), and it cannot be supposed that they know more than does their Queen. A dutiful child delights to be with its mother, and the devout Christian rejoices to address to Mary, the Mother of God, his loving supplications.

2. Another reason why Mary is so highly honored throughout Christendom, is because God has exalted her above all men and angels.

Monarchs grant privileges to the towns where they were born, or where they were crowned; so the King of heaven has conferred special privileges and prerogatives on the Mother who bore Him.

Mary was, in fact, chosen by God to be the Mother of His Son, preserved from the stain of original sin, raised gloriously from the tomb, and crowned Queen of heaven.

No angel, not even the most perfect and greatest of the heavenly host, can say to God as Mary can: "Thou art my Son." O what a marvellous privilege is this! Mary is indeed the *Mater admirabilis*, and that not alone because she is at one and the same time Virgin and Mother, nor because she is Mother both of the creature and of the Creator, but pre-eminently because she gave birth to Him Who was the Author of her being. Mary is the wonder of wonders, and nothing in the universe, God only excepted, is more glorious than she is. Mary's spotless purity, her sinlessness, was first proclaimed by God in paradise (Gen. iii. 15), and afterwards by the archangel Gabriel (Luke i. 28). God said to the serpent, "She shall crush thy head." Had Mary been brought under the dominion of the devil by sin, she could not possibly have been his conqueror. Gabriel saluted Mary as "full of grace." The dignity of Christ alone demanded that His Mother should be entirely free from sin. When God raises any one to a high post, He fits him for it; and the Son of God, in choosing Mary to be His Mother, rendered her by the gifts of grace fit for this exalted dignity (St. Thomas Aquinas). Now we know that no one who built a house for his own use, would first put his greatest enemy in possession of it; much less would the Holy Spirit, Whose temple Mary was to be, allow the evil one to make her his own. The Fathers of the Church and the children of the Church in all ages, have given to Mary the title of immaculate both in their writings and in their prayers; and in 1854 the Holy Father declared her Immaculate Conception to be a dogma of the faith. Mary was therefore free from original and actual sin (Council of Trent, 6, 23); she is compared to a lily among thorns (Cant. ii. 2), a mirror without a flaw (Wisd. vii. 26). She advanced in perfection rapidly and continuously, like the vine (Ecclus. xxiv. 23) that grows higher and higher, till it attains the height of the tree to which it clings. **She** advanced all the more rapidly, because she was so near to the source of all grace, and was the recipient of greater and more abundant graces than other men. Mary was the most holy and perfect of all creatures; and her sanctity surpassed that of all other saints as much as the light of the moon exceeds in brilliance that of the planets. Even in the first moments of her existence, Mary's sanctity was greater than that of the most eminent saints at the close of their life. On account of her exalted sanctity, she is compared to the tower of David (Cant. iv. 4), which rose in majestic stateliness on the highest summit of the mountains about Jerusalem. She is also called the mirror of justice. Of all created beings none ever loved God so intensely as Mary did, or cared so little for the things of earth. As the action of fire causes iron to glow with heat, so the Holy Spirit inflamed the heart of Mary with charity. On account of her great love she is called the house of gold. Mary was adorned with every virtue. She is the mystical rose, for as the rose surpasses all other flowers in the beauty of its coloring and the fragrance of its perfume, so Mary exceeds all the saints in the magnitude of her love for God, and the sweet odor of her virtues. She is the Queen of whom the Psalmist speaks (Ps. xliv. 11), clad in the golden garments of charity, surrounded by a variety of virtues.' "Thus," Suarez declares, "she was dearer to God than all the other saints together." The body of the Blessed Virgin was assumed gloriously into Heaven. It is said that the apostle Thomas, having arrived in Jerusalem too late to assist at her interment, was desirous to see her remains in the sepulchre; but when it was opened nothing was found there but the grave-clothes in which her body had been wrapped. Catherine Emmerich in her visions asserts that Our Blessed Lady died forty-eight years after the birth of Christ, at the age of sixty-four. Having gone from Ephesus to Jerusalem to follow again the footsteps of her Son in the way of the cross, she fell mortally sick and died of grief: hence her tomb was in Jerusalem. The feast of her Assumption is kept throughout the whole Church on the fifteenth of August. No one has ever claimed to possess a relic of her body. Mary shines in heaven with unrivalled splendor. The sun, moon, and stars of our solar system are symbols of Christ, His Mother and the saints. Mary is the Queen of angels, the Queen of all saints. In her more than in any other creature we gain a knowledge of the divine attributes. Most especially we see displayed in her glorious exaltation the infinite goodness of God, Who raises the poor man from the dunghill, that He may set him with princes and elevate him above the choirs of celestial spirits (Ps. cxii. 7. 8).

3. Finally, we entertain this great veneration for Mary, because her intercession is more powerful with God than that of any other saint.

Mary's intercession has immense power with God. On earth her petitions were all-prevailing with Christ, as at the marriage-feast at Cana. And if Christ granted all His Mother's prayers on earth, how much the more will He do so in heaven. When the General Coriolanus could not be prevailed upon by the Senate and priests of Rome to withdraw his army from before the city, he yielded to the entreaties of his mother Veturia, although he knew that to do so

would cost him his life. How much the more will Christ, the great
Lawgiver, listen to the supplications of His Mother! If the prayers
of the saints, His servants, have so much power with God, what
must those of His Mother have! Being the prayers of a mother, they
are less like a petition than a command. St. Bernard declares Mary
to be omnipotent by means of her intercession; there is nothing that
she cannot obtain for us. As at the court of an earthly monarch
he is sure to succeed for whom the queen interests herself, so at
the court of the King of kings those for whom Mary, the Queen of
heaven, pleads, will not be disappointed of their desires. Thus Mary
is our hope; because through her intercession we hope to procure
the blessings which our poor prayers cannot obtain. Hence the
saints speak of her as the dispenser of graces, for all the favors we
receive from heaven come to us through her hands. "God," St.
Peter Damian says, "would not become man until Mary had given
her consent, in order that we might see that the salvation of mankind rested in her hands." She stood beneath the cross that we
might know that without her mediation no one could be made partaker of the merits of the blood of Christ. God the Father sanctions,
Christ grants, and Mary distributes the gifts of heaven to mankind. Thus Mary is the Mother of divine grace. No prayer she
proffers is unanswered. "Who can doubt," exclaims St. Bernard,
"that the Son will listen to His Mother—such a Son to such a
Mother!" Remember how the same saint declares in the *Memorare*
that it is a thing unheard of for any one to implore Mary's aid, and
implore in vain. Even the least and shortest prayer to Mary does not
go unrecompensed; she rewards the slightest intentions with the richest graces. Every time we salute her she does not fail to return our
greeting. She is the Virgin most clement. There is not a trace of
sternness about her; she is all clemency, loving kindness and gentleness. He would be wrong indeed who approached her with trembling.

From time immemorial Christians have been accustomed to
have recourse to Mary in times of affliction and distress.

In the year 1683, when the Turks besieged Vienna, both in the
beleaguered city and throughout Christendom the Rosary was recited to implore the aid of the Mother of God, and a signal victory
was the result. Individual Christians also appeal to Mary for aid
when private troubles press heavily upon them. She is called the
Help of Christians, the Comforter of the afflicted, the Health of the
sick. Christians call upon her in seasons of severe sickness. It is
recorded of St. John Damascene, that when the caliph, enraged with
him for having written in defence of the veneration of images,
caused his right hand to be struck off, the saint prostrated himself
before a statue of Our Lady, and was immediately healed. In the
present day how numerous are the miraculous cures effected at
Lourdes! To Mary also is due the conversion of many sinners who
desire to amend their lives, for upon those who invoke her the light
of the Holy Spirit is shed. Mary is the morning star; as that planet
heralds the sunrise, so devotion to Mary is the forerunner of divine
grace, the gracious influence of the Holy Ghost. She is compared
to the dawn (Cant. vi. 9), because as the shades of night vanish

before the rising sun, so sin departs from the soul that is devoted to Mary. The month of May is dedicated to her, because nature then awakens to a new life, and devotion to Mary brings fresh life to the soul dead in sin. Witness the miraculous conversion of the public sinner, Mary of Egypt, before an image of Our Lady in the Church of the Holy Cross in Jerusalem. Mary is ever desirous to effect our reconciliation with God, far more so than any earthly mother could be to establish peace between two members of her family who were at enmity with each other. Through her intercession Our Lord's anger is easily appeased. Alexander the Great once said: " A single tear from my mother's eyes will blot out many death-warrants." If a man, and a heathen to boot, will speak thus of his mother, what may we not expect from the divine Son of Mary? She is the Refuge of sinners; the Mother of mercy; from her as from an olive tree to which she is likened (Eccles. xxiv. 19), the softening oil of mercy flows. She is our mediatrix; to her we fly in temptation; as the Jews on their entrance into the Promised Land (Numb. x. 35), and in their wars with the Philistines (1 Kings xiv.) carried with them the ark of the Lord to insure victory, so through Mary, the Ark of the Covenant of the New Testament, are we enabled to conquer our spiritual foes. As the star guides the mariner, tossing on the stormy sea, to a safe haven, so Mary guides us over the tempestuous ocean of life to the celestial port. She is compared in Holy Scripture to a plane-tree in the streets (Eccles. xxiv. 19), because as the tree protects the wayfarer from sun and rain, so Mary defends those who place themselves under her care from the assaults of the devil. To the enemy of mankind she is " terrible as an army set in array " (Cant. vi. 3). Various titles are given to Mary to indicate the circumstances in which we may invoke her aid and trust in her succor, such as: Mother of perpetual succor, Mother of good counsel, Mother of dolors, etc.

Devotion to the Mother of God is an excellent means of attaining sanctity here below and eternal happiness hereafter.

No one can fail to observe the filial affection and devotion which all the saints have displayed towards the Mother of God, and the signal success with which God has rewarded this devotion on their part. Among the most prominent of these was St. Bernard of Clairvaux, and in later times St. Alphonsus Liguori, the author of the " Glories of Mary." Mary is the gate of heaven; a ladder connecting heaven and earth, by which the Lord of heaven came down to us, and by which we may ascend up to God. St. Alphonsus declares it to be his persuasion that hell cannot boast of containing one single soul who ever had a true and heartfelt devotion to Mary. St. Bernard asserts that those who honor her daily will assuredly be saved. St. Francis Borgia always feared for the salvation of that soul which had little or no devotion for the Mother of God.

6. THE VENERATION OF IMAGES OF THE SAINTS.

The veneration of sacred pictures and images is as old as Christianity itself. In the Catacombs representations are found of Christ, of the Mother of God with the divine Child, and of biblical scenes from the Old or New Testament, calculated to strengthen the Christians in times of persecution, by reminding them of God's omnipotence and of a future resurrection. With the spread of Christianity the veneration paid to images increased. Pictures, statues, and crosses, were seen not in the churches alone, but on the market-place and highways. In the eighth century the Emperor of the East prohibited the veneration of images; the figures of the saints were broken to pieces or burned, the paintings on the walls of the churches were whitewashed over, and any persons who persisted in venerating images were punished (this was called the iconoclastic movement). The veneration of images answers to a need of our human nature; we respect the portraits of those whom we love or esteem; moreover it is the will of God that man, who lost true happiness for the sake of material things, should regain it by means of material things. The Jews were strictly forbidden to make images or bow down to them (Exod. xx. 4), because they had a strong propensity towards idolatry, and the Son of God had not then become man. In spite of this prohibition there were two golden cherubim, one on each side of the propitiatory in the Holy of holies (Exod. xxv. 18), and we also read of a brazen serpent in the wilderness, whereon the Israelites were commanded to look that they might be healed (Numb. xxi. 8).

By sacred pictures or statues are meant representations of Christ, of the saints, or of the truths of religion.

The manner in which Our Lord is ordinarily depicted is familiar to all of us; the expression of His countenance is grave and benign, His eyes are blue, His hair is of a ruddy brown, curling and parted in the middle, His beard is short, and a burning heart is often placed upon His breast. The Mother of God is represented in various ways: as Help of Christians she holds the divine Child in her arms; as Mother of dolors, the dead Christ is laid across her knees; as Our Lady of the Immaculate Conception she is as she appeared at Lourdes, in a white robe, without her Infant Son; as Queen of heaven (Apoc. xii. 1) with her head encircled with twelve stars and the moon beneath her feet. The most celebrated and well-known pictures of the Mother of God are: (1) The painting in the Church of Santa Maria Maggiore in Rome, supposed to be the work of St. Luke; (2) The Madonna di San Sisto, painted by Rafael; (3) The miraculous picture of Our Lady of Perpetual Succor, painted upon wood, and dating from the thirteenth century, in the Church of St. Alphonsus in Rome. The representations of the saints are easily recognized; they have a nimbus round their head, and are accompanied by emblems either of their office, of the special virtue that distinguished them, or by the instruments wherewith they suffered martyrdom. The four Evangelists are known by their symbols: St. Matthew has an angel in human shape beside him, because his gospel begins with the genealogy of Our Lord; St. Mark has a lion, because he speaks in the opening chapter of a voice crying in the wilderness; St. Luke is accompanied by an ox, because he begins with Zacharias' sacrifice; St. John by an eagle, because his gospel begins with sublime and lofty truths. We also call those sacred pictures which portray some great truth, such as the doctrine of the Holy Trinity, or purgatory; or some event recorded in Holy Scripture. The three divine persons are represented under the form they have assumed when appearing to men. But all delineations of the Godhead do no more than give an idea of certain attributes or actions of the Deity, for it is not within the power of man to make an image of God.

Pictures or statues of saints, by means of which or before which miracles have been worked, are called miraculous images.

There are a great many places of pilgrimage on the continent of Europe where an image of Our Lady is to be seen, by means of which extraordinary favors and graces have been and are obtained. Among these Einsiedeln in Switzerland, Alt-Otting in Bavaria, Kevelaer in the Rhineland may be mentioned. It is also well known that many cures have been effected through devotion to the Infant Jesus of Prague (a wax statue in the church of the Carmelites in that city), especially at the time of the pestilence in 1713. The Empress Maria Teresa had a great veneration for that image; she worked a robe for it with her own hands, richly embroidered with gold. Many of these miraculous images have been preserved from destruction in a marvellous manner; they have, for instance, been in the fire without being burned. Many signal cures have been wrought in a moment, in answer to prayers offered before them. Such miracles are permitted by God as an attestation to the truth of the Catholic Church, and it would be a sin on the part of any Catholic to deny their authenticity. A strict investigation is made of these miracles by the Holy See, and then the statue of the saint is crowned.

Above all representations of the saints or of holy things, we venerate the cross of Our Redeemer.

There ought not to be a single church, or altar, or cemetery, without a crucifix. Such is the honor in which the Church holds the cross of Christ, that she allows no sacrament to be administered, no Mass to be celebrated, no act of divine worship to be performed unless in presence of the crucifix. The cross is seen on the crown of the monarch, on the breast of the bishop, and it is awarded as a decoration to men of merit. The cross is in the hand of the dying Christian when he draws his last breath, and it accompanies him to the grave. This sacred symbol ought to be found in every Christian household; it does not speak well for the inhabitants of a house if none but secular pictures adorn its walls.

1. **We honor the images of the saints by giving them a place in our dwellings; we say our prayers before them, we salute them respectfully, we adorn them with offerings, we make pilgrimages to their shrines.**

The reverence we pay to the image of a saint is not paid to the picture or image itself, but to the individual it represents; that is, to Christ, or some one of the saints. When we adore the cross we adore Him Who died thereon. By showing respect to the portrait of a king, we testify our respect for the monarch, and disrespect manifested to his portrait is a personal affront to himself. When the book of the Gospels is kissed, it is the Word of God therein contained that is venerated. Thus when we kiss our parents or our children, we express the love and fondness of our hearts, and in venerating images, we express our love for the persons they represent. And when incense is burned, or tapers lighted before the images, it is as a symbol of the light of the Holy Ghost and the virtues wherewith the saints were endowed. It is not from the images themselves that we ask help, it is from God, through the intercession of the saints. None but the heathen imagine that there is any virtue or supernatural power in the image itself. Moses did not think that his staff worked miracles, but God Who powerfully assisted him.

2. Through venerating the images of the saints, efficacious and oftentimes supernatural graces are obtained; they are also useful as a means of avoiding distractions in prayer, and affording us a silent admonition.

St. John Damascene says that the Holy Spirit surrounds the images of the saints with a certain halo of grace. Wherever the cross is erected, the malicious designs of the evil one are defeated. How often a soul sunk in sin has been touched and converted by the sight of an image; how often have pictures comforted and encouraged devout persons, especially at the moment of death! While gazing upon an image we pray with greater recollection; images are steps whereby we ascend more easily in spirit to heaven. And as one's prayers, when offered at the shrine of some saint are more fervent, so they are more readily granted; the *ex-votos* hung beside the image testify to the efficacy of the saint's intercession—they are also a constant admonition to us; either by placing vividly before us one of the truths of religion, or exhorting us to imitate the example of the saint. The work of the artist does indeed often prove more influential than the words of the preacher, for the impressions we receive through the ear have less effect upon the mind than those which we receive through the eye. St. Gregory the Great calls pictures the books of the unlearned. In the Middle Ages, before there were any printed books, pictures were widely disseminated among the people. From those times we date the crib, the sepulchre, the stations of the cross, etc.

7. THE VENERATION OF RELICS.

The name of relic is given to the remains of the saints, as well as to objects that have been closely connected with Christ or the saints.

The body of a saint is a relic, or any portion of it, even the most minute particle of bone. These relics are placed beneath or upon our altars; they also pass into the possession of private persons. Those only are *authentic* to which the name of the saint and the episcopal seal is attached. The relics themselves must not be sold, but this prohibition does not apply to the case containing them. From time immemorial those objects also which are closely connected with Our Lord or the saints have been held in high veneration; for instance, the cross of Christ, His tunic, His winding-sheet, the manger wherein the Infant Jesus was laid, Veronica's veil, etc. The holy cross was discovered by the Empress Helena in the year 325, and a portion of it is in the Church of the Holy Sepulchre at Jerusalem. A part of the manger is in the Church of Santa Maria Maggiore in Rome. The seamless coat of Our Lord is in the Cathedral of Treves. (In 1891 it was exposed for six weeks, and two thousand of the faithful came to adore it. During that period eleven authentic cases of miraculous cure took place.) At Argenteuil, near Paris, another garment worn by Our Lord when a child is preserved; it was presented by Charlemagne to the church. The holy winding-sheet is in Turin; Veronica's veil is in St. Peter's at Rome. Several other important relics are preserved in the Cathedral of Aix-la-Chapelle. The whole of Palestine is to the Christian a sacred and precious relic; the seven crusades undertaken to recover it from the Saracens prove how much it was valued in the Middle Ages. The principal holy places are: The place of crucifixion and the sepulchre on Mount Calvary; the scene of Our Lord's agony and the spot whence He ascended on Mount Olivet; the cenacle on Mount Sion, His birthplace at Bethlehem and the holy house of Nazareth, now at Loretto. At all these places churches were erected, mostly by the Emperor Constantine, or his mother, St. Helena. The garments worn by martyrs and the instruments of their execution, the spots where eminent saints were born or are buried, have always been held in veneration. It was formerly the custom to erect churches and altars for the celebration of divine worship over places thus hallowed, especially where the saints are interred.

Relics are deserving of veneration for this reason, because the bodies of the saints were temples of the Holy Ghost, and instruments whereby He worked; and they will rise glorious from the grave.

The Jews regarded a dead body as an unclean thing, but the Christian looks upon it with respect, as having been the dwelling-place of the Holy Ghost, and as being the seed whence the immortal, glorified body will spring at the resurrection. Moreover, as St. Jerome remarks, by honoring the saints, we adore Him for Whom they died. God Himself shows·them honor, for by their medium He works miracles. Many bodies, or portions of the bodies of saints still remain incorrupt and supple, as that of St. Teresa, or St. Francis Xavier; some emit a delicious fragrance; from others an oil distils possessed of healing properties. " God," says St. John Chrysostom, " has divided the possession of the saints between Himself and us; He has taken their souls to Himself, and has left their bodies for us."

1. We honor the relics of the saints by preserving them with reverence, and visiting the spot where they are deposited.

Even among the Jews relics were regarded with reverence. At the exit from Egypt Moses took Joseph's bones with him (Exod. xiii. 19). The early Christians also had great respect for relics. When St. Ignatius, Bishop of Antioch, was torn to pieces by lions, two of his companions came by night and gathered up his bones, carrying them to Antioch. When St. Polycarp, Bishop of Smyrna, was burned alive, the Christians collected his ashes, valuing them more than jewels. At an early date it was customary to erect chapels or altars above the tombs of martyrs, and offer the holy sacrifice over their remains. Relics are usually enclosed in costly reliquaries, richly decorated. It is out of respect for the dead that we lay wreaths on their coffins, and deck their graves with flowers. Relics of great value, such as the portions of the true cross, or of the manger at Bethlehem, are encased in gold or silver; likewise some of the bodies of the saints. From time immemorial pilgrimages have been made to the sepulchres of the saints. For nineteen centuries the faithful have been wont to visit the tombs of the apostles in Rome or the holy places in Palestine. The early Christians flocked in such numbers to the Holy Land that the places in Jerusalem were thronged with devout worshippers. Any one who had not been thither esteemed himself a worse Christian than his neighbors. "We visit the sepulchres of the saints," says St. John Chrysostom, "and prostrate ourselves there in order to obtain some grace which we need."

2. We obtain many blessings from God by venerating relics.

Relics are a source whence spiritual benefits come to us from God. St. John Damascene says: "As water gushed from the rock in the wilderness at God's command, so by His will blessings flow from the relics of the saints." Where the remains of saints or martyrs are interred the snares of the devil lose their potency and obstinate maladies are healed. St. Augustine relates numerous cures effected by the relics of St. Stephen in Africa, besides the raising from the dead of two children. In the Old Testament we read of a dead man restored to life on coming in contact with the bones of the prophet Eliseus (4 Kings xiii. 21). Even in their lifetime the bodies of the saints were instrumental in working miracles. By the shadow of St. Peter (Acts v. 15), and by the handkerchiefs or girdles worn by St. Paul (Acts xix. 12), the sick were delivered from their infirmities. But it must be remembered it is not by the relics themselves that these miracles are wrought, but by God. Hence it is not a superstitious act on the part of pious persons when they visit places of pilgrimage, where God is pleased to work wonders by means of relics or images of the saints.

8. THE EXTRAORDINARY WORSHIP OF GOD.

We can, moreover, honor God by taking an oath or by making a vow.

To take an oath or make a vow is not an ordinary occurrence of our lives; it is only done in peculiar, i.e., extraordinary cases. An oath is taken when human witness or asseveration is not sufficient; a vow is made when we voluntarily pledge ourselves to do something for God. We honor God by an oath, because we thereby acknowledge His omnipotence, His justice, His holiness. And by a vow we offer Him a sacrifice, because we bind ourselves by a solemn promise to perform a work pleasing to God.

The Oath.

Cases sometimes occur in which a man will not believe the word of another. But if a witness comes forward and affirms: " That is so, I myself saw it," then the speaker is more readily believed, and all the more if the witness in question is known to be a man of honor. Now it may occur that a man calls God to witness, that is to say, he appeals to the omniscient God to make known the truth of what is said by His almighty power. In this case his word will be regarded as the word of God. As an official seal gives force to a decree, so the oath is the seal God gives us to corroborate a statement. It is a coin of high value, stamped with the name of the living God. Our Lord took an oath when Caiphas adjured Him by the living God to speak the truth. So did Esau, when he confirmed by an oath the promise he made to relinquish his birthright for the pottage of lentils.

1. To swear or take an oath is to call God to witness that one is speaking the truth, or that one will keep a promise.

In swearing, a man calls either upon God or upon something he holds sacred. If a man swears by God, he makes use of words such as these: As the Lord liveth (Jer. iv. 2); as surely as there is a God in heaven, God is my witness (Rom. i. 9); may God punish me, etc. Or we swear by holy things, such as the holy Gospel, the cross of Christ, the Blessed Sacrament. But as these things are incapable of attesting anything themselves, or of punishing a deceiver, it is in fact equivalent to calling God to witness. Our Lord Himself speaks of swearing by the Temple, by heaven, or by the throne of God (Matt. xxiii. 21, 22). But to use such expressions as: Upon my word, by my honor, as surely as I stand here, etc., is merely emphasizing an assertion, not swearing. An oath may be simple or solemn. A simple oath is between man and man in ordinary intercourse; a solemn oath is taken in a court of law or in presence of official personages. (An oath is administered to soldiers and officers of state.) In taking a solemn oath one is required to kiss the Holy Scriptures, or a crucifix, and to say: So help me God, to intimate that if he departs from the truth, he renounces the divine assistance and the blessings promised in the Gospels. Jews and Mohammedans have their own peculiar ceremonial; the latter raise one finger to show their belief in one God.

2. Christians are not obliged to refuse to take an oath, for it is permitted by God, and pleasing in His sight.

. If swearing were forbidden Christ would not have made use of an oath (Matt. xxvi. 64), nor would God have sworn to Abraham on Mount Meriah that He would multiply his seed as the stars in heaven and as the sand by the seashore (Gen. xxii. 16); nor would St. Paul so frequently have taken God to witness in his epistles (Rom. i. 9; 2 Cor. i. 23). The oath has besides a good object; it serves to put an end to disputes (Heb. vi. 16). It is pleasing to God, because by it we make public profession of faith in His omnipotence, His justice, His omniscience, and thus we honor Him. On this account atheists and social democrats cannot be induced to take an oath. It is God's will that we confirm our word with an oath, when necessary (Exod. xxii. 11). When Our Lord said: " Let your speech be yea, yea, no, no, and that which is over and above these is of evil " (Matt. v. 37), He meant to warn the Pharisees against the habit to which they were addicted of using idle, unnecessary oaths. Catholics need not refuse to take an oath, as some sectaries do; however, no one ought to be compelled to do so. Any one who forces a man to swear when he knows he will swear falsely, is in some way worse than a murderer; for the murderer only kills the body, whereas he who makes another swear falsely, causes the death of a soul, nay, of two souls, his neighbor's soul and his own also, for he is responsible for the other's death.

3. We ought therefore to make use of an oath only when it is absolutely necessary, with deliberation, and in the interests of truth and justice.

When Christ says the oath is of evil (Matt. v. 37), He intends to signify that it is occasioned by man's evil tendencies, and that rash oaths are sinful. Had mankind not fallen from its original state of integrity and justice, there would have been no need for the oath; but since faith and fidelity have vanished, recourse has been had to it. Not until evil prevailed everywhere did swearing become an ordinary practice; when by reason of the general perfidy and corruption no man's word could be relied on, then God was called to witness. St. Augustine compares the oath to a medicine, which must not be taken without good reason; it is to a man's words what the crutch is to the cripple. Consequently it is wrong to swear heedlessly, about trifling matters, as salesmen often do about their wares. Frequent swearing is apt to lead to false swearing. " A man that sweareth much shall be filled with iniquity, and a scourge shall not depart from his house " (Ecclus. xxiii. 12). Wherefore we must make use of an oath as seldom as possible, unless it is required of us by the Government or in a court of law. Our oath must always be true; that is to say, when on our oath, we must always say what we really believe to be true, and we must have the intention of keeping our word. The Roman general Regulus (250 B.C.) affords a fine instance of this. He was taken prisoner in war by the Carthaginians, and after being kept six years in captivity, he was sent to Rome to sue for peace. Before leaving the Carthaginian camp, a solemn oath was administered to him to return thither, provided the Romans would not conclude peace. On arriving in Rome he informed the Senate of the enemy's weakness, and urged them to pursue the war. Then he returned to prison, although every one in Rome, even the pagan high priest, spared no effort to detain him. St. Peter, on the contrary, swore falsely in the outer court of the high priest's palace (Matt. xxvi. 72). Blessed Thomas More, the High Chancellor of England, was thrown into prison by Henry VIII., because he would not concur in the hostile attitude that monarch assumed towards the Catholic Church. He might have purchased his release merely by swearing to conform to what his sovereign decreed. He was advised to do this, mentally applying the words to God, his supreme Sovereign and Lord. But he would not consent, saying he dared not swear falsely.

It is possible, however, that one may swear under a misapprehension, or one may be prevented by illness or misadventure, or some other sufficient cause, from fulfilling a promise made under an oath; in that case no guilt is incurred. Our oath must be premeditated; that is, we must consider well beforehand whether our statement is strictly true, or whether we shall be able to accomplish what we promise. King Herod at the feast swore rashly, for he promised with an oath to give the damsel who danced before him whatever she should ask. At her mother's instigation she asked the head of John the Baptist (Mark vi. 23). We read that forty Jews, in their enmity to St. Paul, swore neither to eat nor drink until they had killed him (Acts xxiii. 12). In the present day Freemasons bind themselves by oath not to express any desire to receive the last sacraments on their death-bed. Such oaths are sinful, and highly displeasing to God.

4. He who swears falsely, commits a grave act of blasphemy, and draws down upon himself the curse of God and the penalty of eternal perdition.

False swearing is also called perjury. He who swears falsely, who confirms by oath a statement he knows to be untrue, or who swears to do something, although he is conscious that he cannot fulfil his promise, is like a man who stamps a forged document with an official seal, an act which cannot escape punishment. Swearing falsely is a mortal sin, whatever be the subject of the oath. The curse of God rests upon the house of him who swears falsely (Zach. v. 3). God often punishes false swearers by a speedy and sudden death. Sedecias, the King of Judah, swore fealty to Nabuchodonosor and broke his covenant. Forthwith God announced to him by the lips of the prophet Ezechiel that he should meet with severe chastisement and die in Babylon (Ezech. xvii.), and in fact Nabuchodonosor took the king captive, put out his eyes, and brought him to Babylon, where he died (4 Kings xxv. 7). Wladislas, King of Hungary, concluded peace with the Turkish Sultan Murad II., and confirmed the treaty with an oath, yet he resumed hostilities against him. He fell in the battle of Warna (1444) with all the flower of his nobility. Perjury is punishable by the law with imprisonment. The Emperor Charlemagne made it a law that all who were convicted of swearing falsely should have their right hand cut off; later on three fingers only of the right hand, wherewith they took the oath, were struck off. Rash swearing is at the least a venial sin; it is a bad habit, and he who is always ready to confirm every statement, whether true or false, by an oath, lives, if he knows the value of his words, in a state of mortal sin. If a man has sworn wrongfully, he must not keep his oath, but deplore it. That is what Herod ought to have done. With regard to breaking an oath, that is to say, the non-fulfilment of a promise made under oath, it may be either a venial or a mortal sin, according as the matter concerned is weighty or not. The same is true of a vow (Suarez).

The Vow (Solemn Promise).

1. A vow is a promise voluntarily made to God, to perform some good action.

The vow is a promise made to God. We call upon God implicitly, if not explicitly when we say: My God, I promise that I will do this or that. A simple intention is not a vow; no one, not even God Himself, can require anything of us because of it. A vow is a promise made of our own free will: no one is bound to make it (Deut. xxiii. 22), and no one can be compelled to make it. A vow made under compulsion is invalid; not so one made under apprehension of danger, or stress of want, for then the act is voluntary. We must only promise what will be pleasing to God; not anything wrong, as did Jephte who, before going to battle, vowed to the Lord that if he was victorious, he would offer as a holocaust whosoever should first come out of the doors of his house. His only daughter came to meet him, and she was sacrificed (Judges xi.). Such a vow is foolish and displeasing to God (Eccles. v. 3), and ought not to be accomplished. Usually something is promised which is not of obligation, a pilgrimage, for instance; but one may also promise something which one is otherwise obliged to do, e.g., to observe the fasts of the Church, to keep the holydays, to be temperate in eating and drinking. In this case failure to keep one's promise is a twofold sin. The owner of a factory, whose only child was dangerously ill, promised before God if she recovered, that he would never have work done on Sundays and holydays. She got well and he kept his word. He was then doubly bound to observe the holydays.

Vows are sometimes accompanied by a condition.

A kind of bargain is made with God. Jacob promised to give tithes of his possessions to God provided He brought him back prosperously to his father's house (Gen. xxviii. 20-22). The processions on the Rogation days originated through a vow made about the year 500 by St. Mamertus, Bishop of Vienna, in time of famine; and about a century later the procession on St. Mark's Day was instituted in consequence of a vow made by Pope Gregory the Great while the plague was raging. The inhabitants of Ober-Ammergau pledged themselves to perform the Passion play every ten years in 1633, at the time of an epidemic. St. Louis of France promised, if he recovered from a severe illness, to undertake a crusade (1248). In the present day many persons promise, in illness or affliction, to visit some place of pilgrimage, to make an offering to some church, to give a statue, to fast on certain days, etc. The celebrated sanctuary of Maria-Zell, which attracts so many pilgrims, is due to a vow made before a battle with the Turks by King Louis I. of Hungary. (1363).

2. The most important vows are the religious vows, that is to say the solemn promise made voluntarily by persons entering a religious Order, to follow the evangelical counsels.

Poverty, chastity, and obedience, are the three vows taken by

Religious. They are very useful, for by them a man entirely gives up the world, in order to serve God better. These vows are most pleasing to God, for those who take them consecrate not only all they do, but their ownselves to God. As St. Anselm says, he who gives the tree gives more than he who only gives the fruit of the tree. Many persons offer oblations to God; a vestment, for instance, candles or flowers; but a better, more perfect oblation is to give one's self to God. The vows of religion are either solemn (so called because the obligations incurred are greater), or simple vows. Solemn vows are those in which there is an irrevocable consecration of one's self accepted by the Church, on the part of one who takes them. What is consecrated to God can never again be employed for secular purposes; with that which is simply dedicated it is otherwise. Thus any one who takes the solemn vows is irrevocably consecrated to the service of God. The Pope alone can release from solemn vows, and that only for weighty reasons. Before taking the solemn vows, i.e., being professed, it is necessary to have spent a year in the novitiate, and have been under the simple vows for at least three years (Pius IX., March 19, 1857). Bishops, or the superior-general of an Order can generally release from the simple vows, and for a less grave cause.

3. A vow renders the good action which we pledge ourselves to perform more acceptable to God. Consequently by means of a vow we obtain a more speedy answer to prayer, and make more rapid progress in the way of perfection.

By a vow we prove our fidelity to God. We also make an offering to God because we thereby bind ourselves to the performance of a good work. Thus, for instance, one who fasts in fulfilment of a vow performs a more perfect action than he who fasts without a vow. Hence it is that the prayers of those who make vows are more speedily granted. After the inhabitants of Ober-Ammergau had made the promise already mentioned, not one more fell a victim to the pestilence. The pious Anna made a vow to the Lord, when she prayed that a son might be granted to her, and she became the mother of the great prophet Samuel (1 Kings i. 11). Why do we see so many *ex-votos* in places of pilgrimage, so many votive offerings in churches? Vows enable us to attain more quickly to perfection (St. Francis of Sales). We thereby gain strength in the practice of virtue, because our will is fortified by the vow. The thought: I have promised my God to do this, is a powerful incentive to the performance of good actions. Many persons of great sanctity have taken vows, as a useful restraint to keep themselves in the fear of God. We may obtain special graces from God by pledging ourselves to make novenas in honor of the saints, to be particularly devout to the Mother of God during the month of May or of October, to perform certain mortifications or good works.

4. He who does not keep a solemn promise, offends against God; and so does he who needlessly postpones the fulfilment of his promise (Exod. xxiii. 21).

If we are bound to keep our word to our fellow-creatures, how much the more ought we to fulfil the promise made to God. " It is much better not to vow, than after a vow not to perform the things promised" (Eccles. v. 4). The debtor is compelled by the law of the land to pay his debts, and can it be supposed that he will go scot free who withholds from God what is His due? The non-fulfilment of a vow may be either a venial or a mortal sin, according to the importance of the matter in question. The guilt is doubled, if at the same time we transgress a command and show disrespect to God, as for instance by violating a vow of chastity. If we are unable to fulfil a promise we are exempt from blame, provided we do our utmost to perform the thing promised.

5. Therefore any one who is desirous of taking a vow, ought to consider well beforehand whether he will be able to keep his word.

A man who wishes to build, first makes an estimate of the cost, to see whether his means will allow him to complete the structure (Luke xiv. 28). No one ought to make a promise for his whole life, without first testing his ability to keep it. St. Francis of Sales made a vow to say the Rosary every day of his life; he often regretted having been so hasty in that promise. In any serious matter it is advisable to consult an experienced priest. For this reason the Church has made the rule that every one who wishes to take the vows of religion, should have a twelve months' noviceship. During that time he can make up his mind as to whether he has a real vocation to the religious life. If he takes the vows without feeling certain about his vocation he has only himself to blame.

6. A Religious who finds himself unable to keep his vows must apply to his Superior to be released from them or have them commuted.

Our Lord said to His apostles: "Whatsoever you shall loose on earth shall be loosed also in heaven" (Matt. xviii. 18). Hence the bishop or other superior is authorized to absolve from vows. The vow is usually commuted for some good work more conducive to the spiritual weal of the individual. There are five vows from which the Holy Father alone can dispense: The vow to enter a religious Order; the vow of lifelong chastity; the vow to visit the tombs of the apostles in Rome; and the vows to make a pilgrimage to Jerusalem (the holy places) or to Compostella (the tomb of St. James). Under certain circumstances the bishop also has power to dispense from these vows: If they have been made conditionally; under some measure of compulsion; without mature deliberation, or in ignorance of what they involved. In a time of jubilee every confessor has power to commute vows for some good work of another nature. One may always do more than one has promised: God will not be displeased, any more than an ordinary creditor, if He is paid more than what is due to Him.

THE SECOND COMMANDMENT OF GOD.

The Second Commandment is this: "Thou shalt not take the name of the Lord thy God in vain;" that is to say, thou shalt not utter it without reverence. By the name of God is not meant the mere word alone, but the majesty appertaining to the Most High.

We owe reverence to almighty God because He is a Lord of infinite majesty, and of infinite bounty.

Reverence is a mixture of fear, love, and esteem. If it was said of a monarch that he had many millions of subjects, that he had an army of a hundred thousand warriors who could take the field at his command, that by a word from his lips he could make the happiness or misery of multitudes, you would fear that monarch. But if you were told of his goodness, his endeavors to promote the welfare of his subjects, you would love and esteem him. So will you feel towards God, if you contemplate His infinite perfections and His great love towards man. Consider the perfections of God! There are upon earth some fifteen hundred millions of human beings; each one of these God knows, preserves, guides. He hears their prayers, He helps them in their necessities; He rewards or punishes them for the most part here below. How vast is the knowledge of this supreme Being! Millions of orbs revolve in space; God has created them all, He maintains them all, He gives them all motion. How boundless is His power! Think of the unseen world alone, peopled by millions of celestial spirits; He knows each one, He preserves each one in existence, He guides and directs each one, and by each and all He is adored. How great is His majesty! "Who is like to Thee among the strong, O Lord? Who is like to Thee, glorious in holiness, terrible and praiseworthy, doing wonders?" (Exod. xv. 11.) On account of the great majesty of God we should fear Him, and should love Him by reason of His infinite goodness. Fear and love are the component parts of reverence.

1. **In the Second Commandment God commands us in the first place to show due respect to His divine majesty. This we must do in the following manner:**

We should frequently call upon the name of God with true and heartfelt devotion, especially at the commencement of all we do and in time of trouble.

Newton, the great astronomer, had the deepest respect for the name of God; he uncovered his head and bowed low whenever it was uttered in his presence. Many devout Christians bow their head when they pronounce the name of Jesus in prayer; the priest does so in celebrating Mass. St. Ignatius, Bishop of Antioch, who when a child is said to have been he whom Our Lord set in the midst of the disciples, at the time that He said "Whosoever shall humble himself as this little child, he is the greater in the kingdom of heaven" (Matt. xviii. 4), loved to repeat the name of Jesus; shortly before his death he said: "This name shall never leave my lips or be effaced from my heart." And, in fact, after his martyrdom, the holy name

was found inscribed on his heart. In the Litany of the Holy Name
we invoke the name of Jesus again and again, because it is the most
powerful of all names, and through it we can obtain all we need. "If
you ask the Father anything in My name, He will give it you"
(John xvi. 23). By the name of Jesus the apostles and saints worked
miracles; St. Peter said to the lame man at the gate of the Temple:
"In the name of Jesus Christ arise and walk" (Acts iii. 6). Christ
promised that in His name devils should be cast out (Mark xvi. 17).
The devils tremble at the name of Jesus; they take flight when they
hear it, even when it is uttered by evil men, so great is its potency.
The name of Jesus is also all-powerful to fill the heart with joy;
it is compared to oil (Cant. i. 2); as oil gives light, alleviates pain,
and affords nourishment, so does the name of Jesus, when we call
upon it. St. Vincent Ferrer declares it to be a defence in all dangers
spiritual and temporal, and the means of healing bodily infirmities.
All graces are combined in this holy name: "There is no other name
under heaven given to men, whereby we must be saved" (Acts iv. 12).
"At the name of Jesus every knee should bow, of those that are in
heaven, on earth, and under the earth" (Phil. ii. 10). An indulgence
of twenty-five days is granted for each invocation of this holy name,
and a plenary at the hour of death for those who have frequently
invoked it during life (Clement XIII., Sept. 5, 1759). To pronounce this name is indispensable for obtaining the indulgence at the
hour of death. Would that every Christian could say with St. Bernard: "The name of Jesus is honey to the taste, melody to the ear,
joy to the heart." No one who clings to mortal sin can devoutly call
on this name: "No man can say the Lord Jesus, but by the Holy
Ghost" (1 Cor. xii. 3). In beginning every wish, before every action
however insignificant, we should call on the name of God, or make
the sign of the cross, with the usual words: "All whatsoever you do,
in word or in work, do all in the name of the Lord Jesus Christ"
(Col. iii. 17). Thus we shall merit the divine blessing, and earn a
reward for every action; Our Lord promises that any one who gives
to another a cup of cold water in His name shall not be unrewarded
(Mark ix. 40). We should also call upon the name of God in the time
of trouble; He has said: "Call upon Me in the day of trouble, I will
deliver thee and thou shalt glorify Me" (Ps. xlix. 15). In the year
1683 the Christians obtained a brilliant victory over the Turks; their
battle-cry was the names of Jesus and Mary. In the hour of death
above all we should breathe the name of Jesus; like St. Stephen
whose last words were: "Lord Jesus, receive my spirit" (Acts vii.
58.)

**2. We ought to show respect for all that appertains to divine
worship; more especially for the servants of God, for holy places,
sacred things, and religious ceremonies.**

We ought to show respect for the ministers of God. In this Count
Rudolph of Hapsburg set an excellent example. One day when out
hunting he met a priest carrying the Blessed Sacrament to the sick.
Instantly he dismounted, and offered his horse to the priest. And
when the latter on his return, gave back the horse to the count, he
would not take it, saying it must thenceforth be devoted to the
service of the sanctuary. The priest predicted that good fortune and

happiness would attend his career, and so it did; nine years later Rudolph was elected emperor. Our Lord bids us reverence His priests; He says: "He that despiseth you, despiseth Me" (Luke x. 16). "Touch not My anointed" (1 Par. xvi. 22). St. John Chrysostom says that the honor shown to the priest is shown to God Himself. God also requires us to show respect to holy places and things. When He appeared to Moses in the burning bush, and Moses approached somewhat near, He said to Him: "Come not nigh hither; put off the shoes from thy feet; for the place whereon thou standest is holy ground" (Exod. iii. 5). Under the Old Dispensation the people were strictly forbidden to touch the Ark of the Covenant (Numb. iv. 15). "Reverence My sanctuary" (Lev. xxvi. 2). Enter into the house of God as if you were entering into heaven, and leave behind you all that savors of earth. "Holiness becometh Thy house, O Lord!" (Ps. xcii. 5.) We should also manifest respect for all religious services. St. Elizabeth of Hungary removed her crown from her head whenever she heard Mass. Out of respect for the Gospel we stand up when it is read, and we preserve a grave demeanor when we approach the sacraments.

3. **We ought frequently to praise and magnify almighty God on account of His infinite perfections and goodness, especially when He reveals His perfections in a special manner, or confers a benefit upon us.**

The three children in the fiery furnace sang a canticle of praise when God preserved them from being hurt by the flames (Dan. iii.). When Tobias recovered his sight, he immediately blessed the Lord (Tob. xi. 17). Remember the *Magnificat*, the song of praise uttered by the Mother of God, and the *Benedictus*, the canticle of thanksgiving pronounced by Zacharias on his cure (Luke i.). Whenever you receive any favor from God, say: *Deo gratias*, "Thanks be to God," or Glory be to the Father, etc., and frequently repeat the salutation: "Let Jesus Christ be praised!" In some parts of Germany and Switzerland, this pious greeting takes the place of the good morning, or good day, in use among us. And if you are prevented by infirmities from praising God with your lips, at any rate praise Him in your heart; for God, Who hears not as we hear, requires not audible sound; He reads the heart, and is content with our good will. "Bless the Lord, O my soul, and let all that is within me bless His holy name. Bless the Lord, O my soul, and never forget all He hath done for thee" (Ps. cii. 1). "I will bless the Lord at all times; His praise shall be always in my mouth" (Ps. xxxiii. 2). "Blessed be the name of the Lord, from henceforth now and forever. From the rising of the sun unto the going down of the same, the name of the Lord is worthy of praise" (Ps. cxii. 2, 3). In praising God, we do the best for ourselves, for thereby we draw down upon ourselves the divine blessings in great abundance.

4. **Furthermore, God prohibits everything which is a violation of the reverence due to His divine majesty; and in particular:**
Taking the name of God in vain.

Many people have the habit of thoughtlessly exclaiming at every trifle that surprises them: "Good Lord! My God!" and the like.

It is a bad habit; correct yourselves of it, and endeavor to correct others also, as it shows a want of due reverence for the name of God. Those who truly love God cannot stand by unmoved and hear His holy name profaned. This careless, flippant use of the name of God or of any other sacred name is at least a venial sin. "Let not the naming of God be usual in thy mouth, for thou shalt not escape free from sin" (Ecclus. xxiii. 10). "The Lord will not hold him guiltless that shall take the name of the Lord his God in vain" (Exod. xx. 7). "We take good care," says St. John Chrysostom, "not to wear out our best clothes by putting them on every day; so we must beware lest we thoughtlessly utter the name of God, which is worthy of our profoundest reverence." The Jews did not venture to pronounce the word Jehovah; they always spoke of "The Lord."

5. Swearing. By this is meant the use of holy names in a moment of anger as an imprecation against certain persons or things.

For instance parents, when angry, wish ill to their children, using the name of God or of heaven; workmen call down evil on the tools they employ. Out of the mouth of a Christian none but blessings should proceed (1 Pet. iii. 9). Should the same mouth wherewith we pray, wherewith we receive the sacred body of the Lord, be employed to curse our neighbor and offend against God?

Almighty God often punishes those who curse others by allowing the curse to be fulfilled.

St. Augustine speaks of a certain mother who cursed her refractory sons, they having gone so far as to strike her. Immediately they were seized with a convulsive movement of the limbs, from which, after wandering through many lands, they were at length cured at Hippo, by touching the relics of St. Stephen. St. Ignatius of Loyola once asked an alms of a Spanish nobleman; the latter flew into a rage, and said: "May I be burned alive if you are not a rogue deserving the hangman's rope." Shortly after, on the occasion of festivities to celebrate the birth of an heir to the throne, a barrel of gunpowder exploded in the nobleman's house, and he was so severely burned that he expired in agony a few days later. Working-people who curse and swear over their work, or call down imprecations upon the horses they are driving, cannot expect their labor to prosper. Thus God rewards those who use bad language: "He loved cursing, and it shall come upon him" (Ps. cviii. 18).

A man who indulges the bad habit of swearing commits many sins, and is in danger of eternal perdition.

As one tells from the language a stranger speaks of what country he is a native, so when oaths flow freely from a man's lips, one may conclude he belongs to hell; there is reason to fear that he does not belong to the kingdom of God, for he talks the language of hell. The Fathers used to consider swearing as a sign of perdition. Those who curse shall perish (Ps. xxxvi. 22); they shall not possess the kingdom of God (1 Cor. vi. 10). Ordinary swearing is a venial sin, provided no serious evil is worked to one's neighbor, yet it is a greater sin than taking God's name in vain, because not only is it a disrespect towards God, but an offence against charity.

6. Indecorous behavior towards persons who are consecrated to the service of God, holy places, sacred objects or actions.

As we treat a priest, in his priestly capacity, so we treat God Himself, for Christ said: "He that despiseth you, despiseth Me" (Luke x. 16). He who abuses or despises a priest is guilty of dishonoring God, and deserves the same chastisement as the Jews who abused and despised the Son of God. St. John Chrysostom says the want of respect for eccleciastical superiors is the source of all evil. How severely the little boys were punished who mocked the prophet Eliseus (4 Kings ii. 24). We also offend God by unseemly behavior in church, laughing, whispering, staring about, lolling, etc. St. Ambrose says of people who behave badly in church that they come with small sins and go away with great ones. Insults offered to God in His house are more offensive to Him than those offered elsewhere; we ourselves resent most of all rudeness shown to us in our own house. This is why the meek and gentle Saviour drove those who bought and sold out of the Temple, saying: "My house shall be called the house of prayer, but you have made it a den of thieves" (Matt. xxi. 13). "If any man violate the Temple of God, him shall God destroy" (1 Cor. iii. 17). The same respect is due to holy things as to holy places. When David was bringing the ark back to Jerusalem, an Israelite named Oza ventured to lay hold of it. God struck him and he died (2 Kings vi. 7). King Ozias was punished with leprosy, because he entered the sanctuary and wanted to burn incense (2 Par. xxvi. 21). To disturb religious services or show contempt for them is also sinful. Of this sin the sons of Heli were guilty when they interfered with the Jewish sacrifices (1 Kings ii.). In the present day sometimes evil disposed persons interrupt sermons, processions, or other services, or insult priests who are taking the Blessed Sacrament to the sick. These offenders are punishable by law as disturbers of divine worship.

7. Blasphemy. Of this sin those are guilty who revile God, His saints, or speak contemptuously of objects connected with His worship.

The Emperor Julian the Apostate always spoke of the Son of God as the Galilean (at that time a word of insult); even at his death, which was occasioned by the thrust of a lance, he is said to have exclaimed: "Thou hast conquered, O Galilean!" Ungodly persons are often heard to utter bitter revilings against God, especially in time of suffering and affliction, as if they did not deserve the trials He sends them. It is blasphemy to speak scornfully of God, or of His actions; or to attribute to a creature what is the prerogative of the Creator. The people sinned thus who when King Herod made an oration to them, cried: "It is the voice of a god and not of a man" (Acts xii. 22). The Jews committed this sin. God says by the mouth of the prophet: "My name is continually blasphemed all the day long" (Js. lii. 5). To speak contemptuously of holy places and things is a kind of blasphemy, as a reflection upon God, Whom we are told to praise in His holy places (Ps. cl. 1).

Sacrilege is another kind of blasphemy. This consists in putting to an improper and degrading use what pertains to the service of God.

The King of Babylon, Baltassar, committed sacrilege when, in a state of inebriation, he commanded the sacred vessels that had been taken from the Temple at Jerusalem, where they were used in the worship of the true God, to be brought to serve as drinking cups at the feast. The mutilation of statues or defacing of crucifixes is a sacrilege. Would it not be considered a treasonable act to treat the crown or the portrait of an earthly monarch with contumely? Again, those who receive the sacraments unworthily, who appropriate to themselves Church property, or who commit a theft in church, come under the same condemnation. It is said that Jews and Freemasons have sometimes obtained consecrated Hosts, which they subjected to horrible profanation. Such conduct is simply satanic.

Blasphemy is essentially a diabolical sin, and one of the gravest transgressions.

Blasphemy may be called a sin peculiar to devils and reprobates, for as the Holy Spirit speaks by the mouth of the good, so the devil speaks by the mouth of the blasphemer (St. Bernardin). The blasphemer is worse than a dog; for a dog does not bite the master who is kind to him when he chastises him, whereas the blasphemer reviles God, from Whom he has received so many benefits, oblivious of the fact that God only afflicts him for his own good. When the saintly Bishop Polycarp was offered his life if he would blaspheme Christ, he answered: " For eighty-six years I have served Him, and He has done me nothing but good; how could I speak evil of my King and Master? " St. Jerome says that all sins are slight in comparison with this, for by all others one offends against God indirectly, but by this sin one offends against the Most High Himself, not against His image. " Whom hast thou blasphemed, against whom hast thou exalted thy voice? Against the holy One of Israel " (4 Kings xix. 22). All other sins arise from human frailty or ignorance, but blasphemy comes from the malice of the human heart (St. Bernard). Other sins bring some advantage to the sinner; pride desires to gain importance, avarice money, intemperance the pleasures of the table. but this sin brings a man no profit, no pleasure. The Jews punished the blasphemer with death. St. Thomas Aquinas declares blasphemy to be a mortal sin, unless it is committed in a hasty moment without deliberation. " Oughtest thou not to fear that fire will fall from heaven upon thee and consume thee, if thou dost venture to asperse the name of the Almighty? Will not the earth open and swallow thee up? Deceive not thyself, O man, thou canst not escape the hand of an omnipotent God! " (St. Ephrem.)

God punishes blasphemy with severe chastisements in time, and with everlasting damnation hereafter; it is also punishable by human law.

" God is not mocked " (Gal. vi. 7). When King Baltassar profaned the vessels of the sanctuary, judgment fell upon him immediately: an unseen hand wrote his fate upon the wall. That same night the enemy entered the city; he was slain and his kingdom became part of the Persian empire (Dan. v.). Sennacherib, the King of Assyria, blasphemed God; shortly after he lost two hundred thousand men in the war against the Hebrews, and was assassinated by his own sons. Michael III., Emperor of Constantinople, made public mockery of the sacraments on the feast of the Ascension; at night there was a tremendous earthquake, and some time later the emperor was murdered. An Israelite cursed God in the wilderness; he was put into prison till Moses had ascertained what was God's will; and the Lord said: "Let all the people stone him" (Lev. xxiv. 14). As a man who throws a stone up to the sky, cannot touch, much less injure any of the heavenly bodies, but may break his own head if the stone falls back upon it, so blasphemous words do no harm to the Being against Whom they are directed; they only fall back upon the head of him who utters them, to his own perdition. Thus the blasphemer whets the sword to pierce his own heart (St. John Chrysostom). Our Lord says that whosoever reviles his neighbor shall be in danger of hell fire (Matt. v. 22); how much more he who reviles God! Under the Old Law, when God was not so well known, it was said: "He that curseth father or mother shall die the death" (Exod. xxi. 17). How much more shall judgment overtake those who in this age of knowledge and enlightenment, curse, not their parents, but the Lord, their God! "They shall be cursed that shall despise Thee" (Tob. xiii. 16). "He that blasphemeth the name of the Lord, dying let him die" (Lev. xxiv. 16). Blasphemy is also punished by the secular authority. St. Louis of France made it a law that any one who blasphemed God should be seared on the lips with a red-hot iron. This was done to a wealthy citizen of Paris, with the result that before long no blasphemous word was heard in the kingdom. St. Jerome on one occasion rebuked an ungodly man for his impious words; when asked why he presumed to do so, he said: "A dog may bark in his master's defence, and am I to stand by silent when God's holy name is blasphemed? I would sooner die than forbear to speak."

8. Simony. This consists in selling spiritualities for money, or the equivalent of money.

In the Middle Ages simony was a common sin; bishop's sees and benefices were sometimes sold to the highest bidder. It is simony to offer a priest money for absolution, to sell relics, to charge a higher price for objects, such as crosses and rosaries, because they have been blessed. This sin takes its name from Simon the magician, who offered the apostles money when he saw that by the imposition of hands the Holy Ghost was given, saying: "Give me also this power, that on whomsoever I shall lay my hands, he may receive the Holy Ghost" (Acts viii. 19). He who is guilty of the sin of simony is excommunicated; to him the words of St. Paul apply: "Thy money perish with thee, because thou hast thought that the gift of God may be purchased with money" (Acts viii. 20). To give money for Masses is, however, not simony; it is much the same as giving some one an alms and asking for his prayers. Nor is the payment of fees to the parish priest for the exercise of his ministerial functions to be reckoned as simony, because these fees are not a price paid for the discharge of spiritual duties, but a contribution towards the maintenance of the priest. Otherwise St. Paul would not have written these words: "They who work in the holy place eat the things that are of the holy place, and they that serve the altar partake with the altar; so also the Lord ordained that they who preach the Gospel should live by the Gospel" (1 Cor. ix. 13, 14).

The object of the Confraternity of the Holy Face is to make reparation for blasphemies and irreverences committed against God.

It is well known that Our Lord miraculously imprinted His sacred countenance upon the cloth handed to Him by Veronica on the way to Calvary. The Emperor Tiberius, when sick, had this cloth brought to Rome, and the mere sight of it sufficed to cure him. Veronica is said to have given it to St. Clement, the fellow-worker with St. Peter, and his successors in the see of Rome. Thus it came to St. Peter's, where it is yet preserved. In 1849, at Christmas, it was exposed, and for three hours it was surrounded by a halo of brilliant light. This cloth still bears the impression of Our Lord's features; they are distinctly discernible, and show how He was maltreated by the barbarous soldiery. In fact, this image affords striking evidence of the irreverence of man towards God. The sight of it inspires us with pious horror and heartfelt contrition. For a long time no copy was permitted to be made of it; this is no longer the case, and the prints of it are now venerated, God making known by miracles and speedy answers to prayer, how highly He approves of this devotion. At Alicante, in Spain, after a long period of drought, a picture of the Holy Face was carried in procession; a tear was seen to roll from the eyes of the picture, and in a few days rain fell abundantly. In Tours a large number of cures were effected in presence of a picture of the Holy Face, and it was there, by means of the exertions of the pious M. Dupont, that the Confraternity of the Holy Face was instituted, its object being to make atonement for sins of blasphemy. In the revelations of St. Gertrude we read that Our Lord said to her: "Those who venerate the image of My humanity (My human countenance) shall be interiorly enlightened by the radiance of My Godhead." And to Sister Saint Pierre, in 1845, He said: "As one can purchase whatever one will with a coin of the realm, stamped with the king's head, so those who adore My countenance will obtain all they desire." Again: "The more you seek to efface from My countenance the marks of disfigurement caused by blasphemers, the more I will restore your soul, defaced by sin, to its original beauty, so that it may appear as if it just came from the waters of Baptism."

THE THIRD COMMANDMENT OF GOD.

On Mount Sinai almighty God spoke, and said: "Remember that thou keep holy the Sabbath day. Six days shalt thou labor and do all thy work" (Exod. xx. 8, 9). The Third Commandment thus contains two injunctions, the command to sanctify the Sunday, and the command to work.

In the Third Commandment of the Decalogue God commands us to sanctify the Sunday and to work six days in the week.

1. THE PRECEPT TO SANCTIFY SUNDAYS AND HOLYDAYS.

In order that amid the many cares and anxieties of life man may not forget God, his final end and high calling, God has enjoined upon him to keep one day in the week holy. As we have certain times set apart for the satisfaction of our bodily necessities, sleeping, eating and drinking, so we have appointed times for meditation upon the eternal truths whereby we may obtain fresh strength for our souls. On holydays we have the opportunity of expiating by prayer what we have done amiss, and of rendering to God the thanks due to Him for the benefits He has conferred on us during the week.

1. God commands us to sanctify the seventh day, because on the seventh day He rested from the work of creation.

In his account of the creation Moses says: "God blessed the seventh day and sanctified it, because in it He had rested from all His work" (Gen. ii. 3). Man, who is made after the image of God, ought to follow the example of the Lord his God; as God ceased from work on the seventh day, so man ought to rest after six days' labor. Man needs this rest after working for six days. Just as one is obliged to sleep for six or seven hours after the work of the day is done, in order to recruit one's bodily powers, so one needs a longer period of rest after six days of labor. At the time of the French revolution, the observance of the seventh day was done away with and the tenth day appointed for the day of rest; but it was soon found indispensable to return to the old order of things. The number seven belongs to the natural order. God, Who set the lights in the firmament of heaven for signs and for seasons and for days and for years (Gen. i. 14), intended the changes of the moon, which occur every seven days, to point out to us the division of time into periods of seven days, of which one was to be a day of rest. Bishop Theophilus of Antioch, writing about the year 150 A.D., mentions the observance of the seventh day as a universal custom. We who are Christians keep the Sunday, the Jews keep Saturday, the Mohammedans keep Friday, the Mongols keep Thursday, the black population of Guinea and Goa keep Tuesday and Monday respectively. The cessation from labor every seventh day foreshadows our eternal rest in heaven (Heb. iv. 9). By solemnizing the day of the Lord we renew and quicken our longing for the unending festival of joy above. The very fact that we wear our best apparel on that day serves to remind us of the celestial happiness that we hope will one day be our portion.

2. God commanded the Jews to keep holy the Sabbath day.

The Sabbath was a joyous festival for the Jewish people, because on that day they were delivered from Egyptian bondage. In addition to this, when God gave the law from Mount Sinai, He enjoined upon

them to sanctify the day by cessation from work: " The seventh day
is the Sabbath; thou shalt do no work on it " (Exod. xx. 10). The
Sabbath was specially suited to be set apart for the public worship
of God, because more than any other day it recalled God's benefits
to His people (Ezech. xx. 12). It was, moreover, typical of the rest
in the sepulchre of the future Messias. The Jews were extremely
strict in their observance of the Sabbath; any profanation of the day
was punished with death, no work of any kind might be done on it.
A man found gathering a few sticks on the Sabbath day was stoned
(Numb. xv. 36). The Pharisees would not allow that it was lawful
to do a good deed on the Sabbath (Matt. xii. 12). No manna fell in
the desert on that day.

3. **Sunday was appointed by the apostles as the day of rest
instead of the Sabbath, because Christ rose from the dead on
a Sunday.**

Sunday is a festival of the Holy Trinity; for on the first day
of the week God the Father began the work of creation, God the Son
rose from the dead, and God the Holy Ghost descended upon the
apostles. The apostles were authorized to transfer the day of rest
from Saturday to Sunday, because it was not so much the observance
of the Sabbath, as the observance of a fixed day in each week upon
which God insisted in the commandment. They were all the more at
liberty to change the day, as the Old Law was but a shadow of the
New. Sunday is called the Lord's Day, because it ought to be devoted
to His service, because on it He rose from the dead. St. Justin (139
A.D.) is the first to make use of the word Sunday: it is a name befitting the day whereon the Lord, like the rising sun, rose from the
grave in the brilliance of His glorified humanity. On this day also
God made the light; the Holy Ghost came down in tongues of fire,
and on this day we receive spiritual enlightenment. The Emperor
Constantine the Great enjoined the observance of Sunday as a day of
rest throughout the Roman empire; and Charlemagne caused those
who violated it to be fined.

4. **We are bound on Sunday to abstain from servile work and
to assist at the public Mass; we ought, moreover, to employ this
day in providing for the salvation of our soul, that is to say by
approaching the sacraments, by prayer, hearing sermons, reading
spiritual books, and performing works of mercy.**

Servile work is that which entails severe physical exertion, and is
exhausting to the bodily strength. It is the work generally done by
servants, menials, artisans, and laborers; in a word the work belonging to the class that serves, hence the name. Markets and all com-
mercial transactions are included in the prohibition; yet in deference
to local customs, the rule is relaxed in some countries. However,
buying and selling must not be carried on during the hours of divine
worship. As God rested on the seventh day, so we ought to rest. As
Christ on Easter Sunday left the grave-clothes in the sepulchre and
rose triumphant, so we ought to lay aside our earthly business, and
on the pinions of prayer soar aloft to God. Physical repose is necessary, because it is impossible for one who is greatly fatigued to pray

well. Public worship is the holy sacrifice of the Mass, generally accompanied by a sermon. In the first centuries of Christianity the Christians were accustomed to assemble on Sundays to hear Mass, and a short exhortation was delivered after the Gospel, as is usual in the present day. There is no act of Christian worship that can compare in dignity and value with the holy sacrifice of the Mass. On Sunday we ought to provide for the interests of our soul; physical rest is ordained in order that we may labor more diligently for our spiritual welfare; and we must not content ourselves with putting on better clothes, but must cleanse and adorn our hearts. The cessation from the work of the week gives an opportunity to the faithful, in compliance with the mind of the Church, to approach the sacraments. They are encouraged to receive holy communion on Sundays and holydays, and to give themselves to prayer; for this reason afternoon services are held, and the churches stand open for private devotions. Our forefathers used to read spiritual books, homilies on the Gospel for the day, and the lives of the saints. Many of Our Lord's miracles of healing were wrought on the Sabbath day—witness the man whose hand was withered (Matt. xii. 10); the man born blind (John ix.); the man that had dropsy (Luke xiv. 2)—although by doing so He gave great offence to the Jews. He intended to teach us to do good work on Sundays.

The work permitted on holydays of obligation is (1), Servile work which is absolutely necessary, especially works of mercy; (2), Light and trifling work; (3), Occupations of an intellectual nature; (4), Reasonable recreation.

′ We are not forbidden to do work that is absolutely necessary. Our Lord does not desire man to suffer on account of the Sunday rest, for He says: " The Sabbath was made for man, and not man for the Sabbath " (Mark ii. 27). All work may be done which is required for the support of life; we may have our food prepared, and are allowed to gather in our crops if the weather threatens their destruction. All work that is indispensable for the public service may be carried on: e.g., the postal service, the railroad, telegraph, and police service. Ecclesiastical authorities have the power to grant special permission for servile work to be done on Sunday, if there is sufficient reason. Christ says: " The Son of man is the Lord of the Sabbath also," and the Church, His representative, can say the same. And as the chief and primary object for which Sunday is instituted is to promote the spiritual welfare and eternal salvation of mankind, all works tending to this end are enjoined upon us. Our Lord says: " The priests in the Temple break the Sabbath and are without blame " (Matt. xii. 5). Works of mercy are also enjoined; nothing is more profitable to salvation than these, for on them our eternal fate depends (Matt. xxv. 35). We have Christ's example and precept also for the performance of charitable works on Sunday: " It is lawful to do a good deed on the Sabbath day " (Luke xii. 12). Some of the saints used to visit the hospitals after Mass, and spend the remainder of Sunday in serving the sick. Yet it must be remembered that only such servile work as is absolutely necessary is permitted, although its object be a charitable one. For if it is lawful to do all servile work without distinction which was for the benefit of the poor, all artisans and laborers might go on with their work, and that would be by no means permissible (Suarez). Necessary works of mercy exempt from the obligation of attendance at public worship; they are in themselves an act of worship (Jas. i. 27). Our Lord says: " I will have mercy and not sacrifice " (Matt. ix. 13). But if it is in any way possible public worship should not be omitted. " These things you ought to have done, and not leave those undone " (Matt. xxiii. 23). What is it right to do if a conflagration breaks out just before the time of Mass, or if there is an inundation? Occupations of an unimportant kind may be engaged in, God does not require us to sit idle on Sundays; besides writing, music, and all mental employments are lawful. Sunday is also instituted as a day of rest; on it we may freely enjoy innocent diversions.

Sins Against the Third Commandment.

The precept enjoining upon us to sanctify the Sunday is transgressed:

1. By doing or requiring others to perform servile work.

The Christian ought to allow his servants and even his cattle, to rest on the Sunday (Exod. xx. 10). Servants, apprentices, and all who are in a subordinate position, ought not to remain in a situation where they cannot fulfil their religious obligations. Servile work is a mortal sin, if it be done for more than two or three hours on Sunday without urgent necessity. Yet hard work, if done for a shorter time, or light work for the same time, is not mortal sin; nor is it so if a not very valid reason is counted on as an excuse, nor again if a servant does what his master, without cogent grounds, requires of him, through fear of evil consequences to himself. In the latter case the sin rests with the master. If scandal is given by doing servile work, even for a short time, it is a grievous sin. Our Lord says of one who gives scandal, " it were better for him that a millstone should be hanged about his neck, and that he should be drowned in the depths of the sea " (Matt. xviii. 6). God threatened the Jews most emphatically, saying that any one who profaned the Sabbath should be put to death: " He that shall do any work in it, his soul shall perish out of the midst of his people " (Exod. xxxi. 14).

2. By carelessness about attendance at public worship.

Entertainments given on Saturday are often the cause why Catholics omit Mass on Sunday. " What folly," exclaims St. Francis of Sales, " to turn day into night and night into day, and neglect one's duties for frivolous amusements! "

3. By indulging in diversions which are over-fatiguing, or which are of a sinful nature.

Games which involve much physical exertion, hunting, dancing, etc., ought to be avoided on Sunday; also those which lead to anything unseemly; brawls, extravagant expenditure, disinclination for work. Worse still, if the amusements are sinful in themselves; for whosoever committeth sin is the servant of sin (John viii. 34), and thus servile work of the most degrading description is done. Woe to him who chooses the day which is consecrated to divine service to offend against God and injure his own soul most deeply. Some people take advantage of the day of rest to indulge more freely in vice. Not unfrequently the devil leaves people in peace all the week, and when Sunday comes he tempts them to all manner of sin, pride and ostentation in dress, gambling, dancing, excess in eating and drinking. In the present day men seem to think most of eating and drinking on the Lord's Day, women of adorning their person. How lamentable is the depravity of mankind, in thus abusing the most sacred institutions! On Sunday the devil of avarice is cast out, but it is as if seven other and worse devils entered in its place; the love of the world and all it entails; the frequenting of convivial scenes, disseverance of the ties of family life, squandering of savings, and dislike of work. "It is far better," St. Augustine says, "that one should occupy one's self with needle-work or field-work on Sunday than indulge in vice." To spend the Lord's Day in worldly vanities amounts to a kind of sacrilege; to desecrate it by sin is worse than plundering the sanctuary.

Motives for the Sanctification of Sunday.

1. God rewards with temporal blessings those who keep holy His day.

Consider the loving kindness of God; it is no toilsome service He requires of you, but that you should rest. There are one hundred and sixty-eight hours in the week. God only demands one day (twenty-four hours) for Himself; must you use this for your worldly affairs? Those who would prosper in their business must consecrate Sunday to the service of God. Christopher Columbus, the discoverer of America, when on his voyage always kept his vessels stationary on Sunday. God often protects in a special manner those who keep holy His day. One of the sailors on board a steamer on the Mississippi refused to shift the cargo—an unnecessary work—on Sunday; he was dismissed in consequence. Shortly after the boiler burst and several of the crew lost their lives; thus the God-fearing sailor escaped. God often increases the gains of those who abstain from the pursuit of their calling on Sundays. A pious friend once persuaded an artisan to desist from working on Sunday, saying he would compensate for the loss thus occasioned. In six months' time he returned, and the artisan acknowledged that far from losing, he had made more money than usual in the interval. Holy Scripture says "God blessed the seventh day" (Gen. ii. 3), that is to say, He made it productive of blessing for us. It is a false argument to allege that the suspension of work on Sunday is prejudicial to the produce of manufactures, for it is an ascertained fact that factory hands do more and better work if they have one day of rest in the seven. A bow never unspanned loses its elasticity; so the workman loses his powers if they are ever on the stretch. Rousseau, no friend to religion, used to say that holidays were essential to the welfare of a nation. In England the observance of Sunday is a strict rule, and see how her commerce has prospered. Some Jews still rigorously keep the Sabbath, and no disadvantages ensue to them.

2. The profanation of the Lord's Day is frequently punished with temporal evils, sickness and poverty.

Because the Jews habitually violated the sanctity of the Sabbath God permitted Nabuchodonosor to destroy Jerusalem and take the people into captivity (2 Esd. xiii. 18). The usual punishment for profaning Sunday and not hearing Mass is to become the captive of vice. Those who work continuously ruin their health; man can no more live without taking repose than without eating. Thus the day of rest is not only a religious duty, but a natural necessity. To those who work on Sundays God says as to the Jews of yore: "I will quickly visit you with poverty" (Lev. xxvi. 16). Those who through greed of gain desecrate Sunday, obtain the very opposite of their aim. The Chinese have no fixed day of rest, and to what a deplorable state of degradation and misery, both physically and morally, they have sunk as a nation!

3. The non-observance of Sunday undermines family life and social relations.

This sin causes the disintegration of the family. If the members of a family neglect public worship, they lose all sense of their duties and fall into evil ways. The father becomes dissolute, the mother indifferent, the children insubordinate. The father does not fulfil his duty to his children; occupied all the week he sees but little of them; on Sunday he has leisure to observe their individual characters, and give them useful instruction. The disintegration of society follows that of the family; the profanation of Sunday is an open violation of God's law; the yoke of the secular law is next thrown off; no respect is shown to the authority of the king, the bishop, the legislator, the parent. Catholics who are careless in regard to the holydays of obligation, gradually lose all sense of their religious duties; they forget God, their final end, and become like heathen. Those who are not found on Sunday among the children of God on earth, will be excluded from His presence to all eternity. By sanctifying Sunday, we lay up for ourselves treasures which will last forever.

2. THE PRECEPT OF LABOR.

Work may be either bodily or mental.

It must not be thought that by those who work, only servants, artisans, operatives, and the like are intended; students, priests, schoolmasters, doctors, etc., are included under the term. The latter do not indeed work with their hands, but with their head; and mental work is far more difficult and fatiguing than physical exertion.

Work was formerly held to be degrading, until it was sanctified by Our Lord.

Among the pagans there were two classes of people: the upper or governing class, and the slaves, the working class. In some states artisans were deprived of civil rights. As work was regarded as a degradation, men used either to join the army, or spend their days in idleness. At Our Lord's coming He gave dignity to labor by His example; He chose a carpenter for His foster-father, and from an early age He worked Himself. In the parable of the laborers in the vineyard He gave His hearers to understand that work was necessary for salvation (Matt. xx.). Many eminent men have not disdained to engage in manual labor. St. Paul earned his own living by the work of his hands (Acts xx. 34), he was a tent-maker (Acts xviii. 3). The monks of old times occupied themselves with agriculture, and in transcribing manuscripts. Work is no humiliation; on the contrary, it is greatly to a man's credit to maintain himself by his own exertions (Leo XIII.). Vice and pride alone really degrade a man. He who serves his fellow-man because it is the will of God, really serves God Who lays the obligation upon him. Christ Himself did not come to be served, but to serve. He who is the servant of another man is more to be respected than he who is the slave of his passions.

1. The obligation to work was laid upon mankind by God after the Fall as a penance.

Previous to the Fall of our first parents work was only a relaxation for man. But after the Fall God said to Adam: " In the sweat of thy face thou shalt eat bread, until thou return to the earth out of which thou wert taken " (Gen. iii. 19).

2. Every individual who can work is bound to work. St. Paul says: " If any man will not work, neither let him eat " (2 Thess. iii. 10).

No man is free from original sin, and on account of original sin we are obliged to do penance, thus all must work. In order to compel man to work, God has ordained that the earth shall not afford ·him nourishment unless it is cultivated. If no one labored all the people on the earth would die of hunger. The rich are not exempt from this obligation; they can give the proceeds of their work in charity. or at least devote them to some good object. Royal personages have often worked costly vestments for the Church; queens and princesses used to spend a great part of their time in this manner. Upon a rich man being once asked why he was always working at something or other, though there was no need for him to do so, he replied: " Do you think almighty God has given me my hands for no purpose? " St. Benedict, in making the rule for his monks, provided that they should be occupied alternately with prayer and work. Nothing but old age, bodily infirmities, and sickness exempt from this universal law. " Man is born to labor and the bird to fly " (Job v. 7). Even the lower animals teach us in this respect; witness the industrious ant (Prov. vi. 6). " We exhort you to work with your own hands, as we commanded you " (1 Thess. iv. 11).

3. Every man is bound primarily to perform the work appertaining to his calling or station.

There are various grades or states of life in human society; there are ecclesiastics, physicians, lawyers, soldiers, married people and unmarried; human society is like a body, each member of which has its own individual functions (1 Cor. xii. 12), or like a clock, in which all the wheels, large and small, work into one another. It is God Himself Who calls every man to his special state, hence we speak of it as his "vocation," and God gives every one the graces necessary to his calling. Thus if a man feels inwardly drawn to one particular state, he ought to obey this attraction, just as the migratory birds obey the motion that teaches them to seek a warmer clime in the autumn. Those who do not follow that interior impulse, but force themselves to embrace a calling for which they feel no inclination, too often share the fate of the birds who do not journey southwards; like them they do not thrive. Parents ought not to compel their children to enter a profession for which they have no attraction. As our vocation comes from God, in fulfilling its obligations we serve Him; consequently the duties of our state ought to take precedence of all others. In some cases we have to leave God for God. The object for which Christ came into the world was to redeem it, and when the time came for Him to fulfil the duties of that vocation everything else was made subservient to it. Remember His words in the Temple when He was twelve years of age (Luke ii. 49), and how He neglected to take food, while conversing with the Samaritan at Jacob's well (John iv. 34). So Moses acted; when God told him on Mount Sinai that the people had sinned grievously, he immediately left converse with God, and returned to the camp (Exod. xxxii. 7).

Careful fulfilment of the duties of one's calling leads to perfection; the neglect of them entails fatal consequences both in time and in eternity.

Those who conscientiously accomplish the duties of their calling are conscientious in all things. Like the principal wheel in a machine, if this goes well, all else goes well; but if it stops, the whole of the works are at a standstill. In the process for canonization, the first inquiry is how the candidate has fulfilled the duties of his calling. It is a mistake to imagine that time and trouble devoted to the duties of one's calling are wasted; on the contrary, there is no speedier means of attaining perfection. Those who, deluded by the devil. neglect their duties for prayer and pious works commit sin. "If a man," says St. Francis of Sales, "does not perform the grave obligations of his state, though he raise the dead and practise all manner of austerities he is in mortal sin and will perish eternally." In vain those pray who will not work; all piety is false which is not subordinated to the claims of our calling, for no state of life, if lawful, is a hindrance to salvation.

4. We must not forget God in what we do; before and during our work we should implore His aid and renew our intention.

God's blessing we need if our work should succeed. Witness the miraculous draught of fishes (Luke v.). Three men with God's blessing will do more work in a day than ten without it. To begin one's work without prayer is as if a soldier went to battle without weapons. St.

Paul exhorts us to renew our good intention in the words: " Whether you eat or drink, or whatsoever else you do, do all to the glory of God " (1 Cor. x. 31). In all our actions we must take aim, like one who shoots at a mark. However long a row of ciphers a child makes on a slate, they have no value whatsoever until a figure is placed before them. So it is with our works: in themselves they are worthless, but if they are performed in God's name, He makes them fruitful and meritorious. And as when writing one dips one's pen from time to time in the ink in order to write on, so we ought to look up to God to gain fresh strength for our work. We should do like the mariner, who looks up at the stars or consults the compass that he may steer his course aright. The angels, while ministering to man, do not cease to gaze upon the countenance of God. As the builder constantly uses square and plumb-line, so all our actions should be measured by the rule of the love of God. " Pray without ceasing " (1 Thess. v. 17). Accustom yourselves to utter ejaculatory prayers at your work and take for your motto the words: *Ora et labora.* Work and pray; and while putting your hand to your work, raise your heart to God.

5. Labor obtains a temporal and an eternal recompense, because it is a kind of divine worship. The temporal recompense is contentment and earthly happiness.

As the law of work was laid upon Adam in paradise by God as an expiation of his fault, when he had acknowledged and confessed it, all who work do the will of God, and perform an act that is pleasing to Him. Work in its character of penance, is more excellent than prayer. St. Francis of Sales, when obliged to curtail his prayers because of the press of business, excused himself by saying: " In this world we must pray by work and action." Work has a bitter root, but the fruit it bears is sweet. It has a temporal reward: the idler finds his time long and is a burden to himself, whereas the industrious is contented and cheerful. He experiences the truth of Our Lord's words: " My yoke is sweet and My burden is light " (Matt. xi. 30). The devil cannot molest the busy man with his temptations; he has no leisure to listen to his enticements, any more than a man will leave some important transaction to go where music and dancing are going on. Work generally insures earthly prosperity. The bees who gather honey all day long in summer, lay up in their hives a store of nourishment for the winter. The industrious man's future is assured. A Roman who had accumulated a large fortune by hard work was accused of magic arts. Being brought before the Senate, he produced his tools and said: " Behold the charms I have made use of. The sweat of my brow I cannot show you." Finally labor, like all other acts of penance, merits an everlasting reward. Our Lord says: " The laborer is worthy of his hire " (Luke x. 7). And St. Paul: " Every man shall receive his own reward according to his labor " (1 Cor. iii. 8). The anticipation of a reward sweetens labor, as we see is the case with all the working classes. They labor for a temporal reward, but we for an eternal. St. Bernard told a monk who was always busily employed, that if he continued to work so zealously he need not dread purgatory. Let us not in our work look so much to what we shall gain by it in time, as to our eternal reward.

For if we only think of present profit we shall work less well, and we shall lose the eternal profit to which we show ourselves indifferent.

The precept of labor is transgressed:

1. By indulging in idleness.

2. By the non-fulfilment of the duties of our station and calling.

3. By omitting to offer to God the work that is done.

The Relaxations Permitted to the Christian.

1. It is lawful for those who work to seek relaxation, for this is a means of renewing one's strength after one's work is done.

The bow never unspanned will break; and the man who works without cessation will become unfit for work. Social convivialities are productive of much good; they promote charity and concord. It is God's will that we should enjoy recreation; He has provided us with pleasures in nature alone; the beauteous coloring, the delicious perfume of the flowers; the song of birds, the various kinds of fruit, etc. Our Lord Himself was a guest at banquets, even at a marriage feast, and He speaks without disapproval of music, etc. (Luke xv. 25).

2. We must not, however, indulge too freely in amusements, and certainly we must eschew all those that are sinful; moreover in all our recreations the thought of God must be present to our mind.

We must not be too great votaries of pleasure, for diversions are not the object of life, they are only a means of renewing our strength after our work. Life is for work, not for play. Excess in everything is harmful; medicine taken in too large doses is injurious, and the best condiments, if too freely used, spoil a dish. So it is with amusements; they are only to be enjoyed when all our duties have been duly performed. The thought of death is a useful check upon indulgence in the pleasures of the senses; if we remember that at any moment our soul may be required of us, we shall be moderate in our use of enjoyments. An exaggerated love of pleasure and craving for excitement prevails in the present day; one festivity and dissipation follows another, and yet everywhere one hears complaints of the evil times. May not the thirst for enjoyment be the cause? Above all, dangerous or sinful pleasures are to be avoided, such as gambling for high stakes, games of chance which are prohibited, slandering the absent, sarcastic speeches, unseemly words, or contempt of holy things. Those who indulge in such pleasures are like thankless children who delight in offending their father. When enjoying innocent pleasures we should think of God, and our high destiny. The Psalmist says: "Be glad in the Lord" (Ps. xxxi. 11). St. Charles Borromeo is said once to have played a game of billiards; when asked what he would do if he was told the

Last Judgment was at hand, he replied: " I should finish the game, for I am playing for the glory of God, and He is present to my thoughts."

THE SIX COMMANDMENTS OF THE CHURCH.

1. The six precepts of the Church are an amplification of the Third Commandment of the Decalogue.

The first precept of the Church enjoins upon the faithful to rest from work on certain days besides the Sunday, to give thanks to God for special graces.

The second precept of the Church ordains the manner in which Sunday and the other holydays of obligation are to be observed.

The third and fourth precepts of the Church oblige us to confess and communicate at least once a year.

The fifth precept bids us support our pastors.

The sixth forbids us to marry non-Catholics, or to solemnize marriage at forbidden times.

2. We are under a rigorous obligation to keep the commandments of the Church, for disobedience to the Church is disobedience to Christ.

Christ has conferred upon the Church the same powers which He Himself received from His Father; He said to His apostles: " As the Father hath sent Me, I also send you " (John xx. 21). When the Church enjoins anything upon us, it is the same as if Christ enjoined it; for He said: " Whatsoever you shall bind upon earth shall be bound also in heaven " (Matt. xviii. 18). In disobeying the Church we disobey Christ; as He told the apostles: " He that despiseth you, despiseth Me " (Luke x. 16). Our Lord speaks of the Church as a kingdom; He also compares it to a fold, to teach us that the children of the Church must obey their ecclesiastical superiors. Every society is authorized to make laws which the members must observe; this the Church does; and by her mouth God makes His will known to us.

He therefore who wantonly violates one of the Church's laws, commits a grievous sin.

Our Lord expressly says that he who will not hear the Church is to be regarded as a heathen (Matt. xviii. 17). Under the Old Dispensation death was the punishment of one who through pride should refuse to obey the commandment of the high priest (Deut. xvii. 12). Thus we see that from the first rebellion against the spiritual authority was a heinous sin.

3. The rulers of the Church are empowered to dispense the faithful from the observance of any of the commandments of the Church for weighty reasons.

Christ said to the apostles: " What you loose upon earth shall be
loosed also in heaven " (Matt. xviii. 18). Some bishops permit meat
to be eaten on Friday when a festival falls on that day. The Pope
has sanctioned the transference of certain holydays to the following
Sunday in some countries.

1. THE FIRST COMMANDMENT OF THE CHURCH : THE OBSERVANCE OF SUNDAYS AND HOLYDAYS.

**1. In the first commandment of the Church the solemn ob-
servance of the holydays is enjoined upon us. There are seven
festivals of Our Lord, five of Our Lady, and three of the saints.**

The early Christians kept a great number of festivals in order to
keep alive the memory of certain events or benefits received from God
as the anniversaries came round. These feasts were instituted that
the events they commemorate might be remembered to all time by
the faithful, and praise and thanksgiving be rendered to God for
them. Unhappily some persons only mark these festivals by providing a more liberal table, as if, St. Jerome remarks, by eating
and drinking one could honor those who sought to please God by
fasting and mortification.

The seven feasts of Our Lord are (1), Christmas (Dec. 25th);
(2), The Circumcision (Jan. 1st); (3), The Epiphany (Jan. 6th);
(4), Easter; (5), The Ascension; (6), Pentecost; (7), Corpus
Christi (the last-named is not a holyday for the United States).

As the nativity and the resurrection of Our Lord and the coming
of the Holy Ghost are events of primary importance, they are celebrated with peculiar solemnity. In European countries the 26th of
December, the feast of St. Stephen, and the two days immediately
following Easter Day and Pentecost, are kept as feasts of devotion.

The five feasts of the Mother of God are: (1), The Immaculate Conception (Dec. 8th); (2), The Nativity of Our Lady (Sept.
8th); (3), The Annunciation (March 25th); (4), The Purification (Feb. 2d); (5), The Assumption (Aug. 15th). Of these festivals the Immaculate Conception and the Assumption are the
only ones now observed as holydays of obligation.

The life of the Mother of God is so intimately connected with that
of her divine Son that the Church commemorates its principal events.
Unlike the other saints, who are commemorated on the day of their
death, because it was their birth to a better life, the day of Mary's
birth is solemnized, because she was born without sin.

The three festivals of the saints are: (1) The feast of St.
Stephen (Dec. 26th), no longer a holyday of obligation; (2),
The feast of St. Peter and St. Paul (June 28th), not a holyday
in the United States; (3), The feast of All Saints (Nov. 1st).
In some lands the feast of the patron saint of the country is

kept as a general holiday. These festivals are either fixed or movable. The former are kept yearly on the same day, the latter vary as to the date of celebration.

The fixed festivals are: The Immaculate Conception, Christmas, the Circumcision, the Epiphany, the Annunciation, St. Peter and St. Paul, the Assumption of and Nativity of Our Lady, the feast of All Saints. The movable feasts are: Easter, which is kept on the first Sunday following the first new moon after the spring equinox, consequently in the interval between the twenty-second of March and the twenty-fifth of April; the Ascension, forty days after Easter; Pentecost, fifty days after Easter; Corpus Christi, the Thursday of the second week after Whitsunday. The Church has instituted some of her festivals as substitutes for the feasts of the Old Testament, which were a foreshadowing of the Christian festivals. Others take the place of heathen festivities; the birth of Our Lord is commemorated in the season when the pagans consecrated the long winter nights to the worship of the sun; the processions in different countries on Candlemas Day is a Christianized form of the torch-light processions held in the first days of February, when the days begin perceptibly to lengthen, in honor of the divinities of the ancients. This the Church did in order to render the evangelization of the heathen more easy, by changing, instead of abrogating, their ceremonies.

2. The holydays of obligation ought to be kept in the same manner as the Sundays; we must abstain from servile work and assist at holy Mass.

The number of holydays of obligation varies in different countries. In some certain festivals have been transferred to the Sunday following, as it was found that holydays recurring too frequently produced the opposite effect to that for which they were instituted.

The Ecclesiastical Year.

The Jews of old used to observe a number of feasts besides the Sabbath in commemoration of important events in their history; e.g., the festival of Easter in memory of the exit from Egypt; Pentecost, in memory of the giving of the law on Sinai; the feast of Tabernacles in memory of their journey through the desert. The Church does much the same; she annually recalls events in Our Lord's life on earth, representing them as vividly as is possible after so long a lapse of time. This is especially the case in the ceremonies of Holy Week.

1. The ecclesiastical year is an annual commemoration and representation of the life of Christ, and of the time before and after His birth.

The Church places these events before us in order that we may meditate upon them and imitate Our Lord's life. In Advent we are called upon to anticipate with the patriarchs of the Old Testament, the coming of the long-expected Redeemer; at Christmas we rejoice with the shepherds at His birth; in Lent we fast forty days with Christ; at Easter we rise again with Him; at Pentecost we join with the disciples in praying for the coming of the Holy Ghost. On almost every day of the year the Church commemorates one or more of the saints; they are like planets, revolving around the Sun of justice. She bids us consider their lives, how they imitated Christ, and thus became patterns of Christian perfection; and she desires to encourage us to imitate Him too. It is besides the intention of the Church that we should implore the intercession of the saints, that we may the more surely be made partakers of the merits of Christ. Finally by weaving these saints' days into the cycle of the ecclesiastical year, she would teach us amid all our earthly occupations to keep our thoughts fixed upon God, doing all, as the Apostle exhorts us, to His glory (1 Cor. x. 31).

2. The ecclesiastical year begins upon the first Sunday in Advent; its three principal feasts are: Christmas, when the birth of Christ is celebrated; Easter, the day of His resurrection; and Pentecost, when the coming of the Holy Spirit is commemorated.

Thus the ecclesiastical year sets forth the glory of the Holy Trinity; it displays the charity of the Father, Who sent His Son into the world; the charity of the Son, Who died for our sakes, and the charity of the Holy Spirit, Who descended to abide with us. Therefore the first Sunday after Pentecost is dedicated to the Holy Trinity; this feast links all the other three together.

Each of these three great feasts has a season of preparation preceding it as well as a subsequent commemoration.

Advent is the season of preparation before Christmas. In the subsequent period we have the feast of the Circumcision, the Epiphany, the Purification, and the Sundays after the Epiphany.

The four weeks of Advent represent the four thousand years during which the coming of the Messias was expected. The Immaculate Conception occurs most suitably in Advent, the eighth of December, for at the birth of Christ the Sun of justice rose upon the world, dispelling the darkness of sin and ignorance; Mary was like the aurora (Cant. vi. 9), heralding the coming day. The period after Christmas is symbolical of the youth of Our Lord, and of the time which intervened before His entry upon His public ministry; His hidden life, that is, at Nazareth.

The forty days of Lent are the preparation for Easter; and the Paschal time lasts during the subsequent forty days before the ascension.

The preparation for Lent includes the three Sundays called respectively Septuagesima (70), Sexagesima (60), and Quinquagesima (50). They were so named because in the early days of Christianity many communities began the fast fifty, sixty, or seventy days before Easter, in order not to have to fast every day of the forty. The Wednesday after Quinquagesima is called Ash Wednesday, because of the ceremony of sprinkling ashes upon the foreheads of the faithful. On Ash Wednesday the season of Lent commences; it is forty-six days before Easter; thus the number of days is completed without the six

Sundays, on which we do not fast. During Lent the public life of Our Lord is set before us, His previous fast, His Passion and death. The forty days which intervene before the ascension represent the forty days He spent on earth after His resurrection. The three days before the ascension are the Rogation days; on these processions are held.

The ten days after the ascension are the period of preparation for Pentecost. The subsequent commemoration lasts for twenty-four weeks, sometimes even longer.

The ten days before Pentecost represent the ten days during which the apostles awaited the coming of the Holy Spirit; the weeks that follow represent the time that shall elapse before the Last Judgment. Consequently on the last Sunday after Pentecost the Gospel read in church is that which foretells Our Lord's coming as our Judge. The feasts of All Saints and All Souls close the ecclesiastical year. This is to signify that we are in unbroken communion with the blessed in heaven and the holy souls in purgatory and that our separation from them is but temporary. All Souls' Day occurs suitably when the face of nature presents an image of death.

3. The aspect of nature corresponds to the three principal festivals.

In Advent, at least for us who inhabit the northern hemisphere, the nights are longer than the days, and the life of vegetation is at a standstill; so it was in the spiritual order before the coming of Christ. After Christmas the days begin to lengthen; just so the birth of Christ brought light to the world. At Easter nature awakens to new life and decks herself with verdure; Christ rises glorious from the dead. At Pentecost trees and meadows are in their full beauty of leaf and blossom; with the coming of the Holy Spirit a fresh era commences for mankind, and fair flowers of holiness are brought forth.

The epistles and gospels, as well as the hymns and sequences of the Mass, are suited to the festivals and seasons of the ecclesiastical year.

The gospels are portions taken from the four gospels, and the epistles from other parts of Holy Scripture. They were originally compiled by St. Jerome.

2. THE SECOND COMMANDMENT OF THE CHURCH.

By the second commandment of the Church the precept of fasting is laid upon us.

Fasting is as ancient as the human race itself. Even in paradise it was enjoined upon man to abstain from the fruit of one tree: moreover, certain meats were forbidden to the Jews; pork, for instance (Lev. xi.). On the Day of Propitiation the Jews were not permitted to taste food for twenty-four hours. Our Lord fasted forty days; so did Moses and Elias before Him; and St. John Baptist, the Precursor, fasted most rigorously. The Church has good reasons for laying the obligation of fasting upon the faithful.

The laws of the Church in regard to fasting are in reality very strict; they have, however, been largely relaxed by the bishops to suit the exigencies of time and place.

The rule of fasting was originally so stringent that on the fast days not only was abstinence from flesh-meat enjoined, but milk, eggs, and butter were also prohibited; and no food was to be taken before sundown. But owing to the increase of constitutional weakness, and still more because of the spread of religious indifference in the course of centuries, the rule has been more and more relaxed. Bishops are empowered to prescribe, each for his own diocese, on what days meat is permitted. Hence the rule varies in different dioceses, and it is well, on going into another diocese, to ascertain what the rule is in that part.

There are three kinds of fasting at present: (1), Abstinence from flesh-meat; (2), Taking one full meal only in the day; (3), Strict fasting, in which both of these are enjoined.

In the second commandment of the Church we are ordered to abstain on all Fridays of the year; and to fast during the forty days of Lent, on the Ember days, and on the vigils of certain feasts.

1. We are forbidden to eat meat on Friday, because on that day Our Lord died for us.

Not only is meat prohibited, but all dishes in the preparation of which it enters. Fish, turtle, and shell-fish may be eaten, also eggs, milk, and butter, in almost all countries. The Church has forbidden the use of meat because Christ sacrificed His flesh for us; also because meat is an article of food easily dispensed with, and yet what men generally like best. Another reason is to remind us that the lusts of the flesh are to be resisted (Gal. v. 19), and these are fostered by eating meat. Some people quote Our Lord's words: "Not those things which go into the mouth defile the man" (Matt. xv. 11), as opposed to this prohibition; but He also said: "The things that come from the heart, those things defile the man" (Matt. xv. 18). Disobedience to the Church comes from the heart, and this it is which defiles, not the actual meat. If Christmas Day falls on a Friday, meat is allowed, because Our Lord would not have us fast at a season of rejoicing (Matt. ix. 15).

In early ages the use of meat was also forbidden on Saturdays.

The original object of this prohibition was to suppress the observance of the Sabbath day, which still lingered among Christian converts. It is now done away with; yet Christians often impose some restriction upon their amusements on Saturday, in view of better sanctifying the morrow.

2. During the forty days of Lent only one full meal is to be taken, as a partial imitation of Our Lord's fast of forty days, and as a suitable preparation for celebrating the festival of Easter.

The forty days of Lent begin on Ash Wednesday, and last until Easter Day; the Sundays alone are not fasting days.

The Lenten fast was instituted by the apostles in commemoration of Our Lord's fast in the wilderness (Matt. iv.). It is a time of penance and of sorrow for sin; hence violet vestments are worn at the altar. It is natural to fast when we are in grief (Matt. ix. 15). We ought also during Lent to meditate upon Our Lord's Passion, which is commemorated in Holy Week, and which usually forms the theme of the Lenten sermons. By fasting and meditation upon Our Lord's Passion we most readily awake within ourselves the grace of contrition and consciousness of sin. The forty days of Lent are also a preparation for the Easter festival. In early times the fast was much more rigorous; the primitive Christians ate no meat all the time, and did not break their fast until the evening. Even in the Middle Ages meat was prohibited; those who ate it were not admitted to the paschal communion (Council of Toledo, 653). Those who broke this law were punished by the secular authority on the ground of contempt for religion. The rule of fasting is made very easy nowadays. All that the Church requires of us is to take only one full meal in the course of the day; a slight refection is permitted in the morning, besides the evening collation. Drinking does not break the fast; yet we must only drink to quench our thirst, not in order to compensate for privations in the way of solid food. No one is required to keep the fast of Lent who has not attained the age of twenty-one years.

3. We ought to keep the fast of the Ember days strictly, in order to implore almighty God to send us good priests, and to thank Him for the benefits received during the past quarter.

The Ember days are three in number, Wednesday, Friday, and Saturday, at the commencement of each quarter (quatuor tempora); of old these were the appointed seasons for ordination to the priesthood.

The Ember days of the winter season fall in the third week of Advent, of the spring quarter in the second week of Lent; in summer in Whitsunweek and in autumn in the third week in September. The Jews were accustomed to fast four times a year (Zach. viii. 19). Christ enjoined upon us the duty of praying for good priests, in the words: " The harvest indeed is great, but the laborers are few. Pray ye therefore the Lord of the harvest that He send forth laborers into His harvest " (Matt. ix. 37, 38).

4. We are also bound to fast on the vigils of certain feasts, in order the better to prepare ourselves for celebrating those feasts.

The better our preparation, the more abundant are the graces we obtain on the feast itself. The early Christians were accustomed to assemble together on the eves of great festivals, to pass the night in watching and prayer, and in assisting at the holy sacrifice of the Mass. This they did because had they held the services in the daytime, they would have been liable to disturbance on the part of the pagans. Our Lord Himself used often to pass whole nights in prayer (Luke vi. 12). When at a later period the attendance at the nightly services fell off, and inconveniences arose, the Popes judged it advisable to transfer the celebration of the vigil to the daytime. The vigil of Christmas is the only one in which the nightly celebration has been retained up to the present time; of all the others nothing survives but the past.

These vigils are the days preceding the three great festivals: that is, Christmas Eve, Holy Saturday, and the Saturday before Pentecost.

The eve of the Assumption is also kept in most dioceses, but the rule respecting the fast varies.

5. It is by no means the desire of the Church that we should fast to the injury of our health, or that we should thereby be hindered from performing the duties of our station.

1. Consequently persons whose health is weak are permitted to eat meat on Friday.

The sick, those who are recovering from an illness, very aged people, and children under seven come within this rule. Children under seven, being incapable of sin, have no need for penance. Persons who have to exert themselves very much, either physically or mentally, are in some dioceses dispensed from the Friday abstinence; this however does not depend upon the nature of their calling, so much as on the constitution of each individual, and the amount of work he has to get through daily. A dispensation is granted by some bishops to those who have to travel on Friday, as well as to those whose meals are provided for them, e.g., servants, students, soldiers; to those also who have to take their meals as best they can, such as railway guards, and to those who are staying for their health at some health resort. The poor may eat meat which is given them as an alms, otherwise they would have to go hungry. Yet all classes of people ought to endeavor to abstain on the strictest fasts, such as Ash Wednesday and Good Friday. Above all, those who eat meat on abstinence days must beware lest they give scandal to others. St. Paul warns the faithful against this: "Take heed lest perhaps this your liberty become a stumbling-block to the weak" (1 Cor. viii. 9), and for his own part he says: "If meat scandalize my brother I will never eat flesh" (v. 13).

2. Persons are dispensed from fasting (i.e., from taking only one meal in the twenty-four hours) who are under twenty-one years of age, or who are constitutionally delicate, or who have continued, strenuous exertion, whether physical or mental.

Young people who have not done growing require more than one full meal a day; of invalids we have already spoken. In the class who are engaged in active and laborious work, we include those who exert themselves for the temporal or spiritual welfare of their fellow-men, such as confessors, preachers, catechists, schoolmasters, nurses, physicians, magistrates, etc., who frequently require to take something to sustain their strength. When the influenza was so prevalent, a general dispensation from fasting was granted. The command to keep ourselves in health is given by God, and is a law of our nature; whereas the precept of fasting is laid on us by the Church; and the law of God is paramount above the law of the Church. Those who cannot fast should substitute for it some other good work. Confessors have ordinarily power to dispense from fasting, and impose some other good work, prayers or alms, in its place.

3. No one ought to carry fasting to an excess, for what God requires from us is our reasonable service (Rom. xii. 1).

He who overdoes fasting is like a coachman who whips his horses into a gallop, and runs the risk of upsetting the carriage; or like an overladen vessel, that is easily capsized. Even some of the saints went to an excess in fasting, and afterwards much regretted it. No one ought to venture to do more than the rule prescribes, without the advice of his confessor. Obedience is far better than self-willed piety. As a rule it is preferable to be temperate every day of the week than to fast rigorously on one or two days. Fasting is intended to destroy the evil lusts of the body, not the body itself. We must deal with our bodies as a parent deals with his child; he does not chastise him when he is docile, but when he is disobedient. Fasting, like medicine, must be used in moderation or it becomes injurious.

6. Fasting is beneficial both for the soul and the body.

The intellectual powers are sharpened by moderation in our food. At Nabuchodonosor's court Daniel ate pulse and drank water, and he surpassed in understanding, knowledge, and wisdom all the wise men of the kingdom (Dan. i.). By fasting the soul is fortified and enabled both to bring the body into subjection (1 Cor. ix. 27), and to overcome the temptations of the devil. The fortress surrenders when the garrison is starved out; so the body, under stress of hunger, yields to the will and the understanding. Our bodies have to be tamed like wild animals. The devil regards the flesh as his best ally; he knows that the enemy at a man's fireside can do him the worst and the greatest harm. By fasting we put our foe in irons, so that he cannot wage war against us. The bird of prey loves a fat prize, he does not make the half-starved one his victim. The athlete who " refraineth himself in all things " (1 Cor. ix. 25), in preparation for the contest, is most likely to conquer. A high degree of virtue is also acquired by means of fasting. It inclines man to prayer; it helps him to overcome himself, to be gentle, patient, and chaste; it makes him resemble the angels, who neither eat nor drink. In the same proportion that the animal part of our nature is lessened, our spiritual nature is invigorated; like the scales of a balance, as one goes down the other rises. Our health is improved and our life prolonged by abstemiousness. It is the parent of good health. The hermits in the Theban desert fasted rigorously and they lived to be a hundred years old. Hippocrates, the father of medicine, reached the age of one hundred and forty years; this he attributed to the fact that he never fully satisfied his appetite. The Wise Man says: "He that is temperate shall prolong his life" (Ecclus. xxxvii. 34); "a moderate man also enjoys wholesome and sound sleep" (Ecclus. xxxi. 24). By fasting we obtain from God the pardon of our sins; witness the Ninivites when they fasted; by it we also work off some of our purgatory. God hears and answers the prayers of those who fast; He heard the prayers of the centurion, who fasted until the ninth hour (Acts x. 30), and sent an angel to him. When Holofernes laid siege to Bethulia, the inhabitants betook themselves to prayer and fasting, and they were delivered in a marvellous manner by Judith. St. Augustine calls fasting and almsgiving the two pinions of prayer. Fasting is a means of earning extraordinary graces, for God has ever been wont to recompense it with singular favors. After Moses had fasted, he was admitted to the honor of conversing with God upon Sinai. After Elias' long fast, God appeared to him upon Mount Horeb (3 Kings xix.). He who fasts, grows more and more spiritual; he is in a measure divinized, hence God vouchsafes to hold intercourse with him (Rodriguez). Fasting is rewarded after death. Moses and Elias were present at Our Lord's transfiguration, because they alone of all the patriarchs had fasted forty days as He did. Hence we see that glory is reserved in a future life for those who fast in this world. In the Preface for Lent the Church sings: "Who by a bodily fast restrainest vices, upliftest our minds, and grantest strength and rewards."

7. Abstinence from food is only pleasing to God if, at the same time, we refrain from sin and perform good works.

Fasting is not in itself an excellent thing (1 Cor. viii. 8), but only as a means whereby the suppression of our vices and the practice of virtue is facilitated. How does it profit a man if he abstains from meat, and by his calumnies destroys his neighbor's reputation? Such a one may be compared to a whited sepulchre, outwardly beautiful, but foul within (Matt. xxiii. 27). The devil does not eat, yet he is unceasingly employed in doing evil. Fasting without prayer is like a lamp without oil, because we only fast to pray better. Fasting without almsgiving is a field without seed; it fosters the weeds of avarice. He fasts for himself, not for God, who does not give to the poor what he denies to himself.

3. THE THIRD AND FOURTH COMMANDMENTS OF THE CHURCH.

1. In the third and fourth commandments the Church enjoins upon us the duty of approaching the Sacrament of Penance and receiving holy communion at Easter.

Holy communion ought to be received often, because it is the food of the soul. That soul will be starved which for a long time does not receive this nourishment. Our Lord says: "Except you eat the flesh of the Son of man, and drink His blood, you shall not have life in you" (John vi. 54). The early Christians used originally to receive holy communion every day; later on only on the three great feasts, Christmas, Easter, and Pentecost. And when in the Middle Ages the fervor of many grew cold, the Council of Lateran (1215), ordained that all Christians who were capable of distinguishing good from evil were obliged to confess their sins at least once a year, and at Easter, at the least, devoutly to receive the Sacrament of the Altar. The Council of Trent expresses the wish that the confession also should be made at Easter, for it says: "Throughout the whole Church the salutary custom prevails of making confession of sin during the holy and most suitable season of Lent; a custom which the Church approves and accepts as pious and most certainly to be retained" (14 C. 5). Holy communion should be preceded by confession, lest any man should approach holy communion in a state of mortal sin; the Easter communion is no exception to this rule. The obligation of the Easter precept is not fulfilled by a sacrilegious communion, nor by an invalid confession. Although the Church only requires every Christian to confess his sins once a year, yet it need hardly be said that if any man has the misfortune to fall into mortal sin, he should go to confession without delay.

2. The time for fulfilling the Easter precept was formerly only two weeks, from Palm Sunday to Low Sunday; it is now extended in almost all dioceses, being from the first Sunday of Lent to Low Sunday, sometimes even to Trinity Sunday.

3. It is fitting that we should receive holy communion at Easter, because it was just before Easter Day, on Holy Thursday, that Our Lord instituted the Adorable Sacrament of the Altar.

At Easter Christ also rose from the dead. If we make a really good confession, we, in a spiritual sense, rise from the dead. For the soul which is in mortal sin is spiritually dead; through the Sacrament of Penance it receives the Holy Spirit again, and spiritual life is again restored to it. At the grave of the risen Redeemer the angel said to the women: "Why seek you the living with the dead? He is not here, He is risen." Would that our guardian angel could say the same of us, when the devil, after Easter, thinks to find us still sleeping in the sepulchre of sin. "You seek the living with the dead, the converted with the sinners; he is not here." "As Christ is risen from the dead, so we may also walk in newness of life" (Rom. vi. 4).

4. The Church allows Catholics to make their Easter confession elsewhere than in their parish church.

The Church is aware that some find it easier to disclose the wounds of their soul to a stranger, and she permits this in order to prevent such persons from approaching the sacraments unworthily. Formerly every one was bound to go to his parish priest as a mark of respect.

5. Christian burial can be denied to a Catholic who has not been in the habit of receiving the sacraments at Easter, and who dies unrepentant.

This is done in the case of one whose neglect of his duty is publicly known, and who has been admonished in vain by his pastor. Before refusing Christian burial, the priest is bound to refer the matter to the bishop; and if time does not allow of this, he takes the most lenient course.

4. THE FIFTH COMMANDMENT OF THE CHURCH.

By the fifth commandment of the Church we are bound to contribute to the support of our pastors.

5. THE SIXTH COMMANDMENT OF THE CHURCH.

Marriage and the penitential seasons.

In the sixth commandment marriage with non-Catholics is forbidden, also the marriage of those who are related within the fourth degree of kindred. Marriages are not to be solemnized during fixed seasons. These penitential times are from the beginning of Advent until the Epiphany, and from Ash Wednesday until Low Sunday.

This rule was made by the Council of Trent (Council of Trent, 24, 10). Formerly the prohibition also included the period between the Monday of Rogation week until the first Sunday after Pentecost; in some countries at the present time it applies to the Rogation days and all fasts throughout the year. Advent and Lent are seasons of penance and sorrow for sin, and festivities ill accord with sorrow. Moreover in Advent the Church proposes the mystery of the Incarnation, and in Lent the mystery of the redemption for our meditation, and it would be unseemly to divert our minds from these solemn subjects by worldly amusements. The bishop can give permission for marriages to be contracted privately during these times; for their public solemnization the authorization of the Holy See is necessary. Concerts are not forbidden, but dances are. Those who transgress this command expose themselves to the judgment God threatens by the prophet: "I will turn your feasts into mourning" Amos viii. 10).

THE FOURTH COMMANDMENT OF GOD.

In the Fourth Commandment God enjoins upon us to honor His representatives upon earth, that is to say, our parents, and both the ecclesiastical and secular authorities.

1. OUR DUTY TOWARDS OUR PARENTS.

1. Our parents are to be honored, because they are God's representatives and our greatest benefactors.

We are all children of Our Father in heaven, and He causes us to be fed and brought up by our earthly parents. Thus parents take the place of God in regard to the education of their children; they are His representatives, and as such, the honor due to Him must be paid to them, for the viceroy can claim the same respect as the monarch who has delegated his authority to him. Those who despise their parents, despise God Himself. St. Augustine, after his conversion, bitterly regretted the disrespect he had shown the mother God had given to him, knowing that thereby he had shown disrespect to God. Our parents are moreover our greatest benefactors. "How much," exclaims St. Ambrose, "has not thy mother suffered on thy account! How many sleepless nights, how many privations, how much anxiety has she not borne for thee! How hard thy father has worked, to provide thee with food and raiment! And canst thou be ungrateful to those who have done and suffered so much for thee?" The Son of God Himself honored His Mother and His foster-father; it is said of Him that He was subject to them. Learn of Him to obey your parents; He honored them, though they were His servants; He loved and respected His Mother, whose Creator He was; He never forgot that as an infant He had lain on Mary's bosom, and had been carried in Joseph's arms.

2. We ought to honor our parents by respectful behavior, love, and obedience.

When God bids us honor our parents. He commands us to love and obey them, for this is included in the reverence we owe them. Love is due to them as our greatest benefactors. It is the first duty of a Christian to compensate his parents for the trouble and the sacrifices his education has entailed on them. The obligation to obey them ceases when there is no longer occasion for it; the duty of loving and respecting them only ends with their life.

Respect towards our parents consists in esteeming them from our heart as God's representatives, and manifesting this esteem outwardly by word and deed.

Esteem for our parents must be heartfelt, otherwise outward manifestations of esteem would be mere dissembling. Christ showed great respect for His Mother at the marriage feast of Cana; for although He told her His hour for working miracles was not yet come, He complied with her request. We must honor our parents even if they are poor and in a humble class of life. Joseph, when Governor of Egypt showed great respect for his aged father. Although he was only a shepherd, he brought him to the king and presented him before him (Gen. xlvii. 7). King Solomon rose from his throne to meet his mother, although she was not of royal lineage; he bowed to her, and made her sit on his right hand (3 Kings ii. 19). Pope Benedict XI. received his mother, who was a poor washerwoman, in the kindest manner when she went to him in the mean apparel of her class. Even if parents do not lead a virtuous life, they still have a claim upon the respect of their children, because of the position they hold in regard to them as God's representatives. The Wise Man says: "Honor thy father in word and work and in all patience" (Ecclus. iii. 9).

Love of our parents consists in kind feelings and kind actions towards them.

We are bound to love our parents, as we are bound to love all men, because they are our neighbor, made in God's image. But this is not enough: They have a right to a special affection on our part, because we are their children, because they love us so tenderly, and confer so many benefits upon us. Are not his parents a child's best friends? Love consists in kind sentiments and kind actions. Joseph showed his affection for his old father; he fell on his neck and embracing him, wept (Gen. xlvi. 29). But kind feelings are not enough. Let us not love in word nor in tongue, but in deed and in truth (1 John iii. 18). Therefore we ought to help our parents in destitution or sickness, and pray for them. The Prussian General Ziethen when a page, was once on guard at night in the king's antechamber. The king, Frederick I., finding he did not answer his summons, went out and found him asleep over a letter which he was writing to his mother, to send her his first earnings (thirty shillings) in the royal service. The king read the letter and was so touched that he put a roll of money in each of the young man's pockets, and the next morning appointed him to the army. When Blessed Thomas More had been put to death for the faith by order of Henry VIII., no one ventured to bury his remains; his daughter Margaret alone braved the tyrant's wrath, and he, respecting her filial devotion, allowed no one to interfere with her. Even among the lower animals we find examples of affection towards parents. The young lions share their prey with the old, and the storks warm those who have lost their plumage through age; they bring them food and assist them to fly. The Wise Man says: "Son, support the old age of thy father" (Ecclus. iii. 18). Remember how Our Lord on the cross provided for His Mother by commending her to the care of St. John (John xix. 26).

Obedience towards our parents consists in fulfilling all their lawful commands, as long as we are under their authority.

"Children, obey your parents in all things" (Col. iii. 20). Just as parents are bound to provide for the education of their children, so it is the duty of children to obey their parents. As in the State some rule and others obey, so it must be in the family; otherwise there can be no domestic order and concord. Virtue is expected of the old; submission of the young. Yet children are only bound to obey when the command is just; if their parents order them to do what is contrary to God's law, and consequently unjust, they must act on the Apostle's words: "We ought to obey God rather than men" (Acts v. 29). St. Hermengild, son of Leovigild, King of the Goths, was imprisoned by his father in a tower in Sevilla, because he would not embrace the Arian heresy. The king promised to restore him to his favor if only he complied with his desire. But the saint replied that he would renounce the crown, his father's affection, life itself, rather than deny his faith. He was accordingly martyred. Several other saints chose rather to disobey the command of their earthly than of their heavenly Father, and thus lost their lives. Parents who require their children to do what is forbidden by the law of God, undermine their own authority; they saw off the bough on which they are sitting. A man ordered his son to work in the fields on Sunday; the lad refused, saying it was forbidden by the law of God. The father rejoined angrily: "You are not a child now, and the commandments are only for children." "In that case," the son replied, "I need not keep the Fourth Commandment which bids me obey you." Children are only bound to obey their parents as long as they are under their control, and they are only bound to obey in matters which come within the sphere of the parental authority, such as their manners and behavior at home and abroad, their companions, etc. Parents have no right to dictate to their children in regard to the calling they shall embrace, for a vocation comes from God. Parents cannot dispose of their children's future, when they are no longer subject to them. St. Francis of Assisi would not let his father make a merchant of him; St. Rose of Lima refused to marry. Yet the advice of parents should always be asked; age gives them greater discernment and experience of life, and they are the best and wisest counsellors a man can have. Holy Scripture exhorts us thus: "My son, hear the instruction of thy father" (Prov. i. 8).

3. Our duty is the same in regard to those who are in authority over us, as it is to our parents; our teachers and governors, masters and employers, and our elders in general.

The old are to be respected by the young. "Honor the person of the aged man, and rise up before the hoary head" (Lev. xix. 32). It becomes the elder to speak first (Ecclus. xxxii. 4). The Spartans entertained great respect for the aged; when an old man could not find a place at the Olympian games, they all rose up to give him a seat. Alexander the Great was one day sitting by a warm fire, when he saw an aged soldier shivering in the cold; he called him in and gave him a place on his own regal couch. Young people ought to heed the counsels of the old, "for of them they shall learn wisdom and instruction" (Ecclus. viii. 9). The old act less on impulse, and consequently more prudently. God appointed a council of seventy ancients for the guidance of the Jews (Exod. iv. 29), and the Roman Senate was composed of old men. Above all, the aged should never be despised, for we too shall become old in our turn (Ecclus. viii. 9). Their infirmities must be borne with: "An ancient man rebuke not, but entreat him as a father" (1 Tim. v. 1).

Transgressions of the Fourth Commandment.

1. He transgresses the Fourth Commandment of God who is disrespectful towards his parents; who behaves rudely to them, is ashamed of them, etc.

Cham mocked at his father, when he lay naked and drunk in his tent (Gen. ix.). For this his father cursed him; his descendants are the negro inhabitants of Africa, and know not the true God.

1. He who is unkind to his parents, who, for instance, hates them, refuses to help them, steals from them, etc.

· The sons of Jacob, after they had sold their brother Joseph, deceived and grieved their father (Gen. xxxvii). Absalom spoke against his father at the palace gates, lied to him, and rebelled against him (2 Kings xv.).

2. He who disobeys his parents, and will not be corrected by them, transgresses this commandment.

The two sons of the high priest Heli disobeyed their father's commands and admonitions (1 Kings ii.).

How Does God Reward the Observance of the Fourth Commandment?

1. God promises long life, happiness, and blessings upon earth to children who honor their parents.

At the giving of the law on Sinai God promised long life as the reward for keeping the Fourth Commandment (Exod. xx. 12). St. Paul holds out the same inducement to the fulfilment of filial duty (Eph. vi. 3). Joseph was obedient to his father; the old man loved him for it but his brethren hated him. Joseph was made Governor of Egypt, and attained the age of a hundred and ten years (Gen. l.). Those who honor their parents honor old age; and as in the providence of God there is generally some connection between the work and the reward, dutiful children usually reach an advanced age. A long life is a great boon to a man; the longer he lives, the more merits he can amass for eternity. Under the Old Dispensation a long life shortened the sojourn of the soul in limbo, consequently it was a greater privilege than under the New Dispensation, when a good death is an immediate transition to eternal life. Certainly many good children die young, but even in this case God fulfils His promise, for instead of life on earth He gives them life eternal, which is far more to be desired. Besides an innocent life is in itself a long life; "a spotless life is old age" (Wisd. iv. 9). God takes many a one out of this world that he may escape contamination: "lest wickedness should alter his understanding" (Wisd. iv. 11). Moreover the blessings which parents invoke upon their children are very powerful. Witness the blessing which the aged Tobias gave to his son when he set out on his journey; the blessings which Noe pronounced upon Sem and Japheth. Honor your parents that their blessing may rest upon you. "The father's blessing establisheth the houses of the children" (Ecclus. iii. 11). "He that honoreth his mother is as one that layeth up a treasure" (v. 5); "The relieving of thy father shall never be forgotten" (v. 15). Hence it comes that dutiful children are generally prosperous, or at least have real contentment. The enjoyment of happiness and peace is more to be desired than wealth. Those who behave well to their parents are blessed in their turn with dutiful children, who are a comfort to them. "He that honoreth his father shall have joy in his own children" (v. 6). Happiness in this world and in the next is the reward God bestows upon children who honor their parents.

2. God threatens to send upon those who do not honor their parents shame upon earth, a miserable end, everlasting damnation.

It is unquestionably a great sin to treat one's greatest earthly bene-factor with ingratitude, and because of the magnitude of the sin the punishment is proportionately heavy. Those who forget their father and mother God will forget, and allow them to suffer reproach (Ecclus. xxiii. 18, 19). As a tree on which there were no blossoms can produce no fruit, so the man who was disobedient in his youth will not be honored in his old age. Bad children frequently come to a miserable end; witness the death of the two sons of Heli, who perished in battle (1 Kings iv. 11), also the fate that overtook the treacherous Absalom, who, having rebelled against his father David, and defeated him, was caught by his long hair in the branches of an oak, and hung there, pierced by three lances (2 Kings xviii.). Bad children are in great danger of losing their souls. If God deals so severely in the Day of Judgment with those who have failed to perform works of mercy towards their neighbor, how much the more rigorously will He judge those who have been unkind to their own parents. The Apostle says that those who are disobedient to parents are worthy of death (Rom. i. 30). The Jewish law pronounced a curse upon him who honoreth not his father and mother (Deut. xxvii. 16). Again, "He that striketh his father or mother shall be put to death" (Exod. xxi. 15). "The eye that mocketh at his mother, let the ravens pick it out and the young eagles eat it" (Prov. xxx. 17). God laid this strict command upon the Jews: "A stubborn and unruly son, who will not hear the commandments of his father and mother, and slighteth obedience; the people of the city shall stone him and he shall die, that all Israel hearing it may be afraid" (Deut. xxi. 18, 21). Those who have not honored their parents, by divine retribution often have unruly children of their own, as experience frequently shows. "By what things a man sinneth, by the same he is tor-mented" (Wisd. xi. 17). Cham despised his father, and his descend-ants were the degraded nations whom God caused to be cast out of Chanaan.

2. OUR DUTY TOWARDS THOSE IN AUTHORITY.

1. God has appointed two powers, the spiritual and the secular, for the direction of human society. To the spiritual power He has committed the guidance of souls, to the secular the main-tenance of peace and order.

Throughout the whole of creation we observe the existence of a certain mutual dependence; the moon is a satellite of the earth, the earth and the other planets of our solar system revolve round the sun; the mineral kingdom supplies nourishment to the vegetable kingdom, the vegetable to the animal, while each and all are for the service of man. Among animals we find the same subordination of some to others; the bees are governed by a queen; the birds, the wild beasts of the forest, the fish in the seas have their leaders, and obey a kind of military rule. In our own bodies we see how one member commands, the others obey. In the spiritual world the same law of dependence exists as in the natural order; there are angels of higher and lowlier rank. In like manner it is the will of God that some men should rule and others be subject. In consequence of original sin, without rulers human society would soon resemble an army without commanders, a disorderly rabble. Governors are to the State what beams are to a wall; without beams the building would collapse; so society would without rulers. When, after the Fall, men began to rage against each other like wild beasts, and the son of the first man slew his brother, God set rulers over men, to restrain them. Our rulers ought in some measure to reflect as in a mirror the divine power and providence watching over mankind. Just as there are two lights in the firmament of heaven, the sun to shine by day, and the moon by night, so two powers are instituted to govern mankind. The spiritual, like the sun, is the superior because it guides man to his eternal goal; whereas the secular authority is primarily concerned with the temporal welfare of its subjects. The earthly interests of the people are entrusted to the ruler, their spiritual interests to the priest. Although the two powers have separate aims, they mutually complete each other. They are like the two golden cherubim, shadowing the Ark of the Covenant with their wings.

2. The highest spiritual authority was given by God to the Pope, the highest secular authority to the monarch of the land; in most countries the people have a share in the secular government.

Both Pope and king receive their power from God. Our Lord said to St. Peter: "Feed My lambs, feed My sheep" (John xxi. 17). Thus the Apostle Peter was constituted Prince of the Apostles, and visible Head of the Church Militant by Christ Himself. The chief rank and spiritual supremacy conferred on St. Peter, is vested, by Christ's appointment, in the person of the Bishop of Rome for the time being. That the head or governor of the State also derives his power from God we learn from the words Our Lord addressed to Pilate: "Thou shouldest not have any power against Me, unless it were given thee from above" (John xix. 11). "By God kings reign and lawgivers decree just things" (Prov. viii. 15). "Hear, ye kings, for power is given you by the Lord" (Wisd. vi. 4). "There is no power but from God" (Rom. xiii. 1). Monarchs usually add the words "By the grace of God" to their title. In all European countries except Russia and Turkey the sovereign consults the will of the Parliament, or representatives of the people.

3. Our duties towards Pope and king are similar to our duties towards God, for they are both His representatives.

The vicegerents of God, both spiritual and temporal, are often called ministers of God (Wisd. vi. 5), or the Lord's anointed (1 Kings xxiv. 7); they are even spoken of as "gods" (Exod. xxii. 28), just as one who fills the place of the king is called the viceroy. The Pope terms himself the servant of the servants of God. We owe to almighty God: Worship and fidelity (First Commandment); reverence (Second Commandment); and service (Third Commandment). We owe to His vicegerents obedience and loyalty, respect and service.

Our duties towards the Supreme Pontiff are these: We are

bound to obey him in spiritual matters, to be loyal to him, to respect his authority, and by prayers and offerings assist him in the arduous duties of his office.

We are under the obligation to obey the Pope in all spiritual matters. All the pastors of the Church and the faithful of every rank and rite are subject to the Pope, and bound to yield him perfect obedience. What the head is to the other members of the human body, that the Pope is to the body of Christ; i.e., the Church (1 Cor. xii. 27). As he is the representative of Christ (2 Cor. v. 20), he declares to us the will of God; he can say: " We are ambassadors for Christ, God, as it were, exhorting by us." The words Christ addressed to the apostles: " He that heareth you, heareth Me " (Luke x. 16), unquestionably apply above all else to St. Peter and his successors. He, therefore, who disobeys the Pope, or turns a deaf ear to his admonitions, cannot please God. Leo XIII. has repeatedly urged upon the faithful the frequent recitation of the Rosary; what is our duty in this respect? We ought, furthermore, to be true and faithful to the Holy Father, for he is not only the Head of the visible Church, but the rock whereon it rests. Those who cast off their allegiance to the See of Rome, as the Greeks did (1053), fall away from God. To them (whom we call schismatics) the words God spoke to Samuel are applicable: " They have not rejected thee, but Me, that I should not reign over them " (1 Kings viii. 7). We must also reverence the Pope. We know that it is Christ's will that we should revere His ministers as Himself; now as the Holy Father is the chief of Christ's ministers, the greatest respect is due to him. On this account the title: " His Holiness " is given to him. It is moreover our duty to assist the Pope by our prayers and oblations; the early Christians prayed for St. Peter when he was in prison (Acts xii. 5), and in the present day his successors are not free from persecution. Let us therefore follow the example of the early Christians. The Pope has, besides, to provide for the many needs of the Church, for the propagation of the Gospel in heathen lands, for the maintenance of ecclesiastical institutions, etc. Thus he requires our pecuniary assistance, and requires it all the more since his temporary possessions have been wrested from him. The alms collected for the Holy Father are called Peter's pence. Catholics are too apt to underrate or overlook the importance of contributing to this object. The enemies of the Church are wont to apply the epithet *ultra montane* to Catholics who are firm adherents of the Holy See, to imply that they are wanting in patriotism, because they recognize as their spiritual sovereign one who is " beyond the mountains " (*ultra montes*); but as a matter of fact good Catholics are good patriots. Origen says: " The more a Christian fears God, the more loyal he is to the emperor." Our duties towards our pastors are the same as towards the Holy Father: we are bound to contribute towards their support. " The Lord ordained that they who preach the Gospel should live by the Gospel " (1 Cor. ix. 14); " The laborer is worthy of his reward " (1 Tim. v. 18).

Our duty towards the ruler of our country requires us to obey all just laws which are issued in his name, to be loyal to him, to hold him in respect, and to support him by our prayers, by the payment of taxes, and by military service if required of us.

We are not only bound to obey the laws of the State because of the penalty incurred by disobedience, but also for conscience' sake, because the commands of the secular authority are the commands of God (Rom. xiii. 2, 5). Remember how willingly Joseph and Mary conformed to the decree of Augustus, and journeyed to Bethlehem to be enrolled (Luke ii.). But if the temporal power commands something which God forbids, we must recall to mind the apostles' words: "We ought to obey God rather than men" (Acts v. 29). The three Hebrew youths in the fiery furnace and the seven Machabees obeyed this precept, likewise St. Maurice and the Theban legion. We are however seldom called upon to do this in the present day. It is our bounden duty to be loyal to our ruler, especially in time of war. Soldiers are required to take the military oath. It is never allowable to rebel against the sovereign authority in the land, for whoso resists the higher powers, resists the ordinance of God (Rom. xiii. 1). We are to be "subject not only to the good and gentle, but also to the froward" (1 Pet. ii. 18). Bad rulers are generally sent by God as a chastisement for the sins of the nation. If the monarch should be tyrannical, we must implore the help of God, and His help will be granted when the people forsake their evil doings. We are also to honor the ruler of our country. "Fear God. Honor the king" (1 Pet. ii. 17). A king is spoken of as "His Majesty," and a royal reception is prepared for him wherever he goes. We ought, moreover, to pray for our rulers. It is acceptable to God that prayers and supplications be made for all that are in a high station (1 Tim. ii.). Besides prayer for our rulers brings a blessing on ourselves, for by it we obtain the passing of decrees beneficial to their people. At High Mass the priest prays for the sovereign ruler. Christ sanctioned the payment of taxes, when He said: "Render to Cæsar the things that are Cæsar's" (Matt. xxii. 21). He paid for Himself and St. Peter the tax levied on every head for the service of the Temple; and in order to do so, He bade St. Peter go to the sea and cast a hook, and in the mouth of the first fish he caught he would find the piece of silver required for the tax (Matt. xvii. 26). It is only just that those who enjoy the peace and welfare which it is the object of the Government to secure, should contribute towards defraying the expenses thus incurred. Besides, the money obtained by taxation is laid out for the good of the nation on public works, the erection of schools and hospitals, the maintenance of the army, of government officials, etc. Thus the members of the body supply food to the digestive organs, whence nourishment is afforded to the whole. It is not right to defraud the State in the matter of taxation. Military service, as required in some lands, is for the maintenance of domestic peace and for the protection of the country from foreign foes. Those who in time of war offer their lives for their fellow-countrymen, receive a great reward from God. Our duty towards the representatives of the sovereign are similar to those towards himself. "Be subject to the king as excelling, or to governors as sent by him; for so is the will of God" (1 Pet. ii. 14).

In addition to all this, the citizens ought to assist their ruler in the government of the country, by choosing as their representatives men of experience and Christian principles.

Not only the representatives of the people, but the electors of those representatives, have a weighty responsibility in God's sight. The former are responsible for the laws they make, the latter for the men they choose to make the laws. In the exercise of his civil rights, it is incumbent on the citizen to obey the will of his Lord and God, for he will one day have to answer for the manner in which he exercised that right. In all human affairs the truths of Christianity must be our guiding light. Let no one therefore assert that religion has nothing to do with politics. Statesmen, public functionaries, senators, members of Congress, Cabinet officers, will all have to give an account of every word they have spoken, every vote they have given. And electors will be responsible for the men they have returned to Congress or the Senate; consequently they should elect men of experience, acquainted with the law, and above all, possessed of Christian principle; for those who are destitute of all religious beliefs cannot be expected to act conscientiously, or adhere to their promises. And since matters closely connected with the essentials of religion are often the subject of debate, it is the duty of Catholics to vote for such candidates as will act justly in dealing with ecclesiastical questions, and have the interests of the Church at heart.

3. If a Catholic, by giving his vote to a candidate who is hostile to the Church, or by abstaining from voting, makes himself in part responsible for the success of that candidate, he has much to answer for.

Catholic electors ought not to return as their representative one who is only a nominal, not a practical Catholic, who regards with indifference or contempt the teaching and ministers of the Church. Before going to the ballot they should ascertain the views of the candidate upon education, marriage, the observance of Sunday, etc.; better not to vote at all than vote for one who is hostile to religion. It is, however, a duty to vote if thereby one can avert evil and promote what is good. Let no man say: My vote is of no consequence; it might turn the scale, and if not, at any rate it lessens the defeat of the non-successful candidate. Those who are not entitled to vote ought to pray that the result of the election may be favorable to the cause of religion and of the country in general.

4. He who grossly offends against either the ecclesiastical or secular authorities has to expect the severe chastisement of God on earth, and punishment in the world to come.

Core and his companions, who rose up against the Jewish priesthood, were swallowed up by the earth, as an example to the people (Numb. xvi.). Remember the deplorable fate of Absalom, who rebelled against the king his father (2 Kings xviii.). Also that of Semei, who not only insulted King David, but disobeyed the mandate forbidding him to cross the brook Cedron (3 Kings ii. 46). High treason is now punished with a long term of imprisonment.

" They that resist the power resist the ordinance of God and purchase to themselves damnation " (Rom. xiii. 2).

3. THE DUTIES OF THOSE WHO ARE IN AUTHORITY.

1. The Christian ought not to strive after a position of authority which he is not competent to fill (Eccles. vii. 6).

In this respect every one may well take example by Moses. He did not aspire to the post of leader of the Hebrew people, but only assumed it when called by God to do so. In fact, at first he would not accept it, deeming himself too weak for its duties. And later on, weary of the office, he desired to be relieved of it. Pope Gregory the Great fled to the forests when he heard that he would probably be elected Pope. Many eminent saints, such as St. Ambrose and St. Augustine, accepted the episcopal dignity most reluctantly. Yet all these men were unquestionably well qualified to fill their respective offices. How great is the presumption of those who strive to obtain some high post for which they lack the necessary strength and talents, and to which they are not called by God! Those who aspire to dignities, to the duties of which they are unequal, are like men who take the helm without knowing anything of navigation; or like those who load their shoulders with burdens heavier than they can carry. Our Lord compares such persons to thieves, who force their way into a sheepfold (John x.). But it is not wrong for one who feels himself competent to fulfil the duties of a post, and knows that he may effect much good if he hold it, to endeavor to obtain it. A Catholic may aspire to the priesthood if he has a vocation, or to a place among the governing powers of the land if he possesses the necessary qualifications.

2. He who is called by God to fill some post of authority, must not on that account think much of himself, but rather consider the responsibility laid on him.

A man may be certain that he is called by God, if an appointment is given him without any effort on his own part to obtain it. When St. Gregory the Great was sought for, and his hiding-place in the forest discovered by the populace, he no longer hesitated to accept the tiara, for he saw it to be God's will that he should do so. St. Alphonsus did not refuse the See of St. Agatha, when Pope Clement XIII. strongly urged him to accept it. Dignities are apparently conferred by the hand of man, but in reality it is God Who bestows them (Matt. xxv. 15). As a gardener guides the water of the spring whithersoever he will, so God influences kings and princes to bestow their favors on those whom He has chosen to be their recipients. " The heart of the king is in the hand of the Lord; as the divisions of waters, whithersoever He will He shall turn it " (Prov. xxi. 1). He is foolish who thinks more of himself on account of the dignity conferred on him, for it makes him no better in God's sight; virtue alone gives a man true worth and distinction. " Earthly greatness," says St. Thomas Aquinas " is fleeting and short-lived; like smoke, it quickly comes and quickly vanishes; it passes away like a dream."

Virtue, on the contrary, brings everlasting glory. Many that are first here shall be last hereafter, and the last shall be first (Matt. xix. 30). Herod was a king, Mary and Joseph were ordinary people; but he was a bad man, whereas they were just and beloved of God. Mary and Joseph now fill glorious thrones in heaven; and where is Herod? Many who now in the gloom of this life appear estimable and great, will in the light of eternity, when the secrets of all hearts are disclosed, be seen to be evil and corrupt. "A most severe judgment will be for those who bear rule" (Wisd. vi. 6). The higher the post, the greater the responsibility. This truth should make the great ones of the earth humble, conscientious, thoughtful. God requires those who are in high places to hold their office as if they had it not; that is, they should regard it as only committed to their keeping for a brief period, and should be ready at any moment to give it up.

3. Those who rule others ought to promote as far as possible the welfare of their subjects, and treat them with impartiality and justice.

As those who are set in authority over others reflect in their person the power of God, they should take Him as their model; besides, they are His vicegerents. The plenipotentiary of the emperor is bound in word and deed to conform to the instructions given him by his imperial master; if he acts on his own judgment, he is reprimanded. Governors ought above all to study the welfare of their subjects; since this is the purpose of their appointment. The princes of the earth are God's ministers for the good of mankind (Rom. xiii. 4). The common weal, not the benefit of a single individual, or of a few, ought to be their object, and they should be ready generously to sacrifice their own interests for the good of their subjects. Christ, the Good Shepherd, laid down His life for His sheep (John x. 11). If a shepherd exposes himself to hardships and dangers for the sake of animals destined for slaughter, what ought not to be done for immortal souls, whom Christ redeemed with His blood, and for whom account must be given? Rulers ought moreover to be impartial, and treat all without distinction, whether rich or poor, with equal kindness, remembering "there is no respect of persons with God" (Rom. ii. 11; 2 Par. xix. 7). "God made the little and the great, and hath equal care of all" (Wisd. vi. 8). He frequently declares Himself to be the helper of the needy and oppressed (Ps. xlv. 2). "The Lord is nigh unto them that are of a contrite heart" (Ps. xxxiii. 19). The more destitute we are of human succor, the more God regards us with His mercy. Consequently rulers ought to befriend the poor and lowly (Is. i. 17). Unfortunately superiors are apt to think themselves justified in going to all lengths, so long as they do not overstep their powers. Some proud men imagine it to be below their dignity to treat their fellow-men as brethren; they think they would thereby forget what was due to them. This is by no means the case. Those who are in authority must beware of acting unjustly, or of allowing themselves to be corrupted by bribes (Exod. xxiii. 8). They must not favor the rich and powerful, and be induced to give unjust judgment, as was the unhappy Pilate. Fearful lest the Jews should accuse him to the emperor, he sentenced Our Lord to death, though he knew Him to be innocent. What he dreaded happened; he was

accused and condemned and banished to France. The curse of God
rests upon unjust judges (Deut. xxvii. 19). Blessed Thomas More
used to say that if his father, whom he dearly loved, came to him with
a grievance, and on the other side was the devil whom he hated more
than words could say, provided the latter was in the right, he should
have justice at his hands. No man should ever be condemned unheard. If any one went to Alexander the Great with a charge against
another, he used to close one ear, saying: "I give one ear to the
accuser, the other to the accused." Even God, Who is omniscient, did
not condemn Adam until He had heard his defence and proved to him
his guilt.

4. Those who are in high places ought to set a good example.

The reason why superiors are bound to set a good example is twofold. On the one hand they occupy a conspicuous position, all eyes
are on them; like a city seated on a mountain, they cannot be hid
(Matt. v. 14). Others imitate them; as is the judge, so also are his
ministers (Ecclus. x. 2). Woe betide them if they lead an evil life!
On the other hand, superiors can effect much more by example than
by precept. Deeds are more eloquent than words. Rulers ought to
pray for their subjects; like the husbandman in the Gospel, they
should entreat the Lord of the vineyard to spare the barren fig-tree
and leave it a year, in the hope that with careful cultivation it
may bear fruit. Pastors are specially bound to pray for their flock,
and to offer the holy sacrifice on Sundays and holydays for the living
and the dead.

THE FIFTH COMMANDMENT OF GOD.

**In the Fifth Commandment almighty God forbids us to destroy
our own life, or that of our neighbor, or to treat the lower animals
with cruelty.**

1. OUR DUTY IN RESPECT TO OUR OWN LIFE.

Many of the ceremonies in the administration of the sacraments,
ceremonies full of meaning, are performed upon the body. By these
the Church intends to inspire us with great respect for our bodies,
and to teach us their high worth and dignity.

**1. Our body was created by God as an abode for our immortal
soul.**

The condition of the soul is often dependent upon the condition of that abode.

When God made the human body out of lifeless earth, it was an
uninhabited tenement; but it was destined to be inhabited, therefore
God created the soul to be its occupant. St. Peter speaks of his body
as a tabernacle which he would shortly have to quit (2 Pet. i. 14). It
fares with the soul in the body as with the inmate of a house. If
the house be unhealthy, the dweller in it falls sick. Our body is like
the shell of an egg; if the shell be injured, the young bird within is
hurt; so if our mortal frame sustains injury, the spirit, the noble

inmate of that dwelling, suffers with it. The Romans had a proverb: A healthy mind in a healthy body. Our body is not our own, it belongs to God (1 Cor. vi. 13). It belongs to God, not only because He created it, but because Christ purchased it with a great price (1 Cor. vi. 20). We are bound to take care of what is the property of another. The tenant of a hired house has no right to damage or destroy that house, so we are not at liberty to injure or destroy our body, the abode of the soul, created by God and belonging to Him. We must not do with our body what we will, but what God wills.

Our body is an implement of the soul, intrusted by God to our keeping, to be made instrumental in amassing merits for eternity.

Like all other instruments, our bodies can be misused. Hence St. Paul warns Christian people not to yield their members as instruments of iniquity unto sin (Rom. vi. 13). As God will require us to give account of the manner in which we have employed the talents given us (Matt. xxv. 19), so we shall have to answer for the employment of the body, which the soul informs and makes instrumental in the performance of the duties of our calling. Our Lord told St. Gertrude that after the resurrection, on the members of the body employed in His service surpassing dignity and excellence would be conferred.

2. Since the life and health of the body are of great importance for the life of the soul and for our eternal salvation, we are bound to take precautions for the preservation of our health and of our life.

By means of cleanliness, temperance, regularity, industry, and the use of remedies in case of sickness.

Health is worth more to us than vast riches (Ecclus. xxx. 16). For the longer we keep our health and our life, the more treasures we can lay up for eternity, where neither the rust nor moth doth consume, where thieves do not break through, nor steal (Matt. vi. 20). If we thoughtlessly do anything to shorten our life, we defraud ourselves of a part of our seed-time. The eagle takes the utmost care of its egg, not for the sake of the shell, but of the young eagle inclosed in the egg; so we should take care of our body because of the soul that dwells within it. Cleanliness is to be observed in our person, our apparel, the rooms we inhabit; temperance in eating and drinking. Abstemiousness promotes health and prolongs life. (See what has been said on the advantages of fasting.) Many men of weak physique naturally, have so increased their strength by abstemiousness that they have been capable of immense activity. St. Paul in his epistles often mentions his bodily weakness. Regularity is to be observed in regard to meals, the time of going to rest and rising in the morning; in one's work and in the arrangement of one's time. Above all, let us never be unemployed. By work we may not only earn our daily bread, but do much towards keeping ourselves in health. Work circulates the blood, and gives an appetite for food. Stagnant water becomes foul, and the blood of the idler is apt to get into a bad state. Yet we must not overtax our strength with work; moderate labor invigorates, excessive toil ruins the powers of our body. Finally, it is our duty to have recourse to remedies in case of sickness. It is sinful, if any one is dangerously ill, not to call in medical aid, and employ remedies. "Honor the physician for the need thou hast of him, for the Most High hath created him" (Ecclus. xxxviii. 1). "The Most High hath created medicines out of the earth, and a wise man will not abhor them" (v. 4). However, if the cure is too costly, or if it involves acute suffering, it may be forborne.

Our solicitude concerning the preservation of our health and of our life must not, however, be so great as to make us forgetful of our eternal salvation.

The good things of time, such as life and bodily well-being, are not intrinsically valuable and to be desired, but only in so far as they are conducive to our eternal welfare. "The Spirit of God does not remain in a man forever, because he is flesh" (Gen. vi. 3), i.e., fleshly-minded. "The wisdom of the flesh is death; it is an enemy to God" (Rom. viii. 6). The more the body is studied and pampered, the more the soul is neglected and ruined (St. Augustine). Hence Our Lord admonishes us: "Be not solicitous for meat and raiment. For your heavenly Father knoweth that you have need of all these things; He feeds the birds of the air, and clothes the lilies of the field, though they labor not: are not you of more value than they?" (Matt. vi. 25, 32).

3. Furthermore we are under a strict obligation to do nothing that tends to destroy health or life.

Consequently it is a sin to rashly hazard one's life, wantonly to injure one's health, or to take one's own life.

1. Those persons generally risk their life without a thought who perform hazardous feats, or who neglect due precautions.

Acrobats, equestrian performers, lion-tamers, and the like commit sin unless they take all necessary precautions to avoid fatal accidents; the professions they follow are objectionable on moral grounds, and even unlawful. Performers of this character are too often dissolute in their manners, and their hazardous feats frequently cost them their life. The same may be said of those who are foolhardy, and wilfully risk their lives in athletic sports, or public games, such as the bull-fights which are the national amusement in Spain. Want of ordinary prudence is also highly reprehensible, as for instance, to cross the line when a train is approaching, by which many have lost their lives, or to stand under a tree, or otherwise expose one's self during a thunderstorm. Again, in the case of infectious disease great precaution is necessary; only the priest, the doctor, and the nurse, should be allowed access to the sick-room. There are other ways whereby one may place one's life in jeopardy: by drinking cold water or taking a cold bath when violently heated; playing with loaded fire-arms; jumping into or out of a train while it is in motion; touching the electric wires with the bare hand, or hanging on behind a carriage as children are wont to do, with the chance of getting their limbs crushed by the wheels. Therefore be prudent and never risk your life rashly.

2. Some persons are in the habit of injuring their health by indulging to an excess in amusements, by vanity in dress, and partaking too freely of unwholesome food.

By excess in amusement is meant frequent playing and dancing all night, smoking and drinking immoderately, etc. " By surfeiting many have perished " (Ecclus. xxxvii. 34). By vanity in dress is meant tight lacing, which by undue pressure upon the vital organs, deranges their action, and has even caused sudden death. The fashion of squeezing the feet into pointed shoes is also injurious. Spirits, if taken in large quantities, or even strong decoctions of tea or coffee, are decidedly prejudicial to the digestion and the nerves.

3. Suicides are generally men who are devoid of religious beliefs, who have got into trouble or committed some great sin, and who despair of God's mercy and assistance; they are sometimes not accountable for their actions, and consequently not to be blamed for them.

King Saul lost all hope when he was grievously wounded and surrounded by his enemies; he then cast himself on his sword (1 Kings xxxi.). The keeper of the prison at Philippi, greatly alarmed at seeing the doors of the prison open, wherein St. Paul was confined, was about to kill himself (Acts xvi. 27). Judas, in despair at the enormity of his crime, went and hanged himself (Matt. xxvii. 5). How often we read of people destroying themselves because they have lost their all at the gambling-table, or because they have ruined their character by embezzling money, or because they cannot obtain the object of their illicit passion. But often madness, or overtaxed nerves, cause men to take their own lives without knowing what they do. Let us beware, therefore, how we hastily judge and condemn them. The prevalence of suicide is however principally and generally to be ascribed to the lack of religion, of a firm belief in a future life, of confidence in God's willingness to aid the unfortunate and to pardon the repentant sinner. Experience teaches that as religion decreases in a land, the number of suicides increases. The ancients considered self-destruction to be dishonorable and blameworthy; they cut off the right hand of the self-murderer, and buried it apart from the body. The Church denies Christian burial to one who has died by his own hand, unless insanity had rendered him irresponsible. The refusal of the burial rites is not intended as a condemnation of the individual, but to express horror of the crime, and to act as a deterrent to others. A man's life is not his own, it belongs to God, Who takes it away at His will (Deut. xxxii. 39). Thus self-destruction is a presumptuous encroachment upon the divine rights, and shows contempt for God, by flinging back at Him His greatest gift to man, which is life. The suicide also defrauds society, whereof he is a member; he wrongs his family, by bringing sorrow and shame upon it; he cruelly injures himself and gives scandal to others. It is even worse to take one's own life than that of another, because in the former case one escapes the punishment of the law. Far from being an heroic deed, it is a most cowardly act; real heroism is shown by bearing bravely the miseries of life. Besides, instead of obtaining relief from suffering, the suicide only falls into what is far worse. The godless press of the day will excuse the self-murderer, saying: He expiated his crime with his life. Instead of expiating a crime, he adds another to it.

4. On the other hand it is not merely right, but even meritorious, to sacrifice one's bodily health or life in order to gain everlasting life, or to rescue one's fellow-man from physical or spiritual death.

All the holy martyrs preferred to sacrifice their life rather than commit sin. By so doing they merited life eternal, for Our Lord says: " He that shall lose his life for My sake shall find it " (Matt. x. 39). Witness Eleazar, the Machabees, St. Lawrence. Missionaries in heathen lands are in constant danger of death, and many of them ruin their health by the hardship and exertions they undergo. St. Francis Xavier, the apostle of the Indies, was, at the close of the day, so exhausted with preaching and administering Baptism, that he could scarcely speak or move his arm. Yet this is not wrong, but most praiseworthy. The same may be said of priests, doctors, and nurses who attend those who have an infectious disease. St. Aloysius and St. Charles Borromeo died of the plague, caught while nursing the sick in the hospital. It is also permissible to risk one's life to rescue any one who has, for instance, fallen into the fire or the water, or to expose one's self in battle for the defence of one's country. And a human soul is of such great value, that all earthly goods, nay life itself, should be sacrificed to save it. Christ gave us an example by dying upon the cross for the salvation of mankind. Of course in performing an heroic act of this nature, we ought not to seek death— that would be sinful—but only to think of the deed itself, of which death may be an accidental accompaniment.

2. *OUR DUTY IN REGARD TO THE LIFE OF OUR NEIGHBOR.*

A strict obligation is laid upon us to avoid everything that may destroy the health or life of our neighbor.

1. Accordingly it is sinful to wish ill to one's neighbor, to injure his health, to challenge him or accept a duel, or to put him to death unjustly and willingly.

1. He who hates his neighbor, wishes him dead; hence hatred often leads to murder.

Hatred suggests revenge. Witness Esau, who sought to kill his brother Jacob (Gen. xxvii. 41); King Saul, who repeatedly endeavored to slay David (1 Kings xxiv.); Joseph's brethren, who would actually have put Joseph to death, had not Ruben interfered (Gen. xxxvii.). There is little distinction to be made between hatred and murder; in God's sight the will is the same as the deed. Hence St. John says: " Whosoever hateth his brother is a murderer " (1 John iii. 15). Our Lord declares that he who is angry with his brother is in danger of the judgment (Matt. v. 22). Real hatred is a mortal sin, whether the evil one wishes to one's neighbor be great or small. However it is no proof of hatred to detest the evil qualities one sees in one's neighbor, or to abhor his conduct, for this is not incompatible with affection for him personally.

2. Men often injure their neighbor's health by quarrels and blows, by the adulteration of articles of food, by dangerous practical jokes, and culpable negligence.

By quarrelling one excites one's neighbor, and deprives him of interior peace and content, thus destroying his well-being. Contention and quarrels cause shedding of blood (Ecclus. xxviii. 13). Blows often cause severe pain or bodily injury. For assault one may be arrested and imprisoned. The practice of adulterating articles of food is only too common nowadays; flour, milk, butter, wine, beer, etc., are mingled with foreign substances, often of a deleterious nature, or a manufactured imitation is sold for the genuine article. As these adulterated goods contain little nourishment, and much that is prejudicial to health, tradesmen who thus defraud the public deserve condign punishment. In the Middle Ages they were burned, together with their falsified wares. Practical jokes, such as tripping any one up, may cause fatal injuries. Culpable carelessness often occasions serious accidents; e.g., furious driving, heedlessness in the handling of fire-arms, neglecting to warn passers-by if anything is likely to fall, etc.

3. Duelling is nothing short of murder. The Church punishes it by excommunicating the combatants, and denying Christian burial to those who are killed (Council of Trent, 25, 19).

By the mere fact of challenging to single combat, or accepting a challenge, a man becomes excommunicated; the same holds good of those who take the part of seconds, or who sanction the duel by their presence. Let no one say, he has given his opponent permission to kill him; he cannot give another a right which he does not himself possess. A Catholic is bound to refuse to fight a duel, even if he thereby incurs the imputation of cowardice, or if he thereby lose the chance of promotion. The duellist is guilty of twofold murder; he intends to kill his antagonist, and at the same time he risks his own life. While he imagines he is repairing an insult to his honor, he loses the respect of all sensible persons, for he shows himself to be enslaved by pride, resentment, and cruelty. Skill in the use of weapons will not avenge an insult; the duellist should seek satisfaction in the law-courts. But let him who would acquire great merit in God's sight, follow the teaching and example of Our Redeemer, and not seek to avenge himself, but bear injustice patiently, for this is the greatest heroism that can be imagined. It is noteworthy that many of the ablest generals and monarchs were strongly opposed to duelling, and prohibited it under severe penalties. It is related of Gustavus Adolphus, that he once yielded to the request of two officers of high rank, and permitted a duel; but at the appointed hour he appeared on the scene with a military escort, and said: "Now fight if you will, but woe betide you if one falls, for the other shall instantly be beheaded." A reconciliation took place at once between the two officers. Frederick II. of Prussia used to expel duellists from the army, saying: "I want brave soldiers, not executioners."

4. Whoso kills his neighbor unjustly and intentionally, commits a heinous sin. Such a one is called a murderer.

Cain was a murderer; he slew his brother Abel. God Himself said that the voice of Abel's blood cried to Him from the earth for vengeance (Gen. iv. 10). The murderer robs his victim of the highest earthly good, his life; he deprives him of the opportunity of gaining merits for eternity, and of preparing himself for death. But a man who kills unintentionally is not a murderer (Deut. xix. 4), yet he is seldom free from sin, as a fatal blow is generally the result of culpable inadvertence. The executioner appointed to carry out the sentence of the judge is not a murderer, since he does not act unjustly.

2. He commits a still greater sin who destroys the spiritual life of his neighbor, either by tempting him to evil or by giving scandal.

"If thou persuade thy neighbor to sin," St. Augustine says, "thou art his murderer." And he who gives scandal is guilty of murder. Nay, even of a greater sin than murder, because the life of the soul is of far more value than the life of the body. If a thousand men were put to death, less harm would be done than if one soul were condemned to everlasting perdition. If the blood of Abel cried to heaven for vengeance on his brother, how much more will the blood of the lost soul cry for vengeance on its murderer. How cursed are they who are the cause of so great a calamity to another! Temptation and scandal are all the more fatal because the evil is handed on from one to another. He who has been led into sin, leads another into it in his turn, as the bird that the fowler has entrapped serves as a decoy to bring others into the snare. Like an avalanche, small in the beginning, but increasing in its course, carrying vast masses of snow with it into the abyss, the tempter drags countless souls with him to perdition. Others corrupt their fellow-men by the scandal they give, as leaven pervades the whole of the flour in which it is placed.

Temptation is the endeavor, by subtle means, to incite a man to sin.

The tempter is like the devil, who by his wiles, led our first parents in paradise to disobey God. He goes to work craftily, like the fisherman who catches fish with a baited hook, or the fowler, who lays traps and spreads bird-lime to ensnare birds. In the case of almost all the holy martyrs before their execution, attempts were made to induce them, either by blandishments and promises, or by threats and torture, to abjure their faith and transgress the commandment of God. What trouble the Proconsul took with the aged Bishop Polycarp; what efforts the King of Bohemia made to force St. John Nepomucene to violate the seal of confession! He offered him a bishopric, he put him to torture, and finally cast him into the Moldau. Those who dissuade others from what is good also deserve the name of tempter. Temptation is the devil's own work. He does not appear in person to seduce mankind, for then every one would recoil from him; he leaves men to do his business for him, and thus attains his end more certainly.

Scandal is given when by some sinful word, deed, or omission, we shock our neighbor, and perhaps cause him to sin.

For instance, a man gives scandal if he is seen in public in a state of inebriation, if he talks indecent talk, makes use of oaths in the presence of children, eats meat openly on Friday, does servile work on Sunday, behaves indecorously in church, publishes ungodly books, decries religion and the ministers of religion in the papers and periodicals, etc. What he does instigates another to do the same; this is true most of all in regard to children, who are sure to imitate anything wrong which they see done by their parents or elders. He who gives scandal is like a man who digs a pit, into which another is likely to fall and break his neck. Scandal is an offence against the love of one's neighbor. That it is a mortal sin we gather from Our Lord's words concerning him who scandalizes others: "It were better for him that a mill-stone should be hanged about his neck and that he should be drowned in the depth of the sea" (Matt. xviii. 6). Again, Our Lord says that at the end of the world His angels shall gather out of His kingdom all who have given scandal, and cast them into the furnace of fire: there shall be weeping and gnashing of teeth (Matt. xiii. 41). But if the scandal given is slight, or unintentional, it is not a great sin, or is no sin at all.

We ought, in as far as possible, to avoid giving scandal, and for this end we must observe the following rules:

1. We ought to abstain from actions which are not only lawful, but good in themselves, which are of counsel but not of precept, if they may possibly give scandal.

If any one is dispensed from the Friday abstinence on account of bad health, he should refrain from eating meat before others, if he knows that they will take scandal at it. And if this is impossible, he should explain to those who are at table with him why he eats it; if they take scandal then, he is not to blame. St. Paul declares: "If meat scandalize my brother, I will never eat flesh" (1 Cor. viii. 13). And the aged Eleazar preferred death to even appearing to eat swine's flesh, lest young persons might be scandalized, and be deceived into thinking he was gone over to the life of the heathen (2 Mach. vi. 24).

2. We must, however, in no case omit any act which is commanded by God, even if others will take scandal at it; yet we should in as far as possible prevent the scandal by some words of explanation or instruction.

By doing what the law of God enjoins on us, we do not give

scandal, but on the contrary, a good example. The fault lies with the one who takes scandal at a good action; no one in fact will do so unless he be corrupted with vice. The obligations imposed by the laws of the Church, such as hearing Mass on Sundays, approaching the sacraments at Easter, may be set aside occasionally, if others will take offence by their observance; yet one should endeavor to obviate this, by explaining the duty to be fulfilled. Purely human laws do not bind as a rule, if great harm may be done by keeping them; for Christ says: "My yoke is sweet and My burden is light" (Matt. xi. 30). Yet it is best to explain matters, and then act boldly; this often prevents difficulties being raised. It is, however, impossible always to avoid scandal, for evil-minded persons take offence at what is well meant. Our Lord bade His apostles not to heed such people: "Let them alone; they are blind and leaders of the blind" (Matt. xv. 14).

3. It is, however, lawful to wound or even to kill our fellow-man, if he threatens to take our life by violence, or anything that is absolutely indispensable to our life, and we have no other means of defence. This is called the right of self-defence.

Self-defence is not wrong, because our object is not to take another man's life, but simply to preserve our own; and the moral worth of an action is determined by that which is, not by that which is not its object. We are permitted to defend, but by no means to avenge ourselves; hence if we can save ourselves by flight, we ought to do so. If it is enough to wound our adversary we must stop short there. Above all, a woman is justified in defending herself against any one who attempts to violate her chastity. We are also permitted to kill any one in order to save the life of a third party; this Moses did when he slew the Egyptian who was striking one of the He-brews (Exod. ii. 12). It is only lawful to put to death one who un-justly seizes our property, if he lays hands on what is absolutely nec-essary to our existence, for then it is our life that we are defending. It is not right to shoot a robber who carries off something of no great value; nor can we plead the right of self-defence if it is only our honor that is wrongfully attacked.

The officers of justice are warranted in punishing evil-doers with death; and soldiers act lawfully in wounding and killing the enemy in time of warfare.

The officers of justice, in as far as they stand in the place of God, have the right to sentence evil-doers to capital punishment. St. Paul says the higher powers bear not the sword in vain, but as avengers to execute wrath upon him that doeth evil (Rom. xiii. 4). The authority of the magistrate is God's authority; when he condemns a criminal, it is not he who condemns him, but God, just as the sword is not answerable for the blow it strikes, but the hand is that wields the sword. Yet the judge must not act arbitrarily; he must only sentence the criminal to death when the welfare of society demands it. Human society is a body of which each individual is a member; and as a diseased limb has to be amputated in order to save the body, so criminals must be executed to save society. As a matter of course the culprit's guilt must be proved; better let the guilty go free than condemn the innocent. It is an error to suppose that the Church advocates capital punishment on the principle of retaliation; an eye for an eye, a tooth for a tooth. This is a principle of Judaism, not of Christianity. The Church does not like to see blood shed, she desires that every sinner should have time to amend. She permits, but does not approve capital punishment. The military profession is not unlawful; we are not told in the Gospels that soldiers were exhorted to leave the army, but only that they were admonished to be content with their pay, and to do violence to no man. God, by the lips of Melchisedech, blessed Abraham after he had made war upon the kings who had robbed Lot (Gen. xiv.). The soldier must not, however, allow himself to treat cruelly those who are disabled in battle. The Church forbids her ministers to use deadly weapons, as this is incompatible with their sacred calling.

4. He who has wrongfully injured his neighbor, either physically or spiritually, is bound to repair the harm done to the utmost of his power.

If any one has been the means of inflicting bodily harm upon his neighbor, he must pay the doctor and all the expenses of his illness, make good the loss of his earnings, etc. If he has killed him he must provide for his family. If he has given scandal to his neighbor, or led him into sin, he must strive to counteract the evil consequences by a good example, prayer, instruction, etc. Unless he does this he will not obtain pardon from God, and the priest's absolution will be invalid.

What are the Reasons which ought to Deter us from Taking our own Life or that of our Neighbor?

1. He who needlessly imperils or seeks to put an end to his own life, is often punished by God with acute bodily suffering here and sometimes by eternal damnation hereafter.

We constantly read of fatalities and sad accidents resulting from foolhardiness in risking one's life. The indulgence of the passions also often brings on some painful malady. On the other hand some saints permanently injured themselves by excessive and unwise austerities and regretted it afterwards.

2. He who takes the life of another is tortured by terrible pangs of conscience, often dies a violent death, and is everlastingly damned.

Cain was a fugitive on the earth after the murder of his brother Abel (Gen. iv. 16). Murderers like him find no rest. As a rule, they die a violent death; either they are sentenced to death by the law, or they destroy themselves, or they fall by the hand of another. Whosoever shall shed man's blood, by man shall his blood be shed (Gen. ix. 6). All that take the sword shall perish by the sword (Matt. xxvi. 52). Divine justice frequently punishes the sinner in the way that he has sinned. The Hebrews in Egypt were commanded to throw their infants into the Nile; the king and all his army were swallowed up in the Red Sea. Retribution speedily overtook those who had condemned Our Lord to death: Judas and Pilate put an end to themselves, and in the year 70, no less than a million of the Jewish people were slain. The persecutors of the Christians in many cases died a violent death: Nero by his own hand, Julian the Apostate on the battle-field. Murderers shall not obtain the kingdom of God (Gal. v. 21); they shall have their portion in the pool burning with fire and brimstone (Apoc. xxi. 8). A similar fate has frequently been known to overtake heresiarchs, and those who by word or writings have undermined the faith of others, and thus incurred the guilt of spiritual murder.

3. He who hates his neighbor loses his peace of mind, and becomes displeasing to God; his prayers are not heard, and his lot is eternal perdition.

One who cherishes feelings of animosity and meditates vengeance is a stranger to peace; he is continually in a ferment; the thoughts of his heart are a perpetual scourge to him. That man can have no concord with Christ, who lives in discord with Christians. If peacemakers are called the children of God, those who stir up strife and dissension are children of Satan. As long as the thorn rankles in the wound, no remedies will heal it, nor will prayer avail the Christian while deadly hatred holds a place in his heart. Our Lord says: "If thou offer thy gift at the altar, and there thou remember that thy brother hath anything against thee, leave there thy offering before the altar and go first to be reconciled to thy brother, and then coming thou shalt offer thy gift" (Matt. v. 23, 24). Feelings of hatred ought to be suppressed at once. Let not the sun go down upon your anger (Eph. iv. 26). A dislocated limb can easily be got back into its place, if this be done promptly, but if some time be allowed to elapse, it becomes a difficult matter to set it right. So it is with hatred; if a reconciliation takes place immediately, the former friendly feelings are restored without trouble; but if it is delayed, anger gets the mastery of us, and we think it beneath us to seek a reconciliation. "If," says St. Augustine, "thy dwelling were infested with snakes, thou wouldst hasten to rid thyself of them; now hatred and enmity are venomous serpents; wilt thou not banish them from thy heart, which is the temple of the Holy Ghost?"

3. OUR CONDUCT IN REGARD TO THE LOWER ANIMALS.

The lower animals are created by God for the service of man.

The benefits we derive from the animals are these: They supply us with what is essential to life, e.g., food, clothing, etc.; they help us in our work, they cheer us by their amusing ways, their song, their beauty, etc. Some instruct us by their example; bees, for instance, incite us to industry, storks to filial affection, sheep to the practice of patience, etc. Moreover they all proclaim the omnipotence, the wisdom, the bounty of their Creator.

In our relations to animals it is our duty to care for their well-being, to refrain from tormenting them, not to kill any useful animal without a special reason, and finally not to treat them with exaggerated tenderness.

We ought to take care for the well-being of animals. "The just regardeth the lives of his beasts, but the bowels of the wicked are cruel" (Prov. xii. 10). Those who keep animals are bound to provide them with necessary food, to keep them clean, and in good condition. Our Lord says: "Not a sparrow shall fall on to the ground without your Father" (Matt. x. 29). This should teach us to care for the welfare of animals. Some treat brute beasts as if they had no feeling, overtaxing their powers, beating them unmercifully, not giving them enough to eat, or depriving them of the one day of rest out of the week which the law of God ordains for them (Exod. xx. 8-11). Those who have to kill animals for the table, and medical men who make experiments with them, ought to be careful to cause them no needless suffering. It is not right, either in the interests of science or for the sake of amusement, to give pain that can be avoided. Wanton cruelty is to be condemned; so is the destruction of harmless or useful animals. Noxious insects and dangerous animals must of course be killed, but others that are not hurtful, but rather useful, should be spared. Finally, animals are not to be pampered and petted over much. There are people who make an idol of some pet animal, preferring it to their fellow-man, and devoting every thought to it. Such persons resemble the ancient Egyptians, who worshipped cats, calves, bulls, etc.

Men who are either cruel to animals or ridiculously fond of them, often are very hard-hearted towards their fellow-men.

Children who take pleasure in teasing animals torment men when they are grown up. All who were tyrants in after years, were cruel to animals in their youth. Criminals have sometimes confessed upon the scaffold that their course of crime began with torturing animals as children. On the other hand we often find people who pamper and show great affection for animals, utterly hard-hearted in regard to their neighbors.

Both extremes, cruelty to animals and foolish fondness for them, are at variance with the order that God has established in the universe.

To torture animals wantonly is an abuse of the sovereignty given to man by the Creator over the brute creation. Man thus becomes a tyrant, and sometimes it pleases God to make him suffer in the same way wherein he made beasts suffer. For instance, a peasant who used to strike his horses on a tender part of the foot, causing them intense pain, was later on crippled by gout in the feet, being confined to his bed for years. He then acknowledged and deplored his fault. The Areopagus of Athens once condemned a child to death who was guilty of wanton cruelty to animals, for they judged that no good could be expected of one who, at a tender age, displayed such evil qualities. Exaggerated fondness and solicitude for animals is also a violation of the appointed order of nature.

THE SIXTH COMMANDMENT OF GOD.

1. In the Sixth Commandment almighty God prohibits everything that might stain our own purity or that of our neighbor.

One cannot enlarge upon sins against the Sixth Commandment, for the mere mention of what is impure takes the bloom off our innocence. Hence St. Paul exhorts the Ephesians: "All uncleanness, let it not so much as be named among you, as becometh saints" (Eph. v. 3). Nevertheless Holy Scripture warns the faithful repeatedly and emphatically against these sins, so the Church cannot pass them by in silence. For this vice perhaps causes the destruction of more souls than any other; in fact among the lost souls in hell, few will be found entirely free from it.

God more especially forbids:
1. Impure thoughts and desires.

Evil thoughts are to be resisted both on account of their sinfulness in themselves, and because they lead to immodest actions. They are like a spark which occasions a great conflagration, unless it be immediately extinguished. St. Jerome compares unchastity to a snake, whose head must be instantly crushed, before it can eject its deadly poison. Evil thoughts must accordingly be banished at once; this is done most readily by diverting the mind, or having recourse to prayer. (See what was said about temptation.) As long as evil thoughts are displeasing to us, they are not sinful; we are only to blame if we take pleasure in them. "Evil thoughts are an abomination to the Lord" (Prov. xv. 26). One ought to flee from unchaste thoughts as one would flee from an assassin, for they cause the death of the soul. Impure thoughts, if entertained, give rise to impure desires, i.e., the wish or longing for the sin suggested. As the tree springs from the root, so evil actions spring from lust. Lust is the consent of the will, and this is as really sinful, as Our Lord says, as is the deed itself (Matt. v. 28).

2. Impure words.

A man whose conversation is unclean has a thoroughly polluted conscience. Unchaste words are a sure sign of unchaste manners. And those who take pleasure in listening to improper conversation, are in great danger of falling into sins of unchastity. St. Louis, on his death-bed, exhorted his son so to regulate his conversation, that if all the world heard what he said, he would not have cause to blush for it. "The tongue is indeed a little member, and boasteth great things" (Jas. iii. 5). "Many have fallen by the edge of the sword, but not so many as have perished by their own tongue" (Ecclus. xxviii. 22.)

3. Impure actions.

These acts are differently designated, according as they are committed by the unmarried (Deut. xxii. 21), the married (Lev. xx. 10), persons related to one another (1 Cor. v. 1), or as they are sins against nature (Rom. i. 26).

4. Immodest looks.

Bold looks are forbidden, because they lead to sin, just as a parent forbids his child to play with edged tools. The sin on which the eye looks with pleasure soon takes possession of the heart. "Many have perished by the beauty of a woman, and hereby lust is enkindled as a fire" (Ecclus. ix. 9). He who observes no custody of the eyes, is like a driver who pays no heed to his horses; he will be carried away and dragged to destruction. Or like a fortress of which the gates are not guarded; the enemy soon effects an entrance through them. David would not have had so much to bewail, if he had kept watch over his eyes. "Look not round about thee in the ways of a city" (Ecclus. ix. 7).

5. Looking at immodest pictures, going to improper plays, and reading books of an immoral tendency.

Immodest pictures and plays corrupt more surely than impure conversation, because what one sees makes a deeper impression than what one hears. The indiscriminate reading of novels is to be avoided; there are many (and these are the most dangerous of all), which under a false semblance of propriety, kindle the passions, and thus do more harm than works of an openly immoral character.

6. Immodesty in dress and excessive finery.

Those who dress immodestly are the devil's instruments for the ruin of souls. Vanity and love of dress are powerful factors in Satan's service; for women who deck their person to attract men dare not presume to say that they are chaste and pure of heart; their very appearance gives them the lie. The longing for admiration does not come from a simple heart; it is a snare to entrap others into vice. It is a bad sign for a woman to be overdressed; those who make their toilet of paramount importance hold virtue cheap. "Let women adorn themselves with modesty and sobriety, not with plaited hair, or gold or pearls or costly attire" (1 Tim. ii. 9).

2. Sins against the Sixth Commandment of God are for the most part very grievous in God's sight and accordingly are severely punished by Him.

Remember the Deluge and the fate of Sodom and Gomorrha. The chastisements God inflicts for the sin of unchastity have already been spoken of under the subject of the deadly sins. From the place given to the Sixth Commandment in the Decalogue it may be inferred that transgressions of this precept are on a par with murder and theft. Unhappily many of the plays performed in the theatre in the present day represent sins against the Sixth Commandment in an attractive light.

THE SEVENTH COMMANDMENT OF GOD.

1. In the Seventh Commandment almighty God forbids us to wrong our neighbor in his goods and property.

By property is meant all that a man needs for his subsistence and all that he possesses as his own: e.g., his money, clothes, provisions, house, land, etc.

1. *THE RIGHT OF POSSESSION.*

1. Earthly goods are necessary to man's subsistence, such as food, clothes, a dwelling-place, money, etc.

1. Consequently every man is justified in striving to gain earthly goods after a just manner, and in possessing them as his personal property.

Since it is the natural right of every man to preserve his own life, he is justified in gaining for himself and keeping as his own, those external goods which are indispensable to his existence. If every moment were occupied in providing for his own maintenance, he would be in the direst destitution, if sickness or misfortune befell him. The natural law prompts him to provide for such contingencies. Besides, were every moment engrossed with the business of self-maintenance, there would be no time to attend to his eternal interests. Furthermore, a man is bound to provide for those who are dependent upon him, and this he could not do if he himself lived from hand to mouth. God commanded our first parents in paradise to "fill the earth and subdue it" (Gen. i. 28). Cain and Abel had separate possessions; each brought of his own to offer sacrifice. All trustworthy information respecting the earliest ages of humanity bears evidence to the possession of personal property. It was necessary that each should have his own, otherwise mankind could not have been at peace. There would have been continual strife and contention. Without the right of possession, the incentive to labor would be wanting. The holding of property is therefore an ordinance of God, just as much as marriage and legal authority. But it cannot be said that the distribution of wealth, as it is under existing circumstances, is in accordance with the will of God. It could not be His will that a small minority should enjoy a superfluity, while an overwhelming majority of His children should live in poverty and destitution. This great inequality is the result of sin.

2. Personal property is justly obtained when it is either acquired by labor or by gift.

Nature does not give man the right to certain goods; the right to possess them must be acquired. It is acquired in the first place by labor. God has ordained that the earth should not yield what is requisite for the maintenance of human life without cultivation. It is a violation of all justice to deprive the cultivator of the soil of what he has won by the sweat of his brow (Lev. xiii.). If the earth is the Lord's and all they that dwell therein, because He is the Maker of it, that which man has made must rightly belong to him. Property as a rule, is gained by work, but sometimes it is a free gift. God Himself bestows property. He promised the land of Chanaan to Abraham and his posterity as a possession (Gen. xii. 7). The patriarchs bequeathed their possessions to their eldest sons by a solemn benediction. In the present day lands and property of all kinds pass into the hands of others by inheritance or bequest. Every man should make a will, in order to prevent disputes should he be suddenly called out of this life. In primitive times property was acquired by taking possession of unowned land; and now valuables, if unclaimed, may be appropriated by their finder.

1. On the other hand, this commandment forbids the acquisition of property by unjust means, i.e., by taking away what belongs to our neighbor.

Property is unjustly acquired by theft, robbery, cheating, etc.

2. The State has not the right to take from any man his personal property, but it is empowered to impose restrictions on the acquisition and disposal of personal property.

The State has not a paramount command over all property. It has a certain right of supervision, but not of disposal. The people do not exist for the Government, but the Government exists for the people; consequently far from wronging any man, it ought to aim at the welfare of each and all of its subjects. Therefore if the State compels an individual to give up his property in the public interest, it is bound to give him compensation. Nor has the State the right to seize ecclesiastical property. To rob a man is theft, to rob God is sacrilege, and for this the penalty is excommunication. Restitution must be made before the Holy See can give absolution. Since it is the business of the secular authorities, under God, to provide for the well-being of their subjects, the Government is empowered by wise legislation, to introduce gradual changes in regard to the holding of property. It can impose such taxes as are necessary for the common weal upon its subjects, in proportion to their means. Thus by heavy taxation of wealthy capitalists it can alleviate the poverty of the working classes. Moreover, St. Thomas Aquinas says this world's riches are only intended for the preservation of human life. This end is not attained if they are already in the possession of individuals; therefore every one is bound of his abundance to assist those who are in want. The superfluity of the rich is the property of the poor. Thus the Government, in exercising its right of guardianship, can do something towards the just distribution of superfluous wealth.

Sins against the Seventh Commandment.

The Seventh Commandment expressly forbids: Theft, robbery, cheating, usury, injuring the property of another, detention of goods that have been found or lent, and the non-payment of debts.

1. Theft is the secret purloining of another man's goods contrary to the rational will of their owner.

Judas was a thief; he had the purse, and appropriated a part of the common money (John xii. 6). Few sins are more common than theft, and this fact may be accounted for in the first place by the covetousness of the human heart, and also by the abundant opportunities afforded for stealing. Occasion makes the thief. But if a man steal when he is starving, or as the only means of saving his life in an extremity, it is not to be reckoned as a sin, provided he has the intention to restore what he has stolen when he is in better circumstances (Prov. vi. 30). Our Lord did not rebuke the apostles when, in passing through a cornfield, they plucked the ears of corn and eat the grain because they were hungry (Matt. xii. 1). To conceal or purchase goods that are known to be stolen is to render one's self a partner in the sin.

2. Robbery is theft accompanied by personal violence.

If a robber kills, or mortally wounds his victim, the crime is said to be robbery with murder. Of this the robbers were guilty who attacked the Jew on the way from Jerusalem to Jericho (Luke x. 30). The forcible extortion of alms is also equivalent to robbery.

3. Cheating consists in injuring one's neighbor in his possessions by crafty means.

For instance, by the use of false weights and measures, the issue of counterfeit coin, the adulteration of food, the falsification of documents, the removal of boundary-marks, smuggling, or arson in view of obtaining the insurance money. "Let no man overreach, or circumvent his brother in business" (1 Thess. iv. 6).

4. Usury consists in making use of the needy circumstances of another to one's own profit (Exod. xxii. 25).

The usurer is called a money-lender, if he lends money at a high rate of interest to one who is in pecuniary difficulties, or a speculator, if he buys up corn and keeps it until a time of scarcity, in order to sell it at a high price. Under the appearance of helping a man in need, the usurer involves him in greater complications. He is like a doctor who instead of strengthening his patient, saps the little force he had; or like a spider that weaves a web more and more closely round the unhappy fly and sucks every drop of its blood. Usurers are murderers of the poor; they take from them their means of livelihood, and thus deprive them of life.

5. Wilfully injuring another man's property, keeping back what one has found or what has been lent to one, and refusing to pay one's debts, is equivalent to stealing.

We may injure our neighbor in his property by setting it on fire, by treading down his crops, damaging his goods, fishing or shooting on his grounds without permission, etc. To keep what one has found, and not to return what has been lent to the owner is theft. Joseph's brethren did well in directly taking back the money they found in their sacks. The more valuable the object one finds, the greater the obligation to give it up to the owner; and if one does not know to whom it belongs, one ought to take steps to discover him. Many people are very careless in returning books, instruments or implements which they have borrowed, and they show displeasure if the owner asks for them. Be careful about lending and very careful about returning. The non-payment of debts also is a kind of stealing. It is a bad thing to get into debt: the debtor is like a man who, when his legs begin to fail him, hobbles onward with a crutch. But it is a sin to borrow and not pay again (Ps. xxxvi. 21). Many people get into debt to satisfy their craving for amusement, to gratify their passions, or for the sake of dressing above their station, and they scarcely think this wrong. Tradespeople sin when they fraudulently declare themselves bankrupts. But most blameworthy of all are those who do not pay their servants and workpeople; this is a sin that cries to heaven. It is theft, and a sort of murder, too, to keep back the wages of a poor laborer, who lives on his daily earnings. "The wages of him that hath been hired by thee shall not abide with thee until the morning" (Lev. xix. 13). "Pay him the price of his labor the same day" (Deut. xxiv. 15). "Owe no man anything, but to love one another" (Rom. xiii. 8).

1. We are in danger of committing mortal sin if we take from our neighbor as much as he requires to support him one day in a manner suitable to his position.

Our sin against our neighbor is greater or less in proportion to the wrong we do him. To steal a few pence from one who is utterly destitute, or a few shillings from a laboring man is a mortal sin; it is equivalent to stealing a considerable sum from a rich man. It is also a sin to take trifling sums repeatedly from the same person, for in time they make a large amount. One ought not to take the smallest thing that is not one's own. Fidelity in small things is most important, for God punishes little sins, and unfaithfulness in small things leads to grave sins. By disregarding petty thefts many a criminal has come to the gallows.

2. *RESTITUTION OR SATISFACTION.*

1. He who has purloined from his neighbor or wronged him in his property, is under a strict obligation to restore the stolen goods or make compensation for the damage done (Lev. vi. 1–5).

A thief is not required to go himself and restore the stolen property to its owner; he may send it by the priest, who is pledged to secrecy, and will give him an acknowledgment of its receipt. On one occasion when Clement Hofbauer, the apostle of Vienna, handed over something that had been stolen to its owner, the latter refused to take it; but Hofbauer rejoined: "It is not wise to allow the thief to retain what he has purloined, or he will think stealing no great offence."

The following rules are to be observed:

1. If the rightful owner of the stolen property is dead, it must be given to his heirs; and if there should be no heirs, it must be given to the poor or devoted to good works.

2. If the thief cannot restore the whole, he must at any rate restore as much as he can.

3. If poverty or other hindrances render the thief unable to make restitution immediately, he must at least resolve to do so as soon as possible, and he must make every effort to fulfil that resolution.

4. If the thief cannot restore even a part of what he has stolen, he ought at least to pray for the individual he has wronged.

2. If any one has unwittingly got stolen goods in his possession, he is bound to give them up to the rightful owner as soon as he becomes aware that they were stolen.

Thus any one who, whether by purchase or gift, has acquired possession of something that was stolen, ought to give it back to its owner. If he does not know that it was stolen, he is said to be a just possessor, but if he does, then he is an unjust possessor. If the former be the case, not only must the stolen property itself be restored, but also whatever may have been gained by it without any labor on his part; if the latter, any loss the rightful proprietor may have sustained through the loss of his property must also be made good. At any rate it is well to refer the matter to one's confessor, and follow his counsel, for he stands towards us in the place of God.

3. He who refuses either to give up the stolen property or to compensate for the loss sustained, will not obtain pardon of his sins from God, nor absolution from the priest.

" He that will not render what he hath robbed, shall die everlastingly " (Ezech. xxxiii. 15). It was not until Zacheus had declared his determination to make full restitution of all unjust gains, that Our Lord called him a son of Abraham (Luke xix. 9). As long as one who has wronged his neighbor refuses to make reparation, though he entreats the divine pardon with tears, though he seeks to appease the divine justice by fasts and penances, his sin will not be remitted. " Such a one," St. Augustine says, " does not do penance, but only counterfeits it." Without restitution there is no forgiveness. St. Alphonsus relates the story of a rich man who had gangrene in the arm, and was near death. The priest urged him to restore the property he had acquired unjustly; he refused on the plea that by doing so he would leave his three sons penniless. The priest bethought him of a stratagem. He said he knew of a means of cure, but it was a costly one. The sick man declared no sum would be too great to procure it. The priest replied that some living person must allow his hand to be burned and while raw, laid on that of the sufferer. The three sons were called, but neither of them would do this for their father. Then the priest said: " See, none of your children would hold his hand in the fire a few moments for you, and you are willing to endure the tortures of hell-fire to all eternity for their sakes." This opened the sick man's eyes; he went to confession and made restitution.

What are the Reasons which ought to Deter us from Transgressing the Seventh Commandment?

The heathens of old held theft in abhorrence, and punished it very severely. The Anglo-Saxons (in the sixth century) used to cut off the hands of thieves; in Hungary they were sold as slaves. The Jews inflicted condign retribution on a thief; the man who at the taking of Jericho in spite of the prohibition carried away some of the spoil, was stoned to death by God's command (Josue vii.). In former days the laws of the Church in regard to the sin of stealing were extremely rigorous; even for a petty theft restitution had to be made, and besides it was expiated by fasting for a year on bread and water. God Himself inflicts heavy chastisements on those who take what belongs to another, no matter how trifling the thing stolen; for whether it be great or small, the will to defraud is the same, and it is to the will He looks.

People who wrong their neighbor in his property generally come to shame and poverty, often die unrepentant, and are in danger of everlasting damnation.

Confusion is upon a thief (Ecclus. v. 17). Stealing does not bring a man to honor, but to prison. Thieves are generally caught, sooner or later. Stealing is the way to poverty. Ill-gotten goods bring no blessing. He who steals another man's goods will lose his own, for when that which he acquired unjustly is taken from him, that which was honestly acquired will go too. Stolen goods are like fire, which not only vanishes in smoke, but reduces everything near it to ashes. When the Jews returned from the Babylonian captivity, there was great scarcity in the land. Some of the people profited by it to become rich; but when Nehemias came from Babylon to Jerusalem he was exceedingly angry, and rebuked the usurers. He shook his clothes before all the people, and called upon God to shake every man out of his house and out of his possessions, who did not restore what had been unjustly exacted, so that what he had got by usury might vanish as the dust (2 Esd. v. 1-13). "He that soweth iniquity shall reap evils" (Prov. xxii. 8). "The riches of the unjust shall be dried up like a river" (Ecclus. xl. 13). "Woe to him that heapeth together that which is not his own" (Hab. ii. 6). Injustice is even the cause of the fall of whole nations (Ecclus. x. 8). Where are the ancient and mighty kingdoms of Babylon, of the Medes and Persians, of the Greeks, and the great empire of Rome? They came to ruin because they sought to extend their limits unjustly. Look at the state of Italy in the present day; since the Holy Father was robbed of his temporal possessions the taxation has been excessive, and a large portion of the population are starving. Furthermore thieves often come to a miserable end. Remember Judas' wretched fate; what misery of mind, what torture of soul he endured before he hanged himself in despair! (Matt. xxvii. 5.) Those who have stolen or embezzled money are rarely brought to repentance, because they are unwilling to restore what they have taken. Even upon their death-bed they will not hear of making restitution. Beware, therefore, of allowing yourself to touch what belongs to another.

Moreover, if at the Last Day he will find no mercy who has not given
of his substance to the needy, how much the more pitilessly will he
be judged who has actually taken from his neighbor what was his
(St. Augustine). Thieves and the covetous shall not possess the kingdom of God (2 Cor. vi. 10). The Mohammedans consider that he
who so much as plucks an ear of corn from his neighbor's cornfield,
has done a disgraceful thing, and will go to hell. The dread of everlasting damnation deters many from committing acts of injustice.
Of this the following story affords an example. A poor widow who
had been defrauded of a plot of land belonging to her by a rich man,
asked to be at least allowed to carry away a basket of earth. The man
consented with a scornful smile; when the basket was filled, she further requested him to help her up with it on to her back. The rich
man attempted to raise it, but it was too heavy for him to lift.
"There," said the widow, "if you find this basket of earth too great a
weight, how will you bear the burden of the whole field for all eternity?" This remark made such an impression on the rich man that
he gave the land back to the woman. Fools indeed are they who play
away their chance of heaven for the sake of earth's transitory riches!
"What doth it profit a man if he gain the whole world, and suffer the
loss of his own soul?" (Matt. xvi. 26.) By stealing you may obtain
money, but you lose God. You think of the gain; forget not the
loss.

The honest man will prosper upon earth (Ps. xxxvi. 25).

Tobias affords a model of upright conduct. Although he was blind
and reduced to poverty, when he heard the bleating of a kid that
had been given to his wife, he immediately said: "Take heed, lest
perhaps it be stolen; restore ye it to its owners, for it is not lawful
for us either to eat or to touch anything that cometh by theft" (Tob.
ii. 21). God restored him to sight, and he lived forty-two years
longer (Tob. xiv. 1). The Lord will not afflict the soul of the just
with famine (Prov. x. 3). His ears are open unto his prayers (Ps.
xxxiii. 16). Justice exalteth a nation (Prov. xiv. 34). Honesty is the
best policy.

THE EIGHTH COMMANDMENT OF GOD.

**In the Eighth Commandment God forbids us to detract from our
neighbor's honor, or bear false witness of any kind**

1. THE PROHIBITION AGAINST INJURING OUR NEIGHBOR IN HIS HONOR.

**1. A good reputation is a precious possession, for it enables
us to gain riches for time and for eternity.**

An honorable reputation, or a good name, consists in being well
thought of, and well-spoken of by our fellow-men. The opposite of
honor is shame. "A good name is better than great riches; and good
favor is above silver and gold" (Prov. xxii. 1). A good reputation is
the best thing on earth; it is a talent entrusted to us by God, for he
who has a good reputation can do a great deal of good, because he
has influence over others. The esteem of others is essential to real

happiness; who can enjoy his life if he knows that he is despised by his fellow-men? A man without a penny will often get an excellent post merely because he has a good character. And those who are highly thought of are more careful to lead an upright life than those who have no reputation to preserve. An honorable name is to a man what the peel is to an apple; while it is whole, the apple keeps sound for a long time, but if the skin is once cut, the fruit rots quickly.

2. Above all we ought to strive to acquire a good name among men, and for that reason we ought to let our good works be known, and we ought to defend our character if it be aspersed to any great extent.

It is God's will that we should strive after honor, for He implanted within us feelings of honor and an abhorrence of disgrace. To suppress this instinct would be to act at variance with His appointment. Hence we ought to perform our good works openly. Our Lord expressly enjoins this upon us when He says: " So let your light shine before men that they may see your good works and glorify your Father Who is in heaven " (Matt. v. 16). Our good works should be like a sweet odor, pleasing to men as a perfume is to the nostrils (2 Cor. ii. 15). Good works are the best means of defending our good name, and silencing the tongue of detractors (1 Pet. ii. 12). We ought to consider what may be good not only before God, but also before men (2 Cor. viii. 21). " Let your modesty be known unto all men " (Phil. iv. 5). " From all appearance of evil refrain yourselves " (1 Thess. v. 22). It need hardly be said that our good works must not be performed in view of pleasing men, and courting their praise, or we shall receive no reward from God (Matt. vi. 2). It is our duty to defend ourselves when our name is aspersed. All manner of accusations were brought against the early Christians; some of their ablest men published " apologies " and sent them to the emperor. Our Lord did not disdain to justify Himself, when, for instance, it was said of Him that He cast out devils by the aid of the prince of the devils (Matt. xii. 27); or again, when a servant of the high priest struck Him (John xviii. 23). St. Paul repeatedly spoke in his own defence, before the council and the governor (Acts xxii. 26). Yet it is not well to be over-sensitive about one's honor, and go to law about trifles. An amicable adjustment of differences and reconciliation, is better than quarrelling and bringing accusations. To be very touchy in regard to one's honor is likely to give an appearance of truth to the slander, for it looks as if we were not quite sure of ourselves; besides it provokes the calumniator to go to greater lengths. After all, a man whose life is without reproach need not fear the permanent loss of his good name; only the evildoer, if he fall into disgrace, cannot retrieve his character. It is just the same as with one's hair; shave it off and it grows again quickly; but if it is pulled out by the roots, the bare place remains. David rightly compares the tongue of the slanderer to a sharp razor. In the matter of self-defence one must know how to keep the medium. Strong and generous characters are not affected by trifles; they bear them in silence, only giving expression to their just anger in matters of importance. St. Francis of Sales tells us that only when grave and dis-graceful crimes are imputed to us, such as no man can allow himself to be charged with, should we take steps to clear ourselves. Finally, be it remarked, much more can be done by bearing an affront patiently than by displaying great anxiety about our good name. Many eminent servants of God, by the calmness with which they bore the revilings of godless men, were the means of converting their accusers.

Yet we ought not to strive too anxiously to obtain the esteem of men, or else we shall lose the friendship of God as well as the esteem of men; moreover in some cases it is impossible to enjoy at the same time the favor of God and the favor of men.

He who is over-solicitous to obtain honor among men, makes this, and not God, his chief aim. Such a one is arrogant and ambitious, and will consequently be humbled by God (Luke xiv. 11). How deeply the proud Absalom was humbled! Likewise the ambitious Emperor Napoleon. Honor is a capricious goddess: if we run after her, she flies from us; if we fly from her, she pursues us. She allows no force to be put upon her; but there is a price at which she may be purchased, and that is uprightness and humility. It is impossible to serve God and to please men (Gal. i. 10). All who lead a truly Christian life are despised and reviled by men (1 Cor. iv. 13; 1 Pet. iv. 14), and even counted as fools (1 Cor. iv. 10). There are some silly people who mete out honor or disgrace not by the standard of virtue, but by things that are of no real value; riches, position, dress, etc. But whatever your exertions, you cannot please at all times, and all persons.

3. Furthermore, we ought to refrain from everything that may wound our neighbor's honor. Thus suspicion, detraction, slander, and abuse are forbidden, also listening with pleasure when our neighbor is spoken against.

Suspicion implies malice of *heart;* detraction, slander (both of which are directed against the absent) and abuse (which is directed against one who is present), are sins of the *tongue;* listening with gratification when another is evilly spoken of, is a sin, if it is in the evil speaking that we take pleasure.

1. Suspicion consists in supposing evil of one's neighbor without reasonable grounds.

The Pharisee in the Temple took for granted that the publican was a sinner and how greatly he was mistaken (Luke xviii.)! Job's three friends thought he must needs be ungodly merely because he was afflicted by God. Simon the Pharisee thought the Magdalen, when he saw her at Our Lord's feet, was still a sinner, but he deceived himself; she was then a penitent (Luke vii. 39 *seq.*). When St. Paul, shipwrecked on the island of Malta, lighted a fire, a viper, coming out of the sticks, fastened on his hand; in consequence of this the inhabitants of the island instantly judged him to be a murderer, pursued by divine vengeance (Acts xxviii.). A goldsmith had an apprentice who bore a very good character. One day he found two precious stones concealed in a hole in the wall close to the boy's head. He directly accused him of theft, chastised him soundly, and drove him out of the house. Soon after he again discovered two stones in exactly the same place. He watched, and found they were put there by a magpie which he had in the house, and deeply regretted his rash judgment, when it was too late to repair his fault. If he had detected the boy in dishonesty, he would not have done wrong in suspecting him. People judge of others by themselves; for the affections are apt to mislead the understanding. He who is not evil himself does not lightly think evil of others, whereas a bad man readily concludes his neighbor to be as bad as himself. Molten metal takes the shape of the mould into which it is poured; so every man's judgment of what he sees and hears takes its shape from his own feelings. The most wholesome aliments disagree with the man whose digestion is out of order; thus a corrupted mind always takes an evil view of things, while a good man puts the best construction on everything. " I would far rather err," says St. Anselm, "by thinking good of a bad man than by thinking evil of a good man." " Charity thinketh no evil " (1 Cor. xiii. 5). The just man, in whom dwells the spirit of love, even when he sees an action which is unquestionably reprehensible, does not allow his thoughts to dwell on it; he leaves the judgment of it to God. This is what St. Joseph did, in regard to his spouse, the Blessed Virgin (Matt. i. 19). " Let none of you imagine evil in your heart against his friend " (Zach. viii. 17). Trust others, if you would have others trust you. Trust engenders confidence, and mistrust the want of it.

2. Detraction consists in disclosing the fault committed by another without necessity.

This sin, the lessening of our neighbor's reputation, is an act of injustice towards him. For if he is really guilty of some secret sin, still he has not lost the good opinion of others, and of this we rob him if we publish his misdeeds. We are not justified in robbing a man of the esteem he enjoys, even though he has no right to it, any more than in taking from him money which he has gained unjustly. Nor must we speak evil of the dead. Let nothing but what is good be said of the departed. Some people, like hyenas, who tear from their graves and devour dead bodies, deface the memory of the dead by their malicious words and bring to light faults long since forgotten. Like insects which alight, not on the sound part of the apple, but on the decayed portion, detractors do not enlarge on the virtues of the deceased, but they pitilessly dwell upon their faults. They may be compared to dogs who prefer carrion to fresh meat, for they pass over the good which they cannot help seeing in their neighbor, and care to keep alive the remembrance of his failings. The sin of detraction is one most frequently met with. " Rarely," says St. Jerome, " do we find any one who is not ready to blame his neighbor's conduct." This comes from pride, for many people imagine they exalt themselves in proportion as they decry others. Detraction is a hateful sin. It is an ugly and shameless thing to do, if one goes to a stranger's house and spies into every corner; but how much more so to scrutinize and criticize our neighbor's course of life!

Mud should be covered over, not stirred up, for no one can touch it
without defiling himself. " O fool! " exclaims St. Alphonsus. " Thou
dost declaim against the sin of another, and meanwhile, by evil
speaking, dost commit a far greater sin than that thou blamest in
thy neighbor." Besides the detractor in disclosing the faults of
another, discloses his own, for he shows that he has no charity. However, to speak of another man's sin is not wrong, unless one has the
intention of lowering him in the eyes of others; it is not detraction
to tell some one else of it in order to prevent a repetition of the sin.
One may also blame the fault of another, if this may be useful to
a third person; but it must be done from a sense of duty, and the
sin rather than the sinner is to be condemned. The crime of any
malefactor who has been brought to justice may be freely spoken of,
as it is already made public. Tale-telling is a form of detraction;
it consists in repeating to another what a third person has said of
him. Tale-telling ruins the peace of families, and is a fruitful
source of feuds. It is worse than ordinary detraction because it
not only destroys the reputation of one's neighbor, but puts an
end to friendly relations and brotherly love. Therefore God says:
" The whisperer and double-tongued are accursed " (Ecclus. xxviii.
15).

3. Slander consists in attributing to one's neighbor faults
of which he is not guilty. If the accusation is made publicly
it is called a libel.

Slander or calumny is taking away a man's good name. Putiphar's wife accused Joseph to her lord of having attempted to lead
her astray (Gen. xxxix.). The Jews accused Our Lord before Pilate
of having perverted the nation and forbidden to give tribute to the
emperor (Luke xxiii. 2). Exaggeration of another's fault also comes
under the head of calumny. The motives that actuate the slanderer
are generally revenge, hatred or ingratitude; his sin is twofold, for
he lies, and at the same time destroys his neighbor's reputation.
" He that backbiteth secretly is like a serpent that biteth in silence."
Some slanderers accompany their calumnies with a jest, or accentuate
them with a witty or amusing speech. This is the greatest cruelty
of all, for the slander which might have passed in at one ear and
out at the other, is then firmly lodged in the mind of all who hear it.
Again, slanders that are prefaced by words of eulogy make more
impression on the hearer, just as an arrow flies with more force and
penetrates more deeply if the bow be drawn back first. Of such
persons David says: " The poison of asps is under their lips " (Ps.
xiii. 3).

4. Abuse consists in making public the low opinion which
one has of another.

In evil speaking one makes known a man's fault behind his back,
abuse utters it in his presence. Abuse therefore stands in the same
relation to detraction as robbery to theft. While detraction and
slander undermine the good opinion others have of a man, abuse
aims at depriving him of the outward respect that is shown him.
Semei reviled King David; he called him a man of Belial, and threw

stones at him (2 Kings xvi. 5). The Jews reviled Our Lord; they called Him a Samaritan, and said He had a devil (John viii. 48). If two men quarrel, the one who is in the wrong usually resorts to abuse. The one who is in the right does not need such weapons; truth conquers of itself. Sneers and sarcasms are a form of this sin. Their object is to make a man ridiculous before others and put him to confusion. By such unkind speeches one may deeply wound one's neighbor, and fill him with bitter resentment. "The stroke of a whip maketh a blue mark, but the stroke of the tongue will break the bones" (Ecclus. xxviii. 21).

5. He who takes pleasure in listening to detraction commits the same sin as the speaker to whom he listens.

He who asperses his neighbor's good name kindles a fire, and he who listens to him throws fuel on it. Were it not for the latter, the former would soon be silent. St. Ignatius says we should not talk about our neighbor's faults did we not find eager listeners. St. Bernard says he cannot decide which is more blameworthy, the man who slanders his neighbor, or he who lends his ear to the slanderer; the only difference is that one serves the devil with his tongue, the other with his ear. What do I care to know that such a one is a wicked man? The knowledge only does me harm. How much better to spend one's pains on scrutinizing one's own conduct. Our Lord exhorts us to do this: "Cast first the beam out of thine own eye, and then thou shalt see clearly to take out the mote from thy brother's eye" (Luke vi. 42). It is those who are blind to their own faults who are most keenly alive to the faults of others. Never listen to detraction. St. Augustine had these words inscribed upon his dining-table: "There is not place at this table for those who love to defame their neighbor." "Hedge in thy ears with thorns, hear not a wicked tongue" (Ecclus. xxviii. 28). Slander is a three-edged sword; at one blow it inflicts three wounds; it wounds the slanderer, for he commits a sin; it wounds the slandered, because he is robbed of his good name; it wounds the hearer, for he also falls into sin. And since the slanderer injures the soul of him who listens to his calumny, he imitates the serpent, whose poisoned words were the means of driving Eve out of paradise.

4. He who has injured his neighbor's reputation is strictly bound to restore his good name; either by apologizing, if the offence was committed in private, or by publicly retracting his words, if they were spoken before others.

Any one who has unjustly diminished his neighbor's reputation, is bound to make satisfaction, according to the nature of the offence. It is not enough to draw the arrow out of the wound, the hurt must be healed; nor is it enough to desist from evil-speaking; the injury done must be set right. That is bitter to human nature, for it requires no slight self-humiliation. Moreover, it is almost impossible fully to make amends for calumny; it is easy to break a seal, but difficult to repair it so that no one can perceive that it has been broken. An ink-spot is soon made on a sheet of paper, but no efforts will remove all traces of the blot.

5. Those who do not endeavor to repair the harm they have done by slandering their neighbor, cannot obtain pardon from God, nor absolution from the priest.

What are the Reasons which should Deter us from Injuring our Neighbor's Good Name?

1. **He who is severe in his judgment of his neighbor, will in his turn be judged severely by God.**

Our Lord says: "Judge not, that you may not be judged" (Matt. vii. 1). "For with what measure you mete, it shall be measured to you again" (v. 2). "Condemn not and you shall not be condemned" (Luke vi. 37). A monk who on account of delicate health had not been very regular in the performance of his religious duties, displayed great cheerfulness when his death drew near. On being asked the cause of this, he replied: "I have never judged any one, even when I had just cause for complaint; therefore I hope that God will not judge me."

2. To judge one's fellow-man is to commit an offence against God, for it is an usurpation of His rights.

"There is one Lawgiver and Judge; but who art thou that judgest thy neighbor?" (Jas. iv. 12.) "Who art thou that judgest another man's servant?" (Rom. xiv. 4.) Only He Who is omniscient can claim the right to judge others, for the intrinsic evil of an action depends upon the intention of the heart, and that is hidden from man.

3. He who robs another of his good name is often severely punished by God upon earth; not unfrequently he is overtaken by the same calamity which he sought to bring on his neighbor.

A man of evil tongue shall not be established upon the earth (Ps. cxxxix. 12). Jezabel, the wife of King Achab, suborned two wicked men to falsely accuse Naboth, who would not· give up his vineyard to the king, of blasphemy. Retribution eventually fell upon her; she was thrown from the palace window, trampled upon by horses and eaten by dogs (3 Kings xxi.). It is now no uncommon thing for the slanderer to meet with the self-same fate which he prepared for another, as the following story shows: St. Elizabeth. Queen of Portugal, had a favorite page, who used to distribute her alms. One of the king's servants, who was jealous of the large share of the queen's favor enjoyed by that page, calumniated him to the king, one day when he was out hunting. The king believed the calumny; and going up to a lime-kiln which he saw in the forest, he said to the proprietor: "To-morrow I shall send a young man hither, who will ask you whether you have executed the king's orders; seize him instantly and cast him into the kiln." On the following morning the king dispatched the queen's page to the lime-burner with the message agreed upon. On his way thither the young man passed a church, and as the bell was ringing for Mass, he went in and assisted at the holy sacrifice. Meanwhile the servant who had slandered him, curious to know his fate, followed him, as he thought, to the lime-kiln, and on arriving, eagerly asked if the king's orders had been executed. Almost before he had uttered the question, he was thrown into the furnace. When the queen's page shortly made his appearance, he was told that the royal behest had been obeyed, and the workmen expected a reward. On his return to the palace, the king was astonished and horrified, and saw clearly that he had been foully deceived. "He hath opened a pit and dug it, and he is fallen into the hole he made" (Ps. vii. 16).

4. He who indulges a habit of detraction is in danger of losing his soul.

The pulse does not always correctly indicate the progress of a fatal disease, but if the tongue becomes black, it is a sure sign of approaching dissolution. So many people are assiduous in their prayers, are diligent churchgoers, and are considered to be pious, but their tongue, wherewith they blacken the character of others, infallibly indicates the mortal disease of their soul. To blast a man's reputation is a great sin, because his good name is better than great riches (Prov. xxii. 1). It is a kind of murder, because it destroys a man's life as a citizen, i.e., his social standing, which depends on the repute in which he is held. It is also sinful because thereby one causes distress to one's neighbor. The man of honor values his good name above everything. He would rather part with his money, with all he possesses, with life itself, than lose his honor. Hence we may conclude how grievous a sin is detraction. "Railers shall not possess the kingdom of God" (1 Cor. vi. 10). "Detractors . . . are worthy of death" (Rom. i. 32). "Whosoever shall say to his brother, thou fool, shall be in danger of hell fire" (Matt. v. 22). The magnitude of sins against one's neighbor depends upon the harm that is done. On account of this, it matters greatly who the individual is who slanders his neighbor; if he be a man of position and respectability, the sin he commits is liable to be grievous, for the esteem in which he is held gives weight to his words. In the case of one who is known to be a tattler, on the other hand, the sin is slight. Again it makes a difference who the individual is whose name is aspersed. The higher his position, and the greater the respect due to him, the worse is the sin. It is but a venial sin to speak against one who has already lost his character. But let the evil speaker beware, for if he has not already fallen into mortal sin, he is on the high road to it.

2. THE COMMAND AGAINST UNTRUTHFULNESS.

God is truth itself; consequently He forbids every kind of falsehood, especially lying, hypocrisy, and flattery.

God is true (John iii. 33). It is impossible for God to lie (Heb. vi. 18). Our Lord says: "I am the way and the truth and the life" (John xiv. 6). Hence God commands: "You shall not lie" (Lev. xix. 11). "Putting away lying, speak ye the truth every man to his neighbor" (Eph. iv. 25). Let your conversation be upright and truthful, if you would show yourselves to be the children of Him Who is the Father of truth and truth itself.

1. He is guilty of lying who says what is not true with the intention of deceiving others.

Lying is a misuse of speech. Speech was not given to man in order that he might deceive others, but as a means whereby he might communicate to them his thoughts. The conditions under which lies are commonly told are these: Under stress of circumstances, to avert some evil from one's self or from others, as when St. Peter in the outer court of the high priest's palace said: "I know not the man" (Matt. xxvi. 72); in jest, to amuse others; or for the sake of injuring some one, as Jacob did when he deceived his father in order to obtain his paternal benediction (Gen. xxvii.). But to relate a fictitious narrative, or make use of a fable for the instruction of others is no untruth, for it is done without an intention to deceive. Our Lord Himself employed parables in teaching. A liar is like counterfeit coin, which appears to be what it is not.

2. Hypocrisy or dissimulation is acting a lie; we commit this sin when we speak or act differently to what we think and feel.

Judas kissed Our Lord in the Garden of Olives, as if he were His greatest friend, but he only did so to betray Him (Matt. xxvi. 49). King Herod said to the three kings: "When you have found the Child bring me word again, that I also may come and adore Him" (Matt. ii. 8). But he thought in his heart that when he knew where the Child was, he would have Him put to death. Those are hypocrites who make an outward profession of piety while in reality their lives are far from irreproachable. They are like Satan, who can assume the form of an angel of light. To feign sanctity in this manner is worse than to sin openly. Some appear very devout in church, they cross themselves and smite their breasts, but all the while their thoughts are far away; they are dissemblers. The hypocrite is like a dunghill covered with snow, which hides what it really is. Our Lord compared such men to whited sepulchres, outwardly beautiful, but within full of foulness and dead men's bones (Matt. xxiii. 27); also to wolves in sheep's clothing (Matt. vii. 15).

3. Flattery consists in praising another immoderately to his face, against one's own conviction for the sake of advantage.

King Herod Agrippa was highly gratified by the flattery of the Tyrians and Sidonians, when they exclaimed, on hearing his oration: "It is the voice of a god and not of a man." But the angel of the Lord forthwith struck him, and he was eaten by worms (Acts xii. 22, 23). Flatterers speak contrary to their conviction; they deride a man behind his back while they praise him to his face. The flatterer only seeks his own advantage. He is like the cat which purrs, and the dog which fawns on his master to get a piece of meat. Crafty people cringe to others if they think anything can be gained. Flatterers frequent the presence of the rich, for from the poor they get nothing; they are like the locusts which do not come in the winter, or where the land is barren, but they alight in cultivated places, where there is plenty for them to devour. Flatterers praise immoderately, i.e., they ascribe excellences to a man which he does not possess, or they exaggerate his good qualities and palliate his misdeeds. They are dangerous acquaintances, because they hide a man's faults, instead of endeavoring, as a true friend would, to correct them. It is a matter of indifference to them whether they do harm or good, if they only get themselves into favor; they are like a cook who cares not whether the dishes he prepares are wholesome or the contrary, so long as they are tasty and please the palate. Flattery feeds sin as oil feeds a flame; it is a nursery of vice. Isaias exclaims, addressing flatterers: "Woe to you that call evil good and good evil" (Is. v. 20). Let us therefore be on our guard, if any one appears unusually complaisant and begins to praise us. Our Blessed Lady was troubled at the salutation of the angel.

What are the Reasons that should make us Refrain from Untruthfulness?

1. The liar is like the devil and displeasing to God.

He who forfeits the confidence of his fellow-men causes a great deal of harm and is capable of committing all manner of evil deeds.

The liar resembles the devil, for the devil is a liar and the father thereof (John viii. 44). Remember how the serpent in paradise lied to Eve. Liars are children of the devil, not by nature, but by imitation. The liar is displeasing to God. God is truth itself, and therefore He abhors the liar. Our Lord did not speak as sharply of any one as of the Pharisees. And why? Because they were hypocrites (Matt. xxiii. 27). From every class of sinners He gave an example of one who was saved; e.g., Zacheus among usurers, the good thief among highwaymen, Magdalen and the Samaritan at Jacob's well among profligate women, Saul among persecutors of the Church, but not one single individual among liars and hypocrites did He mention as having sought and found pardon. Many a time God punished liars severely; witness Ananias and his wife Saphira, who for their falsehood fell dead at St. Peter's feet (Acts v.) and Giezi, the servant of Eliseus, who was struck with leprosy for his lies and avarice (4 Kings v.). "Lying lips are an abomination to the Lord" (Prov. xii. 22). The liar forfeits the trust of his fellow-men. The shepherd who cried "Wolf" when no wolf was near, found he was not believed when his flock was really attacked; his comrades had been so often deceived that they did not heed his cries. A liar is not trusted when he speaks the truth; he is hated by God and man. Liars often do a great deal of harm. The spies who went to view the Promised Land deceived the Israelites by their false report, and alarmed them so that they blasphemed God, wanted to stone the two spies who spoke the truth, and clamored to return to Egypt. See what mischief those men wrought: God declared His intention to destroy the people (Numb. xiii.). Jacob deceived his father and obtained his blessing fraudulently; his brother Esau threatened to kill him and Jacob was obliged to take to flight. "He that hath no guard

on his speech shall meet with evils" (Prov. xiii. 3). The liar falls
into many other sins. "Show me a liar and I will show you a
thief." Where you find hypocrisy, you find cheating and all manner
of evil practices. A liar cannot possibly be God-fearing. The Holy
Spirit will flee from the deceitful (Wisd. i. 5). All the piety and
devotion of one whose words serve to conceal, not to express his
thoughts, is a mere sham; do not associate with such a one, lest he
corrupt you with his ungodly ways. "Lying men are without honor"
(Ecclus. xx. 28). "The just shall hate a lying word" (Prov. xiii. 5).

**2. The pernicious habit of lying leads a man into mortal sin
and to eternal perdition.**

Lying is in itself a venial sin; but it can easily become a mortal
sin if it is the means of doing great harm, or causing great scandal.
He who indulges the habit of lying runs no small risk of losing his
soul, for God withdraws His grace from those who deceive their
neighbor. "The mouth that belieth killeth the soul" (Wisd. i. 11).
A thief is not so bad as a liar, for the thief can give back what he
has stolen, whereas the liar cannot restore his neighbor's good name,
of which he has robbed him. "A thief is better than a man that is
always lying; but both of them shall inherit destruction" (Ecclus.
xx. 27). A lie is a foul blot in a man (v. 26). The soul of the liar
is like a counterfeit coin, stamped with the devil's effigy; when at the
Last Day, the Judge shall ask: "Whose image is this?" the answer
will be "the devil's;" and He will then say: "Render unto the devil
the things that are his" (St. Thomas Aquinas). The Lord will
destroy all that speak a lie (Ps. v. 7). Liars shall have their portion
in the lake burning with fire (Apoc. xxi. 8). Our Lord uttered a terrible denunciation of the Pharisees because of their hypocrisy (Matt.
xxiii. 13).

Lying is consequently forbidden, even if it may be the means
of effecting much good.

St. Augustine says it is just as wrong to tell a lie for your neighbor's advantage as to steal for the good of the poor. Not even to save
one's own life or the life of another, is a falsehood justifiable. St.
Anthimus, Bishop of Nicomedia, would not allow the soldiers who
were sent to arrest him, and who were enjoying his hospitality, to
save him by a lie; he preferred to suffer martyrdom. We must not
do evil that there may come good (Rom. iii. 8). The end does not
justify the means. The enemies of the Jesuits allege that they teach
and act upon the principle that the end justifies the means, but this
has never been proved against them. It was the philosopher Voltaire
who proclaimed that doctrine, for he said: "Lying is only reprehensible when it causes mischief; it is a virtue when it is a means of
effecting good."

A falsehood told in jest is not wrong if every one can see
at once that it is not meant in earnest.

If any one says: "How delightfully mild it is to-day!" when the
cold is exceptionally severe, no one will call this a sin. But if a
foolish joke produces lamentable results, the case is different. A

gentleman once told a peasant who was at a distance from home, that he had heard his cottage and half the village where he lived was burned down; he only meant to make an "April fool" of him, but the poor man took the news so much to heart that he fell down dead. As a rule it may be said that every lie, however trifling it may appear, injures either ourselves or our neighbor, for it is a departure from truth and uprightness; there is always a certain duplicity about it, even if it be only a joke. Let your speech be truthful and honest, as becomes children of Him Who is truth itself.

It is, however, lawful to give an evasive answer to one who causes us embarrassment by asking a question he has no right to ask.

We are under no obligation to answer a question which another has no right to ask. We may return an evasive or an ambiguous reply, or refuse to give any at all. St. Athanasius, Bishop of Alexandria, was concealed in a vessel on the Nile, when the soldiers of the Emperor Julian overtook and stopped it. On their inquiring where Athanasius was, his servant replied: "He is not gone far, if you make haste you will soon take him." The soldiers went onward on their quest, and the bishop escaped. The archangel Raphael himself told Tobias that he was Azarias, the son of a distinguished Jew, whose form he had assumed (Tob. v. 18), because, had he revealed his true nature, he could not have fulfilled the commission intrusted to him by God. If an impertinent person presumes to ask a professional secret of us, we make reply unceremoniously "I do not know," i.e., "it is not mine to tell." In this sense Our Lord stated that He did not know when the Day of Judgment would be (Mark xiii. 32). If any one whom we cannot trust wants to borrow money of us, we are justified in saying: "I have not any," that is, "to lend you." Again we may return an evasive answer if some one in authority, in the absence of proof, tries to force a confession of guilt from us, for no man is obliged to incriminate himself. In many cases we should refuse to give an answer. St. Firmus, Bishop of Tagasta, concealed in his house two young men, whom the emperor had unjustly condemned to death. The officers of justice came to the bishop, and demanded to be told where the young men were hidden. The prelate refused to answer; he was put to torture, but this availed nothing: "I can die," he said, "but I cannot make others miserable." The emperor hearing of his heroic conduct, pardoned the young men. Our Lord did not answer all the questions Pilate put to Him. It will be understood that ambiguous replies must only be given when considerations of the glory of God, the good of our neighbor, or the exigencies of our own position renders them necessary. When our neighbor has a right to the truth, we must answer simply and openly, in buying and selling, for instance, or drawing up an agreement. It would be grossly unjust if persons about to marry were to deceive one another by equivocating about money matters and other things.

3. Whoso is really upright is like almighty God, is pleasing in His sight, and is esteemed by his fellow-men.

Christ says: "I am the truth" (John xiv. 6). Therefore the lover of truth is like unto Him. The lover of truth is well pleasing to God. Our Lord said in praise of Nathanael that he was: "An Israelite indeed, in whom is no guile" (John i. 47). The lover of truth is esteemed by his fellow-men. On one occasion when Cæsar Augustus was making a triumphal entry into Rome, he happened to hear that among the captives there was a heathen priest, who had never been convicted of a lie. Immediately he ordered him to be liberated. St. John Cantius was once stopped by robbers who, after taking his purse, asked if he had any more money about him. The saint replied that he had not. After he had gone a few steps on his way, he remembered that he had some pieces of gold sewn up in his clothes; he hastened after the robbers and gave them to them. The thieves were so astonished that they restored all that they had taken from him. See how highly pagans and robbers esteem truthfulness! Thus it is always best to acknowledge one's fault freely, for thereby one obtains forgiveness, or at least a mitigation of the punishment due to it. It is said that Washington, when a boy, hacked with a chopper a beautiful cherry-tree which his father greatly prized. His father was extremely angry when he saw what was done, and asked the boy if he was the culprit. He replied: "Yes, father. I will not tell a lie. I did it." This candor pleased his father so much that he did not punish the boy. We may, perhaps. sometimes have to suffer through speaking the truth, but the suffering is far outweighed by the approval of a good conscience. "He that walketh sincerely, walketh confidently" (Prov. x. 9). Our Lord exhorts us to be simple as doves (Matt. x. 16). Guile is not half so profitable as simplicity. It is therefore our wisest course to be candid and truthful.

3. THE MEANS OF PREVENTING SINS OF THE TONGUE.

It is the opinion of the Fathers of the Church that a third part of all the sins committed in the world are sins of the tongue.

Sins of the tongue can be best avoided by checking talkativeness, and being guarded in our speech; moreover by making excuses for those whom we hear spoken against, and not repeating what is said of them.

We must not indulge the love of talking too freely. St. Augustine says that silence is the best preventive of sins of the tongue. He who knows how to keep silence will speak wisely. "He that keepeth his mouth, keepeth his soul; but he that hath no guard on his speech shall meet with evils" (Prov. xiii. 3). "In the multitude of words there shall not want sin" (Prov. x. 19). While all the organs of the senses are open to sight, God has enclosed the tongue behind a double wall, the lips and the teeth, to warn us to be circumspect in our speech. You should be as careful in choosing the words you speak, as in selecting the food you eat. Holy Scripture compares the tongue to a sharp knife, because we ought to be as cautious in our use of it as the surgeon in the use of his knife, when he has to perform an oper-

ation on the human body. We should speak with all the more deliberation because what is once said cannot be as if it had not been said.
We can no more recall the words we have spoken than we can the
arrow we have let fly from the bow. Our Lord says: "Every idle word
that men shall speak, they shall render an account for it in the
Day of Judgment" (Matt. xii. 36). Nay, He will even judge us by
our words, for He adds: "By thy words thou shalt be justified, and
by thy words thou shalt be condemned" (v. 37). "Death and life are
in the power of the tongue" (Prov. xviii. 21). Furthermore, if any
one is spoken evil of in our presence, we ought to life up our voice
in his defence. Holy Scripture says: "Open thy mouth for the
dumb" (Prov. xxxi. 8), that is, for him who, being absent, cannot
defend himself. If therefore, you hear the misdeeds of another
spoken of, endeavor to show that he did not act from a bad motive;
if that is impossible, then make excuses for the act on the plea of
violent temptation, ignorance, or human frailty, and thus, at any rate,
mitigate the harshness of the judgment passed on it. Or one may
mention something to the credit of the person in question. This was
St. Teresa's invariable practice, and no one dared in her presence to
utter a word of detraction. One may also express one's disapproval
by looking very grave, and thus putting the detractor to shame. It
will have the effect of shooting arrows at a rock, the shaft will rebound upon the marksman. "The north wind driveth away rain,
as doth a sad countenance a backbiting tongue" (Prov. xxv. 23). It
is also advisable at once adroitly to change the conversation, and thus
prevent the calumniator from pursuing the subject. By tolerating
detraction one participates in the sin. We should never repeat anything depreciatory which we hear said of our neighbor. "Hast thou
heard a word against thy neighbor? Let it die within thee, trusting
that it will not burst thee. As an arrow that sticketh in a man's
thigh, so is a word in the heart of a fool" (Ecclus. xix. 10, 12). Be
very cautious in speaking of your neighbor, lest unawares you may
blight his whole future.

THE NINTH COMMANDMENT OF GOD.

See what is said concerning the Sixth Commandment; and respecting the Sacrament of Matrimony; also the words of Our Lord in
Matt. v. 28, and of St. Paul, 1 Cor. x. 6.

THE TENTH COMMANDMENT OF GOD.

**In the Tenth Commandment God forbids us to endeavor to pos-
sess ourselves of the property of another by unlawful means.**

In God's sight the will is equivalent to the deed. Evil desires are
sinful as well as evil deeds, as the act is accomplished in will. Therefore transgressions of this commandment must not be omitted in
confession (Council of Trent, 14, ch. 5).

1. SOCIALISM.

1. In our own day a large proportion of the so-called Socialists or social democrats aim at depriving their fellow-men of their private property by unjust means.

Social democracy, or the rule of the people (Demos) proposes to reconstruct human society. It is of recent origin, being first started in Germany in 1840, and propagated some ten years later by the notorious Jew, Marx. In 1862 another Jew named Lasalle was very successful in spreading socialistic doctrines, so much so that in 1878, a special law was passed for the suppression of Socialism. Associations and meetings were prohibited, publications advocating its principles were seized, and the leading agitators were banished from several of the large towns. From that time forward the work of propagation was carried on covertly, in the workshop and clubroom, meetings being held in the woods, and pamphlets circulated privately. In 1880 a Socialistic Congress was held in Zurich, attended by members from all the countries of Europe to arrange a general programme for the universal upheaval of society and subversion of the existing order of things. Since then the system has made steady progress, and assumed a revolutionary character. Those who resort to open acts of violence in order to accelerate the disintegration of society are called anarchists. Switzerland is a hot-bed of Socialism, and there the principal organs of the society are printed. Socialism has gained ground chiefly on the continent of Europe.

1. The object of Socialists is this: They want all private property to be confiscated by the State, and capital and labor equally distributed among the members of the State; moreover many of them would do away with religion, authority, social order, and family life.

The fundamental principle of Socialism is: All property has been unjustly acquired. Consequently in the new republic no one is to possess personal property, but is to be provided for out of the public funds. Every one must work, and with the proceeds of his labor purchase what he needs. In the new republic of the extreme Socialists there is to be *ni Dieu ni maitre*, neither the ordinances of religion nor the institutions of law. These men openly declare themselves to be atheists and republicans; they say religion concerns the individual alone. The intercourse of man and woman is to take the place of wedlock; the children are to belong, not to their parents, but to the State, to be educated at the public expense; a public kitchen is to supersede the domestic hearth. Prisons will not be needed, for there will be no criminals, since all crime comes from the possession of private property. These principles have spread chiefly among the irreligious, who care only for the gratification of their appetites, and the lower orders, the proletariate, who, in the division of property, have nothing to lose and all to gain. They are mostly held by certain ones of the laboring class who have been thrown by peculiar circumstances into the arms of Socialism.

2. The origin and development of Socialism is chiefly to be ascribed to the increasing poverty of the working classes, the greed of gain and immoderate craving for enjoyment among the rich, and finally, the decrease of religious feeling in all classes of society.

As in the human body disorders for the most part originate in the stomach, so discontent among the people generally arises from material want. The prevailing destitution among the lower orders is partly due to the employment of machinery. Machines can produce, in a few days, more than a hundred workmen can in a month, and goods can be manufactured at a far cheaper rate by machinery than when made by hand. Consequently hundreds are thrown out of employment. Through the introduction of machinery, wealth has accumulated in the hands of the manufacturers, and the number of the poor and discontented has increased, from day to day, swelling the ranks of Socialism. The employers, striving to make larger profits, in many cases do not treat their workpeople according to the maxims of the Gospel; they reduce their wages to a scanty pittance (the market value of labor being so low); they require them to work for a lengthened period; they heed not the bodily health of those they employ, and even destroy their sense of religion and morality. These and other evils naturally have the effect of rendering the workmen irreligious and discontented. Factory hands, employed constantly in working machinery, are apt to lose their mental vigor and independence, they perform their task mechanically, and are easily beguiled and misled. The exhaustion produced by long hours of labor disinclines them to raise their hearts to God, thus they neglect their prayers. The wretched state of their homes, where several families live crowded together on account of poverty caused by the low rate of wages, adds to their moral degradation. Moreover, the sight of the rich man's greed of money on the one hand, and his extravagant expenditure and love of luxury on the other, excites the envy of the poor man, and arouses in him the desire to satisfy his idea of happiness at the cost of the capitalist. Thus God punishes the rich in the way that they have sinned; the Socialist is the scourge wherewith He chastises them. In the present day the Christian faith is more and more undermined by an irreligious press, by godless associations—notably the Freemasons—and in some lands by antichristian legislation; witness the exclusion of religious instruction from the schools. What wonder if the belief in God and a future life grows dim, the divine commandments are unheeded, and the people, craving for happiness in this life, seek to wrest his wealth from their richer neighbor!

3. If the dangers wherewith Socialism threatens us are to be averted, the condition of the laboring classes must be ameliorated; the rich must be liberal towards the poor, and religion must regain her place in the hearts of the people.

Coercive measures will do no more good to the Socialist than random blows will correct a naughty child. If anything is to be done for him, it must be done through kindness. Above all, the em-

ployer must deal with his workpeople according to the principles of
Christianity and justice. Ketteler is right when he says: " If for one
day we all acted in conformity with the teaching of the Gospel, all
social evils would be at once swept away." The employer must pay
his men properly, that is, their wages must be sufficient to support
a Christian family suitably to their station, provided they are thrifty,
industrious, and virtuous. The position of the workman must be
secured; he must not be treated as a chattel, only to be employed as
long as a good profit is to be got out of him. As the workman pays
taxes, he is entitled to the privilege of the franchise. Opportunities
of improving his mind should be afforded to him by the institution of
libraries, evening classes, and the formation of workingmen's clubs,
which the Holy Father strongly advocates. Legislation must also interfere to prevent the undue growth of the proletariate, through the
absorption of lesser industries by the manufactories, and the accumu-
lation of capital in the hands of a few plutocrats. The rich ought, as
the Apostle says, " to give easily and communicate to others " (1 Tim.
vi. 18). Now more than ever the rich are bound to give alms, otherwise they will be rigorously judged. But religion affords the most
effectual means of combating Socialism. Social democracy is too often
nothing but the absence of religious belief. Its chief dogma is the
non-existence of God and of a future life, its chief commandment
the gratification of the senses. Moreover, religion alone can give the
poor the spirit of contentment, so essential to their happiness.

4. Some of the socialistic theories could not possibly be
realized; others might indeed be carried out, but they would
be attended by fatal consequences.

The universal equality which Socialists propose to bring about,
is an utterly impracticable idea, especially in regard to property.
For if the State apportioned to every one the exact amount required
for his livelihood, what more probable than that one would spend it
all, and another put a part by. Thus an inequality would immediately
arise; and to enforce the surrender of a man's savings would be sheer
tyranny. The same endless variety which we see in nature, exists
among mankind. Differences of age, of sex, of health, of physical
power and mental endowments, above all of character and of manners cannot be effaced, and from these, differences of position and of
possessions are inseparable. Just as in an army all the soldiers
cannot be officers nor all privates, so all members of society cannot
stand on the same level. Some must manage the business of the
State, or occupy themselves with military affairs, and they must
naturally hold a higher rank than the other members of the State,
because they work more exclusively for the common weal. The happiness the Socialist dreams of is not attainable upon earth. Whatever the exertions that may be made to ameliorate the lot of man
here below, none can succeed in eliminating from it suffering, sickness, and death. Sorrow and suffering are the portions of mankind;
a life of peace and enjoyment is not for this world. True happiness
is not to be found in sensual pleasures, but in God. While the whole
world lasts, crime, vice and poverty cannot be banished from it. Our
Lord says: " The poor you have always with you " (John xii. 8).

And in regard to the proposed absorption of individual property by the State, this could not be accomplished without serious disturbances, for who would be willing to surrender his property without a struggle? And were community of goods once introduced, tranquillity would not be attained; the oppressed minority would, out of revenge, commit fearful outrages. Besides, laborious and industrious individuals would not be content, as they would gain nothing by their industry; thus the working classes would lose instead of gaining. Socialistic theories could only be realized if men were like the lower animals, destitute of the love of liberty and the desire for improvement. Socialism would cast a blight upon culture and destroy all stimulus, all motive for the exercise of inventive genius. Few would exert themselves to make progress and aim at perfection if they knew their achievements would bring them no reward. In the socialistic republic all would be slaves. No man would exert himself to do better than another, if he knew all was provided for him; there would be a premium upon slothfulness and negligence. Experience has shown the evils brought upon mankind by the example of communities which have had their goods in common, and which have been noted for their crimes and have come to an ignominious end. But although the dreams of the Socialist are mere fantasies of the brain, yet, like much else that is undesirable, they are not without a certain use. As a hurricane tears down what is rotten and crazy, so Socialism points out the weak points in the social structure, and compels our rulers to institute the needful reforms. Attention has been drawn pre-eminently to the exploitation of the laborer by the capitalist, and the claims of the poor have been brought into notice. Yet the harm done by Socialism is far greater than any possible good it may indirectly produce.

2. All who endeavor by unlawful means to deprive their neighbor of his personal property, live in a state of mortal sin.

The mere fact of coveting what belongs to another is a sin. We know that all sins bring others in their train, and this is no exception to the rule. St. Paul says that the inordinate desire of money is the root of all evils (1 Tim. vi. 10), and the utterances of Socialists at their gatherings prove the truth of these words. Their speeches often abound with virulent attacks upon all in authority, on the Pope, on priests, and civil magistrates. Some go so far as to assert that perjury in a court of law is permissible, if it furthers their own interests. We know the crimes of which anarchists have been guilty, dynamite outrages and assassinations. Let it not be said in behalf of their principles that the early Christians had all things in common, for the voluntary sharing of goods is quite different to what the Socialists propose to enforce. The fundamental principle of Christian charity, which urges to almsgiving is this: "Brother, what is mine is thine;" whereas the Socialist says: "Brother, what is thine is mine." Again, the Socialists point to the religious Orders, where all is the property of the community; they say what is possible for them is possible in the State of the future. There is, however, no analogy between the two; for voluntary poverty and obedience form the basis of the religious life, while in the State of the future sensual gratifications are to be encouraged and enjoyed.

XI. THE WORKS OF MERCY.

1. *THE VALUE OF EARTHLY GOODS AND THE USE TO BE MADE OF THEM.*

1. Earthly riches do not of themselves make us better in God's sight.

It is not the possession, but the good use of earthly goods which makes us truly rich. It is in his moral qualities, in virtue and not in his wealth, that man's real dignity and greatness consist. Let not the rich man arrogate anything to himself because of the abundance of the goods he possesses. The grave teaches us the worthlessness of earth's treasures, for we can carry nothing with us out of the world (1 Tim. vi. 7). When Crœsus, the rich king, showed all his treasures to the sage Solon and asked if he did not consider him a happy man, the sage replied: "No man is to be pronounced happy before his death." Crœsus was displeased by this answer, but when, defeated and a prisoner, he stood beside the funeral pyre, he acknowledged the truth of the words. Let us not therefore strive eagerly to acquire riches on earth, but obey the injunction of Our Lord: "Lay not up to yourselves treasures on earth, where the rust and moth consume and where thieves break through and steal" (Matt. vi. 19). How admirable is Solomon's prayer: "Give me neither beggary nor riches; give me only the necessaries of life" (Prov. xxx. 8). St. Paul says: "Having food and wherewith to be covered, with these we are content" (1 Tim. vi. 8). Remember Christ teaches us to ask day by day our daily bread.

2. Earthly goods have their value, however, because with them we can earn eternal felicity.

On the one hand earthly riches contribute to our temporal welfare; they relieve us of many cares and anxieties, may render our life pleasant, and give us a certain ascendancy over our fellow-men. The man of wealth is a small potentate. They are also a means of salvation. This may be inferred from the words Our Lord addross to those on His right hand at the Day of Judgment (Matt. xxv. 34). "Your property was not given you," says St. John Chrysostom, "that you might live in luxury and revelry, but that you may help the poor." Money should therefore be regarded as a means of doing good, for it is only good when turned to good account.

3. God is the Lord of all earthly riches; we are only His stewards.

"The earth is the Lord's, and the fulness thereof" (Ps. xxiii. 1). "The silver is Mine and the gold is Mine, saith the Lord of hosts" (Agg. ii. 9). Thus when we give alms, we distribute what belongs to another, not to ourselves.

4. Earthly riches should consequently only be employed in accordance with the commands of God.

We are not even at liberty to make what use we choose of the senses and members of our body; we must employ them as God ordains. It is exactly the same with our property. And how are we to employ our property according to the will of God? We must employ it to His glory and for the welfare of our fellow-men. As the steward has to give an account to his master, so we shall have to give an account to God; He will reckon with us concerning the use of the talents entrusted to us (Matt. xxv. 14). At our death He will say to us: "Give an account of thy stewardship" (Luke xvi. 2).

2. THE PRECEPT TO PERFORM WORKS OF MERCY.

1. Christ has strictly enjoined upon us to assist our neighbor who is in need with our earthly goods; for He will only grant everlasting happiness to those who have helped their fellow-men who were in need.

At the Last Judgment Our Lord will, as He tells us, set some men on His right hand and others on His left. To those on His right He will say: "Come, ye blessed of My Father, possess you the kingdom prepared for you from the foundation of the world. For I was hungry and you gave Me to eat; I was thirsty and you gave Me to drink; I was a stranger and you took Me in, naked and you covered Me; sick and you visited Me; I was in prison and you came to Me." Then shall the just answer Him, saying: "Lord, when did we see Thee hungry or thirsty or a stranger, and ministered to Thee?" And Our Lord shall answer them: "Amen I say to you, as long as you did to one of these, My least brethren, you did it to Me." And to those on His left hand He shall say: "Depart from Me, you cursed, into everlasting fire! For I was hungry and you gave Me not to eat; I was thirsty, and you gave Me not to drink." Then they also shall answer Him in like manner as the just. And He shall answer them: "As long as you did it not to one of these least, neither did you do it to Me" (Matt. xxv. 31-46). The poor must win heaven by patience, the rich by works of mercy. One gladly parts with the lesser for the sake of keeping the greater; one submits to have a foot or an arm amputated in order to save one's life. So must you give up the lesser, in order not to lose the greater, which is eternal felicity.

1. The rich are chiefly bound to assist the needy.

To whom much is given, of him much shall be required (Luke xii. 48). The rich ought of their abundance to supply the wants of the poor (2 Cor. viii. 14). They ought to sustain the poor, as the elm supports the vine. The elm is a stately tree, but it produces no fruit; the vine is a creeping plant, and unless it clings to something, its branches trail on the ground and its fruit is apt to be spoiled. But if it casts its tendrils round the elm, and clings to its trunk, it will grow up and flourish. The rich man is like the elm; his wealth alone gives him no claim to an eternal reward, but by the help he renders to the poor he will purchase for himself everlasting treasures. But if the rich do not give willingly, they imperil their eternal salvation. Our Lord says: "It is easier for a camel to pass through the eye of a needle, than for a rich man to enter into the kingdom of heaven" (Matt. xix. 24). The rich run risk of shipwreck, like a vessel that is too heavily freighted. They are reluctant to part with their money because they think the enjoyment of the present is real happiness; they mistake the shadow for the reality, and value the false more than the true. In the hour of death they will discover their sad mistake, as a bird resting upon a limed bough only finds that he is a captive when he attempts to fly away. The rich man, when the moment comes for him to pass from time into eternity, will feel how bitter has been his deception, like one who awakens from a delightful dream to find his happiness a delusion (Ps. lxxv. 6). Therefore God has made the way to the attainment of riches a difficult and thorny path, as a farmer plants a quickset hedge round the field that he does not want trodden down.

2. Even the poor man can help his neighbor who is in need.

Tobias says: "If thou hast much, give abundantly; if thou hast little, take care to bestow willingly a little" (Tob. iv. 9). If any one gives a cup of cold water out of charity to his neighbor, provided that is all he can give, it will count for as much as when Zacheus the publican gave the half of his goods to the poor. The poor widow in the Temple gave more with her two mites, than all the rich who cast their gifts into the treasury (Luke xxi.). The widow of Sarephta gave Elias the last remainder of her oil (3 Kings xvii. 12).

3. He who has not helped his neighbor who is in need, will find no mercy with God.

St. James says: "Judgment without mercy to him that hath not done mercy" (Jas. ii. 13). The rich man was buried in hell, because he gave no alms. "He that stoppeth his ear against the cry of the poor shall also cry and not be heard" (Prov. xxi. 13). He who refuses to relieve the necessitous defrauds them of their own. St. John Chrysostom says the rich man who is hard-hearted is no better than a thief, for he stores in his chests treasures that belong to others. He who keeps exclusively to himself the gifts Providence has bestowed on him, creates himself the murderer of those who perish from want. It is not enough to say we have never wronged the poor. By not giving alms we incur the penalty due to those who take from their neighbor that which is his.

2. The assistance we give to the needy, of whatever nature it may be, is an alms, or work of mercy.

These works are called works of mercy, because in performing them we are actuated by feelings of compassion or mercy.

3. The works of mercy are either spiritual or corporal, according as the necessities we relieve are spiritual or corporal.

The corporal wants of our neighbor are: Food, drink, clothing, shelter, liberty, health, or life. What can we do to supply him with these? His spiritual wants, the needs of the soul, are: The knowledge of the truth (for which instruction or counsel is required); a good will, through lack of which he offends God or his fellow-man (which calls for correction, patient endurance or forgiveness); a joyful spirit (in lack of which he needs consolation). If we can do little or nothing to succor and solace our neighbor, we must pray for him, that God may come to his aid.

3. THE SEVERAL WORKS OF MERCY.

1. The corporal works of mercy are: (1), To feed the hungry; (2), To give drink to the thirsty; (3), To clothe the naked; (4), To harbor the stranger; (5), To visit the sick; (6), To ransom the captive; (7), To bury the dead.

(1), To feed the hungry. Abraham entertained the three men; Christ fed five thousand people; St. Elizabeth of Hungary gave all the contents of her granaries to the poor in a time of famine; St. Louis of France provided a dinner daily for a hundred and twenty poor men, and sometimes waited on them himself. (2), To give drink to the thirsty. The Samaritan woman gave Our Lord water to drink at Jacob's well; Rebecca drew water for Eleazar. Wine and medicine come under this category. (3), To clothe the naked. Tabitha at Joppe made garments for destitute widows; St. Martin gave half his cloak to a beggar; Christmas gifts to poor schools are works of mercy. (4), To harbor the stranger. Hospitality is a duty enjoined upon us by St. Paul when he says: " Hospitality do not forget; for by this some, not being aware of it, have entertained angels " (Heb. xiii. 2). Both Abraham and Lot were privileged to receive angels in human form beneath their roof. The Good Samaritan took the man who had been wounded by robbers to an inn. Martha and Mary received Our Lord into their house as their guest. The monks of St. Bernard perform a work of mercy when they rescue travellers who have met with accidents, and carry them to their hospice, where they nurse them until they recover. When travelling was more dangerous than at present, they were the means of saving many lives. (5), To ransom innocent captives. Abraham delivered Lot out of the hands of the robbers; the Christians in Damascus rescued St. Paul out of prison; in the Middle Ages the Order of Ransom was founded for the release of Christians taken prisoner and held in slavery by the Turks. More than a million Christian slaves regained their liberty on the payment of a sum of money, or by others taking their place. Cardinal Lavigerie also established a guild for the liberation of slaves in Africa.

(6), To visit the sick is only to be reckoned as a work of mercy, when the object of the visit is to afford spiritual or temporal relief to the sufferer.

The visit Job's friends paid him was no work of mercy. That of the Samaritan to the wounded Jew was on the other hand, most meritorious. Several religious Orders have been founded for the express object of nursing the sick in hospitals or elsewhere; witness that of the Christian Brothers, founded by St. John of God (1617), and that of the Sisters of Charity, founded about the same time by St. Vincent of Paul. The self-sacrifice of Catholic priests in taking the last sacraments to the dying, especially at the time of an epidemic, is most emphatically a work of mercy. We read of the Emperor Joseph II. that he was asked one day by a poor boy in the street for a florin, that he might get a doctor for his mother. The emperor gave him the money, and asked where he lived. He then went to see the sick woman, who took him for a doctor, and he wrote a prescription for her. Shortly after his departure the doctor whom the boy had called in made his appearance. On opening the paper to look at the supposed prescription, he read these words: " Woman, your visitor was the emperor. Take this paper to the palace, and fifty ducats will be paid you."

(7), To bury the dead. It is a particularly meritorious work of mercy to provide the dead with decent burial, to follow the body to the grave, or to erect a stone to his memory.

Tobias used to bury the dead at the time of the persecution of the Jews under Sennacherib. The inhabitants of the city of Naim accompanied the bier on which the young man was carried to the grave. Joseph of Arimathea and Nicodemus laid the body of Our Lord in the sepulchre. In burying the dead we do him a service which he can never requite. " We ought," says St. Augustine, " to show respect to the bodies of Christian people, because they have been the instrument employed by the soul." In some localities the pernicious custom prevails of making funerals an occasion for feasting and revelry. This is most unseemly, and a waste of money which might be spent for the benefit of the soul of the deceased. Besides it is the means of stifling the grace of God, which exercises a salutary influence on the soul through the solemn ceremonies of an interment.

In addition to the seven corporal works of mercy already enumerated, there are others, e.g., the distribution of money, the rescue of one in danger of death, giving assistance in case of accidents, etc.

King Pharao's daughter performed a work of mercy when she saved the life of the infant Moses; so did Veronica when she gave her veil to wipe Our Lord's countenance. In fact every kind word or act, if spoken or done to our neighbor because we see Our Lord in him, is a meritorious work. Our Lord Himself says that a cup of cold water given in His name shall not go unrewarded (Mark ix. 40).

2. The spiritual works of mercy are: (1), To instruct the ignorant; (2), To counsel the doubtful; (3), To admonish sinners; (4), To bear wrongs patiently; (5), To forgive offences willingly; (6), To comfort the afflicted; (7), To pray for the living and the dead.

One may instruct the ignorant either in religion or other useful knowledge either by word of mouth or by writing good books. The holy apostles, and the evangelizers of the different nations, performed a work of mercy, as in the present day do all the missionaries to heathen lands, besides all preachers, catechists, confessors, Christian writers and teachers. To co-operate with God for the salvation of

souls is the highest of all works. Those who impart religious instruction to others will have a more exalted place, and enjoy a
greater degree of glory in heaven. Daniel says: "They that instruct
many to justice shall shine as stars for all eternity" (Dan. xii. 3).
Those who collect money for foreign missions also perform a work of
mercy. To counsel the doubtful is another of the spiritual works of
mercy; but the counsel given must previously be maturely considered, and not forced upon one's neighbor. Joseph gave good advice
to Pharao; Christ to the rich youth; Gamaliel to the council.

We ought to admonish the sinner, provided we can do so
without prejudice to ourselves, and provided a good result may
be anticipated.

He would indeed be cruel, who seeing a blind man on the brink
of a precipice, did not warn him of his danger; and yet more blameworthy would be he who, having it in his power to save his brother
from everlasting death, will not take the trouble to rescue him.
God will require us to give an account for the soul of our neighbor,
if we omit anything we might have done to further the work of his
salvation. "We call a man's attention," says St. John Chrysostom,
"to a stain upon his clothes, but we do not tell him of stains upon
his soul; which, if not washed away, will be his eternal ruin." Noe
preached penance to the Ninivites. The good thief admonished his
fellow culprit. Admonition is like salt; it makes the wound smart
more, but it heals it. Thus reproof is not agreeable but useful.
If by administering a rebuke we shall bring trouble on ourselves,
we are not obliged to give it; no one is required to love his neighbor
more than himself. (It is however the bounden duty of those who
are in authority to admonish those under them of their faults;
justice, not charity, requires it.) Nor are we called upon to correct
others if no good will come of it. Who would be so unwise as to
rebuke a man who was intoxicated? Rebuke him by all means, but
wait until he is sober.

In admonishing sinners we should observe the rule Christ
gave us.

First we are told to rebuke our brother when we are alone with
him. If he will not hear us, we must rebuke him in the presence of
two or three witnesses. If that is useless, we are to tell his superiors
(Matt. xviii. 15-17).

We must admonish our neighbor with gentleness and
charity.

The greater the gentleness and tact wherewith a reprimand is
administered, the more effect it produces. If our admonition is to be
of use, it must fall on the heart like a gentle rain upon the earth;
for it is the still, quiet rain that sinks into and fertilizes the soil,
whereas a violent, sudden downpour only breaks up the surface of the
ground and rushes away. The bitterness of the reproof should be
tempered with kindness and charity, as sour fruit is sweetened with
sugar and cooked to render it digestible. Before rebuking any one,
it is well to mention something praiseworthy in his conduct, and
afterwards to speak a word of encouragement. If the rebuke is harsh

and severe, it will do no good, only harm. Rough reproaches will
not bring a man to a better mind, any more than kicks will put a
wanderer in the right road. They will only drive him in the opposite
direction. The sinner will not resolve to amend his ways unless he
feels that the admonisher has his welfare sincerely at heart. The
Christian must treat his erring brother as the coachman treats a
timid horse, which is not to be managed by the violent use of the whip,
but by a gentle hand on the rein.

" He who causeth a sinner to be converted from the error of
his ways shall save his soul from death, and cover a multitude
of sins " (Jas. v. 20).

We are told that the Evangelist St. John took the greatest
trouble to save an unhappy youth whom he had converted, and who
afterwards became a highwayman. He went after him to the mountain fastnesses, and called to him: " Why, my son, do you fly from
your father, from a defenceless old man? Fear not; I will myself
implore pardon for you of God, and make satisfaction for you."
These kind words touched the heart of the prodigal. We cannot
offend Christ more deeply than by robbing Him of the souls He has
redeemed; nor can we honor Him more than by bringing back to
Him those which have gone astray. There is nothing upon earth
to compare with the value of a soul. " If thou wert to give vast sums
to the poor," says St. John Chrysostom, " the merit would be nothing
in comparison with that of having converted one sinner." He who
converts a sinner deserves an infinitely greater reward than he who
rescues a king's son from death; for he saves a son of the King of
heaven, and saves him not from temporal, but from eternal death.

When we bear wrongs patiently, we benefit not ourselves
only, but also our fellow-man; we prevent him from going to
greater lengths, and make it easier to bring him to a sense of his
wrongdoing.

David bore Semei's abuse patiently, and after a time he acknowledged his sin and implored the king to pardon him. We lose nothing
if we suffer wrong patiently, for when our innocence is proved, our
forbearance will be richly rewarded. It is also most meritorious, as
St. Teresa says, not to justify one's self when one is blamed. Unhappily too many people are like the hedgehog, which rolls itself into a
prickly ball the moment it is touched, for at the first fault-finding
word they break out into excuses and exculpations. However it is incumbent upon us to protect ourselves from false accusations, when to
bear the injustice in silence would be productive rather of evil than of
good. Slight affronts should not be heeded, but one ought not to
allow a heinous crime to be falsely laid to one's charge.

By forgiving offences willingly is meant that we do not seek
to avenge ourselves on those who offend against us, but treat
them kindly, and are ready to confer upon them any benefit
within our power.

Joseph's conduct towards his brethren affords a beautiful example
of this virtue; instead of revenging himself on them, he embraced

them and kissed them and loaded them with gifts. If we willingly forgive those who trespass against us, God will forgive our transgressions, as we are told in the fifth clause of the Our Father.

We can comfort the afflicted by showing them heartfelt sympathy, by suggesting grounds of consolation, or by succoring them in need.

Evincing sympathy towards those in trouble is called condoling with them. We may suggest comfort to the poor and afflicted by reminding them of the watchful care of God's providence, of the happiness that awaits them in heaven; to the sinner we may speak of the divine mercy and compassion. We shall do still better, if we relieve them in their distress. Thus Our Lord comforted the widow of Naim, and the sisters of Lazarus. Grief is a mental malady: " The sadness of a man consumeth the heart " (Prov. xxv. 20). To console the sorrowing is as much a good work as to nurse the sick. Words of comfort in a time of affliction are as welcome as rain in the time of drought.

To pray for the living and the dead is a work well pleasing in God's sight. It benefits at the same time both them and us. God enjoins upon us especially to pray for our parents and benefactors, for the Pope, and the ruler of our country, for the bishops and clergy, and also finally for our enemies.

St. Paul declares that it is good and acceptable in the sight of God, that prayers be made for all men, for kings particularly, and those that are in high stations (1 Tim. ii. 2, 3). Furthermore we read in Holy Scripture: " It is a holy and a wholesome thought to pray for the dead, that they may be loosed from their sins " (2 Mach. xii. 46). Far from being losers, we are greatly the gainers if we offer prayer to God for others, for we thereby increase our merit, and draw down upon ourselves the blessing of God. Before Judas Machabeus gained the decisive victory over Nicanor, he caused sacrifices to be offered for the warriors who should fall in battle. Prayers offered for others sometimes seem to be fruitless. On one occasion when St. Gertrude complained that no improvement was discernible in the persons for whom she prayed, Our Lord said to her: " No sincere prayers are in vain, although the effect they produce may be imperceptible to the eye of man." Abraham interceded for Sodom, Moses for the people, the Christians for St. Peter when he was in prison. At the Last Supper Our Lord prayed for His disciples and for the whole Church, and on the cross He prayed for His enemies. Let us follow the example He gave us. When we recite the Our Father we pray for all men; we say, " Give us our daily bread, etc."

4. IN WHAT SPIRIT SHOULD THE WORKS OF MERCY BE PERFORMED ?

1. We ought not to do good to our neighbor in order to be seen and praised by men, for in that case we have our reward on earth (Matt. vi. 1).

Nor should we do good to our neighbor in the hope that he will requite our kindness (Luke xiv. 12).

Our Lord says: "When thou dost give alms, let not thy left hand know what thy right doth" (Matt. vi. 3). The saints, as a rule, gave alms secretly. St. Nicholas threw money to the poor out of his window at night; others performed works of mercy under cover of the darkness. The less reward we get on earth for our good works, the greater will be our recompense after death. Hence, as Christ exhorts us, we should do good by preference to those who cannot repay us: the poor, the maimed, the lame, the blind (Luke xiv. 13). Nor must we expect to be thanked. God is repaid with ingratitude and so are the charitable among men. Yet we ought not on this account to desist from doing good, for it is in showing kindness to the unthankful that true charity consists.

2. We must do good to our neighbor for Christ's sake.

Christ lives in His people. This we learn from His own words at the Day of Judgment. Thus we must see God in our neighbor. St. Magdalene of Pazzi placed works of mercy before prayer: "When I engage in mental prayer," she said, "God assists me; but when I do good to my neighbor, I assist God, for He regards what I do to my neighbor as done to Him."

3. We should do good to our neighbor promptly and pleasantly.

We ought not to postpone giving alms until the morrow, if we can do it at once (Prov. iii. 28). What is given promptly has a double value. He that showeth mercy, let him do it with cheerfulness (Rom. xii. 8). God loveth a cheerful giver (2 Cor. ix. 7). We ought not to upbraid the poor (Ecclus. xviii. 18). Those who are harsh to the poor are like a surgeon who in healing one wound makes another. We ought not to question the poor at too great length; we should rather give of our own accord, without waiting to be asked. Nor ought we to hold ourselves aloof from the poor. If almighty God permits us to proffer our petitions to Him at all times, and is always ready to grant them, surely we who are but dust and ashes, ought not to do less for our brethren. The Emperor Rudolph of Hapsburg used to say: "Every one can have access to my presence. I was not chosen emperor that I might live in seclusion."

4. We are only required to give alms of our superfluity.

In no wise are we bound to deprive ourselves of what is necessary for our subsistence or to keep up our position. Our Lord says: "Yet of that which remaineth give alms" (Luke xi. 41). Theologians are of opinion that it is sufficient to give a small percentage of one's yearly savings.

5. We must only give alms out of what is our own, and only give to those who are really poor or who are unable to work.

Some people think they will give alms at another's expense; they take from one what they give to another. Such almsgiving, which is an act of injustice, is abhorrent to God. Therefore let a man who is in debt pay his creditors, instead of giving alms to the poor. Justice comes before generosity. " How manifestly unjust it would be to take the coat off one man's back to give it to another; it is no less unjust to give in alms money which thou owest to another" (St. John Chrysostom). As well might a thief, when brought to trial, offer the judge a part of the stolen property; he would only insure his conviction. "And canst thou hope to gain the favor of God by giving alms of what is not thy own?" (St. Augustine.) To give to those who are known to be idle and addicted to drink, is to encourage them in sin; but it is better to err on the side of charity than of severity. When the Master of the house is so liberal, it ill becomes His steward to be niggardly. As all shipwrecked sailors without distinction are received in a port, so we should not sit in judgment upon those who have fallen into poverty, but hasten to help them in their misfortune.

6. In giving alms, preference should be shown to our relatives, our fellow Catholics, and those who are in the greatest need.

St. Paul exhorts us: "Let us do good to all men, but especially to those who are of the household of the faith" (Gal. vi. 10). For what we give to the poor we give to God, as we know from Christ's own words. The money bestowed in alms is lent to the Lord and He will repay it with high interest.

5. OF WHAT BENEFIT ARE THE WORKS OF MERCY TO US?

1. Almsgiving obtains for us the remission of our sins; that is to say the sinner obtains the grace of repentance, while the just man receives the pardon of venial sin, and the remission of the temporal penalty.

) Our Lord therefore says: "Blessed are the merciful, for they shall obtain mercy" (Matt. v. 7). "Water quencheth a flaming fire and alms resisteth sins" (Ecclus. iii. 33). St. Ambrose exhorts the sinner to employ his money to ransom his soul. Daniel gives similar counsel to King Nabuchodonosor (Dan. iv. 24). By almsgiving the sinner obtains actual graces, which gradually bring about his conversion, or sometimes he obtains extraordinary graces. Cornelius, a heathen centurion at Cæsarea, was the recipient of great graces as the reward of his prayers and alms; an angel was sent to him, and he was converted by the preaching of St. Peter. "A merciful man doeth good to his own soul" (Prov. xi. 17); almsgiving is a means whereby we may escape eternal perdition. The archangel Raphael expressly told Tobias: "Alms deliver from all sin, and from death, and will not suffer the soul to go into darkness" (Tob. iv. 11). "He who has made the poor man happy," says St. John Chrysostom, "will not himself suffer misery." God will not allow a man who has shown mercy to be lost; He will grant him the graces necessary for his conversion. St. Jerome declares that he has never known one who in his lifetime was liberal to the poor, to make a bad end; for the charitable have many to intercede for them. The just man obtains the remission of what is due to his sins by almsgiving; for St. Thomas Aquinas says the satisfaction made by alms is greater than that which is effected by prayer and fasting.

2. By almsgiving we obtain an eternal recompense, provided that at the time we are in a state of grace.

It is related of the German Emperor Louis II. that he lost his way in a forest when hunting one day. Late at night he reached a village presbytery, and begged the priest to give him a night's lodging. The priest entertained the stranger most hospitably; the next day the latter took leave, after thanking his host. Some weeks later a messenger presented himself at the priest's humble dwelling, and handed him a letter stamped with the imperial seal; it announced his nomination to the see of Münster. In like manner your heavenly King will reward your alms hereafter in a manner which you little anticipate. Alms are like seed cast into the ground; they are not lost, but yield an abundant harvest. The ant lays up a store for the winter; by giving alms we lay up treasures for the life to come. Thus we exchange what is temporal for what is eternal; we purchase everlasting possessions with our earthly pelf. Success in trade consists in buying cheap and selling dear; we too are engaged in commerce, and for a mere trifle, a piece of bread, even a cup of cold water, we purchase for ourselves heaven. When the new continent was discovered, the aborigines exchanged silver and gold for things of no value to the Europeans who landed on their shores. So we obtain the good things of God in return for the worthless goods of earth. "Give, then, to the poor that which thou canst not keep, in order to obtain that which thou canst not lose" (St. Augustine). Even in this life almsgiving produces a feeling of happiness. A youth was one day walking through a wood with his tutor, when he saw a pair of boots which a woodcutter at work at a little distance had taken off. The boy wanted to hide them, but his tutor suggested that rather than do that, he should put a piece of money in each. When the poor man went back to get his boots, he found the coins, and falling on his knees, thanked God and invoked blessings on the unknown benefactor who had helped him in dire distress. The money was the exact sum he needed to pay his rent. The boy, who had watched what occurred, turned to his tutor and exclaimed: "I never felt so happy in all my life." Truly a blessing attends works of mercy.

3. Almsgiving brings down upon us temporal blessings: God increases our means and gives us bodily health.

"He that is inclined to mercy, shall be blessed" (Prov. xxii. 9). "The blessing of the Lord maketh men rich" (Prov. x. 22). God declares that he that giveth to the poor shall not want (Prov. xxviii. 27). Our Lord says: "Give, and it shall be given to you" (Luke vi. 38). The widow of Sarephta gave generously to Elias. For this she got back far more than she gave to the prophet, for her little store of meal and of oil was not diminished until the time of scarcity was over (3 Kings xvii. 14). A nobleman of Granada, who had bestowed a large alms on St. John of God, went to him the same day disguised as a mendicant, and asked for money. The saint gave him all that he had received from him a few hours before. Thereupon the nobleman restored ten times the amount, and was his greatest benefactor during the rest of his life. God acts in a similar way; if we give to the poor even a portion of what He has bestowed on us, we shall receive it again with interest. A tree grows all the better for being pruned; so the rich will increase in goods if they part with some of their wealth, in acts of charity. St. Paula gave a great deal to the poor, though she was the mother of five children; when her relatives remonstrated with her, she said: "The best inheritance I can bequeath to my children is the blessing of heaven, which almsgiving draws down on us." God gives bodily health to those who are bountiful to the poor. The archangel Raphael was sent to heal Tobias because he had performed so many works of mercy (Tob. xii. 14). Tabitha was raised from the dead by St. Peter because of the good works and almsdeeds which she did (Acts ix. 36, *seq.*). David exclaims: "Blessed is he that understandeth concerning the needy and the poor; the Lord will deliver him in the evil day" (Ps. xl. 1). Throughout the Scriptures we constantly find instances of blessings being the reward of almsgiving.

4. Almsgiving is a means of obtaining a speedy answer to prayer.

The angel said to Cornelius: "Thy prayers and thy alms are ascended for a memorial in the sight of God" (Acts x. 4). Listen to the voice of the poor, if you would have God listen to your voice. By nothing do we gain access to God so readily as by showing mercy. Alms, like fasting, is one of the wings on which prayer soars to heaven.

5. By almsgiving we make the poor our friends; they pray for us, and their prayers have great power with God.

The ancients of the Jews besought Our Lord on behalf of the centurion at Capharnaum who had built them a synagogue; and immediately He complied with their request (Luke vii. 3-5). The poor of Joppe prayed for Tabitha; she was restored to life (Acts ix. 39). God Himself declares that the prayer of the poor is always heard (Ps. xxi. 25; lxviii. 34). The petitions of those who are in heaven are, however, more effectual. Thus Our Lord bids us: "Make unto you friends of the mammon of iniquity, that when you shall fail, they may receive you into everlasting dwellings" (Luke xvi. 9). Therefore never refuse an alms to the poor.

XII. THE DUTY OF GRATITUDE.

Our Lord says: "It is better to give than to receive." And why? Because the one who receives is bound to give thanks, whereas the giver has a right to a reward.

1. For every act of mercy done to us, we are bound to render thanks first to God and then to our benefactor; for God requires of us that we should be grateful for the benefits we receive.

It is our duty to be grateful; i.e., to show our sense of the benefit conferred upon us, and to endeavor to repay our benefactor. Gratitude is due to almighty God in the first place, because from Him comes down every best gift and every perfect gift (Jas. i. 17). Men are His servants, the instruments He employs; therefore we owe thanks to them in the second place. Whenever Our Lord received a favor from His heavenly Father He raised His eyes to heaven, and said: "Father, I thank Thee." This He did at the raising of Lazarus (John xi. 41). He never rose from table without giving thanks; after the Last Supper a hymn was said. All the saints did the same. David exclaims: "What shall I render to the Lord for all the things that He hath rendered unto me?" (Ps. cxv. 3.) The first words Tobias uttered when he was cured of his blindness were these: "I bless Thee, O Lord God of Israel, because Thou hast chastised me and Thou hast saved me" (Tob. xi. 17). Noe's first act when he came out of the ark was to build an altar to the Lord and offer sacrifice ·(Gen. viii.). Columbus, when he beheld the continent of America, gave thanks to God; and in gratitude to Him he gave the name of _San Salvador_ to the first island on which he set foot, and erected a cross on its shores. Accustom yourself to repeat the words _Deo gratias_ or the _Gloria Patri_ whenever any benefit is conferred on you. It is also incumbent on y· to return thanks to your human benefactors as well as to God. ᴗavid wished to take with him to Jerusalem and entertain at his court the wealthy old man who provided him with sustenance in the camp during the period of Absalom's rebellion. And on Berzellai declining the honor, on account of his advanced age, the king took h·s sons with him instead, and showed them every kindness; and on his death-bed he bade Solomon to be mindful of his obligations to their father, and let them eat at his table (3 Kings ii. 7). Tobias wished St. Raphael to accept half of all the things they had brought back from their journey (Tob. xii. 5). Even brute beasts show gratitude: witness the well-known story of Androcles and the lion. It is the will of God that we should in all things give thanks (1 Thess. v. 18). Our Lord was much displeased with the nine lepers because they did not turn back to thank him (Luke xvii. 17). Almighty God frequently complains by the mouth of the prophets of the ingratitude of mankind: "The ox knoweth his owner, and the ass his master's crib; but Israel hath not known Me" (Is. i. 3). St. Paul repeatedly exhorts the Christians to give thanks (Eph. v. 20; Col. iii. 15).

2. By our gratitude we obtain fresh favors, whereas ingratitude brings misfortunes upon us.

The husbandman scatters fresh seed in the fertile soil, knowing that it will yield an abundant harvest. God acts in a similar manner: nothing pleases Him more than thankfulness for His benefits. Gratitude for past favors prepares us for favors to come. God notices and takes especial care of those who acknowledge and appreciate His gifts (Ps. xlix. 23). Ingratitude, on the other hand, dams up the stream of divine grace; he deserves no fresh favors who is not at the pains to return thanks for those he has received already. Ingratitude is a hindrance to salvation; St. Bernard expresses the opinion that nothing is so displeasing to God as unthankfulness, especially on the part of His own favored children. He that rendereth evil for good, evil shall not depart from his house (Prov. xvii.

13). Judas had received the greatest kindness from Our Lord, yet he betrayed Him, and how terrible was his end ! The grateful soul is a friend of God; whereas the devil takes possession of the thankless.

Ingratitude is a mark of ill-breeding and a bad disposition.

It is vain to look for gratitude from the world; its votaries take as their right the benefits conferred on them; they repay them with ingratitude, nay, more, they return evil for good. How thankless was Achitophel, who after sitting at King David's table, and basking in the royal favor, joined in Absalom's revolt! Of this David complained bitterly (Ps. liv. 13 *seq.*). Those who are ungrateful to their fellow-men are yet more so towards God. "He who loveth not his brother whom he seeth, how can he love God Whom he seeth not?" (1 John iv. 20.) However trifling the gift may be, show yourself thankful for it.

XIII. THE POVERTY OF THE CHRISTIAN.

God does not distribute talents to all alike; to one He gives five, to another two, to a third only one (Matt. xxv). It is in wisdom that He thus acts; for if the same were given to all, every one could stand alone, and there would be no need of mutual good offices. What opportunity would there be for the exercise of brotherly love, what occasions of merit?

1. Poverty is no disgrace in God's sight; to be poor in virtue and in good works is the only thing of which one need be ashamed, for it leads to eternal damnation.

In the eyes of eternal Truth poverty is not the slightest shame (Lev. xiii.). Our Lord Himself being rich, became poor (2 Cor. viii. 9). He Who was the King of heaven and of earth passed His life in constant privations; He had not where to lay His head (Luke ix. 58). What could exceed the poverty of His birthplace! A man may be poor in this world's goods and exceedingly rich before God; and on the other hand, a man may be rich in earthly possessions and utterly destitute before God (Luke xii. 21). "The fear of God is the glory of the rich" (Ecclus. x. 25). Virtues, not earthly treasures, constitute true riches. "He," says St. Augustine, "is not rich who possesses chests full of silver and gold, but he in whom God dwells, who is the temple of the Holy Ghost."

2. The poor save their souls more easily than the rich.

Our Lord declares that it is easier for a camel to pass through the eye of a needle, than for a rich man to enter into the kingdom of heaven (Matt. xix. 24). Wealth affords its possessor the means of gratifying every inordinate desire. It is otherwise with the poor; they have not this occasion of sin. Just as a traveller goes on his way more easily if he is not encumbered with baggage, so the poor man is less impeded on his journey to the goal whither he is bound. The pugilist overthrows his opponent with greater facility when he is stripped to the waist; so the poor man is better prepared to resist the temptations of the devil. Consequently many of the poor will have a higher place in the kingdom of heaven than their richer brethren. Christ says: "Many that are first shall be last, and the last first" (Mark x. 31). Lazarus after his death was carried to Abraham's bosom, while Dives was buried in hell.

3. God often sends poverty upon a man for his salvation.

Many, if they were rich, would misuse their wealth, lead a vicious life, and be eternally lost. This God foresees, and therefore He takes their earthly possessions from them. "Poverty and riches are from God" (Ecclus. xi. 14). St. Antoninus, Archbishop of Florence, saw angels descending and ascending around a certain house; on hearing that the inmates were a poor widow with three daughters, he made them a liberal allowance. Later on he saw evil spirits coming and going about that same house; he made inquiries and learned that the people he had assisted now led an idle and dissolute life. Thereupon he immediately withdrew his gift. God deals in like manner with us. What does the schoolmaster do if he sees one of his scholars playing with a toy instead of learning his lesson? Or a father, if he sees a knife in the hand of a very young child?

4. The poor are beloved by God.

Those who are unhappy and forsaken in this world are especially dear to God. Christ calls the poor blessed (Matt. v. 3). He invites all that labor and are burdened to come to Him, that He may refresh them (Matt. xi. 28); the oppressed and persecuted are the objects of His peculiar favor (Matt. v. 10). These truths ought to serve as an encouragement to the poor, and repress the pride of the opulent and powerful. To the poor first of all the Gospel is preached (Matt. xi. 5). The offerings of the poor are more acceptable to God than those of the rich. Our Lord said the widow's mite was of greater value than all the gifts that the rich cast into the treasury (Mark xii. 41-43). God promises to hear the cry of the oppressed (Jas. v. 4). The poor shepherds were privileged to see the Infant Christ, not the rich Pharisees and Scribes. There is no respect of persons with God (Rom. ii. 11). Poor and rich are alike His children (Prov. xxii. 2).

5. The poor man who leads an upright life will never be forsaken by God; nay, more, he will enjoy happiness and contentment in this world.

God Who feeds the birds of the air, and clothes the lilies and grass of the field, will also provide for man, who is of so much more value than they (Matt. v. 25-30). God does not allow the just to want the necessaries of life. Our Lord says: "Seek ye first the kingdom of God and His justice, [i.e., be solicitous for your salvation and keep the commandments] and all these things [i.e., the wherewithal to live] shall be added unto you" (Matt. vi. 33). David says: "I have been young, and now am old, and I have not seen the just forsaken, nor his seed seeking bread" (Ps. xxxvi. 25). When we read that by God's permission, just men, such as Job, Tobias, Joseph, fell into destitution and distress, we also read that in God's good time they were restored to ease and plenty. Virtue is generally attended by temporal blessings here below (Ps. cxi. 2-3). A poor man may be very happy despite his poverty. Happiness by no means consists in the abundance of things that one possesses (Luke xii. 15), but in interior peace and content, and these the just man enjoys, whether he be rich or poor. St. Paul speaks of himself as having nothing, and yet possessing all things (2 Cor. vi. 10).

6. The poor are not warranted in wresting from the rich the alms which they have a right to expect; they should rather bear their lot patiently and rely on help from God.

The duty of giving alms is not required by *justice*, except in cases of dire necessity. It is a duty of Christian *charity*, consequently no man can lawfully be compelled to give. The Fathers of the Church constantly exhorted the rich to give alms. "Thou art master of thy property, and canst give or not give at thy will," St. Jerome said to the rich: "Distribute a portion of thy wealth. But if thou refusest, I cannot force thee. I can only entreat." The poor can however demand that their labor be sufficiently remunerated. Doubly indeed is that poor man to be commiserated who forsakes God and transgresses His law; for in that case he has nothing in this life, and after death everlasting perdition awaits him.

B. GOOD WORKS, VIRTUE, SIN, VICE.

Hitherto the will of God (the commandments) has been the subject treated of. In the following pages we shall speak of the fulfilment of the divine will and the transgression thereof. Good works are the result of the accomplishment of the divine will; sin is the result of the violation of it. By the repeated performance of good works the habit of virtue is formed; by repeated acts of sin, the habit of vice.

I. GOOD WORKS.

1. The name of good works is given to such voluntary actions on the part of man as are in conformity with the will of God, are performed for the love of God, and consequently will be rewarded by God.

No action, however excellent, is to be called a good work unless it is voluntary. The compulsory fast of a criminal in prison is not a good work; nor in fact is any action which is not in accordance with the will of God. To spend one's time in reciting long prayers, instead of accomplishing the duties of one's station, is not a good work, but a sin. Nor do works which fail in any one particular to correspond to the will of God deserve to be called good works, or to receive a reward. Those actions again, which are not performed for the love of God are not good works. God requires a pure motive on our part. For instance, to give an alms to an importunate beggar merely to get rid of him is not wrong, but it is not a perfect good work. It is an imperfect or natural good work, because it is done from natural motives. But an action performed for God's sake, because it is the will of God, for love of Christ, in view of an eternal reward or for fear of everlasting punishment, is a perfect, or supernatural good work, and will bear fruit, because it is done in union with Christ (as the branch bears fruit that abides in the vine, John xv. 4), and participates in His merits. A plain woollen cloth has a certain worth, but if it be dyed a rich purple color, its value is greatly enhanced. So the good works we perform are of little worth unless they are done for God's sake. Then they are crimsoned with

434

the blood of Christ, precious in God's sight, and deserving of a celestial recompense.

Actions, although good, if performed for merely natural motives, are worthless in God's sight.

The Pharisees in Christ's time are a striking instance of this, for they did good works to be seen of men and praised by men. Our Lord blames them for this, and says: "They have received their reward" (Matt. vi. 2). If a man subscribes to some charitable object, in order to get his name into the papers, or to get some office of trust, he does not perform a good work, or one deserving of reward. Such works are like a great, empty package which, when put into the balance at the Judgment Day, will have no weight at all. " Man seeth those things that appear, but the Lord beholdeth the heart" (1 Kings xvi. 7). It is the intention to which one must look, not the external act; this may appear to be good, but if it is not done in some way in view of our final end, it is worse than useless. He who seeks his own glory in what he does is a thief, for he robs God of what is His due. Some people say we ought to do good for its own sake. They are mistaken, for the act itself is not our highest aim, but a means towards the attainment of that end. We ought to do good for God's sake.

A good work has all the more value in God's sight, the less it is done in hope of earthly reward.

He who does good to the poor who cannot requite him, does a work which is great in God's eyes, however contemptible it may be in the eyes of the world, because it is done for God. Good works which cost us a great sacrifice are more valuable than others. For this reason Abraham's obedience in promptly offering his only son at God's command was so highly praised. Therefore what we do in spite of outward contradiction or inward opposition has more worth before God. Thus the value of our works depends entirely upon whether they are or are not done for the love of God. He does not consider the magnitude of the work, but the amount of love wherewith it is performed.

2. The good works most pleasing in God's sight are these: Prayer, fasting, and almsdeeds.

By these works the centurion Cornelius merited the praise of the angel (Acts x.), and Tobias the approval of Raphael (Tob. xii. 8). In the sermon on the mount Our Lord lays special stress on these works (Matt. vi.). Prayer includes every kind of divine worship, the reception of the sacraments, hearing Mass, attending sermons, etc. Fasting is not merely abstaining from food, or some sort of food, but the repression of sensual desires in general, e.g., restraining curiosity, the avoidance of idle conversation, denying one's self some pleasure. As alms may be reckoned every service rendered to one's neighbor, pre-eminently the spiritual and corporal works of mercy.

Prayer, fasting, and almsgiving are the principal means of

attaining perfection, because they combat the three evil appetites, the concupiscence of the flesh, the concupiscence of the eyes, and the pride of life; and thus the soul is enabled to rise more freely to God.

By prayer the pride of life is suppressed, by fasting the craving for sensual enjoyment, by almsgiving the desire for earthly riches. Thus by prayer, fasting, and almsdeeds, more than by anything else, we shake off the bonds of earth and consequently draw nearer to God.

3. Even the most trifling works are pleasing to God if they are done with the intention of promoting His glory.

St. Paul exhorts us: " Whether you eat or drink, or whatsoever else you do, do all to the glory of God" (1 Cor. x. 31). This includes work, recreation, sleep, etc. Midas, King of Phrygia, is said to have asked of the gods that whatsoever he touched might be turned to gold. This power is granted to the Christian; for by purity of intention all his good works do in reality become golden, i.e., supernatural, and consequently highly valuable and meritorious. The intention determines the worth of every action. Witness the kiss Judas gave Our Lord; a kiss is a token of love and friendship, but his evil intention made it a vile action. The intention is to the action what the root is to the tree. If the root is healthy the tree flourishes and its fruit is good; but if the root is unsound, the sap does not circulate or the fruit mature. The decorations of the streets when a monarch makes his entry into a city, are a matter of no moment to him, except in so far as they display the affection and loyal devotion of his subjects. So it is with the actions we perform for the glory of God. Be careful therefore to direct your intention every morning, and renew it occasionally throughout the day. An action without a good intention is like a body in which the life is extinct.

4. Good works are necessary to salvation.

Our Lord says: " Every tree that doth not yield good fruit shall be cut down and cast into the fire" (Matt. iii. 10). At the Last Judgment He will require good works of us. Remember the parable of the barren fig-tree (Luke xiii. 6); of the ten virgins (Matt. xxv.), and of the talents (v. 16). God is not satisfied with mere integrity of life (which consists in not being guilty of murder, or theft, or cheating, or evil practices of any kind). At the Last Judgment many will be sentenced to everlasting misery, not because they have done what is evil, but because they have not done what is good. St. John Chrysostom says that to do no good is tantamount to doing evil. Heaven is the recompense of labor; he that has done no work can claim no guerdon. If you had a servant who did not indeed steal your goods, but who neglected his work, would you not dismiss him? Look to it, therefore, that you appear not before God with empty hands. Every man has three friends: (1), Money, which is taken from him by death; (2), Relatives, who part from him at the grave; (3), Good works, which alone follow him to the judgment seat of God (Apoc. xiv. 13). By good works we may make sure our calling and election (2 Pet. i. 10). Good works are like bulwarks which protect the city from hostile incursions. On account of our good works God grants us the grace of perseverance, or, if we fall into grievous sin, actual graces to bring us to repentance (2 Par. xix. 3). The prophet Nathan was sent to David after he fell into sin; Our Lord looked with compassion on St. Peter after his fall.

5. Through good works the sinner obtains the actual graces which are necessary for his conversion; the just man obtains an increase of sanctifying grace, eternal felicity, and the remission of the temporal penalty of sin; furthermore his prayers are heard, and sometimes earthly blessings are bestowed on him.

The good works performed by the sinner contribute to his conversion. When our hemisphere is turned towards the sun, we experience light and warmth. So it is with the sinner; when by good works he turns from creatures to the Creator his mind is enlightened, his heart is softened, and he enters upon a new life. The prayer of the sinner, although without merit, earns the grace of pardon; it has power with God, not on account of the merit of the petitioner, but on account of the divine promise: " Every one who asketh receiveth." The good works of the sinner will not in themselves be rewarded hereafter, but are only conducive to his conversion. By his good works the just man obtains an increase of sanctifying grace and eternal felicity. Our Lord says: "Every branch in Me that beareth fruit, My Father will purge it, that it may bring forth more fruit" (John xv. 2). " To every one that hath shall be given, and he shall abound" (Luke xix. 26). By these words Christ signifies that the sanctifying grace which he already possesses will be increased. He also receives new actual graces. Christ promises as the reward of good works a hundredfold and life eternal. As the good works of the just are rewarded hereafter they are called *living* works. The more good works he has done in time, the greater will be his felicity to all eternity. Our Lord says: " The Son of man shall come in the glory of His Father with His angels, and then will be rendered to every man according to his works" (Matt. xvi. 27). St. Paul declares: " He that soweth sparingly shall reap also sparingly " (2 Cor. ix. 6). The Council of Florence asserts that all the redeemed in heaven enjoy the beatific vision of the triune God, but in a different degree of perfection, according as their merits are greater or less. Good works cancel the penalty due to sin, because on account of original sin it is difficult to man to perform them, and the devil seeks to deter him from them. The monks of a certain convent, having risen early to pray, beheld to their astonishment a number of demons approaching, who said to them: " If you will but betake yourselves to your beds again, we will immediately go away." Inasmuch as good works are onerous to perform, they make satisfaction for sin, and appease the retributive justice of God; inasmuch as they conduce to the honor of God and the welfare of our fellow-men, they are meritorious, and serve to glorify the remunerative justice of God. They also exalt the loving kindness of God, for they procure for us a gracious answer to our petitions. The temporal reward of good deeds consists generally in the increase of riches, the improvement of health, the prolongation of life, the esteem of men, and above all interior peace and joy, etc.

He who commits a mortal sin, loses the merit of the good works he has done in the past.

"If the just man turn himself away from his justice, and do iniquity, all his justices that he hath done shall not be remembered" (Ezech. xviii. 24). But when the sin has been washed away in the Sacrament of Penance, the good works of the past are revivified, as the leaves come out again in the spring sunshine. It is not so with sins; once forgiven, they are effaced completely. How great is the mercy of our God!

6. We can apply to others, either to the living or to the dead, the merit of our good works.

Thus we can offer the holy sacrifice of the Mass, communion, fasts or almsdeeds for others. In this manner the good work, inasmuch as it be satisfactory or propitiatory, benefits another; the merit of it, however, remains with the doer. Nor is it wholly lost to us as a satisfaction for sin, for in applying it to another we perform a work of mercy, and works of mercy procure for us remission of sin and entitle us to an eternal reward. Hence we see that in applying good works to others they are of twofold value.

7. We ought to let our good works be seen of men, in order to set them a good example.

In the life of St. Pachomius we see how powerful is the effect of good example. When a soldier, he was quartered in a Christian family. Here he was treated with the greatest kindness, and the behavior of all the members of the household was so exemplary, that he was vastly impressed by it, and was led to inquire into and finally embrace the Christian religion. Pachomius was an active promoter of monasticism in Egypt. Our Lord admonishes us to let our light shine before men, so that they may see our good works, and glorify Our Father Who is in heaven (Matt. v. 16). It is His will that our influence should make itself felt by those around us; that by our light we should illumine the darkness, and become teachers and guides to our brethren. The Christian should not only be a burning but also a shining light, that he may be of use to others. At the same time all works of an extraordinary nature should be hidden, such as praying with one's arms outspread, rigorous fasting, etc. All singularity is to be avoided, it is a fault whereby piety is made ridiculous and contemptible. But those works which are binding on all, such as the reception of the sacraments, should not be done in secret. If Christ denounced those who give scandal, what a rich blessing must be in store for those who by their edifying and virtuous life lead others into the right way!

8. We ought to make diligent use of our earthly riches, as well as of our life here below, for the performance of good works.

We ought to make friends by means of our wealth, that after our death they may receive us into everlasting dwellings (Luke xvi. 9). On how short a span of this transitory life our whole eternity depends! (St. Jerome.) " We ought to work while it is day; the night cometh when no man can work " (John ix. 4). The period of man's existence upon earth is his seed-time. The lost in hell would give up all the treasures of the world, for one short moment to spend as they please in which to reconcile themselves with God. How foolish are those who pursue sensual pleasures instead of doing good works ! They are like men who, in a gold mine, pick up stones and earth instead of the precious metal. You are sorry if perchance you have spent a small sum of money unwisely, but you consider it no matter for regret to have wasted a whole day in the service of the devil. The hour will come when we shall become alive to the inestimable value of time, but alas, it will come too late!

II. VIRTUE.

1. Virtue consists in proficiency in the practice of good works and the tendency of the will towards what is good, resulting from persevering exercise.

By good deeds is meant whatever is done in obedience to the will of God, or is pleasing in His sight. By practice in writing, painting, athletic and other sports, etc., proficiency and dexterity is attained, and the will becomes disposed towards the action in question. Practice makes perfect. Habit is second nature. It is difficult to break off any habit to which we have accustomed ourselves. One or two isolated good deeds do not constitute virtue, any more than two or three vines constitute a vineyard.

Certain good qualities or propensities, the gift either of nature or of grace, are often called by the name of virtue.

There are natural, inborn good qualities, dispositions or virtues. Many men are naturally meek, obedient, liberal or honorable. Hence it is that some of the heathen were distinguished for their virtues. There are also supernatural dispositions, which are imparted by the Holy Spirit when we receive sanctifying grace, that is, the Sacrament of Baptism or of Penance. The Holy Spirit renders us capable of accomplishing what is good for the love of God. This supernatural capability is something more than a mere qualification for the performance of what is good; a certain inclination thereto is also given us. But this disposition or inclination is not the same as proficiency or ease in the exercise of virtue; the latter must be won by practice. The capabilities imparted by the Holy Ghost stand in the same relation to actual virtue as the seed does to the plant, or the gift of one of the senses, e.g., the sense of sight, to the use of that sense. The good dispositions imparted by the Holy Spirit are also called *infused* virtue, and the proficiency attained through practice is called *acquired* virtue. The powers imparted by the Holy Spirit do not at once cause us to act aright; it is requisite for us to employ them frequently in order to gain proficiency in virtue.

2. It is only perfect virtue, i.e., those acts of virtue which are performed for the glory of God, which will be rewarded after death.

God does not merely require of us good deeds, but a good intention in accomplishing those deeds. Only when done with good intention, with a view to His glory, are they pleasing to Him, and entitled to a reward. Without the love of God there is no true virtue. The actions we perform for the love of God are acts of perfect, supernatural, Christian virtue. There are, as we have seen, natural virtues, which are inspired by earthly motives and are not done with a view to the glory of God. These only receive a temporal recompense (Matt. vi. 2), and have no value for the kingdom of heaven (Matt. v. 20). The difference between natural and supernatural virtues may be compared to the difference which exists between objects which are merely gilt, and those that are fashioned out of solid gold.

3. **Virtue can only be acquired and increased by dint of struggle and self-conquest; for many obstacles have to be encountered, inward hindrances, the evil proclivities of the human heart, and outward hindrances, the contempt and persecution of men.**

Nothing else is wanted to cause a boat which is launched on a fast-flowing river, to be carried away by the stream and swallowed up in the waters, than that the rowers should cease to ply their oars; but if the boat is going against the current, strenuous exertion on the part of the crew is required to bring it to its destination. So it is with man; he needs but to give way to the frailty of his corrupt nature to be borne to eternal perdition; but to contend against the force of his passions, the seductions of the world, and the temptations of the devil, and guide his bark to the haven of everlasting felicity, calls for no slight effort on his part. "The kingdom of heaven suffereth violence" (Matt. xi. 12). The path of virtue is a difficult ascent, not an easy descent. Virtue is won not in times of peace, but of warfare. Many appear to be virtuous, but are not so in reality, because their virtue costs them nothing. Those who desire to attain proficiency in an art, or dexterity in a trade, must give themselves much trouble in learning it. Only in proportion as you do violence to yourself will you make progress in virtue. The most formidable obstacles have to be overcome at first, afterwards advancement becomes more easy. And as we advance in virtue, it brings happiness, and thus we are stimulated to greater efforts. But suffering is inseparable from virtue; wherefore he who shrinks from sufferings and persecution will never be rich in virtue. "He who fears the world," says St. Ignatius, "will never accomplish anything worthy of God's acceptance; for nothing great can be done in God's service without provoking the enmity of the world." He who strives in earnest to attain to virtue, will necessarily be humble, for he will feel his own frailty, as one who climbs a steep ascent becomes conscious of his bodily weakness. Consequently the most virtuous are the most humble.

4. **Virtue procures for us real happiness both in time and in eternity.**

The Greeks related of Heracles, one of their heroes, that at a spot where two roads met he found two maidens awaiting him, Pleasure and Virtue. The former spoke flattering words to him and promised him a life of enjoyment. The latter gravely warned him that many sorrows awaited him, but they would be followed by an everlasting reward. Heracles wisely followed where this one guided him. Sin, although it leads to perdition, is unquestionably most alluring; virtue is difficult and laborious, but it is attended with blessings. The fear of the Lord, the practice of virtue, is the way to attain true happiness even on earth (Ps. cxxvii. 1). "Much peace have they that love Thy law" (Ps. cxviii. 165). Above all, the virtuous man will have joy at his latter end (Ecclus. vi. 29). How joyfully St. Paul spoke of his approaching dissolution (2 Tim. iv. 7). Nothing can really harm one who loves God; all things, however adverse they appear, work together unto good (Rom. viii. 28). Many temporal blessings are bestowed on him (Ps. cxxvii. 4); he is compared by the Psalmist to a tree planted by running waters. A virtuous life contributes to one's physical well-being; the practice of virtue, moreover, enlightens the understanding, and gives intelligence of the teaching of Christ. He Himself says: "If any man will do the will of God, he shall know of the doctrine whether it be of God" (John vii. 17). The practice of virtue entitles us to eternal salvation (Ps. xxxvi. 29). Godliness has promise of the life that now is and of that which is to come (1 Tim. iv. 8). Virtue makes us rich and honorable in God's sight. She is to be preferred before kingdoms and thrones, and riches are nothing in comparison with her (Wisd. vii. 8). It is a treasure which cannot decay or be stolen from us (Matt. vi. 20). Noble ancestry, high position, does not make us renowned before God; virtue alone procures for us immortal honors, eternal riches, never-ending felicity.

5. Virtue makes us resemble God, and admits us to the friendship of God.

If we are humble, gentle, generous, and otherwise virtuous, we shall be like to almighty God, in Whom is the perfection of every virtue. We should therefore be careful to study the divine attributes, that we may imitate them and become true children of our heavenly Father. The virtuous man is a friend of God, for Our Lord says: "Whosoever shall do the will of My Father that is in heaven, he is My brother, and sister, and mother" (Matt. xii. 50). Similarity of tastes and feelings makes men friends. Virtue renders us beautiful in God's sight. Physical beauty is deceitful and vain (Prov. xxxi. 30); true beauty is that of the heart. All the glory of the king's daughter is within (Ps. xliv. 14). This loveliness is not apparent now, but it will be made visible one day. In winter all the trees are bare, though they are not lifeless, but when the summer comes they are clothed with verdant foliage. So the virtuous now appear insignificant and contemptible, for their true glory, their inner life, is hidden from human ken. But when this life is done, those who were counted dead shall shine as the sun in the kingdom of their Father (Matt. xiii. 43), while the wicked who were deemed happy shall mourn and weep. Virtue alone makes us true Christians. The seal of Baptism is not enough, nor even the sacerdotal robe. A Christian without virtue is a husk without a kernel, a spring without water, a vine without grapes. In vain do we call ourselves Christians, if we are not imitators of Christ.

The Different Kinds of Christian Virtue.

One and the self-same virtue has reference to different objects and consequently receives different names.

Many virtues, such as liberality or prudence, are lauded by men of the world; others, such as meekness, humility, love of one's enemies, are regarded by them with contempt. In some virtues the understanding is the chief factor, as in faith; in others, the will, as in temperance.

1. The virtues that unite our soul to God are the three theological virtues: Faith, Hope, Charity.

These three virtues are symbolized by a flame; faith is signified by the light it emits, hope by its upward tendency, and charity by the heat it radiates. A tree is also an emblem of these virtues: faith is its root, hope its stem, charity its fruit. Faith lays the foundation of the temple of God, hope raises the walls, and charity crowns the structure. The cross is a symbol of faith, the anchor of hope, while charity is denoted by a burning heart. The greatest of these virtues is charity (1 Cor. xiii. 13). Without charity, faith and hope are valueless, for God only grants eternal felicity to those that love Him.

1. The three theological virtues are manifested in the following manner:

The effect produced by the virtue of Faith is to make us believe in the existence of God and in His divine perfections.

The effect of the virtue of Hope is to make us look for eternal salvation from God, as well as the means that are necessary for its attainment.

The virtue of Charity causes us to find satisfaction in God, and to seek to please Him by keeping His commandments.

2. These virtues are fitly termed theological, because God Himself is their object, their motive, and their Author.

God is the object of faith; that is to say, we believe what God has revealed, and all that has reference to God Himself, to His being, His attributes, His works and His will. God is the motive of faith, for we believe that which He has revealed because He is omniscient and the highest truth. God is the object of hope; for we hope for eternal happiness after death, to see God and enjoy Him forever. God is the motive of hope, for we hope for eternal felicity because He is almighty, most bountiful, and faithful to His promises. God is the object of charity, for all our love centres in Him. God is the motive of charity, since we love Him because He is supreme beauty and sovereign goodness. God is also the Author of the three theological virtues, as the following reasons demonstrate:

3. We receive the three theological virtues to render us

capable of performing good works simultaneously with sanctifying grace.

When the Holy Spirit enters into the soul, He transforms the
powers of the mind, so that it can rise to God with greater facility.
When He comes and imparts to us sanctifying grace, a light shines
in our heart that awakens faith and hope (2 Cor. iv. 6), and a fire
is ignited, that kindles a flame of charity (Rom. v. 5). This action
of the Holy Ghost within the soul is called the infusion of the three
theological virtues. The three theological virtues are infused into
the soul (Council of Trent, 6, ch. 7). The infusion of these virtues
has a similar effect as have the rays of the sun in imparting light
and warmth to the atmosphere. God does not force these virtues upon
us; the freedom of the will is in no wise interfered with. The power
of exercising the three theological virtues is imparted in Baptism,
and if it be lost, it is given again in the Sacrament of Penance. As
the seed lies dormant in the bosom of the earth, until, under the
influence of sun and rain, it germinates and grows, so the three
theological virtues at first lie dormant in the soul of the child until
he attains the use of reason, and through the action of grace and
religious instruction they are developed and come to sight (in works).
The baptized child resembles one who is asleep, who possesses the
power of sight, but sees nothing, until he awakens from sleep and
makes use of that power. So the power to exercise faith, hope, and
charity are latent in the soul of the child, until with the use of
reason they are brought into play, and their existence is made apparent.

4. We ought to make acts of the three theological virtues
frequently in the course of our life, especially before approaching the sacraments and at the hour of death.

The means of making acts of the three theological virtues is to
place before the mind the object and the motive of these virtues. In
doing so, it is well not to employ the usual formula, but to express
one's self in one's own words. Every time we make the sign of the
cross, utter a prayer, or do a good deed, we make implicitly at least,
an act of one or more of these virtues.

2. Those virtues which have the effect of bringing our actions
into conformity with the moral law, are called moral virtues.
These we gain for ourselves by our own exertions and the assistance of divine grace, after we have received sanctifying grace.

These virtues are called moral virtues, because they order our
actions in a manner pleasing to God. As the three theological virtues perfect our interior being, so the moral virtues perfect our exterior. The three theological virtues have immediate reference to
God, the moral virtues bear in the first place upon our neighbor or
upon ourselves. Liberality, for instance, has reference to our neighbor; temperance in eating and drinking to ourselves exclusively. The
three theological virtues were infused into us with sanctifying grace,
whereas we have to gain for ourselves the moral virtues at the cost
of our own labor, and with the timely aid of divine grace. At Bap-

tism, it is true, our will is disposed by the inspiration of the Holy Ghost to the practice of the moral virtues; yet the habit of their practice must be acquired by repeated good deeds, and the conquest of our evil proclivities. At Baptism the seed of moral virtue was implanted in the field of our heart; we must diligently cultivate that field if the seed is to bear fruit. At the same time we need the sun of God's grace, the vivifying influence of the Holy Spirit, or our labor will be in vain.

3. The principal moral virtues are the seven capital virtues: Humility, obedience, meekness, liberality, temperance, chastity, diligence in what is good.

Humility concerns our honor, obedience our liberty, meekness and patience the attitude of the soul, liberality has reference to our property, temperance in eating and drinking and chastity to our bodies, diligence in what is good to our work. Among these virtues meekness and liberality ought pre-eminently to mark the Christian, and for this reason Christ speaks of His followers as sheep or lambs, because the sheep is the most patient and harmless of animals. The seven capital virtues are opposed to the seven capital or deadly sins.

4. All the moral virtues proceed from the four cardinal virtues: Prudence, justice, temperance, and fortitude (Wisd. viii. 7).

The four fundamental virtues are called cardinal virtues, from the word *cardo*, a hinge, because all our moral actions turn on them as a door turns upon its hinges. They are called fundamental virtues because the whole fabric of virtue rests upon them; they are the cornerstones of the edifice of Christian virtue. The four cardinal virtues are inseparable parts of each and every virtue; on them all the moral virtues rest, for instance moderation in eating and drinking and meekness spring from temperance, diligence is what is good from fortitude, etc. These four virtues may be said to be the parents of every other virtue. Prudence is a virtue of the understanding, justice of the will. Temperance and fortitude support the will. Prudence fixes its gaze upon heaven; temperance seeks what is eternal and employs temporal things only as a means of attaining what it seeks; fortitude allows no obstacles to hinder it from attaining its goal. The philosophers of antiquity recognized the value of temperance and fortitude; they asserted that to renounce and to endure was the compendium of all worldly wisdom, for they considered that the practice of these two virtues would preserve a man from sin and conduct him to supreme felicity.

1. Prudence is the capacity of the intellect to apprehend the good things of eternity and the means of attaining to them.

That is the truest prudence which can best distinguish what is divine from what is human. The prudent man always looks to his final end. Like a wise merchant who thinks continually of what profit he can make, the Christian's thoughts are fixed upon gaining riches for eternity. The serpent looks out afar, and exposes its body if only it can shield its head: so the Christian keeps the end of life always in view, and scorns earthly things in order to preserve its true treasure. Our Lord bids us " Be wise as serpents " (Matt. x. 16). How cleverly the saints contrived to carry out their undertakings and obtain the end they desired! St. Paul displayed this prudence when he made use of the superscription he saw at Athens: " To the unknown God," to afford him an opportunity of preaching the Gospel (Acts xvii.). Prudence is a most important virtue, for the will is guided by the reason. If the understanding is not capable of judging between good and evil, the will deviates from the right way and transgresses the commandments. Prudence is said to be the eye of the soul (St. Thomas Aquinas). Without the light of the eye we cannot find our way, nor without prudence can we discern the path to heaven. Without the eye we cannot make full use of our limbs, nor without prudence can we practice virtue aright. Prudence is the rudder that directs the course of the vessel; without it we shall make shipwreck of virtue. The contrary of prudence is worldly wisdom (Luke xvi. 8), or the wisdom of the flesh. The wisdom of this world consists in discerning what will bring a man temporal advantage or sensual enjoyment; this wisdom is foolishness with God (1 Cor. iii. 19).

2. Justice is the steadfast inclination of the will towards that which is just.

Justice makes us willing to walk in the narrow path of the commandments; the just man dreads the slightest deviation from it. The foster-father of Christ was termed a just man. (The word just is often used to signify that one is in a state of grace, but in this sense it is not employed here.) The just man is upright, he gives to every one his due; to God he gives worship, to the authorities obedience; to his subordinates he metes out rewards and punishments; to his equals he shows fraternal charity. But as both from within and without he encounters opposition and obstacles, he needs temperance and fortitude to sustain him and regulate his actions.

3. Through temperance man only makes use of temporal good things, in so far as is necessary for the attainment of those which are eternal.

For instance, a man does not eat or drink more than he needs to support life and preserve health and fulfil his duties. He does not strive with excessive eagerness after honors, pleasures, or other sensual enjoyments. He is like the eagle, that has its eyrie on the heights, and only descends to the valley in search of food. We should use this world as if we used it not (1 Cor. vii. 31). Would that every one could say with St. Francis of Sales: " I desire very little, and that little I desire but little." Temperance does not, however, consist in refusing one's self what is necessary, and thus unfitting one's self for good works; such temperance lacks prudence.

4. Fortitude enables a man to make sacrifices willingly for the sake of attaining eternal riches.

He who possesses the virtue of fortitude does not allow himself to be intimidated by ridicule. threats. or persecution. He is ready even, if need be, to suffer death. On the other hand he endures patiently all the afflictions that come upon him. In this he resembles the diamond that no stone can break. Fortitude is more strikingly displayed in bearing great suffering than in undertaking great achievements, for suffering is more difficult than doing. An example of heroic fortitude is given us by the mother of the Machabees with her seven children, who " esteemed torments as nothing " (2 Mach. vii. 12); by Abraham, who was ready to offer up his son Isaac; by Pope Leo the Great, who fearlessly went to meet Attila, the King of the Huns. No saint was ever a coward. The holy martyrs showed fortitude in its highest degree. There is the spurious fortitude of the reprobate; when a man cannot be made to desist from the love of transitory things by the chastisements of the Creator and pursues them at the cost of his life.

5. All perfect virtues spring from the love of God and are inseparably united together by that same love (1 Cor. xiii.).

As all the different branches of a tree grow from the same root, so the various virtues spring from the love of God. All virtue is rooted and grounded in charity (Eph. iii. 17). Charity may be called the queen of virtues, because it incites the will to the performance of good deeds; as flowers of various hues are bound together to form a wreath, so the different virtues form a harmonious whole; only they cannot be severed one from the other, and the bond that unites them so closely is charity.

Therefore he who is devoid of charity towards God does not possess a single perfect virtue; while he who has charity possesses them all, if not all in the same degree.

The love of God may fitly be compared to the sunshine. When in winter the sun withdraws its rays, the face of nature loses its beauty; so in the absence of charity, virtue loses its supernatural beauty. But it is quite possible to possess imperfect. natural virtue without the love of God. For every man has by nature a certain inherent knowledge of what is good, and a desire for what is good, by reason of which he can perform many a good action and by habit acquire ease in the performance of it. One may also possess imperfect moral virtues without the love of God; this was the case with the pagans of antiquity, and now we often meet with people who are naturally gentle, abstemious, liberal, etc. Moreover, one may even possess imperfect theological virtues without the love of God. For faith can exist without hope. and both faith and hope without charity (Council of Trent, 6, 7, 23). For faith and hope can only be lost by falling into the sins opposed to them; faith is lost through unbelief, hope by despair. But he who possesses the love of God possesses all and every virtue, if not all in an equal degree. As soon as the sun shines upon the earth, the flowers, the meadows, all things are once more decked in their former beauty; so when charity fills the soul, it will be adorned with all virtues; supernatural divine virtues, worthy of an eternal recompense. All the saints possessed every single perfect virtue that there is, but they excelled in one more than in the others. Job possessed patience in a high degree, David the virtue of forgiveness, Abraham obedience, St. Aloysius was remarkable for purity, St. Francis of Sales for meekness, St. Ignatius for zeal.

He who is lacking in one single perfect virtue is devoid also of all the others, for he has not the love of God. And he who possesses but one single perfect virtue, possesses all.

One virtue alone is either no virtue at all, or an imperfect one. For instance, a man who is given to anger possesses neither the virtue of meekness, nor of liberality, nor of humility, nor any other. It is only natural virtues that are alone. For instance one may meet with an avaricious man who is gentle and meek.

6. The greatest and noblest of all the virtues is charity.

Because it alone unites man to God, it alone gives value to the other virtues, and it alone will last beyond the grave.

The three theological virtues hold the highest place among the virtues because they have direct relation to God. Charity is the greatest of them, as St. Paul declares (1 Cor. xiii. 13). It takes precedence of all the rest, as fire does of the other elements, as gold of the other metals, as the seraphim do of the other angelic choirs—charity unites man to God. Our Lord says: "He that loveth Me shall be loved of My Father, and I will love him; we will come to him and will make our abode with him" (John xiv. 21, 23). Again, St. John says: "He that abideth in charity, abideth in God and God in him" (1 John iv. 16). Charity alone gives value to the other virtues. St. Paul declares that to speak with tongues, to possess all knowledge, to have the gift of prophecy and of miracles, to perform almsdeeds and austerities, profits nothing, for all these are worthless unless inspired by charity (1 Cor. xiii. 1-3). Charity lasts beyond the grave; St. Paul tells us: "Charity never falleth away" (v. 8). Faith on the other hand passes into the vision of God; hope into the enjoyment of God. The moral virtues do indeed remain in the life to come, but in another and more excellent manner, for eternal blessedness does not destroy the perfection human nature has attained.

7. The virtues can always be increased.

Virtue resembles an estate, situated on the highest point of a mountain. He who is ascending this mountain is sometimes nearer, sometimes farther from the summit, and there are many travellers before and many behind him. For we do not always possess the same degree of virtue, neither do all men possess it in an equal measure. If any one has attained so high a degree of virtue that his state approximates to that of the blessed in heaven—nay more, if to a certain extent he becomes like unto God, that virtue is termed heroic. Heroes, among the ancients, were men who had achieved more than ordinary mortals could accomplish. For the beatification or canonization of any individual it is necessary to prove that he practised the three theological and the four cardinal virtues in the fulfilment of the duties of his calling in an heroic degree. Heroic virtue is neither understood nor appreciated, but rather contemned by those who do not live a godly life.

The three theological virtues are increased through the increase of sanctifying grace.

That the increase of the three theological virtues is possible, we learn from the collect of the Thirteenth Sunday after Pentecost, in which the Church prays: "Almighty and everlasting God, give unto us an increase of faith, hope, and charity." If the atmosphere receives more light and heat from the sun, we see more clearly and experience more warmth. In like manner when grace is augmented in the soul, the power of belief becomes stronger and we are stimulated to the exercise of charity. We also find that frequent acts of the three theological virtues serve to increase them; or if they do not immediately produce this effect, they dispose the soul to growth in virtue.

The moral virtues are increased by frequently performing good actions, and also by the increase of sanctifying grace.

Frequent acts will increase the facility in the practice of good, while the increase of grace will render the will more disposed towards what is good. The more proficiency we attain and the greater the measure of sanctifying grace we receive, the greater will be our moral virtues. We should endeavor to increase at least in one virtue, for the increase of one will be accompanied by the increase of all the rest. We can and ought to cultivate more especially that virtue for the exercise of which our circumstances afford most opportunity, or for which we have a particular admiration. The more we advance in our favorite virtue, the greater progress we make in every other virtue.

8. All perfect virtue is lost immediately upon falling into mortal sin, for thereby the love of God is lost, without which there can be no perfect virtue.

He who suffers shipwreck (1 Tim. i. 19), loses all that he has; and so the man who falls into mortal sin loses all the perfection in virtue and all the merits he has acquired. However great the proficiency attained in the practice of virtue, the freedom of the will is not impaired; man is always liable to sin. "He that thinketh himself to stand, let him take heed lest he fall" (1 Cor. x. 12). Remember how David sinned, and St. Peter fell. Virtue is far more easily lost than won. How swiftly a stone rolls down hill, and yet how slowly it is rolled up! One single mortal sin suffices to obliterate virtue, just as one string out of tune in an instrument spoils the melody. Yet suffering is not of itself calculated to destroy virtue. Virtue is like a precious pearl, which if it falls into the mud retains its pristine beauty unmarred. In fact virtue stands out in stronger relief in the season of affliction; just as the stars shine at night and are not seen by day, or spices give out their aroma most freely when they are crushed. The outward semblance of virtue often remains when one has committed a grievous sin, but it then resembles a corpse, for the soul, the life, has departed from it. One may, therefore, be extremely pious, and yet corrupt at heart.

The perfect virtues will be diminished if one desists from the practice of good.

He who makes a parade of his virtues is in danger of losing them. The man who carries his treasures openly on the highway is sure to be robbed of them. As the display of gold or costly apparel invites the thief, so the display of virtue attracts the devil, who seeks to take it from us. Moreover, sweet-scented things lose their perfume if they are exposed to the air. Consequently, if we cannot avoid doing good in the sight of man, let our only desire be to please God. Unless we are constant and persevering, we shall gradually fall off in virtue. Trees that are continually transplanted cannot grow properly, much less bear fruit; on the contrary, they are likely to wither and die. So continual change of place, of position, of office, is highly prejudicial to progress in virtue.

III. SIN.

1. He who wittingly and willingly transgresses one of God's commandments is guilty of sin.

Adam and Eve in paradise transgressed the commandment of God; they knew it well, and no one, not even the serpent, compelled them to violate it. Thus they committed a sin. The commandments of God are principally the Ten Commandments, and the precept to do works of mercy, besides all other precepts enjoined upon us in God's name. The commandments either enjoin or prohibit some act, therefore they are divided into sins of commission and sins of omission. As the divine law is for the safeguarding of the majesty of God, or for our own welfare or the good of our neighbor, we sin in transgressing that law, either against God, our neighbor, or ourselves. Sin is nothing else but revolt against and disobedience to God (Rom. iv. 15; 1 John iii. 4). The sinner throws off the yoke of God, saying: "I will not serve" (Jer. ii. 20). He attacks God, he would fain destroy Him, that He might no longer see and punish his transgressions. When we commit sin, we take up arms against God, we crucify again the Son of God (Heb. vi. 6), by making the Redeemer's blood of no avail. The malice of the sinner pains Our Lord more deeply than all the sufferings of His Passion, just as the loss of his wages is more grievous to the workingman than all the toil he has gone through. How foolish it would be of any one in the world to offend an individual on whom his whole future happiness depended; how much more foolishly then do we act, when we make Him our enemy Whose aid is indispensable to us for all things and at all times, and on Whom our eternal salvation depends. If your life was at another man's mercy, would you venture to insult that man? Remember your existence depends entirely upon the will of God; it hangs as by a thread, at any moment He could cast you back into the nothingness whence you came, and yet you do not fear to provoke His anger. Miserable mortals that we are, we cannot tolerate the slightest indignity offered us by our fellow-men, who are our equals, and yet we ourselves show the utmost disrespect to the Lord of heaven!

It is not counted as a sin if we commit an evil action, of the sinfulness of which we are ignorant, through no fault of our own, nor if our will does not consent to the evil deed.

450 Good Works, Virtue, Sin, Vice.

Noe's intoxication was guiltless, because he was not aware of the inebriating qualities of wine. If one eat meat on Friday, forgetting that it is Friday, it is no sin. But it is quite otherwise if it is in consequence of a long-continued habit of sin that one fails to see the guilt of an action, or if one's ignorance of its sinfulness is due to culpable negligence. " It is one thing," says St. Gregory, " not to know, another to wish not to know; for he who closes his eyes that he may not see the truth is a despiser of the law." . Those who in the present day avoid hearing sermons will have no excuse before God. We do not commit sin so long as we do not consent to what is evil. The early Christians had incense forcibly thrust into their hands, and were compelled to cast it upon the altar; were they to blame? Evil thoughts are suggested by the devil, but if we do not consent to them, we commit no sin, any more than we are responsible for what we do in our dreams. We should not allow these thoughts to disquiet us, but simply put them out of our minds. But actions done without our will most certainly are sinful, if we are to blame for the cause of those actions. The misdeeds of a drunken man are unquestionably sins, if in any way he foresees them as a consequence of his intoxication.

2. Sin is in its essence an unlawful turning towards the creature and turning away from God.

St. Bonaventure says that turning towards creatures is the source of all sin. Earthly creatures are only a means for the attainment of everlasting felicity; they are in no wise the final end of man. It is with them as with drugs; used in moderation they are beneficial, but used immoderately they are injurious and a hindrance in the way of our salvation. Therefore God only allows us to use creatures within a certain limit, and in fact only in so far as they are necessary or helpful to our eternal happiness; for instance, He permits us to take such nourishment as is needful for the support of nature, but forbids excess in eating and drinking; He permits us to have possessions of our own, but not to take what belongs to our neighbor. He who uses creatures to a greater extent, or otherwise than God ordains (doing violence to the creature, Rom. viii. 22), wanders away from God and from his final end; he prefers transient joys to eternal bliss (Wisd. ii. 1-9). Thus a child, if a lump of sugar and a piece of gold be offered him, chooses the sugar. The sinner forsakes God, the fountain of living waters, and digs to himself broken cisterns that can hold no water (Jer. ii. 13). Sin is a species of idolatry; for the sinner worships the creature in the place of the Creator; his sin is his god. By sin man becomes the servant of the creature, he becomes dependent upon creatures; he is like a fish caught upon a hook, and held fast by it. Whosoever committeth sin is the servant of sin (John viii. 34). He is worse than a servant, for a servant can run away; but the servant of sin cannot escape from sin; he carries it with him whithersoever he goes.

3. Sin is the one only evil upon earth; it robs man of the supernatural beauty of the soul, it makes him resemble the devil, and brings misery upon him even while he is on earth.

Sin is the one only evil in the world. We mortals are accustomed to regard the sufferings and contradictions of this life as evils, whereas they are graces in reality; since, far from separating us from God, they bring us nearer to Him. Through sin man becomes worthless in God's sight; through sin, he, who is made of nothing, returns to his original nothingness. St. John Chrysostom says: "Many consider eternal damnation to be the greatest of all evils; but for my part, I always assert that to offend Jesus Christ is a far greater evil." Sin is a greater evil than the annihilation of the world, nay, of a million worlds, with their countless inhabitants. Sin is the only real disgrace. When it was said to St. Francis Xavier, the apostle of the Indies, who bore the title of Apostolic Legate, that it was a degradation to him to wash his own linen, he replied: "Nothing degrades the Christian except sin." Through sin the supernatural beauty of the soul is lost. As a white robe is soiled and stained if it comes into contact with the mud of the streets, so the soul loses her supernatural beauty, which consists in sanctifying grace, and contracts a hideous stain, through the inordinate love of creatures. On some one observing to St. Francis Chantal, when she was nursing a leper, that she might easily take the disease, she answered: "I fear no leprosy but the leprosy of sin." Sin renders man like to the devil. Sinners are imitators and followers of the devil (Wisd. ii. 25). They are made one with him by sin. "He that committeth sin is of the devil" (1 John iii. 8). They even become his children by sin (v. 10). Our Lord said to the Pharisees in the Temple: "You are of your father the devil, and the desires of your father you will do" (John viii. 44). Sin makes the misery of man even while he is on earth. If the heavenly bodies forsook their orbits, they would be dashed to pieces; if the train becomes derailed, a catastrophe ensues. So God's rational creatures, the human race, are overtaken by disaster if they transgress the law God has laid down for them. The sinner rebels against the rules of his own reason, the rules of society, the rules that govern the universe; for this he has to endure the reproaches of conscience, the penalties of the law, and the chastisements of God.

THE DEVELOPMENT OF SIN.

A house does not fall all at once; at first a few drops of rain that are scarcely noticed soak into the walls, soften the mortar and loosen the stones; presently the whole building collapses. The devil sets to work in a similar way to destroy the soul. We learn from Eve's example how sin begins.

Sin arises generally in the following manner:

1. First of all an evil thought comes into the mind, which in itself is not sinful. (Temptation.)

Within the heart there are two masters, whose characters are diametrically opposed; what one praises, the other blames. One of these is concupiscence, the other conscience. Hence when an evil thought comes into the mind, a struggle immediately arises: conscience admonishes and holds us back, concupiscence incites and urges us to evil. We can no more prevent bad thoughts from coming into the mind, than an island in mid-ocean can prevent the waves from dashing on its shores; but as the island resists the force of the breakers, so we can withstand the assaults of temptation. We must instantly turn our thoughts elsewhere; by means of prayer, or the remembrance of death or of judgment. "In all things remember thy last end, and thou shalt never sin" (Ecclus. vii. 40). Or we may recall to mind the terrible consequences of sin. What is of the greatest importance is to turn one's thoughts at once; a fire just lighted is easily extinguished, a disease may be arrested in its first stage. Slay your enemy while he is young and feeble. Stifle evil thoughts at their birth; banish them the moment they present themselves.

2. If evil thoughts are not instantly expelled, they awaken in the mind complacency in what is evil, and that is already a venial sin.

Complacency or satisfaction in what is evil, may also be a mortal sin if we willingly take pleasure in something which is forbidden under pain of mortal sin. The evil thoughts which the devil puts into our mind may be compared to eggs; as after a period of incubation the young bird is produced from the egg, so sin is produced from evil thoughts if they are cherished in the breast and regarded with complacency. "When concupiscence hath conceived, it bringeth forth sin" (Jas. i. 15). "Evil thoughts are an abomination to the Lord" (Prov. xv. 26). Forget not that God is omniscient; He sees all your thoughts. He knows them better than you do yourself, and at the judgment they will every one be disclosed.

3. The evil desire next arises; this has a turpitude corresponding to that of the sinful action towards which it is directed.

An evil desire is an act of the will, or deliberate consent. That which proceeds from the heart (i.e., the will), that is sin (Matt. xv. 19). Before God the will to sin counts as the deed of sin. He who entertains an evil desire has committed the sin already in his heart (Matt. v. 28). He who has consented to a mortal sin is like a stag, fatally wounded by the huntsman, which, if it escapes capture, cannot escape death. Evil desires may be compared to the little worms which perforate the keel of a vessel and render it unseaworthy, if they do not cause it to sink. So evil desires arrest the course of the good and pious on their voyage to the celestial haven, or even cause them to sink into the nethermost abyss. Many evil desires are mortal sins (Council of Trent, 14, c. 5). He who knows not how to tame his evil lusts, is like a rider whose horse takes fright and bolts, dragging him through bogs and morasses, for he will be drawn into mortal sin and finally cast into hell. How unhappy are you, if you cherish sinful desires in your heart!

4. Finally comes the resolution to commit the sin.

The evil concupiscence was merely a wish or longing for the sinful object. The resolution is a final decision to adopt the means necessary to the attainment of that object. Up to this point the sin is still an interior sin.

5. If occasion then presents itself for the sin, the exterior act is committed.

An exterior sin is attended by worse consequences than an interior sin; it augments the malice of the will, destroys the sense of shame, often gives scandal, brings misery on the sinner, and is more severely punished by God. A king has intrusted the defence of a fortress to his general. A messenger is sent in disguise to this general, bearing a letter, in which a large sum of money is offered him if he will surrender the fortress. Three courses of action are open to the general; either he will reject the offer and have the messenger hanged for a spy; or he may enter into negotiations with him at first, and presently break them off; or he may open the gates to the enemy. Our soul is that fortress; we are its commandant and our adversary is the devil. He sends out envoys seeking by all manner of promises and representations to estrange us from God. If we indignantly reject his advances, our loyalty to God is thereby confirmed; if we take pleasure in his suggestions, we begin to fail in fidelity to God and deserve punishment; but if we commit the sin, we surrender our soul to the devil, who enters in with all his satellites. After mortal sin, the soul is in a state of sin. When water is once frozen, it remains a block of ice, until it is melted by heat. Thus it is with the man who falls into mortal sin; he continues in a state of sin until he is brought to repentance. Hence we say: That man lives in sin, or, he died in his sins, etc.

6. By the repetition of exterior sins the habit of sin, or vice, is contracted.

If mortal sin be repeated many times the habit of sin is formed; that is to say the sinner acquires a certain proficiency in wickedness, and the will is permanently inclined to evil. The Fathers point to the three instances in which Christ raised the dead as exemplifying mortal sin in its three stages: interior sin, exterior sin, and the habit of vice. Whoso only sins in his heart, is like the daughter of Jairus, who lay dead within the house; he who commits sin outwardly, is like the young man at Naim, who was carried out of the city gates; while he who is given up to vice is like Lazarus, who had lain several days in the grave. In the first two instances Our Lord merely bade the dead arise, in the last He was troubled in spirit, He wept, He caused the stone to be removed and called loudly into the interior of the sepulchre. This He did to signify the great difficulty of reawakening one who is sunk in vice to the life of the Spirit.

7. Every outward sin and every vice brings, as its own punishment, other sins and vices of a different nature in its train.

The grace of God departs from every man who has fallen into mortal sin. Not so temptation. In fact the evil enemy bestirs himself the more to bind his captive more tightly. Now since temptation cannot be overcome without God's grace, the sinner falls lower and lower, from one sin to another. The sins which follow upon a sin may therefore be called the chastisement of sin. Holy Scripture expresses the withdrawal of grace in words such as these: "God blinded the eyes, or hardened the heart of the sinner" (e.g., Pharao). "God delivered him up to a reprobate sense" (Rom. i. 28).

8. If any vice is firmly rooted in the soul, it oftentimes brings after it sins of the worst type, and those that are said to cry to Heaven for vengeance; finally it produces complete obduracy in the sinner.

He who has for a lengthened period been given over to a life of sin, does not shrink from the greatest excesses. And just as perfection in virtue procures for mortal man upon earth happiness which is almost that of heaven, and exalts him to union with God, so there are different grades in vice, by which the soul descends to the condition of the reprobate and her complete separation from God is consummated. Finally he who is the slave of vice is often inspired by a bitter hatred against God, and wilfully and of set purpose resists the influence and action of the Holy Spirit; and at last by final impenitence commits the sin against the Holy Ghost which cannot be forgiven.

THE KINDS OF SIN.

There are different kinds of sin.

Circumstances which alter the nature of a sin must be specified in confession (Council of Trent, 14, 5).

All those sins which violate different commandments, or which are opposed to different virtues, are distinct in their nature one from the other; as also are those sins by which one and the same commandment is transgressed, or which are opposed to one and the same virtue, in different ways.

For instance, theft and lying are two different kinds of sins, because by theft the Seventh, by lying the Eighth Commandment, is broken. Pride and avarice are sins of a different kind, because they are opposed to two different virtues, humility and liberality. Theft and cheating are two sins of a different nature because they violate the Seventh Commandment in two several ways. Presumption of God's mercy and despair are two sins of a different nature, because they are opposed to the virtue of hope in two different ways.

1. Sins are generally divided into sins of word, of thought, and of deed.

Hatred and murder are two different kinds of sin, because the Fifth Commandment is transgressed by them in two different ways, by thought and by deed. Boasting in speech and ostentation in dress are two different kinds of sin, because they offend against the virtue of humility in two different ways, by word and by deed.

2. A distinction also exists between our own sins, and the sins in which we co-operate.

Our own sins are those which we ourselves commit.

The sins in which we co-operate are those which we do not indeed commit ourselves, but for which we are to blame. We may be accessory to another's sin by command, counsel, consent, praise, assistance, defence; by provocation or by silence, or by abstaining from punishing the ill done, although we might and ought to have prevented it.

The sinner is like a man with the leprosy; he leads others into sin as the leper infects others with his loathsome disease. In that case the guilt of their sin lies at his door. If a man sets fire to a house, he is to blame for the conflagration; if he gives his neighbor poison, he is answerable for his neighbor's death. The same is true of us if we lead any one into sin, or even if we do not endeavor to prevent the sin. To leave a crime unpunished is to teach others to commit it. If the bodyguard of an emperor were to hear that an attempt had been made on the person of their imperial master, they would be sorely alarmed, for they would know that to allege that they had no part in it would be of no avail as an excuse; in like manner we shall have good cause for apprehension, if through our cowardice or negligence an affront has been offered to the divine majesty. He who might prevent an evil deed and does not do so, is to blame for that deed. In illustration of this remember how Herod commanded the murder of the holy innocents. Aaron consented to the Israelites' demand and made the golden calf. The Jews were pleased because Herod had put the Apostle James to death; this induced him to apprehend St. Peter, with the intention of executing him also (Acts xii.). Saul assisted the men who stoned Stephen, by taking care of their garments. Job's wife provoked her husband to anger and impatience; Tobias' wife did the same. Heli, the high priest, did not rebuke his sons for their misdeeds nor correct them; for this God reprimanded him by Samuel's mouth (1 Kings iii.). Those, too, who, being members of a council, through human respect do not protest against the passing of unjust decrees, are guilty of sin; the prophet compares such persons to dumb dogs, not able to bark (Is. lvi. 10).

Earthly potentates, legislative bodies, parents and superiors, employers of labor, editors of periodicals, and publishers, may easily render themselves guilty of the sin of others.

If the ruler of a nation enters upon an unjust war, is he not answerable for all the crimes which are perpetrated in that war? Who is to blame when laws are passed antagonistic to religion, whereby the salvation of many is imperilled? Who is to blame when the daily papers are the means of stirring up national and religious animosities and rousing the spirit of persecution? Whose in such cases is the greater sin?

He who is to blame for another man's sin deserves punishment quite as much as if he had committed the sin himself.

He who tempts another to sin is perhaps the more blameworthy of the two. Remember that God punished Eve more severely than Adam, because she led him into sin. Even to this day the consequences of original sin weigh more heavily upon the weaker than upon the sterner sex. To tempt others to sin is also a sin against charity. It is like the devil who, not content with being evil himself, seeks to make others evil. For this reason Our Lord exclaims:

" Woe to that man by whom the scandal cometh. It were better for
him that a millstone should be hanged about his neck, and that he
should be drowned in the depth of the sea " (Matt. xviii. 6).

THE COMPARATIVE MAGNITUDE OF SIN.

1. All sins are not equally great.

Our Lord compares some sins to camels, others to gnats (Matt.
xxiii. 24); or again He compares some to motes, others to beams
(Matt. vii. 3); He contrasts the depth of ten thousand talents with
that of a hundred pence (Matt. xviii. 23 *seq.*). He said to Pilate:
" He that hath delivered Me to thee hath the greater sin " (John. xix.
11).

1. A sin is all the greater the more important is the object
it injures, the clearer the knowledge of the sinfulness of the
deed, and the greater the liberty of action enjoyed by the doer.

In the first place, much depends on the value and importance of
the object against which the evil act is directed. If God is thereby
offended, it is much more sinful than if the offence were against one
of our fellow-men. Or if it be directed against a man's life, it is
worse than if his property alone was attacked. A great deal depends
also on the knowledge possessed of the sinfulness of the action.
Sin is much greater in a Christian than in a heathen. If a priest
commits a sin, it is worse for him than for an ordinary man,
little versed perhaps in religious matters, because the priest has a
closer knowledge of the will of God. Our Lord says: " The servant
who knew the will of his lord and did not according to his will, shall
be beaten with many stripes; but he that knew not, and did things
worthy of stripes, shall be beaten with few stripes " (Luke xii. 47, 48).
The greater your knowledge, the more rigorously will you be judged,
if your life is not holy in proportion to your knowledge. The more
abundant the graces bestowed on you, the more heinous your transgression. Finally much depends upon whether a man has or has not
been a perfectly free agent. Any one who was intimidated, or who
was exposed to fierce temptation, is far less culpable than one who
was free to act as he pleased. St. Peter's denial was consequently
a lesser sin than Judas' betrayal of Our Lord.

2. Circumstances of person, cause, time, place, means, object, or the evil consequences of a sin may enhance its guilt.

For instance: it is worse for a monarch to sin openly than for one
of his subjects; offences committed in the presence of several persons
are graver than if they were done in secret; to work hard all day long
on Sunday is more sinful than to work for one hour only. Robbery
with violence is a greater sin than surreptitious purloining; to take
from a poor man is a greater sin than to steal from a rich man. It
is far more wrong to steal in church than out of it.

2. Many sins are so great that they separate us entirely from
God, and deprive us of His friendship; they are called mortal or
deadly sins. Sins of lesser moment are called venial sins.

Some diseases only weaken the bodily strength, others destroy life. It is the same with sin; some sins only impede the soul in her efforts to attain her final end, others again extinguish within her sanctifying grace, the life of the soul. In our intercourse with our friends, it often happens that some difference arises; if the offence is but slight, it does not seriously affect our friendship; if it is grave, it puts an end to the friendship. Holy Scripture speaks of some sins whereby the grace of God is completely lost (as David's sin), and of others into which the just man may fall seven times, that is frequently (Prov. xxiv. 16), without ceasing to be a just man (Council of Trent, 6, 11). Again, it speaks of sins which exclude from heaven, by which eternal punishment is incurred, and of others which have not these fatal consequences. St. Paul reckons among mortal sins, idolatry, murder, covetousness, drunkenness, etc. (1 Cor. vi. 9; Gal. v. 19.) In the present day there is no sin so grievous but it finds some ready to palliate and excuse it. Beware lest you be led astray by the false maxims of the world; hold fast by the word of God, the teaching of the Church. God, not the world, will one day be your judge. Mortal sin is so called because it causes the death of the soul; the soul does not, it is true, cease to exist, but it loses the presence of the Holy Ghost. As the body dies when the soul departs from it, so the soul dies when God departs from it. Thus mortal sin may to a certain extent be said to be spiritual suicide. Venial sin is so called, because it is easily forgiven. Yet venial sin must not be underrated. It cannot withdraw us from the way which leads to God, but it can arrest our progress in that way. Venial sin is, moreover, an offence against the infinite majesty of God. St. Jerome says no offence against Our Lord God, however slight, is to be thought of little moment. The destruction of the heavens and the earth would be a lesser calamity than one venial sin. Many theologians assert that the blood of all the martyrs and all their merits would not suffice to make satisfaction to the divine majesty for one venial sin; only the precious blood of Christ can do this.

Mortal and venial sin differ essentially from each other.

Mortal sin is like a severe wound, from which a man rarely recovers, whereas venial sin is a slight wound, which at the most makes him ill. By mortal sin the axe is laid to the root of the tree; by venial sin a cut is made in the bark, which may perhaps prove prejudicial to its growth.

It is an exceedingly difficult and dangerous matter to decide whether a sin is mortal or venial. Only one thing is certain:

Mortal sin is not possible unless God is no longer the final end towards which our intention is directed.

It is difficult and dangerous to decide what is mortal and what is venial sin. It is often impossible to determine about any act whether it is a mortal or a venial sin. "Let no one presume," says St. Alphonsus, "to assert any sin to be mortal, unless he is quite certain of it; otherwise he may lead men to despair, and even cast them into hell; instead of raising them out of the mire of sin, he will plunge them the deeper into it." No man can be guilty of mortal sin, unless

God has ceased to be the centre towards which all his affections converge. Mortal sin is a turning away of our whole being from God, and a turning to creatures as our ultimate end.

3. He commits a mortal sin who consciously and of his own free will does grievous dishonor to God or wrong to his neighbor in a weighty matter; who does injury to his own life, or to the life, the property, or the reputation of his neighbor.

Idolatry, heresy, blasphemy, perjury, serious desecration of Sundays and holydays, come under the category of mortal sins, because they are a direct affront to the majesty of God. To injure one's health slightly through thoughtlessness is a venial sin; suicide is a mortal sin. A man who beats his neighbor commits a venial sin, but if he injures his body to any great extent, it is a mortal sin. To steal a halfpenny is a venial sin, to defraud one's neighbor of a large sum of money is a mortal sin. To disclose the faults of another without necessity is a venial sin, but to lodge a false accusation against him is a mortal sin, because in that case the wrong done him is in an important matter. We cannot commit a mortal sin, unless we are conscious of the sinfulness of the act. Thus children who have no conception of the abominable nature of some act which as a rule is a mortal sin, cannot be guilty of grievous sin. It is also requisite that a man should act of his own free will. One who perhaps does a very sinful deed under the mastery of intense fear, having been intimidated by threats, can scarcely be said to have committed mortal sin. A man may also be so distracted in consequence of illness that he scarcely knows what he does. Beware then how you pass judgment upon your neighbor's misdeeds; you are not omniscient!

4. He commits a venial sin who only injures something of trifling consequence; or who, though he injures something of great importance, injures it very slightly, or does so almost unconsciously and to some extent unwittingly.

Yet that which is ordinarily only a venial sin, may become a mortal sin; if, that is to say, great scandal is given thereby, or great harm done, or if the venial sin is committed out of contempt for the law.

Attacks upon religion or upon a man's good name in the public journals can scarcely be reckoned as venial sins, as they give rise to great scandal and occasion no small mischief. If a man were to do wrong and say boastingly, I do it precisely because it is forbidden, he is guilty of grievous sin.

Venial sins if repeated may become mortal, if they are the means of doing great harm.

He who steals a trifling sum time after time from the same person does very wrong, if the small sums mount up to a considerable figure. As water that gradually filters through a tiny leak in the vessel finally causes it to sink, so venial sins affect the destruction of the soul. Many fibres of hemp twisted together form a strong rope fit to hold back a mighty ship; so a number of venial sins form a cord that keeps the soul back from journeying towards heaven.

5. **All mortal sins are not of equal magnitude, nor are all venial sins of the same importance. The most heinous sins are the sins against the Holy Ghost, and those that cry to heaven for vengeance.**

6. **He commits a sin against the Holy Ghost who persistently and wilfully resists the action of the Holy Ghost.**

It often occurs in the course of one's life, that the Holy Spirit incites us to prayer or other good works, and by reason of distractions or the cares of this world we do not obey His voice. This is not, however, the sin against the Holy Ghost. That sin is only committed when a man persistently and wilfully withstands the inspirations of the Holy Ghost and dies in an attitude of resistance to Him. The Pharisees and Scribes were perfectly aware that Christ was the Messias; they were convinced of it by the miracles He worked, by the excellence of His doctrine, by the sanctity of His life, by the fulfilment of the prophecies, by His own utterances, but their arrogant pride did not allow them to recognize Him, for then they would have been obliged to alter their lives. Although they knew better, they declared Him to be possessed of the devil (John viii. 48), His works to be the work of the devil (Matt. xii. 24), and persecuted Him as much as was within their power. Thus they resisted the known truth. King Pharao knew the exit of the Israelites from Egypt to be the will of the true God, from the intrepid conduct of Moses and the wonders he wrought; yet in spite of Moses' admonitions he adhered to his own will. He hardened his heart against salutary exhortations. Freemasons will not allow a priest to approach them when they are on their death-bed. "They stop their ears, not to hear, and make their heart as the adamant stone" (Zach. vii. 11). They persist of set purpose in impenitence. The Holy Ghost acts like a man who finds his enemy asleep in the snow, and wakes him, lest he should die of cold. But the sleeper, far from being grateful for this act of kindness, thrusts away his benefactor, and settles himself again to sleep. Thus he who sins against the Holy Ghost, refuses to be aroused from his spiritual torpor by the influence of grace. He may also be likened to a sick man, who not only will not have his wounds healed, but accelerates his own death.

The sin against the Holy Ghost is for the most part the result of a wicked course of life.

It belongs essentially to mortal sin to darken the understanding, and alienate the will from God. The more sins a man commits, the more his understanding is darkened, and the more his will, already estranged from God, is hardened, until at length he finds himself in a deplorable state of blindness and impenitence. The soul is like a room of which the shutters are closed; sin prevents the light of the Holy Spirit from penetrating into it. Holy Scripture says of Pharao that God hardened his heart (Exod. ix. 12). That is, He allowed his heart to become obdurate, as the penalty of his sins. Like ill weeds, which not merely continue what they are in spite of fair weather and fertilizing rains, but grow all the more rank on account of these favorable conditions, the wicked only become worse under the gracious influences of the Holy Spirit. A pillar that is straight stands all the firmer if a weight be placed upon it, but if once it leaves the perpendicular, pressure upon it will cause it to fall. So if the heart is upright, the teaching of wisdom confirms it in integrity, but the depraved heart only sinks lower in vice. A neglected education, bad books, or pride, are often the cause of the heart being closed against the action of the Holy Spirit. The heathen persecute missionaries and put them to death, because they are so blinded by idolatry that they will not renounce their foolish ideas. Anti-Christian periodicals are the means of prejudicing many of their readers against the doctrine and practice of holy Church. Pride caused the so-called Old Catholics to refuse to accept the dogma of Papal Infallibility when it was defined by the Vatican Council in 1870.

Whosoever has committed the sin against the Holy Ghost cannot obtain forgiveness of sin from God, and for this reason: Because he thrusts from him the grace of conversion.

Our Lord says: " The blasphemy against the Holy Ghost shall not be forgiven, neither in this world or in the world to come " (Matt. xii. 32). The sick man cannot be cured of his malady if he refuses to take the remedy which is known to be unfailing; nor can the soul recover from its sickness if it reject grace, the infallible means of cure. Final impenitence is the only offence which God will not pardon; it is a greater insult to Him than sin itself.

Those who sin against the Holy Ghost often come to a miserable end here, and are consigned to eternal damnation hereafter.

The sin against the Holy Ghost is not a sin of frailty, it is a sin of diabolical malice, and therefore it is deserving of more severe punishment. King Pharao, with all his army, was drowned in the Red Sea (Exod. xiv.); the Jews, who rejected and even killed the prophets (Matt. xxiii. 37), had to expiate their impenitence bitterly in the year 70, on the destruction of Jerusalem by the Romans, when there came upon them the tribulation Our Lord predicted, "such as had not been from the beginning of the world, neither shall be " (Matt. xxiv. 21). A clever physician continues to prescribe for his patient although his medicines produce no immediate improvement, trying to save him by every expedient his skill can devise; but if the patient cannot be induced to swallow the drugs, and even goes so far as to throw them out of the window, the physician discontinues his visits. God acts in a similar manner towards the sinner who resists actual grace; He forsakes him entirely. To him may be applied the words the prophet Samuel addressed to King Saul: "Because thou hast rejected the word of the Lord, the Lord hath rejected thee " (1 Kings xv. 26). He who has committed the sin against the Holy Ghost cannot be saved, because at the hour of death he is without the indwelling of the Holy Spirit and sanctifying grace. His spiritual condition is that of the reprobate.

7. Sins that cry to heaven for vengeance are sins of great

malice. They are: wilful murder, oppression of the poor, defrauding laborers of their wages, and the sin of Sodom.

These sins are of so abominable a nature, that every man's feelings must revolt against them. When Cain killed his brother Abel, God said to him: "The voice of thy brother's blood crieth to Me from the earth" (Gen. iv. 10). Every nation on the face of the earth punishes murder with exceptional severity, generally by the execution of the criminal. The oppression of the helpless Israelites in Egypt was a sin that cried to heaven (Exod. iii. 7). The Pharisees were guilty of this sin; they oppressed the poor and prayed long prayers (Matt. xxiii. 14). God expressly forbade the Jews to injure the widow and orphan (Exod. xxii. 22; Ecclus. xxxiv. 26). To keep back the wages of the needy (Deut. xxiv. 14), is a sin that cries to heaven, also on some pretext or other to defraud them of the whole amount (Jas. v. 4). In the Middle Ages an action brought by a working man took precedence of all others in the law courts, and judgment was given within three days. The sin of Sodom takes its name from the inhabitants of Sodom, who were guilty of unnatural sins, by reason of which they were destroyed by God, Who rained down upon them brimstone and fire (Gen. xix. 24). The Dead Sea is still a mournful memorial of their sin; one so shameful that it must not be named among us.

In the present day sins that cry to heaven are sometimes committed by employers, in their conduct towards their defence-less workpeople.

Many employers make their people work in unhealthy and over-crowded rooms, unheated in winter time; they do not allow them a proper interval for rest and for their meals; they do not pay them enough to enable them to live decently; they require of them more work than they can do, and of a kind which they have no right to demand of them. The exploitation and oppression of the laborer has in our day given rise to the abuses of social democracy.

8. A distinction must be made between venial sins and imperfections. Imperfections are faults which are due not to a bad will, but to human frailty.

Uncivil manners, lies told in joke, involuntary distractions in prayer, etc., are imperfections. "Venial sins," says St. Francis of Sales, "arise from a bad will, imperfections do not." But, although imperfections are not actually sins, yet they are wrong and ought to be avoided.

THE CONSEQUENCES OF SIN.

Mortal sin makes a man supremely unhappy. Many are the scourges of the sinner (Ps. xxxi. 10). God calls to the sinner, saying: "Know thou and see that it is an evil and bitter thing for thee to have left the Lord thy God" (Jer. ii. 19). A man who has forsaken God meets with a similar fate to the man who went from Jerusalem—the dwelling-place of the living God—down through rough ways to Jericho. The punishment of sin follows immediately upon it, although the Day of Judgment is not yet come.

1. Mortal sin deprives a man of sanctifying grace, and delivers him into the power of the devil.

The Holy Ghost departs immediately from one who has committed a mortal sin. As the dove will not remain in unclean places, so the Holy Ghost will not remain in a heart that is defiled by mortal sin. The ungodly say to God: " Depart from us " (Job xxii. 17). Mortal sin is a thief, for if it gains access to the soul, it robs it of grace, its most precious treasure. It is the death of the soul; a man killeth indeed through malice (Wisd. xvi. 14). Sin when it is completed, begetteth death (Jas. i. 15). Thus there are men who live and yet are dead. " Sinners," says St. John Chrysostom, " are dead while they live, and the just live after they are dead." " Thou dost weep," says St. Augustine, " over a body from which the soul has departed, but not over a soul from which God has withdrawn Himself." When God abandons the soul, the devil enters into it. By mortal sin the temple of the Holy Ghost is transformed into a den of robbers, the sister of the angels into the companion of fallen spirits. As a ship that has lost her rudder is driven about at the mercy of the current, so the soul that has lost divine grace is driven by Satan into perdition. Sin gives the devil power over the soul, for through sin man places himself under servitude to obey the devil (Rom. vi. 16). As every one thinks he may treat a widow as he chooses, as she has no one to protect her, so the demons do not hesitate to set upon the sinner; they cry: " God hath forsaken him; pursue him and take him, for there is none to deliver him " (Ps. lxx. 11). The loss of sanctifying grace entails upon the sinner the following terrible consequences: (1) He loses the supernatural beauty of the soul and becomes unclean before God; (2) He loses charity towards God and towards his neighbor; (3) His understanding is completely darkened, and his will immensely weakened; (4) He loses the merit of all the good works he had previously performed, and none of those which he does in a state of mortal sin gain for him a reward hereafter; (5) Finally, he is liable to fall into other mortal sins.

Through mortal sin we lose the supernatural beauty of the soul and become unclean before God.

Mortal sin is to the soul what decay is to an apple; the rottenness destroys the color, the scent, the flavor of the fruit, all, in short, that gives it worth and beauty; so sin robs the soul of all that makes it fair and precious. It would be a sore blow to a bride if she were to be so much disfigured by a severe illness as to become an object of repulsion to her betrothed; it is much the same with the soul that is guilty of mortal sin; she is thereby so much disfigured that Christ, her Spouse, regards her with aversion. Through mortal sin charity to God and to one's neighbor is lost. When the earth travels away from the sun, winter sets in; so the heart of man becomes cold when it is estranged from God by mortal sin; the flame of charity is then extinguished. The understanding is completely darkened by mortal sin. As heavy clouds hide the light of the sun from our sight and involve us in darkness, so mortal sin obscures the eye of reason, and renders us incapable of perceiving the brightness of the Sun of justice. A man who has fallen into mortal sin perceiveth not, as the Apostle says, the things that are of the Spirit of God (1 Cor. ii. 14). As a mirror covered with mildew no longer reflects the objects presented to it, so the soul which is sunk in sin can no longer receive the impressions of divine grace. The sinner is blinded, and fails as fully to see the misery and danger of his condition as one who wanders in the darkness of night beside a quarry; were the sinner in a state of grace, and enlightened by the Holy Spirit, he would be no less startled and alarmed at his spiritual condition than the traveller would be on perceiving in the daylight what a perilous path he had trodden. By reason of this blindness sinners are often gay and light-hearted in spite of their deplorable state. As the maniac laughs frantically while he tears his own flesh, so our erring brethren make merry while in their madness they inflict serious injury on their soul. A living body feels the prick of a needle; not so a corpse. Thus it is with the soul: As long as it preserves its life, it is sensitive to the least sin; but if it be dead, it experiences no stings of conscience, even if it be guilty of grievous crimes. Through mortal sin the will is immensely weakened. When the cold is extreme one's limbs are benumbed and paralyzed; so by mortal sin man loses the power to do what is good. He is held captive by mortal sin, as a bird is by bird-lime. Through mortal sin we lose the merit of all the good works we have previously performed. God says by the mouth of His prophet: "If the just man turn himself from his justice and do iniquity, all his justices which he hath done shall not be remembered" (Ezech. xviii. 24). The just man who falls into mortal sin, may be compared to a merchant who has accumulated great treasures, and whose vessel founders just as he enters the harbor. Mortal sin sweeps away at one stroke all our good works and our merits, as a sharp frost cuts off all the fair flowers in one night, or as a hailstorm ruins the crops of a whole year. He who falls into mortal sin earns no reward in heaven for the good works he performs while in a state of sin. As a branch cut off from the vine withers away and bears no fruit, so a man who has lost sanctifying grace can do no works that are meritorious. The apostles labored all night and took nothing; so the sinner during the night of sin cannot, in spite of his utmost exertions, gain any merit for heaven. The soul of a sinner is like a desert where nothing grows, but which is the haunt of reptiles and beasts of prey. How desolate is that spot where God is not! how parched without the dew of heaven, how sterile without the vivifying Sun of grace! One mortal sin makes it easy to commit others. When the soul has left the body, decomposition begins; and spiritual decay soon sets in when the Holy Spirit has departed from the soul. A grievous sin which has not been effaced by penance is the precursor of many others, which follow it as its punishment. "The man," says St. Augustine, "who persists in his iniquity, adds sin to sin."

2. Mortal sin brings down upon the sinner both eternal damnation and temporal chastisement.

By mortal sin we incur eternal damnation. As one throws away an apple that is rotten throughout, so God repudiates the soul that is stained with mortal sin. He who has fallen into mortal sin has lost the wedding garment, i.e., sanctifying grace; he will be cast into the exterior darkness (Matt. xxii. 13). Mortal sin is an act of high treason against the King of kings. This crime of high treason is punished on earth by a long term of imprisonment; as the majesty of God infinitely exceeds that of any earthly monarch, the punishment of mortal sin is of eternal duration. The man who commits mortal sin is as foolish as Esau, who for one mess, sold his first birthright (Heb. xii. 16), since for the sake of a momentary gratification he relinquishes his title to the kingdom of heaven. Blessed Thomas More, when sentenced to death, would not be persuaded to acknowledge the royal supremacy, for he said: "How foolish should I be, were I to barter everlasting honor and felicity for the transient happiness of a few fleeting years." Mortal sin brings temporal chastisements upon the sinner. God sends earthly punishments to restore the spiritual health of the sinner. The temporal penalty most certain to follow upon mortal sin is interior disquietude. Mortal sin destroys the serenity, the cheerfulness of the soul, as a high wind disturbs and ruffles the smooth surface of a lake. "The wicked are like the raging sea, that cannot rest" (Is. lvii. 20). Apprehension and terror follow mortal sin like its shadow. He who lives in mortal sin, carries hell about with him (St. John Chrysostom). Remember the fate of the fratricide Cain (Gen. iv. 14). The sinner's evil conscience daily calls to him: "Where is thy God?" (Ps. xli. 4.) What peace can the sinner enjoy when he knows that an almighty arm is uplifted against him? A flash of lightning, a peal of thunder, affects the sinner as much as the devout prayers of the faithful; in every sound he thinks to hear his sentence of condemnation. God has ordained that inordinate passions should be their own punishment. Spiritual consolations and sensual gratifications can no more co-exist than fire can mingle with water. Those who delight in worldly vanities are not capable of tasting spiritual joys. Mortal sin, moreover, brings temporal misfortunes on the sinner. Of this our first parents afford a striking example. They were driven out of paradise, condemned to labor in the sweat of their face, and made subject to death, because of their sin. The most ordinary consequence of sin is sickness; hence Our Lord said to the man whom He had cured: "Sin no more, lest some worse thing happen unto thee" (John v. 14). Want is sometimes the punishment of sin; witness the prodigal son (Luke xv.). The loss of property and of reputation are also consequences of sin, as is the case with thieves and drunkards. The guardian angels cease to protect those who give themselves up to sin. St. Basil says that as smoke drives away bees, so sin causes our good angel to depart. If a slave betrays his master, not his master alone, but all the members of his master's household are enraged with him. As David's servants were angry with Semei, who threw stones at the king, so the holy angels are displeased with the sinner who offends God. How great is man's folly! He is afraid of eating anything deadly, but he does not fear deadly sin, which causes the death of the soul.

THE CONSEQUENCES OF VENIAL SIN.

Venial sin is a slight thing in itself, but it deprives us of much that is good; just as a hair, if it gets into the pen, spoils the best handwriting.

1. Venial sin gradually leads to mortal sin, and eventuates in the loss of sanctifying grace.

Venial sin makes mortal sin easy. As a spot of decay in an apple gradually spreads until the whole fruit is rotten, so the man who does not heed venial sins will soon fall into mortal sin. As sickness precedes death, so venial sins precede mortal. He who begins by neglecting trifling faults, will end by committing grievous sins. Venial sins may be compared to the dust which settles on our clothes, and if it be not brushed off will spoil them in the end; it is the moth that frets away the garment of sanctifying grace. God permits those who make light of venial sin to fall into mortal sin as the chastisement of their negligence. "Avoid small sins," says St. John Chrysostom, "for they will grow into great sins." "He that is unjust in that which is little is unjust also in that which is greater" (Luke xvi. 10). As one who wants to cleave a log of wood makes a small incision, and then drives in the wedge, so the devil tempts us first to commit slight offences, and gradually leads us to greater transgressions. Venial sin is all the more dangerous because it deprives us of many actual graces, without which we cannot overcome the assaults of temptation. A mirror when covered with dust cannot reflect an image clearly, and the mirror of the soul, if its surface be obscured by the dust of venial sin, is almost impervious to the rays of the Sun of justice. A personage of distinction cannot be expected to approach a man who is frightfully disfigured by some cutaneous disease, much less to embrace him, or even suffer him to kiss his hand; so God will not admit you to His friendship or delight you with His consolations if your soul is defaced by venial sin. Venial sin lessens our diligence in the pursuit of what is good. A trifling indisposition often incapacitates us for the performance of the duties of our calling; in like manner venial sin weakens the will and indisposes it for good works. It diminishes the force of charity, and makes a man lukewarm in the service of God. To him may be applied the words of Holy Scripture: "Because thou art lukewarm, and neither cold nor hot, I will begin to vomit thee out of My mouth" (Apoc. iii. 16).

2. There are temporal penalties due to venial sin, and these will come down upon us either on earth or after death in purgatory.

Zachary was struck dumb because he would not believe the message of the angel (Luke i. 20); Moses was not allowed to enter the Promised Land because of his incredulity (Numb. xx. 12). Ananias and Saphira fell dead at St. Peter's feet in consequence of the deception they practised. Those who at their death are in a state of venial sin, will have to pass through the fires of purgatory in order to expiate them before gaining admittance to heaven. On this ac-

count the saints inflicted severe penalties upon themselves for the
least sin. Venial sin must needs be a great evil, since God, Who is
a merciful and gracious Father, punishes it with such rigor, namely
by temporary exclusion from His kingdom, and prolonged suffering
in purgatory.

IV. VICE.

**1. Vice is proficiency in the practice of evil, and the confirmed
tendency of the will towards evil which is acquired by habitual
sin.**

Everything is evil which is contrary to the will of God. A horse
when put into harness for the first time, tries to shake off the collar. By
degrees he became accustomed to it, and in time, when led out of
the stable, he goes of his own accord to be placed between the shafts,
although he has to undergo toil and fatigue. So man becomes accustomed to the servitude of sin. A dog who is trained to the chase
will in his eagerness outrun his master; so the man who is habituated
to sin, makes more haste to sin than the devil does to incite him
thereto.

The habit of vice is easily formed, but it requires a great
struggle to give it up, and the longer a man has indulged in
vice, the more difficult that struggle becomes.

Nothing is so easy to learn and so difficult to unlearn, as are
vicious practices. The vicious drift down with the stream, the virtuous swim against the current. Good works are arduous to perform,
but it is easy enough to do evil. To cast off the yoke of vice requires a hard battle. It is easier to fall into a pit than to get out of
it again. The devil entangles the sinner in his toils, as the spider
makes the fly fast in his web. When the sinner tries to shake himself free, he finds the flimsy web has become a heavy chain. As a
vessel which has got loose from its moorings in a river is swept
downwards, snapping like threads the ropes that hold it, so neither
admonitions nor any considerations whatever prevail to arrest the
downward course of a man who is addicted to vice, when he is carried
away by his passions. The longer he goes on in sin, the stronger will
be the habit formed, and the more difficult his conversion. The
deeper a nail is knocked in, the harder it is to pull out; so the longer
a man persists in sin, the greater the effort needed to break off the
habit. Those who shrink from jumping over the stream while it is
a mere rivulet, will find themselves unable to cross when it has become a wide river. The repetition of a sin forms a habit, the habit
becomes a necessity, and ere long it is impossible of eradication.
This impossibility leads to despair and eternal damnation (St. Augustine).

A man who is addicted to vice cannot amend of his own
power; he needs the mighty assistance of divine grace. Nor
can he amend all at once; a long and strenuous exertion of the
will is required to achieve his conversion. Furthermore he must

commence by combating one fault only, that very one to which he is most prone.

The snows do not melt unless the warm breath of spring passes over them, nor can man rise superior to his sins without divine grace. Those who have fallen into the pit of sin can only be lifted out of it by the help of God's grace. An old tree whose roots have run deep into the soil, cannot be torn up or bent down by ordinary means, so powerful graces are needed to effect the conversion of a hardened sinner. Remember the circumstances of St. Paul's conversion. For eighteen years St. Monica continued to weep and pray for her son's conversion. The sinner must first of all implore the aid of divine grace, or he will never be able to reform; better still if others will intercede for him. A man cannot all at once throw off the yoke of vice; constant and persevering exercise of the will is necessary. Habit must be overcome by habit. A physical ailment of long standing takes a long course of treatment for its cure, and the maladies of the soul can only be removed by patient resolution. For even after the Sacrament of Penance, a propensity to the long-indulged sin still remains; evil passions are ready to spring up again unless one is ever on one's guard. If one who is addicted to vice desires to reform, he must grapple first with one fault; and precisely that one which has most dominion over him. A bundle of wood cannot be broken unless the sticks are drawn out one after another and broken separately; the same course must be pursued in regard to our vices. If one is overcome, all the others are in great measure subdued. A military commander who is about to fall upon a hostile army, makes the attack at the point where the enemy is strongest, because if he takes that position, the conquest of the remainder will be an easy matter. Thus, if we overcome our dominant fault, we shall soon obtain the mastery over the lesser ones. If every year we rooted out one vice, we should soon become perfect men. Unhappily too many Christians only correct their lesser failings and allow their dominant fault to grow and flourish; or they rid themselves of one vice and become enthralled by another, like servants who leave one master only to take service with another.

2. Habitual sin makes a man supremely unhappy, because it deprives him completely of sanctifying grace, subjects him entirely to the dominion of the devil, and brings down on him many temporal judgments as well as eternal damnation.

The Holy Spirit does not dwell in the heart where vice reigns. Respectable people will not enter a tavern which is the resort of the drunken and dissolute, for the good have no fellowship with the evil. God will not make His abode in the sin-stained soul of the sinner. As one would rather live in the humble cottage, provided it be clean, than in a palace that was unclean and infected, so God will not visit the soul which is defiled and infected with the pestilence of sin. The vicious are completely under the dominion of the devil. The Roman emperor Valerian, having been taken prisoner by the King of Persia, was forced by the latter to make himself his footstool when he dismounted from his horse. Thus man, the son of the King of heaven, falls under the thraldom and servitude of the devil by the practice of vice. The just man is ever free, though he wear the chains of a slave; the sinner is ever enslaved, even on the throne; and every vice in which he indulges adds one more to his degrading fetters. A course of vice brings great misery upon a man in this life; loss of property, of health, of reputation; besides anxiety, discontent, etc. Sometimes God sends public calamities for the chastisement of nations that have sinned. Sin makes nations miserable (Prov. xiv. 34). Was not Attila, the King of the Huns, surnamed " the scourge of God "? Those who are the servants of vice shall not possess the kingdom of God (1 Cor. vi. 9, 10). " If you live according to the flesh, you shall die " (Rom. viii. 13). They who do the works of the flesh shall not obtain the kingdom of God (Gal. v. 19). When the fatal results of sin come upon the sinner, he makes good resolutions; but before long he is again led astray. Each time he repeats his sin his power of resisting it is lessened. Finally it works his ruin both for time and for eternity.

The wicked do not possess sanctifying grace, consequently their understanding is greatly obscured, and their will greatly weakened.

The understanding of the sinner is completely clouded. As cataract destroys the bodily sight, so vice obscures the eye of the soul. The passions which make their home in the heart of the sinner cloud his spirit and darken his intellect. As one who looks through a colored glass sees everything colored, so one who is the slave of his passions cannot judge of things aright; he views them in a false light. Nor can he attain a true knowledge of himself; his mind is like troubled water. which reflects one's countenance in a distorted manner. The habitual sinner is so blinded that he regards abhorrent vices as virtues, and is angry if his attention is drawn to his evil habits, their disgraceful nature, and their fatal consequences. Reason is, however, never completely dethroned by the rebellious passions. The will of the sinner is greatly weakened; he becomes powerless for good. The more a man sins, the weaker he becomes. If one who has fallen into a deep sleep is called to awake or otherwise roused, he opens his eyes, and makes an effort to rise up; but overcome by drowsiness, he sinks back on his pillow. So it is with one who is sunk in the slumber of sin. He may be seriously admonished; death, hell, judgment, and eternity, set before him; he listens to it all, acknowledges it to be true, and makes some slight effort to amend; but the habit of sin and the love of the world hold him captive; he presently relapses into sin. It is almost as impossible for one who lives in habitual sin to do good as for the Ethiopian to change his skin (Jer. xiii. 23). The habitual sinner ceases to struggle against sin. One is annoyed to see the first spot on a white garment; but after a second and a third and many others, one considers it as soiled, and one does not care what stains it contracts.

3. The most ordinary sins are the seven capital sins: Pride, disobedience, anger, avarice, intemperance in eating and drinking, unchastity, sloth.

These are the seven sinful proclivities of the human heart, which are the origin of every sin. All other sins take their rise from them, as from their source. They are called vices, because they are productive of permanent disorder in the soul. They are also simply called sins, because their outward manifestation may be venial or mortal sin, according as the offence is in a more or less weighty matter. One isolated act of a sin does not prove that sin to be habitual. They are called capital sins, because each one of these propensities is the head or centre whence other sins proceed. They are like commanding officers, who come at the head of a whole army of sins to lay waste the heart. Each one is a poisonous root which will bear deadly fruit. The seven deadly sins in their turn originate in temptations to ambition, avarice, and luxury (1 John ii. 16). A full enumeration of the principal sins is not possible, because the dispositions of every individual are utterly different, and the evil tendencies vary no less. Some reckon melancholy and vain-glory to be capital sins; envy is often placed among them, or again it is not mentioned as being the offspring of covetousness. Pride is universally acknowledged to be the queen of sins; to it is given the precedence over all the other sins. He who is under the permanent dominion of a capital sin is a server of idols (Eph. v. 5), because he makes a creature (self, a fellow-being, gold, the pleasures of the table, etc.), his final end. Such a one serves Mammon and not God (Matt. vi. 24). As the seven deadly sins close the portals of heaven against us, they may be compared to the seven nations which opposed the entrance of the Israelites into the Land of Promise (Deut. vii. 1). They are the seven devils whom Our Lord cast out of Mary Magdalen (Mark xvi. 9); the seven wicked spirits who enter into the man who has lost sanctifying grace (Luke xi. 26); they are the seven fatal diseases of the soul, which end in death. Pride resembles madness, disobedience blood poisoning, anger fever, covetousness consumption, intemperance dropsy, unchastity the plague, sloth paralysis. He who will be a friend of God must divest himself of these vices. Before we lay out a beautiful garden, the thorns and weeds must be rooted up. So those who desire their own sanctification must first eradicate their faults.

V. THE FORGIVENESS OF SIN.

1. There is no man upon earth without sin; consequently there is none who does not need the forgiveness of sin.

"If we say we have no sin, the truth is not in us" (1 John i. 8). The just man falls seven times (Prov. xxiv. 16). God permits us to fall into venial sin again and again, to keep us humble. As we sin daily, we must daily ask for the forgiveness of sin in the Our Father. Only by reason of an exceptional privilege, such as was bestowed by God upon His blessed Mother, can mortal man pass the period of his sojourn upon earth without committing venial sin (Council of Trent, 6, 23); nay more, without the succor of special grace it is impossible to avoid venial sin for any length of time. The highest perfection of which human frailty is capable is this: Not to commit any sin, even venial sin, with deliberate intention.

2. We can obtain forgiveness of sin, because Christ merited it

for us by the death of the cross; and because He gave power to forgive sins to His apostles and their successors.

There is nothing more consoling for mankind upon earth than the forgiveness of sins, for nothing causes us more misery than sin. Even in pagan times Socrates looked forward hopefully to the advent of a mediator who would teach mankind in what manner remission of sins was to be obtained. Christ earned the grace of forgiveness for us by His sacred Passion and death upon the cross (Council of Trent, 6, 7). Christ is the Lamb of God, Who taketh away the sins of the world (John i. 29). In Him we have redemption through His blood, the remission of sins (Col. i. 14). Christ is the propitiation for our sins, and not for ours only, but also for those of the whole world (1 John ii. 2). Christ conferred the power to forgive sins only upon the apostles and their successors. He Himself exercised this power in the case of Mary Magdalen, Zacheus, the good thief; when He healed the paralytic He said expressly: "That you may know that the Son of man hath power on earth to forgive sins, I say unto thee, Arise, take up thy bed, and go" (Matt. ix. 6). This same power which He possessed Our Lord gave to the holy apostles, when, after His resurrection He said to them: "Receive ye the Holy Ghost. Whose sins you shall forgive they are forgiven them, and whose sins you shall retain, they are retained" (John xx. 23). He therefore who would have his sins forgiven must address himself to the bishop or to the priests whom Christ has appointed. In the Catholic Church alone is remission of sins, for she alone has received the Holy Ghost as a pledge of this grace (St. Augustine).

3. Mortal sin is remitted by Baptism and penance, venial sin, and the temporal penalties due to it, by good works done in a state of grace. These good works are: Prayer, fasting, almsgiving, hearing holy Mass, receiving holy communion, use of the sacramentals, gaining indulgences, forgiving offences.

Baptism is the ship in which we embark on our voyage to heaven; if we commit mortal sin we are like men who are shipwrecked. The only hope for them of being saved is in laying hold of a plank, and clinging firmly to it; so for the Christian, the only means of reaching the port of eternal salvation is through the Sacrament of Penance. Not prayer, fasting, nor almsgiving in itself can procure for man the forgiveness of mortal sin; these can only lead to penance, by which sin is washed away. Angels and archangels have no power to alter this; nay, "The Redeemer Himself does not forgive sin without penance" (St. Augustine). Good works, do, however, avail for the expiation of venial sin. Thus St. Augustine declares: "A single *Pater Noster* said from the heart, will obliterate the venial sins of a whole day." Venial sins can also be remitted by the use of holy water, indulgences, prayers, communion, the blessing of a bishop, etc.

4. There is no sin too great for God to forgive here below, if it be sincerely repented of and humbly confessed.

God makes this promise to the contrite sinner: "If your sins be as scarlet, they shall be made white as snow; and if they be red as crimson, they shall be white as wool" (Is. i. 18). God makes no distinction between sinners; He permits the priest to forgive every sin without exception. Therefore no man is so godless and wicked but he may yet hope to obtain forgiveness, provided he is sincerely sorry for his transgressions. In fact God receives the sinner more graciously the greater his sin has been, just as a fisherman pursues his work more gladly, the bigger the fish he catches. The sin against the Holy Ghost is the only one which admits of no forgiveness, because the man who sins against the Holy Ghost is the man who will not amend. The fault does not rest with God, but with the man; for even if he acknowledges his sin he will not abandon it, and consequently does not bewail it. Without contrition and change of heart there is no forgiveness.

5. A sin once forgiven is effaced forever, even if the sinner falls again into mortal sin.

This is not the case with good works. They are reckoned again to a man's account, if he makes his peace with God. See how merciful is God almighty!

VI. TEMPTATION.

1. **Temptation is the action of the evil spirit upon our soul, in order to induce us to sin; he excites within us the concupiscence of the eyes, or the pride of life.**

Remember the temptation of Eve in paradise, and the threefold temptation of Our Lord in the desert. All the saints were greatly tempted: St. Hugh, Bishop of Grenoble, was tempted to blaspheme; St. Francis of Sales was tempted to despair; St. Francis of Assisi was tormented by suggestions of impurity. Some saints experienced temptations against the faith; some temptations lasted for years. God tempteth no man (Jas. i. 13); He simply permits man to be tempted. It is the devil who hammers at you when you are tempted. "Our wrestling is against the spirits of wickedness in high places" (Eph. vi. 12). On earth we are surrounded by robbers; many of us are overcome and wounded by them. The conflict with the spirit of evil is a more critical struggle; it is carried on covertly, and against a more powerful adversary—one who spares no pains and knows no shame; who, when he is repulsed, returns all the more defiantly to the attack. For six thousand years he has tempted mankind; such long practice has made him perfect. He excites within us concupiscence of the flesh, or concupiscence of the eyes, or the pride of life (1 John ii. 16). In this threefold manner he tempted Our Lord. Many temptations come upon a man through no fault of his own (witness Job); some are the result of culpable negligence (witness Eve). The evil enemy as a rule attacks our weak point, our affection for creatures. Like a fowler, he attracts the birds to his net by offering them the food they like best. Physical infirmities give the devil more power over us; every one knows how apt the sick are to be fretful, impatient and exacting. The devil sets to work craftily. He transforms himself into an angel of light (2 Cor. xi. 14); that is, he de-

ceives us by assuming an appearance of candor and piety. His arti-
fices prove his weakness; he would not resort to them were he powerful enough to do without them.

Temptation is not in itself sinful, only acquiescence in the
suggestions of the tempter is sin.

Hence we ought not to be alarmed and uneasy when we feel the
incentive to sin, but we should trust in God's help, saying: " O Lord,
make haste to help me! Jesus and Mary be my help!" To tremble
in the hour of temptation betrays a want of confidence in the divine
assistance; the devil will assail the fearful soul only the more fiercely.
Unless we remain calm, we cannot possibly conquer. Those who lose
their composure are like a bird caught in the net; the more it flutters
and tries to escape, the more it becomes entangled in the meshes.
Our Lord promises us: " In your patience you shall possess your
souls" (Luke xxi. 19). The good Christian is like a soldier, who as
a rule rejoices when war breaks out, in the prospect of gaining rich
booty.

**2. God allows us to be tempted out of mercy, for the good
of our souls.**

As the schoolmaster examines his scholars in order to give them
a good testimonial, so God deals with the souls of men; He allows
us to be tried by temptation to give us the opportunity of manifesting our loyalty to Him, and acquiring a claim to the recompense He
promises us. Thus He has only our welfare in view. The tempter
however, the evil enemy, means no good to us; he aims at our ruin,
as the history of Job testifies. Temptations may therefore be said to
be a mark of the divine favor. The archangel Raphael said to
Tobias: " Because thou wast acceptable to God, it was necessary
that temptation should prove thee" (Tob. xii. 13). God sends temptations to those whom He trusts; hence it is that those who fear Him
are more sorely tempted than other men. The devil does not tempt
those who are already in his power, but those whom he fears will
elude his grasp or who may be injurious to him. St. Ephrem in a
vision saw a large city, the inhabitants of which were very corrupt;
only one devil was sitting on the wall, and he was half asleep. But
in the desert he saw a whole swarm of devils busily engaged within
the cell of a hermit. Thus the fact that a man is greatly tempted
proves him to be a friend of God, and a stranger to, an enemy of
the devil. Pirates do not attack an empty ship, but one which they
know to be returning home with a valuable cargo. A king does not
take up arms against loyal subjects, but against rebels who resist
his authority. Temptations have besides the following advantages:
They rouse us from a state of tepidity (they are what the spur
is to the horse); they cleanse us from imperfections, as the stormy
sea throws out foreign substances; they make us humble, by acquainting us with our frailty; they increase our strength, as a high wind
makes the tree strike deeper root; they augment our charity, as the
breeze makes the flame burn more fiercely; they afford us a means
of expiating sin in this life; finally, they add to our glory hereafter,
as the beauty of a jewel is enhanced by polishing. Thus we see that
the tempter does us good service, and his temptations are steps in the

ladder which leads to heaven. Therefore let him who is tempted rather pray for strength to resist the temptation than for its entire removal. We read that St. Paul thrice besought the Lord that the angel of Satan might depart from him, and asked in vain (2 Cor. xii. 8).

God permits every man to be tempted, but He never permits us to be tempted beyond our strength.

Temptations must come to every man. No one can be crowned unless he has conquered; no one can conquer unless he fight, and no one can fight without an adversary. Hence temptations must come. For this reason God subjected the angels to a probation, and also our first parents. And subsequently to the Fall trials have been the lot of mankind (witness Job and Tobias). " The life of man upon earth is a warfare " (Job vii. 1). The Apostle compares the Christian to one who runs in a race (1 Cor. ix. 25). " Yet God will not suffer us to be tempted above that which we are able to bear " (1 Cor. x. 13). The devil can only tempt man within the limit God sets him, as we learn from the history of Job. And when God permits violent temptations to assail us, He gives grace sufficient to enable us to withstand them (2 Cor. xii. 9). The stronger the temptation, the more abundant is the grace; the greater the danger, the more potent the divine assistance. No sinner can venture to say as his excuse that the temptation was too great for him to resist.

3. We ought to protect ourselves from temptation by assiduous work, by keeping our thoughts fixed upon God, and by continual self-conquest.

In order to hold a fortress against the enemy two things are necessary: (1) Strong fortifications and well-guarded gates; (2) In case of attack valiant defence. In like manner we must protect our soul, to prevent the entrance of the evil enemy. Our fortifications will be: Continual occupation; this is the surest means of holding temptations aloof. Thieves do not break into a house where work is going on. Idleness is the parent of crime. We shall also find it easy to resist temptation, if we keep our mind fixed on God. A traveller journeying towards a fixed destination meets with few difficulties on his way, whereas the vagrant, wandering hither and thither, is sure to get in trouble. So it is with the Christian who makes God his final end, and one who has no aim in life. Hence Christ exhorts us: " Watch ye and pray, that you enter not into temptation " (Matt. xxvi. 41). Wolves do not approach a watch fire and the devil leaves those alone who are on their guard. When Moses stood with arms uplifted to God, Israel was victorious; but when through weariness he let them fall, that moment the enemy prevailed. The majority of the sins good people commit come from forgetfulness of God's presence; the habit of self-control also greatly helps us to conquer temptation. He who is accustomed to repress his impulses is like a soldier, well trained in the use of arms before he goes to battle. Practice in self-conquest strengthens the will. But attachment to creatures makes a man an easy prey to the devil; just as one who carries a heavy load cannot run away when robbers attack him.

4. When we are tempted we ought to betake ourselves immediately to prayer, or think of our last end, or of the evil consequences of sin.

If the enemy dares to attack the fortress in spite of the ramparts raised about it, it behooves us to defend it manfully. When assailed we must instantly assume the defensive; for of all things it is most important to repulse the first onslaught. The greater our determination, the sooner will our adversary be discouraged. If we falter, he will force an entrance, and gain the mastery over our imagination. He acts like soldiers, who when they have taken the enemy's guns, instantly turn them upon him. St. Jerome says that he who does not resist immediately is already half conquered. A conflagration can be extinguished at the outset, but not later on. A young tree is easily bent, not an old one. But since we can do nothing in our own strength, we must strive to obtain divine grace. Wherefore let him who is tempted have recourse to prayer; let him imitate the apostles when a storm arose on the sea of Genesareth; or the child who, when he sees a large dog coming, runs to his mother. He who neglects prayer in the time of temptation is like a general, who, when surrounded by the enemy, does not ask for reinforcements from his monarch. Adam fell into sin because when he was tempted he did not look to God for help. We should say a Hail Mary, or at least devoutly utter the holy names of Jesus and Mary. " These holy names," St. John Chrysostom declares, " have an intrinsic power over the devil, and are a terror to hell." At the name of Mary the devils tremble with fear; when she is invoked their power forsakes them as wax melts before the fire. Prayer is the weapon wherewith to ward off the assaults of our spiritual foe; it is more potent than all the efforts of the demons because by prayer we procure the assistance of God, and nothing can withstand His might. Prayer is exactly opposed to temptation for it enlightens the understanding and fortifies the will. The sign of the cross and holy water have also great efficacy against the spirit of evil. He flies from the cross as a dog flies at the sight of the whip. Holy water derives its efficacy from the prayers of the Church. St. Thomas Aquinas and many other saints frequently made use of the sign of the cross with excellent results. St. Teresa on the other hand constantly employed holy water. It is well to sprinkle the sick and dying with holy water, and we should never omit to take it on entering a church. A second means of conquering temptations is to turn our thoughts elsewhere, above all to think of the last things: of death, of the judgment, of eternal punishment. " Remember thy last end and thou shalt never sin " (Ecclus. vii. 40). Or we may consider the terrible consequences of sin. The Romans used to say: " Whatever thou doest, act wisely and think of the end." In some cases, especially when temptations against the faith or against purity present themselves, the wiser course is to despise the temptation rather than grapple with it. Proud people, like the devil, are soonest got rid of by ignoring them altogether. If the passer-by takes no notice of the dog, he soon leaves off barking. If one keeps still the bees do not harm him, but if one drives them off, then they sting. Again, we may follow Our Lord's example, and resolutely forbid the tempter to remain. Christ repulsed him with the words: "Begone, Satan" (Matt. iv. 10). St. James bids us: "Resist the devil and he will fly from you" (Jas. iv. 7). The devil is like an angry woman, who blusters if she sees that her husband is afraid of her, but who gives way directly if he exerts his authority. One may also retort upon the tempter by quoting the word of God, as Our Lord did (Eph. vi. 17). St. Peter says: "Whom resist ye, strong in faith" (1 Pet. v. 9). Another means of overcoming temptation is by humbling ourselves before God. "To the humble He giveth grace" (1 Pet. v. 5). St. Augustine in the hour of temptation was accustomed to exclaim: "Thou knowest, O Lord, that I am but dust and my frailty is great." When we are pressed hard by temptation, it is well to confess to the priest those sins of our past life of which we are most ashamed; this is a sure means of repelling the severest temptations. It is advisable to acquaint one's confessor with all one's temptations. Satan would have us keep silence concerning them, whereas it is God's will that we should discover them to our superiors and spiritual guides, for if sinful thoughts are disclosed, the temptation is already half overcome. To open its griefs gives, moreover, great relief to the troubled heart.

5. He who has conquered temptation will receive more graces from God.

When we have driven away the spirit of evil, the holy angels come and console us. We read that when the tempter had left Our Lord angels came and ministered to Him (Matt. iv. 11). Fierce temptations are generally the precursors of special marks of the divine favor. Therefore, let us see that we make a good use of temptations, one and all. They are like examination at a school; examinations are not held every day, so the opportunity of gaining a prize does not come within the reach of the pupils every day.

VII. OCCASIONS OF SIN.

1. By occasions of sin are meant such places, persons, or things which as a rule are the means of leading us into sin, if we go in quest of them.

For instance, the society of the dissolute, the perusal of antireligious books are an occasion of sin to every one; so is the drinkingsaloon to the drunkard. Occasions of sin may be compared to a plague-stricken person, who gives the contagion to all who approach him; or to fire, which burns all that it touches, or to a stone in the way, which causes many to stumble.

Occasions of sin may be voluntary or involuntary.

The drinking-saloon is a voluntary occasion of sin to the inebriate, because nothing obliges him to frequent it; but to the landlord himself it is an involuntary one.

2. To expose one's self heedlessly to an occasion of sin, is in itself a sin; it entails the loss of divine grace and leads to mortal sin.

Every one knows it is wrong to carry a burning torch into a place where hay, straw, and other inflammable materials are stored. To delight in occasions of evil and to fall into sin, St. Augustine declares to be one and the same thing. St. Peter sought the company of the enemies of Christ in the high priests' palaces and he fell, for God withdrew His grace. "He that loveth danger shall perish in it" (Ecclus. iii. 27). "He that toucheth pitch shall be defiled with it" (Ecclus. xiii. 1).

3. **He who finds himself in circumstances which are an occasion of sin to him, and does not instantly leave them, although it is in his power to do so, commits a sin; he will be deprived of the assistance of divine grace and will fall into mortal sin.**

In paradise Eve sinned by not going away from the tree. St. Augustine says our first parents ought not to have so much as touched the forbidden fruit. Cleomenes, King of Sparta, was once urged by a foreign prince to betray his country for a large sum of money. The king's little daughter, hearing what was proposed, exclaimed: "Father, go quite away or the stranger will corrupt thee." The king instantly left the room and would not suffer the stranger to enter his presence again. Let us be equally prompt in forsaking occasions of sin.

4. **He who refuses to give up what is to him an occasion of sin, cannot expect to obtain pardon of sin here, or eternal salvation hereafter.**

One who so acts has no contrition, that determinate turning away from creatures and turning to God, which is an indispensable condition for forgiveness of sin. Hence one who might give up an occasion of sin without great difficulty and does not do so, must not expect absolution from the priest. It is otherwise if giving up the occasion of sin involves loss of reputation, of property, of the means of livelihood; but even then he must promise either to abstain from the sin, or avoid the occasion of it. We know from Our Lord's words that hell awaits those who will not forsake the occasions of sin: "If thy hand or thy foot scandalize thee, cut it off and cast it from thee. It is better for thee to go into life maimed or lame, than having two hands or two feet, to be cast into everlasting fire" (Matt. xviii. 8); that is to say, although any object be as dear to you as your hand or your foot, you must separate yourself from it, if it is an occasion of sin to you, or hell will be your portion. "What sacrifices men will make," says St. Augustine, "to preserve their mortal life; they shrink from no expense, no humiliation; yet they will make no sacrifice for life immortal." As a man consents to the amputation of his hand or foot if it is a question of saving his life, so the sinner must detach himself from what he loves best, in order to save his soul. Traders will cast all their merchandise into the sea to save the ship and their own lives from destruction; so we must part with all to which our heart clings most fondly, rather than imperil our eternal salvation.

Hence even the greatest saints did not venture lightly to expose themselves to the danger of sin.

Their watchword was: "Safety is in flight." It is said that St.

Peter on the outbreak of the persecution, fled from Rome, fearing lest he should again be tempted to deny Christ; not until Our Lord appeared to him outside the city gates did he venture to expose himself to the danger. And shall those who are the slaves of their senses consider vigilance to be superfluous? Will one who cannot swim dare to plunge into the water?

Those, however, who by reason of their calling or any other necessity, are compelled to expose themselves to occasions of sin, must put their trust in the protection of the Most High.

Officials, priests, doctors and others are often compelled by the duties of their office to incur many dangers. If they do not tempt God by presumption, they may count upon the assistance of His grace; but not so those who in an uncalled-for manner and without just cause expose themselves to the risk of sin.

5. The most common and the most dangerous occasions of sin are: liquor saloons, dancing saloons, bad theatres, bad periodicals, and bad novels.

Some one may perhaps ask: Is one expected to live like a recluse or a misanthropist? St. Augustine answers this question: "Better and holier people than thou have forsworn those amusements; canst not thou do the same? The Christian's pleasures are not taken from him, they are changed and ennobled." Again he says: "How sweet it is to renounce the vain enjoyments of the world! I shrank from the obligation to forego them, and now I rejoice in having lost them." "The worldling," says St. Bernard, "sees our afflictions, but he knows not our consolations." Those are no true joys which are not in God.

1. The liquor saloon is principally dangerous for those who go thither every day, and spend a long time there.

There is nothing sinful in frequenting a saloon as a recreation after the day's work; in fact taverns are necessary for the entertainment of travellers. But one ought to be careful as to the character of the house one frequents, so as not to associate with hard drinkers, or men whose conversation is unseemly. Unfortunately those who spend much of their time in the saloon are apt to acquire the habit of drinking and gambling, to be involved in quarrels, and to neglect the duties of their calling.

2. The dancing saloon is chiefly a source of danger to those who carry dancing to an excess, or who have already been led into sin by it.

In the art of dancing there is nothing evil or reprehensible; it is in itself nothing more or less than an innocent means of enjoyment and relaxation, and of promoting good feeling and friendly intercourse among men. Among the Jews the dance was often made a part of divine worship; we read that when the Ark of the Covenant was removed, David danced with all his might before the Lord (2 Kings vi. 14). The Hebrew maidens performed round or processional dances on many religious festivals (Judg. xxi. 21; Exod. xv. 20);

and St. Basil and St. Gregory the Great state as their opinion that
the angels move in the solemn measures of the dance before the
throne of God in heaven. However the rule must be strictly observed
of not dancing at prohibited times (in Advent or Lent) nor with persons of improper character (as is often the case at public balls), and
of not taking part in dances which outrage modesty and decorum,
as some do in the present day. Young people must, however, be
warned against indulging in this amusement inordinately, as it has
a tendency to arouse sensuality, to excite the passions, and lessen the
sense of Christian modesty. Living as they did in heathen times,
the Fathers of the Church denounced dancing in no measured terms.
On the occasions of weddings, entertainments, or family gatherings, when dancing is proposed as the evening's amusement, it would
be unfriendly to refuse to take part. But those for whom dancing has
often proved an occasion of sin, must if possible eschew it for the
future; they may allege as an excuse that it is injurious to them.

3. The theatre is a source of danger to those who frequent it,
because some theatres are a school of vice rather than of virtue.

When dramas of an elevating and edifying nature are put upon the
stage, plays in which virtue and innocence triumph, and heroic devotion to religion, the love of one's country, the love of one's neighbor,
are held up to admiration, and the misery and shame attendant upon
crime depicted in its true colors, the theatre becomes a school of
morals. But good plays are rare: they ill suit the taste of the present
day; and often they would be acted to an empty house. The majority
of plays, more especially on the continent of Europe, are of a ques-
tionable tendency; in France, in Italy, vice—some illicit affection—
is often represented upon the stage as attractive and delightful, while
virtue is uninteresting and despicable. Even the freethinker Rousseau says that in the theatre our evil propensities are too often fostered and encouraged, our power to resist the force of our passions
is diminished, we learn to regard work as irksome, and useful employment as distasteful. Moreover, it cannot be denied that the heated
atmosphere of a crowded house and the late hours are prejudicial to
the health of the habitual play-goer.

4. Bad periodicals are dangerous to all who read them; their
effect is to gradually undermine the faith and awaken discontent
in the minds of those who read them regularly; and whoever
takes such journals, declares himself an enemy to religion.

The society papers of the day pander to the popular taste. Scandals in high life, political feuds, animadversions on the conduct of
prominent persons, sneers at religious ordinances, the defence of
wrong-doers, such is the *pabulum* too often provided for the reader.
The writers in such papers are frequently those who have fallen low
in the social scale, and the editors are in many cases Jews. The
Holy Father has said that a large proportion of the countless evils
of the day and the unhappy condition of society are to be ascribed
to the journals that issue from the press, and he exhorts the faithful to endeavor to counteract their corrupting influence by upholding
those that are of an opposite tendency. Not only may this be done
by subscribing to some Christian periodical, lending it to others,

asking for it at reading-rooms and hotels, but by contributing letters and sending advertisements to journals of whose principles we approve. He who underrates the importance of the press displays little knowledge of the times in which he lives. The press is a gigantic power, especially since it has taken the telegraph and telephone into its service, and can thus supply the reader with the latest intelligence from all parts of the world. The daily papers are therefore taken in and eagerly read by all classes of society. And since, in addition to the latest news, they pronounce a verdict upon all questions of the day, concerning religion, politics, science, art, commerce, etc., the press is the great educator of the masses, the source whence the people derive their information and form their opinions. The press may well be said to be the organ of public opinion. Even as early as the commencement of the present century, when the press first began to be developed, the Emperor Napoleon spoke of it as a sixth great European power. He expressed himself thus because he was sensible of the influence exercised by the Rhine *Mercury*, which had just been started by Görres. Hence we learn how important a duty it is to support and encourage the Catholic press.

5. Bad novels are dangerous to all, for the novel-reader acquires a false and exaggerated view of life.

Indiscriminate novel-reading must be avoided, for a large proportion of works of fiction present poison in a golden goblet. Crime and vice, sins of immorality, are not only justified; they are arrayed in the most fascinating garb, depicted in the most charming colors. Thus they rouse and inflame the dormant passions of the human heart. A novelist once while being shown over a prison, was addressed by two young fellows. "You ought to be wearing these handcuffs instead of us," they said to him, "for it was through you that we got here." Many works of fiction are, it is true, of a perfectly harmless character. But even at the best the habitual reader of romances is transported into an unreal world, and is rendered incapable of judging justly of the world of actuality. Books of general interest, such as the lives of saints and of distinguished personages are far preferable to romances, for the facts they contain bear the stamp of truth, and are much more improving to the mind than fiction is.

VIII. THE SEVEN PRINCIPAL VIRTUES AND THE SEVEN PRINCIPAL VICES.

1. HUMILITY.

1. The humble man is he who acknowledges his own nothingness and the nothingness of all earthly things, and comports himself in accordance with this conviction.

The heathen centurion at Capharnaum displayed great humility when he said to Our Lord: "Lord, I am not worthy that Thou shouldst enter under my roof, but only say the word and my servant shall be healed" (Matt. viii. 8). Notwithstanding his position, his wealth, his good works—he had built the Jews a synagogue—he thought nothing of himself. Humility is twofold; it consists of humility of the understanding, by which a man becomes conscious of his own abjection, and humility of the will, which causes him to manifest his consciousness in his conduct; he humbles himself, and takes the lowest place. That would be false humility which was merely external, not heartfelt. St. Bonaventure defines humility as voluntary self-abasement resulting from the knowledge of our own frailty.

We learn humility by the consideration of the infinite majesty of God and the transitory nature of earthly things.

The poor man feels his poverty most keenly when he compares himself with his opulent neighbor. St. Augustine prayed for the knowledge of God, that he might thereby know himself. The majesty of God is most apparent in creation. In the firmament of heaven are many million orbs far surpassing in magnitude our earth, which is but a speck of dust in the universe. How insignificant then is each individual man! Must not the pride of every one be humbled at the sight of the endless myriads of worlds that people space, and which no man can count? And what is one single man among the hundreds of millions that inhabit the earth, not to speak of those that have lived in the past, and will live in the future. All earthly things pass away like a shadow and have no value before God. " The grave," says St. John Chrysostom, " is the school wherein we learn humility." Let no man pride himself on his riches; he may lose them in a single night; he must lose them at his death. Let no man pride himself on his physical beauty, for it may be disfigured by disease, and after death will be the prey of worms. Let no man pride himself upon his knowledge; how soon he forgets what he has learned, and how immeasurable is the amount of what he does not know! A philosopher of antiquity used to say: " All I know is that I know nothing." " If it seem to thee that thou knowest many things and understandest them well enough, know at the same time that there are many more things of which thou art ignorant " (Imitation, Book 1, ch. 2). Besides all our knowledge is ignorance compared with the infinite wisdom of God. Let no man pride himself upon earthly honor, for to-day the people cry " Hosanna," and to-morrow " Crucify him." How shortlived is the power and prestige of earthly potentates (witness Napoleon). Let no man pride himself even upon the graces he has received from God, for they may be withdrawn at any moment, and they increase his responsibility. Neither let him pride himself upon his good works, for God has no need of his goods (Ps. xv. 2). After we have done all, we are unprofitable servants (Luke xvii. 10). Whatever therefore a man may possess, he in reality possesses nothing or next to nothing. The humble man is no hypocrite; he only forms a just estimate of things.

The humble man conducts himself in the following manner: He delights in abasement, he does not attach his heart to transitory good things, he trusts wholly in God, and does not fear man.

The humble man delights in abasement; he never unnecessarily attracts attention to himself, i.e., he avoids ostentation and singularity in his demeanor and deportment, in his conversation, his gestures, at prayer, in dress, at table. He never seeks to make his humility conspicuous by downcast eyes, a slouching gait, a dejected mien; he is humble of heart, like Our Lord; he only allows his humility to be observed when occasion requires, and then only simply and unaffectedly. He is not always calling himself the chief of sinners; uncalled for self-blame generally betokens pride. Furthermore he hides his talents, for he knows that what man reveals God conceals, and what man disclaims, God proclaims. St. Anthony of Padua concealed his great erudition until God made it known. The humble man does not think himself better than others; he esteems others above himself (Phil. ii. 3). He does not publish the failings of others, he does not choose the highest place (Luke xiv. 10); on the contrary, he rejoices in being slighted, despised, humiliated, knowing that for this God will exalt him (Luke xiv. 10). Thus it was with the publican in the Temple (Luke xviii. 13); the humble man aspires only after eternal treasures, and does not attach his heart to what is transitory. Earthly good things, riches, dignities, pleasures, the praise of men, do not allure him; he is aware that he is none the better for them in God's sight, and they may prove his ruin. Earthly sufferings, contempt, reproaches, ridicule, persecution, do not dishearten him; he glories in them, because they enable him to earn heaven. He despises contempt, because it cannot harm him. Thus St. Paul writes: "To me it is a very small thing to be judged by you, or by man's day" (1 Cor. iv. 3). The humble man trusts in God alone. Conscious of his own weakness he does not confide in his own strength, but only in the aid of divine grace; as Joseph did when required to interpret Pharao's dream (Gen. xli. 16). He does not take to himself the credit even of his virtues and good works, but ascribes all to God, knowing that it is God Who worketh in Him; as the sun calls vegetable life into being upon the earth. Yet he is ready to acknowledge the favors God confers on him, saying with the blessed Mother of God: "He that is mighty hath done great things to me" (Luke i. 49). The recognition of these favors makes him grateful to God and increases his love of God. "No one," says St. Teresa, "will do great things for God, who does not know that God has done great things for him." The humble man does not fear men, because, far from being cast down by any humiliation he may meet with at their hands he rejoices in it. Besides he knows that he is in God's safekeeping, and to them that love God all things work together for good (Rom. viii. 28). Discouragement and pusillanimity are not characteristics of true humility.

2. Christ gave us in Himself the grandest example of humility, for He, being the Son of God, took the form of a servant, chose to live in great lowliness, was most condescending in His intercourse with men, and finally, voluntarily endured the ignominious death of the cross.

Christ emptied Himself, taking the form of a servant, i.e., human nature (Phil. ii. 7). In the Sacrament of the Altar He even takes the form of bread. And at the baptism of Our Lord the Holy Spirit assumed the shape of an animal, the dove. The prophets, in predicting the coming of Christ spoke of Him under the designation of the Lamb of God. Thus we see how almighty God humbles Himself. Our Lord lived in great lowliness; He chose for His birthplace not a royal palace but a stable; for His Mother, not a queen but a poor maiden; for His foster-father a humble carpenter; for His dwelling-place an obscure town; for His apostles, not the philosophers and sages of the world, but simple and unlearned fishermen. In His intercourse with men Our Lord was most condescending; He encouraged children to approach Him, He even conversed with sinners (e.g., the Samaritan woman, Mary Magdalen, the woman taken in adultery); at the Last Supper He washed His disciples' feet, and made not the slightest objection to go to the house of the centurion, when the latter entreated Him to cure his servant (Matt. viii. 7). Crucifixion was at that time the most ignominious death by which a man could die, yet Christ chose that very death for Himself; showing by His own actions that humility is the royal road to God.

In His teaching also Our Lord exhorts us constantly to the practice of humility. "He that is the greatest among you shall be your servant" (Matt. xxiii. 11), and again: "When you shall have done all these things that are commanded you say: We are unprofitable servants" (Luke xvii. 10).

Moreover He commends humility in the parable of the Pharisee and the publican (Luke xviii. 13). On one occasion he took a child and said: "Whosoever shall humble himself as this little child, he is the greater in the kingdom of heaven" (Matt. xviii. 4). He presents Himself to us as a pattern of this virtue: "Learn of Me, because I am meek and humble of Heart, and you shall find rest to your souls" (Matt. xi. 29). Finally, He promises that the humble shall be exalted (Luke xiv. 11), and shall enter into the kingdom of heaven (Matt. v. 3).

3. Humility leads to great sanctity, to exaltation, and to everlasting felicity.

Furthermore through it we obtain enlightenment of the understanding, true peace of mind, forgiveness of sin, a speedy answer to prayer, and are enabled to overcome temptation without difficulty.

God is with the humble. If any one has a lowly opinion of himself, and considers himself inferior to others, it is an unfailing proof that the Holy Spirit dwells within him. In the first place the humble man attains a high degree of perfection. The more humble he is, the more perfect he is, and vice versa. Well-filled ears of corn bend downwards, the thin ears hold their heads aloft. Empty vessels make the most sound. "He who thinks much of himself," says St. Teresa, "thinks much of little; he who thinks little of himself, thinks little of much." Humility is the surest test of sanctity. St. Philip Neri was once sent by the Holy Father to a convent in the vicinity of Rome one of whose inmates enjoyed a reputation for sanctity, in order to test the truth of that report. As soon as he entered the parlor, he requested the nun in question to clean his boots, which were covered with mud. She replied in no very courteous manner that she was unaccustomed to such work. St. Philip returned to the Pope and said: "She is no saint and works no miracles, for she lacks what is most essential, humility." Humility leads to exaltation. Our Lord says: "Every one that exalteth himself shall be humbled, and he that humbleth himself shall be exalted" (Luke xiv. 11). No man can ascend who has not first descended. "Be humbled in the sight of God and He will exalt you" (Jas. iv. 10). The blessed Mother of God attributed all the graces she received from God to her humility: "He hath regarded the humility of His handmaiden; for behold, from henceforth all generations shall call me blessed" (Luke i. 48). Honor pursues him who flies from her, humility leads to everlasting felicity. Our Lord says: "Blessed are the poor in spirit, for theirs is the kingdom of heaven" (Matt. v. 3). The gate of heaven is narrow, and only little ones, i.e., the humble, can pass through. Humility is also a means of obtaining enlightenment of the mind through the Holy Spirit. The humble alone can enter into the spirit of Our Lord's teaching. He Himself says: "I confess to Thee, O Father, Lord of heaven and earth, because Thou hast hid these things from the wise and prudent and hast revealed them to little ones" (Matt. xi. 25). St. Peter says: "God resisteth the proud, but to the humble He giveth graces" (1 Pet. v. 5). The communications of the Most High are with the simple (Prov. iii. 32), that is, He enlightens his mind. Hence it is that the poor and unlearned sometimes have a truer knowledge of the things of God than the learned. The shepherds were informed of Christ's birth, the Scribes and Pharisees were not. He must stoop who desires to draw water out of the fountains of God's grace. St. Teresa says that one day in which we humble ourselves before God is more fruitful in graces than many days spent in prayer. The humble man attains true peace of mind. Our Lord says: "Learn of Me, for I am meek and lowly of Heart, and you shall find rest to your souls" (Matt. xi. 29). The humble are not lifted up by prosperity nor cast down by adversity. The humble man obtains forgiveness of sins. The publican who smote upon his breast and said: "God, be merciful to me a sinner," went down to his house justified (Luke xviii. 13). The humble man obtains a speedy answer to prayer. "The prayer of him that humbleth himself shall pierce the clouds" (Ecclus. xxxv. 21). The humble man overcomes temptation without difficulty. Humility is the most powerful weapon wherewith to vanquish the devil. It is the virtue he most fears, for it is the only one which he is unable to imitate.

2. THE OPPOSITE OF HUMILITY : PRIDE.

1. He is proud who overestimates his own worth, or the value of his earthly possessions, and shows openly that he does so.

The giant Goliath was proud; he exalted himself overmuch (1 Kings xvii.). Many a one overrates the worth of his body, is proud of his fine physique, the beauty of his features; others overrate the worth of their wealth, their learning, their birth, the

virtues they imagine themselves to possess, etc. The proud man resembles the devil, or a drunkard, for pride is a kind of intoxication
which fills one with strange fancies and makes one talk in a foolish
manner and do irrational things. Pride is like a bubble that looks
large, but whose size is deceptive; it is a color which fades in the
sun, for the proud will appear in all their native vileness when, after
death, they stand in the light of the Sun of justice. They are like
the frog in the fable who puffed himself out in the hope of appearing
as large as the ox.

The proud man manifests the undue opinion he has of himself in the following manner: He tries to attract notice by his
conversation and his dress, he strives after honor, distinctions,
and earthly riches, he despises the assistance and grace of God,
and relies only on himself and on earthly things.

Pride is a mimicry of God. The proud man desires to appear
greater than he is. If he has done anything good, he boasts loudly of
it, as a hen cackles when she has laid an egg. Sometimes he speaks
depreciatingly of himself, but only in the hope of hearing others
praise him the more. He slanders others and thinks evil of them,
as the Pharisee did in the Temple (Luke xviii. 11). Pride makes
itself manifest in dress; the proud dress above their station, they
dress showily, in the latest fashion, and wear a great many unnecessary ornaments. The people who attach so much importance to dress
are not as a rule the most virtuous. They are extravagant, hard-
hearted to the poor, and deceitful, for by dressing unsuitably to their
class they give themselves out for what they are not. Love of dress often
leads to worse sins, for those who spend so much care on the adorn-
ment of their person lose sight of their final end, and lead a godless
life. He who stands well in God's sight has no need of choice and
costly apparel; good and holy people have generally dressed in a
simple, quiet manner. The Emperor Heraclius found that he could
not carry the true cross, which had been recovered from the Saracens,
back to Jerusalem, until he had laid aside his rich garments; an unseen hand held him back. One ought however to dress properly and
suitably to one's position, and have a strict regard to cleanliness.
The proud pursue honors as boys hunt after butterflies; and wl. n
they have gained them, they exult as loudly as if they had achieved
something wonderful, although they have nothing to boast of in
reality; for the honor and applause of men are like the morning dew,
glittering with rainbow tints, but quickly disappearing in the sun,
or like smoke which the wind carries away. How foolish are they
who covet earthly glory! The proud man despises the help and grace
of God, and relies upon himself alone, trusting in the things of earth.
He is his own deity. "The beginning of the pride of man is to fall
off from God" (Ecclus. x. 14). The proud neglect prayer and the
ordinances of religion; they are not sensible of their own sinfulness
and misery, or if they are they will not apply to the physician, but
try to heal themselves. Hence it is that God is the enemy of the
proud. "God resisteth the proud" (1 Pet. v. 5). Pride is hateful
before God and man (Ecclus. x. 7).

2. **Pride leads to all manner of vices, to degradation here and**

eternal damnation hereafter; it also destroys the value of all our good works.

Pride leads to all manner of vices. Pride is the beginning of all sin (Ecclus. x. 15), the parent of vice; many and evil are her progeny. Pride leads more especially to disobedience (witness Absalom); to cruelty (as in Herod's case, to the murder of the innocents), to apostasy (as with Luther, who was offended because he was slighted at Rome); to strife, envy, ingratitude and impurity. God punishes secret pride by open sin. He permits the proud to fall into sin in order that they may be humbled and amend. He who has vanquished pride has vanquished all other vices. When Goliath fell, the Philistines took to flight; when the root is torn up the tree withers. Pride leads to degradation. "He that exalteth himself shall be humbled" (Luke xiv. 11). The lightning strikes what is highest; a lofty tree is often struck down by the bolt. Apply that to the proud. Aman, the chief minister of the King of Persia, persecuted the Jews and arrogated to himself regal honors; he ended by being hung on a gibbet (Esth. vii. 10). King Herod was delighted at being called a god; he was eaten of worms and died (Acts xii. 22). God hath overturned the thrones of proud princes (Ecclus. x. 17). He often chastises the pride of nations, and even destroys them altogether (witness the fall of the Roman empire). God even abolishes the memory of the proud (Ecclus. x. 21) (witness the destruction of the tower of Babel). Abasement and disgrace follow in the footsteps of pride. Pride also leads to eternal damnation. It was the cause of the angels being cast out of heaven, and our first parents being expelled from paradise. As one scale in a balance drops as the other rises, so those will be abased in the world to come who exalt themselves in this world. Pride destroys the value of our good works. The proud have received their reward already (Matt. vi. 5). Pride pulls down the structure that justice raises. As a drop of gall spoils the flavor of the most delicious wine, so pride ruins virtue. It is like the little worm that caused Jonas' ivy to wither. Whatever good a man may have done, if he pride himself upon it, he is utterly destitute.

3. OBEDIENCE.

1. Obedience consists in being ready to fulfil the behest of one's superior.

Thus obedience does not merely consist in doing what is commanded, but in being ready and willing to do what is commanded. Many obey, but obey grudgingly; in that case obedience is no virtue. Moreover obedience is not a virtue unless it is for God's sake that one subjects one's will to that of another. Abraham was a pattern of obedience when he offered up Isaac. The Son of God Himself practised obedience, for He was subject to two of His creatures, Mary and Joseph. The Creator of all things obeyed an artisan, the Lord of glory a lowly maiden. Who ever heard or saw anything to compare with that? Christ was moreover obedient to His heavenly Father even to the death of the cross (Phil. ii. 8). By the obedience of one many shall be made just (Rom. v. 19). "I admire," says St. Francis of Sales, "the Infant of Bethlehem; He is all-powerful, and yet does whatever He is told without a word."

1. Children are required to obey their parents, or those who hold the place of parents to them, wives their husbands, servants their masters, and all men those who are placed in authority over them, whether ecclesiastical or secular rulers.

In order to unite all His creatures to a harmonious whole God has established a certain relationship between them, and mutual dependence. The moon revolves round the earth and the planets of our solar system around the sun. The angels stand in the same relationship to one another as men do on earth. In the Fourth Commandment God enjoins upon children obedience to their parents; this is due to them as being God's representatives. St. Paul says: "Children, obey your parents in all things" (Col. iii. 20). And again: "Those who are disobedient to parents are worthy of death" (Rom. i. 30). Teachers are the parents' representatives. Wives must obey their husbands, for so God has appointed. He said to Eve after the Fall: "Thou shalt be under thy husband's power, and he shall have dominion over thee" (Gen. iii. 16). The very origin of the woman proves her subjection to man, for she was made of his flesh, and thus belongs to him. As a mark of inferiority the woman's head must be covered (1 Cor. xi. 7). St. Peter teaches servants their duty towards their masters in the following words: "Servants, be subject to your masters with all fear, not only to the good and gentle, but also to the froward" (1 Pet. ii. 18). Our Lord admonishes us to obey our ecclesiastical superiors, saying: "Whoso will not hear the Church, let him be to thee as the heathen and the publican" (Matt. xviii. 17). Because of the obedience required of Christians, he calls them sheep and those who are set over them pastors. We ought also to obey the secular authorities, because they have their power from God. St. Paul says: "There is no power but from God, and those that are, are ordained of God. Therefore he that resisteth the power, resisteth the ordinance of God" (Rom. xiii. 1, 2).

2. Yet obedience has certain limits; we are not required to obey our superiors in matters that are not within their jurisdiction, and we ought not to obey them if they command us to do what the law of God forbids.

(This subject is fully treated of under the head of the Fourth Commandment.)

2. Obedience is the most difficult and at the same time the most excellent of all the moral virtues (St. Thomas Aquinas).

Obedience is the most difficult of virtues because all men are naturally inclined to command, and disinclined to obey. "Obedience," says St. Bonaventure, "is the sacrifice of one's own will, and it is a great sacrifice for man, when what is commanded is contrary to his inclination and to his advantage." By obedience the understanding does penance; it is a kind of moral martyrdom. Original sin is the cause why men are under the yoke and dominion of one another. Where sin enters freedom is dethroned, and servitude takes its place. Obedience is the most excellent of all virtues. Man can offer to almighty God nothing greater than the submission of his will to that of another for God's sake. Obedience is the most acceptable burnt-offering that we can sacrifice to God upon the altar of the heart. Obedience is better than sacrifices (1 Kings xv. 22); and for this reason, in a sacrifice we offer the flesh of another; in obedience the oblation is our own will, our own self.

3. By our obedience we accomplish the will of God most surely, and we attain certainly and quickly to a high degree of perfection.

By obedience we accomplish the will of God most surely, for our superiors are God's representatives, therefore their commands are God's commands. Thus we serve as to the Lord and not to men (Eph. v. 7). We ought not to consider who it is who issues the behest, but only the will of God which is made known to us by the mouth of our superior. He who obeys will not be required to give an account of what he has done; the one who commands has to do that. Obedience gives value to all that we do. The simplest action done out of obedience has greater value in God's sight than the most austere works of penance. Eating and sleeping, if done in obedience to the will of God, are more pleasing to him than the voluntary fasts and vigils of the hermit. By obedience we attain certainly and quickly to a high degree of perfection. Obedience is the means of avoiding many sins. It is the antidote to pride. By the practices of the other virtues we combat the spirits of evil, by obedience we vanquish them. And this is just, for since they fell through disobedience, by our obedience we show our superiority to them. St. Augustine calls obedience the greatest of virtues; it is the parent and source of every other virtue. St. Teresa declares that no path leads so quickly to the summit of perfection as the path of obedience; hence the evil enemy endeavors by all means to deter us from the practice of this virtue. Obedience is the key that opens the portals of heaven, the ship that carries us into the celestial harbor. Disobedience closed heaven and opened hell; obedience on the other hand opens heaven and closes hell. "Learn," says St. Francis of Sales, "to comply willingly with the wishes of thy equals, and thus thou wilt learn to fulfil cheerfully the commands of thy superiors." Above all, when you have to obey, obey promptly, do not stop to deliberate; for reasoning is only a hindrance to obedience. Remember that Eve began to waver as soon as she allowed herself to argue about the divine command.

4. DISOBEDIENCE.

1. Disobedience consists in not fulfilling the commands of one's superiors.

Our first parents in paradise are an instance of disobedience. He who does not obey his superiors, is like a palsied limb, which does not move as the will commands.

2. Disobedience brings temporal misfortune and eternal misery upon man.

Even in this world misery is the result of disobedience. Think of the fatal consequences of original sin! Adam's offence was the means of bringing evil upon all his posterity. Pharao's disobedience brought sad calamities upon himself and his subjects; remember the plagues of Egypt and the destruction of the king and his army in the Red Sea. The prophet Jonas had bitter cause to rue his disobedience. Eternal perdition is also the consequence of disobedience. God rejects the disobedient, as the money-changer rejects a counterfeit coin. The disobedient must expect a severe sentence in the Day of Judgment, for in despising their superiors, they have despised, not them, but Him Whose representatives they are. Disobedience deprives us of all merit. No virtue is acceptable to God if it is marred by the stain of disobedience; it then is changed from a virtue to a vice. Disobedience also deprives us of many graces which we might have obtained through obedience.

5. PATIENCE, MEEKNESS, PEACEABLENESS.

PATIENCE.

1. Patience consists in preserving one's serenity of mind amid all the contrarieties of this life for the love of God.

Some persons are patient in order to make themselves admired. Many on the other hand, accept cheerfully only a part of their suffering: e.g., they will endure sickness patiently, but they cannot endure to be a burden to others on account of it. That is not being truly patient. Our Lord affords us the most exalted example of patience in His Passion. Our heavenly Father also exhibits Himself to us as a model of patience, for He bears with sinners, even with those who provoke His justice, as perjurers and blasphemers do. Job and Tobias were remarkable for their patience. The patient man is like a rock in the ocean, on which the waves break. Again, he may be compared to a lamb, which does not utter a sound when it is slain.

The trials of life in which it specially behooves us to maintain our tranquillity of mind are: Sickness and reverses, relapse into sin, the pressure of many and onerous duties appertaining to our calling.

Sickness and reverses are not really calamities; they are graces. God sends them upon us for the good of our souls. We ought therefore to welcome them. We must not be irritated with ourselves if by reason of our frailty we relapse into our old sins, and thus are forced to acknowledge that there is more of the human than of the angelic nature about us. We must have as much patience with ourselves as with our fellow-men. Our Lord says: " Bring forth fruit in patience" (Luke viii. 15). We must not lose our equanimity when our work is pressing and difficult. Excitement creates haste, and hastiness always does harm, just as an overflowing stream, or violent rain, destroys and devastates. We ought to imitate the angels who minister to man without disquiet or hurry. We ought also to wait with patience for the end of our life and our entrance upon eternal felicity (Rom. viii. 25).

Tranquillity of mind is displayed by not yielding to anger, or to sadness, or complaining to any great extent and calling for the commiseration of others.

We ought not to yield to anger. Anger obscures the reason and makes an act unjustly. "The anger of man worketh not the justice of God" (Jas. i. 20). Nor ought the tribulations of this life to render us sad. There is indeed a sadness which is pleasing to God, that which is caused by the loss of eternal things. Our Lord says: "Blessed are they that mourn, for they shall be comforted" (Matt. v. 5). But the sorrow of the world, i.e., that of the worldling over the loss of mundane things, worketh death (2 Cor. vii. 10). "Sadness hath killed many, and there is no profit in it" (Ecclus. xxx. 25). It is, however, allowable to complain on account of severe physical or mental suffering, so long as we submit to the will of God. Our Lord uttered complaints upon the cross; our heavenly Father frequently complained of the conduct of sinners by the mouth of the prophets. But a medium must be observed; we must not lament over trifles, nor let our complaining be prolonged or exaggerated; to do so is to evince selfishness or cowardice. Complain to God as long and as loudly as you will, for your complaints are an appeal to Him for help, and consequently are pleasing to Him. But if you fill a fellow-creature's ear with the sad tale of all your care, he will soon weary of your conversation. Not so God; He is ever ready to hear you, and to impart to you such consolation as will cause you to forget all your sorrow. Our Lord says: "Come unto Me, all you that labor and are burdened, and I will refresh you" (Matt. xi. 28).

2. Patience produces many virtues and leads to salvation.

St. Teresa says that if we bear slight things patiently, we shall acquire courage and strength to bear great things. The patient man displays fortitude equal to that of the martyrs. Patience is the guardian of all the virtues, for there are obstacles to be encountered in every good work, and they can only be overcome by patience. St. Gregory the Great declares that by unwavering patience the crown of martyrdom may be acquired without the sword. The patient man is greater than he who works miracles. Patience leads to salvation. "In your patience you shall possess your souls" (Luke xxi. 19). Fragile things are not so likely to be broken if they are wrapped in wool, nor are our souls so likely to be lost if they are safeguarded by patience. The patient man is like a ship at anchor in a peaceful harbor, protected from the stormy waves of the ocean.

3. If we would bear with patience the trials of life, let us place Our Lord's Passion before our eyes; let us also consider that sufferings are a favor from God.

Think upon the Passion of Christ. He drank of the bitter cup, in order to overcome our repugnance to drink of it; He suffered first, that we might not fear suffering. Frequently think of Christ crucified; your sufferings cannot be compared with His, either in intensity or in number. A soldier scarcely feels his hurt, if he sees his general to be severely wounded. "Let the sick man," says St. Francis of Sales, "offer his pains to God, and pray Him to accept them in union with the sufferings of Christ." Remember the words the archangel Raphael said to Tobias: "Because thou wast acceptable to God, it was necessary that temptation should prove thee" (Tob. xii. 14). Without suffering there is no salvation, for "through many tribulations we must enter into the kingdom of God" (Acts xiv. 21). As the bitter pill is coated with sugar to render it palatable, so when we look forward to the rich recompense in store for us the chalice of suffering loses its bitterness. The laborer could not labor all day long without the anticipation of the wages to be paid him, and the thought of our eternal reward enables us to bear the trials of life with patience. Think of the martyrs, and of others who have greater afflictions than you, and your thorns will lose their sharpness. Beware of losing merit by impatience; remember that you must suffer, either willingly or unwillingly; if you suffer willingly, you will earn great merit; if unwillingly, you do not diminish, but only add to your suffering. Patience is displayed pre-eminently by meekness and peaceableness.

MEEKNESS.

1. Meekness consists in showing, for the love of God, no irritation when wrong is done us.

Many persons are meek through timidity or for convenience' sake, but that is no virtue. One who is meek does not excite himself when he is wronged, i.e., he bears injustice in silence, and is polite and obliging to the offender. There is something divine in meekness. God Himself is infinitely long-suffering; He does not exert His almighty power against transgressors. He bears with the sinner, and gives him ample time for repentance. God appeared to Moses in the burning bush (Exod. iii.), to Elias He spoke by the whistling of a gentle wind (3 Kings xix. 12). This was not without a deep significance. The Holy Spirit also assumed the form of a dove, and Our Lord proclaimed Himself by the mouth of the prophets to be the Lamb of God (Jer. xi. 19). Who can fail to be astonished at the meekness of God when we behold the Redeemer upon the cross? Meekness is agreeable to the Lord (Ecclus. i. 35). God chose Moses on account of his meekness and sanctified him (Ecclus. xlv. 4).

2. By meekness we gain power over our fellow-men, we attain peace of mind, and eternal salvation.

Our Lord says: "Blessed are the meek, for they shall possess the land" (Matt. v. 4), that is they shall gain command over others. Those who are meek gain the affections of their fellow-men, and render them kindly disposed. If one who is incensed against another is met with meekness, his anger vanishes as darkness is dispelled on the rising of the sun. A mild answer breaketh wrath (Prov. xv. 1). Bad men may be won by kindness. He who subdues anger within himself will be able to conquer it in others also. A good example of the effect of meekness is given by the conduct of Blessed Clement Hofbauer when he was collecting alms for orphan children in Warsaw. Going up to a group of men at a card table in an hotel he asked them for a donation. One of the card-players spat in his face. Hofbauer quietly wiped his face, and said: " That, sir, was for myself; I ask you now for something for my poor children." The man was greatly ashamed, and gave Hofbauer all the money he had about him; what is more, a few days later he went to him and made a general confession. St. Francis Xavier was stoned by the Indians while he was preaching. He went on without taking the slightest notice. The Indians who had thrown the stones were so amazed at his meekness that they were the first to be baptized. He who has complete mastery over himself will find all the world subject to him. Far more is done by meekness than by anger. " One catches more flies," says St. Francis of Sales, " with an ounce of honey, than with tons of vinegar." If two hard substances strike against one another, a loud crash ensues, but if a hard substance comes against what is soft, scarce a sound is heard. One must bear with the irate as one bears with the sick, for anger is a moral malady. " Anger resteth in the bosom of a fool " (Eccles. vii. 10). By meekness we gain peace of mind. For Our Lord says: " Learn of Me, for I am meek and lowly of Heart, and you shall find rest to your souls " (Matt. xi. 29). Consequently the meek are always cheerful. By meekness we gain eternal salvation. The land promised by Christ to the meek is heaven (Ps. xxxvi. 11). There was a servant who could not control his angry temper, despite all his master's rebukes and admonitions. One day the latter promised him half a dollar if he would not utter an angry word all day long. The man refrained from a single outburst, although his fellow-servants were extremely provoking. When his master gave him the half dollar at night, he said: " If you can conquer yourself for the sake of so paltry a sum, how is it that you cannot do so in view of an eternal reward?" These words had the effect the speaker desired; he had no cause to complain of the man in future.

3. Meekness can only be acquired by the diligent practice of self-control.

St. Francis of Sales, naturally of a choleric temperament, attained in the course of twenty years such perfect mastery over himself that he was thought to be phlegmatic by nature.

4. We ought to behave with meekness towards those with whom we live, and superiors ought to be gentle towards their inferiors.

It is especially incumbent upon us to be meek in our intercourse with those with whom we live. Some do not observe this rule; they are angels abroad and devils at home. Superiors ought to show meekness towards their subordinates; but meekness in them is called gentleness. More is done by gentleness than by severity. For the human mind is so constituted that it resists force and yields to mildness. Superiors should be rigorous to themselves and lenient towards those under them. Meekness was the chief characteristic of the apostles. Our Lord said to them: " Behold, I send you as sheep in the midst of wolves " (Matt. x. 16). It ought also to be the chief characteristic of the Christian; for Christ speaks of the faithful as sheep (John x. 1), or lambs (John xxi. 15); both these animals are remarkably gentle.

PEACEABLENESS.

1. Peaceableness consists in willingly making a sacrifice for the sake of remaining at peace with one's neighbor, or reconciling one's self with him.

Abraham was content to take the worst portion of the land, in order to keep the peace with Lot's servants (Gen. xiii.). St. Francis of Sales was unjustly expelled from a lodging he had taken in Rome; he quitted it without a murmur, and the next night a hurricane destroyed the house. St. Ignatius of Loyola, when returning from Palestine, was rudely refused a passage in the ship on which he wished to embark. That vessel sank on its way to Europe; the one in which he sailed got safely to port. Peace is invaluable to mankind. The angels who announced the birth of Christ could wish nothing better to man (Luke ii. 14). Our Lord promised to give His peace to His apostles (John xiv. 27), and He saluted them with the words: " Peace be to you " (John xx. 26). This was also the salutation He placed upon their lips when He sent them forth to preach (Matt. x. 12). All the good things of this world cannot please us, if we are not at peace, for without peace we can enjoy nothing. Peacemakers are like God; He is not the God of dissension, but of peace (1 Cor. xiv. 33). He is the Lord of peace (2 Thess. iii. 16). The prophets foretold His coming as the Prince of peace (Is. ix. 6). And at the birth of Christ the temple of Janus was closed, because peace reigned everywhere.

2. Peacemakers enjoy the special protection of God, and receive a hundredfold as the reward of all that they give up for the sake of peace.

Our Lord says: " Blessed are the peacemakers, for they shall be called the children of God " (Matt. v. 9). God will replace a hundredfold all that we surrender for the sake of peace. We have seen how St. Francis of Sales and St. Ignatius were saved from disaster and death through their love of peace. Not only in this world, but also in the life to come, does God reward us for all that we do for His sake (Mark x. 29). Forgiveness and forbearance are better than contention and complaining.

3. Hence every one ought to be willing to make concessions for the sake of peace, and as far as lies in his power, to avoid all that may engender strife.

We ought to put up with a great deal for the sake of peace. " Bear ye one another's burdens " (Gal. vi. 2). Many people are peaceable as long as no one interferes with them, and all goes on in accordance with their will; but the slightest contradiction irritates them terribly. Such people are like stagnant water, which is all well enough as long as it is left alone; but stir it up, and it emits a most unpleasant odor. We ought also carefully to avoid everything that may stir up contention. One should never contradict any one without a good reason. St. Teresa bids us never to enter upon a strife of words about matters of no importance, especially at one's own fire-side. A ship in which the timbers are not well joined will sink; so every community will fall to pieces whose members are not welded together with the bonds of love. However, one must not for the sake of peace omit or give up anything which God commands; that is not the peace God desires; hence Our Lord says: "Do not think that I came to send peace upon earth; I came not to send peace but the sword" (Matt. x. 34). Some people will not let you be at peace with them unless you acquiesce in their evil deeds, such peace is unlawful.

6. THE OPPOSITE OF MEEKNESS: WRATH.

1. Wrath consists in exciting one's self about something at which one is displeased.

The man who is in a rage is more like a beast than a man. His countenance is distorted, he gnashes his teeth, raises his voice, gesticulates wildly, stamps with his feet and knocks things over, etc. Were he to look in the glass, he would hardly know himself. Those who are of a choleric temperament carry their anger about with them everywhere, as the viper does its venom; they are like a surly dog which barks and bites if you do but touch him; like flint that gives out sparks when it is struck; like an empty vessel which cracks when put on the fire. Were the vessel full of water, it would not break; were the heart full of grace, its patience would not give way. Angry people always put the blame of their anger on others, but experience proves that they give way to irritability when they are alone. Zeal for God's glory is called just anger; such was the anger Our Lord displayed, when He drove the sellers of doves and the money changers out of the Temple (John ii.), or Moses, when, returning from the Mount, he saw the people worshipping the golden calf. Just anger is not really anger; it is the offspring of charity, and like charity, is patient, kind, calm, and not actuated by hatred. Just anger is quite lawful. "Be ye angry and sin not" (Ps. iv. 5). That anger alone is sinful which desires to take personal revenge.

2. Those who indulge anger injure their health, temporarily lose the use of reason, make themselves hated, and incur the danger of losing eternal salvation.

How foolishly those act who are transported with anger! They punish themselves for another man's fault. Anger is prejudicial to the health and shortens one's life. It causes the gall to overflow, and poisons the blood. The man who is in a rage is like the angry bee which loses its sting, or like a volcano, that widens its crater and burns itself out. Anger exhausts the body in every part. When a man is in a rage, he trembles in every limb, his heart beats high, his tongue falters, his face burns, his eyes glow like fire, he shouts aloud. Anger cherished in the breast destroys life as the worm at the root of a tree. "Envy and anger shorten a man's days" (Ecclus. xxx. 26). Many men have had a stroke brought on by anger, some have fallen down dead through rage. If anger is so hurtful to the body, what must it be to the soul! Anger temporarily deprives a man of the use of reason. Every violent emotion troubles the understanding. The mind of an angry man is like the surface of the sea when lashed into fury by the waves; it reflects nothing distinctly. Aristotle compares the effect of anger on the mind to that of smoke in the eyes, or it may be compared to a fog, through which it is impossible to see things in their true proportions. Anger is an intoxication, a temporary madness; for one who is thoroughly enraged is not master of his own actions. Hence St. Francis of Sales, speaking of one who was mad with anger, said: "Lord, forgive him; he knows not what he does." Thus in his anger a man will act most unjustly; he will do what he afterwards regrets. The anger of man worketh not the justice of God. Men in their anger are worse than wild beasts, for the lion when he is enraged does not fall upon his companion lions, whereas the irate man vents his wrath upon his fellow-men. He is worse than the evil spirits, for they live in amity with one another, although they are the authors of all dissension. And how men rage against one another! Whence come blows, murders, feuds, lawsuits? A man who is easily provoked to anger is hated by his fellow-men; he is as little welcome as a hurricane or a waterspout; every one avoids an angry man as every one gets out of the way of a mad dog. He has no friends: "Be not a friend to an angry man, and do not walk with a furious man" (Prov. xxii. 24). Men are easily led by calm reason, but they resist if an angry man attempts to domineer over them. It is easier to deal with a brute beast than with a man who is prone to anger, for the beast may be tamed, but with the wrathful man one is never safe. He who gives way to wrath is in danger of eternal damnation, for he deprives himself of grace. The Holy Spirit does not dwell in the heart where anger abides, for where anger is there is no peace. As the inhabitant of a house constructed of wood is in constant danger of having it burnt down, so the choleric man is in constant danger of injuring his soul and being cast into everlasting fire. In fact hell has already begun for him, since he is a prey to unceasing agitation and unrest.

3. Anger must be overcome in the following manner: We must never speak or act when we are angry, but if possible, betake ourselves to prayer. If in our anger we have injured any one, we should make amends for the wrong done without delay.

One must never speak nor act when one is angry. One should do as mariners do; when a storm arises they cast anchor, and wait until the tempest is over. St. Francis of Sales, on being asked how he could remain so imperturbably placid in regard to persons who were raging with anger, replied: "I have made an agreement with my tongue never to utter a word while my heart is excited." A heathen philosopher once counselled the Emperor Augustus to repeat the twenty-four letters of the Greek alphabet when he felt within him the ebullition of angry passions. "Let every man be slow to speak and slow to anger" (Jas. i. 19). Silence is an act of patience; this enables one to conquer. When the excitement is allayed, one can act as one thinks best. Prayer is very efficacious as a means of dispelling anger. When we feel the rising of passion within us, we should do as the apostles did when a storm arose on the lake. They went to Our Lord for succor. If we do so, God will command the waves of anger to be still, and calm will ensue. The saints counsel us to repeat silently an *Ave Maria* as a means of driving away the devil who tempts us. Or one may recite the *Gloria Patri;* at any rate we must have recourse to prayer immediately, for if we delay, our anger will gain ground, and will not be easily quelled. If we have offended any one in our anger, we should make amends by extreme politeness. "Let not the sun go down upon your anger" (Eph. iv. 26). Wrath frequently begets hatred. "It is better," says St. Francis of Sales, " never to let anger into thy heart, than to keep it within the bounds of prudence and moderation; for it is like a viper which if it once gets its head through a hole, slips its whole body through; and once admitted, it is no easy matter to drive it out."

7. *LIBERALITY.*

1. Liberality consists in being ready and willing, for the love of God, to give pecuniary assistance to those who are in need.

He who relieves the needy in order to elicit the praise of others has no claim to the virtue of liberality, for he is not actuated by the love of God. Even the poor may be liberal, for liberality does not depend upon giving largely, but upon giving with a good will; it is the disposition of the giver that makes the gift great or small. The liberal man is like God, for by showing mercy we resemble our heavenly Father, Whose mercy is perfect and infinite. The heathen sage Seneca used to say: "He resembles the gods who distributes to the poor."

2. By liberality we obtain forgiveness of sin, an eternal reward, and temporal blessings, besides a speedy answer to prayer and the friendship of our fellow-men.

This subject has already been considered. The liberal man rejoices those on whom he bestows his gifts, as the sun gladdens the earth with its rays. Christ could not employ a more forcible argument to urge us to perform works of mercy than by saying that what was given to the poor was given to Him.

8. *THE OPPOSITE OF LIBERALITY: AVARICE.*

1. Avarice consists in an inordinate craving for riches, which makes a man not only strive after them, but refuse to give any portion of his goods to the poor.

We call it an inordinate desire for riches when a man strives to gain far more than he really requires for himself and his family, and is never content, however much he possesses. Thus he is cove-tous. He is like a vessel without a bottom, that is never full, however great the quantity of liquid that is poured into it. He is like the wolf that is always hungry; like the fire, that ever requires a fresh supply of fuel; like hell, which is never satisfied. Avarice does not consist only in acquiring fresh riches with eagerness, but in greedily retaining what one already has. He who clings tenaciously to the property he has accumulated, is niggardly or penurious; he who grudges every little outlay, is a miser. We meet with covetous per-sons both among rich and poor. Among the wealthy one often finds money without avarice, and among the poor avarice without money. "The covetous is a worshipper of idols" (Eph. v. 5), for gold is his god. To this deity he devotes all his thoughts and all his care, all his efforts and aspirations, the sweat of his face; he even sacrifices to it his spiritual welfare and his eternal salvation. As the angels find their highest felicity in the contemplation of the Godhead, so the rich delight in nothing more than in handling and counting their money. How great a sin is this, which subjects us to the dominion of those things which were created for our service!

2. The avaricious are miserable both in time and in eternity; for the sake·of money they commit all manner of sins, they lose the faith and their peace of mind, they are cruel to themselves and hardhearted to their neighbor, and finally perish eternally.

The desire of money is the root of all evils (1 Tim. vi. 10). The devil hides behind money-bags as a snake conceals himself in a hedge; and he bites you with his venomous fangs when you greedily clutch at gold. He who accumulates riches and does not give to the poor is like a fount, which, if no water is drawn from it, becomes foul; for a man's wealth will not benefit him if no portion of it is distributed to the needy. They that will become rich fall into temptation and into the snare of the devil, and into many un-profitable and hurtful desires, which drown men into destruction and perdition (1 Tim. vi. 9). For the sake of money the covetous fall into all manner of sins. "Such a one setteth even his own soul for sale" (Ecclus. x. 10). Greed of money fills the houses with thieves, the market with cheats, the law courts with perjurers, the eyes of the poor with tears, the prisons with criminals and hell with the reprobate. For money Judas betrayed his Lord and Master. Not until the Judgment Day will it be revealed how many lives have been sacrificed to this false god. The covetous lose their faith. St. Leo the Great says that the greatest of all the evil arising from covetous-ness is the destruction of faith. The avaricious are so absorbed in the pursuit of material gain that they cannot give a thought to their spiritual welfare. You cannot serve God and mammon (Luke xvi. 13). A rich merchant lay on his death-bed, and a priest stood at his side, urging him to repentance. After setting before him the gravity of his state, the priest held up a silver crucifix before him. The dying man fixed his eyes upon it with a softened expression, and the priest rejoiced, thinking the man's heart was touched. But no; the only words that escaped his lips were these: "What do you consider that cross to be worth?" The covetous loses his peace of mind; he lives in perpetual anxiety lest he should lose his wealth.

If riches increase, they are a burden to their owner; if they decrease, they torture him. The covetous is cruel to himself; the miser grudges himself the necessaries of life; he often endures the greatest privations. "He consumes his own soul, drying it up" (Ecclus. xiv. 9). He is like the oxen who carry the corn to the garner, and themselves feed on hay and straw. The justice of God often avenges on the miser the tears of the destitute by bringing him to poverty. The covetous is hardhearted towards his neighbor. He has no feeling for the suffering of others, he shows no compassion, he gives them no succor. His heart is as hard as the anvil, which is not softened by all the blows rained down upon it; for however great the need of his neighbor, the miser is never moved to pity. The covetous only think of what they can get from every one; as the shark devours all the fish that come in his way, so the covetous man ruins his neighbors. "He that gathereth together by wronging his own soul gathereth for others" (Ecclus. xiv. 4), who will squander his riches. The miser is an object of hatred to others. Califas, King of Babylon, had stored a vast quantity of gold, silver, and precious stones in a tower; when he refused to part with a portion of these for the benefit of his army, the soldiers shut him up in the tower, bidding him satisfy his hunger and quench his thirst with the treasures he had been so eager to amass. The covetous will be eternally damned. The Apostle includes them among those who will not possess the kingdom of heaven (1 Cor. vi. 10). Our Lord says: "It is easier for a camel to pass through the eye of a needle, than for a rich man to enter the kingdom of heaven" (Matt. xix. 24). It is a remarkable fact that the ancient poets identified Pluto, the god who reigned supreme in the infernal regions, with Plutus, the god of riches, as if to show that avarice leads to hell. The lover of money gets no good to himself; he undertakes long journeys, he exposes himself to labor and perils for the sake of gain, and when death comes what has he of it all? For all his wealth he has nothing but a shroud, a few planks, and a few feet of earth; while he leaves his property to his smiling heirs, who ridicule the contemptible parsimony he practised.

3. The surest means whereby the avaricious can conquer the greed of gain, is by forcing themselves to give alms. They ought besides to meditate frequently on the poverty of Christ, and the ephemeral nature of earthly possessions.

Since the best method of correcting a vice is by exercising the opposite virtue, avarice will be cured by liberality. "What," asks St. Augustine, "can so effectually counteract avarice as the poverty of the Son of God? Consider, O miser, that thy Lord and thy God, Who came down to earth from heaven, would not possess any of the riches at which thou dost clutch so eagerly. He loved poverty and lived in poverty; and, thinkest thou, ought a miserable mortal to desire ardently what the Lord of all creation despised?" Remember also that we must part with all our earthly possessions at our death. We brought nothing into this world, and certainly we can carry nothing out (1 Tim. vi. 7). That which you leave behind at your death will pass into the hands of others, who will perchance make a bad use of it to their own damnation. "The most effectual medicine for the disease of avarice," says St. Augustine, "is to think daily of death." True riches are not earthly possessions, but virtues; pursue them (1 Tim. vi. 11), for they are treasures which thieves cannot steal or moth and rust corrupt. Why, then, busy one's self about the acquisition of evanescent treasures?

9. TEMPERANCE IN EATING AND DRINKING.

1. Temperance consists in not eating and drinking more than is necessary, and not being either too greedy or too dainty in regard to the nourishment one takes.

Temperance teaches us not to eat or drink more than is needful to support life. A sage of antiquity used to say: "We do not live to eat, but we eat to live." One who is temperate does not fully satisfy his appetite, or take what is injurious to his health; he has regular, fixed hours for his meals. He eats such things as are set before him (Luke x. 8), and is not angry when a dish is badly served. What concerns him most is to have food which suits his digestion and gives him strength for his work.

2. Temperance is highly advantageous to soul and body; it improves the health, lengthens life, strengthens the faculties of the mind, fosters virtue and leads to everlasting life.

Moderation at table is advantageous both to body and soul and is the source of many virtues. We are travellers on earth, and we shall expedite our arrival in the celestial country, if we only make such use of the things of this world as is indispensable to enable us to proceed on our journey.

3. Diligent meditation on the truths of our holy religion will assist us to form a habit of temperance.

He who sustains his mind with spiritual aliments will not care greatly for the food of the body; for fleshly desires are suppressed when the love of celestial things fills the heart. As Our Lord said: "Not in bread alone doth man live," etc. Let us lift our eyes up to heaven, lest we should be allured by the baits of earth. Above all, think on the privations many of the poor endure, of the privations Our Lord endured. There are thousands of poor who think themselves fortunate if they only have sufficient bread and water to still their hunger and quench their thirst. How kind God has been to you in giving to you so much more than to them, and how ungenerous it would be on your part, if you abused His liberality for the gratification of your palate. If He vouchsafed for your sake to feel the pangs of hunger, how much the more ought you to be abstemious for your own interest.

10. INTEMPERANCE IN EATING AND DRINKING.

1. Intemperance consists in eating and drinking much more than is necessary, and in being greedy or dainty in regard to one's food.

"Food ought to be looked upon as a medicine to sustain the body," says St. Augustine, and by no means made use of for the gratification of the palate. Intemperance is displayed by sumptuous feasting (witness Dives); excess in drinking, e.g., Baltassar; greediness, e.g., Esau in regard to the pottage of lentils; daintiness, e.g., the Israelites in the wilderness, who longed for the flesh-pots of Egypt (Exod. xvi. 3). The glutton and the drunkard are more contemptible than brute beasts, for the latter leave off eating when they have had enough, and the glutton does not do this. Those who eat with great avidity are like birds of prey, which in their voracity swoop down upon their victim the moment they decry it. Intemperance is productive of much harm. We must not forget that had the apple not been attractive to the appetite death would not have come upon the human race.

2. By intemperance a man injures his health, weakens his mental faculties, destroys his reputation, and reduces himself to poverty; falls into vice, often comes to a miserable end, and is eternally lost.

Intemperance destroys the health. The fire goes out when too much coal is heaped upon it, and the stomach is ruined when it is overloaded with food. Excess in drink is as prejudicial to the system as excessive rain is to agricultural districts. Dyspepsia, loss of appetite, dropsy, apoplexy, are the results of want of moderation in eating and drinking. Many lose their reason by indulgence in strong drinks, and end their days in a madhouse. By surfeiting many have perished (Ecclus. xxxvii. 34). Over-indulgence in the pleasures of the table has a bad effect on posterity. Physicians assert that there is an innate weakness in those that are the offspring of drunkards. Intemperance weakens the mental faculties. Intoxication obscures the mind as a fog obscures the sun. The intemperate cannot raise their hearts to God, any more than a bird that has gorged itself with food can soar aloft to the sky. Intemperance also weakens the will; it renders us incapable of resisting temptation and avoiding sin, just as a ship too heavily laden cannot outride a storm. It also destroys a man's reputation; Noe, when drunk with wine, became an object of derision to his own son. Thus a man when in liquor makes a fool of himself, talks nonsense, and is mocked even by children. The Lacedemonians used to show drunken Helots to young people that they might learn to despise this degrading vice. Intemperance reduces men to poverty. The drunkard squanders in one day the wages earned by many days of work, and renders himself incapable of labor. "A workman that is a drunkard shall not be rich" (Ecclus. xix. 1). Intemperance leads to all kinds of sins, to immorality and godlessness. As in a morass all manner of weeds grow rank, so evil lusts grow and flourish in an over-fed body. Those who eat and drink immoderately waste their money, feel disinclined to prayer at night on account of the inertia produced by excess, and in the morning because of headache and sensations of discomfort; they miss Mass on Sundays, contract debts, live in discord with their families, and fall into sins of impurity. Remember that Herod had been feasting when he caused John the Baptist to be beheaded; Baltassar had been drinking deeply when he desecrated the sacred vessels of

the sanctuary; the rich man in the Gospel who refused a morsel of
bread to Lazarus fared sumptuously every day. Intemperance leads
to uncleanness and godlessness; the glutton and drunkard forget
their final end; they have no understanding for the truths of
religion; "the sensual man perceiveth not those things that are
of the Spirit of God" (1 Cor. ii. 14). A sudden and miserable end
often overtakes those who indulge in strong drink. Our Lord thus
warns such persons: "Take heed to yourselves, lest perhaps your
hearts be overcharged with surfeiting and drunkenness and the cares
of this life, and that day come upon you suddenly" (Luke xxi. 34).
As we live, so we die. Holofernes was asleep, exceedingly drunk,
when Judith cut off his head (Judith xiii.); the voluptuous Baltassar
was sleeping off the effect of his revels when the enemy made their
way into the city (Dan. v.). The death of individuals who perish in
this manner is all the more deplorable because they die unrepentant
and without the last sacraments. Those who are addicted to excess
seldom correct themselves; they may amend and abstain for a time,
but too often they relapse into their former sins, and eternal perdition is their fate. The rich man was buried in hell. Our Lord says:
"Woe to you that are filled for you shall hunger" (Luke vi. 25).
Drunkards shall not possess the kingdom of God (1 Cor. vi. 10).
"He that soweth in his flesh, of the flesh also shall reap corruption"
(Gal. vi. 8). Think of the flames of hell, and you will be able fully
to subdue the impulses of nature. Resolve never to omit a short
prayer before and after meals; to take what is set before you so as to
check daintiness, and never to eat to satiety.

11. CHASTITY.

**1. Chastity consists in preserving the mind and body free from
everything that might stain their innocence.**

St. Stanislaus Kostka left the room instantly if a single objectionable word was uttered in his presence. St. Aloysius did the
same. Many persons have given up all they had, even their life, in
order to preserve the virtue of chastity; witness Joseph in Egypt,
St. Agnes, St. Agatha, and other saints. Chastity is a superhuman
perfection; it is divine in its origin, for God brought it to earth
from heaven. Those who practise this virtue are like the lily (Cant. ii.
1). Every tiny insect that rests upon the snowy petals of the lily
mars its dazzling whiteness and disfigures its beauty; so the mere
thought of evil is a stain upon the mind of the man who lives
chastely. Rough handling spoils the fair lily and causes it to wither,
so the man who lives chastely suffers from indiscriminate intercourse
with those around him. The lily grows upright, straight and slender:
so the man who lives chastely must ever look upwards and tend
towards heaven. The lily fills the whole house with its fragrance;
so the man who lives chastely edifies all with whom he associates by
his good example.

Those who lead a chaste life resemble the angels and are
most pleasing in God's sight.

Those whose life is pure are angels in human form. Chastity is an angelic virtue; by it men become like the angels. Chaste souls are in fact superior to the angels, because they have the flesh to combat, which the angels have not; they preserve angelic purity in spite of the continual temptations of the devil. What differentiates the angels from men is not their virtue, but their bliss. The purity of the angels is more blissful; that of man is stronger because it is the result of struggle. We learn from the lives of the saints that angels delight in the company of chaste mortals, thus proving that they regard them as their equals. The devils know that through chastity man recovers the angelic dignity which he lost, hence they strive assiduously to instil impure thoughts into his mind. Men who live chastely are extremely pleasing to God. Christ when on earth showed a predilection for chaste souls; He chose a pure virgin for His Mother, a man of angelic purity for His foster-father; the Baptist, who was purified in his mother's womb, was His precursor; the chaste John was His favorite disciple, privileged at the Last Supper to rest upon His breast; at the foot of the cross two pure souls stood; and He loved little children because of their innocence. "He that loveth cleanness of heart shall have the King for his friend" (Prov. xxii. 11). God calls the chaste soul by the endearing title of friend, of sister, of spouse (Cant. iv. 6-8). The Son of God so delighted in virginity that He chose to be born of a virgin, and to give to man an example of it in His own person. The pure also enjoy the esteem of their fellow-men in a high degree. Even the heathen respected chastity. The Romans had their vestal virgins, who during their service in the temple, a period of thirty years, lived in celibacy. When they appeared in the streets, public honor was shown them, and if they chanced to meet a criminal on the way to execution, he was immediately pardoned. If pagans respected those of their daughters who preferred virginity to the married state, ought the Christian to look with contempt on the virgin who from supernatural motives does not marry? "O how beautiful is the chaste generation with glory, for the memory of it is immortal: because it is known both with God and with men" (Wisd. iv. 1).

2. Those who lead a life of chastity possess the sanctifying grace of the Holy Spirit in abundant measure; they will be happy here on earth, and will enjoy special distinction in heaven hereafter.

Purity of heart is health to the soul; it also gives light to the understanding. The chaste are like a crystal without flaw, or a clear, gently-flowing stream, in which the face of heaven is mirrored. Purity of heart, interior brightness and angelic freedom aid to the attainment of wisdom; it imparts knowledge to savants and teachers, to philosophers and theologians. It was through his spotless purity that St. John the Divine penetrated so deeply into the sublime mysteries of the faith, that, in the commencement of his Gospel, he soared as on eagle's pinions, to gaze upon the Godhead. Purity enables a man to gaze undazzled upon the Sun of justice. It also endows the soul with heroic courage. Judith, a weak woman, displayed such heroism at the siege of Bethulia, that she went into the enemy's camp and beheaded Holofernes. Holy Scripture says of her, "For

thou hast done manfully and thy heart has been strengthened, because thou hast loved chastity" (Judith xv. 11). The pure of heart
easily acquire other virtues; they are happy even in this world. Chastity possesses an indescribable attraction and intrinsic sweetness;
it affords enjoyments far more delightful than sensual pleasures.
Purity is also health to the body; virginal purity is an earnest and
foretaste of the immortality of the glorified body. He who lives
chastely generally enjoys better health and lives to an advanced
age. Sometimes God in His wise providence withdraws pure souls
from earth in their youth; if so, He takes them away lest wickedness should alter their understanding or deceit beguile their souls
(Wisd. iv. 11). Those who lead a chaste life will enjoy special distinction in heaven. Virginal souls will be near to the throne of God;
they will stand around the Lamb and follow Him whithersoever He
goeth. They will sing a new canticle that no man could say (Apoc.
xiv.). God will crown the chaste souls (Cant. iv. 8), that is, He
will confer upon them a special and singular glory. The chaste generation triumpheth forever (Wisd. iv. 2). Virginal souls will have
their portion with the Blessed Virgin. Even here on earth God
chooses them as the recipients of His revelations, to them He discloses His secrets, to their petitions He turns a gracious ear. Queen
Esther obtained from her royal consort all that she asked because
of her fidelity and attachment to him; so the heavenly Spouse grants
the petitions of all chaste souls.

3. It is the bounden duty of every man to preserve chastity
inviolate until he embraces the married state.

This is enjoined by God in the Sixth Commandment of the
Decalogue. Among the Jews a breach of chastity was punished by
stoning (Deut. xxii. 21). The Romans buried alive any vestal virgin
who violated the vow of virginity. See how severe a penalty the law
of Jews and pagans inflicted upon those who outraged chastity !

4. The following means should be employed for the preservation of chastity: We should be temperate, accustom ourselves
to exercise self-control, receive the sacraments frequently, pray
devoutly to the Mother of God, love to meditate upon the truths
of religion, especially upon the presence of God and the four
last things; finally we should observe moderation in frequenting
the ballroom and the theatre, and be guarded in our intercourse
with persons of the opposite sex.

St. Augustine declares that the preservation of chastity is the
greatest victory achieved by the Christian, and requires the hardest
struggle. The Fathers of the Church call it a martyrdom; a blood-
less martyrdom, it is true, but not on that account the less sublime.
For the martyr's agony is short, and admits him immediately to
celestial glory; whereas the safe-guarding of chastity demands a
prolonged, a lifelong conflict. Self-control has been enlarged upon
under the head of the means of attaining perfection in general.
We may particularize the necessity of bridling the tongue and observing custody of the eyes. St. Augustine says that tattlers and

busy-bodies are in great danger of losing their purity. Death comes up into the soul through the window of the eyes (Jer. ix. 21). The lion is said to be tamed by blindfolding him; so we can subdue our evil proclivities by strict custody of the eyes. Fasting is another aid to the preservation of purity; the flesh is tamed, just as animals are, by depriving them of food. "Be not drunk with wine," says the Apostle, "wherein is luxury" (Eph. v. 18). "Feasting fosters fleshly lusts," says St. Ambrose, "and wine heats the blood and inflames the passions of young men." Prayer and the sacraments are means of grace without which it is impossible to conquer one's self. "It is a mistake," says St. John Chrysostom, "to imagine that one can in one's own strength vanquish concupiscence and preserve purity; by God's mercy alone can the passions of nature be controlled." No man can otherwise be continent, unless God give it him (Wisd. viii. 21). Through confession and communion the will is strengthened and man is enabled to avoid sin. The Adorable Sacrament of the Altar is the corn of the elect, and a wine springing forth virgins (Zach. ix. 17). The wine of earth is prejudicial to purity, the wine of heaven produces purity. Devotion to the Mother of God is also most efficacious; to how many young people has it proved the means of maintaining themselves in innocence, like the angels! Segneri speaks of a dissolute youth whom a priest in the confessional told to recite three *Ave Marias* every morning in honor of the immaculate purity of Our Lady; after some years the young man returned to the priest, and informed him that to this practice he owed his complete conversion. Meditation upon the truths of religion destroys the taste for sensual pleasures. "Walk in the Spirit, and you shall not fulfil the lusts of the flesh" (Gal. v. 16). Those who delight themselves in God care for no other joys; after tasting spiritual joys, those of earth are insipid and even abhorrent. He who remembers that God is present everywhere and sees everything will not do what is displeasing in His sight. Witness the conduct of Joseph (Gen. xxxix. 9), and Susanna (Dan. xiii. 35). Do not deceive yourself with the hope that your sin will remain hidden, for God is omnipresent, and from Him nothing can be concealed. "In all thy works remember thy last end and thou shalt never sin" (Ecclus. vii. 40). If the flame of impurity blazes up within you, think of the eternal fire, and that thought will quench it. St. Martinian, a hermit in Palestine, when tormented by temptations, thrust his feet into the fire; and when he screamed with the pain, he asked himself, since he could not bear that feeble flame, how could he endure the everlasting burning of hell-fire? The subject of dancing and theatre-going has already been treated of. Unrestrained and familiar intercourse with persons of the opposite sex is to many a source of danger. Undue familiarity between young men and women is as likely to inflame the passions as straw is to blaze up when brought into contact with fire. One cannot be too careful in this respect. Love your own fireside. "If the candle is to be kept alight," says St. Thomas Aquinas, "it must be put into a lantern; so if you mean to live chastely, beware of going too much abroad."

12. UNCHASTITY.

1. Unchastity consists in thoughts, words, or deeds, which are destructive of innocence.

If the chaste resemble the lily, the unchaste resemble a thorn-bush, which tears one to pieces. It was in order to expiate sins of impurity that the Redeemer of the world suffered Himself to be cruelly scourged, and crowned with thorns.

Unchaste persons are like the brute beasts; they are unlike God and displeasing to Him, and are regarded with contempt by man.

Impurity degrades man to the level of the brute beast. The unchaste prefer the gratification of their lusts to the joys of paradise. To them the words of the Psalmist may be applied: "Man when he was in honor did not understand; he hath been compared to senseless beasts, and made like to them" (Ps. xlviii. 21). Pride is the sin of angels, avarice is the sin of man, and lasciviousness that of the brute. It is most degrading to humanity, which is brought so near to the Deity by the Incarnation of the Son of God, to be unduly subject to any dominion but that of God. By unchastity man loses his likeness to God. Through this sin man defiles the image of God in which he was created and commits a grievous offence against the Most High. It is because no other sin defiles a man as this does, that it is called by the name of impurity, or uncleanness. The unchaste are extremely displeasing to God. In primitive ages, when mankind fell into various sins, even that of idolatry, God bore with them patiently; but when they fell into impurity and sank even deeper in that vice, their wickedness was so abhorrent to Him, that it repented Him that He had made man upon the earth (Gen. vi. 6). St. Philip Neri possessed the gift of discerning the chaste from the unchaste by the sense of smell; to the former a sweet odor attached, whereas the latter stunk in his nostrils. Those who violate their chastity are thus spoken of by the prophet Jeremias: "How is the gold become dim, the finest color is changed. The noble sons of Sion, they were clothed with the best gold, now they are esteemed as earthen vessels. They that were fed delicately have died in the streets" (Lam. iv. 1, 2, 5). The unchaste lose the esteem of their fellow-men; "they are trodden upon as dung in the way" (Ecclus. ix. 10).

2. Unchaste persons do not possess the sanctifying grace of the Holy Ghost, they are severely chastised by God in this life, and after death are condemned to eternal perdition.

The indulgence of evil lusts is a bait the devil throws out, and those who swallow the alluring morsel are drawn by him to destruction. The end of this sin is bitter as wormwood, and sharp as a two-edged sword (Prov. v. 4). St. Jerome declares that the fruits of this sin are more bitter than gall. Since the unchaste are without the light of the Holy Spirit, their understanding is completely darkened. When man descends to the level of the beasts, he loses that intelligence which distinguishes him from the brute; he becomes like the horse and mule, which have no understanding (Ps. xxxi. 9). " The sensual man perceiveth not these things that are of the Spirit of God" (1 Cor. ii. 14). Through yielding to this sin, King Solomon lost his wisdom, and was so blinded by folly that he turned aside to follow the gods of the heathen (3 Kings xi.). The will is weakened by the sin of impurity; it creates a sort of paralysis in regard to good works, and thus amendment is rendered most difficult. The unchaste is a prisoner who has forged iron fetters for himself. Impurity is a snare of the devil, and those who are caught in this net can hardly escape ever from its meshes. It leads moreover into many other sins: Jealousy, hatred, murder, etc. The terrible consequences of this sin are seen in the case of Henry VIII.; it was the cause of his rupture with Rome, and the apostasy of the English people. Unchastity is severely punished in this life; peace of mind is lost, the bodily health is impaired. " Every sin that a man doth is without the body, but he that committeth fornication, sinneth against his own body " (1 Cor. vi. 18). The voluptuary soon loses the bloom of youth, and becomes prematurely aged. Special chastisements, moreover, overtake those who violate chastity; the Deluge was sent on the earth on account of that sin (Gen. vi. 7), and the Lord rained down brimstone and fire upon Sodom and Gomorrha because the transgressions of the inhabitants in the same respect had become exceedingly grievous (Gen. xviii. 20). And if in the present day God does not visit impurity with the same condign punishment, it is because an infinitely fiercer fire, an infinitely more rigorous chastisement, is reserved for sinners of our own time. Fornicators, we are told, shall not possess the kingdom of God (1 Cor. vi. 9). " Neither fornicators nor unclean hath inheritance in the kingdom of Christ and of God" (Eph. v. 5). Of the heavenly Jerusalem it is said there shall not enter into it anything defiled (Apoc. xxi. 27). The soul of the fornicator shall be taken away out of the number (Ecclus. xix. 3). If you live according to the flesh you shall die (Rom. viii. 13). The gratification is momentary, the penalty is eternal.

3. The best means of avoiding the sin of impurity is flight.

Remember how Joseph acted (Gen. xxxix.). There are other means of avoiding this sin, such as the reception of the sacraments. devotion to the Mother of God; yet the best of all is instant flight from temptation. The Apostle says that we ought to resist all temptations to sin, but from impurity he bids us flee—fly fornication (1 Cor. vi. 18). In battling with sensual temptations cowards gain the victory; they seek safety in flight.

13. ZEAL IN WHAT IS GOOD.

1. Zeal in what is good consists in working out one's salvation with all earnestness and fervor.

Unless zeal springs from the love of God it is valueless. It must also be discreet, or it will do more harm than good. He whose zeal is without discretion is like a man who is gathering up the cockle in a field, roots up the wheat together with it (Matt. xiii. 29). Blind zeal is only pernicious. If Alexander the Great performed such great achievements for the sake of earthly renown, what ought not we to do, who aspire to eternal glory! We ought each day so to serve God as if it were the first day of our consecration to His service. We should be like the merchant, who never thinks he has made enough money, but is continually on the watch for fresh gains; or like the traveller who does not look back upon the way he has traversed but only onward to the goal before him. He who is zealous in what is good avails himself as far as he can of the means of grace the Church affords for his sanctification; he is assiduous at prayer, he frequently approaches the sacraments, he listens attentively to the Word of God, and reads spiritual books. He neglects no opportunity of doing good works; he never refuses an alms to the poor man, he conscientiously observes the fasts of the Church, he devotes his free time to prayer. Moreover he who is zealous in what is good cheerfully makes sacrifices for God; he is glad when he is ridiculed or persecuted for his faith; he rejoices in the sufferings that come to him from God; he will give up anything rather than commit sin; he is even ready to lay down his life for Christ, if need be. He who is zealous in what is good exerts himself also for the salvation of others. He strives to deter his subordinates, his friends, his relatives, from sin; he admonishes them and prays for them; he prays besides for the conversion of heretics and sinners; how much the saints did in this way! Zeal is like fire which spreads to all around, both far and near.

2. Without zeal in what is good we cannot be saved, for the kingdom of heaven suffereth violence.

Our Lord says: "Not every one that saith to Me, Lord, Lord, shall enter into the kingdom of heaven" (Matt. vii. 21), and in another place He says: "The kingdom of heaven suffereth violence, and the violent bear it away" (Matt. xi. 12). Of those who run in a race only he who perseveres will receive the prize (1 Cor. ix. 24). Let us not imagine that it is an easy matter to be saved. Eternal felicity is spoken of as a kingdom, the city of God, the house of God, paradise, a crown. All these things can only be acquired by a fierce battle, or for a large sum. Only those who have had a long training can obtain a high salary. Yet the kingdom of heaven is bought cheaply; the price paid for it comes infinitely short of its value. Without zeal and energy nothing good can be accomplished. God allows obstacles to be placed in the way of every good work, to test our will. No good work can be performed without some sacrifice; no virtue can be gained without a struggle. "The greater violence thou offerest to thyself, the greater progress thou wilt make" (Imitation, Book 1, ch. 25). We cannot expect our prayers to be heard, unless we persevere in spite of all hindrances. Remember the example of St. Monica, and the blind man by the wayside (Luke xviii. 35).

14. THE OPPOSITE OF ZEAL : SLOTH.

1. Sloth consists in shunning everything that conduces either to our temporal or eternal well-being, provided it be toilsome.

Sloth displays itself either by indolence, dislike of work, and the non-fulfilment even of the duties of one's calling; or by tepidity in and indifference to what is good and conducive to one's spiritual welfare. The slothful man displays distaste for all good works. We find life and movement and activity in all nature; the celestial hosts laud and magnify the Most High continually; the heavenly bodies revolve unceasingly in space; trees and herbs grow to their appointed size; the tiny ant lays up a store in summer, the busy bees make honey and do not suffer drones to live; and shall man alone be an idler, an exception to all creatures whom instinct teaches to abhor idleness? " Go to the ant, O sluggard, and consider her ways " (Prov. vi. 6). The indolent postpone all work to a future day, and only pursue sensual pleasures. To-morrow, to-morrow, not to-day, is their cry. The lukewarm Christian wills and does not will; he would fain have the wages God gives, but he will not work for Him; as soon as it is a question of putting force upon himself he shrinks back. Yet the slothful think they do more than others, for while the fervent look at those who do better than themselves, to learn humility, they on the contrary look at the good, not in others but in themselves. Hence the slothful never attain perfection. Great sinners have been known to become great saints, but the lukewarm never.

2. Idleness leads to all kinds of vice; it brings misery in this life and eternal damnation in the life to come.

Idleness hath taught much evil (Ecclus. xxxiii. 29); it is in fact the source of every evil habit. Man is like the earth: if a field be not sown with good seed, a crop of weeds spring up and grow apace; so if man has no useful occupation, his natural activity turns to all manner of mischief. Iron rusts when it is not used; water when stagnant becomes foul; and man, corrupted by idleness, becomes the abode of evil passions, and falls into manifold temptations. The busy man is assailed by one demon, the unemployed by a hundred. Idleness ruins the young, for it destroys all that is good in them. The man who does nothing all day long is like the trunk of a tree, without foliage and without fruit. Idleness brings misery in this life. Holy Scripture says of the slothful: " Want shall come upon thee and poverty " (Prov. vi. 11). St. John Chrysostom declares idleness to be the parent of poverty and the root of despair. It also brings a man to eternal damnation. Idleness is in itself a sin. A servant may not steal, or drink, or be insolent; but if he has the fault of being lazy, his master will dismiss him from his service. God acts in the same manner. " Every tree that bringeth not forth good fruit shall be cut down and cast into the fire " (Matt. vii. 19). The servant who refuses to trade with the talents his lord has confided to him, shall be cast into the exterior darkness; there shall be weeping and gnashing of teeth (Matt. xxv. 30). The idler cannot indeed hope that heaven will be his portion, for Our Lord says: " Call the laborers and give them their hire." God does not love those who love their own ease. He expressly states that those who are lukewarm, neither cold nor hot, He will vomit out of His mouth (Apoc. iii. 16), that is to say, He is disgusted with them. Our God is a consuming fire, and He delights in the adoration of the seraphim, who are inflamed with burning love. An open unbeliever is less abhorrent to Him than a tepid Christian.

3. Those who are inclined to indolence should think frequently of the reward, both temporal and eternal, of industry, and thus they will overcome their distaste for work.

" Look not, O Christian," says St. Augustine, " on the labor that it costs thee; look rather to the rest and the joys which God promises thee; see how infinitely they outweigh all thy toil." " In doing good let us not fail; for in due time we shall reap, not failing " (Gal. vi. 9).

C. CHRISTIAN PERFECTION.

I. THE ASPIRATION AFTER CHRISTIAN PERFECTION.

No builder leaves an edifice half-finished. If he has begun to construct a house, he does not rest until it is completed. An artist does not hand in the portrait he has painted until every feature is faithfully delineated. Let the Christian do likewise; when once he has undertaken the work of his own sanctification, and is in a state of grace, let him strive to bring the edifice of virtue to completion, and form himself to a true image of God. Our aim should be to make progress every day.

1. God requires of all the just that they should aspire to Christian perfection.

God desires the sinner to be converted, the just to strive after perfection. The duty of aspiring after perfection is included in the precept of charity, for it requires us to love God with all our strength. And what else does that mean but continual advancement in the path of virtue? "He that is just let him be justified still, and he that is holy let him be sanctified still" (Apoc. xxii. 11). Our Lord lays this injunction upon us: "Be you therefore perfect, as also your heavenly Father is perfect" (Matt. v. 48). The will of God is none other than our sanctification. He who does not aim at the attainment of Christian perfection, is in danger of losing his soul. The vessel that does not stem the stream will drift downwards. Where there is no progression there is retrogression; no man can stand still on the path of virtue. "As soon," says St. Augustine, "as thou art content with thyself, and thinkest thou hast done enough, thou art lost." We should aim at the highest degree of sanctity, imitating the trader, who is wont to ask the highest possible price for his wares.

2. The most sublime example of Christian perfection is found in Our Lord. After Him, the saints are also patterns of perfection.

Christ says: "I am the way, the truth and the life" (John xiv. 6). When the rich youth asked Our Lord what he was to do in order to be perfect, the answer given him was: "Follow Me" (Matt. xix.

509

21). St. Paul bids us: "Put ye on the Lord Jesus Christ" (Rom. xiii. 14). As an apprentice watches his master at work, that he may learn to work like him, so we ought to keep our eyes fixed on our Master Christ. The saints meditated unceasingly on the life and Passion of Our Lord. He is the Christian's pattern. The saints are also examples of perfection, for they imitate Christ; their life is a copy of His life. St. Paul exhorts the Corinthians: "Be ye followers of me" (1 Cor. iv. 10), and he enjoins on the Hebrews the necessity of imitating the saints (Heb. vi. 12). The Church commemorates one or more of the saints on each day of the ecclesiastical year, in order to incite us to their imitation. The saints stand in the same relation to Christ as the stars do to the sun; He surpasses them all in perfection. Thus it is easier for us to imitate the saints; we know that it is impossible for us ever to attain to the perfection of which Christ sets us the example, but the sanctity of the saints is within our reach. And here it must be remarked that almost every saint excelled in the practice of one particular virtue. Also that the actions of each were suited to and in conformity with the circumstances, the environment in which they were placed; e.g., their calling, their means, their bodily strength and natural temperament. Every one ought to choose for his model a saint whose position and calling were similar to his own.

3. The perfection of the Christian consists in charity towards God and his neighbor, and in detachment of heart from the things of this world.

"Love is the fulfilling of the law" (Rom. xiii. 10). Charity is the bond of perfection (Col. iii. 14). St. Augustine, when asked how sanctity of life was to be attained, answered: "Love God, and do as thou wilt;" meaning that he who truly loves God will do nothing that displeases Him. St. Francis of Sales says that the only true perfection is to love God with our whole heart and our neighbor as ourselves; all other perfection is spurious. St. Thomas Aquinas defines sanctity as the fervent surrender of one's self to God. Sanctity does not consist in the outward observances of religion, in long prayers, in fasting and almsgiving; these are but means to its attainment. Nor does sanctity consist in complete freedom from sin; it is evinced rather by constant and energetic resistance to sin. For God frequently permits even saints to fall into sin to keep them humble. Least of all does sanctity consist in extraordinary works, which the world regards with astonishment and admiration. We do not read of the Mother of God ever having performed extraordinary works, or St. Joseph, the foster-father of Christ. In the ranks of the saints a great number will be found who never shone in the sight of the world; their life was hid with Christ in God (Col. iii. 3). The love of God is always accompanied by hatred of the world, abhorrence of its sinful, sensual delights. If any man love the world, the charity of the Father is not in Him (1 John ii. 15). The love of God and the love of the world are like the scales of a balance; as one rises the other falls. As charity increases in the heart sinful affections die out. As one who would climb to the top of a tower must ascend the steps that lead to it, so if we would reach the summit of perfection, we must detach our hearts as completely as possible from earthly things. The greater our hatred of the world, and our proportionate charity towards God and our neighbor, the greater the degree of perfection we have attained.

4. He who makes Christian perfection his aim will attain it surely but slowly.

Our Lord says: "Blessed are they that hunger and thirst after justice for they shall have their fill" (Matt. v. 6). A sincere desire for perfection and an untiring effort to attain it will not be unsuccessful. The desire for it is already half the battle; for an energetic desire gives force and courage, makes labor light, daunts the enemy, makes a man pleasing to God and obtains grace. On St. Thomas Aquinas being asked how one could make sure of attaining sanctity, he replied: "By a resolute will." No one has ever attained sanctity without fervently desiring it, any more than proficiency in an art or science has ever been acquired by one whose wishes were not eagerly set upon it. But progress towards Christian perfection is very slow. Our sanctification is not the work of a single day. No one, unless he be peculiarly privileged by God, can reach perfection in a short time. It is the same in the spiritual as in the natural order: A plant does not spring up and blossom in a night, the infant does not grow to man's estate in a single day. The process of healing is a slow one; indeed the slower the surer. So it is with our sanctification. There are three degrees in the way of perfection; that of the beginners, who still retain a strong affection for mortal sin; that of the advanced, who cannot abstain from venial sin, and who, because of attachment to earthly things, are still in a state of warfare; and the perfect, whose heart is completely detached from earth and given to God, and who consequently are entirely at peace within themselves. These three degrees are also known as the purgative, the illuminative, and the unitive way. They correspond in the supernatural life to the three stages of man's natural life; childhood, the period of mental and physical weakness; adolescence, the period of development; and manhood, the period of maturity. St. Ignatius enjoins upon beginners meditation on the four last things; on the advanced, consideration of the Passion of Our Lord; on the perfect, contemplation of the divine goodness and of celestial joys. There is no end to the way of perfection, for the love of God is without limit. "He who is just, let him be justified still, and he that is holy, let him be sanctified still" (Apoc. xxii. 11). It is, however, within the power of man to approach very near, while still on earth, to the state of the blessed in heaven.

5. There is no state or calling of life in which Christian perfection is not possible.

Saints are formed in every class, from the highest to the lowest. To love God and one's neighbor is within every one's power. "How easy a thing it is," says St. Bonaventure, "to love God; there is nothing laborious, nothing disagreeable involved in it." In fact nothing is more delightful to the heart than to love God. From other good works a man may excuse himself, saying: "I cannot fast; I have not the means to give alms;" but no one can say: "I cannot love." Pious practices must be proportioned to the powers and adapted to the occupations and duties of the individual. St.

Francis of Sales compares piety to a fluid, which takes the shape of the vessel in which it is contained.

II. GENERAL MEANS FOR THE ATTAINMENT OF PERFECTION.

In order to make sure of attaining Christian perfection, the following means should be adopted.

1. Fidelity in small things.

By this greater graces are obtained and grave sins more easily avoided.

In the natural order we see how great things are evolved out of what is apparently insignificant. How small the acorn is, and yet it contains the germ of a mighty oak! So it is in the spiritual order. Pay heed, therefore, to small things; do not despise even the least; be careful to avoid every untrue word, every word that may give offence; never utter lightly the name of God. To him who is faithful in small things God gives great graces; to him Our Lord says: "Well done, good and faithful servant; because thou hast been faithful over a few things, I will place thee over many things" (Matt. xxv. 21). He who, on the other hand, is unfaithful in small things, loses many graces and is punished by God. Moses was not permitted to enter the Promised Land because he doubted God's promise, and Zacharias was struck dumb for his incredulity. Many of the saints were deprived of consolations, and visited by aridity, because of slight faults. He who is faithful in small things is not as likely to fall into heinous sins; for Our Lord says: "He that is faithful in that which is least is faithful also in that which is greater; and he that is unjust in that which is little, is unjust also in that which is greater" (Luke xvi. 10). Hence whosoever is attentive to small things makes rapid progress in virtue. "If thou wouldst become great," says St. Augustine, "begin with that which is little." Grains of sand form a mountain, a number of trees make a forest. "He that contemneth small things shall fall by little and little" (Ecclus. xix. 1). Little infidelities to grace often cause great mischief, and embitter a man's whole life. A spark will occasion a vast conflagration, and a small leak will cause a ship to founder. So it is with small sins. Judas began with purloining, and ended by becoming a traitor and a suicide; Cain first gave way to jealousy and then slew his brother. Contempt of trifles shows secret pride.

2. A habit of self-control.

We should not encourage curiosity, nor stare out of windows; we should avoid useless or loud talking, refrain from complaining of the weather or of our health; from eating between our meals, from finding fault with what is provided for us, from too long indulgence in sleep, from eagerness to join in conversation, from speaking of ourselves, from contradicting others. These and similar acts of mortification cost no great effort. The saints practised far more severe ones, but in this they are not to be imitated by all. St. John the Baptist led a life of extreme self-denial. St. Paul says of himself:

" I chastise my body and bring it into subjection; lest perhaps when I have preached to others, I myself should become a castaway " (1 Cor. ix. 27). Self-control is a sort of abstinence; it is far more profitable than merely abstaining from food. He who can rule himself is a king; for instead of being led captive by his passions, he dominates them. Self-conquest is the mark of a true Christian. Our Lord says: " If any man will follow Me, let him deny himself " (Mark viii. 34); that is to say, he that will be My disciple must practise self-abnegation. St. Paul also says: " They that are Christ's have crucified their flesh with the vices and concupiscences " (Gal. v. 24). A fish that is alive swims against the current; a dead one is carried along by it. Hence you can easily ascertain whether you have the life of the Spirit in you, or whether you are dead; ask yourself whether you stem the tide of your sinful desires, or if you are carried away by it.

By the practice of self-control the understanding is enlightened, the will strengthened, and the soul finds peace.

" We have a law in our members fighting against the law of our mind " (Rom. vii. 23). Our members that are upon the earth must accordingly be mortified (Col. iii. 5). The flesh is continually at war with the spirit, and we must continually be at warfare with the flesh. He who does all that is allowed, will soon proceed to do what is not allowed (St. Augustine). But if we deny ourselves what is lawful, it will be easy for us to abstain from what is unlawful. The most perfect among us will fall into sin if he ceases to practise self-denial, as a field that is uncultivated produces a crop of weeds. Self-control enlightens the understanding. All that we deny to our carnal senses is repaid a hundredfold to our spiritual senses. " Let us," says St. Basil, " stifle our fleshly desires, in order that our spiritual sense may become keener, and our interior vitality and peace be augmented." Self-control fortifies the will. If the will be strong, carnal impulses are quickly subdued, and the temptations of the devil easily overcome. Mortify yourself in matters that are apparently of little moment; you will thereby learn to conquer where great things are at stake. The mortified man is like an oak, which will break, but will not bend; the unmortified is like a reed, shaken with the wind (Matt. xi. 7). By self-control we acquire true peace of mind. There is no quiet in a house the door of which stands open to all comers, and there is no peace in the soul if the senses are not kept in custody. Our disorderly affections are like a storm at sea; they raise a tempest in the soul and perturb the mind. But if you know how to command the winds of passion, a marvellous peace and great calm will ensue. He who for the love of God has renounced all carnal lusts will enjoy the sweetest consolations of the Holy Spirit. He who is master of himself will not easily be provoked to wrath. Self-control is the parent of meekness and patience.

3. Abstinence from all that is superfluous, especially in regard to eating and drinking.

Among superfluities we reckon splendid dress, costly furniture, theatre-going, giving and taking part in entertainments, banquets, etc. Those who take great delight in such things will never attain perfection; the Holy Ghost will not dwell in a heart that is filled with the love of earthly things. He who would enter upon the path of virtue and perfection must begin by diligent mortification of his appetite. No gourmand can be a good soldier of Christ. Those who eat and drink more than is necessary are in danger of losing grace and succumbing to temptation. Hence Our Lord says: "Woe to you that are filled" (Luke vi. 25). And St. Peter exhorts the faithful thus: "Be sober and watch; because your adversary the devil as a roaring lion goeth about, seeking whom he may devour" (1 Pet. v. 8). Talkativeness is also to be avoided. An unrestrained tongue is a sign of conceit and folly. As a doctor judges of a man's bodily health by the state of his tongue, so one may judge of the health of the soul by the words the tongue utters. From the ring of a vessel one can perceive whether it is full or empty; so by the conversation of a man it may be seen whether his mind is empty or well-stored. He that setteth bounds to his tongue is knowing and wise; a fool multiplieth words. The temperature of a room is speedily reduced if the door be left open; so the love of God cools in the heart of one whose lips are ever unclosed for idle gossip, and the sanctifying grace of the Holy Spirit departs from the soul. Incontinence of speech is a fruitful source of contention. "If any man offend not in tongue, the same is a perfect man" (Jas. iii. 2). Mortification of the tongue is indispensable to the attainment of sanctity. "If any man bridle not his tongue, that man's religion is vain" (Jas. i. 26), even though he seem to be God-fearing. "He that hath no guard on his speech shall meet with evils" (Prov. xiii. 3). For this reason St. Paul bids us: "Shun profane and vain babblings" (2 Tim. ii. 16). Speech is silver; silence is gold. Yet we must beware of being too chary with our words, or our silence might appear contemptuous. In this as in all else, a wise medium should be observed.

4. Order and regularity.

For this is conducive to peace of mind and rapid advancement in sanctity.

"Let all things be done decently and according to order" (1 Cor. xiv. 40). It is well to have a fixed time for rising and retiring to rest, for meals, for work. for recreation, etc. We should endeavor to keep order in all around us, for thus we shall save much time and trouble. St. Augustine says that order leads to God, for all that He ordains is regulated in perfect order. Behold the beautiful order that reigns in the starry firmament. Order must be maintained in all institutions. schools, convents, etc. It is remarkable how many men who have had military training have reached an eminent degree of sanctity.

5. Unremitting prayer.

By this means many temptations are held aloof, and graces in abundant measure obtained.

As fortifications defend a garrison against the attacks of the enemy. so prayer without ceasing protects us from the devil. Our Lord admonishes us: "Watch and pray, that ye enter not into temptation " (Matt. xxvi. 41). St. Paul bids the faithful: " Pray without ceasing " (1 Thess. v. 17). Unremitting prayer is a sure means of drawing down the Holy Ghost from on high. The more a plant enjoys the sunshine, the better it will grow and the more luxuriantly will it blossom; in like manner the more often the soul draws near in prayer to the sun of divine grace, the greater will be its increase in perfection. All the saints were instant in prayer. Blessed Clement Hofbauer was accustomed to recite the Rosary while walking through the streets of Vienna. St. Alphonsus used to say that the saints owed their sanctity more to their prayers than to their works. Habituate yourself to ejaculatory prayer; it will refresh you and help you on your way as an occasional draught of wine does the traveller.

6. Frequent confession and communion.

Sins once properly confessed, are, it is true, forgiven; yet it is advisable, though not obligatory upon us, to accuse ourselves of them repeatedly.

The saints used to confess again and again the mortal sins of which they had been guilty. The confession of the sins of our past life serves to keep us humble. And if, after confession, we frequently approach the holy table, we shall increase in perfection, as a tree which is planted near running waters grows to great height. We admire the sanctity of the early Christians; let us remember that they communicated daily. It is said of them that they persevered in the communication of the breaking of bread (Acts ii. 42).

7. Reading attentively the life of Our Lord and the lives of the saints, and meditation on the truths of religion.

By reading the lives of the saints we shall feel ourselves powerfully incited to imitate their example. We shall ask ourselves, as St. Augustine asked himself: " If these and those could do so much, wherefore canst not thou do the same? " The saints loved to study the lives of the saints and to imitate them; so a draughtsman looks long and often at the picture he is about to copy. However, we must not imagine that with our love of God, so poor, so faint, we can all at once imitate the sublime actions of the saints, or it will be as if a crow were to attempt to imitate the song of the nightingale. The most profitable plan is for us to read the life of a saint whose position corresponded to our own, and learn from it practical lessons. The lives of the saints are the maxims of the Gospel put in practice. Meditation on the truths of religion is supremely useful; it enlightens our understanding, stimulates the will to the pursuit of what is good, and gives us peace of mind. The truths of religion are like a fire, standing near which we receive light and warmth. They impart nourishment to our souls; they are a food that satisfies. Remember Our Lord's words to the Samaritan woman (John iv. 13). The world would not be as bad as it is if there were not so few who consider the truths of religion in their heart (Jer. xii. 11). Through meditation the saints attained sanctity.

8. Love of solitude.

In solitude we obtain many actual graces; we are preserved from temptation and from sin, and grow in virtue.

Our Lord was wont to take Himself to solitary places, to a mountain (John vi. 15), to the desert (Luke v. 16), or the Mount of Olives (John viii. 1), where He spent a long time in prayer.   Until He was thirty years of age He led a hidden life.   We know also that many holy men withdrew into solitude and devoted themselves to spiritual exercises.   St. Benedict passed three years in a cavern among the mountains.   St. Ignatius of Loyola dwelt for a considerable time in the cave of Manresa.   Those who are now unknown, whose life is hid with Christ in God, will one day appear with Him in glory (Col. iii. 3, 4).   St. John Chrysostom says the life of the recluse is that of an angel upon earth.   In solitude we obtain many graces; there the Holy Spirit speaks to the heart (Osee ii. 14).   One cannot hear a sweet melody in the midst of din and tumult; God's voice can only be heard by those who flee from the world.   The further the soul lives from all worldly tumult, the more familiar does she become with her Creator (Imitation, Book 1, ch. 20).   In solitude alone is true contentment to be found.   Were the recluse to leave his cell, he would perceive that the world is a field in which more vexation than pleasure is to be reaped.   Solitude is a preservative from temptation and sin, as the harbor shelters the mariner from storm and shipwreck.   While Adam was alone he did not sin; it was after he had Eve for a companion. The sage Seneca used to say: " As often as I have been among men, I have returned less a man."   Solitude helps to maintain and increase virtue.   Choice spices only retain their aroma when shut up; they lose it if exposed to the air.   Virtue is more easily preserved in solitude than amid the noise and bustle of the world.   He who frequents the drinking saloon, who goes to every place of amusement, who, in a a word, enjoys life, will not enjoy true peace of heart, will not attain perfection.   But however great the advantages of seclusion, we must not be unsociable, and withdraw altogether from the society of our fellow-men; we must mix with them freely whenever duty bids, or charity calls upon us to do so.   Our Blessed Lady visited her cousin Elizabeth, to congratulate her.   Let us hold aloof from the world in spirit, not in bodily presence.

III. SPECIAL MEANS FOR THE ATTAINMENT OF PERFECTION.

1. He who aspires to a higher degree of perfection must follow the three evangelical counsels: Perfect obedience. perpetual chastity, and voluntary poverty.

These three virtues are called counsels because they were not enjoined upon us by Our Lord as a command, but as a counsel.   There is no sin incurred in not following them.   It befits the law of the New Testament to contain counsels as well as precepts, for in it God makes Himself the Friend of man. and in this character He does not command but commend.   The New Law is a law of liberty, the Old Law was one of servitude.   By following the evangelical counsels we offer an oblation to God of our will, our body, our property.   They are the three arms of the cross on which we are crucified with Christ.   To follow them is a lifelong martyrdom; a martyrdom less terrible than that of the sword, but more painful because of its duration. Those who follow these counsels will attain a higher degree of glory. That which is done voluntarily, not under compulsion, deserves a greater reward.

1. Perfect obedience consists in the complete subjection of one's will to that of a superior.

Christian obedience, that is, obedience to the ecclesiastical and secular authorities, is binding upon every man. But this obligation does not extend to all our actions; it leaves us free in many respects. For instance, the spiritual authority requires us to hear Mass on Sundays and holydays, to approach the sacraments at Easter, etc.; but it leaves us at liberty to fulfil our duty in what church and at what hour we please. Perfect obedience, on the contrary, requires us to obey in everything. This voluntary obedience is the greatest sacrifice we can make for God; if we fast, give alms, or sacrifice our reputation for God's sake, we give to God only a part of ourselves. But he who sacrifices his will has nothing more to give; he immolates himself to God. Obedience to a superior is neither irrational nor degrading to man, for he subjects himself voluntarily once and forever to the will of one who is placed over him by the will of almighty God; he is like a traveller who unquestioningly proceeds in the direction to which the signpost points. It is a difficult matter to know one's self, but it is easy for another to know and guide one.

2. Lifelong chastity consists in abstaining from marriage and from all unclean desires.

The Sixth Commandment of the Decalogue obliges every one to subdue his evil concupiscences. This counsel requires those who follow it to abstain from wedlock; they lead on earth an angel's life. In fact in this respect man surpasses the angels in excellence, for the latter have no carnal impulses to combat. The Council of Trent (C. 24, 10), declares the single state to be higher than the married state; it is therefore better to be unmarried (1 Cor. vii. 38). The reason of this is because conjugal intercourse fosters man's lower nature, and the care of providing for a family engrosses him in material interests.

3. Voluntary poverty consists in the renunciation of all earthly possessions.

To give of one's own to the needy is the bounden duty of all. But it is an immeasurably greater sacrifice if, for the love of God, we renounce all earthly possessions and voluntarily embrace poverty, to which so many hardships are attached. The voluntary poverty of the Christian bears no resemblance to the voluntary poverty of the pagan philosophers. The latter despised riches from earthly considerations; they wished to be quit of the cares attending them. The Christian on the other hand makes himself poor in order to serve God better, and thus attain more surely to the possession of eternal treasures. There is, besides, involuntary poverty, when a man is destitute, or in straitened circumstances. Again there is poverty of spirit, which is required of all men; it consists in acknowledging that whatever wealth, distinctions, or learning we may possess, we are poor in the sight of God. But now we are speaking of voluntary poverty; he who is poor for Christ's sake is exceeding rich (St. Jerome).

2. These three counsels are called the evangelical counsels; because Our Lord gave them to us when He preached the Gospel, and followed them Himself.

Our Lord counselled perfect obedience in His conversation with the rich young man; perpetual chastity in His discourse on the indissolubility of marriage; voluntary poverty in the afore-mentioned conversation with the rich young man.

We read that Christ said to the rich young man: "Come and follow Me" (Matt. xix. 21); i.e., come and let your conduct be guided by Me completely. This is perfect obedience. And when He was speaking about the indissolubility of marriage, He said that there were some who remained unmarried for the kingdom of heaven's sake; adding: "He that can take it let him take it" (Matt. xix. 12). By these words He counselled perpetual chastity. Finally He said to the young man: "If thou will be perfect, go, sell what thou hast and give to the poor" (Matt. xix. 21). This was voluntary poverty.

Our Lord Himself practised the counsels; for He sought not His own will but did the will of Him that sent Him (John v. 30). He led a life of celibacy and extreme poverty.

The poverty of Christ was perfect; He chose a stable for His birthplace, a poor virgin for His Mother, a lowly artisan for His fosterfather; He had nowhere to lay His head (Matt. viii. 20).

3. The evangelical counsels lead to higher perfection, because by their means the three evil concupiscences in man are completely destroyed and the chief obstacles in the way of his salvation are removed.

In following the evangelical counsels, we do not combat this or that evil tendency; we tear up all bad passions by the root, and lay a solid foundation for the edifice of virtue. All sins spring from the threefold concupiscence: The concupiscence of the eyes, the concupiscence of the flesh, and the pride of life; i.e., the inordinate longing for riches, for sensual gratifications, and for honor (1 John ii. 16). As in medicine some remedies are drastic and others mild, so it is with the remedies for these evil concupiscences. Prayer is a cure for pride, fasting for sensuality, almsgiving for avarice; these are mild remedies. But let him who desires a radical cure adopt the three evangelical counsels. By obedience pride will be thoroughly subdued: concupiscence of the flesh by chastity, concupiscence of the eyes by poverty. The counsels are a means of removing the chief obstacles in the way of our salvation. By following them we shake off the fetters of earth, and thus advance more swiftly towards our final end. That earthly possessions are a formidable hindrance to those who would follow Christ, we gather from the story of the rich young man (Matt. xix.). Socrates compares riches to a long robe, which prevents one from walking quickly because one's feet get entangled in it. The traveller proceeds on his way much more rapidly if he has nothing to carry. What is said about riches is equally true in reference to wedlock. He that is married is solicitous for the things of the world, that he may please men; he that is unmarried is solicitous for the things that belong to the Lord, how he may please God (1 Cor. vii. 32). He who is detached from earthly things can fix his eyes on heaven and contemplate the Sun of justice with unclouded vision, and gain a more profound knowledge of divine things. Let no one say that the wealthy can do more good to his fellow-men, and gain more merit, than one who embraces voluntary poverty. The former gives but a part, the latter gives the whole. And consider what immense good has been done, in spite of their poverty, by those who have given up all.

The evangelical counsels are, however, not in themselves perfection, they are but a means towards its attainment.

The highest perfection is the highest degree of charity towards God. To adopt the counsels does not make a man perfect, for it is possible to pledge one's self solemnly to do something and then not fulfil one's promise. A certain man sent his two sons to work in his vineyard. The one said: "I will not," but afterwards being moved with repentance he went. The other said: "I go, sir," and he went not (Matt. xxi. 28-30). There are many in a state of perfection who are very much the reverse of perfect. And those who profess to follow the counsels, and yet give way to love of eating, to anger, avarice, love of ease, or other sins, are all the more culpable; just as a messenger would be who, although he had no weight to carry, dallied on his way, and made no attempt to reach his destination.

4. Not every one is called of God to follow the evangelical counsels; for Our Lord says: " All men take not this word, but they to whom it is given " (Matt. xix. 11).

Those are called to whom God gives the desire of this grace; and who are ready to make any effort to obtain it. Let not those who are not called to follow them hold the evangelical counsels in contempt. "If the ring does not fit thy finger," says St. Francis of Sales, "do not on that account cast it into the mire."

5. The members of religious Orders are bound to follow the evangelical counsels, and likewise all persons living in the world who have taken a vow to do so.

As a servant has to serve his master by reason of the duties he has taken upon himself, so the Religious is bound to strive after the highest perfection by following the counsels, by reason of the vows he has made. The religious Orders originated in this wise: St. Anthony the Great assembled around him in the Thebaid a number of disciples, who lived in separate cells, and occupied themselves with prayer and manual work, and followed the evangelical counsels. St. Pachomius (348 A.D.) collected these anchorites under one roof, and gave them a fixed rule. Thus the first cloister was established upon an island near the mouth of the Nile. The monastic life was introduced into Palestine and Syria by the Abbot Hilarion, whose disciples numbered some three thousand, and into Asia Minor by St. Basil (379 A.D.), Archbishop of Cæsarea. St. Martin, Bishop of Tours, and St. Benedict, were the founders of monasticism in the West in the fifth and sixth centuries. Thus the Orders arose for men and women; communities who led a regular life in accordance with the teaching of Christ. The men were called monks, from the Greek *monachoi,* hermits; the women *nuns,* i.e., virgins. The principal Orders are: The Franciscans, founded by St. Francis of Assisi (1226); the Dominicans, by St. Dominic (1216); the Jesuits, by St. Ignatius of Loyola (1556); the Order of Mercy, by St. John of God (1550); the Lazarists, by St. Vincent of Paul (1660); the Redemptorists, by St. Alphonsus Liguori (1787), besides many others. Each Order has its special mission: the care of the sick, the instruction of youth, foreign missions, etc. Religious are under the obligation of remaining in one place, either in a particular house (monastery) or a part of a house (enclosure). They are all subject to a superior, who is generally elected for three years. Each Order has a habit peculiar to itself. Admission to the Order is by profession, i.e., taking the vows; previous to being professed, a novitiate of at least one year has to be passed through. The religious Orders are very numerous at the present time in America and still more in Europe, excepting Germany, whence they are banished for the most part. It is an act of tyranny on the part of the State to forbid community life; it is depriving subjects of their natural rights. Besides, the religious Orders are not merely an ornament to the Church, they are an essential part of the Christian commonwealth. The suppression of the religious Orders by the secular power is a mutilation of the body corporate. The religious state affords more security of salvation than a secular life; the means of grace can be employed more easily, more regularly; the religious are safeguarded from many occasions of sin which cannot be avoided in the world, through the supervision of the superior and also by the habit they wear. But those who do not live up to their religious profession, nor keep their vows, fall into a disorderly life and go swiftly to perdition. It is a mortal sin not to keep the vows. This causes St. Augustine to say: "As I have never met with a better man than a really good monk, so I have never seen a more wicked man upon earth than a bad Religious." Most of the Orders have, as history proves, done great work for humanity, especially by works of mercy and the encouragement of learning. The Benedictines in the Middle Ages cut down the primeval forests and cultivated the untilled soil. The contemplative Orders also contributed much to the furtherance of godliness and piety by their valuable writings. All the monastic houses were noted for their liberality to the poor. It cannot be denied that in some conventual houses in the Middle Ages laxity and self-indulgence prevailed, but on these the scourge of God fell. Persons living in the world often take a vow of chastity. Remember the example of St. Agnes; she suffered torture and martyrdom rather than break her vow by marrying the son of the Proconsul. The other two evangelical counsels are not suited for those who live in the world.

The secular clergy are pledged to obey their bishop and lead a life of celibacy.

The secular clergy are bound to obey their bishop; this obligation is imposed on them when they are admitted to the sub-diaconate; as also is the obligation of reciting the Breviary. The celibacy of the clergy was first made obligatory at the Synod of Elvira, in 306. During the three first centuries there was no need of this law, because priests voluntarily abjured marriage, out of respect for the sacredness of their office. Only at times when the lack of priests was most keenly felt, were married men admitted to the priesthood; but after ordination no one was permitted to marry. Only in isolated and very rare instances, for weighty reasons, has the Pope been known to dispense priests from their vow; and then they had to give up their benefices, and were debarred from all exercise of their sacerdotal functions. Yet they were required to recite the Breviary until death. In the Middle Ages Pope Gregory VII. made a determined stand against the marriage of priests, prohibiting those who had wives from performing any ministerial work. The Council of Trent (24, 9), declared the marriage of priests to be invalid. The apostles, after their vocation, left all they had; the great prophets, Elias, Eliseus, Jeremias, St. John Baptist, lived a celibate life. A parish priest must devote himself wholly to the salvation of souls; he must administer the sacraments to the sick at the risk of his life, he must assist the poor, admonish his flock, and offer the holy sacrifice of the Mass with a pure heart.

IV. THE EIGHT BEATITUDES.

Those who scrupulously keep God's commandments are happy even on earth. Hence Our Lord (Matt. v. 3-10), pronounces the following beatitudes:

1. Blessed are the poor in spirit, for theirs is the kingdom of heaven.

This is the meaning of these words: Blessed are they who, however great their wealth, their dignity, their health, their learning, acknowledge that before God they are poor, for in this life they enjoy celestial peace and after death are partakers of eternal felicity.

The poor in spirit are not the fools, but the humble. They are those who have the spirit of a little child. The rich in spirit are the proud, who think much of themselves because of all they possess. Yet the rich man may be poor in spirit, if he acknowledges that all his riches are valueless in God's sight. And a poor man is not poor in spirit if he pride himself on some quality or other that he possesses. But as a rule, the rich are not, and the poor are, poor in spirit. The poor in spirit enjoy celestial peace, for Our Lord declares that theirs is the kingdom of heaven. They are like rocks, externally barren and unproductive, but containing within rich veins of pure gold; for while they appear to the eye of man bereft of all joys they possess consolations of which the world knows nothing. The poor in spirit are admitted to eternal felicity. Heaven belongs to the poor in spirit, as the pearl belongs to the man who has purchased it at a goodly price; for the poor in spirit, by their renunciation of all earthly things, have bought heaven at the cost of all they possessed.

2. Blessed are the meek; for they shall possess the land.

The meaning of these words is this: Blessed are they who preserve their composure (are not provoked to anger by the wrong done to them); for they will rule their fellow-men (they will conquer the hearts of men) and after death they will enter into heaven.

(See the instruction on meekness.)

3. Blessed are they that mourn, for they shall be comforted.

The meaning of these words is this: Blessed are they who lament but little over the loss of transitory things, for God will impart to them such consolation that they will forget their sorrow; and after death He will bestow upon them celestial and eternal joys.

They that mourn are therefore not those who mourn over the loss of earthly things, e.g., the enjoyment of some pleasure. Sorrow such as that is a sign that the heart is not detached from the things of earth; it profits us no more than a plaster would heal a wound if it were laid beside, instead of on it. Sorrow is only a cure for sin. Unless our sorrow is on account of sin, it will only be harmful; as a moth doth by a garment and a worm by the wood, so the sadness of a man consumeth the heart (Prov. xxv. 20). Sadness incapacitates the soul for action; it has the same benumbing effect upon it as excessive cold has upon the body. A season of gloom and depression is an opportune moment for the devil; he avails himself of it to tempt us and make us fall, as birds of prey go out by night in quest of spoil. Hence Holy Scripture exhorts us to be cheerful. The joyfulness of the heart is the life of a man, and a never-failing treasure of holiness (Ecclus. xxx. 23). But sorrow for sin, whether our own or that of others, is pleasing to God, and is succeeded by joy and gladness. What happiness awaited the prodigal son when he returned home, after deeply deploring his sin! What joy the penitent thief experienced when Our Lord promised him paradise! What joy Magdalen felt when Christ pardoned her and commended her love! and David when, after he had bewailed his transgression (Ps. l.), the prophet announced to him that he was forgiven! Mourning for sin can hardly be called sadness, because it is not incompatible with interior gladness. St. Jerome says: "In spite of penitential tears and heart-rending sighs I am sometimes so joyous that I fancy myself already with the angels." Nor is sorrow on account of the trials Providence sends us reprehensible; it too leads to joy and consolation. This was the sorrow Our Lord felt on the Mount of Olives, at the approach of His Passion; and an angel appeared to Him, strengthening Him. This was the sorrow the widow of Naim felt when her son was carried out for burial; and Our Lord consoled her grief by restoring him to life. The apostles mourned when Christ left them and ascended into heaven, and immediately two angels came to comfort them. When God has happiness in store for us, He invariably sends some trial first to make us more humble, more grateful for His gifts; thus light is more welcome after darkness, health is better appreciated after sickness. They that mourn will also be comforted hereafter. "God shall wipe away all tears from their eyes, and death shall not be any more, nor mourning, nor crying, nor sorrow" (Apoc. xxi. 4). "They that sow in tears shall reap in joy" (Ps. cxxv. 5).

4. Blessed are they that hunger and thirst after justice; for they shall be filled.

The meaning of these words is this: Blessed are they who strenuously strive after truth and moral perfection, for they shall attain it, and shall be satisfied by the beatific vision of God in heaven.

The centurion Cornelius sought after truth with prayer, fasting, and alms; God instructed him first by an angel, and subsequently by the mouth of St. Peter. The pagan philosopher Justinus made a careful study of all the systems of philosophy in order to discover the truth, and God employed an old man on the banks of the Tiber to teach him the doctrines of Christianity. He who strives earnestly after sanctity will surely attain it. Clement Hofbauer, a baker's apprentice, set his heart upon becoming a priest; he attained his end in spite of all hindrances, and has been beatified. A man who is tormented by hunger or thirst will do anything to obtain relief, as Esau relinquished his birthright; the saints acted in like manner, counting no exertion too great, no sacrifice too costly, in order to satisfy the hunger of their soul. This spiritual hunger and thirst, the craving for increase of knowledge and growth in holiness is attended by joy and causes no uneasiness to the soul. The aspiration after justice renders us fit to receive the communication of divine grace, for by fervent desires our heart is enlarged. Eternal felicity also awaits those who strive after justice; here below they never think they have reached their goal, they never say they have done enough. They hunger continually; and a never-ending hunger merits never-ending satisfaction.

5. Blessed are the merciful, for they shall obtain mercy.

The meaning of these words is this: Blessed are they who help their neighbor who is in need, for they will obtain from God pardon of their sins, and will be leniently judged at their death.

(See what has been said on the usefulness of works of mercy.)

6. Blessed are the clean of heart, for they shall see God.

The meaning of these words is this: Blessed are they whose heart does not cling to the things of earth, for they will have a clearer perception of God in their lifetime, and after death will behold Him face to face (1 Cor. xiii. 12).

The proud, the covetous, the intemperate, are not clean of heart, for the things of time and sense, honors, riches, the pleasures of the table, hold a place in their heart. Only those who are conscious of no habitual sin can be said to be clean of heart. What enabled St.

John the Evangelist to penetrate so deeply into the mysteries of religion, to gaze upon the sublimity of the Godhead? "The sensual
man perceiveth not these things that are of the spirit of God" (1 Cor.
ii. 14). "Wisdom will not enter into a malicious soul, nor dwell in
a body subject to sins" (Wisd. i. 4). Truth does not reveal itself
to the unclean, but from a pure heart it cannot be hid (St. Bernard).
As a sheet of paper must be clean, upon which one is about to write,
so that heart must be pure from carnal desires upon which God will
set His seal by the action of the Holy Ghost.

7. Blessed are the peacemakers, for they shall be called the
children of God.

The meaning of these words is this: Blessed are they who
make sacrifices for the sake of peace, and who promote peace
among others; for here below they enjoy the special protection
of God, and hereafter they will receive the reward of their self-
conquest.

(See the instruction upon peaceableness.)

8. Blessed are they that suffer persecution for justice' sake;
for theirs is the kingdom of heaven.

The meaning of these words is this: Blessed are they who
have to suffer at the hands of their fellow-men for the sake of
their faith, or of some Christian virtue; for even in this life
they will be filled with interior joy, and after death a high degree of felicity will be theirs.

What indescribable happiness St. Stephen felt while he was being
stoned; he saw the heavens opened and Christ standing in the glory
of God (Acts vii. 55). St. Lawrence, who was broiled upon a red-hot
gridiron in Rome, must have experienced similar consolations, for
while he was enduring the torture he joked, saying to the pagan
governor: "I am roasted enough on this side; now turn me over to
the other." St. Paul declares: "I exceedingly abound with joy in
all our tribulation" (2 Cor. vii. 4). How could the martyrs have
suffered torments so terrible with such equanimity, unless they had
been mingled with celestial consolations? Our Lord says of those
who suffer for His sake: "Your reward is very great in heaven"
(Matt. v. 12). Persecutions are the precious stones wherewith the
crowns of the saints are adorned in heaven. You must suffer with
Christ here, if you would reign with Him thereafter. There is no
greater honor upon earth than to suffer for God. The order in which
the beatitudes are enumerated indicates the existence of three degrees, or stages, in the spiritual life. (1), All sinful inclinations
must be combated, by means of humility, meekness, sorrow for sin;
(2), Our sanctification must be effected by means of striving after
perfection and the practice of works of mercy: (3), We must be
united to God, by cleanness of heart, by peaceableness, and patient endurance of suffering. The beatitudes begin with the promise of
the kingdom of heaven, and with it they end. This is to signify that
eternal felicity is the reward of all the intervening beatitudes. _ What

is promised to the poor in spirit as their reward under the name of the kingdom of heaven, is the same as the land which the meek are to possess, the comfort promised to those who mourn, the satisfaction which is to be the portion of those who hunger and thirst after justice, the mercy to be obtained by the merciful, the contemplation of God which the clean of heart are to enjoy, the adoption of the peacemakers as the children of God, and the kingdom of heaven which belongs to the persecuted. The Church has appointed the eight beatitudes to be read as the Gospel on the feast of All Saints, because it was the prospect of this eternal reward which urged the saints onward on the path of virtue.

The worldling counts those as fools whom Christ declares to be blessed.

The world has its own maxims, which are utterly opposed to those of the Gospel. (1), Riches constitute the greatest happiness, poverty is the greatest misery. If a man has anything at all, he must make a show with it, or the world will not think much of him; (2), One ought not to put up with anything; (3), Happy is the man who is free from care and sorrow; (4), One must look to it that one makes a lot of money; (5), Let every one study his own advantage; (6), Let us eat and drink, for to-morrow we die; (7), One must take up arms in one's own defence, whenever one is wronged; (8), Blessed are they who have nothing to suffer. Well indeed might St. Paul say: "The wisdom of this world is foolishness with God" (1 Cor. iii. 19).

PART III.: THE MEANS OF GRACE.

I. THE HOLY SACRIFICE OF THE MASS.

1. ON SACRIFICE IN GENERAL.

Since the most important of all the means of grace, the holy Mass, is a sacrifice, it is necessary first of all to speak of sacrifice in general. The word " to sacrifice " means to offer something valuable to some person as a token of affection for, or dependence on that person; or to surrender something that we prize for the sake of another. If a father gives all he has to his sons to enable them to pursue their studies, and himself lives in straitened circumstances, he is said to make a great sacrifice for his children. When a soldier marches to battle for the defence of his country at the risk of life and limb, he is said to sacrifice himself for his country. By a sacrifice to God is signified something given up to God. Out of love to Him the poor widow cast into the treasury the last two mites which she possessed; in doing this she made a great sacrifice for God's sake (Mark xii. 43). Tobias did the same, when in captivity he distributed alms to his poorer fellow-countrymen, and at peril of his own life buried the bodies of the slain (Tob. i.). The Jews made a sacrifice, when after the giving of the law, they brought gold, silver, precious stones, purple, etc., to Moses for the making of the tabernacle (Exod. xxxv.). We are told in Holy Scripture that to keep the commandments, to depart from injustice, and to do mercy, is to offer sacrifice (Ecclus. xxxv. 2-4). The essential part of a sacrifice is the surrender or renunciation of some object which we highly prize. Of old, if any one desired to accentuate his surrender of the object he valued, he used to destroy it completely; thus rendering it impossible for him ever to recover possession of it. The sacrifices offered by Cain, Abel, and Noe, were of this nature. Abel slaughtered and burned the firstlings of his flock; his brother Cain offered of the fruits of the earth gifts unto the Lord (Gen. iv. 3, 5). Noe, on leaving the ark, took some of the animals and offered them as holocausts upon the altar he had built (Gen. viii. 20).

1. Hence the word sacrifice signifies the voluntary surrender
526

or the destruction of an object which we value, to give honor to God as our supreme Lord.

It is no uncommon thing among men to present a valuable present to some one as a sign of respect or an act of homage. Subjects not unfrequently offer the best produce of their land or their skill to their monarch. So we ought to give to God what we most value. And as in a State there are certain honors which it is the exclusive prerogative of the ruler to receive, so the offering of sacrifice is an act of homage which can be paid only to God.

2. There are bloody and unbloody sacrifices.

As may be seen from the sacrifices of Cain and Abel, the oblation offered in sacrifice varied according to the nature of the possessions of him who offered it. Either a victim, such as an ox, a lamb, a dove, was taken from the animal kingdom (this was a bloody sacrifice, because the blood of the victim was shed), or an oblation was taken from the vegetable kingdom, some species of food, such as flour or fruit, or drink, wine, for instance (this was an unbloody sacrifice, because it was without shedding of blood). The animals used to be slaughtered, their blood poured upon the altar, and their flesh either consumed entirely by fire, or eaten in part by the priests and Levites. The fruits of the earth were either burned or eaten; wine was poured as a libation on or before the altar.

3. The intention of a sacrifice may be to give honor to God, to give thanks to Him, to entreat a favor, or make propitiation.

The offering of a sacrifice gives outward expression to the feelings of the heart. The man who has a due knowledge of God, who knows Him to be the almighty Creator, the wise and bountiful Preserver and Ruler of the world, will be penetrated with sentiments of respect, of gratitude, of confidence, and of contrition. And since it belongs to the nature of man to manifest outwardly what he feels inwardly, he will evince these sentiments by the surrender,—the renunciation or destruction—of some object that he values. These sentiments are essential to a sacrifice—without them it would be mere hypocrisy—consequently the sentiment of compunction is of itself sometimes designated a sacrifice (Ps. l. 19). Sacrifices of praise used to be offered daily in the Temple; Noe's sacrifice was a sacrifice of thanksgiving, while the sacrifices which Judas Machabeus caused to be offered before going to battle were deprecatory sacrifices; those offered for the warriors who fell in the fight were expiatory sacrifices (2 Mach. xii. 43).

4. The custom of offering sacrifices has existed in all times and among all nations of the world.

Sacrifices have been customary from time immemorial. They were offered by Cain and Abel, the children of the first man and the first woman. They are found among Jews and Gentiles. The Jewish high priest offered an oblation morning and evening in the name of the people; first he burned incense upon the altar, then he offered an unbloody sacrifice consisting of flour, oil and frankincense (Lev. vi.

14), and finally a sacrifice in which was shedding of blood, the victim being a lamb of one year old, without blemish, together with an oblation of food and drink (Exod. xxix. 38). On the Sabbath day two lambs of a year old, together with bread and wine, were immolated in addition to the daily oblation (Numb. xxviii. 9). Special sacrifices were also appointed for certain feasts. The heathen nations also offered sacrifices, but their ideas on the subject were perverted, for they offered human sacrifices, and not to the true God, but to idols. Hence St. Paul says: " The things which the heathen sacrifice, they sacrifice to devils and not to God " (1 Cor. x. 20). We read in Holy Scripture that the King of Moab took his oldest son and offered him for a burnt-offering upon the wall, in order to obtain help against the Israelites (4 Kings iii. 27). The Phœnicians and other Asiatic people used yearly to immolate young children to their god Moloch, the brazen statue of the deity being made red-hot, and the children cast into its arms. The custom of offering human sacrifices formerly prevailed to a great extent in Mexico; it is said that the number of victims slaughtered yearly amounted to no less than twenty thousand. Human sacrifices are not yet entirely abolished, they are still customary among savages, notably among some African and Indian tribes. How sad is the condition of man without the Christian faith!

5. The chief motives which urge mankind to offer sacrifice are: The consciousness of sin and the desire for reconciliation with God and because God often required or sanctioned the sacrifice.

The consciousness of sin was a powerful incentive to man to offer sacrifices. St. Paul says: " In them there is made a commemoration of sins every year " (Heb. x. 3), and again: " Without shedding of blood there is no remission " (Heb. ix. 22). God not unfrequently showed His approbation of sacrifice; He testified His acceptance of Abel's offering (Gen. iv. 4). Of Noe's (Gen. viii. 21), of the holocaust offered by the prophet Elias, which was consumed by fire from heaven (3 Kings xviii. 38). On many occasions God required a sacrifice, as that of Isaac (Gen. xxii.). He gave minute directions concerning the sacrificial offerings to the Jews by Moses' lips (Lev. i.-vii.; xvi.; xxii.). The knowledge that God approved of and even demanded sacrifices from man was a potent motive inducing him to offer them.

6. The sacrifices of the Jewish nation, more particularly that of the paschal lamb and the victim of expiation, were typical of the great sacrifice that the Redeemer was to offer on Mount Calvary.

In the Old Testament everywhere there is shedding of blood; this was typical of the blood of Christ, whereby we are purified. On the great Day of Atonement one of the ceremonies consisted in this: The high priest laid both his hands upon the head of one of the goats which were to be offered up for the people, confessing at the same time the iniquities of the children of Israel, and praying that they might light upon the head of the animal; thereupon the goat was turned out into the desert, to express symbolically that the sins of the people were taken away out of God's sight. Since the Jewish sacrifices were but a foreshadowing of Our Lord's expiatory sacrifice, they ceased after this was offered, as had been foretold by the prophets (Dan. ix. 27; Osee iii. 4). Nor were the sacrifices of the heathen anything more or less than a seeking after the true sacrifice of atonement; the victims were without blemish, a pure and spotless oblation; moreover everywhere the persuasion seemed to prevail that " it is impossible that with the blood of oxen and goats sin should be taken away " (Heb. x. 4), or that the Deity should be propitiated by any other similar victims. A victim of infinite value was needed to reconcile God with man.

2. THE SACRIFICE OF CHRIST UPON THE CROSS.

1. The sacrifice which reconciled God with man was that which Christ offered upon the cross.

The life of Our Lord upon earth may be said to have been one uninterrupted sacrifice. This sacrifice was commenced at the Incarnation, for then He divested Himself of His divine dignity that was His as Son of God, and took the form of a servant (Phil. ii. 7). He gave up His free will, becoming obedient to His heavenly Father unto death, even to the death of the cross (v. 8). This sacrifice was continued throughout His whole life. He relinquished all earthly possessions; He Himself says: " The foxes have holes and the birds of the air have nests, but the Son of man hath not where to lay His head " (Matt. viii. 20). He often denied Himself the food of the body; for instance, on the occasion of His converse with the Samaritan woman, He said to His disciples, when they pressed Him to take some refreshment: " My meat is to do the will of Him that sent Me, that I may perfect His work " (John iv. 34). Even when wearied with His apostolic labors He denied Himself rest; we read that not unfrequently He went up into a mountain, and passed the whole night in prayer to God (Luke vi. 12). He willingly renounced honor, saying: " I seek not My own glory " (John viii. 50). He bore scorn and derision in silence, especially when brought before His judges (Luke xxiii. 11). He allowed Himself to be put on a par with murderers, and crucified between two thieves (Mark xv. 27). He suffered a notorious criminal to be preferred to Him (Matt. xxvii. 17). Finally, upon the cross, He surrendered all that He had, even His life itself, for He said: " Greater love than this no man hath, that a man lay down His life for His friends " (John xv. 13). Well might He exclaim immediately before His death: " It is consummated! " The actual sacrifice of propitiation began with Our Lord's Passion, and ended with His death upon the cross. On the cross He gave His body to be offered up. It was not, it is true, slain, divided and burned with fire like the bodies of other victims, but it was cruelly tortured and deprived of life. While hanging upon the cross the Redeemer might echo the words of the Psalmist: " I am a worm and no man. I am poured out like water, and all My bones are scattered " (Ps. xxi. 7, 15). It was in reference to this expiatory sacrifice made by the Redeemer that the prophet spoke of the Messias as a lamb brought to the slaughter. When John the Baptist saw Christ approaching, he exclaimed: " Behold the Lamb of God; behold Him Who taketh away the sins of the world! " (John i. 29.) And St. Paul says: " Christ, our Pasch, is sacrificed."

The sacrifice of the cross is, however, differentiated from every other sacrifice by the fact that in it the officiating Priest is the Victim Himself; also because the value of this sacrifice is infinite.

Christ Himself, as St. Augustine says, was both Priest and Victim. The soldiers were only instruments of which it pleased Him to make use. Had He willed otherwise, they would have had no power at all over Him. This He made manifest on Mount Olivet, for at the word: " I am He," they fell to the ground. The soldiers could not indeed have been the sacrificers, because by putting Christ to death they did not perform a work pleasing to God, but committed one of the greatest of all crimes. Christ was immolated, because it was His will to be immolated (Is. liii. 7). Not all the sacrifices offered under the Old Testament had power to reconcile God and man; their value was but finite. St. Paul says: " It is impossible that with the blood of oxen and goats sin should be taken away " (Heb. x. 4). These sacrifices could only serve as a means of recalling sin to men's minds, and awakening compunction; they had no cleansing power. With the sacrifice Christ offered it is quite otherwise.

2. The sacrifice of Christ upon the cross was a vicarious sacrifice for the sins of all mankind, and a sacrifice of superabundant value.

Christ suffered in our stead. Of Him the prophet spoke when he said: " He was wounded for our iniquities, He was bruised for our sins " (Is. liii. 5). Christ, the second Adam, the Head of the human race, suffered for His members. The Good Shepherd gave His life for the sheep (John x. 15). We know by the experience of daily life that vicarious atonement is possible. Not only property, but disgrace or glory may be bequeathed to posterity. A family, nay more, a whole nation, will be proud of a great man born in their midst, and on the other hand, nations are sometimes severely chastised for the sins of a single individual. Original sin has become the heritage of humanity, and in like manner the merits of one man may become the heritage of all mankind. Christ made atonement for the sin of the whole human race, original as well as actual sin. The apostle says: " He is the propitiation for our sins, and not for ours only, but also for those of the whole world " (1 John ii. 2). Christ is the true Paschal Lamb, the sacrifice of which did not liberate one nation from the yoke of Pharao, but the whole human race from the servitude of Satan. Although Christ died for all, yet all do not receive the benefit of His death; only those to whom the merit of His Passion is communicated (Council of Trent, C. 6, 3). Christ's atonement was more than sufficient; He suffered beyond what was necessary. A single drop of His blood would have sufficed to wash away the sins of all mankind, for He is very God, and the least of His actions is of infinite value. Christ suffered more than it is possible for any human being to suffer. Hence He cried aloud upon the cross: " My God, My God, why hast Thou forsaken Me? "

Our Lord suffered so much in order to show how much He loves us, and how greatly God is offended by sin.

A single word of Christ would have fully sufficed to redeem us, but it was not enough to make manifest the love of God. It is because of the great love Christ displays towards us, that we venerate the most Sacred Heart of Jesus. The heart is the centre of the physical life; from it the blood flows into every part of the body, maintaining its vitality. And since there is an intimate connection between body and soul, the heart is spoken of as the centre of the spiritual life, whence all the thoughts and feelings take their rise. Hence we say: " My heart rejoiced, my heart is grieved, etc." The heart is regarded pre-eminently as the seat of love. When we venerate the Sacred Heart of Jesus, we call to mind His exceeding great love for us, and are stimulated to return love for love. God made use of a French nun at Paray-le-Monial, named Margaret Mary Alacoque, to propagate this devotion. Our Lord appeared to her repeatedly, showing her His Heart pierced by the lance, emitting flames of fire, surrounded by a crown of thorns—to signify the pain sinners cause to Our Saviour—and surmounted by a shining cross. Our Lord intimated His desire that pictures of this Heart should be exposed for veneration, and promised signal blessings to all who should practice this devotion. He also commanded the festival of the Sacred Heart to be kept on the Friday after the octave of Corpus Christi. This day is a most appropriate one, for it was on a Friday that Our Lord by His death gave the greatest possible proof of His love, and His Heart was pierced by the lance. Moreover the Adorable Sacrament of the Altar affords abundant testimony to the love of the Saviour, for as the sun's rays are focussed in a lens, so the rays of the sun of divine love are concentrated in the Sacrament of the Altar. Hence the feast of Corpus Christi is a special memorial of the love of Christ for man. The devotion to the Sacred Heart, opposed at the outset, as are all works that are of God, spread rapidly over all the earth, and was attended by signal blessings. Another reason why Our Lord suffered so much was that He might be a pattern to us in suffering: " Christ suffered for us, leaving you an example " (1 Pet. ii. 21). He Himself said: " I have given you an example " (John xiii. 15).

3. The graces which Christ merited for us by His death are communicated to us by the means of grace; that is to say, the holy sacrifice of the Mass, the sacraments, the sacramentals, and prayer.

The means of grace are the channels whereby the divine Redeemer conveys to us the graces He merited for us upon the cross. His side was opened that the means of grace might thence flow out. It is because the Church, through the medium of the appointed means of grace, communicates to the faithful the graces flowing from the cross of Christ, that in dispensing them she always makes use of the sign of the cross.

He who neglects the use of the means of grace cannot be saved, in spite of Christ's death.

Medicine cannot work a cure unless the sick man swallows it. "He Who made thee without thyself," says St. Augustine, "will not save thee without thyself." The devil makes strenuous efforts to deprive men of the means of grace. He acts like the General Holofernes, who when besieging the town of Bethulia cut off the aqueducts, in order to reduce the inhabitants through want of water; for he deters the faithful from drinking from the channels of grace, by inspiring them with indifference or aversion towards them.

3. THE INSTITUTION, NATURE, AND PRINCIPAL PARTS OF THE MASS.

At the Last Supper the Son of God changed bread into His body, and wine into His blood; He then gave both to the apostles, bidding them eat and drink the same.

We are told that after the washing of the feet Our Lord sat down at the table, took bread in His hands, looked up to heaven, gave thanks, blessed it, broke it, and gave it to His apostles, saying: "Take ye and eat; this is My body." And after the apostles had received the body of Christ, He took the chalice in which was wine, gave thanks, blessed it, and gave it to His disciples, saying: "Drink ye all of this, for this is My blood; the blood of the new, the eternal covenant, the mystery of faith (a mystery for the trial of our faith), which shall be shed for you and for many for the remission of sins. Do this for a commemoration of Me." (These are known as the words of consecration.)

After the consecration, the species or appearance of the bread and wine still remained the same.

The body of Christ had not the appearance of flesh, but the appearance of bread; it had the smell, the taste, the color, the weight, etc., of bread; the species was in fact retained. Nor did the blood of Christ bear the appearance of blood, but of wine; it had the smell, the taste, the color, etc., the ordinary appearance of wine. (This subject will be enlarged upon in the instructions concerning the Adorable Sacrament of the Altar.)

1. The Son of God offered a sacrifice at the Last Supper, because He gave His body and blood to be offered up, in order to reconcile His heavenly Father with man.

At the Last Supper our blessed Lord instituted a visible sacrifice, in order thereby to represent the bloody sacrifice which was to be offered once upon the cross, and to preserve the memory thereof unto the end of the world. Our Lord indicated to us that He intended at the Last Supper to institute a sacrifice, by choosing for this act the very time when the paschal lamb was slain and eaten. Moreover the words He made use of were almost identical with those which Moses spoke on the institution of the Old Covenant. We read that Moses, after the giving of the law on Mount Sinai, slaughtered an animal, and sprinkled the blood upon the people, saying: " This is the blood of the covenant which the Lord hath made with you" (Exod. xxiv. 8). As Our Lord's words were similar to these, it follows that in His case also there was a sacrifice. Again it is a significant fact that Our Lord caused His Passion and death to follow immediately after the Last Supper; by this He would have us know that they were one and the same act. The sacrifice begins with the consecration, when Christ assumes the form of bread and wine; for He then divests Himself of the splendor of His divine glory, and conceals His infinite majesty. Nay, more, not only does He conceal His divine grandeur, He also conceals His human presence. " Christ, the King of heaven and of earth, reduces Himself by the words of consecration to a condition of abasement which is almost equivalent to annihilation. Not even a trace can be perceived of that regal dignity with which His humanity was invested, and which inspired men with reverence and awe. At His birth at Bethlehem He was at least in the likeness of man, but here He seems to be nothing but a morsel of bread." By this profound self-abasement Our Lord reconciles us to His Father, Who is justly angry with us; for there is no better means of appeasing one whom we have offended than by humbling ourselves before him. King Achab averted the punishment of which he was warned by the prophet Elias, by humbling himself before God (3 Kings xxi. 27); the Ninivites did the same. The sacrifice is not consummated until the species of bread and wine are consumed. Thus it was with the sacrifice Our Lord made upon the cross; He suffered first, His body being torn and mangled; then death came, and His human existence was ended. The sacrifice was accomplished; He spoke the words: "It is consummated!" Hence it will be seen that the unbloody sacrifice of the altar is in every respect a faithful representation and a true repetition of the bloody sacrifice of the cross. What the death of Christ was then, the reception of the sacred elements is now. Thus St. Paul says that those who eat this bread and drink the chalice show the death of the Lord (1 Cor. xi. 26). Moreover the separate forms of bread and wine symbolize the destruction of Christ's human nature, for the body and blood of Christ are separated one from the other upon the altar, as they were upon the cross, when the blood flowed out of His body through the countless wounds. We also gather that the object of this unbloody sacrifice is the reconciliation of man with God, from the words Our Lord uttered at the Last Supper. " This is My blood," He said, " which is shed for the remission of sin." This unbloody sacrifice is therefore like the sacrifice of the cross, truly a propitiatory sacrifice (Council of Trent, 22, 2). We are not, indeed, redeemed anew by it, for we are redeemed by the bloody sacrifice, but the fruits of redemption are applied to our souls by this unbloody sacrifice. Nor is this unbloody sacrifice of itself sufficient to reconcile men to God without their own co-operation: but it has the effect of awakening them to a sense of sin, exciting them to contrition, inducing them to confess their sins and avoid them in future.

1. The apostles had, and their successors have, the power of offering the same sacrifice, for the Son of God at once com-

manded and empowered them to do so, when He said: "Do this for a commemoration of Me" (Council of Trent, 22, 1).

When Christ gave His twelve apostles His flesh to eat and His blood to drink, He commanded them to immolate Him in lieu of the usual sacrificial victims. God had enjoined upon the Jews to slay a paschal lamb every year, in remembrance of their deliverance from Egyptian slavery, and in like manner it was His will that a special sacrifice should be offered in commemoration of the death of Christ upon the cross, and the redemption of mankind from the servitude of the devil (Council of Trent, 22, 1).

2. This sacrifice was foretold in the Old Testament both by types and prophecies.

Several sacrifices in the Old Testament were types of the true sacrifice; the offering made by Abel, to which the Lord had respect (Gen. iv. 4), because it was offered by faith in the future Redeemer and His true oblation (Heb. xi. 4); the sacrifice of Abraham, who in obedience to God's command offered his son Isaac upon Mount Moria, without shedding his blood (Gen. xxii.), and above all, the sacrifice of Melchisedech, the King of Salem (i.e., the king of peace), who offered bread and wine (Gen. xiv. 18). These three sacrifices are mentioned in the Mass, immediately after the consecration, when the priest beseeches God to look propitiously upon our gifts, as He was graciously pleased to accept the gifts of Abel, Abraham, and Melchisedech. The holy Mass was also foretold by prophecies. David predicted that the Messias would be a priest forever, according to the order of Melchisedech (Ps. cix. 5). The prophet Malachias foretold the holy Mass to the Jews who, after their return from captivity, performed the sacrificial ceremonies in a careless manner, saying: "I have no pleasure in your sacrifices, saith the Lord of hosts; I will not receive a gift of your hands. For from the rising of the sun even to the going down, My name is great among the Gentiles; and in every place there is sacrifice, and there is offered to My name a clean oblation" (Mal. i. 10, 11).

3. This sacrifice was offered by the apostles, and it has since been offered by their successors, the bishops and priests of the Church.

Even in apostolic times the Christians were accustomed to assemble together, on Sunday particularly, for breaking of bread (Acts xx. 7, 11). St. Paul repeatedly mentions the chalice of benediction which was blessed and given to the faithful, and the bread whereof they partook (1 Cor. x. 16; xi. 26). He says: "We have an altar whereof they have no power to eat who serve the tabernacle" (Heb. xiii. 10). It is recorded that the Apostle Andrew when urged by the proconsul to offer to the gods, said to him: "I offer daily to the almighty and true God, not the flesh of oxen or the blood of rams, but the immaculate Lamb of God; and when all the congregation of the faithful have received His sacred body, the same Lamb that was immolated is still unconsumed and lives forevermore." St. Justin, in one of the apologetic writings he addressed to the Roman emperor, speaks of the different parts of the Christian sacrifice, the reading and explanation of Holy Scripture, the oblation of bread and wine, the consecration and transformation of the sacred elements, and their distribution to the people. The oldest of the Fathers of the Church mention the sacrifice of the Mass. St. Irenæus, Bishop of Lyons (202 A.D.), says: "The oblation of the New Covenant is the Lord's Supper; Christ instituted it as at once a sacrifice and a sacrament, and throughout all the world the Church offers this sacrifice." St. Cyprian, Bishop of Carthage (258 A.D.), says: "In the Church the priest offers the same sacrifice which Christ Himself offered," and again: "Day by day, in times of persecution and of peace, we offer the sacrifice whereby the faithful are prepared to give themselves as sacrificial victims by a martyr's death." Pope Leo the Great says: "The one oblation of the body and blood of Christ is substituted for all the former sacrifices." The frescoes in the Catacombs bear witness to the offering of the holy sacrifice, likewise the most ancient liturgies, the altars, chalices and vestments, which would not have been needed had not the Mass been celebrated. Some of these are still preserved, among them the wooden altar at which St. Peter and his successors for nearly three centuries said Mass. Until the tenth century no heretic dared to impugn the holy sacrifice. Luther attacked it most vehemently, at the instigation of the devil, as he himself confessed.

2. We call the sacrifice instituted by Our Lord at the Last Supper holy Mass, or the sacrifice of the Mass.

In the first centuries of Christianity the catechumens and penitents used to be sent away out of the church at the commencement of the sacrifice. The Latin for dismissal is *missio* (*missa*).* Hence it came to pass that the ceremonies consequent to the dismissal of the catechumens were called the *missa*, the Mass. This expression is used by Pope Pius I. as early as the second century; it also occurs frequently in the writings of St. Augustine and St. Ambrose. Another explanation of the word *missio* (mission) is that it denotes the sending of Our Lord from heaven to earth at the moment of the consecration, and again the sending of the sacred Victim up to heaven by the faithful in the hands of angels; as St. Bonaventure says: "First of all God sends His Son down to us upon the altar, then the Church sends Him up to the Father, to make intercession for sinners." The sacrifice of the Mass must be clearly distinguished from the Sacrament of the Altar. In the latter Christ is present as an object of our worship and as our spiritual sustenance; in the former He is also our Victim and the means of our salvation.

1. The sacrifice of the Mass is the chief and central act of Catholic worship.

Several of the sacraments and the sacramentals can only be administered in connection with the Mass. It stands in the same relation to the other services of the Church as a jewel does to its setting. It is a reservoir wherein the streams of grace are collected which flow from the sacrifice of the cross, and whence they are poured out upon mankind through the channels of the sacraments. The holy Mass is

---

* The true derivation of the word *missa* is wrapped in obscurity. The derivations given in the text are conjectural.

the sun of grace, day by day rising upon the world, the bright rays of which, in the prismatic colors of the seven sacraments, form the fair rainbow, the emblem of peace, the connecting link between heaven's riches and earth's poverty. The dignity of holy Mass surpasses by many degrees that of the sacraments, for they are only vessels of mercy for the living, whereas the Mass is an inexhaustible ocean of divine liberality for the living and the dead. In the holy Mass man has a foretaste of heaven upon earth, for in the sacred Victim he has before him the Creator of heaven and of earth, he even holds Him in his hands. The sacrifice of the Mass contains in itself as many mysteries as there are drops in the ocean, stars in the firmament, flowers upon the earth. Take this sacrifice away from the Catholic Church and you leave nothing but unbelief and error. Were holy Mass not of such surpassing excellence the devil would not have aroused so many enemies against it among heretics.

2. The sacrifice of the Mass is a *catholic* sacrifice in the true sense of the word, for it is and will be offered unceasingly throughout the whole earth until the end of time.

At the present time some 350,000 Masses are celebrated daily on our globe; there is not an hour in the day in which Mass is not being said. Thus the words of the prophet are literally fulfilled: "From the rising of the sun until the going down, in every place there is sacrifice" (Mal. i. 10). Mass will be celebrated until the Day of Judgment (1 Cor. xi. 26). Not any or all of the adversaries of the Church, not Antichrist himself, will be able to suspend the offering of the holy sacrifice. The last Mass said will be on the last day of this world's existence. This is what Our Lord meant when He said: "I am with you all days, even to the consummation of the world" (Matt. xxviii. 20).

3. What takes place in the sacrifice of the Mass is this: The priest at the altar, as the representative of Christ, offers up bread and wine to almighty God; he changes these substances into the body and blood of Christ, and destroys them by consuming them.

Thus it is not the priest, but Christ Himself, Who in the Mass is the sacrificing Priest.

From the words of the consecration it is evident that the priest is only an instrument of which Our Lord makes use, for the priest says: "This is My body, this is My blood," although he does not change the bread and wine into his own body and blood. It is not the man who causes the oblation upon the altar to be changed into the body and blood of Our Lord, it is Christ Himself; Christ, our High Priest, Who is holy, innocent, undefiled, separate from sinners, purer than all the celestial spirits (Heb. vii. 26). Hence the sacrifice of the Mass does not lose its value, supposing the officiating priest should be living in sin. The Council of Trent declares that the sacrifice of the Mass cannot be defiled through the unworthiness or malice of him who offers it. "This oblation is holy," says St. John Chrysostom, "be the priest what he may; for man does not consecrate, but Christ."

Christ is also the Victim which is immolated in the Mass.

Christ is the Priest Who offers the sacrifice, and He is likewise the Victim which is offered. The Priest and the Victim are one and the same. Christ our Paschal Lamb, once immolated upon the cross, is daily immolated anew upon our altars. Christ offered Himself, because among all the treasures of heaven and of earth He could find nothing that could serve as a worthy oblation to be offered to the Blessed Trinity. The sacred humanity of Our Lord is the most precious, the most perfect work of God. Even the inexpressible beauty of the Mother of God is, in comparison to the humanity of Christ, as a flaming torch beside the noonday sun. Even the graces and prerogatives which God has bestowed upon the angels and the saints, all taken together, fall far short of the graces and excellences appertaining to the sacred humanity of Christ. By reason of its intimate union with the Godhead it is enriched with boundless treasures and endowed with infinite dignity.

4. There are three distinct parts in the sacrifice of the Mass: the offertory, the consecration, and the communion.

The sanctuary bell is rung at the consecration and the communion, and also between the offertory and the consecration, at the *Sanctus.*

1. What takes place at the offertory is this : Bread and wine are offered to God and blessed.

The priest takes the paten whereon the Host is placed, and elevates it, offering the Host to God. Then he takes the chalice, pours into it wine and a little water, elevates it, and offers it likewise to God. He next invokes the Holy Spirit and blesses the oblation with his hand. This is called the offertory, because the actual sacrificial act does not begin until the consecration. For if the priest who was celebrating should chance to fall sick, or any accident should occur, if it was before the consecration he could break off the Mass, but not after the consecration; in that case he must take the communion immediately, and then leave the altar. And supposing the priest were to die after having consecrated, another priest must proceed with the Mass, even were he not fasting; but if the priest who was celebrating died before the consecration, it would not be necessary to go on with the Mass. What does this prove ? The name of offertory is given to this part of the Mass because in early times the offerings of bread and wine were made by the faithful. The bread is prepared from wheaten flour; it is unleavened, because the bread Our Lord used was unleavened, and also because it denotes the purity of the body of Christ; it is round in shape, to symbolize the eternal nature of Christ, without beginning and without end. A large Host must be used at Mass, unless only small ones can be had. The wine must be prepared from the juice of grapes; a little water is mixed with it, because this was done by Christ. The water and the wine are also in commemoration of the water and blood which flowed from His riven side.

2. What takes place at the consecration is this: The bread is changed into the body, and the wine into the blood of Christ; and they are then elevated in the sight of the people.

The consecration is effected by means of the words Our Lord uttered at the Last Supper.

At the consecration something similar occurs to that which occured when Elias offered sacrifice on Mount Carmel, when the fire of the Lord fell, and consumed the holocaust (3 Kings xviii.); in that case however the agent was natural fire, whereas at Mass it is the supernatural fire of the Holy Ghost. As natural fire changes wood into glowing embers, so the Holy Spirit effects the transubstantiation of the oblation by words of fire. Hence from the earliest times it was customary in the East—as we learn from ancient liturgies—to call upon the Holy Ghost to come and effect the change. At the moment of consecration the heavens are opened at the word of the priest, and Christ, the King of heaven, descends from above with His courtiers, the angels, who wait upon their Monarch. He descends from heaven upon our altars as swiftly as the eyes on being opened perceive at once the most distant objects. At the moment of consecration, the Incarnation of the Son of God takes place anew, and in the same manner as when, at the salutation of the angel, Mary was overshadowed by the Holy Ghost. As the Blessed Virgin then spoke but a few words, so now the priest utters but a few words, and the Son of God comes down from heaven at his summons. It is because Christ becomes man again in the Mass, that at the conclusion the words: " The Word was made flesh, and dwelt among us," are read; and when the *Credo* is sung at High Mass, special emphasis is given to the sentence: *Incarnatus est, de Spiritu Sancto, ex Maria Virgine; et homo factus est.* The birth of Christ is also repeated in the Mass, with this difference, that Christ is not born corporally, as at Bethlehem, but spiritually; that He is not now clad in mortal flesh, but arrayed in His glorified body, resplendent with the five sacred wounds. It is on account of this spiritual birth that the Church appoints the *Gloria in excelsis,* the song of praise sung by the angels at Bethlehem, to form part of the Mass, and that Our Lord has appeared many times after the consecration under the form of an infant. An appearance of this kind is said to have been the means of converting the Saxon chief Wittekind, who, when at war with the Emperor Charlemagne, entered the enemy's camp in disguise, and was present when Mass was said. The same announcement may be made to us Christians as was made by the angels to the shepherds of yore: " Behold, I bring you glad tidings of great joy, for to-day is born to you a Saviour."

3. What takes place at the communion is this: The priest receives the body and blood of Christ, and oftentimes administers the body of Christ to the faithful.

Before the priest communicates the people, the *Confiteor* is repeated and at the end he absolves and blesses the faithful; then taking the sacred vessel containing the Hosts in his hand. he holds one up in the sight of the people, saying: " Behold the Lamb of God, behold Him Who taketh away the sins of the world;" and then repeats three times: " Lord, I am not worthy that Thou shouldst enter under my roof; say but the word and my soul shall be healed." To each of the communicants, when administering holy communion to him, he says: "May the body of Our Lord Jesus Christ preserve thy soul to life everlasting, Amen;" having previously made the sign of the cross over him with the sacred Host, to signify that it is the crucified Redeemer Whom he gives to him. The Hosts that remain after the communion of the people are reserved in the ciborium, which is placed in the tabernacle. In each of these Hosts which were consecrated in the Mass Our Lord remains present. They are used to give communion at other times than in the Mass. Communion may be given at any time when it is allowable to say Mass; but not on Good Friday, nor on Holy Saturday until after the communion of the priest. If there should not be enough Hosts for the intending communicants, the priest may divide them, or in extreme cases, a particle may be broken off the large Host.

4. THE CEREMONIAL OF THE MASS.

1. **In the course of time many ceremonies of deep significance grouped themselves around the holy sacrifice of the Mass, which were not to be omitted without absolute necessity.**

As early as the third century, certain prayers and ceremonies were added to the essential part of the sacrifice of the Mass. The service began with psalms sung by the people (at the present time the priest says the psalm *Judica me* at the foot of the altar); this was followed by the petition for mercy (the priest now recites the *Confiteor* at the foot of the altar, and the *Kyrie Eleison* standing in front of the altar). Then came the thanksgiving for the pardon of sin (now the *Gloria* is said immediately after the *Kyrie*). The officiating bishop next turned to the people and pronounced the salutation: *Dominus vobiscum*, "the Lord be with you," and then with extended arms offered a prayer in the name of the people (the collect). After this one of the acolytes read a portion of one of the epistles, then a portion taken from one of the gospels, as is done in the present day, the congregation standing meanwhile, and the bishop gave a short explanation of the gospel of the day. When this was ended, one of the ministers, generally the deacon, called upon the catechumens (i.e., the Jews or heathen who were under instruction for Baptism) to leave the church; if he did not feel sure about any one who remained, he required the watchword of him, that is, he made him repeat the confession of faith, that was known only to the Christians. This division of the Mass, up to the Creed, was the preparatory part, and used to be called the Mass of the catechumens. At this point the actual sacrifice of the Mass began. The faithful presented offerings of bread and wine, from which the deacons took what was required for the Mass; this the bishop then offered to God and blessed (the offertory). He then washed the fingers with which he had touched the bread, and one of the acolytes called upon the people to pray for the catechumens who had just departed, for the clergy and the Church in general, for friends and for foes. (The *Orate Fratres* is now said by the priest.) Then followed a prayer of thanksgiving, in imitation of Our Lord, Who gave thanks before consecrating the elements (the preface of the present day, which ends with the *Sanctus*, an ascription of praise to the Holy Trinity), and all present prayed, as had been enjoined upon them, for the Pope, the bishop, the emperor, invoking the intercession of the Mother of God, of the apostles and holy martyrs. Then came the consecration, the ceremonial for which was the same as it is now; the people prostrating themselves in lowly adoration at the elevation of the Host and of the chalice. The prayer for the dead came next, some of the martyrs being commemorated; the *Pater Noster* was said aloud, and the *Agnus Dei* three times: " O Lamb of God, Thou that takest away the sins of the world, have mercy upon us." Upon this the communion followed, the bishop received the body and blood of Christ, and gave communion to the faithful; they crossed their hands, the sacred Host being placed on the palm of the left hand. During the communion appropriate psalms were sung (the priest now recites some verses from the psalms at the right hand side of the altar, which are called the post-communion). The Hosts that remained over were placed in a chest, or a vessel in the shape of a dove beside the altar. After a concluding prayer, the bishop saluted the people with the words, *Dominus vobiscum,* and dismissed them, saying: *Ite, missa est:* " Depart, the Mass is ended." The blessing being given, the commencement of St. John's Gospel was generally read, in which occur the words: " The Word was made flesh," and : " He came unto His own, and His own received Him not," the former being an allusion to the presence of Our Lord in the holy sacrifice, the latter having reference to the sin of those who, without good reason, absent themselves from Mass. In the course of the Mass, which, if a low Mass, lasts from twenty-five to thirty minutes, the celebrant has to observe no less than five hundred ceremonies, such as bowing down, smiting his breast, making the sign of the cross, etc. All this ceremonial is intended to impress the faithful more deeply with the majesty of so great a sacrifice; also to incite them to the contemplation of those most sublime things that are hidden in the Mass (Council of Trent, 22, 5). Each of the ceremonies has its own special meaning.

2. The whole story of the Redemption is symbolically represented by the ceremonies of the Mass.

The opening prayers, said by the priest at the foot of the altar, and at a little distance from it, are emblematic of the 4000 years during which man was comparatively far from God, and looking for the redemption. The *Kyrie,* repeated nine times, and the *Gloria,* signify the book of Christ, and the song of praise sung by the nine choirs of angels at Bethlehem; the *Orationes,* the youth of Our Lord, which was passed in prayer and seclusion from the world. The Epistle, the carrying across of the missal, the Gospel and the Creed, are to remind us that the Gospel was first preached to the Jews, and being rejected by them, was proclaimed to the Gentiles, many of whom believed and were baptized. The offertory represents Our Lord's preparation for His Passion and His willingness to surrender His life. The preface, which ends with the words: " Blessed is He that cometh in the name of the Lord, Hosanna in the highest," represents Christ's entry into Jerusalem; the prayer for the living, His prayer for the Church before the Last Supper. The five crosses which the priest makes over the oblation are symbolical of the five times that

Our Lord was mocked, before Annas, Caiphas, Herod, Pilate, and once again before Herod. The elevation of the bread and wine, of His lifting up on the cross; the five crosses made from time to time over the elements, of the five sacred wounds. The seven petitions of the Lord's Prayer represent the seven wounds upon the cross; the breaking of the Host, the death of Christ, when His soul and body were parted. When the priest says the *Agnus Dei* and strikes his breast, it recalls the action of the soldiers and others present upon Calvary, who, amazed at the stupendous convulsions of nature, struck their breasts, while the centurion exclaimed: "Indeed this man was the Son of God!" (Luke xxiii. 48; Mark xv. 39.) The communion represents the burial of Christ; the *Dominus vobiscum*, twice repeated, His salutation of the apostles on His twofold appearance to them after His resurrection; the words of dismissal, *Ite, missa est*, His ascension, when He sent His apostles forth to evangelize the world, and blessed them for the last time; and the Last Gospel, the propagation of the Gospel after the descent of the Holy Ghost. Thus the Mass is seen to be a brief compendium of Our Lord's life; in one half hour all is depicted which He did during thirty-three years upon earth (Cochem).

5. THE RELATION WHICH THE MASS BEARS TO THE SACRIFICE OF THE CROSS.

1. The sacrifice of the Mass is a living renewal of the sacrifice of the cross, for in the Mass, as upon the cross, Christ immolates Himself.

Only in the Mass He sacrifices Himself in an unbloody manner under the appearance of bread and wine, whereas on the cross He sacrificed Himself in a bloody manner as man.

Since it is impossible for the faithful to be present at Our Lord's sacrifice of Himself upon the cross, He has provided a means whereby they can at least assist at the repetition of that sacrifice, and gain the same merit that would have been theirs had they actually stood beneath the cross on Calvary. The Son of God foresaw that, despite all His bitter Passion, many millions of mankind would not be saved; for their sake He offered Himself to His heavenly Father, expressing His readiness to hang upon the cross, not for three hours only, but until the Last Day; and as this could not be, He devised in His wisdom a plan whereby He could daily suffer anew in a mystical manner, in the holy sacrifice of the Mass, and anew move His Father to compassion. The Mass is consequently no mere image of the sacrifice of the cross; it is not a bare memorial of it, it is the self-same sacrifice which was consummated on Calvary (Council of Trent, 22, 3), and accordingly it is of the self-same value and of the self-same efficacy. In the Mass the Passion and death of the Son of God take place again in a mystic manner, His blood is shed afresh. In it He displays His wounds to His heavenly Father, to save man from perdition; He sets before Him the bitter anguish He endured at His death as vividly as if His Passion were but just ended. To say Mass therefore, is to immolate the Son of God anew in a mystic manner. The principal ceremonies of the Mass demonstrate, as we have seen, that the oblation once offered upon the cross is renewed upon the altar.

2. In the sacrifice of the Mass all the sacrifices made by Our Lord are also renewed.

In the Mass Christ does not only sacrifice His humanity, as upon the cross, but with it He offers all that He did and suffered during the thirty-three years of His life on earth, placing it all forcibly before the Holy Trinity, though with all lowliness. The prayers which He sent up to heaven while on earth are all repeated and summarized, as it were, in the Mass, and presented to God the Father with the same urgency as if they were but just uttered. All this He offers for the salvation of each individual who is present at the Mass. Our Lord said once to St. Mechtilde: " I alone know and fully understand how I offer Myself daily upon the altar; it surpasses the comprehension of the seraphim and cherubim, and all the heavenly hosts."

6. THE PROFIT TO BE DERIVED FROM THE HOLY SACRIFICE OF THE MASS.

1. By means of the holy sacrifice of the Mass the fruits of the sacrifice of the cross are applied to us in most abundant measure; more particularly we obtain thereby forgiveness of sin, certitude that our prayers are heard, temporal blessings, and eternal rewards.

Every Mass is productive of the same fruits, the same profit to the soul as that which resulted from the death of Our Lord on Good Friday. And since the sacrifice of the Mass is identical with the sacrifice of the cross, it follows as a necessary consequence that its effects are the same (Cochem). The death and Passion of Christ are the treasury, the Mass is the key that unlocks it. The cross is the tree of life laden with celestial fruits, and by the Mass those fruits are given to us. In the sacrifice of the Mass we are made partakers of the merits of Christ; they are, it is true, applied to us by the other means of grace, but far less freely and abundantly. At the time of Mass God gives lavishly; from no other source do the streams of grace flow so copiously as from the altar. In the Mass, the Son of the most high God comes down from the gardens of paradise, bringing to us from thence celestial riches and treasures of infinite value. In the Mass the heavenly Father gives us His Son; "and hath He not with Him, also given us all things?" (Rom. viii. 32.) If you, O Christian, knew how to profit by the Mass, by it you might become richer than all the creatures of God can make you ! One must be in a state of grace in order to receive most of the sacraments, otherwise one cannot share in Christ's merits, and one incurs the guilt of mortal sin; but it is not necessary to be in a state of grace to hear Mass; the sinner does not commit a fresh sin by doing so; on the contrary he gains the grace of conversion.

1. The forgiveness of sins consists in this: Through the sacrifice of the Mass sinners obtain the grace and gift of penitence (Council of Trent, 22, 2), while the just obtain the remission of venial sin, and of the temporal penalty due to sin.

That remission of sin is effected by the Mass, we learn from Our Lord's words when He consecrated the chalice (Matt. xxvi. 28). The Mass is above all a propitiatory sacrifice; thereby it is differentiated from the Old Testament sacrifices. They only cleansed from legal impurities, not from sin (Heb. x. 1); the oblation of the New Testament alone has power to remit sin (Heb. ix. 9). Upon the cross Christ cried: "Father, forgive them" (Luke xxiii. 34), and at Mass He utters the same petition on behalf of all who are present. As the blood of Abel cried to heaven for vengeance, so the blood of Christ calls to heaven in the Mass for mercy, and the voice of His well-beloved Son has more power with God than that of Abel had (Heb. xii. 24). In the Mass Christ is our Advocate with the Father, the propitiation of our sins (1 John ii. 1). Our Lord once said to St. Mechtilde: "My condescension in the Mass is so great, that there is no sinner, however great, there present, to whom I will not gladly grant forgiveness, if only he asks Me for it." Just as men are pacified by a gift, and induced thereby to condone offences committed against them—remember how Jacob on returning home approached his brother Esau with a present, to allay his wrath—(Gen. xxxii. 20)—so God allows His anger to be appeased by the oblation of holy Mass. That holy sacrifice rescues the sinner from eternal perdition. As the sun disperses the clouds and makes the face of nature bright, so holy Mass gladdens the Church of God. The effect of holy Mass upon the sinner is not immediately perceived; God brings about his conversion in an opportune moment, when his heart is open to the influence of grace. At the time of Our Lord's crucifixion few were moved to repentance; not until Pentecost, when the hearts of many were softened by the preaching of Peter, did the effect of the sacrifice of the cross become apparent. Many are gradually converted through divine grace, without knowing that this is owing to the power of holy Mass. The Holy Ghost acts upon the hearts of those who assist at Mass as He acted upon the centurion and some others who stood beside the cross of Christ, and who acknowledged: "Indeed this man was the Son of God." The lights about the altar are emblematical of the graces of the Holy Spirit, which are communicated in rich abundance to those who hear Mass devoutly. It would not be meet for one who had served at the table of a monarch to go away hungry, and it cannot be supposed that one who had heard Mass piously should be allowed to depart without spiritual nourishment. As when the mouth eats the whole body is refreshed, so the faithful communicate spiritually at the communion of the priest, although they do not actually receive the Lord's body. The just obtain remission of venial sin through the sacrifice of the Mass, because the treasures of the infinite satisfaction Our Lord made to His heavenly Father are offered for them in it. "Venial sins," says Cochem, "melt away at Mass like wax before the fire." The Council of Trent (22, 1), declares that by the sacrifice of the Mass we obtain the remission of the sins we daily commit. If, as St. Augustine asserts, one Our Father said from the heart will expiate the venial sins of a whole day, how much the more are they expiated by the holy Mass? The Mass is also a sacrifice of atonement for sins of which we are not conscious. Father Cochem tells us that one Mass will do more to pay the temporal penalty due to sin than the severest penances. Moreover the divine chastisements are averted by holy Mass. When God sent a pestilence upon Israel during David's reign, and seventy thousand of the people died, the prophet told the sorrowing king to offer a holocaust and burnt-offerings to appease the anger of God. No sooner was this done than the plague was stayed. Now if the sacrifice of oxen and sheep availed to arrest the divine judgments, what cannot the sacrifice of the Mass effect? "If," says Cochem, "thou dost often hear Mass, thou mayst hope that thy purgatory will be short and not severe, because by frequently assisting devoutly at holy Mass, thou hast to a great extent expiated thy sins." Consider how quickly the penitent thief, who witnessed the sacrifice of Our Lord upon the cross, was admitted to heaven.

2. The prayers we offer during Mass will surely be heard, because they are aided by the prayer of Our Lord and of the angels who are present.

When we hear Mass, our prayers are strengthened by Our Lord's prayers, and His prayers are never offered in vain, for the Father heareth Him always (John xi. 42). The holy angels await the time of Mass, in order to proffer their petitions on our behalf with greater urgency and more hope of success. As the sacrifice of the Mass is more excellent than any other act of worship, so the prayers offered during Mass are more efficacious than any others. St. Francis of Sales says that prayers offered in union with the divine Victim have an inexpressible power; favors can be obtained at the time of Mass which can be obtained at no other. "Let him who is always complaining that he cannot pray aright," says Cochem, "go to Mass, that Christ may pray for him and instead of him, and supply what is wanting to his prayers." How foolishly those act who say at home the prayers they might say at Mass!

3. Through the holy sacrifice of the Mass temporal blessings are obtained, especially these: God protects us from misfortune, assists us in our work, and blesses us in our temporal substance.

He who has heard Mass devoutly will succeed in all things during the remainder of the day. The favorite servant of Queen Elizabeth of Portugal escaped apparently certain death through hearing Mass. St. Philip Neri was accustomed to offer the holy sacrifice before commencing any important undertaking, because he thereby insured its success. You are strengthened to meet the troubles of the whole day, if you have been near your Redeemer in the morning at holy Mass. God assists those in their work who have heard Mass with devotion in the early morning. St. Isidore, a farm-servant at Madrid, used to rise daily at a very early hour, in order to hear Mass before going to his work. When his master, at the instigation of his fellow servants, blamed him for doing this, he replied: "If you find that I get through less work than the others, take something off my wages." The master observed him narrowly, and was soon convinced that Isidore did a great deal more than the other men, for an angel at his side assisted him in his labor; and thenceforward he did not attempt to hinder him from going daily to Mass. God also adds to the worldly possessions of those who make a point of hearing Mass. By increasing their property He gives them the occasion of earning more merits. He does not fail to recompense even unrepentant sinners who go to Mass. Since they are not in a position to receive an eternal reward, God, Who of His infinite bounty does not permit the least good work to go unrewarded, either confers some good fortune upon them, or protects them from misfortune.

4. We cannot obtain an eternal recompense through hearing Mass unless we are in a state of grace.

"Every Mass thou hearest," says Father Cochem, "perceptibly increases thy future felicity." As one who is mounting a flight of stairs comes higher at each step, so he who hears Mass ascends one degree higher in heaven. The higher he mounts, the nearer he comes to God; the more clearly he knows Him, the more dearly he loves Him, the more ineffable is his enjoyment of Him. And for all the hardships you have to endure by reason of going to Mass, early rising, exposure to cold, etc., you will be abundantly requited in heaven. A man who had given up going to Mass on week-days, on account of the distance, once beheld in a dream an angel following him on the way to the church, and counting every step he took, in view of his future reward. After he had that dream, he again attended Mass regularly. How unwise are those who neglect the holy sacrifice of the altar! The early Christians valued holy Mass aright, and were ready to lay down their lives rather than be deprived of it. What a responsibility for us, now that it is such an easy matter, that it costs us nothing to go to Mass. The burnt-offerings of the Jews were costly; they were required to sacrifice at once a sheep and a goat, or if poor, two doves; and we have an all-efficacious sacrifice without price. "Let us therefore go with confidence to the throne of grace" (Heb. iv. 16).

2. Those who participate in the fruits of the holy sacrifice of the Mass are: First, the individual for whom it is celebrated; then the priest and all who are present; finally, all the faithful, both living and dead; moreover the holy sacrifice gives joy to all the angels and saints.

First and foremost, the individual for whom the Mass is said benefits most by it. The priest is at liberty to apply the actual fruit of the Mass to whomsoever he will. From time immemorial it has been customary in the Church to give a fixed sum to the priest, that he may say the Mass for a certain intention. The money is not given to pay for the Mass, for the value of the Mass is beyond all price, but as an alms towards the maintenance of the priest, and to defray the expenses of divine worship; to pay the server, to purchase candles, etc. In early times the priest was not paid in money, but in kind;

the people brought him wine, oil, bread, etc.; not until the Middle Ages did it become usual to give money. The amount to be given is fixed by the bishop; it varies in different countries. No priest is allowed to ask more, unless the Mass is wanted at a very early hour, or a sung Mass is desired, or the priest has to go a long distance. The priest who celebrates Mass derives greater benefit from it than do those who hear it, because of his closer proximity to the Author of all grace. A monarch pays more attention to the envoy of his subjects than he would to one of the people who have deputed him to speak for them; and God, in like manner, regards the priest at the altar not as a sinful mortal, but as the ambassador empowered to speak in the name of the Church and as the representative of His Son; consequently his prayer has more power with God. All who are present at Mass are spiritually sprinkled with the blood of Christ. Could you see the beauty and the brilliancy of a soul thus sprinkled with His blood, you would be ready to fall down and adore it. By reason of the communion of saints, the whole Church is benefited by the holy sacrifice. It is an embassy to the Holy Trinity, bringing a gift of inestimable value. If a deputation from a town offers a present to their monarch, all the inhabitants take part in offering it. So all Christendom has its share in the Mass, although at the sacrificial act its representatives are few in number; on this account the priest says in the prayers of the Mass that he offers up this sacrifice of praise for the whole Church, for all who pay their vows to the eternal, living and true God (prayer after the *Sanctus*). Every priest offers the sacrifice of the Mass for the salvation of the whole world; without it, destruction would long ago have come upon the earth by reason of the multitude of man's transgressions. The faithful departed benefit more particularly by holy Mass. Our Lord's death upon the cross was of immediate profit to the dead, for He directly went down to limbo, to set free many who were there. It is the same now; whenever a Mass is said, several souls are released from purgatory; the angels hasten to open for them the gate of their prison. Moreover the holy sacrifice gives joy to the angels and saints. Since the blessed desire above all things the glory of God and the salvation of mankind, they experience inexpressible delight when they see that in the Mass highest honors are paid to the Holy Trinity, and the spiritual welfare of man is powerfully promoted. The angels and saints also rejoice because their names occur in the holy Mass; they exult with the exultation of warriors who, having been companions of their monarch in the fight, are not forgotten in the triumph of his victory. And if even from the Jewish sacrifices a most sweet odor rose up to heaven (Numb. xxviii. 2). how much more must this be the case with the oblation of Christ. The fragrance of His blood goes up on high to refresh and invigorate the blessed denizens of heaven. For this reason the angels descend from the realms above to assist at Mass; as on Christmas night they came down to Bethlehem, singing songs of praise, to adore the new-born Infant in the manger, so now they stand around the altar at the time of Mass, because the only-begotten Son of God is again made flesh. When God brought in the first begotten into the world, He said: "Let all the angels of God adore Him" (Heb. i. 6). Remember, when you hear Mass, that you are in the company of countless celestial spirits.

7. THE CELEBRATION OF HOLY MASS.

1. The holy sacrifice of the Mass is only offered to God; it may be offered to Him with a fourfold intention; by way of atonement, of petition, of praise, or of thanksgiving.

When we offer sacrifice, we acknowledge that He to Whom we offer it is the Author of all being, the sovereign Lord of all things, and that we consequently owe Him homage. The sacrificial act is therefore an act of adoration, which can be offered to no created being, be he saint or angel. No one has ever offered sacrifice except to the true God, or to one whom he erroneously supposed to be the true God. Under the Old Dispensation there were various sacrifices: Sin-offerings, burnt-offerings, sacrifices of praise, etc.; we have but one sacrifice, which answers all these ends. To make atonement is pre-eminently the object of the sacrifice of the Mass; this is the chief intention for which it is celebrated. The sacrifice of the Mass has also an immense potency if we would ask for anything; no gift or favor is too great to be obtained by means of it. For what we implore is something finite, something created, whereas what we offer is something divine, something infinite. It cannot be imagined that God, Who is so generous that He richly rewards a cup of cold water given in His name, will not reward us when we offer Him the chalice containing the blood of His divine Son. St. Bonaventure says: "If a commander is taken prisoner, he is not liberated until a large sum has been paid for his ransom;" now in holy Mass we can say: "Behold, O eternal Father, Thy only-begotten Son, Whom all the earth cannot contain, is now a prisoner in our hands; we will not release Him until that which we earnestly implore of Thee has been granted to us for His sake." The holy sacrifice of the Mass is also a sacrifice of praise. That alone can be praised which is praiseworthy; the more good there is in a man, the more praise can be given to him. God is the supreme and infinite Good; all the creatures He has made cannot praise Him enough. "Glorify the Lord, exalt Him as much as you can, for He is above all praise" (Ecclus. xliii. 32). Yet there is one means whereby we can worthily praise God, and that is by the sacrifice of the Mass. Upon the altar Christ praises the Godhead as He ought to be praised, as neither angel nor saint, much less mortal man, is able to praise Him. One single Mass gives more glory to God than all the angels and saints in heaven are capable of rendering Him; the glory given Him is as much greater as God is more exalted than His creatures (Cochem). In no way can God be more honored than by the spotless Victim upon the altar; Christ instituted the Mass for this end, to enable the Church to give glory to God. Another intention for which Mass may be celebrated is to give God thanks. "If any one has done thee a kindness," says Cochem, "thou art bound to make him a fitting return, unless thou wouldst appear ungrateful." Now consider what countless benefits we have received from God; think how admirably He has made the earth, fashioned man; how He provides continually for our sustenance. Think, above all, of the work or redemption, the institution of the sacraments, and of the many graces He has conferred on us. Will we not say with Tobias: " What wages shall we give Him, or what can be worthy of His benefits?" (Tob. xii. 2.) See, you have the sacrifice of the Mass; therefore it is in your power to make a worthy return for the divine benefits. For as Our Lord gave thanks to God at the Last Supper, so He now gives thanks in the Mass; and the thanksgiving offered by God is infinite, surpassing in value that of all angels and all mankind. If the whole company of heaven and all good men on earth were to unite with you in one unceasing act of thanksgiving, you would not give God as much thanks as is rendered to Him in one Mass by His divine Son. How great is the love of God towards us! Not only does He lavish innumerable benefits upon us. but at the same time He places within our reach an excellent means of repaying worthily the great blessings we have received.

2. The holy sacrifice of the Mass may also be offered in honor of the angels or saints.

When we offer holy Mass in honor of the saints, it is the same as when a play is acted in honor of a prince. Although no allusion may be made in it to the prince, yet he accepts it graciously. Even so the blessed take special delight in the Mass when it is celebrated in their honor, although the Passion of Christ alone is re-enacted in it, and it is offered solely to God (Cochem). When offered in honor of the saints, the Mass is essentially a sacrifice of thanksgiving and of petition; for we give thanks to God for the graces bestowed on the saints, and beseech Him to grant us grace through their intercession. When Mass is celebrated with this intention, the accidental glory of the saints is increased, but not the degree of happiness they enjoy. St. Gertrude often had Mass said in honor of the saints, and they generally appeared to her to thank her. During the Mass she was permitted to see them shining in greater glory, arrayed in garments more resplendent. The renewed presence of her Son upon earth also gives the Mother of God a thousand times more joy than all the psalms, litanies, prayers, you could recite in her honor; and doubtless she will show you special favor if you hear or celebrate Mass in her honor.

3. The holy sacrifice of the Mass can also be offered for the souls of the departed, who have been members of the Catholic Church, and have not died in a state of mortal sin.

The Council of Trent expressly declares that the sacrifice of the Mass may be offered for the dead (C. 22, 2). It is unquestionably true that the departed may be assisted by holy Mass; that God is thereby induced to deal with them more leniently than their sins deserve (St. Augustine). From the earliest ages of Christianity it was customary to offer the holy sacrifice for the faithful departed. and give them a memento in every Mass, as is done now after the consecration. Tertullian states that this was the practice of the apostles themselves. We know that Monica begged St. Augustine to remember her at the altar of God after her departure. " She was not concerned." says St. Augustine, " about the embalming or preparing of her body for burial; she was not solicitous about her sepulchre or the monument to be raised to her memory; her only anxiety was that intercession should be made for her at the altar." What a contrast to Christians in the present day! Holy Mass may not be publicly celebrated for non-Catholics, such as Jews and Protestants, after their death. "We cannot," says Pope Innocent III., "hold communion after their death with those with whom we held no communion during their life." To offer the holy sacrifice for such persons by name, as we do for Catholics, would be out of harmony with Catholic teaching. It is, however, permitted to offer up holy Mass privately even for non-Catholics, and it will avail them if they were free from mortal sin at the time of their death.

4. The holy sacrifice of the Mass can, however, be offered for the living, whether Catholics or non-Catholics.

Holy Mass may be said for the living; we know that it is well to pray for our brethren when we are present at the holy sacrifice, and in every Mass a memento is made for the living. Father Cochem tells us that prayer for others is far more efficacious if offered during Mass, and we can even obtain the conversion of sinners by saying Mass, or having Mass said for them. No better assistance than this can be given to the sick and dying. We may also offer the holy sacrifice for unbelievers during their lifetime, because Christ died for all men, and the Church intercedes for infidels, e.g., on Good Friday. The greater the number of persons for whom a Mass is said, the less profit does each individual derive from it. For this reason priests are strictly forbidden to accept more than one gratuity for one Mass. From time immemorial Mass has been offered for individuals, for it could not be supposed that a Mass which is said for hundreds or thousands of people could profit each one as much as if it were said for him alone.

5. Not the priest alone, but all the faithful who are present at Mass, may offer the holy sacrifice for a special intention.

The people who are present when Mass is celebrated offer it with the officiating priest. The priest offers the sacrifice in his own person, the people offer it by his hands. Hence St. Peter speaks of Christians as a kingly priesthood (1 Pet. ii. 9), and the Jews of old were called a priestly kingdom (Exod. xix. 6). In the prayers of the Mass the priest includes the people with himself as those who offer the oblation (*Orate Fratres*); in fact the priest must of necessity have some one to offer it with him, for on no account is it permitted to say Mass without a server, who represents the people. And as those who assist at Mass are fellow-sacrificers with the priest, it follows that their prayers have the same power as his. The faithful ought therefore, whenever they hear Mass, to offer it for some definite intention. This may be done either at the commencement of the Mass, or at the offertory, or immediately after the consecration. Take heed, O Christian, that in the Mass you frequently offer up the divine Victim to His heavenly Father; the more often you do this, the more abundantly will you be enriched. Those who neglect thus to offer the holy Mass in word or in thought, lose much that they might gain. The due blessing of Mass does not consist in merely being present at it, but in uniting one's self in spirit to the priest who offers it.

8. *THE VALUE OF THE SACRIFICE OF THE MASS.*

1. As the holy sacrifice of the Mass is an oblation of infinite value, to celebrate or to hear Mass is a good work which surpasses all other good works in excellence.

An oblation is nothing else than a gift we offer to God. Now the value of a gift is proportionate to the dignity of the giver and the costliness of the gift. Thus it is with a sacrifice; the more holy the sacrificer and the more precious the victim, the greater is its importance in God's sight. Hence it is that the value of the sacrifice of the Mass is infinite, for the priest and victim are none other than He of Whom God the Father said: "This is My beloved Son, in Whom I am well pleased" (Matt. iii. 17). The glory given to God in the Mass is greater than that which accrues to Him from all the good works of the saints, for the glory they give Him is finite, whereas the glory He receives in the Mass is infinite; it is an honor paid not by angels or men, but by Christ Himself. "Christ alone," says Cochem, "knows the greatness of the divine majesty; He alone knows what is due to the Most High; He alone is capable of rendering to the divine majesty the honor that appertains to Him; all that angels and men can do for the glory of God scarcely deserves notice in comparison with what Christ does." No sacrifice is an act of such profound abasement as the sacrifice of the Mass, for in it the all-glorious Son of God abases Himself to the utmost upon the altar, making Himself appear less than man. In presence of the sacrifice of the Mass, all the sacrifices of the Old Testament vanish as do the stars when the sun rises, for those sacrifices were only acceptable to God inasmuch as they foreshadowed the oblation of Christ on the cross, with which the Mass is identical. Therefore to hear or celebrate Mass is a good work of greater excellence than any other. As the sun exceeds the planets in radiance and vivifying power, so to hear Mass devoutly is much more important, more profitable to us, than any other good work. "If," says St. Laurence Justinian, "you place all your good works, prayers, fasts, alms, mortifications in one scale, and a single Mass in the other, you will find the latter far outweighs the former." For by the practice of penance we offer to God gifts that are purely human, but when we hear Mass with due devotion, we offer Him gifts that are divine; we offer Him the body of Christ, the blood of Christ, the wounds of Christ, the Passion of Christ—nay, the only-begotten Son of God Himself. The Council of Trent declares that no more holy and divine act can be performed by the faithful than the sacrifice of the Mass. To hear Mass, as a good work, is more profitable than mental prayer, which is the highest form of prayer, because in meditation we represent to ourselves Christ as present, whereas in the Mass He is really present in person.

2. Offering or hearing Mass has more value as a good work in proportion to the worthiness and devotion of priest and people.

The sacrifice of the Mass has a twofold virtue. The one it has of itself, quite independently of the worthiness of the priest. By the sacrifice of the Mass the virtues of Christ's Passion and His merits are applied to our souls in a totally different manner to that of any other works. Hence a man in no wise loses the fruit of the holy sacrifice if it is offered for him by a priest who is unworthy. Just as the efficacy of the sacraments does not depend upon the character of the priest who dispenses, so the oblation of a bad priest has the same intrinsic value as that of a good priest (St. Thomas Aquinas). Yet on the other hand, the Mass regarded as a good work performed by a believing Christian, has a secondary virtue which depends upon the sanctity and fervor of priest and people. The holier the priest, the more profound his devotion, the more acceptable is the sacrifice he offers, and the greater is the benefit accruing from it. Thus it is far preferable to hear the Mass of a good priest than of a careless one, for the piety and sanctity both of the minister himself, and the faithful who join with him in offering the sacred oblation, enhance its beneficial effect as a good work and incite those present to greater devotion.

9. DEVOTION AT HOLY MASS.

When we are conversing with any one, we give him our whole attention, and do not think of other people. So when we hear Mass, when we are in the presence of God, we should fix our thoughts on Him, and for the time forget everything else. This we should do all the more because to hear Mass is the highest and holiest act of worship we can perform, and if we do this carelessly, it will be without benefit to ourselves.

We ought to be very devout at Mass; that is, we ought to banish from our minds all that may cause distraction, and endeavor to unite our supplications to those of the priest, especially in the three principal parts of the Mass.

As it is only at the cost of great toil that miners extract precious stones from the bowels of the earth, so we cannot make the hidden treasures of grace contained in the Mass our own unless we take pains to assist at it with the utmost attention and devotion.

1. Whispering, laughing, looking about at the time of Mass must be carefully avoided; moreover it is unseemly to come to Mass overdressed.

It may be said of our churches, where God is present upon our altars, what God said to Moses out of the burning bush: "The place whereon thou standest is holy ground" (Exod. iii. 5). We gather from the indignation Our Lord manifested in regard to those that bought and sold in the Temple (Matt. xxi. 13), how abhorrent to Him is indecorous behavior in the house of God. The house of God is a house of prayer. You would not allow yourself to chatter and laugh, nor even to sit down in the presence of an earthly monarch; with how much greater awe and reverence ought you to behave in the presence of Him Who is above all kings and emperors, the Son of the most high God! Seven hundred priests and Levites ministered in the

Jewish Temple of old; they slaughtered victims daily for the burnt-offerings; and all went on in silence so profound that it might have been imagined that one priest only was in the Temple. Alexander the Great once was offering sacrifice to one of the heathen gods; a young nobleman stood by holding a lighted torch; before the function was ended the torch burned down and scorched his hand, but such was his reverence for the act of sacrifice that he would not allow himself to fling it away. How much more ought Christians to avoid everything that would disturb the solemnity of this sublime sacrifice! The early Christians remained motionless at Mass, so that it was as still as if no one were in the church. It has always been customary to kneel during Mass, at any rate from the consecration until after the communion. A pious empress, who was in the habit of kneeling throughout the Mass, was once begged not to fatigue herself in this manner: " What," she replied, " would you have me sit in the presence of my Lord and God, when my servants do not venture to sit in my presence? " St. Elizabeth of Hungary used always to remove her crown while she heard Mass. Those who behave irreverently at the holy sacrifice deserve condign punishment; they certainly derive no profit from it. It is also most unseemly to come to Mass dressed to excess, in the height of the fashion. St. John Chrysostom animadverts severely upon women who apparently go to Mass to attract attention, and show off their fine clothes. " Thou popinjay! is this finery," he says, " befitting a contrite sinner, who comes to entreat pardon? Such garments are more suitable for the ballroom than the church." St. Ambrose says the more admiration such persons gain from men, the more they are despised by God. Some Popes and holy bishops have ordained that women should come veiled to church: St. Paul seems to have made the same rule for his converts, remarking that nature provided them with a veil, by giving them long hair (1 Cor. xi. 5, 14).

2. When assisting at the holy sacrifice, we ought to unite our supplications to those of the priest, but it is not necessary to use the same prayers as he does.

Meditation upon Our Lord's Passion is the best method of hearing Mass, because in holy Mass the sacrifice of the cross is re-enacted, and it was instituted as a commemoration of the death of the Redeemer.

Those do wrong who repeat the prayers of the Mass out of a prayer-book in a formal manner, with their lips, not with their heart. There is nothing reprehensible in refraining altogether from vocal prayer during Mass if we substitute for it mental prayer. Those who repeat vocal prayers must take care not to disturb others by whispering. The five sorrowful mysteries of the Rosary are a very suitable devotion for Mass, because Our Lord's Passion is thus set before us.

It is well to have a little singing during Mass, as it is conducive to devotion, is in itself a prayer, and promotes the glory of God.

Sacred music is most useful in exciting devotion. St. Augustine says: " How many tears I have shed, when hymns and canticles were sung to Thee, O my God! What emotions were aroused within me, when the church re-echoed with sweet melodies! Each note fell upon my ear like soothing balm, carrying conviction of Thy truth to my heart, and kindling within me the ardor of devotion." Music is, moreover, an efficacious prayer; it is a heartfelt and fervent prayer, for the feelings of the heart gain force when the voice expresses them in song. The Fathers of the Church cannot say enough in commendation of the use of vocal music in church; they say that it appeases the wrath of God, drives away the spirits of evil, attracts the angels, and leads the Holy Spirit to visit the heart of the singers; that on the wings of song the soul is aided to soar on high, that the voice of song awakens in the mind a longing for heavenly things, that it melts the heart and causes the sinner to shed tears of contrition and compunction. Vocal music is also an appropriate accompaniment to the sacrifice of the Mass; for it affords a means of expressing and manifesting the intense feeling, the deep emotions evoked by an attentive consideration of what is being enacted upon the altar. And since it is in song that the heart gives vent to her inmost feelings most freely and touchingly, it is the most perfect and fitting means of honoring the divine majesty. As often as Holy Scripture speaks of giving glory to God by the lips of angels or saints, it is described as a sublime and exalted song of praise. Therefore vocal music may almost be said to be an integral part of the solemn celebration of the holy sacrifice; the Church could more readily dispense with magnificent structures, rich coloring, costly vestments, precious vessels, than with singing, for it is the language in which utterance is given to her prayers. We read that at the Last Supper Our Lord and His apostles sang a hymn, after which they went out unto Mount Olivet (Matt. xxvi. 30). And we know, from the testimony of the earliest writers, that the Christians of primitive times were wont to sing during the celebration of holy Mass; for the first Christian annalists employ the expression: " Sing to Christ a canticle of praise," as synonymous with offering the holy sacrifice. In the present day some parts of the Mass are appointed to be sung by the priest. It is, however, important that the singing at Mass should be as far as possible in harmony with the prayers recited by the priest and with the festival of the day; for congregational singing is not a mere accompaniment to, an accessory of the Mass, but a means whereby the people take part in the service and join with the priest who officiates at the altar. But the singing should not be continuous, for this is disturbing to devotion. The Holy See has expressly forbidden the singing to go on during some parts of the liturgy, as at the consecration, and when benediction is given with the Blessed Sacrament.

3. At the three principal parts of the Mass we should to a certain extent suspend our private devotions, and fix our attention upon what is done upon the altar.

It is evidently the intention of the Church that we should discontinue our private prayers or singing during the canon of the Mass and at the communion, as a bell is rung to call our attention to it. At the offertory the priest says: " We offer unto Thee, O Lord, the chalice of salvation," and the faithful ought on their part to make an act of offering, to verify his words.

In the course of the Mass we are required to do as follows: When the priest commences the Mass, we should make the sign of the cross, and direct our intention.

The priest also offers the Mass for a definite intention. Ask yourself for what intention you should offer the holy sacrifice. In some places it is customary for the people to stand when the priest goes up to the altar, as a mark of reverence to him as Christ's representative.

At the Gospel all stand up, out of respect for the word of God; we should at the same time cross ourselves on forehead, lips, and breast, to testify our belief in, and our readiness to confess and follow the teaching of the crucified Redeemer.

At the offertory we ought to offer to God the oblations upon the altar, ourselves, and all that we possess.

At the *Sanctus* we ought to give praise to God, and hail the coming of the Son of God Who is about to descend upon the altar. The words of the *Sanctus* are like the thrice holy of the angels (Is. vi. 3), and the cries of the people at Our Lord's entry into Jerusalem (Matt. xxi. 9).

At the consecration we ought to kneel and adore the Redeemer Who comes down from heaven upon the altar.

Imitate at the consecration what you see the priest do; he falls upon his knees, and reverently adores the Lord and God Whom he holds in his hands. Do as the three kings did in presence of the Infant Christ, or as the apostles on Mount Thabor. When the priest elevates the Host, look upon it with veneration; Our Lord once revealed to St. Gertrude that those who did so would have greater joy hereafter in the contemplation of God. If looking upon a brazen serpent in the wilderness brought healing (Numb. xxi. 9), what must it not do for us to gaze in faith upon the sacred Host! It is not well to drop one's head immediately, as if one would hide one's self. For what purpose does the priest elevate the sacred Host and hold it up on high but that we may behold it ? Every one should remain perfectly silent, in trembling awe, when the King of kings comes to be immolated for the faithful and given to them as their spiritual sustenance. Before Him the choirs of angels move, covering their faces, singing songs of praise with great jubilation. "The Lord is in His holy temple; let all the earth keep silence before Him" (Hab. ii. 20). Some people keep cold and unmoved at the consecration, just as if Our Lord were not present; they are like a man who, when a friend comes from a distance to visit him, does not so much as bid him welcome on his arrival, but leaves him standing as if he were a stranger. The whole court of heaven makes preparation for the consecration, and we miserable mortals look on with indifference, scarcely seeming to heed what is enacted upon the altar. Oh! did God but open the eyes of our soul, what marvels would be disclosed to our spiritual sight! But because we do not perceive with our senses the abasement of the Son of God, we think little of it, whereas the angels gaze on it with trembling.

4. It is an excellent practice immediately after the consecration to make to our heavenly Father a definite act of offering of His divine Son sacrificed upon the altar, and of His Passion and death.

The priest officiating at the altar recites a prayer of offering. We may use some such words as these: "I offer Thee, O heavenly Father, Thy well-beloved Son, here present upon the altar; I offer Thee His sufferings and cruel death, beseeching Thee to have compassion upon the souls in purgatory" (or any other intention, such as the recovery of a sick person, or in thanksgiving for favors received). How pleasing it is to the eternal Father, when you honor Him in this manner! How rich a return will He make for the gift you present to Him! If any man possessed the whole world, and offered it to almighty God, he would not give Him so great a gift as when he humbly offers to Him His beloved Son in the Mass. The power of Christ's precious blood is all-prevailing to appease the wrath of God; by it we can obtain the conversion of sinners and the deliverance of souls from purgatory. Even the most grievous sinner may hope to obtain pardon, if he offers up the Passion and death of Christ to His divine Father. This may be done at other times than at Mass, but with less efficacy.

5. At the communion if we do not communicate actually, we ought to do so spiritually.

The early Christians communicated daily; but now few Christians lead so perfect a life as to be able to communicate daily. When the priest gives the blessing we should cross ourselves, at the same time imploring the blessing of God and giving thanks for the graces we have received. At the Last Gospel we should do the same as at the first.

6. It is not possible to hear two or more Masses at the same time; therefore when in church we ought to follow one Mass attentively, and not more than one.

We should endeavor, if we are present when several Masses are being said, to hear the one which is said where we can see it best, and follow that alone. In some dioceses it is the rule that if several Masses are celebrated simultaneously, the bell should be rung at one altar only, and that the principal, or at any rate the most conspicuous one. Yet though we cannot hear more than one Mass at the same time, if we are where several are being said, we profit in a certain measure by all, since every priest prays for all who are present.

10. *THE OBLIGATION OF HEARING MASS.*

1. Every Catholic is bound, under pain of mortal sin, to hear the whole of one Mass devoutly every Sunday and holyday of obligation.

(See the second commandment of the Church.)

1. Those persons who could not go to church without great injury to themselves, or who have some urgent work of mercy to perform, are excused from hearing Mass.

Those are dispensed from hearing Mass who by going to church would incur serious personal injury. Thus the sick who cannot go to church are excused, likewise those whose health is so delicate that they cannot go without at least the risk of falling ill; or those who by going would be in danger of being set upon by ruffians; others again who live more than three miles from a church, or at too great a distance to go in bad weather. A king once observed that on a stormy December morning the church was almost empty, whereas in the evening, though the snow was falling heavily, the theatre was crowded. " Alas," he exclaimed, " people are ready enough to make sacrifices for pleasure, but for God they will make none." Working-people are also excused if they would lose their employment by leaving their work to hear Mass, or they may stay away occasionally, if by going they have great disagreeables to put up with from the people they live with, though they should endeavor rather to bring them to a better mind. One member of a household may remain at home to keep the house; those, again, are excused from attendance at Mass who have works of mercy to perform, such as nursing the sick, taking care of young children, preparing the meals for other inmates of the house, etc.

2. We have not heard a whole Mass, unless we have been present in the church during the three principal parts of one and the same Mass.

It is requisite to be present at the three principal parts of the Mass; if one of these is omitted through negligence, the obligation is not fulfilled; if, for instance, we do not come in before the offertory, or if we leave before the communion. It does not suffice to hear one Mass from the consecration to the end, and another from the commencement to the consecration. What Christ has joined together, let not the Christian put asunder. He who comes in after the offertory must stay for the whole of another Mass. Moreover one must be present inside the church; it will not suffice to sit or stand outside, unless the church should be so overcrowded that it is impossible to get inside. How potent is the prayer of an assembled multitude; for where two or three are gathered together in Christ's name, there is He in the midst of them (Matt. xviii. 20). St. John the Almoner, Patriarch of Alexandria in the seventh century, put a stop to the bad habit his flock had contracted of remaining outside during Mass-time. One Sunday, instead of vesting for Mass, he went out and sat with the people outside the church, to their great astonishment. "Where the sheep are, there the shepherd must be," he observed. "While you stay here, I shall do the same; if you go in, I will go too." After this rebuke no one was to be seen outside the church at Mass-time.

3. Those only can be said to hear Mass devoutly who banish from their mind all that may cause them distraction, and who unite their petitions to those of the priest, especially at the three principal parts of the Mass.

4. It is permissible to assist at the holy sacrifice of the Mass on Sundays and holydays in any church; but it is desirable to go to one's parish church.

The Council of Trent admonishes the faithful to be frequent in their attendance at their parish church, at least on Sundays and the greater festivals. On those days the priest offers the holy sacrifice for all his parishioners, both living and dead, and adapts his sermons to the needs of his flock; furthermore in the parish church notices are given out of marriages, of fast days, of ecclesiastical festivals and ordinances. The faithful ought to become acquainted with their parish priest, who is their pastor and spiritual father, in the house of God. There is however no law which makes it binding upon Catholics to hear Mass in their parish church.

2. To hear Mass on week-days, if possible, is a highly commendable practice, for it may be the means of gaining the greatest graces.

If the holy sacrifice were celebrated in only one place in the world, and offered only by one priest, with what longing would Christian people hasten to that spot! But now that there are many priests, and Christ is daily offered up in many places, how much is our lukewarmness and negligence to be deplored, which has thereby arisen (Imitation. Book iv., ch. 1). Some people consider the half hour they take from their work to hear Mass as a loss of time; this is, however, not so, for they do their work better and more quickly through having been to Mass. Has not Our Lord said: "Seek first the kingdom of God and His justice, and all these things shall be added unto you" (Matt. vi. 33)? "If," says Cochem, "a shower of gold fell from the clouds, thou wouldst surely leave thy work and hasten into the street to gather up the coins. Only a fool would stop indoors. And thou art a fool if thou dost through indifference or negligence omit to hear Mass, when a stream of heavenly treasures is poured out from on high. Through neglecting holy Mass one loses far more than one would gain by a whole day's work. Arrange thy business therefore, if thou canst, so as to allow of thy hearing Mass daily. And if it is impossible for thee to go thyself, give an alms to some poor person to hear Mass for thee; he will do so gladly, and thou wilt reap the greater benefit." For, as is the case with every good work, we may apply to others the merit of hearing Mass without being losers ourselves. For the priest, in the canon of the Mass, supposes that those who are present who with him offer up the holy sacrifice, do so for their families and friends as well as for themselves. Do not allow human respect to keep you from serving Christ, for if you are ashamed of Him, He will also be ashamed of you (Luke ix. 26). When King Louis of France was told that people talked about his habit of hearing one or even more than one Mass daily, he replied: "How careful people are about my time; if I spent twice as long at play or out hunting, they would not have a word to say about it." The Blessed Thomas More was accustomed to say, in connection with hearing Mass daily, that he esteemed it his greatest honor to render that mark of respect to the King of kings.

11. THE TIME WHEN MASS IS TO BE CELEBRATED.

1. The holy sacrifice of the Mass is generally to be celebrated between sunrise and noon, and at midnight on Christmas Eve.

Mass may be said before sunrise under exceptional circumstances, such as the priest's going on a journey, or in order to give working-people the opportunity of hearing Mass before commencing the day's labor; or it may happen that after the consecration of a church, or a confirmation, the holy sacrifice is not commenced before twelve o'clock (noon). The early Christians celebrated Mass at night, in order to escape the persecution of the heathen. And in later years it was customary to offer the holy sacrifice during the night several times in the course of the year; at Christmas, on Holy Saturday, on St. John Baptist's Day, and on Ember days.

2. On Sundays and holydays of obligation the holy sacrifice of the Mass is offered at a convenient hour in all parish churches, and almost always on week-days also.

Every Catholic priest is bound to say Mass on Sundays and holy-days (Council of Trent, 23, 14). Those who have the care of souls are, in virtue of their office, under the obligation of offering the holy sacrifice every Sunday and holyday for their parishioners, both living and dead. These Masses which are binding on those who have the cure of souls are called parochial Masses, and must be said at the hour when the parishioners are best able to come to church.

3. No priest may, as a rule, say Mass more than once daily; but on Christmas Day all priests are allowed to say three Masses. And by the permission of the bishop some parish priests who have a large congregation are allowed to duplicate, that is, say two Masses on the same day.

In the commencement of the Middle Ages it was customary for priests sometimes to say one Mass after another, but this gave rise to many abuses. By a decree of Pope Innocent III. the clergy were forbidden to say more than one Mass daily, except on Christmas Day, when three might be said. It is not, however, obligatory on priests to say three Masses on Christmas Day, any more than it is upon the laity to hear three. Priests who have a large parish obtain permission from the bishop to duplicate, if the church is too small for all the parishioners to hear one and the same Mass.

On the other hand no priest may say Mass on Good Friday. And on Holy Thursday and Holy Saturday only one solemn Mass is to be celebrated in the parish church.

The only exception to this rule is made when the feast of the Annunciation falls on Thursday in Holy Week. If it falls on Good Friday or Holy Saturday, it is transferred to the Monday in Low Week.

12. THE PLACE WHERE MASS IS TO BE CELEBRATED.

1. The apostles offered the holy sacrifice on a table in a dwelling-house.

(See Acts ii. 46; Col. iv. 15.) To this day the table whereon St. Peter offered the holy sacrifice may be seen in the Church of St. John Lateran in Rome. The Council of Nice (325), speaks of the holy table on which the priest immolates without bloodshed the Lamb of God, Whose body and blood is the spiritual food of Christians. A table was used because it was on a table that the holy Mass was instituted by Our Lord on Holy Thursday; that table, made of cedar-wood, is still preserved in Rome. Another reason for using a table was that it could be easily hidden or removed in times of persecution.

2. In the time of the great persecution of the Christians, the holy sacrifice was offered on the tombs of the martyrs in subterranean passages (the Catacombs).

It is from this that the altar to this day has the form of a tomb, and that relics of the saints are deposited in it. Another reason why relics are placed in the altars is to denote the communion we hold with the saints in heaven, and it is on account of the relics being there that the priest frequently kisses the altar. When the Church had emerged from the Catacombs, the churches were erected by preference upon the spots where the saints and martyrs were interred (witness St. Peter's in Rome), and eminent ecclesiastics were buried in the crypts. Hence arose the custom at funerals of having the body in the church when the requiem is sung. And the lights which are burned during divine worship date from the time when the Christians assembled to hear Mass in dark, subterranean chambers. The burning lights also symbolize divine grace, which enlightens and vivifies, and which is communicated at no time so freely as during holy Mass. The candles upon the altar signify, furthermore, the presence of Him Who is the Light of the world, the God-man, Who enlightens us by His word.

3. When the period of persecution was over, the holy sacrifice of the Mass was offered in churches upon altars of stone.

In old times a table or mound was formed of stone, and decked as an altar. Noe, on coming out of the ark, built an altar, and the other patriarchs did the same. In the Temple at Jerusalem there were two altars, the altar of burnt-offering in the outer court, and the altar of incense in the sanctuary. Altars must be either composed entirely of stone, or a stone, blessed by the bishop and containing relics, must be let into the top. On this the chalice and paten are placed, to signify that Christ is the foundation and cornerstone on which the Church rests (Ps. cxvii. 22), and a threefold linen cloth must be spread upon the altar, both because Our Lord was wrapped in a linen cloth when He lay in the sepulchre, and also to absorb any drops of the precious blood that might perchance fall from the chalice. On every altar there must be a cross, because the sacrifice of the cross is renewed there, and also two candlesticks with wax tapers. The altar is generally placed so that the officiating priest looks towards the east; the reason of this is because when he celebrates the Mass he lifts his heart and hands to Him Who is the source of spiritual light. The altar is raised, both to denote its dignity, to enable all who are in the church to see the ceremonies, and also because the great oblation of our redemption was offered upon an eminence visible from afar.

Churches are usually built on a height, or in the centre of a township. The styles of ecclesiastical architecture are many and varied.

A hill, or some eminence, used to be selected as the site of a church, because of old high places were considered sacred; under the Old Dispensation God frequently manifested Himself to mortals on a mountain; Our Lord often withdrew to a mountain to pray, and the Temple of Jerusalem, the type of the Christian Church, was situated upon a mountain. On an eminence one is more disposed for prayer and recollection; one is further aloof from the noise of the busy world, one feels nearer to God. Christ Himself said His Church was to be built upon a rock, and He was crucified upon Mount Calvary. When churches are situated in the centre of a town or village, it should remind us that in the Blessed Sacrament the Good Shepherd loves to dwell in the midst of His sheep. The Church of St. Peter in Rome is the largest basilica in the world.

Both the external and internal arrangements of churches are adapted to awaken and aid devotion.

In regard to the exterior, the church is larger and higher than ordinary dwelling-houses, because it is the house of the most high God. It looks toward the east, because it is destined for the worship of the Sun of justice. It is built in the form of a cross, because the sacrifice of the cross is re-enacted within its walls, and the doctrine of the Crucified preached. It has a spire, pointing to heaven, our home, to admonish us to " seek those things that are above " (Col. iii. 1). Bells are hung in the tower to summon us to divine worship or call us to prayer; the spire is surmounted by a cross, the emblem of salvation, whereby God is reconciled with man. The interior of the church is divided into three parts; the porch, where in former days the catechumens and penitents used to kneel, and which ought to remind us of the preparation necessary before entering the church;

the nave, which is the part appropriated to the faithful, wherein, as in Noe's ark, they are saved from eternal perdition; and the choir, where the singers formerly sat, but which is now set apart for the clergy. It is separated from the body of the church by a rail or communion table. At the entrance of the church we see the holy water stoup, reminding us that we ought to approach God with pure hearts; in the interior is one or more altars; over the high altar is the tabernacle wherein the Blessed Sacrament is reserved, and before which the sanctuary lamp is kept perpetually burning, to symbolize the Light of the world there present. There are also pictures and statues of saints and angels, who assist unseen at the sacred offices, besides the font, and all the other furniture of a church, with which every Catholic is familiar. The " dim religious light " that pervades the building, owing to the colored glass of the windows, reminds us that here below we understand the things of God only in a dark manner. Those people who say that it is unnecessary to go to church, because they can say their prayers anywhere, should consider that in the churches Our Lord is actually present upon our altars, that the atmosphere of the sacred edifice disposes us to recollection, and that petitions offered there have more power than those offered elsewhere.

The consecration of a church is performed by the bishop, but a church can, with the permission of the bishop, be employed for divine service without consecration.

~ By God's command Moses had to anoint the tabernacle with the oil of unction (Exod. xl. 9), and Solomon's Temple was dedicated by that monarch himself. When King Antiochus had profaned the Temple by setting up idols within it, it had to be cleansed and dedicated anew; this was the origin of the feast of the Dedication (1 Mach. iv. 54). It appertains to the office of a bishop alone to consecrate churches, but he may give leave for Mass to be said in any building set apart for the purpose. The principal ceremonies of the consecration of a church are as follows: The bishop first prostrates himself before the principal entrance, and recites the Litany of the Saints; then rising up, he goes three times around the outside of the building, sprinkling the walls with holy water; each time that he passes the door he knocks upon it with his crozier; finally he makes the sign of the cross upon the threshold with the crozier to signify that nothing can resist the force of the cross, and enters the church, where he falls on his knees and invokes the Holy Spirit. He then draws the letters of the Greek and Latin alphabets upon the pavement of the church, which is strewn with ashes, to signify that all the nations of the earth are called into the Church of Christ; next he goes round the interior of the building three times, sprinkling the walls with holy water, and three times up the centre and across it; this is in honor of the Holy Trinity, and of the crucifixion of Christ; afterwards he anoints the walls in twelve places, where lighted tapers are affixed, in memory of the twelve apostles who spread abroad the light of the Gospel, and then proceeds to consecrate the altar. From time immemorial the anniversary of the dedication of a church formed a yearly festival in the parish, but abuses having crept in, one festival was appointed for the whole Church, the third Sunday in October, to be kept as the feast of the Dedication. If any grievous crime is committed in a church, such as murder, or suicide, and it is known publicly, the sacred edifice must be instantly closed and dedicated anew. This must also be done if a church is rebuilt, either wholly or to such an extent that the walls are in great part pulled down. Only under most exceptional circumstances, in time of war, or if a church is burned down, or at open-air festivals, may Mass be said outside the church, and express permission from the bishop must invariably be obtained. For saying Mass on board ship, the sanction of the Holy See is necessary. On such occasions a portable altar, blessed by the bishop, is used; that is, a square stone slab, large enough to admit of the chalice and Host being placed upon it.

13. THE VESTMENTS AND SACRED VESSELS USED AT MASS.

He who is granted an audience of an earthly monarch dresses himself in full dress out of respect to that monarch; and the priest, when he appears before the King of kings at the altar, is arrayed in suitable vestments. These vestments show that he does not act of his own power, but as the representative of Christ. God Himself gave directions concerning the vestments which were to be worn by the priests under the Old Testament (Exod. xxviii. 4). The vestments to be worn by the Christian priests were prescribed by the apostles.

1. The vestments which the priest wears in the celebration of Mass consist of (1), the amice; (2), the alb; (3), the girdle; (4), the maniple; (5), the stole; (6), the chasuble.

The amice is a white linen cloth laid about the head and shoulders. Formerly it used to be placed over the head like a hood, to keep the priest from distractions at Mass. The alb is a white linen garment, reaching from head to foot. In the East it was customary to wear a white robe on festival occasions, as for instance, when invited to a wedding. In the parable of the marriage-feast, Our Lord makes mention of the "wedding garment" (Matt. xxii. 12). The girdle is a cord which fastens the alb together, so that it may not inconvenience the priest in walking. It is said of the young Tobias, when he was seeking a companion for his journey, that he found a young man, standing girded, as it were ready to walk (Tob. v. 5). Our Lord also says: "Let your loins be girt" (Luke xii. 35). The maniple was at first a linen cloth which was worn on the left arm, representing the cloth wherewith Our Lord's countenance was wiped. The stole is a long band of silk which hangs down from the neck and is crossed on the breast. It is the special sign of the sacerdotal office, therefore the priest wears it whenever he exercises his priestly functions. The chasuble is a garment which covers the priest before and behind, reaching down to the knees; in early times it was a kind of mantle, with only one opening, through which the head was passed, whence came the name *casula*, a little house. At other times than at Mass the priest wears a short alb or surplice, or a cope. At High Mass the deacon and sub-deacon wear special vestments, called dalmatics.

2. The various portions of the sacerdotal vestments are commemorative of Our Lord's Passion, and also serve to remind the priest of the duties of his office.

The amice represents the cloth with which the soldiers muffled Our Lord's face when they struck Him; the alb represents the white robe in which Herod arrayed Him in mockery; the girdle, the cords wherewith He was bound; the maniple, Veronica's handkerchief; the stole, the rope laid about Our Lord's neck after His condemnation; the chasuble, on the back of which is a cross, the cross He bore on His shoulders. The amice reminds the priest to observe custody of the eyes; the alb betokens purity of heart; the girdle, abstemiousness, purity, and self-control; while the stole signifies his dignity as a priest, and the chasuble the heavy responsibilities that rest upon him.

3. The principal things which are used in saying Mass are: The chalice, the paten, and the missal.

The upper part of the chalice must be of gold, or silver, gilt inside. The paten is a small plate, whereon the sacred Host is laid; it must be gold or silver-gilt. Both chalice and paten must be blessed by the bishop. The missal contains the prayers that are said in every Mass, and those which vary according to the seasons and days of the ecclesiastical year. The ciborium somewhat resembles a chalice; it has a cover, and in it the consecrated Hosts are reserved for the communion of the faithful. The monstrance is sometimes used for the exposition of the Blessed Sacrament. Some worldlings are inclined to say as Judas did, when Magdalen anointed Our Lord's feet: "To what purpose is this waste?" when they see the care and money expended by Catholics on the sacred vessels and furniture of their churches. They should, however, consider how greatly the beauty of God's house impresses the beholder and conduces to devotion; and that it is, moreover, only right to give what is most precious and beautiful for the service of God. Why should the house of God be less richly adorned than the mansions of the wealthy?

14. THE COLORS OF THE VESTMENTS.

The Jews made sacerdotal vestments of various colors by God's injunction for use in the Temple, white, scarlet and purple being the prevailing colors. Among the heathen the priests wore garments of dazzling whiteness, hence the Christians, who were converts partly from Judaism, partly from paganism, wished to provide similar colored vestments for divine worship. Besides, from the revelations of St. John, the Church learned that the celestial spirits who serve God in heaven standing about the throne, are arrayed in brilliant hues, so as to resemble a rainbow (Apoc. iv.). Thus the Church Militant imitates the Church Triumphant in the use of colors in her services. And again, as the face of nature changes with the varying seasons, so the different emotions evoked by the various seasons of the ecclesiastical year find expression in the use of different colors.

1. In the vestments worn by the priest at Mass, the Church makes use of five colors: white, red, green, purple, and black.

White is emblematic of innocence and purity, and of the eternal bliss to be enjoyed hereafter; red, the color of fire and of blood, betokens love and martyrdom. Green signifies hope, and violet or purple, faith and penance. Black is an emblem of death.

1. White is the color used on the feasts of Our Lord, of the Blessed Virgin, of the angels, and of confessors.

Christ is the Light of the world and perfect purity; the Mother of God was free from the stain of original sin. The angels dwell in everlasting light and perfect sanctity; the confessors let the light of their good works shine before men. On the nativity of St. John Baptist white vestments are worn, although he was martyred, because he was sanctified before his birth.

2. Red is the color used at Pentecost and on the feasts of martyrs.

At Pentecost the Holy Ghost, Who kindles the fire of charity in our hearts, came down upon the apostles in tongues of fire. The martyrs shed their blood for Christ, and thus manifested the greatness of their love for Him. Red is also used on the feasts of the holy cross, because Our Lord shed His blood upon the cross.

3. Green is used on the Sundays after the Epiphany and after Pentecost on which nothing special is commemorated.

On the Sundays after Epiphany the Church commemorates the youth of Christ, and His entrance upon His public ministry, which brought hope to the world; after Pentecost she celebrates her own springtime, the germination of the grain in the kingdom of God.

4. Purple is used in Advent and Lent, and upon vigils and Ember days.

Advent is the season in which faith looks for the coming of the Saviour; Lent is the time of fasting and penance. Purple is worn in administering the Sacrament of Penance, Extreme Unction, and Baptism, until after the anointing of the person to be baptized.

5. Black is used on Good Friday and at Masses for the dead.

There is generally some white about black vestments, to indicate that the souls of the departed will soon enter upon eternal joys. At the obsequies of young children white is used because they die in innocence.

2. These colors not only depict the course of Our Lord's life on earth, but serve as a constant admonition to us to lead a pious life.

The colors in use in the Church, which, as we have seen, coincide with each event commemorated as it recurs in the cycle of the ecclesiastical year, are, besides, a continual lesson to the Christian. Let the white vestments remind you that the Church calls on her children to strive after holiness; let the sight of the red kindle in you the love of God, while the green bids you raise your heart and fix your hopes on heaven. The sight of the purple will remind you that you must do penance; the black will recall the thought of death, urging you to prepare for your last end and also to pray for your departed friends.

15. THE LANGUAGE OF THE MASS.

In celebrating the holy sacrifice of the Mass the Church makes use of the Latin language.

1. The Latin language is well adapted for the services of the Church, because it is both venerable and mysterious.

The Latin language is venerable on account of its origin and its antiquity; it is the language in which the praises of God resounded from the lips of Christians during the first centuries. It is a sublime and solemn thought that the holy sacrifice is now offered in the same language, nay, with the very same words as it was offered in times long past in the obscurity of the Catacombs. There is also an element of mystery about the Latin tongue; it is a dead language, not understood by the people. The use of an unknown tongue conveys to the mind of the vulgar that something is going on upon the altar which is past their comprehension, that a mystery is being enacted. In the first centuries of Christianity a curtain used to be drawn during the time from the *Sanctus* to the communion, to conceal the altar from the sight of the worshippers. This is now no longer done, but the use of an unknown tongue has something of the same effect, by inspiring awe into the minds of the common people. It is a striking fact that Jews and pagans made use, in the worship of the Deity, of a language with which the multitude were not conversant. The Jews made use of the ancient Hebrew, the language of the patriarchs; we do not find Our Lord or the apostles censuring this practice. The Greek Church, both orthodox and schismatical, employs the old form of the Greek language for divine service, not that spoken at present. The same language is in use in the Russian (so-called orthodox) Church, not the vernacular, which is a Slavonic dialect.

2. The use of the Latin language in her services is most advantageous for the Church; it serves to maintain her unity and preserve her from many evils.

The use of Latin is a means of maintaining unity in the Church, as well as uniformity in her services, for the use of one and the same language in Catholic churches all over the surface of the globe, is a connecting link binding them to Rome, and making one nations which are separated by diversity of tongues. Latin, as the language of the Church, unites all nations, making them members of God's family, of Christ's kingdom. The altar on earth is a type of the heavenly Jerusalem where a great multitude of all peoples and tongues stand around the throne, praising God. If Latin were not the official language of the Church, deliberations and discussions among bishops assembled at the councils, the mutual exchange of opinions between theologians would be impossible. Moreover, the use of Latin, the language of ancient Rome, is a constant reminder of our dependence on the Holy Roman Church; it recalls to our minds involuntarily the fact that thence, from the Mother Church, the first missionaries came who brought the faith to our shores. The use of a dead language is a safeguard against many evils; it is not subject to change, but remains the same to all time. Languages in daily use undergo a continual process of change; words drop out, or their meaning is altered as years go on. If a living language were employed in divine worship heresies and errors would inevitably creep into the Church, and sacred words would be employed in an irreverent or mocking manner by the unbeliever. This is prevented by the use of Latin, at any rate as far as the unlearned are concerned. Yet the Church is far from desiring to keep the people in ignorance of the meaning of her religious services; the decrees of the Council of Trent (22, 8), strictly enjoin upon priests to explain frequently the mysteries and ceremonies of the Mass to the children in schools, and to adults from the pulpit. But as a matter of fact, it is by no means necessary for the people to understand every detail of the ceremonial of the Mass. "If," says St. Augustine, "there are some present who do not understand what is being said or sung, they know at least that all is said and sung to the glory of God, and that is sufficient for them to join in it devoutly." Moreover, experience teaches that the fact of the prayers being in Latin does not at all hamper or interfere with the devotion of the faithful, or lead them to absent themselves from the services of the Church. Besides, the sermons are always delivered in the vernacular; it is often used at the opening services and to some extent in administering the sacraments. The reason why the whole of the Mass is in Latin is because it is a sacrifice, not an instruction for the people. The greater part of the prayers are said by the priest secretly, so that were they in the mother tongue, they would be inaudible to the people. Furthermore, the celebration of Mass consists more in action than in words. The actions of the priest, the whole ceremonial, speaks a language intelligible to all. And if, as some would wish, all the services were conducted in the language of the country, persons of another nationality, not conversant with other languages, might be led to drop their religion on leaving their own land. Another evil consequent upon such a change would be a lessening of the respect felt for the holy sacrifice, as was proved at the time of the reformation, when the prayers of the Mass were, to a great extent, translated into German and English.

16. SINGING AT MASS.

1. The singing of which the Church makes use as an accompaniment to the Mass, is what is known as the Gregorian chant.

This may be heard at High Mass, when the priest sings the preface or the *Pater Noster*, and when he begins the *Gloria* or *Credo*. This style of music is called Gregorian, because it was brought to perfection and introduced into general use by Pope St. Gregory the Great. It is believed that it was by divine inspiration or through direct revelation that the saint did so much in the interests of Church music. This chant is marked by extreme gravity, tranquil solemnity, majestic dignity. It is free from all rapid movements, florid passages, all striving after effect. It is the language of another, a higher sphere, it is truly the voice of prayer and of praise. In the Gregorian style special attention is paid to the text, the words of which are plainly audible; the beautiful, subdued melody holds a secondary place. This style of chanting is not hampered by restrictions of time and measure, and that gives it the irresistible power it possesses over the feelings, as an eloquent discourse carries away the heart. Gregorian music undergoes no change; like Latin, the language of the Church, it is always and everywhere the same. Hence it admirably corresponds to the nature and characteristics of the Church, particularly her unity and universality. Many devout Christians prefer this style of singing to any other, because it is a stimulus to recollection and devotion.

2. In addition to the Gregorian chant we have in our churches congregational singing, hymns in which the people join. Instrumental music, as an accompaniment to the singing, is played on the organ, violin, or other musical instruments.

Congregational singing had its origin in the first centuries, when the vernacular was the language of religion, and the people joined in some portions of the liturgy that was chanted. But when, in the fifth century, the Teutonic tribes overran Italy, and the national languages took a new form, and the people could no longer join in those parts of the liturgy which were sung in Latin, hymns to be sung in the vulgar tongue were introduced. The singing of hymns and canticles was more popular in Germany than elsewhere. Hymns full of sterling piety for processions, pilgrimages, and anthems in honor of Our Lady were composed and set to simple but splendid melodies. Luther was the ruin of Church music. He took advantage of the national love of psalmody and employed it as a means of propagating his erroneous tenets; it is said that he perverted more Catholics by his psalm-singing than by his preaching. The "chorales" to which he gave the principal place in divine worship were of so exciting a nature that it is said that while singing them, many a one felt himself urged to use his fists as well as his voice in spreading the new teaching. The Catholics of that period met Luther on his own ground; they too composed hymns in defence of the doctrines he attacked. This was the cause of a lamentable deterioration both in the spiritual songs themselves, and in the time and measure of the melodies to which they were sung, an effect which is felt to this day. Congregational singing during Mass should only be allowed in moderation, so as to leave every worshipper free to enter into the spirit of the holy mysteries, and not interfere with the private devotions of any one present. Instrumental music in churches enables us to lift up the heart to God with greater facility. Delight in the melody disposes the mind of the weaker brethren to deeper devotion, and is an aid in raising the thoughts from the natural to the supernatural. It must, however, be remembered that instrumental music is only an accessory; it is an accompaniment to vocal music, and serves to accentuate the words that are sung. In divine worship the simple words of prayer alone, or in their more solemn form of sacred music, are of main importance, because they are the outcome of the heart; the orchestral accompaniment is an accessory that can well be dispensed with. The playing ought never to drown the singing, or render the words sung unintelligible. Still less ought the instrumental music be calculated rather to please the ear than to touch the heart and awaken pious emotions, for in that case it would be a hindrance, not a help to prayer. For the earthly-minded Jews instrumental music was necessary on account of their weakness; for only through the pleasures of the senses could they be stimulated to strive after nobler aims. In the early days of Christianity no instrumental music was heard at the time of divine worship, for the Christians would not have their prayers mingle with the notes of instruments which were associated with pagan dances and idolatrous ceremonies. Organs were first used in churches in the eighth century; in the sixteenth century, when kings and princes who were patrons of music had orchestras attached to their courts, we find instruments of various kinds, violins, flutes, etc., in the churches. Later on, professional bandmasters were engaged to conduct the choirs in churches, and unfortunately they introduced secular melodies into the house of God, and in the performance of these compositions no heed was paid to the sacred words of the liturgy. Among those who contributed most to the reform of Church music was Palestrina, the Papal choirmaster in the Vatican; he composed several Masses of a solemn and dignified character, in which due prominence was given to the words. His name is immortalized by the *Missa Papæ Marcelli.* A contemporary of his of Dutch origin, Orlando di Lasso, choirmaster of the Lateran Church in Rome, asserted himself in the same direction. He was called the "king of composers," and was the author of eight hundred secular compositions, besides fifteen hundred sacred works. The finest of the latter is the seven penitential psalms arranged for five voices, in which the feelings of penitence and compunction are expressed in a masterly manner. Gabrieli, organist of St. Mark's in Venice, and Allegri, are also celebrated composers. The *Miserere* (for Holy Week), written by the last named, with nine parts and a double score is much esteemed. These masters promoted vocal music without an accompaniment, more than instrumental music, for which they did little. Instrumental music owes much to the composer Bach, a native of Eisenach (1750), whose sacred music is distinguished by its serious, religious tone. Towards the close of the eighteenth century instrumental music was brought to great perfection by Haydn, an Austrian, who composed fifteen Masses; he died in 1809 in Vienna; Mozart, a native of Salzburg, who attracted attention as a boy by his musical talent, composed fifteen Masses before he was eighteen years old; he died at the age of thirty-five in Vienna; and Beethoven, a native of Bonn, who wrote two Masses of prodigious length; he died in 1827 in Vienna. The works of these composers cannot be considered as models of what sacred music ought to be: they do not reflect the spirit of the Church in the Gregorian music. They may express feelings of devotion, otherwise they differ little from secular compositions, and bear the stamp of the age in which they were written. In recent times much has been done for the improvement of Church music by the Society of St. Cecilia, founded in 1867 at Regensburg, the object of which is to train choirs, to raise congregational singing to a higher level, and introduce instrumental music of a nature to correspond with the liturgy of the Church. The rules of this Society were confirmed by Pope Pius IX. in 1870.

17. HEARING THE WORD OF GOD.

At the miraculous multiplication of the loaves, Our Lord caused the bread to be distributed to the people by His disciples (Matt. xv. 36). And now He employs His ministers to dispense to the faithful the spiritual bread, the word of God. This bread is given to them freely (2 Cor. xi. 7).

1. The word of God is said to be the food of the soul, because it sustains the life and strength of the soul, as bread does that of the body.

The Fathers of the Church speak of the word of God as the food of the soul. Our Lord Himself says: "Not in bread alone doth man live, but in every word that proceedeth from the mouth of God" (Matt. iv. 4). The manner in which the word of God acts upon the soul is by enlightening the understanding and inciting the will to do what is good. In the darkness of this life it shows us the path to heaven, as a lantern enables the traveller to find his way by night. The word of God reveals to us the stains upon our soul, as a mirror shows us the marks upon our countenance. When St. Augustine had attended the sermons of St. Ambrose at Milan, he said: "That man opened my eyes." The word of God stimulates the will to what is good. The fable tells us that Orpheus played the lyre with such a wonderful charm, that the sounds he drew from it fascinated the most savage mortals, tamed wild beasts, and even recalled the dead to life. This is true of the word of God; by it whole nations sunk in heathendom, degraded below the level of the beasts, have been converted, and civilized, and rescued from eternal death. St. Anthony the hermit embraced the life of an anchorite in consequence of having heard a sermon on Our Lord's words to the rich young man. "Are not·My words as a hammer that breaketh the rock in pieces?" (Jer. xxiii. 29.) The word of God strikes the heart like a thunderbolt. The thunder of the divine menaces awakens those asleep in sin, indifferent as to their salvation. The word of God banishes sin. "It acts on the soul," says St. Jerome, "as a plough on the soil, loosening the hardened surface, rooting up the thistles of vice." The word of God kindles the flame of charity in the heart of man; like fire, it consumes the rust of sin, it promotes the growth of virtue; or it may be compared to the gentle rain that cometh down from heaven to soak the earth and water it, and make it to spring, and give seed to the sower and bread to the eater (Is. lv. 10).

He who shows indifference towards the word of God exposes himself to the risk of spiritual death and eternal damnation.

Just as a man who refuses to take food will surely die, so those who do not hear the word of God, which is the food of the soul, incur spiritual death. In this life we are travellers on the long and dangerous journey from time to eternity; and as the traveller who walks by night without a lantern strays from the right road, so we shall not reach the end of our journey without the light of God's word to illumine our mind and guide us to our final end. The word of God is the sun of the soul, without which the spiritual life will droop and fail, as nature would if deprived of the vivifying warmth and radiance of the sun.

2. Hence it is the duty of every Christian either to hear sermons frequently, or to read spiritual books and make a practical application of what he hears or reads.

The Council of Trent orders that there should be a sermon in every parish church on Sundays and festivals. As it has long been customary to have the sermon after the Gospel, all who go to Mass on those days hear a sermon as a matter of course. Consequently there is no special injunction to hear sermons. Preaching was the principal occupation of Our Lord and the apostles (Luke iv. 43; Mark xvi. 20), and the greatest saints have generally been able and zealous preachers. The preached word has more force and effect than what is read in books. The Bible history, the lives of the saints, or books of meditation are much to be recommended; these are preachers to whom we may listen at any hour. Spiritual books are a mirror in which we discern our own feelings, and the virtues of which we stand most in need. Experience shows how much good may be done by reading them; witness the well-known conversion of St. Ignatius Loyola, or of St. John Columbinus, a nobleman and burgomaster of Sienna. One day, returning home from the town-council at noon, he found dinner was not quite ready. His wife gave him a volume of the lives of the saints to while away the time of waiting; at first he threw it aside, but presently opening it, he read the history of St. Mary of Egypt. This touched him so deeply that he became a changed man; from thenceforth he led an austere and saintly life. If we would profit by what we read, we must read with deliberation, and not too much at a time; and above all, be careful in the choice of books. Many books are like fungi, not food, but poison; "evil communications corrupt good manners" (1 Cor. xv. 33). Moreover one must make a practical application of what one hears or reads. As food only nourishes the body when it is properly digested, so the word of God does not profit the hearer unless it be received into the heart and meditated upon. And as when we have been walking in a beautiful garden, inhaling the perfume of the flowers, we like to take away with us a few fragrant blossoms, so after spiritual reading we should retain a few thoughts as a spiritual bouquet to refresh us during the day. Unfortunately people do not think over what they hear or read; they are like a man who beholds his own countenance in a glass and goes his way, presently forgetting what manner of man he is (Jas. i. 23, 24). This is so because either they are distracted by worldly cares (the seed falls on the wayside), or they are prejudiced against the word of God (the seed falls upon a rock), or their hearts are full of corrupt inclinations and unruly passions (the seed falls among thorns) (Luke viii.).

To apply the word of God to another, not to one's self, is reprehensible; or to listen to a preacher as the Pharisee did, merely in a critical spirit; or again to refuse to obey the word of God, because the example of the preacher does not correspond to his teaching.

We ought to apply the sermons we hear to ourselves. Some are so busy in apportioning what they hear to others, that they leave nothing for themselves. It is recorded in the life of St. Anthony of Padua, and those of other saints, that when they preached against the follies of the day, gambling and love of dress, men brought their cards and dice, women their cosmetics and finery, and burned them in the presence of the preacher. It is not eloquence, but truth, that should attract us in a preacher. If we listen to the simplest discourse in a docile spirit, we are sure to learn something from it. Others will not obey the word of God because the preacher does not practise what he teaches. St. Augustine compares those who will not follow the counsels of a preacher because he himself does not act upon them, to travellers who, coming to a wooden guide-post, will go no further on the road pointed out to them because the guide-post itself is stationary. The preacher is but the instrument of which the divine husbandman makes use to sow His celestial seed. Look not at the poverty of the vessel containing the seed, but at the excellence of the grain, and the majesty of the husbandman.

3. Those who are assiduous in hearing sermons or reading spiritual books, will not have great difficulty in attaining eternal salvation.

Our Lord says: " He that is of God, heareth the words of God " (John viii. 47). " Blessed are they who hear the word of God, and keep it " (Luke xi. 28). We delight to hear men speak of those whom we love; therefore, if we rejoice to hear of God, we must have the love of God in our hearts, and those who have divine charity are in a state of grace. Appetite is a sign of health; so the desire for spiritual nourishment is a sign that the soul is in a healthy condition, that is, in a state of grace. A disgust for food shows the body to be sick, and a distaste for the word of God indicates a bad state of the soul.

The profit to be derived from a sermon is proportioned to the enlightening grace of the Holy Spirit present in the hearts of the preacher and his hearers.

This is why the assistance of the Holy Ghost is invoked before the sermon. It is God, not the preacher, Who speaks to the heart. The preacher planteth only and watereth, it is God Who giveth the increase (1 Cor. iii. 7). However splendid the equipments of a ship, she cannot sail unless the wind is favorable; so it is with the preacher; however great his erudition and eloquence, unless the Holy Spirit imparts unction to his words, they avail nothing. An officer of distinction, who had heard all the best preachers of France, once went to hear the sermon of a simple but pious village priest, the Curé d'Ars. When asked what he thought of the discourse, he answered: " Hitherto I have only been pleased with the orator, now I am displeased with myself." It is said that St. Francis of Sales converted seventy thousand heretics by his preaching. When we see a beautifully executed piece of penmanship, we do not praise the pen, but the hand that guided it; in like manner it is not to the preacher who delivers an excellent discourse that praise is due, but to the Holy Ghost Who spoke by his lips. The word of God does not always bear fruit immediately, it is like the grain of mustard-seed (Matt. xiii.), which after a considerable time grew up and became a large tree. Sometimes it produces no fruit at all. Our Lord speaks of three cases in which the seed perished and only one in which it bore fruit; when it bears fruit the amount is not always the same.

II. THE SACRAMENTS.

On the Day of Pentecost the Holy Spirit manifested His coming by a visible and audible sign; the tongues of fire indicated the enlightenment of the apostles and the gifts of tongues; the mighty wind the power imparted to them. In like manner, it is the good pleasure of Our Lord to convey graces to us by means of sensible signs. He ordained for the communication of graces the use of such words and objects as clearly signify the grace bestowed; for the washing away of original sin He ordained that water should be poured on the head (because water cleanses) and at the same time a form of words used which indicates that it is done by the power of the Holy Trinity. In order to impart to us the gifts of the Holy Spirit, light and fortitude, He instituted the laying on of hands, with prayer and anointing with oil (oil being used to give light and warmth).

1. The sacraments are sensible signs instituted by Christ, by means of which the graces of the Holy Spirit are communicated to us.

In every sacrament there is: An appropriate ceremony, called the matter, and a form of words, which accompanies the sign or ceremony; and besides, there is the grace conveyed. The sign, or visible part of the sacrament, not only signifies what is effected in the sacrament, but effects what is signified. They are, therefore, practical signs; they may also be termed instruments, and the graces conveyed through them the effect of those instruments. The signs of the sacraments are like Our Lord's humanity, and the graces conveyed like the Godhead concealed beneath this humanity. The word sacrament (*sacramentum*) means something holy and also mysterious, because in early times holy things were hidden from the knowledge of the heathen.

Sensible signs were instituted by Our Lord for this purpose: that the graces conferred by their means might be made duly apparent, and thus recognized by man.

As water cleanses from impurity and extinguishes fire, the use of water signifies that our souls are cleansed and the fire of hell is quenched for us. As oil gives light and strengthens the body, its use in Confirmation indicates plainly that our souls are enlightened and fortified by the Holy Spirit. Thus the practical effect of the sacrament may be known by the sensible sign. Our Lord made use of distinct signs in conferring graces and benefits, although a thought, a word on His part, would have sufficed; He touched the eyes of the blind man (Matt. ix. 29); He touched the leper (Matt. viii. 3); He breathed on the apostles and said to them: "Receive ye the Holy Ghost" (John xx. 22). Under the Old Dispensation likewise, God bestowed His favors through signs; witness Moses' rod, the brazen serpent, the gall of the fish wherewith Tobias' sight was restored, the cure of Naaman by washing in the Jordan. Sensible signs were instituted by Our Lord for the purpose of humbling the pride of man. Man, who aspired to be as God, is now dependent for the recovery of the grace he lost upon what is lowest in creation, lifeless matter. As for the sake of what is sensible man renounced heaven, it is meet that by use of what is sensible he should rise again to that which is suprasensible. Sensible signs are, in fact, required by the nature of man. If we were pure spirits we could dispense with corporal signs for the communication of spiritual gifts, but as we are composed of body and soul, we have need of them.

In addition to the signs instituted by Christ, certain ceremonies have been appointed by the Church, in order to indicate still more perceptibly the graces conferred, and to increase the devotion of those who dispense and those who receive the sacraments.

The various significant ceremonies are like a mirror, wherein a man sees the reflection of what goes on within his soul. The benefits God bestows on us are more deeply impressed upon our minds by the accompanying ceremonial; it also deepens the devotion of both the dispenser and the recipient of the sacrament. If an earthly monarch is seen by his subjects in all the grandeur of his regal dignity, attended by the grandees of his court, they think more of him than when he is in ordinary attire. The sacraments are not dispensed in a bare and informal manner, but are accompanied by the accessories of a rich and solemn ceremonial; this is not only to make a greater impression upon mortals, but to give greater glory to God. The ceremonies also constitute a certain preparation for the reception of the sacraments; they prepare the soil of the heart, that the good seed may bear more abundant fruit. The ritual is not precisely the same in all dioceses, local custom having added some rites which cannot well be abolished, but the Roman *ritus* is the one universally followed. The ceremonies of the Church may be omitted in case of necessity, as in Baptism when there is danger of death.

2. Christ instituted seven sacraments: Baptism, Confirmation, Holy Eucharist, Penance, Extreme Unction, Holy Orders, and Matrimony.

The doctrine of the seven sacraments is as old as the Church herself. All the sects that fell away from the Church in the early centuries retained the seven sacraments, as did the Greeks and Romans at a later period. The institution of seven sacraments is, it is true, not mentioned in Holy Scripture, but it is not said that there were more or less. On this point Tradition is sufficient authority. The seven sacraments answer exactly to the needs of the soul, which resemble to a certain extent the exigencies of the body. The life of the soul begins at Baptism, it is fortified by Confirmation, brought to perfection by the Holy Eucharist; if the life of the soul be lost, it is restored by Penance and Extreme Unction; it is kept up by Holy Orders and Matrimony from generation to generation.

Through the seven sacraments we receive divine grace at the very time of our life when we are most in need of it.

These times occur at birth, at our entrance into youth, when we have lost the friendship of God, when we embrace a new state of life, and at the hour of death. As at sea there are islands and harbors, where the mariner can cast anchor and take in supplies; as there are roadside inns where the traveller can pause to rest and recruit his strength, so on the weary journey of life the sacraments are provided to afford support and refreshment now and again to the pilgrim.

3. By the three sacraments, Baptism, Confirmation, and Holy Orders, there is imprinted upon the soul a certain spiritual and indelible mark or character, on account of which they cannot be repeated (Council of Trent, 7, 9).

The indelible mark or character consists in a special consecration and dedication to Christ. By this mark the angels know whether a man is one of God's family, and if so, they give him particular protection. This mark is not effaced by mortal sin, it never can be removed from the soul. Consequently these three sacraments can never be received a second time, not even by one who has apostatized from the faith and has been received back into the Church. These three sacraments will be like a seal upon the soul in a future life; they will be a cause of eternal glory and rejoicing to the blessed; to the reprobate they will be a source of shame and confusion.

4. Two of the sacraments, Baptism and Penance, are instituted principally with the object of conferring sanctifying grace where it was not already given; the five others with the object of increasing that gift.

The holy sacraments are the wine and oil of the Samaritan in the Gospel, for the maintenance and restoration of the health of the soul. Baptism and Penance are called sacraments of the dead, of those who are spiritually dead, because they were instituted for those whose spiritual life is destroyed by mortal sin. The five others are sacraments of the living, because they were instituted for those who are in a state of grace. It is, however, possible for sanctifying grace to be increased by Baptism and Penance, if through earnest amendment of life and heartfelt contrition a man has merited to receive the Holy Ghost previous to Baptism or confession, like the centurion

Cornelius, on whom, and on whose household, the Holy Ghost was poured out while St. Peter was preaching (Acts x. 44). So also one may go to confession without being guilty of mortal sin and thereby acquire more grace.

Each sacrament has besides its own individual object, and confers a grace peculiar to itself.

Thus Baptism confers the grace to live according to the precepts of the Gospel; Confirmation, to confess the faith fearlessly; the Holy Eucharist, to make progress in the supernatural life; Penance preserves us from relapse into sin; Extreme Unction is a remedy; Holy Orders and Matrimony confer the graces appropriate to those states in life. Such is the great practical efficacy of the sacraments, and yet how little we appreciate their value! What efforts, what sacrifices, people make to keep or to regain their bodily health! And yet they will not employ the simple, easy means within their reach for preserving the health of their soul, which is far more important.

5. Due preparation must be made before receiving the sacraments, in order to obtain the graces they convey.

Any one who approaches the Sacrament of Baptism or Penance without a thorough change of heart, or who receives the other sacraments in a state of mortal sin, commits the terrible sin of sacrilege, and will not obtain the graces of the Holy Spirit until the hindrance to grace has been removed.

On this account in the early ages of Christianity a two years' probation was required before admission to Baptism, the object of this being to give the heathens time to reform their life. St. Peter in his preaching insisted on the necessity of penance and sincere conversion (Acts ii. 38; iii. 19). To this day the Church requires those who approach holy communion to go to confession first. How reprehensible is the conduct of those who, from force of habit, or because of some special indulgence, go to confession without purposing a serious amendment of life! "The sacraments," St. Augustine says, "are the salvation of those who use them aright, the damnation of those who misuse them." That which is meat to the healthy is poison to the sick. Infant baptism is the only case in which no previous preparation is necessary. And if any one is so unhappy as to receive one of the sacraments sacrilegiously he may yet participate in the grace of the sacrament, if the obstacle to it be removed. The sacraments are like the sunshine; it cannot penetrate into a room of which the shutters are closed, but as soon as they are opened, it streams in, warming it and illumining it. In like manner a sacrament, if received unworthily, need not be received again; on amendment of life, its gracious influences are freely exercised. This rule does not hold good in regard to the Holy Eucharist; if it be received by one who is in mortal sin, the grace of it is lost, even if the sinner returns to a state of grace. The more worthy the recipient, the greater the graces conferred by the sacrament. The drier the wood, the more freely it burns. If the vessel taken to the spring be clean, the water contained in it will be pure.

There are two indispensable conditions which the Church imposes on those who approach the sacraments: They must be qualified to receive them, and desirous to receive them.

The power of assimilating food is dependent upon certain organs of the human body; even so certain qualifications are necessary for the reception of the sacraments. An unbaptized person is incapable of receiving any of the other sacraments; a child who has not reached the age of reason cannot receive the Sacrament of Penance; Extreme Unction cannot be given to one who is in robust health; no one under the age of twenty-three can receive Holy Orders. If a sacrament is administered to any one against his will, it is invalid. The Church has never sanctioned the action of secular rulers who have compelled their subjects to be baptized, as was done in early times. Thus now at Baptism the question is asked: "Wilt thou be baptized?" The last rites of the Church are, it is true, administered to persons who are unconscious, before death; but only if it be supposed that they would have wished for the sacraments had they been conscious. The baptism of infants is justified on these grounds.

6. Supposing the priest who administers the sacrament to be unworthy, the graces of the Holy Spirit will still be communicated by means of the sacrament.

The entire efficacy of the sacraments is derived from the merits of Christ, not those of the priest who dispenses them. It is out of the power of man to confer what is divine. The sacraments are essentially holy in themselves, not because they are administered by one who is holy. Nor is the grace of the sacraments lessened by the evil life of the priest. God is wont to make use of unworthy instruments. The minister is but the dispenser of the mysteries of God (1 Cor. iv. 1). A leper can act as porter as well as a healthy man, provided he has the key of the door. A judge may be, as a man, worse than the criminal before him, yet he can pass sentence on him. The coin of the realm has the same value in the hand of a bad as of a good man. The wine is the same, whether it be drunk out of an ordinary glass or a gold goblet. So it is with the sacraments; the Donatists, who asserted the contrary, were heretics. If the sacraments could only be administered aright by good priests, one would never have any certainty in regard to them.

The Church imposes two indispensable conditions on those who administer the sacraments: they must make use of the prescribed sensible sign without any essential alteration at the same time as the form of words, and they must have the intention to do what the Church does.

If wine, for instance, were employed instead of water for baptizing, the visible sign would be essentially changed, and it would be no baptism at all. Or if one were to say: "I baptize thee in the name of Christ," the audible sign would be essentially changed, and it would be no baptism. But the wrong pronunciation of some word —by a foreigner perhaps—would not interfere with the efficacy of the sacrament. In the prescribed form of words is pronounced some time before or after the water is poured upon the head of the person to be baptized, the baptism is not valid; the two actions must be simultaneously performed. When Protestants baptize, their baptism is valid, if they have the intention to do what the (true) Church does, and are careful to adhere to what is prescribed.

1. BAPTISM.

Even heathen nations, such as the Egyptians, Greeks, and Romans, made use of water to cleanse their souls and render them pleasing to the Deity. The Jewish law enjoined purifications, to cleanse from various legal uncleannesses (Lev. xii.-xv.). Before the giving of the Ten Commandments the people were to be sanctified and wash their garments (Exod. xix. 10). John the Baptist baptized in the desert those who promised amendment of life, to signify the remission of sins which they would gain by their penitential works. The baptism of Christ is of a different nature; it has a transforming power, for it washes away sin and confers the gift of the Holy Ghost (Matt. iii. 11).

1. This is what takes place at Baptism: Water is poured upon the head of the person to be baptized, and at the same time the words appointed by Our Lord are repeated; the person is thereby cleansed from original sin and all other sins, he is gifted with habitual and sanctifying grace, and becomes a child of God, an heir of heaven, and a member of the Church.

At our baptism much the same takes place as at Our Lord's baptism: like Him, we have water poured upon our head, and certain words are spoken ("I baptize thee in the name of the Father, and of the Son, and of the Holy Ghost"); the Holy Ghost descends upon us (although not in the form of a dove), we are made temples of the Holy Ghost and endowed with sanctifying grace; God the Father says: "This is My beloved son, in whom I am well pleased" (we are made children of God), and the heavens are opened (we are made heirs of immortality). Again, much the same takes place at our baptism as at the cleansing of Naaman (4 Kings v. 14); we are washed with water, and delivered from the leprosy of sin, both original and actual. So again much the same takes place at our baptism as at the passage of the Israelites through the Jordan (1 Cor. x. 2); we pass through the water of Baptism into the promised land, the Church of which we become members. Those on whom sanctifying grace has been bestowed, are in virtue of that bestowal children of God and heirs of heaven. Only the baptized have the right to call God their Father, hence in early times the Lord's Prayer was not taught to the unbaptized. St. Louis of France used to say: "I think more of the private chapel where I was baptized, than of the Cathedral of Rheims where I was crowned; for the dignity of a child of God, which was bestowed on me at Baptism, is greater than that of the ruler of a kingdom. The latter I shall lose at death; the other will be my passport to everlasting glory." It is because man is cleansed from sin by baptism that St. Paul exclaims: "There is therefore now no condemnation to them that are in Christ Jesus" (Rom. viii. 1). The words of St. Peter on the Day of Pentecost show what is the effect produced by Baptism: "Do penance, and be baptized, every one of you in the name of Jesus Christ, for the remission of your sins; and you shall receive the gift of the Holy Ghost" (Acts ii. 38). St .Paul speaks of Baptism as "the laver of regeneration and renovation of the Holy Ghost," whereby "being justified by His grace we may be heirs according to hope of life everlasting" (Titus iii. 5, 7). Again he says: "In one spirit were we all baptized into one body" (1 Cor. xii. 13).

Baptism was instituted by Our Lord at His own baptism and enjoined upon the Church at His ascension.

Our Lord caused Himself to be baptized in the Jordan in order to sanctify water and impart to it a cleansing power. The manifestation of all the three persons of the Holy Trinity at the time of His baptism showed that the sacrament was to be administered in the name of the three divine persons. Christ also told His apostles at His ascension to go, "baptizing all nations in the name of the Father, and of the Son, and of the Holy Ghost" (Matt. xxviii. 19).

2. Baptism acts spiritually as water does materially.

It cleanses us from the stains of sin, it extinguishes for us the flames of hell and of purgatory; it imparts to us a new life, it quenches the thirst of the soul, it gives us strength to fulfil the commandments, causes us to bring forth fruit to life eternal, and makes us members of Christ's mystical body.

Every one knows that in the natural order water cleanses the body, puts out fire, and recalls to consciousness one who has fainted; that it invigorates the human frame and gives fertility to the soil. The water of Baptism does the same in the spiritual order. Every new-born infant has the stain of original sin attaching to him, and every adult has, in addition, that of actual sin. These sins vanish at the laver of regeneration as a spark disappears if it falls into the ocean. On this account no penance is enjoined on the newly-baptized. Any one dying immediately after baptism, goes straight to heaven if he has at the time no attachment to venial sin, thus escaping purgatory and hell. And since the person baptized receives the Holy Ghost, and with Him sanctifying grace, a new life begins for him, the life in God. Thus Baptism is the birth of the soul, whereas the other sacraments are its food or its medicine. Baptism is also called regeneration, because it is the commencement of another and a new life. When the water is poured upon the exterior, an interior change takes place; the individual becomes a new creature—from sinful he becomes just. In Baptism true peace of mind is acquired through the indwelling of the Holy Ghost. The early Christians used to feel the same interior happiness after baptism that we feel after making a good confession. It may truly be said that the water of Baptism quenches the thirst of the soul. Furthermore, when the Holy Ghost enters into the soul at Baptism, He enlightens the understanding and justifies the will. When Saul, the persecutor of the Christians, was baptized, there fell from his eyes as it were scales (Acts ix. 18), indicating that his spiritual blindness was at an end. Baptism also confers strength to resist the temptations of the evil enemy. Yet the corrupt proclivity remains, and man is ever subject to temptations, as the Hebrews, when they had escaped from servitude by the passage of the Red Sea, were still exposed to the attacks of their adversaries in the desert. As the will is fortified by Baptism, we are better able to perform good works. He who has received the Holy Ghost possesses divine charity (Council of Trent, 6, 7), and by charity we abide in God, and are closely united to Him (John xiv. 23; 1 John iv. 16). Hence, having received the Holy Ghost and with Him divine charity, we are in Baptism made one with Christ (Gal. iii. 27); we are united to Christ as members to the head; "your members are the members of Christ" (1 Cor. vi. 15). We are made members of the one great body of which Christ is the head and the life; all the graces which we receive as members of the Church proceed from Christ. Hence He is rightly termed the lifegiving Head of the Church, for in one Spirit we were all baptized into one body (1 Cor. xii. 13, 15). In Baptism we are cut off from the stock of the old sinful Adam, and grafted into Christ as new creatures; we are no longer of the posterity of the old Adam, but of the posterity of Christ. Baptism is compared to the door of Noe's ark. See how marvellous are the effects of this sacrament! The grace of Baptism is of all the gifts of God the most excellent, the most exalted, the most precious. Who, being unbaptized, would not desire Baptism?

3. Baptism is indispensably necessary to salvation. Hence children who die unbaptized cannot enter heaven (Council of Trent, 7, 5).

Our Lord says: "Unless a man be born again of water and of the Holy Ghost, he cannot enter into the kingdom of heaven" (John iii. 5). He makes no exception, not even in the case of infants. St. Basil says Baptism is the vessel wherein we embark for the celestial port. Baptism is no less indispensable in the spiritual order than water in the natural order, and since it is so indispensable, God has made it very easy. Nothing is absolutely necessary but water, which may be had everywhere; every one can baptize in case of need; newborn infants may be baptized; and for adults the simple desire is sufficient, if actual baptism is impossible. And since Baptism is of such urgent necessity for salvation, it follows that infants dying unbaptized cannot attain eternal salvation. For every child coming into the world has the taint of original sin, and has not sanctifying grace, without which no man can enter heaven. Yet, although infants dying without baptism are excluded from participation in celestial joys, the divine Judge does not consign them to the torments of hell, because they have never committed actual sin; they enjoy a certain natural happiness without physical suffering or mental sadness; they are cheerful as those are with whom all goes well on earth. But the happiness which is their portion bears much the same relation to everlasting felicity as the feeble light of a candle does to the brilliance of the noonday sun. Thus parents who through negligence allow their children to die unbaptized have much to answer for. The eternal salvation of the infant is entirely dependent on the free will of its fellow-man, especially near relatives. St. Augustine mentions the relics of St. Stephen having been efficacious in restoring to life a dead child in order that it might receive Baptism.

4. Hence it follows that parents ought to have their children baptized immediately after their birth, because new-born infants hover between life and death.

Infant baptism has been customary since apostolic times. St. Alphonsus says that if parents, without an urgent reason, neglect to have their children baptized within ten days after their birth, they incur the guilt of mortal sin.

5. In case of necessity any one can administer baptism, and without the usual ceremonies.

Nurses often baptize weakly infants. The baptism by Jews and heretics is valid, provided it is correctly administered, that is, if water be poured on the child's head (or some other portion of the body) and at the same moment the formula is repeated: "I baptize thee, etc." If the child lives, he should be taken to the church later on for the usual ceremonies. If it be surmised that through overhaste, or some other cause, the first baptism was not properly performed, the priest must baptize the child again, conditionally.

In the majority of cases only priests should administer Baptism, and that in the church with the prescribed ceremonial.

In the early ages of Christianity only the bishop, or a priest whom he empowered to act for him, had the right to baptize. But when the dioceses became larger, and it was impossible for the bishop to go about continually to administer that sacrament, the power to baptize was made a part of the priests' office. As a matter of fact in the present day only the priest of the parish possesses this right, unless he authorizes another to act in his stead. Originally Baptism was only administered in baptistries, or small stone chapels containing all that was necessary for baptism, situated either in close proximity to the principal church of the diocese, or in the interior of the building. About the seventh century infant baptism became universal, and adult baptism of rare occurrence; fonts containing blessed water were then placed in the church where the bishop officiated. Baptism in private houses was strictly forbidden, but in the case of the children of kings and princes it might be administered in the palace-chapel. So sacred and solemn a ceremony ought to be performed in a consecrated place. In the present day the bishop's permission must be obtained for the administration of Baptism in a private house.

6. If baptism by water is impossible, it may be replaced by the baptism of desire, or by the baptism of blood, as in the case of those who suffer martyrdom for the faith of Christ.

The Emperor Valentinian II. was on the way to Milan to be baptized when he was assassinated; St. Ambrose said of him that his desire had been the means of his cleansing. The patriarchs, prophets, and holy men of the Old Testament had the baptism of desire; their love of God was ardent, and they wished to do all that He commands. God accepts the will for the deed; in this He manifests His superabundant loving kindness. But all the temporal penalties of sin are not remitted by the baptism of desire. Martyrdom for Christ's sake is the baptism of blood. This the holy innocents received, and the Church commemorates them as saints. All unbaptized persons who suffer martyrdom for the Christian faith, for some act of Christian virtue, or the fulfilment of a Christian duty, also received the baptism of blood. Witness St. John Baptist; or St. Emerentiana, who, while yet a catechumen, was found by the pagans praying at St. Agnes' tomb, and was put to death by them. The Church does not pray for the unbaptized who suffer death for Christ; for He Himself says: " He that shall lose his life for Me, shall find it " (Matt. x. 39).

7. In the early ages of the Church solemn Baptism was administered on three days of the year: Holy Saturday, the eve of Whitsunday, and in the East on the eve of the Epiphany.

Baptism used to be administered in the night preceding Easter and Whitsunday. It was administered at Easter, because it is a spiritual resurrection, and therefore appropriate to the season; at Pentecost, because on the first day of Pentecost three thousand persons were baptized, and because the Holy Spirit is given in Baptism; on the eve of the Epiphany because the Church commemorates the baptism of Our Lord in the Jordan on that day. Individuals were also baptized at other times, the sick, for instance, or converts who were thoroughly versed in Christian doctrine. The water to be used in Baptism is solemnly blessed on Holy Saturday and on the eve of Pentecost to this day; the ceremonial is elaborate and impressive; it is accompanied by prayers and chants, and many beautiful symbolical ceremonies, such as the mixing of the chrism, breathing upon the water, dipping the paschal candle into it, etc.

In the first ages of Christianity, religious instruction preceded Baptism; the candidates for Baptism were called catechumens.

Any one who desired to become a Christian had to present himself to the bishop, who questioned him closely, and if he thought him worthy admitted him into the number of the catechumens. He laid his hands upon him, as a sign that he was soon to receive the Holy Ghost; he made the sign of the cross upon his forehead and breast, to signify that he must believe the teaching of our crucified Lord, and shape his life thereby; finally he put salt on his lips, to denote preservation from the temptation of sin. The candidate was then a catechumen of the first class; for two years he was instructed in biblical history, the Ten Commandments, the precepts of charity, and allowed to be present at Mass until the creed. At the end of the second year, he became a catechumen of the second class: that is, he was obliged to fast in Lent, to hear sermons, to confess his sins in public and undergo various exorcisms, anointings and other symbolical ceremonies. In the last week before Baptism was administered, after Palm Sunday, that is, the candidates were taught the doctrine of the mystery of the Holy Trinity, the Apostles' Creed and the Lord's Prayer. All these ceremonies previous to Baptism have been retained until the present day.

Immediately before Baptism the candidate had to take a solemn vow to believe and follow the teachings of Christ. (The baptismal vow or covenant.)

Standing with his face towards the west, he renounced the devil and all his works (the worship of idols and the corrupt practices of the heathen), and the pomps and vanities of the world. Then turning towards the east, he promised to believe and follow the teaching of Christ. This promise is known as the baptismal vow; it is also called a covenant, because God at the same time promises the assistance of His grace to fulfil the promise made, and to reward those who keep it with eternal felicity after death. The baptismal vow resembles the military oath taken by the soldier, for at baptism we are enrolled under the banner of Christ, and promise to fight against the adversaries of God. The baptismal vow also resembles the marriage treaty concluded between those who are wedded at the altar, for the soul then promises fidelity and love to her celestial Bridegroom. It is well for those who have been baptized in their infancy to renew their vows at certain times after they have attained the age of reason, particularly before approaching the sacraments. St. John Chrysostom used to renew his vows in the hours of temptation, saying: "I renounce the devil and give myself wholly to Christ." In the time of persecution the early Christians were accustomed to solemnly renew their vow once a year, to strengthen themselves in the faith. One could wish that this was done now. Christians who have been unfaithful to their vows will, at the Last Judgment, hear from the lips of Our Lord the appalling words: "Thou wicked servant, out of thine own mouth will I condemn thee, by the promise thou didst once solemnly make to Me."

Formerly baptism was generally by immersion, but oftentimes water was sprinkled or poured upon the individual.

The priest and the godfather, or in the case of women, the godmother, led the person to be baptized by the hand down the steps, and plunged him three times under the water, while the priest pronounced the words prescribed by Our Lord. The threefold immersion was in honor of the most Holy Trinity; it was also in commemoration of the burial of Christ and His rising again, and was intended to signify that the old, sinful man was buried, and the new man had arisen (Rom. vi. 3, 11). In the later centuries baptism by immersion was abolished, and the custom of sprinkling almost exclusively adopted.

The name of a saint was given to every one at the baptismal font; this was his baptismal or Christian name.

The individual baptized was placed under the special protection of a saint or angel, who was to serve him as a model. Socrates of old used to advise parents to give the names of virtuous persons to their children in order to encourage them to imitate their example. Alexander the Great used to say to soldiers who had the same name as himself: " Either take another name, or see that thou dost credit to my name." The addition of the name of some saint was to indicate that the person baptized had been made a child of God, and incorporated into the company of the saints. On occasions when God bestowed particular favors on one of His servants, the name was sometimes altered; as Abram became Abraham, Simon was called Peter, Saul was changed to Paul. The Church does not approve of heathen or fantastical names being given to children. Priests cannot give such names in Baptism, though they enter them in the register. The name of a saint may often prove an incentive to him who bears it, to lead a Christian life.

When Baptism is administered with the usual ceremonies, which is called solemn Baptism, the person baptized must have a godfather or godmother, or one of each, but not more.

The obligation of a sponsor is to see that the person baptized keeps the faith and leads a Christian life. In appointing sponsors, the Church acts like a man who lends money; he requires securities. A child when born into the world, requires a nurse to bring it up; so one who is baptized needs some one to watch over his spiritual growth. The sponsors have also to provide for the Christian instruction of their godchild, if the parents neglect their duty in this respect, or are removed by death. Now that children receive regular religious teaching at school, the responsibilities of the sponsor are virtually almost nothing; still he should endeavor to influence his godchild for good, if necessary. A spiritual affinity is contracted between the sponsors and the person baptized and his natural parents, which the Church regards as an impediment to marriage. Hence the number of godparents is limited to two, to prevent difficulties arising. One sponsor is indispensably necessary. If a man, he must be at least fourteen years old; if a woman, twelve is the lowest age admissible; the sponsor, if there be but one, must be of the same sex as the person baptized, and a Catholic (non-Catholics can only be allowed as witnesses). The sponsor ought to have been confirmed, and be known to lead a good life; the parents of the child cannot possibly act as his sponsors, nor members of a religious Order, because they cannot, if necessary, replace the parents. At baptism the sponsor, holding the infant on his right arm, awaits at the entrance of the baptistry the coming of the priest, who asks the name the child is to receive, and interrogates him by name thus: " What dost thou ask of the Church of God?" The answer is: " Faith and life everlasting, which it obtains for me." The priest then performs the same ceremonies as were prescribed for the reception of a catechumen; afterwards he lays his stole upon the child (as a sign of his ecclesiastical powers), and admits both him and his sponsor into the church, when the Apostles' Creed and the Lord's Prayer are recited. Next the person to be baptized, or if he be an infant, his sponsor, takes the baptismal vows; to the three first questions addressed to him he replies: " I renounce them," and to the three last, " I believe." The baptism then takes place, and presently the priest dismisses the party with a valedictory benediction: " Go in peace and the Lord be with you."

The beautiful ceremonies following upon Baptism denote the dignity conferred upon the newly baptized, and the obligations resting upon him.

The priest anoints the person or child on the top of the head with chrism in the form of a cross, to remind him that he is now a Christian, an anointed one. This unction also recalls his royal dignity as a son of the King of heaven; it admonishes him to overcome the concupiscences of the flesh (Gen. iv. 7). Moreover oil, being a mild substance, reminds him to practice meekness, and exercise the works of mercy; it also signifies the illuminating and justifying grace of the Holy Spirit. In former times the newly-baptized used to put on a white robe which they wore in the church for a week, until Low Sunday, as a symbol of the robe of baptismal innocence, and of the wedding-garment of sanctifying grace, which they were to keep unspotted until death. On the present day a white cloth is laid upon the newly-baptized. A lighted candle is then given to the person baptized (or to the sponsor, if an infant). This is to denote the light of the Holy Spirit, which he has received, and recalls the words of Our Lord: " So let your light shine before men, that they may see your good works, and glorify your Father Who is in heaven " (Matt. v. 16). It also indicates that the portals of the city of eternal light are opened to him. All these ceremonies have a sanctifying influence, and consecrate him who receives them to be a fitting temple of the Holy Ghost.

Formerly the person baptized was confirmed immediately afterwards, and admitted to holy communion.

He was also fully instructed in the doctrine of holy Mass, the sacraments, and prayer, the so-called *disciplina arcani.* Previous to Baptism he would not have understood them, as he was without the enlightening presence of the Holy Ghost. See how great the esteem in which religious instruction was held!

2. CONFIRMATION.

Confirmation is so-called from its effect, which is to confirm and strengthen in the faith those who receive it; it is also spoken of as the laying on of hands (Acts viii. 17), from the nature of the ceremonies. Our Lord had given the Holy Spirit to His apostles before His ascension, yet they were timid and fearful, and did not lose this timidity until the Day of Pentecost, when the plenitude of the Spirit was poured out upon them. So we receive the Holy Ghost at our baptism, but not in all His fulness; this we receive at our Confirmation. On the Day of Pentecost the Holy Ghost came down upon the apostles under sensible signs, tongues as of fire and a mighty wind; so in Confirmation the visible sign is the imposition of hands, the audible sign the prayers repeated by the bishop. At Pentecost the apostles received the seven gifts of the Holy Spirit, pre-eminently the gift of fortitude, and the extraordinary gift of tongues; it is the same with us at Confirmation, only the gift of tongues is not now given. What the Day of Pentecost was to the apostles, Confirmation is to the Christian.

1. The ceremonial of Confirmation is as follows: The bishop lays his hands upon the candidates and anoints each one severally with chrism upon the forehead, with prayer; and those who are so anointed receive the gift of the Holy Ghost, especially courage to profess their faith.

The bishop extends his hands over the persons to be confirmed, while he invokes the Holy Spirit with His sevenfold gifts, to indicate that a supernatural power is communicated to them; he then goes to each one separately, and laying upon his head four fingers of his right hand, with the thumb of the same hand he makes the sign of the cross with chrism on the forehead of the person to be confirmed, giving him thereby to understand that he must never be ashamed to profess himself the disciple of a crucified Saviour, saying meanwhile: " I sign thee with the sign of the cross and I confirm thee with the chrism of salvation. In the name of the Father, and of the Son, and of the Holy Ghost, Amen." Then he gives him a slight blow upon the cheek, to teach him that he must be ready to suffer persecution for the faith, saying: " Peace be with thee." In conclusion the bishop gives to all his blessing. The chrism is composed of olive oil and balm of Gilead; it is solemnly blessed by the bishop in the cathedral church on Maundy Thursday.

The apostles administered Confirmation, as at Samaria and Ephesus.

The holy apostles Peter and John laid their hands on the Christians at Samaria, and they received the Holy Ghost (Acts viii. 11-17). St. Paul did the same at Ephesus. At that time when Confirmation was administered, it was generally accompanied by extraordinary gifts of the Holy Ghost, such as the gift of tongues and of prophecy (Acts xix. 6). At the laying on of hands the Holy Ghost was wont to manifest His coming by visible signs, so that the apostles needed not to make use of chrism. Originally oil alone was employed; not until the sixth century was balm mingled with it. The oldest writers and Fathers of the Church speak of the Sacrament of Confirmation. Pope Urban, in the third century, says: " All the faithful ought, after baptism, to receive the Holy Ghost by imposition of hands, in order that they may become perfect Christians." St. Augustine remarks that it must not be concluded, because the gift of tongues is no longer given, that the Holy Ghost is not communicated by imposition of hands. It was only given in early times for the more rapid propagation of the Gospel. The Council of Trent expressly declares Confirmation to be a true sacrament, not a mere rite, which formerly was appended to Baptism, nor a public profession of faith in presence of the faithful.

2. The supernatural effect of Confirmation is similar to the natural effect of oil.

It creates within us a spirit of meekness; it increases, that

is, our charity towards God and our neighbor, it enlightens
our understanding, strengthens our will, preserves our soul
from the corruption of sin, and fills us with the sweet odor of
virtue.

Oil softens what is hard, it adds vigor to the frame, it diffuses
an agreeable light. Balm is a preservative against putrefaction, and
emits a fragrant smell. Confirmation increases our charity towards
God and our neighbor, or, in other words, it increases sanctifying
grace, and imparts to us the fulness of the divine Spirit. Hence
Confirmation is the complement of Baptism; in Baptism we are made
the temples of the Holy Ghost, in Confirmation we receive Him in
all His plenitude of graces. In Baptism we are made soldiers of
Christ; at Confirmation our weapons are handed to us. Those who
have been confirmed enjoy a greater degree of glory in heaven than
the unconfirmed. This is why, in early times, Confirmation was administered to infants. The enlightenment of the mind consists in
giving man a sense of the worthlessness of the goods and pleasures of
this world, and inspiring him with an abhorrence of them. By Confirmation our thoughts and aspirations are directed towards heaven;
from earthly, man becomes heavenly, from sensual, spiritual; he becomes a perfect Christian. By Confirmation timidity is dispelled
and courage imparted. Before the Day of Pentecost the apostles were
faint-hearted as children; after that day they were bold as lions. The
Holy Spirit produces a like change in those who are confirmed: they
can say: " I can do all things in Him Who strengtheneth me " (Phil.
iv. 13). St. Vincent is of opinion that at the end of the world Antichrist will spare no effort to deter Christian people from receiving
the Sacrament of Confirmation, as in that case they would more readily apostatize from the faith. And since Confirmation confirms the
will, it makes it easier for those who have received it to resist temptation, and thus avoid sin. If such a one should fall into mortal sin,
he will incur a rigorous chastisement, like a soldier who deserts to
the enemy's camp. And the stronger the will, the less difficult does
the practice of virtue become. Confirmation tends especially to render us humble and meek, as the oil and balm denote: for balm sinks
into the liquid into which it is poured, symbolizing humility, and oil
always floats on the surface, teaching man to rise superior to the
vexations of life by unfailing meekness. Holy Scripture speaks of
virtue as a good odor (2 Cor. ii. 15), because those who are virtuous
are as pleasing to God as a sweet perfume is to us.

**3. Christians ought to be confirmed at the age when they pass
from childhood to youth, because at that period temptations
thicken around them, and they need strength of will to resist
them.**

It is not well to administer the Sacrament of Confirmation before
a child has attained the age of seven years, and the use of reason.
The most suitable age is about twelve; it should not be deferred
longer than the age of fourteen, but it is impossible to fix an exact
time, as in large dioceses the bishop can only visit the more remote
parishes at long intervals.

It is a grievous sin wilfully to omit to receive the Sacrament of Confirmation.

To do this is to act like a traveller who, having to pass along a dangerous road, refuses to accept the means of defence offered to him; what wonder if he have to pay a high price for his folly! Although Confirmation is not absolutely necessary to salvation, yet God punishes contempt of this sacrament severely. The Fathers of the Church ascribe all the misery of Novatus, who became a teacher of heresy and ended his days in wretchedness, to his having neglected to be confirmed. In early times parents who did not have their children confirmed had to do penance for three years. Let it be enough for us to know that it is Christ's will that all should be filled with the Spirit (John vii. 37).

4. The candidate for Confirmation ought previously to go to confession and, if possible, to holy communion; for to receive this sacrament one must be in a state of grace.

For any one in mortal sin to receive Confirmation is as if a precious and delicate substance were poured into an unclean vessel. It it not obligatory on one who is unquestionably in a state of grace to go to confession before Confirmation. In the early ages of the Church it was the custom to confirm very young children, as is now done in Greece and in Spain. In many dioceses children are confirmed before they make their first communion, provided they are eight years old and have been to confession, in order that they may not lack the graces Confirmation imparts at the time when they most need them. St. Charles Borromeo established this rule throughout his diocese.

The candidate for Confirmation must be well instructed in the doctrines of the faith, and prepare himself to receive the Holy Ghost by retirement and prayer.

He should in this respect imitate the apostles, who spent the ten days before Pentecost in persevering prayer (Acts i. 14). On this account several Synods decreed that candidates for Confirmation should be placed under instruction for a week previously; that each day in that week they should repeat seven Our Fathers and seven Hail Marys in honor of the Holy Ghost, and that they should keep the eve of their Confirmation day as a fast. Every one must be provided by his parish priest with a certificate, to certify that he is properly prepared for the reception of this sacrament. Without this the bishop will not confirm him.

5. Confirmation is usually administered about Whitsuntide, as the bishop visits the whole of his diocese at intervals of a few years.

In the first centuries of the Church Confirmation was, as a rule, administered at Easter and Pentecost, because it followed immediately upon Baptism. St. Jerome relates that in his time (about the commencement of the fifth century), the bishops used to take long journeys for the purpose of confirming those who had been baptized by a priest or a deacon. An ordinary priest cannot administer Confirmation unless he be expressly authorized and empowered to do so by the authority of the Pope; they are thus empowered in missionary dioceses, which are of too great extent for the bishop to traverse, and where the converts would be in danger of relapsing into paganism unless they were confirmed in the faith as soon as possible. As in erecting a building the whole of the work is done by the workmen, the finishing touch alone being put by the architect, so in the spiritual fabric it devolves upon the bishop to administer Confirmation, whereby the top-stone is put to the edifice (St. Thomas Aquinas). This sacrament appears more imposing when administered by the bishop in person.

The person confirmed receives the name of some saint at his Confirmation.

When Confirmation followed immediately upon Baptism, no other name was added to that given in baptism. But when in after years, the convert got into the habit of retaining his heathen name after Baptism, he was made to take the name of some saint at his Confirmation, on whom he was to look as his model in the spiritual warfare, as a soldier looks to his general. And he whom he chose for his pattern on earth he was to invoke as his intercessor in heaven. Besides this heavenly guide, the Christian has at Confirmation an earthly guide.

The person to be confirmed must also have a godfather or godmother.

The gladiator who is about to enter the arena requires some one to instruct him in swordsmanship and assist him with his counsel; so it is at Confirmation. In all the difficulties of life the godparent ought to be ready to support and help his godchild; he ought to do his utmost to induce him to keep within the paths of virtue; and the godchild ought to feel that he must not rely too much on his own powers, but must seek counsel from others. A spiritual relationship exists between the two, which constitutes an ecclesiastical hindrance to marriage. The sponsor chosen ought to be one who has himself been confirmed, a person of blameless life, older than the one to be confirmed, and of the same sex; not, if it can be avoided, the same who stood sponsor for him at the baptismal font.

Those who present themselves to the bishop to be confirmed must be simply and suitably dressed.

The Holy Spirit does not take up His abode in the heart that is enslaved by the pride of life. God resisteth the proud (1 Pet. v. 5). Some, on going to be confirmed, think more of their dress than of the sacrament they are about to receive. It is no longer required of the candidates for Confirmation that they should be fasting, in fact, this would not be possible now, as the ceremony often lasts a long time. They should be dressed simply, their forehead being uncovered; each one should have a prayer-book, and the necessary certificate. Adults kneel, children either stand or kneel, to receive the sacrament; behind each one stands the sponsor, his right hand on the right shoulder of his godchild. All must be present in the church before the bishop extends his hands over all in general, after that the door is closed and no one else admitted. Nor must any one depart before the bishop gives the final blessing, although it does not constitute an integral part of the sacrament. After receiving Confirmation, one must be careful not to drive away the Holy Spirit by feasting and diversions. " Grieve not the Holy Spirit of God " (Eph. iv. 30). The chief reason why the faith of Christians is so cold in the present day is because so little is now thought of the Sacrament of Confirmation.

3. THE HOLY EUCHARIST.

Institution and Nature of the Holy Eucharist.

Our Lord promised the Jews at Capharnaum that He would give them His flesh to eat and His blood to drink (John vi.).

After the miraculous multiplication of the loaves and fishes the people went in search of Christ, and found Him in the synagogue at Capharnaum. They wanted Him to give them bread again; but He promised to give them the bread of immortality. When they asked Him for it, He answered: " The bread that I will give is My flesh." And when they refused to believe His words, He added: " Except you eat the flesh of the Son of man, and drink His blood, you shall not have life in you. He that eateth My flesh and drinketh My blood, hath everlasting life, and I will raise him up at the Last Day. For My flesh is meat indeed, and My blood is drink indeed " (John vi. 52-56).

Our Lord fulfilled this promise at the Last Supper; He changed the bread into His body, and the wine into His blood and gave it to the apostles (Matt. xxvi. 28).

The apostles did not, however, see the body of Christ under the appearance of flesh, for the accidents of the bread remained, i.e., its color, taste, smell, weight. Nor did they see His blood otherwise than as wine, because the accidents of the wine were retained; the substance only was changed. So the shell of an egg remains the same while what is contained within it is changed into a living bird.

1. The body of Christ under the appearance of bread, and the blood of Christ under the appearance of wine, is called the Most Holy Sacrament of the Altar.

Here again we find the three essentials of a sacrament. The visible sign is the form of bread and of wine, the audible sign is the words of Christ; the invisible grace is the reception of the body and blood of Christ; the institution of this sacrament took place at the Last Supper. The visible form portrays the invisible grace: the bread prepared with water and the flour of wheat, and baked with fire, represents the body of Christ which was subjected to cruel suffering; the wine, the juice pressed from the grape, represents the blood of Christ, which flowed from the wounds of His sacred body.

The bread is unleavened, to denote the purity of Christ's body; it is round in shape, because it conceals Him Who is without beginning and without end (Heb. vii. 3). Water is mixed with the wine, to signify the intimate union of the Godhead and manhood in His person. Bread and wine being the principal means of nourishment for the body, signify that the body and blood of Christ are the chief sustenance of the soul. This Sacrament is called the Most Holy Sacrament of the Altar, because the change of substance takes place upon the altar; it is called the Blessed Sacrament, because in it not only are the graces of the Sacrament received, but the Author and Giver of all grace; and it is besides the most exalted and sublime of all the sacraments. It is called the Bread of heaven, the Bread of angels, because Our Lord comes down from heaven to be our food, a food which makes men like to angels.

We speak of this Sacrament as the *Sacrament of the Altar,* because the priest, standing at the altar, does the same by Christ's command which He Himself did at the Last Supper.

Our Lord commanded the apostles: "Do this for a commemoration of Me" (Luke xxii. 19). On this account the priest pronounces exactly the same words over the bread and wine which Our Lord uttered at the Last Supper, thereby changing the bread into the body, and the wine into the blood of Christ.

The Most Holy Sacrament of the Altar is reserved in the tabernacle in every parish church.

The tabernacle, which stands in the middle of the high altar, is made of wood, marble or brass, gilt inside, and lined with white silk curtains. In earlier times it was situated beside, not above the altar. The name of tabernacle, or tent, is given to it, from the sacred tent of the Israelites; and the mysterious cloud that accompanied them on their journey, was a type of the tabernacle of God in which He dwells with men (Apoc. xxi. 3). A lamp is kept burning continually in the sanctuary before the tabernacle, to indicate the place where the Blessed Sacrament is reserved, and also to symbolize the Light of the world. It is, besides, emblematic of the perpetual adoration the angels pay to the God present upon the altar. In the Temple at Jerusalem there was a candlestick with seven branches in which lights burned continually. Our divine Lord is thus ever present with mortal men; as He Himself declares: "I am with you all days, even to the consummation of the world" (Matt. xxviii. 20). He is as truly present with us as with the saints in heaven; the only difference is that they behold Him face to face, whereas He is hidden from our sight beneath the eucharistic veils. The manna preserved in the ark was a type of the hidden God present in our tabernacles (Exod. xvi. 33).

2. The presence of the body and blood of Christ under the appearance of bread and wine is a mystery, because our feeble reason cannot comprehend it.

Our Lord conceals Himself under the appearance of bread and wine in order to test our faith, whether we believe His words rather than the testimony of our senses. If we saw what we believe. faith would have no merit. Moreover, if we were to behold Our Lord in all the majesty of His glorified body, radiant with light, we should be struck with alarm, and dazzled, as those are dazzled who look with the naked eye on the noonday sun. Even the apostles could not bear the unveiled brilliance of the glorified body at Our Lord's transfiguration, for they fell to the ground upon their faces. And Moses covered his face, when God appeared to him in the burning bush. We cannot trust our senses even in natural things, for they often deceive us. For instance, an oar half in the water looks as if it were broken; objects seen from a distance appear quite small. Faith teaches us to believe that as the food we eat is assimilated to our body, as the moisture of the earth is changed into the sap of the vine and the juice of the grape, even so, and far more, by the power of His word, can Christ change bread into the substance of His body, and wine into His blood. He, Who by His almighty power can create things out of nothing, can surely effect a change in what already exists. He Who can cause the earth to bring forth bread, can change that bread into His own body. Many different heretics have contested the truth of this doctrine of the real presence of Christ in the Sacrament of the Altar, and endeavored to attach a different meaning to Our Lord's words: " This is My body." But in the course of centuries almighty God has worked many striking miracles in confirmation of the truth. Consecrated Hosts have remained unconsumed in the midst of fire; they have remained suspended in the air without support; the place where they were concealed has been disclosed by a bright light hovering around it; blood has flowed from the sacred Host during Mass; Our Lord has appeared in it in the form of an infant, etc.

It has been the firm belief of Christians in all ages that the bread and wine are converted into the body and blood of Christ.

St. Augustine says: " Our Lord held Himself in His own hands, when He gave His body to the disciples." St. Cyril: " If Christ changed water into wine on one occasion, He can also change wine into His blood." And when He asserts that it is His body, who shall dare to gainsay it? It was a calumny commonly brought against Christians by the heathen that they killed and ate the flesh of a child at their ceremonies.

3. It is most true that under the species of bread, as also under the species of wine, Christ is present, God and man, whole and entire.

Where the body and blood of Christ are, there He must be present, not in part, but in His whole person; for now He hath risen from the dead to die no more, and consequently the body can no more be separated from the blood than the body and blood can be separated from the soul of Christ. Our Lord's words: " This is My body which is given for you," and: " This is My blood, which shall be shed for many," demonstrate that it is His living body, His living blood, that are present under the appearance of bread and wine, and therefore the living, not the dead Christ Who is present upon the altar. As a whole landscape may be seen in the pupil of the eye, so Christ is contained whole and entire in the sacred Host.

4. Our Lord is present in every particle, however minute, of the consecrated bread and wine.

We have seen that Christ is present in every Host, and when the priest breaks the Host, He is equally present in every fragment of it. If a magnet be broken in pieces, each part forms a separate magnet with the property of pointing to the north. And if a mirror is broken, in each portion one's face is reflected. But the body of Christ is not multiplied; His body is but one, animated and pervaded by His divinity, which fills all space. It is not increased by each fresh consecration, nor diminished by the numbers who receive it. As the light of a candle is not lessened, however many other candles are lighted at its flame, so Our Lord's body suffers no diminution when it is given to thousands of communicants. Thus St. Andrew said to the proconsul at Achaia: "I daily offer upon the altar to the almighty and true God the immaculate Lamb of God. And when all the faithful have received His sacred body, the Victim that was slain is yet alive and unconsumed."

5. Christ is present in the consecrated elements as long as the accidents of bread and wine remain.

Our Lord is not only present in the Sacrament of the Altar at the moment of communion, but both before and after the Host is consumed. Had this been otherwise, He would not have said: "Take and eat this, for this is My body." And He is present in those who receive the sacred Host as long as the accidents of bread remain unconsumed. Thus after communion we bear in our body the body of Christ.

6. The duties of the Christian in regard to the Holy Sacrament of the Altar are these: He ought to visit it frequently, to adore it, and to receive it.

We ought to visit the Blessed Sacrament frequently. In this respect the shepherds and the three kings, who came to worship the Infant Saviour in the manger, set us an excellent example. The saints spent many hours in prayer before the Blessed Sacrament. Cardinal Bellarmine, when a student, was accustomed whenever he passed by a church to go in and say an Our Father. When asked why he did this, he replied: "It would be ill manners to go by a friend's house without a word of greeting." He was distinguished while yet a youth for his great wisdom. Access to Our Lord is not denied us; the church door stands open, and from the tabernacle the voice of Our Lord calls to us: "Come unto Me, all you that labor and are burdened, and I will refresh you" (Matt. xi. 28). St. Teresa declares that Our Lord in the Adorable Sacrament of the Altar affords us far more satisfaction than can be derived from the whole world, with its festivities and pleasures. In His presence the sorrowful are comforted, the foolish learn wisdom, the feeble are strengthened, and the poor are enriched. Wheresoever the body shall be, there shall the eagles also be gathered together; and in like manner the faithful should hasten to the Blessed Sacrament, the food of the soul. The saints loved to drink of this river of paradise, as the hart pants to quench his thirst at the fountains of water. Unwise indeed are they who in the hour of need, choose rather to seek human aid, to pour their troubles into a human ear; they do not betake themselves to the church, to Christ, Who is so willing, so able to help them.

The Church admonishes us to pay homage to the Holy Sacrament of the Altar by the sanctuary lamp; by the bell rung at Mass and when the Viaticum is carried to the sick, by the processions of Corpus Christi, and by frequent Expositions of the Blessed Sacrament.

It is customary on entering or leaving a church to genuflect before the Blessed Sacrament; to kneel down reverently at the consecration, and when benediction is given with the Blessed Sacrament. In former times people used to kneel whenever they met a priest carrying the sacred Host to the sick; it is related of Rudolph of Hapsburg that once when he was out hunting, he met a priest going to give communion to a dying man; immediately he dismounted, and kneeling by the roadside, gave his horse to the priest; nor would he allow the animal to be again used except in the service of the Church. Before receiving holy communion, we ought to make an act of adoration of the Blessed Sacrament. Unhappily many among us possess no living faith; they pass by the Most Holy Sacrament of the Altar with cold indifference. The procession of Corpus Christi was instituted by Pope Urban IV. in 1264, with a view to increase our faith in the presence of Christ in the Blessed Sacrament, and the Exposition of the Forty Hours has the same object. The Confraternity of the Perpetual Adoration is intended to keep up the worship of the Blessed Sacrament uninterruptedly; each member has to spend at least one hour every month in adoration before the altar. This Sacrament was instituted by Our Lord immediately before His death in order to give it greater importance in our eyes, as we treasure more the last gift of a dying friend. If the Jews were not permitted to behold, much less to touch, the Ark of the Covenant, which was a type of the Adorable Sacrament of the Altar, what dread ought we not to feel in presence of the reality!

Christ invites us to receive the Most Holy Sacrament of the Altar when He says: " Except you eat the flesh of the Son of Man and drink His blood, you shall not have life in you " (John vi. 54).

The reception of this Sacrament is known as communion, that is, union with Christ. In communion we receive Our Lord, as Zacheus did, into our house. In the Scriptures there are many types of the Holy Eucharist; for instance, the tree of life in the midst of paradise, which gave immortality to our first parents; the manna; the paschal lamb; the bread that gave Elias strength to go the forty days' journey to Mount Horeb; the miraculous multiplication of the loaves; the water made wine at the marriage of Cana. And holy communion is itself an earnest of the spiritual food wherewith we shall be nourished in heaven.

The faithful receive the Holy Eucharist under the form of

bread only; the priest alone, at Mass, receives it under both kinds.

The priest at the altar offers an oblation, the very same as the one Christ offered on Calvary. On the cross Christ shed almost all His blood, so that His body and blood were separated one from the other. The two several species of bread and wine in the Mass signify this separation of Our Lord's body and blood. The faithful, on the other hand, do not sacrifice the Victim, but receive the Sacrament; it is unnecessary for them to receive the chalice, as Our Lord is contained wholly under either species. He Himself says: "He that eateth this bread shall live forever" (John vi. 59). There are many reasons for withholding the chalice from the laity; the precious blood might easily be spilled in passing from one to another; there is the difficulty of procuring wine in some places; the difficulty of reserving it and bearing it to the sick; and some people cannot bear the taste of wine. Communion in both kinds was, it is true, enjoined on the laity by the Holy See in the fifth century, but this was only done to combat the error of the Manichees, who declared wine to be an invention of the devil and wholly to be avoided. And in 1433 the chalice was for a time given to the laity, to induce the followers of Huss to return to the unity of the Church.

The Necessity of Holy Communion.

1. The Holy Sacrament of the Altar is the nourishment of our souls.

Consequently the reception of this Sacrament is an indispensable means whereby to attain spiritual perfection or sanctity here, and eternal life hereafter.

The Holy Eucharist is the nourishment of our souls; on it our spiritual life is dependent. Our Lord says: "He that eateth Me, the same also shall live by Me;" and again: "Except you eat the flesh of the Son of man and drink His blood, you shall not have life in you" (John vi. 58, 54). Holy communion is therefore essential to our progress in sanctity, and to the final attainment of eternal life. As the bodily health cannot be maintained without nourishing food, so spiritual health cannot be acquired and preserved without holy communion. St. Francis of Sales tells us that there are two classes of men who need holy communion: the perfect, that they may not decline in perfection, and the imperfect, that they may become perfect; the strong, that they may maintain their strength, and the weak, that they may acquire strength. The early Christians communicated daily, and this it was that gave them constancy, and fortitude to suffer martyrdom. As a rule the saints communicated frequently. Yet it must not be supposed that frequent communion is in any way a mark of sanctity, or the reward of sanctity; it is only a means of acquiring it.

Therefore those who rarely receive holy communion will not make rapid progress in perfection.

The consciousness that even after confession we are unworthy to receive Our Lord, ought not to deter us from going to communion. The Church puts the words of the heathen centurion upon the lips of the intending communicant. No mortal can ever be worthy to receive a God. Yet it must be remembered that Christ did not institute the Holy Sacrament of the Altar for angels, but for men. Those who are conscious of their own misery, and desire to remedy it, will feel the need of frequent communion. Our daily failings ought not to hold us back; on the contrary, they ought to incite us to approach the holy table, that we may be delivered from them. For holy communion purifies the soul from venial sin, and weakens the force of evil concupiscence. Nor ought the absence of sweetness and consolation deter us from communicating; "how unwise would be the man," says St. Ignatius, "who refused to eat his bread, and chose to die of hunger, because it was not spread with honey." Again, who would wait until he was warm before going to the fire? "He who censures the practice of frequent communion," says Ségur, "does the devil's work." The saints have always advocated frequent communion, and it has been urged on the faithful repeatedly by the Holy See.

Those who wilfully neglect holy communion for a lengthened period, incur the risk of spiritual death here and eternal damnation hereafter.

The soul cannot live without food any more than the body. Yet as certain saints have existed without taking any corporal sustenance, so others have lived for years without holy communion. St. Mary of Egypt, for instance, who spent forty years in the desert; and several anchorites, such as St. Paul and St. Anthony. The Holy Spirit, who led them into the wilderness, replaced all that holy communion could have been to them. Yet most, if not all, were communicated before their death. Every one, however, if he be prevented from receiving communion, is bound to make a spiritual communion; that is, he must desire to communicate, and must do so actually, whenever opportunity offers.

2. We are bound under pain of mortal sin to communicate at least once a year, and that at Easter; also in case of dangerous illness. It is, moreover, the wish of the Church that the faithful should, if possible, receive holy communion on Sundays and holydays.

In the first ages of Christianity the Christians communicated daily. About the middle of the third century it became necessary to enjoin upon the faithful to communicate three times a year, at the three great festivals. In the Middle Ages people grew careless, some absented themselves from the holy table for years; consequently in the Lateran Council (1215) the Church decreed that every Catholic who had come to the age of reason, should receive holy communion at least once in the year, and that at Easter; those who failed to obey this precept were to be deprived of Christian burial. Children are to be admitted to holy communion as soon as they can distinguish the heavenly food from the earthly, and it can confidently be assumed that they will receive this Holy Sacrament with due reverence and devotion. It is not well to postpone the first communion until children have reached the age of fourteen years, as it is most important that it should take place while their innocence is still unstained. In the Middle Ages children were allowed to make their first communion when they were seven years old. The Christian is also bound to receive holy communion if he be in danger of death. Hence the communion given to the sick is called the Viaticum, the sustenance of the traveller on his last journey. The sacred Host must not be administered to any one who cannot swallow, or who is subject to vomiting. If the illness is of prolonged duration, the sick man may receive communion two or three times during its course, if he desire to do so. Holy communion may also be given to children who are in danger of death, provided they have attained the use of reason (seven years of age), although they have not previously approached the sacraments. The priest must briefly instruct them in the chief truths of the faith, and the sacraments they are about to receive. Furthermore, it is the desire of the Church that the faithful should, in as far as is possible, communicate on all Sundays and holydays. The Council of Trent would fain indeed that at each Mass the faithful who are present should communicate, not only in spiritual desire, but also by sacramental participation of the Eucharist, that thereby a more abundant fruit might be derived to them from this holy sacrifice (Council of Trent, 22, 6). Now it is of obligation that every Catholic should hear Mass on all Sundays and holydays, hence it may be inferred that they should receive holy communion on all those days at the least. Many Fathers and Doctors of the Church urge frequent communion on the faithful. "We give our bodies nourishment several times a day," says St. Charles Borromeo, "and shall our souls receive nourishment only once a year?" It is the duty of those who have the cure of souls to exhort the faithful to the practice of frequent, if not daily communion, as the soul, like the body, will languish without nourishment.

The confessor must not, however, recommend frequent communion to all indiscriminately; he must have due regard to the spiritual state and the manner of life of each individual.

St. Alphonsus says that there are but few who may not be admitted to communion once a month. Weekly communion must only be permitted to those who keep themselves free from mortal sin, and give no scandal in their daily life; who, that is to say, have not the character of being tattlers, slanderers, quarrelsome, etc. Weekly communion is sometimes almost a necessity for persons who are constantly tempted to mortal sin, for by it they obtain the power to resist. Daily communion must only be granted to those who are earnestly striving after perfection, who courageously resist venial sin, and who ardently desire holy communion. Such persons should seek to lead a blameless life; they must have sufficient time at their command to make their preparation and their thanksgiving with due deliberation, and they must have intelligence of divine things. The daily communicant is not obliged to go to confession every day, for holy communion cleanses from venial sin; it is only obligatory upon him to go to confession previously if he is conscious to himself of mortal sin (Council of Trent, 13, 7), but as a rule he is expected to avoid all such sins. For one who leads a worldly life, or who is not bent upon overcoming his faults, such as irascibility, vanity, love of gossip, etc., frequent communion would be exceedingly hurtful; for holy communion is like a fire, which, if it does not purify, consumes everything in its flame.

The priest must not administer holy communion to persons who are not able to distinguish this supersubstantial bread from ordinary food, or of whom it may be surmised that they will receive it without reverence and devotion.

Thus children who have not attained the use of reason are not admitted to holy communion. If exceptions to this rule have been made in former days, it was because of the exigencies of the times. Children must also be thoroughly instructed in faith and morals before making their first communion. Idiots and lunatics are incapable of communicating; the latter may, however, have lucid intervals, or recover their reason at the approach of death.

The Effects of Holy Communion.

Holy communion is of great benefit both for the soul and the body. " The divine King," says St. Alphonsus, " is accustomed to reward royally all those who entertain Him well."

Holy communion acts spiritually, as bread and wine act materially.

Bread and wine, i.e., material food, (1), Assimilates itself to the body; (2), Maintains life, promotes growth; (3), Dispels fatigue and weakness and imparts strength to the body; (4), Affords a certain satisfaction by pleasing the palate; (5), And influences the mind by the medium of the body. In a similar way the action of holy communion upon the soul may be described.

1. By holy communion we are united most closely to Christ. Our Lord says: " He that eateth My flesh and drinketh My blood, abideth in Me, and I in him " (John vi. 57).

Holy communion is, as it were, a continuation of the Incarnation. By His Incarnation Our Lord united Himself to mankind in general, by holy communion He unites Himself to each individual member of the human race. As two pieces of wax when melted are amalgamated with each other, so completely does Our Lord make Himself one with us in holy communion. He is in us and we are in Him. St. Augustine says that those who receive Our Lord frequently assume His nature, are, as it were, transformed into Him. By communion Christ changes our nature into His own, as leaven changes a quantity of flour. There is this difference between the spiritual food we receive in communion and the ordinary food of the body; the latter is less powerful than our nature, and is assimilated by it; the former is more powerful than our nature, and consequently it converts that nature

into its own. Our nature is ennobled by communion, as a wild tree
is ennobled by being grafted with a cultivated tree. Holy communion
also unites us to one another; all Catholics by means of it are made
one body, as St. Paul says: "For we, being many, are one bread, one
body, all that partake of one bread" (1 Cor. x. 17). The Fathers
speak of communion as the general union of all the faithful in
Christ and with one another (*communis, unio*). Hence it is called
"the sign of unity, the bond of charity, the symbol of concord"
(Council cf Trent, 13, 8).

**2. Holy communion imparts actual graces, and also maintains
and increases sanctifying grace in the soul.**

At each communion fresh actual graces are obtained, that enlighten the understanding and strengthen the will. Holy communion
acts like the rising sun, dispelling darkness and bringing light. It
imparts strength as did the bread of which Elias partook (3 Kings
xix.); and power to withstand temptation and to practice virtue.
Holy communion gives to the timid the courage of lions; St. John
Chrysostom says that the devils tremble when they see lips reddened
with the blood of the Lord. Those who have great trials and sufferings to endure ought to communicate often to acquire strength. It
was because the early Christians were so cruelly persecuted that they
used to fortify themselves so often by receiving holy communion;
thence they gained courage to confront martyrdom. Whenever they
knew that some danger had to be encountered, they approached the
Holy Sacrament of the Altar, for they were conscious that otherwise
their force would fail them. Those also who are exposed to violent
temptations ought to communicate often, for holy communion has
even more power than had the blood of the paschal lamb sprinkled
on the doorposts, to deliver from the destroyer. Holy communion
preserves the life of the soul, as bread and wine do that of the body;
for it maintains within us sanctifying grace, which gives vitality to
the soul. Hence Our Lord says: "He that eateth Me, the same also
shall live by Me;" and again: "If any man eat of this bread, he shall
not die" (John vi. 50, 58), that is to say, he will not fall into mortal
sin, and thus destroy the life of the soul. Holy communion is also
the means of keeping us from relapse into mortal sin; it is an antidote
against the poison of sin (Council of Trent, 13, 2). Those who communicate frequently persevere in grace; for where God is often present, the enemy of God can find no permanent abode. Holy communion also increases sanctifying grace in the soul; and since the
degree of felicity we shall enjoy hereafter is dependent on the measure
of sanctifying grace we possess here, it follows that holy communion
conduces to the augmentation of our eternal happiness.

**3. The force of evil concupiscence is lessened by holy com-
munion, and we are freed from venial sin by means of it.**

Physicians order nourishing food for those who are infirm, that
they may gain strength. There is an aliment cf surpassing excellence
well calculated to remove spiritual infirmities and impart vigor to
the soul. He who communicates frequently will feel less sharply the
stimulus of anger, envy, uncleanness, and other evil propensities.
Holy communion quenches the flame of concupiscence; it is the corn

of the elect and the wine springing forth virgins (Zach. ix. 17). It cleanses us from venial, but not from mortal sin; like fire which consumes wood and straw, but does not burn stone or iron. It is the food and the medicine of the soul; now food and medicine are beneficial to the sick, but in no wise to the dead. Therefore if after confession we commit some venial sin, it is not necessary to go to confession again before approaching holy communion.

4. Holy communion often affords much refreshment to the soul.

The manna is said to have had a pleasant taste, like honey. In holy communion, St. Thomas Aquinas says we taste sweetness at its true source. In the prayer said before benediction is given with the Blessed Sacrament, it is declared to contain within itself all sweetness (Wisd. xvi. 20). The greater the worthiness of the communicant the greater is the sweetness he experiences in holy communion; but sometimes God withdraws all consolation, even from the saints.

5. Holy communion sanctifies the body, and implants in it the germ of a future glorious resurrection.

The temporal penalties of sin are cancelled by holy communion according to the measure of our devotion. If those who did but touch the hem of Our Lord's garment were cured of whatever infirmities they labored under, how much the more shall we be healed of our spiritual sickness, who have the privilege of receiving Christ into our breast? St. Louis Bertrand used to advise the sick to receive holy communion as a means of recovering bodily health. Our Lord says: "He that eateth My flesh and drinketh My blood, hath eternal life, and I will raise him up at the Last Day" (John vi. 55). The body of Christ is the seed of immortality for our flesh. Communion represents to us the tree of life, which stood in the midst of Eden.

The graces above named are the portion of those who receive holy communion frequently, and prepare themselves carefully for it.

The best means of learning to receive Our Lord well is to receive Him often, for in everything it is practice that makes perfect.

Preparation for Holy Communion.

1. We must make a suitable preparation of body and soul before receiving holy communion.

We must endeavor, before approaching holy communion, to render ourselves as much like Our Lord as possible; for unless we resemble Him spiritually no union between Him and us will be practicable. Liquids cannot mingle one with another, without they are of the same nature; thus wine and water can be mixed, but not water and oil. The better our preparation for holy communion, the more plentiful the graces we receive from it. Those who make a bad preparation for communion, or none at all, draw down on themselves the divine anger. Such persons lose all reverence for the Holy Sacrament of the Altar; in fact their faith in the presence of Our

Lord under the eucharistic veils dies out altogether. He who approaches holy communion merely from force of habit, cannot expect to receive anything from God.

2. The manner in which we should prepare our soul is this: We must cleanse our souls from mortal sin by confession, perform good works, and adorn ourselves with the virtues.

When a monarch visits a town it is previously cleansed and decorated. We should do the same when the King of kings comes to us; we should purify our conscience by confession and adorn our soul by good works. St. Paul says: " Let a man prove himself, and so let him eat of that bread and drink of that chalice " (1 Cor. xi. 28). We must examine our conscience before approaching holy communion, and that not merely in regard to greater transgressions, but also minor offences. The apostles laid their garments upon the ass, before they made Our Lord sit thereon; so we should deck ourselves with virtues when we prepare to receive Him in communion. Some people think more of communicating upon certain festivals, than of purifying their hearts by confession, although this is of far greater importance. Wherefore it is not he who communicates often, or he who communicates seldom, who should be esteemed, but he who communicates with a clean heart.

To receive holy communion when one is conscious of having committed a mortal sin, is to incur the guilt of sacrilege.

He who receives holy communion in a state of mortal sin profanes the Holy Sacrament; he is guilty of the body and blood of the Lord (1 Cor. xi. 27), that is, his sin is the same as if he had put Our Lord to death. The unworthy communicant acts like the Philistines, who took possession of the ark and placed it close to the image of their god Dagon, for he introduces Christ where Satan is. Holy communion is like the light, which is salutary to good eyes, but hurtful to those that are diseased; so the Lord's body is a medicine, giving spiritual health to the pure of heart, but spiritual death to the unclean and evil. Holy communion is like the pillar of the cloud, enlightening the Israelites but enveloping the Egyptians in darkness (Exod. xiv. 20). Wherefore if any man call to mind a mortal sin before he communicates, let him go to confession at once, if by any means he can do so. If it be impossible, he may communicate, but he must confess the sin in question the next time he goes to confession; for as it was not wilfully omitted, it was remitted with the rest by the sacerdotal absolution.

The consequences of a sacrilegious communion are very terrible; it produces spiritual blindness, obduracy of heart, and brings upon the sinner chastisements both temporal and eternal.

Satan enters into the unworthy communicant, as he did into Judas after his sacrilegious communion (John xiii. 27). If the possession of the ark brought such grievous afflictions upon the Philistines; if the profanation of the sacred vessels by Baltassar was so bitterly expiated (Dan. v.), what must be the punishment of those who lay violent hands on the body of the Lord? The Apostle tells us that infirmities and death are no unusual chastisements of unworthy communicants (1 Cor. xi. 30). Remember the awful fate of Judas. Terror, despair, hatred of God, the torments the lost suffer in hell, begin on earth for the unworthy communicant. He who comes to the marriage feast (holy communion) without a wedding garment (sanctifying grace), shall be cast into exterior darkness (Matt. xxii). St. Paul warns the Christians of communicating unworthily when he says: " He that eateth and drinketh unworthily eateth and drinketh judgment to himself, not discerning the Lord's body " (1 Cor. xi. 29).

All that is absolutely required for the worthy reception of holy communion is to be in a state of grace; but it is greatly to be desired that all unruly attachment to earthly things should be completely given up before approaching the Holy Sacrament of the Altar.

" If you are in a state of grace," says St. John Chrysostom, " why do you not go to communion, which was instituted with the object of enabling you to continue in that state? " The more we are detached from earthly things the greater will be our charity, and the greater our charity the more abundant will be the graces we receive in communion. Thus the avaricious, the ambitious, the intemperate, all who indulge their evil tendencies, will derive little benefit from holy communion. A pure heart is the only fit dwelling for the God of purity.

Prayer, acts of self-denial, the works of mercy, are the good works which we ought to practise before going to communion.

At least half an hour ought to be spent in prayer before holy communion. It is advisable to hear Mass first. On the previous day we should be specially abstemious at table, deny ourselves worldly pleasures and amusements, avoid idle conversation, etc. It is well also to perform some works of mercy. " If thou givest earthly food to Christ (in the person of His poor)," says St. Augustine, " He will in return give thee celestial food."

Those who receive holy communion ought to possess these virtues in particular: Faith, hope, charity, humility, and meekness.

It is usual before communion to make acts of the three theological virtues and also of contrition. The Church herself seeks to awaken these sentiments in the heart of the communicant; for after the *Confiteor* has been said by the sinner, the priest implores the pardon of God, and when elevating the sacred Host he repeats the words of St. John Baptist: " Behold the Lamb of God, etc.," as well as those of the centurion: " Lord, I am not worthy, etc." Children generally are made to renew their baptismal vows before making their first communion. Before communicating we ought to make an act of faith, for Our Lord always required a lively faith in those on whom He bestowed graces and for whose sake He worked miracles. Thus we read that He said to the blind men: " Do you believe that I can do this unto you? " and until they answered in the affirmative He did not heal them. We ought also to make an act of hope before communicating. When Our Lord was on earth He never sent any one away empty who came to Him in trustful confidence. The woman who had been afflicted for twelve years was made whole immediately upon touching the hem of His garment in faith (Matt. ix. 20). We ought also to make an act of charity before communicating; for the greater our love to God, the greater is His generosity towards us. He must be received with love Who out of love gives Himself to us. "Love Him," says St. Augustine, "Who for love of thee comes to unite thy mortality to His immortality." We ought also to humble ourselves before God before communicating, considering His majesty and our misery, and deploring our sinfulness, for God resisteth the proud, but to the humble He gives grace (1 Pet. v. 5). Meekness is also necessary in those who communicate, for without it we cannot be pleasing to the Lamb of God.

3. Our body must be prepared for holy communion by fasting from midnight; by dressing in a neat and suitable manner, and by a reverent deportment at the time of communion.

The heavenly food must be taken before the earthly, for precedence is always given to the noblest and most excellent. The body of Our Lord when taken down from the cross was laid in a sepulchre wherein never yet had any man been laid. Our bodies must also be cleansed; Christ washed the apostles' feet before giving them communion. The Israelites were even commanded to wash their clothes before the Ten Commandments were delivered to them. External cleanliness is supposed to represent inward purity. The guests at a marriage have to appear in wedding garments, and shall we come to the Lord's Supper in soiled apparel? At the table of an earthly monarch a certain etiquette has to be observed; how much the more should we behave with reverence when approaching holy communion.

Only in the case of those who are in danger of death may holy communion be received after taking food.

Necessity knows no law. Those who are dangerously ill may receive holy communion repeatedly by way of Viaticum; but those who are sick, and not in danger of death, must communicate fasting.

It is necessary to obtain an express permission from the Pope for any one who is not dangerously sick to take anything before communicating.

The permission in question is only granted to kings and emperors before their coronation; to aged and infirm priests who are obliged to say Mass, and yet cannot fast without serious injury to their health; to sick priests who are not under the obligation of celebrating Mass, but yet are allowed to do so two or three times in the week; and certain of the laity who are sick, but in this case the permission only extends to five or at most six times in a month. For this privilege application must be made to the Holy See through the bishop of the diocese, and the permission as a rule, applies to liquid, not solid food. If any one inadvertently eats or drinks anything before going to communion, he must not communicate on that day.

Our dress should be clean and suited to our station when we go to communion; that is to say, we should put on better things than those in daily wear, but not dress showily.

To attach importance to dress when approaching the holy table, would lead us to overlook what is essential, and mar devotion. Shabby clothes are no shame to the wearer; Christ was poor and He loves the poor. He looks at the interior, not the exterior of a man.

Our demeanor should be reverent when we go to communion; we should avoid singularity and everything prejudicial to devotion.

When the priest repeats the words: *Domine non sum dignus,* the intending communicant should strike his breast, and rising from his knees, go slowly up to the altar-rails without looking about him; when the priest advances to give him the sacred Host, let him raise his head, close his eyes, open his mouth, and put his tongue forward as far as the underlip; then let him swallow the Host as soon as possible, and after a few moments' pause return reverently to his place.

Behavior after Receiving Holy Communion.

After receiving communion we should make our thanksgiving, and proffer our petitions to almighty God, praying for the Pope, for the authorities, secular and ecclesiastical, for our relatives, friends, and benefactors, and for the holy souls in purgatory.

Our thanksgiving ought to last at least a quarter of an hour. Priests recite the *Benedicite* after Mass. To leave the church after communion without thanksgiving would be a very rude act; how ill-mannered would he be thought who, when invited to the table of one far above him in rank, did not so much as thank his host! To do so is to be like Judas who, after receiving communion, immediately went out. St. Philip Neri once sent two acolytes with burning tapers to accompany a person whom he observed thus hurrying from the church. We ought also to present our petitions to God after communion. Queen Esther pleaded with King Assuerus on behalf of the Jewish people after the banquet, for she knew this was the most favorable moment to make her request, and it was granted her (Esther vii.). There is no better time for us to hold converse with God than when He is present with us as our Guest. Our prayers have far more weight with God after communion than at any other time, because they are sanctified by the presence of Our Lord. We have not Him always with us (Mark xiv. 7). " How much those lose," exclaims St. Alphonsus, " who neglect to implore graces after receiving holy communion! "

No food should be taken until at least a quarter of an hour after receiving communion, when the species of bread are consumed.

It is not well to indulge in worldly amusements on the day of communion, for by doing so we lose the graces we have received. We shall do better if we go to a church, and thus return the visit Our Lord has graciously vouchsafed to pay us.

Spiritual Communion.

Spiritual communion consists in awakening within the heart a lively desire to receive holy communion.

To make a spiritual communion is a matter of no difficulty; it is enough to recollect one's self for a few minutes, to place one's self in spirit before the tabernacle, and to say: "Lord Jesus, come, I beseech Thee, into my heart."

We ought to make a spiritual communion during Mass, more particularly at the communion of the priest, and also when we pay a visit to the Blessed Sacrament.

We may even communicate spiritually every hour of the day, the oftener the better. For this there is no need to fast beforehand, nor to obtain permission from our confessor.

Spiritual communion is the means of enriching the soul with many and precious graces.

Actual communion is compared to a golden, spiritual communion to a silver vessel. Our Lord, when on earth, did not heal those only to whom He went in person, but those also who were absent, and who ardently desired His presence. Remember how He acted in regard to the centurion's servant; He does the same now as He did then (Cochem). The Council of Trent says (13, 8): "Those who eat in desire that heavenly bread, are by a lively faith which worketh by charity, made sensible of the fruit and usefulness thereof." Spiritual communion is the best preparation for sacramental communion. Our Lord did not come to earth until His advent was ardently desired; and in like manner He is reluctant to visit the soul that does not earnestly long to receive Him.

4. THE SACRAMENT OF PENANCE.

The Nature and the Necessity of Penance.

As soon as the fish swallows the bait, he feels the smart. So it is with the sinner. Yet what God has laid upon us as a chastisement He has made the means of our salvation; He sends suffering as the chastisement of sin; but by suffering we can be delivered from sin.

Interior sorrow for sin, accompanied by sincere turning from creatures and turning to God, is generally called penance.

As a matter of fact, our whole life ought to be one continued penance. Our Lord says: "Unless you shall do penance, you shall all likewise perish" (Luke xiii. 3). And again: "Woe to you that now laugh, for you shall mourn and weep" (Luke vi. 25). He often threatens those who only desire to enjoy life, with eternal perdition (John xii. 25). No man, even should he not be conscious of any sin, ought to depart out of this world without doing penance (St. Augustine). St. Jerome says we can no more attain everlasting life without penance, than we can get at the kernel of a nut without breaking the shell. The greatest saints used to perform severe penances for their slightest faults.

Our Lord instituted the Sacrament of Penance on the day of His resurrection, when He spoke these words to His apostles: "Whose sins you shall forgive, they are forgiven; and whose sins you shall retain, they are retained" (John xx. 23).

With these words Christ on the one hand imparted to the apostles the power to remit sins, and on the other laid upon the faithful the injunction to confess their sins to a priest in order to obtain the remission of them. The conditions under which forgiveness of sins is to be obtained, are indicated in the following instances: (1), the cure of the man sick of the palsy (Matt. ix.); sin is a spiritual paralysis; when sin is forgiven, a penance is imposed on the penitent, as the paralytic was commanded to carry his bed; (2), The cleansing of the leper (Matt. viii.); sin is a spiritual leprosy; the sinner must show himself to the priest, who will declare him to be clean by God's authority; (3), The absolving of the penitent Magdalen, who cast herself at Our Lord's feet, and heard from His lips the words: "Thy sins are forgiven thee" (Luke vii.). The sinner now acts as she did; filled with contrition, he casts himself at the feet of Christ's representative, and obtains the pardon of his transgressions.

1. In the Sacrament of Penance the repentant Christian confesses his sins to a duly authorized priest, who, standing in the place of God, pronounces the absolution by means of which they are forgiven.

The method of confession is this: The penitent, kneeling down in the confessional, makes the sign of the cross and receives the priest's blessing. He recites the first part of the *Confiteor*, then accuses himself of his sins, and repeats the concluding part. The priest asks him any questions that may be necessary, gives him a short instruction, sets him a penance, gives him absolution and dismisses him with his blessing. The penitent then withdraws to one of the benches to say his penance, and prepare for communion, if he is about to communicate. The words of the sacerdotal absolution are these: " I absolve thee from thy sins in the name of the Father, and of the Son, and of the Holy Ghost." The absolution is a judicial act (Council of Trent, 14, 9). Like the lightning, it consumes the sin at a flash. Even when the priest withholds the absolution, he gives the blessing. A crucifix always hangs in the confessional, sometimes a picture is added, calculated to excite contrition, such as the prodigal son, the repentant Magdalen, the sorrowing Peter, etc. In very old confessionals one may sometimes see a rose carved, as an emblem of the silence which is binding upon the confessor. The ancient Romans used to suspend a rose over the dining-table, to warn their

guests not to indulge in any confidential conversation in the presence
of strangers.

**2. The Sacrament of Penance is indispensably necessary for
those who have fallen into sin after Baptism, for without this
sacrament they are unable to recover the justice they have lost
(Council of Trent, 14, 1; 6, 29).**

" The Sacrament of Penance is, for those who have fallen after
Baptism, as necessary unto salvation as Baptism itself is for those
who have not yet been regenerated " (Council of Trent, 14, 2). Hence
the Fathers term this sacrament: " the second baptism," or " the
plank after shipwreck." By Baptism we embark upon the ship that
is bound for the port of salvation. By mortal sin we are shipwrecked;
and in this case our only hope of rescue is by clinging to a plank.
The Sacrament of Penance is that plank. No one who has been
bitten by the old serpent, the devil, can be cured, unless he discovers
his hurt to the physician. Through pride the sinner places himself
at a distance from God; only by humility can he return to God.

The man who has fallen into mortal sin ought to approach
the Sacrament of Penance as speedily as possible.

A dislocated limb must be set right at once; if not, a swelling
forms and the cure becomes difficult. If a vessel leaks, the pumps
must be set at work immediately, or the water will cause the ship to
sink; if a house is on fire, the conflagration must be got under
promptly, or the house will be burned down. If any one has taken
poison, he must swallow an emetic forthwith, or he will lose his life.
So it is with mortal sin. The Church does not appoint a fixed time
for the forgiveness of sin; the sinner may at any time make his
peace with God. Do not presume upon the long-suffering of the Most
High! The longer you postpone your penance, the more rigorously
will you be judged; the more severe will be your punishment. Those
who put off repentance until the hour of death, often have no opportunity allowed them to reconcile themselves with their Maker (Job
xxii. 16). It is the just penalty of sin that he who would not do what
is right when he could, cannot do it when he will. Our Lord says:
" You shall seek Me and shall not find Me " (John vii. 34). No one
knows how soon the time of grace may end. It is a sorry thing when
a man begins to buy what he needs just as the yearly market is over.
One of the thieves upon the cross was forgiven, that nobody might
despair; but only one, that nobody might presume, and put off repentance until the hour of death. St. Bernard declares death-bed
repentances to be, not examples, but miracles of grace. Those who
postpone repentance will meet with the fate of the fig-tree which
Our Lord, finding no fruit on it, cursed. " Trust not," says St.
Augustine, " to the morrow; for thou knowest not whether there will
be any morrow for thee." Contrition, moreover, is of little value
when a man has no more opportunity to sin; in that case you do not
abandon sin, but sin abandons you. Finally, on the approach of death,
the sinner in his alarm becomes bewildered and frightened; he is like
a traveller who, just as night closes down, discovers that he has lost
his way. Besides this, the long habit of sin deprives a man of the

power to do penance; he is like one who has slept heavily, and, though he wishes to get up, cannot pull himself together and rise from his bed. No one considers it safe to sleep in a half-ruined house, yet, frail as is your body, you do not scruple to live on, for weeks, months, nay, years, in a state of mortal sin.

3. Let no one be deterred by a feeling of shame from confessing his sins; the priest dare not, under any pretext, reveal what is said in the confessional, and he is ever ready to receive the contrite sinner kindly.

Furthermore, let him who is ashamed to confess to the priest now, remember that one day he will be put to confusion before the whole world, and condemned to endless misery.

The priest dare not, even to save his life, disclose the secrets of the confessional. We shall speak further on of the seal of confession. The penitent is always received with kindness by the priest. Some one who had confessed several grievous sins to St. Francis of Sales, afterwards said to him: "What can you think of me now?" The saint replied: "I think you must be a very holy person, for only the saints have made so good a confession." Nothing gives a priest greater joy than to see that a penitent has made a full and sincere confession of all his misdeeds, for then he knows that his conversion is real. The priest is like a fisherman, who, the bigger the fish he catches, the better pleased is he. God frequently calls those who have themselves been great sinners to the care of souls, in order that they may deal more gently with transgressors. For he who knows himself to be guilty of heinous offences will be lenient towards those who have also offended. Shrink not, therefore, from confessing your sins to one who is himself a sinner; who perhaps is more deeply stained than you are. Christ did not give the power of the keys to angels, but to men. He who is ashamed of confessing to the priest will one day be put to confusion before the whole world, and be condemned to endless misery. To such a one God says: "I will show thy nakedness to the nations, and thy shame to kingdoms" (Nahum iii. 5). Far better is it to confess one's misdeeds to the servant of God, who has compassion with the sinner, than to be put to shame in the sight of all men; far better willingly to acknowledge them once for all, than to do so compulsorily throughout all eternity. What man conceals, God reveals; what man confesses, God suppresses. Who would not rather go to confession here, than burn forever in hell? It is the devil who makes us timid and shamefaced in regard to confession. When we are about to sin he takes all fear from us, but when it is a question of acknowledging our offences, he inspires us with alarm and embarrassment. How else can it be explained that men who on the battle-field face death without fear, tremble on approaching the confessional? The early Christians did not hesitate to confess their sins openly before all the faithful; St. Augustine wrote a book of confessions, in which he acquaints all the world with his transgressions. As the sick man, if he has any sense, will gladly swallow the bitter potion which he hopes will restore him to health, so he who is spiritually sick ought not to shrink from the penance, however severe, which will cure the malady of his soul.

4. He who from a sense of shame conceals a mortal sin in confession, does not obtain forgiveness, but only adds to his other sins that of sacrilege; and exposes himself to the grave risk of dying impenitent.

Moreover all his subsequent confessions are invalid, so long as he does not confess over again all the sins of which he has been guilty since his last valid confession.

The devil acts like the wolf, who seizes the lamb by the throat, that it may not cry out; the devil stops the sinner's mouth, that he may not confess his misdeeds. He who conceals one mortal sin in confession does not obtain forgiveness. If all the locks on a door are unfastened except one, the door cannot be opened; so it is with the soul; unless every mortal sin, those locks of the soul, are subjected to the power of the keys, wielded by the priest, the door of reconciliation cannot be unclosed. Moreover, to conceal a mortal sin in confession is to commit the grievous sin of sacrilege, which is a profanation and contempt of divine things. By concealing one sin, a man also embitters his life. Sin unconfessed is like indigestible food, which lies in the stomach and ruins the health. "Sin concealed," says St. Augustine, "scourges the conscience, lacerates the heart, and fills the soul with anguish and terror." Whoso lies in the confessional deceives himself, not God. To conceal a mortal sin in confession is to merit the danger of dying impenitent. Sin concealed is fatal to the life of the soul; it is like a wound which bleeds inwardly and causes death. St. Antoninus, Archbishop of Florence, speaks of a woman who purposely omitted a mortal sin in confession, and then made a sacrilegious communion; later on she repeatedly went to confession with the intention of revealing that sin, but every time failed to do so, through a false shame. Even when she lay on her deathbed, she could not prevail upon herself to mention the long-concealed sin. Just before breathing her last, she shrieked aloud: "I am damned, for ever since my youth I have concealed a mortal sin!" What a terrible thing it is, thus to abuse the Sacrament of Penance! One sacrilegious confession renders all subsequent ones invalid. In order to return to a state of grace, under such circumstances, it is necessary not only to confess the sin wittingly concealed, but all the other sins mentioned in the first invalid confession, as well as all that have been subsequently committed, whether they have been confessed or not. It is the same with confession as with a sum in arithmetic. If one has made the omission of a single figure in the first row, the total will be wrong, and the whole must be reckoned up over again. In the same way, if a man has buttoned his coat wrong at the top, all the other buttons must be undone to set that one right. Hence St. Bonaventure gives this advice: "Begin with the sin which it costs thee most to confess, and afterwards all the rest will come easy to thee." When once the general is slain, the whole army will speedily be routed. If you find it very difficult to confess any sin in particular, say at least to the confessor: "There is something more, but I cannot bring myself to tell it."

The Confessor.

1. No priest can give absolution who has not received the faculties for hearing confessions from the bishop of the diocese.

To none but the apostles and their successors did Our Lord give the power to forgive sins. To them alone did He say after His resurrection: "Receive ye the Holy Ghost. Whose sins you shall forgive, they are forgiven them; and whose sins you shall retain, they are retained" (John xx. 23). He commanded the apostles to loose the bands of Lazarus, after he had risen from the grave, to indicate that to them was given the power to unbind. This power is called the power of the keys, because by it the gates of heaven, closed against the sinner, are reopened to him. Thus the confessor is the doorkeeper of heaven. The bishops can confer the right to forgive sins to such priests as they deem fitted to hear confession. A priest, as a rule, has faculties for the whole diocese in which the bishop has given him an appointment.

2. Priests who are duly authorized to hear confessions have not power to absolve from all sins, since there are certain sins which the Pope or the bishop has reserved to himself for judgment. (Council of Trent, 14, 11).

They can only absolve from these sins if jurisdiction be delivered to them by the Holy See or the bishop of the diocese.

These are called reserved cases. The bishops are accustomed to reserve to themselves the absolution from more heinous crimes, such as apostasy, perjury, murder, arson; the object of this is to deter the faithful more effectually from the commission of such crimes. Secular magistrates cannot pass sentence on all criminals; many cases have to be sent up to a higher court for judgment. But at the point of death all priests may absolve all penitents whatever from every kind of sin or censure (Council of Trent, 14, 7). In places of pilgrimage the priests can usually absolve in cases reserved for the bishop; and in many dioceses they are empowered to do so during missions, at Easter, or when a general confession is made.

3. In the confessional the priest stands in the place of God; therefore the penitent is bound to yield him obedience.

If Our Lord Himself sat in one confessional, and an ordinary priest in another, the one would not remit sins more fully than the other. Why is this? We call the priest who hears confessions "Father" because he represents our heavenly Father. For the same reason he deals with the penitent gently and indulgently, like a father. We must obey the confessor, for it is not a man whom we obey in his person, but God, Who has said: "He that heareth you, heareth Me." If we obey our confessor, we may be sure that we shall not have to give account of our actions to God; for should the confessor be at error, there is no blame attaching to the penitent; he cannot do wrong in obeying. Those who would make progress in perfection should obey their confessor as they would obey the voice of God, even should the practice of some devotion or penance be forbidden them. St. John of the Cross says that to rebel against the dictum of the confessor manifests pride and want of faith.

In the confessional the priest exercises three functions: The office of a teacher, a physician, and a judge.

In his office of teacher the priest has to instruct the penitent if he perceives that he is in ignorance of something important for him to know. Like a guardian angel, he directs the traveller in the right way. In his office of physician he listens to the penitent, who is sick with the disease of sin, while he gives an account of his condition, as the physician listens to the patient describing his bodily pains. He gives him the remedy to effect his spiritual cure, as the physician prescribes medicines for those who are sick in body. In his office of judge, he must decide whether the penitent is or is not to be absolved; in the former case he gives him absolution, in the latter he withholds it.

4. Under no possible conditions may the priest repeat anything out of the confessional.

This obligation to secrecy is called the seal of confession. Not even to save his life may the priest reveal what has been said in confession. St. John Nepomucene could not be prevailed upon either by menaces or torture to disclose the queen's confession to King Wenceslas. That monarch accordingly ordered him to be thrown into the Moldau, and five lights floating over the water marked the spot where his corpse lay. Not even to avert a terrible calamity may the priest reveal what has been said in confession. A king once asked the court chaplain whether, if any one confessed that he intended to assassinate the king, he would make it known. "On no account," the clergyman replied. "Then," said the king, "my life is not safe." "It would be less so," the priest rejoined, "but for confession, and the seal of confession." The obligation of secrecy also exists in regard to the penitent. A priest's servant once confessed to him that he had stolen his corn; the priest was obliged to leave the key in the barn-door the same as before. The seal of confession must be observed no less strictly in a court of justice, for the divine law is higher than human law. The penalty for violating the seal is deprivation for the remainder of the priest's life, besides severe ecclesiastical punishments. We hear from time to time of bad priests who apostatize, but never has one been known to fall so low as to break the seal of confession. The obligation of secrecy is for the protection of the penitent as well as to safeguard the Sacrament of Penance. The penitent may give the priest permission to make use of what he has told him in confession, but the confessor must be very chary of availing himself of that permission. He must only do so when something really important is at stake, and there is no risk of thereby bringing confession into discredit. The seal of confession does not bind the priest if any one speaks outside the confessional of what he has previously confessed.

5. Every Catholic is perfectly free to choose his own confessor.

The slightest coercion in regard to confession is forbidden, for fear of leading any one to conceal a sin. St. Teresa says: "Oh, what mischief the evil one is enabled to do, if force is put upon any one in regard to confession!" Accordingly no one is obliged to go to confession to his parish priest (unless it be at Easter, as is the rule in some places); every one is at liberty to approach the sacraments wherever he chooses, and the priest may not refuse to hear any man's confession because he belongs to another parish. Monks are required to go to confession to a member of their Order. Nuns have their confessor appointed by the bishops; yet besides the ordinary confessor, the bishop or other superior has to offer them twice or thrice a year an extraordinary confessor whose duty it is to hear them (Council of Trent, 25, 10). No one can prevent them from making their confession to him.

Whoso desires to make progress in perfection must place himself under the guidance of some particular confessor (St. Philip Neri).

If a man wants to learn a profession or trade, he must have a master to instruct him; how much more he who wishes to acquire that most difficult of all professions, Christian perfection! He who would ascend a high mountain must have an experienced guide; how much more he who would scale the heights of Christian perfection! Choice should not be made of a confessor without mature deliberation and fervent prayer. For twenty years St. Teresa failed to find a spiritual Father who understood her; she persevered in prayer, and St. John of Avila was sent to her. A wise confessor should be chosen; one would not consult the first doctor one met with about one's bodily ailments; nor in legal difficulties would one take the advice of any but a good solicitor. And should one use less precaution in a matter on which one's eternity depends? One must also choose a confessor in whom one has entire confidence. The devil ruins many souls by sowing distrust between the penitent and his confessor. One's confessor should not be changed without good reason, any more than one would leave a doctor who has attended one for long, and who knows one's constitution. It is, however, well to go to some one else occasionally, so as not to get into servile subjection to one individual.

The Effects of Penance.

It is not any easy matter to do penance; confession, the sincere acknowledgment of sins of which we are ashamed, in itself requires great self-conquest. On this account penance is liberally rewarded by God. Confession is, moreover, an act of profound humility, and to the humble God giveth grace (1 Pet. v. 5).

By worthily receiving the Sacrament of Penance we obtain the following graces:
1. The guilt of sin is remitted and the debt of eternal punish-

ment; yet there remains the debt of temporal punishment to be discharged (Council of Trent, 6, 30; 14, 12).

God says in Holy Scripture: "If the wicked do penance for all the sins which he hath committed, he shall live, and not die. I will not remember all his iniquities that he hath done" (Ezech. xviii. 21). Thus Our Lord said to Magdalen: "Thy sins are forgiven thee" (Luke vii. 48). To those who confess their sins Christ is not a judge, but an advocate and protector. In the Last Judgment the sins that have been expiated by penance will be no more remembered against the sinner; they alone will be hidden, when all else is revealed. Seneca used to say: "He who repents of the wrong he has done is no longer guilty." Through the absolution the debt of eternal punishment is changed into a temporal debt. God acts like the monarch who commutes capital punishment into imprisonment for a term of years. Holy Scripture furnishes many examples in which God imposed a penalty for sin forgiven: He forgave Adam, yet He cast him out of paradise and laid severe penances upon him. Moses, who offended God by not believing His word, was pardoned, but not permitted to enter the Land of Promise (Numb. xx. 12). The Jews who murmured in the wilderness were forgiven upon Moses' intercession, but were condemned to die in the desert (Numb. xiv.). David was forgiven when he had committed two mortal sins, but the child that was born to him died (2 Kings xii. 14). No sin is left unpunished; either we punish ourselves by doing penance, or God lays chastisements upon us. For every sin satisfaction must be made either in this world or in purgatory; the more we have sinned here, the more we shall suffer hereafter. Our transgressions are rightly called debts; as debts must be paid, so sins must be blotted out.

The debt of temporal punishment for sin must be discharged either in this world or in purgatory.

In this world we make satisfaction by performing the penances enjoined on us by the priest in confession; by works voluntarily undertaken, such as prayer, fasting, almsdeeds, or other pious acts, and also by bearing patiently the punishments inflicted on us by God; for instance, accepting death willingly, and finally by gaining indulgences (Council of Trent, 14, 13).

God in His wisdom never leaves sin wholly unpunished, lest we should think lightly of it (St. Augustine).

At baptism all the punishment due to sin is remitted, but in the Sacrament of Penance this is not so. Sin committed after baptism is much more grievous than that which is committed before; those who sin before baptism sin in ignorance, but after baptism in malice, for they have been enlightened by the Holy Spirit, and consequently have a better knowledge of sin. Those who are regenerate, moreover be it remembered, when they sin knowingly violate the temple of God (1 Cor. iii. 17). and are guilty of breaking their promise; for by sin on the one hand they banish the Holy Ghost Who dwells within them, and on the other hand they break the solemn vows taken at baptism. A good father forgives his child's disobedience the first time, if he promises amendment; but if the child repeats the offence, his father forgives him, but does not this time let him go unpunished. God acts in a similar manner; at baptism He remits both the sin and its penalty, but afterwards He is not so indulgent to the transgressor.

The more perfect our contrition, the greater will be the amount of the punishment remitted to us.

"Many sins are forgiven her, for she loved much," Our Lord said of Magdalen. Sometimes God touches the heart of man so profoundly that his contrition avails for the complete remission both of sin and its penalty.

2. The Holy Spirit returns to the repentant sinner, and imparts to him sanctifying grace; and the merits of all the good works he formerly performed while in a state of grace are restored to him again.

The contrite sinner, like the prodigal son, receives a beautiful robe, sanctifying grace, and a ring is placed on his finger, a token of divine charity. Traces of our sins will, it is true, always be apparent on the white robe of sanctifying grace, but having been washed out by penance, they will not disfigure its beauty. Penance is a ladder whereby we may ascend again to the place whence we have fallen. The heart that is full of sin is the habitation of swine; by penance it becomes the dwelling-place of the Most High. Penance is a crucible wherein base metal is changed to silver. It would indeed be a miracle, if by a single word some one were to make the black skin of the negro white. Yet a greater wonder is worked by the words of absolution, spoken over the penitent sinner, for thereby the soul, which through sin was black as ink, becomes white as snow. When the sinner is restored to a state of grace, as a matter of course he is again a child of God, an heir of heaven, capable of performing meritorious works. Another effect of penance is that the merit of all good works done formerly in a state of grace is recovered. For the merit of all those works was lost through mortal sin (Ezech. xviii. 24); not because God withdrew their merit on account of the mortal man, but because man made them of no effect. So a meadow, parched by long drought, recovers its verdure under the influence of gentle rain and soft sunshine.

If before confession we are already in a state of grace, we receive an increase of grace.

Any one who is free from mortal sin, or who has perfect contrition, is in a state of grace before confession. The greater the degree of sanctifying grace we possess here, the higher will be our degree of glory hereafter; hence let no one say it is useless for him to go to confession, as he has no mortal sin on his conscience. Those who speak thus are, alas! too often living in mortal sin.

3. Through the indwelling of the Holy Ghost we obtain great peace of mind, nay, great consolations, if our conversion be sincere.

Penance gives us peace of mind. The Holy Ghost is a comforter (John xiv. 26). When we have relieved our soul by confession, a deep peace ensues, as the sea became calm as soon as the sinful prophet Jonas had been cast out of the ship. The Sacrament of Penance distils balm on the wounds of the soul; it relieves us of a heavy burden. The restoration of one's peace of mind often has a beneficial effect upon the body, and contributes to the recovery of health. Hence the saints used to exhort the sick to receive the sacraments. To the contrite sinner great consolations are often given. Our Lord says: "Blessed are they that mourn, for they shall be comforted" (Matt. v. 5). On the return of the prodigal son, his father caused the fatted calf to be killed, and a merry banquet was held, with music and dancing (Luke xv.). Thus God acts with regard to the repentant sinner whose conversion is real; He makes him to abound in consolations and spiritual delights. In fact the grievous sinner seems in reality to fare better than the just man; remember what the elder son said to his father respecting the reception given to the prodigal (Luke xv. 29). By these consolations God encourages us to walk more resolutely in the toilsome path of virtue; for the penitent has a sharp conflict to wage with his corrupt nature. When first we enter upon the way of holiness, God lavishes these consolations upon us; later on He withdraws them, lest they should prove prejudicial to us. Therefore we ought to render Him thanks when He deprives us of them.

4. The Holy Spirit imparts to us the strength necessary to overcome sin.

The converted sinner is like one recovering from an illness; his former strength has to be regained. By penance the broken limb is set, and its power restored. The might of the Holy Spirit is communicated to the newly-converted, to enable him to resist evil. Confession serves to keep us from falling into sin in future, as well to cleanse us from past offences. Converted sinners are generally faithful and zealous servants of God. On this account Our Lord says that "there is joy in heaven upon one that doth penance, more than upon ninety-nine just persons" (Luke xv. 7). Which is to be preferred, the soldier who has evaded the battle, or the one who has fled from the field, but returns to the attack, to repair his fault, and has valiantly routed the enemy? The former is the tepid Christian, the latter the fervent penitent.

Yet these graces are only given if the Sacrament of Penance is received worthily; they are given abundantly if the sacrament is received frequently.

The more often a house is purified the cleaner it is; so it is with the soul of the Christian. The more frequently he goes to confession, the more thoroughly he casts off the yoke of the devil; for as a bird does not generally return to build its nest again in a place whence it has been driven away, so the evil one is not so prompt to molest the soul whence he has been expelled by confession. Confession once a year suffices to make one a member of the Catholic Church, but it is not sufficient for the welfare of the soul. As well might one expect a house to be clean that was only swept out once a year. The Christian who only goes annually to confession is like Absalom, who only had his hair polled once a year (2 Kings xiv. 26); in the hour of temptation he is in danger of being caught and held fast, as Absalom was in the branches of the oak.

The Worthy Reception of the Sacrament of Penance.

No rule can be laid down here, as in regard to holy communion, concerning the time to be employed in preparation. The reality of our contrition, not the length of our previous preparation, is what is of true importance. However, a few minutes are not enough. "Noe was a hundred years building the ark," says St. Thomas Aquinas, "and thinkest thou in a brief moment to construct the ark which is to save thee from temporal and eternal perdition?"

In order to receive the Sacrament of Penance worthily, we must do as follows:

Since we sin in our heart, by our lips, and in our actions, we must atone for it by the sorrow which is felt in the heart, expressed by the lips, accomplished in our actions. We must do as the prodigal did: as soon as he experienced the gracious operation of the Holy Ghost, he thought over his misdeeds, and acknowledged them (examination of conscience). He saw how ungrateful he had been towards his father, and was truly grieved at heart (contrition). He determined to return to his father and begin a fresh life at home (resolution of amendment). He went back to his father, fell at his feet, confessed his fault and implored forgiveness (confession). He said he would no longer take the place of a son, but of a servant (satisfaction). The father fell on his neck and kissed him (absolution). Then followed a joyous repast (communion).

1. We must examine our conscience, i.e., we must carefully consider what sins we have committed and not yet confessed.

We must make as careful a scrutiny as if we were immediately to appear before the judgment seat of God. If our examination is insufficient, the Sacrament of Penance may conduce to our damnation, rather than to our salvation. Yet we must not be over-anxious, as some scrupulous persons are, for God does not require from us what is out of our power. The examination of conscience is most important, for by it we learn to know ourselves, and this is the beginning of all improvement. One can no more acknowledge and overcome a fault of which one is not aware, than one can cure a malady of the existence of which one is ignorant. Most men are wanting in self-knowledge. There are many who search into the secrets of nature, who observe the course of the stars and the laws of motion, but who know nothing about themselves, and never look into their own heart. They are to be commiserated, despite their learning and their fame, because they pay no heed to their most glaring faults. The Creator has placed a book in the hands of every man, his conscience; study this book diligently, for of all your library it is the only one which you can take with you into eternity. Self-knowledge leads to the knowledge of God.

Before examination of conscience let us invoke the aid of the Holy Spirit, that He may enlighten us.

We can find a thing that is in a dark room much more quickly if we bring a light with us; and it is the same when we search out our sins. When the sun shines into a room we notice a thousand motes which were unobservable before; so the soul, when illuminated by the Spirit of God, sees the slightest imperfections. Self-knowledge is a gift of God, which we can obtain by prayer alone. The eye sees everything but itself; it is the same with our spiritual sight; it is quick in discerning the faults of others, and slow to see its own. It is well to examine one's conscience in solitude, for there the Holy Spirit speaks to the heart (Osee ii. 14).

When examining our conscience we must put aside self-love and earnestly endeavor to acquaint ourselves with our faults.

Many sick people will not allow that there is anything serious the matter with them, and sinners often do the same. This arises from self-love, and self-complacency, on account of the advantages they imagine themselves to possess, both natural and acquired. Some even count their faults as virtues; they think arrogance to be manliness, deceitfulness to be prudence, etc., like some mothers who are so infatuated about their children that they think all their faults to be praiseworthy qualities. In examining his conscience, let a man look on himself as his own enemy; enemies have a sharp eye for one another's feelings.

In examining our conscience, it is well to go through the Ten Commandments, the precepts of the Church, and the deadly sins.

Children may ask themselves: (1), Have I forgotten my prayers or been inattentive at them? (2), Have I uttered the name of God, or spoken of holy things irreverently, or said any bad words? (3), Have I done servile work on Sundays or holydays of obligation? have I missed hearing Mass, or behaved badly in church? or eaten meat on Fridays? (4), Have I been rude or disobedient to my parents? (5), Have I been unkind to others, struck them, or led them to do wrong? provoking them to anger? (6), Have I indulged any thought, or spoken any words or done any deeds of impurity? (7), Have I ever taken what was not mine, and if so, given it back to the owner? have I injured or deceived any one? (8), Have I told a falsehood, accused any one wrongly, abused any one, or told of his faults? (9 and 10), Have I coveted another person's goods? or been proud, given way to anger, or greediness, or been idle at school or at work?

In regard to mortal sins, we must remember how often we have been guilty of them.

All the mortal sins of which the penitent is conscious after a diligent examination of himself, must needs be enumerated in confession (Council of Trent, 11, 5, 7). If the exact number of times cannot be remembered the approximate number must at least be stated.

It is not necessary, though it is advisable, to examine one's self in regard to venial sins.

Venial sins, though rightly and profitably declared in confession, may be omitted without guilt (Council of Trent, 14, 5). The most usual defect in the examination of conscience is that the penitent keeps back certain shameful sins, and is careful to search out slighter ones. Such persons are like the Pharisees, who strain out a gnat and swallow a camel (Matt. xxiii. 24). Hence it is that many do not benefit at all from frequent confession. How many apparently pious people will take their sins with them to eternity!

We must also consider whether there are circumstances which alter or aggravate the sin we confess.

All those circumstances which change the quality and nature of the sin are to be explained in confession (Council of Trent, 14, 5). For instance, if a man has taken another's goods by violence, it is not enough to say: "I stole;" for robbery with violence and theft are two different sins. If anything was stolen in a church, this must also be mentioned.

We ought to examine our conscience every evening in order to render our examination easier before confession.

If a man will not do the necessary repairs of his house as they are wanted, it will become dilapidated and require thorough renovation; so it is with the soul, if its condition is not continually seen to and amended. If a master looks through his steward's accounts daily, they do not get into disorder, and we must do the same with our conscience if we would keep it right. Daily examination is very profitable; it guards us from falling into mortal sin. If a merchant makes up his debit and credit account every day, he is not liable to get deeply into debt. Daily examination keeps our conscience pure, and conduces to moral perfection. St. Ignatius asserts it to be more important than prayer. If a king knew that his enemies were concealed in a certain quarter of his dominions, he would assuredly search out their hiding-place and frustrate their schemes. You have foes within you, your unruly passions; search them out daily, and vanquish them with the sword of sorrow. It is not enough merely to gain a knowledge of our faults, we ought earnestly to deplore them and endeavor to overcome them by good resolutions.

2. We must truly repent of our sins, that is, we must grieve from our heart that we have offended God by them, and the thought of offending Him must be abhorrent to us.

As instances of true contrition, we may mention Magdalen, who fell at Our Lord's feet weeping (Luke vii.); St. Peter, who after he had denied Christ, went out and wept bitterly (Matt. xxvi. 75); David, who when the prophet Nathan had awakened him to a sense of sin, lay upon the ground and did neither eat nor drink (2 Kings xii.), but cried: "Have mercy on me, O God, according to Thy great mercy; and according to the multitude of Thy tender mercies blot out my iniquity. A contrite and humbled heart, O God, Thou wilt not despise" (Ps. l.). Repentance, unless accompanied by trust in God's mercy, would be despair. Remember Judas' repentance. True contrition is also sorrow of soul. An external action alone, such as the recitation of a certain formula of prayer, wailing like that of the Jewish women, rending of garments (Joel ii. 13), do not constitute repentance. Exterior grief without inward grief is mere hypocrisy. But interior heartfelt contrition shows itself exteriorly, for we mortals can rarely prevent all outward manifestation of what we feel inwardly. True repentance has reference to God; hence we call it supernatural, because it proceeds from faith in an unseen, supernatural world. Sorrow for sin because of its disastrous consequences is no true contrition; it is a natural sentiment, without merit before God. The cruel King Antiochus Epiphanus bewailed his wicked deeds when he was eaten by worms; but not because he had offended God (2 Mach. ix. 13). In like manner a gambler, a drunkard, a criminal who is arrested, may regret his folly when he perceives the evil resulting from it. Temporal calamities may be the occasion, but not the motive of our sorrow. True repentance implies profound detestation of sin, or a complete abandonment of sin; it is more a matter of the will than of the feeling. "If," says St. Augustine, "that which formerly caused thee joy and pleasure, now fills thy soul with bitterness, and that which formerly thou didst enjoy is now a torture to thee, then know that thy repentance is real." That is true conversion when a man turns to God with his whole heart, and detaches himself completely from earthly things. Penance is worthless if it produces no amendment. To him who is truly penitent, the thought of offending God is abhorrent. Repentance is not real if every evil affection without exception is not given up. What does it profit thee to break every other chain, if one remains, binding thee to hell? (St. Augustine.)

True contrition often manifests itself in tears.

It was so in the case of Magdalen in Simon's house (Luke vii. 38), and of St. Peter when he had denied Our Lord (Matt. xxvi. 75). The apostle's sorrow was lifelong; it is said that his tears made two furrows on his cheeks. Penitential tears are not indispensable, but they are very efficacious; they render forgiveness more sure. The tears of the penitent are the most forcible language he can use; they compel God to forgive him. Penitential tears wash away the stains of sin; they are a kind of baptism, only the cleansing waters come from within, not from without. They enlighten the mind, as rain clears the sky. The more we weep for sin the more clearly we perceive its turpitude, and our tears lead to a fundamental amendment of life. As medicinal springs heal bodily sickness, so tears cure the maladies of the soul. They bring interior consolation; they refresh the soul as dew does the plant. The tears of the penitent give joy to the angels and drive away the devils; they have much the same effect on them as holy water has.

The means of awakening true contrition is to reflect that by our sins we have grievously offended the infinite majesty of God, and have displeased our loving Father, our greatest Benefactor.

Contemplate the myriad stars in the firmament of heaven, consider the countless number of human beings upon earth, the innumerable hosts of spirits in the realms of space, and thence conclude how infinite is the divine greatness. And you have offended this sovereign Lord! Consider furthermore the greatness of your heavenly Father's love for you, in that He gave what was dearest to Him, His only-begotten Son for you. How shameful to offend so loving a father! Remember also all that the Son of God suffered in your stead. Consider too, the innumerable benefits which throughout your life you have received from God; health, food, clothing, etc., all these things are His gifts, which, when He sees fit, He withdraws from the ungrateful; how instead of showing your thankfulness to God, you have often grieved Him, and repaid His benefits with ingratitude.

The contrition which arises from the love of God is called perfect contrition. Perfect contrition reconciles man with God immediately, before the Sacrament of Penance be actually received (Council of Trent, 14, 4).

Let us suppose that a father sends his two boys into a town to make some purchases. They loiter and play on the way, and are late by several hours. On reaching home, they are frightened; one of them begins to cry, because he is afraid he will be whipped for his negligence; the other boy cries because he knows he has vexed his father. The second boy is an example of perfect contrition, the first of imperfect. He only has perfect contrition who is sorry for his sin because he has thereby offended God. Of this we find examples in David, St. Peter, Magdalen, the publican in the Temple; all these transgressors were speedily forgiven. Perfect contrition is, as may be gathered from Our Lord's words to Magdalen (Luke vii. 47), as a matter of fact, nothing more or less than fervent charity towards God, the operation of the Holy Spirit dwelling in man; and he in whom the Holy Spirit dwells, possesses sanctifying grace and is free from mortal sin. The least degree of perfect contrition suffices instantly to cancel the debt of sin (St. Thomas Aquinas). And if one who is not in mortal sin awakens perfect contrition, the effect is to increase sanctifying grace and remit the temporal punishment due to sin. Perfect contrition is accompanied by the desire of confession; yet it is not necessary to go to confession at once; it is enough to do so when the precept of the Church enjoins this upon one. In fact, it is not indispensable to perfect contrition that the desire for confession should be explicit; it is enough that the penitent should be ready to go to confession when the obligation arises.

We should make an act of perfect contrition from time to time in the course of our life, particularly in the hour of death, or if our life is in danger.

If, in travelling by land or sea, we should perceive an accident to be imminent, let our first thought be to make an act of perfect contrition, and our reconciliation with God will be complete. It happened once that the father of a family broke a blood-vessel. A messenger was instantly dispatched to summon a priest, but meanwhile the youngest child, who had recently made his first communion, perceiving that his father's life was fast ebbing away, took a crucifix from the wall, and holding it before the dying man's eyes, repeated aloud an act of perfect contrition. Tears filled the father's eyes; he expired before the priest came, but he was safe for all eternity. It is probable that at the time of the Deluge, and the destruction of Sodom and Gomorrha, some persons were saved from eternal perdition by an act of perfect contrition. If you should have the misfortune to offend God grievously, make an act of contrition immediately. Do not go to rest at night, or begin the day's work, or start on a journey, without in this manner making your salvation sure. It is no difficult matter to awaken true contrition, if one has a good will. Under the Old Dispensation it was the only means of obtaining remission of sin; and every Christian is bound, under pain of mortal sin, to make an act of perfect contrition in the hour of death, in case he is conscious of sin and cannot go to confession again. Only those find it hard who neglect all the ordinances of religion; they are like a clock which will not go, even when wound up by sanctifying grace, because the works are rusty from disuse. A special interposition of Providence, or a miracle of grace is needed to enable such persons to awaken perfect contrition. Cardinal Franzelin was so impressed with the immense value of perfect contrition, that he declared were he to go as a preacher from land to land, it should be the principal theme of his discourses.

The consideration that we must expect the just judgments of God on account of our sins, also disposes us to true contrition.

Remember the punishment of the rebel angels, of our first parents, of the population of Sodom, of Noe's contemporaries, etc. Reflect upon the awful pains of hell. And even if you do escape hell, there is the fire of purgatory to be endured; there the least punishment far exceeds all that one can suffer on earth, even the tortures inflicted on the martyrs. None but great saints have been exempted from this chastisement. How then can you expect to elude it? How terrible a thing it is to offend God!

The contrition which arises from fear of God is called attrition, or imperfect contrition. When the contrition of the penitent is imperfect, forgiveness of sin is only obtained through sacerdotal absolution.

The contrition of the Ninivites was imperfect, when, smitten with fear at the preaching of Jonas, they did penance (Council of Trent, 14, 4). The penitent who is actuated by fear alone, retains a certain attachment to sin, though he may abstain from the outward act. Hence his repentance is less efficacious. Imperfect contrition is like a tiny spark, which must be fanned by confession and the priest's absolution, before it consumes the chaff of sin.

Confession without contrition does not obtain the divine forgiveness.

Whoso goes to confession without sorrow of mind, detestation of sins committed, and the purpose of not sinning in future, but merely from force of habit and not from consciousness of sin, derives no benefit from the act. The husbandman who scatters seed on untilled soil, labors in vain; in like manner the words of absolution are inefficacious in regard to one whose heart is unprepared, and who will not renounce sin. Confession without contrition is like a gun loaded without shot, an ear of corn empty of grain; it is like the barren fig-tree Our Lord cursed; for on the tree of penance confession is but the leaves, while contrition is the fruit. St. John Chrysostom compares the man who goes to confession without contrition to an actor in a play. From the story of the prodigal we gather that confession alone is not everything; the father scarcely heeded what his son said, but as soon as he perceived his heart was changed, he hardly let him finish speaking, but clasped him in his arms.

3. We must make a firm resolution, that is, we must steadfastly determine with the help of God to desist from all sin, and to avoid the occasions of sin for the future.

The purpose of amendment is an essential part of true contrition (Council of Trent, 14, 4). The resolution to sin no more arises out of contrition, as water issues from a spring. So long as the will retains its attachment to sin, neither mortal nor venial sin can be remitted. All men are not thus resolute, for many do not adhere to their resolutions. They act like a woman, who, when her husband dies, makes a terrible outcry, extolling loudly the excellent qualities of the deceased, and protesting vehemently that she will never marry again; but in a very short time, oblivious of her asseverations, she gives her hand to another man. Those who in time of illness or of adversity form good resolutions, but do not carry them out, are like the wolf who retreats to the wood when he hears the dogs bark and the shepherds cry out, but remains a wolf none the less. A good resolution is like a nail driven fast into a wall; but the resolutions of too many resemble a nail badly knocked in, which falls out as soon as anything is hung upon it. The way to hell is paved with good resolutions, which have not been carried out. All men will not determine to renounce every sin. St. Sebastian promised to heal the proconsul if he would destroy all the idols in Rome; the proconsul did this, with the exception of a little idol of gold, an heirloom in his family, which he concealed. The saint consequently could not cure him, and he told him the reason. Many sinners do the same; there is one darling sin which they will not give up, and therefore they cannot break away from the devil and become the friends of God; for God's sake everything must be renounced. The penitent must also seriously avoid all occasions of sin. The man who merely dislikes his neighbor, contents himself with eschewing his company; but if he has a thoroughgoing hatred for him, he gets rid of everything that can remind him of him; he holds aloof from his friends and relatives, he destroys his portrait, the presents he has received from him, etc. Thus must the penitent act who has a real detestation of sin; he must avoid all and everything that leads to sin, or that reminds him of sin. Those who wish to do better, but will not avoid the occasion of sin, are like one who sweeps away the cobweb, but does not kill the spider; thus a fresh web is soon spun. Or he is like a gardener who cuts off the weeds and does not root them up; in a little time they are greener than ever. Too often sinners who confess their sins but will not give up the occasion of sin transgress more deeply than before. If you would keep the flies from your table, you must remove the sweet dishes that attract them; so if you would keep free from sin, you must keep far from you the occasions of sin. Good resolutions are no use without the divine assistance, any more than the corn can fructify without rain and sunshine. Hence we must not trust to our own strength, but in the grace of God.

Our resolution should have reference to one particular sin, and that the one to which we are most attached.

It is impossible to carry out many resolutions at a time. To attempt this is like endeavoring to roll several large stones up hill all at once; we shall succeed with none. It is enough if we set ourselves resolutely to overcome one fault, for in doing so we shall combat all the others, just as while curbing one restive horse, we check the others who are harnessed with it. If we did but root out one vice every year, we should soon become perfect men.

4. We are under the obligation of confessing our sins, that is, we must secretly to the priest enumerate all the mortal sins of which we are conscious, accurately, simply and humbly; with the number of times we have committed them, besides all that is necessary to make known the nature of the sin (Council of Trent, 14, 5, 7).

It is not necessary, but it is salutary and profitable to confess venial sins.

If a mortal sin has been forgotten in confession, it must be mentioned the next time.

Confession must be made secretly, that is, we must speak in so low a tone that no one near, besides the priest, shall hear what is said. Confession must be accurate. We should avoid the use of general terms; for instance, it is not right to say: I have transgressed the Third, Fifth or Seventh Commandment; I have not loved God with my whole heart; I have sinned in thought, word and deed. Such phrases are unmeaning. Yet, while entering into particulars, everything should be told as briefly as possible, every superfluous detail being avoided. Any one who has been accessory to our sin is not to be mentioned by name. Simple: Ambiguous expressions, attempts at self-justification, cannot be allowed in confession; the penitent must be simple and candid, as a crystal is clear and transparent. To seek to justify one's self is to act like our first parents in paradise, who shifted the blame from their own shoulders, and were punished more severely for it. "Accuse thyself, and God will excuse thee; excuse thyself and God will accuse thee" (St. Augustine). Humble: The penitent must not take offence if the confessor reproves or questions him. In the confessional the priest is in the place of God, the penitent is but a miserable sinner. King Louis IX. once said to a priest, who timidly addressed him as " Your Majesty "; " I am not a king here, nor are you a subject; I am a child, and you are a father." The Empress Constantia once sent for the Abbot Joachim, and wanted him to hear her confession while she remained seated on her throne. But the abbot said: "If thou art to be in the place of Magdalen, and I in that of Christ, thou must leave thy throne and kneel at my feet; otherwise I will go away at once." If the priest perceives that the confession is not entire and complete, he asks questions; just as the customs officer, if he thinks that a traveller has articles on which duty has to be paid, does not satisfy himself with yes or no, but searches his luggage. If the penitent is unable to speak, for instance, if he is deaf and dumb, or extremely ill, he must make his confession by signs, or the deaf-mute may make it in writing. Absolution can never be given to any one at a distance, though it is besought by letter or by a messenger. It is enough if all mortal sins are confessed. For if the beams are burned away, the planks will probably be consumed with them, but the reverse is not the case. Unfortunately, people are too apt to confess venial and conceal mortal sins. Yet it is profitable to confess venial sins, for thereby a portion of the temporal penalty is cancelled, and greater peace of mind is acquired, since in regard to some sins we cannot decide with certainty whether they are mortal or venial. Those who cannot accuse themselves of any mortal sin, must at least confess some venial sins, or a sin of their past life, otherwise they cannot receive absolution. All mortal sins must be declared, unless under exceptional circumstances, such as the penitent being at the point of death, in imminent danger (on a sinking ship), too ill to speak more than a few words, or in a hospital where his confession may be overheard. In such cases an incomplete confession is permissible. All the mortal sins of which we are conscious must, as has been said, be enumerated in confession; yet it may occur that one is forgotten; if so, it must be mentioned next time, and we need not distress ourselves if we do not remember it until after communion, for our confession was not sacrilegious. We must also declare as nearly as possible how often any mortal sin has been committed.

5. Satisfaction must be made: i.e., we must perform the penance enjoined upon us by the confessor.

The debt of temporal punishment is in no wise remitted by the Sacrament of Penance. For God is not more merciful than He is just; therefore works of penance are imposed on the penitent, whereby he may discharge the debt of temporal punishment due to his sins. Works of penance are not only for the punishing or avenging of past sins, they are also a medicine. The sinner is like a wounded warrior; it is not enough to extract the bullet from the wound; bandages and balsam must be applied to heal it. The priest does not merely deliver the penitent from the guilt of sin, he enjoins on him suitable and salutary satisfaction, which shall act as a remedy against relapse. As a rule, he imposes on him penances exactly opposed to his evil propensities; almsdeeds on the avaricious, fasting on the intemperate, and so forth. Nothing is more efficacious in eradicating sin than prayer, almsgiving, and fasting, because the concupiscence of the eyes, the concupiscence of the flesh, and the pride of life, are overcome by the practice of the opposite virtues.

The confessor generally enjoins upon the penitent, prayer, almsdeeds, and fasting, as works of penance, in order that he may thereby discharge the temporal penalties, and weaken the power of evil tendencies (Council of Trent, 14, 8).

In former times most rigorous penances were imposed; e.g., fasting on bread and water, abstinence from meat and wine, the nonreception of holy communion, and the like. These penances were not for a few days, they lasted months and even years, nay, many were lifelong. Some penitents withdrew to the desert to live a life of penance, as did St. Mary of Egypt. Nor were these penances only imposed for grievous sins, but for comparatively slight transgressions, such as the omission of Mass, neglect of the rule of fasting, misbehavior in church, etc. Nowadays the penances imposed are very different; they bear no possible proportion to the punishment we have merited. It is well therefore to undertake some voluntary penances, that we may not suffer in purgatory hereafter, as will be shown presently.

The confessor also directs reparation to be made for any injury that has been done, and the suppression of all that may cause scandal.

He obliges those who have stolen other people's goods to make restitution; those who have wronged others by slander to retract their words and make an apology. He deals gently with the penitent, and does not require from him what he cannot or will not perform.

The works of penance imposed by the confessor ought to be conscientiously performed in union with the satisfaction of Our Lord Jesus Christ.

By the performance of our sacramental penance (that enjoined by the priest), we discharge more of our debt than by works voluntarily undertaken. The former have the virtue of obedience; they would lose their value if they were knowingly altered, therefore they must be done with scrupulous exactitude. If they cannot be performed, this must be told to the priest in the next confession. They must also be performed without delay, for they have no efficacy in remitting sin or earning grace unless the penitent is in a state of grace, and this is most certain immediately after confession. Still there is no obligation to say one's penance before approaching holy communion, but we must not put off saying it until there is a danger of our forgetting it. Whoso neglects to perform his sacramental penance loses many graces, and violates the obedience he owes to the priest as God's representative; but he does not thereby render his confession invalid. He is like a sick man who, when the physician has gone, will not take the medicine he prescribed. He shows moreover, that he does not think seriously of amending his life. All our works of penance are of themselves without merit; they derive their sufficiency from the merit of the satisfaction made by Christ. For this reason the Church concludes all her petitions with the words: *Per Dominum nostrum Jesum Christum.* Our works cannot, nevertheless, be dispensed with, for Christ has only merited for us what was beyond our reach; He has opened heaven to us again, it behooves us through the satisfaction we make to appropriate to ourselves what He merited for us. We know that only if we suffer with Him shall we also be glorified with Him (Rom. viii. 17).

We should, besides, make satisfaction by punishments voluntarily undertaken of ourselves; and also by bearing patiently the temporal scourges inflicted of God (Council of Trent, 14, 9).

We ought to perform voluntary penances as well as those enjoined on us. The man who owes a thousand dollars does not deem himself out of debt when he has paid three or four hundred; he cannot rest until the whole debt is paid off. So we must labor continually to discharge our debt. Divine justice can only be satisfied by long and continuous penance. " Chastise thyself," says St. Augustine, "if thou wouldst not have God chastise thee." By a little labor here we can avert great pains hereafter. The whole life of the Christian ought to be a perpetual penance (Council of Trent, 14, 9). " Attach no credit," says St. John of the Cross, " to the man who decries penance, although he may have the gift of miracles." While we do penance, we may count upon the assistance of grace. Patience under suffering is an effectual means of making satisfaction; the merit of suffering does not consist in the amount we bear, but the manner in which we bear it. Comparatively slight afflictions borne patiently will have far more value as expiation for sin than much greater works undertaken of our own free will. Happy those to whom it is given to expiate their sins on earth, for the fires of purgatory are infinitely worse than anything we suffer here, and they do not contribute to our future felicity; they are simply punitive, not meritorious. Another most profitable means of making satisfaction is the willing acceptance of death at the hand of God. Since Christ died for us, death is not now regarded so much in the light of a chastisement, and by nothing can we merit so greatly as by accepting it willingly.

The works of penance which we perform and the sufferings we bear patiently do not only cancel the temporal punishment due to our sins, but they contribute to the increase of our eternal happiness.

The satisfaction we make here obtains not only pardon from God, but also a reward. All suffering is the penalty of sin, but by God's mercy it is also a ladder whereby we may ascend to heaven. How vast is the mercy and loving kindness of God!

General Confession.

1. By a general confession is meant the confession of all the sins we have committed within a considerable period of time.

Dwelling-houses are swept and cleaned every week, but at longer intervals a thorough cleansing is necessary; the ceilings are white-washed, the floors are scrubbed. It is the same with our soul; we cleanse it frequently during our lives by confession, but occasionally we purify it more fully by a general confession.

2. A general confession is profitable because it produces in us greater self-knowledge, deeper humility, increased tranquillity of conscience, and obtains many graces from God.

It produces greater self-knowledge, because it brings many hidden sins to light. If we fish with a rod or a net, not many fishes are caught, for they shelter themselves under the banks; but if all the water is drawn off the pond, all the fish come to sight. The difference between ordinary confession and a general confession is much the same. It also deepens humility. A small troop of soldiers attacking the enemy has not the same force as the whole army; so the sins we confess from time to time have not the same power to humble our pride as the whole array when disclosed by a general confession. It increases tranquillity of conscience. When a steward has to make up his accounts to his master, he is afraid lest some error should be de-tected; but when they are all looked over and found correct, his mind is at rest. So it is with confession. It also obtains great graces from God. Just as a beggar excites more commiseration if he tells the full tale of his woes, so man appeals more strongly to the com-passion of God, and obtains more graces from Him, if he humbles himself by the acknowledgment of all his misery and frailty. With many persons a general confession has inaugurated a new life. Hence we may conclude that it is a means of obtaining a large meas-ure of grace.

3. A general confession is indispensable, if an invalid con-fession has once been made; it is also advisable in the case of persons who are entering upon a new state of life, or who are in danger of death.

What has already been said upon concealment of sins in confession need not be repeated here. People about to be married, or clerics on the eve of ordination, ought to make a general confession. What consolation for the dying to know that the affairs of their soul are all well-ordered! Scrupulous persons should be forbidden to make a general confession; for them the practice of obedience is more salutary.

Confession a Divine Institution.

1. Confession of sins was instituted by Our Lord, and has been the practice of the Church in all centuries.

Confession was practised under the Old Dispensation, not indeed as a sacrament, but as foreshadowing the sacrament. The first confession was made in paradise; God was the Confessor, Adam and Eve were the penitents. God called upon Cain to make a confession;

he refused to do so and was cursed in consequence. David confessed his sin and was forgiven. Under the law of Moses a certain form of confession was customary among the Jews (Numb. v.-vii.). The people who came to John the Baptist to be baptized confessed their sins (Mark i. 5). Christ, Who did not come to destroy the law, but to fulfil it (Matt. v. 17), confirmed and perfected the existing practice of confession, and attached many graces to it.

1. On the day of His resurrection Our Lord gave to the apostles and their successors the power to forgive and to retain sins. It is obvious that in order that this power may be exercised aright, it is necessary for the sinner to reveal the state of his soul.

The words of Our Lord are these: " Whose sins you shall forgive, they are forgiven them; and whose sins you shall retain, they are retained " (John xx. 23).

2. Even in the apostles' time the Christian converts came to them, " confessing and declaring their deeds."

Thus they came to St. Paul in Ephesus (Acts xix. 18). St. John also states that by confession of sin pardon may be obtained (1 John i. 9).

3. In the writings of the Fathers and Doctors of the Church in the first centuries Christians are frequently exhorted to confess their sins, many appropriate and beautiful similes being made use of in illustration.

Tertullian, St. Basil, St. Gregory the Great and others compare the sinner to a sick man, who, if he would be cured, must declare his symptoms or exhibit his festering sore to a skilful and experienced physician. So the sinner must apply to the dispenser of the divine mysteries and confess his sins that he may obtain remission. St. Augustine says: " It is not enough that a man acknowledge his sins to God, from Whom nothing is hidden; he must also confess them to the priest, God's representative." Pope Leo I. censured the custom of public confession as too rigorous, asserting that secret confession was quite sufficient. It is noteworthy how often the Fathers warn Christians against concealing a sin in confession. Even Protestants cannot contest the fact that confession was practised both in the first centuries of Christianity and in the Middle Ages; in regard to the latter, history affords abundant evidence, for the very names of the confessors of distinguished Christian rulers are recorded.

4. Confession was also retained by the earlier heretical sects which fell away from the Church.

This fact affords unquestionable proof of the antiquity of confession. But we find the practice in a perverted form among sectaries; for instance, it is said that in the Russian Church the priest is bound to inform against any one who confesses crimes of a Nihilistic character. What a contrast to the rules of the Catholic Church!

5. It is impossible to prove confession to be of human institution.

The name of the inventor or originator is generally attached to every human institution or discovery. But those who deny the divine origin of confession, cannot say in what land and at what epoch this custom—than which none other is so difficult and wearisome, and at the same time so unremunerative for the priest—was first introduced. Protestants do, it is true, allege that it was introduced at the Lateran Council in 1215, when confession once a year was made obligatory for the faithful; but who would be so foolish as to conclude, because a father bade his son pay him a visit regularly once every year, that until then he had not been in the habit of ever visiting him?

2. The institution of confession affords us proof of the infinite mercy and wisdom of God.

How easy it is for us, who on account of our sins are like criminals condemned to death, to obtain pardon from God! He does not require of us severe sufferings, a pilgrimage to Jerusalem, or the like; nothing but the confession of our sins to any one of His ministers whom we may select, and who is pledged to strictest secrecy. No earthly monarch was ever so indulgent to transgressors. What exertions a prisoner confined in a subterranean dungeon will make to regain his liberty! For a whole year he will work at filing through a bar or loosening a stone. The spiritual prisoner need take no such pains to recover his freedom; such is the unfathomable bounty and mercy of God. The infinite wisdom of God is also exhibited in the institution of confession. The skill of an experienced physician is shown by the fact that he not only relieves the patient, but by the employment of a remedy opposed to the disease, eliminates its cause. Now we know that all transgressions come from pride; it is, as St. Thomas Aquinas declares, the source of all sin; confession is diametrically opposed to pride, it is a humiliation for the sinner. Thus God manifests His wisdom by appointing a practice easy and simple in itself, and yet most painful to human nature; for confession requires no slight conquest of self.

The Advantages of Confession.

Confession is extremely useful both to individuals and to society in general.

1. Confession is profitable to the individual inasmuch as he derives from it self-knowledge, delicacy of conscience, interior peace, strength of character, and moral purity.

By comparing all that he has done or left undone with the law of God's commandments, the penitent learns to know his own heart. His conscience also speaks more clearly. By frequent confession the law of God is more deeply impressed on the heart of man; when tempted to sin, the commandment he is about to break presents itself to his mind. The mere thought of confession also acts as a deterrent from sin; some persons abstain from sin because they could not bear to tell it to the priest. Experience proves how great a relief confession is to the mind of one who has committed a grievous sin. The impulse to confess one's misdeeds is inherent in human nature; confession answers to this feeling, and the assurance of pardon affords the greatest consolation. Confession also increases strength of character, for by it we learn to overcome ourselves. Moreover the Holy Spirit enlightens our understanding and fortifies our will, and the more steadfastly the will is inclined to what is good, the more strength of character we shall possess. Confession, being in itself an act of humility, cannot fail to make a man humble, and humility is the foundation of all moral perfection. Proud people have the greatest aversion to confession. It is a means of freeing ourselves from the fetters of the devil, for by telling the truth when it would be so easy to deceive, and the temptation to conceal is often experienced, we throw off the yoke of the father of lies, and turn to Him Who is eternal Truth. And the less power the devil has over a man, the more easily he will draw nigh to God. The first step in amendment of life is to go to confession. " Before applying thyself to good deeds," says St. Augustine, " confess thy misdeeds."

   2. Confession is profitable to society at large because it is a means whereby disputes are settled, stolen property is restored, crimes are prevented, and vice effectually suppressed.

Absolution is not given to the penitent who refuses to forgive his neighbor or make restitution of property wrongfully obtained. The reason why non-Catholics often prefer Catholic servants and are willing to let them go to confession is apparent. The priest in the confessional spares no pains to dissuade those who come to him from carrying out any evil designs they may have formed, and tells them what measures they must take to master their passions. More is done in the confessional than in the pulpit for the furtherance of morality, for what is said in private has more effect that what is said in public. Pope Pius V. used to say: " Give me good confessors and I will reform the whole world." If the discovery were made that confession was practised by one of the pagan nations of antiquity, too much could not be said in praise of so excellent and wise an institution; but because it is practised in the Catholic Church, and appointed by the living God, it is termed foolish, tyrannical, and degrading.

The Sin of Relapse.

When the Ark of the Covenant, we are told, was carried to the brink of the Jordan, the water left off flowing downwards, and stood together in a heap. But no sooner had the ark passed over, than the waters returned into their channel and ran on as they were wont before (Josue iii.). So it is with many a Christian. When they have received the sacraments, they restrain their passions a little; but before long they again give them free rein, and sin even more deeply than ever. " Many," says St. Jerome, " begin well, but few persevere." " They put their hand to the plough and then look back " (Luke ix. 62). They are to be compared to the sow that was washed and returns to her wallowing in the mire (2 Pet. ii. 22), or to the dog that returneth to his vomit (Prov. xxvi. 11).

1. **He who after his conversion relapses into mortal sin, is in danger of dying impenitent, because the devil acquires great power over him, and the influence of the Holy Spirit is lessened.**

It is impossible for those who were once illuminated, and were made partakers of the Holy Ghost, and are fallen away, to be renewed again to penance (Heb. vi. 4). The backslider finds it difficult to regain the right road. Relapse into sin is like the relapse of a convalescent; the disease from which he suffered has more hold on him than before. Our Lord says of such a one that the unclean spirit returns to him and takes with him seven other spirits more wicked than himself (Luke xi. 26). The devil deals with the backslider as a prudent warder does with a prisoner who has once escaped; he guards him more watchfully than before. The backslider grieves the Holy Spirit of God (Eph. iv. 30); nay he drives Him away, and violates the temple of God (1 Cor. iii. 17). Thus the sin of relapse renders a man unworthy of the assistance of divine grace. He does not deserve to be cured who opens his wounds afresh. A prince will not readily readmit a man to his favor, who despite all protestations of fidelity has proved himself a traitor. The sin of relapse is severely punished by God. Our Lord said to the man whom He had healed: " Sin no more, lest some worse thing happen to thee " (John v. 14).

2. **If any one should relapse into mortal sin, let him forthwith repent and go to confession; for the longer penance is delayed, the more difficult, the more uncertain conversion will be.**

The backslider ought to act as St. Peter did when he had denied Christ; he went out and wept bitterly (Matt. xxvi. 75). If fire breaks out in a house, it can be extinguished at once if help is at hand; and if the backslider does penance immediately, his sin may be pardoned; nay more, his fall may even obtain for him a greater measure of grace. In the case of some saints, their fall produced in them a greater accession of fervor, and the depth of their contrition obtained for them a higher degree of grace. But the longer penance is postponed, the worse it will fare with the sinner. It is the opinion of the Fathers that as almighty God has appointed beforehand the number of talents to be confided to every individual, so He has fixed the number of sins which shall be forgiven to each; when this number is complete, there is no more pardon to be found. St. Augustine says that the long-suffering of God bears with the sinner up to a certain point; after that he cannot obtain 'forgiveness. In his first illness the infidel Voltaire repented; but he presently fell into greater wickedness than before, and his end was a dreadful one.

3. **If, through frailty, we fall into venial sin, we must not be disquieted on that account, but humble ourselves before God.**

To be vexed and out of temper with one's self shows pride; we cannot tolerate the sight of our own imperfections. It is of no use to

be angry because we are men, not angels; in that way we only per-
petuate our faults. "If," as St. Francis of Sales says, "we are
angry with ourselves for being angry with another, we feed our
anger instead of stifling it." No one is able throughout his whole
life to avoid all sins, except by a special privilege from God, as the
Church holds in regard of the Blessed Virgin (Council of Trent, 6,
23). God permits us to fall into venial sins to keep us humble. He
does like the mother who lets her child run alone in a soft meadow,
where a fall will do him no harm; but on a rough road she carries
him in her arms. So God upholds us in great dangers by His almighty hand, but in slight matters He leaves us more to ourselves.
Hence we must act like children, when they fall; they cry a little
and get up again; so we must at once bewail our fault, acknowledge
our misery, renew our trust in God, and go on as before. Thus our
sins may be made of profit to us; they ought to humble, not to dis-
courage us (St. Francis of Sales). It is impossible to keep the linen
we wear perfectly clean, but we can have it washed when it is soiled.
It is equally impossible to keep our soul free from all stains, yet
it is in our power to cleanse it when we have fallen into sin. The
just man falls seven times, but he shall rise again seven times (Prov.
xxiv. 16).

**4. Since we cannot possibly continue in a state of grace until
death without the special assistance of the Holy Spirit, let us
fervently implore of God the grace of final perseverance.**

In addition to sanctifying grace the just man needs actual grace,
in order to persevere in justice. As the most healthy eye cannot see
without the light of the sun, so the best of men cannot live aright
without the operation of grace. The justified are not able to persevere in justice received without the special help of God (Council
of Trent, 6, 22). Without the assistance of grace we should quickly
relapse into our former sins, and into yet worse ones, just as creation would fall back into nothing if not preserved in existence by
God. The gift of final perseverance is the greatest gift we can receive from God, for all other graces are valueless without it. "He
that shall persevere unto the end, he," and he only, "shall be saved"
(Matt. xxiv. 13). It is useless to lay the foundation of a house if
the structure is not to be finished. "The Christian," says St.
Augustine, "will not be questioned about the commencement, but the
end of his life." St. Paul made a bad beginning, but a good end.
Judas began well, and ended by betraying Our Lord, to his own
damnation. The gift of final perseverance will not be denied to him
who humbly implores it.

By good works also we may make sure our calling and election (2 Pet. i. 10). Unremitting prayer, and heartfelt devotion
to the Mother of God are besides excellent means to enable us
to persevere in justice.

The more good work we have done the less need we fear damnation. Hence the prophet said to Josaphat, the King of Israel: "Thou
didst deserve indeed the wrath of God, but good works are found in

thee" (2 Par. xix. 3). Why were David and St. Peter treated by God with such favor and indulgence after their fall? Because of the good works they had previously performed. Unremitting prayer is also an excellent means of persevering in justice. As birds continually move their wings in the air, to keep from falling to the ground, so we should soar to God on the pinions of prayer, lest we fall into mortal sin. Our Lord enjoins on us "always to pray" (Luke xviii. 1). There is nothing more certain to preserve us throughout our life in the grace of God than unceasing prayer. Hot water does not get cold if it be placed close to the fire, neither does the warmth of divine charity die out of our heart if we keep it near to God by frequent ejaculatory prayers. And since all graces come to us through the hands of the Mother of God, we cannot doubt that the gift of final perseverance, the greatest of all graces, will only be obtained through her intercession on our behalf. "If thou dost enjoy Mary's favor," St. Bernard declares, "thou art sure of salvation."

INDULGENCES.

It has already been explained that by the Sacrament of Penance the debt of eternal punishment due to the sinner is remitted, but not the temporal. This he must discharge either in this world by sickness, adversity, temptation, persecution, voluntary works of penance, and the like, or in the fires of purgatory after death. This is exemplified by the holy penitent, Mary of Egypt. For seventeen years she led a sinful life; after her conversion she did penance in the desert for seventeen years. Her penance consisted in horrible temptations, in hunger and thirst, in sufferings from exposure to cold and heat. It was the same with other penitents.

1. God has granted to the Church the power, after the reconciliation of the sinner with God, of changing the punishments yet remaining due to sin into works of penance, or of remitting them altogether.

Our Lord conferred on St. Peter in particular, and on all the apostles in general, the power to remove whatever hindered the admission of the penitent to heaven. To St. Peter He said: "Whatsoever thou shalt loose on earth, it shall be loosed in heaven" (Matt. xvi. 19), and to the apostles He said: "Whatsoever you shall loose on earth shall be loosed also in heaven" (Matt. xviii. 18). Now since mortal sin excludes from heaven permanently, and the temporal penalty of sin temporarily, power to remit both one and the other is vested in the Head of the Church and in the bishops. We read that certain Christians of Corinth, who had been excommunicated for their vices, were pardoned by St. Paul in the name of Christ (2 Cor. ii. 10), after they had testified to the sincerity of their compunction. When the Church remits temporal penalties, she does not cancel them altogether; she supplies what is lacking from the treasury of the infinite merits of Christ and of the saints. Many members of the Church have performed penances over and above what was due to their sins, and the store of their merits, owing to the satisfaction made by Christ, is so vast in extent, that it far exceeds the penalties due to the sins of all living (St. Thomas Aquinas). In these merits all participate who belong to the communion of saints; and the distribution of them was entrusted by the Son of God to St. Peter, who is the doorkeeper of heaven. Thus it will be seen that no one is actually exempted from the payment of his debt, since what is still due is paid out of the treasury of the Church.

1. Hence at the time of the great persecutions, the Church used to lay upon repentant sinners public penances for the expiation of the temporal punishment of sin, and afterwards commute them into lesser ones, or remit them altogether, if the penitent manifested a sincere intention of amendment, or a martyr interceded for him.

The Christians of early ages were mostly recent converts from heathenism, and needed rigorous treatment. Public penance generally consisted in exclusion from the company of the faithful; the excommunicate were only allowed to kneel in the vestibule of the Church and hear the first portion of the Mass; they were not permitted to receive holy communion, and as a rule, were not absolved until the expiration of their term of penance. During that time on fixed days they had to fast on bread and water. This public penance usually lasted seven years; it was only imposed for grave offences, such as apostasy, giving the Holy Scriptures into the hands of pagans, etc.; for heinous crimes such as murder, the period was still longer. For lesser transgressions a fast of forty days was the ordinary penance. But the Church knew that the design of God is not so much to chastise the sinner as to detach him from earthly affections and lead him to amend; thus, if the penitent showed by his conduct that his conversion was not superficial, but real, it was deemed unnecessary for him to do further penance. Consequently the penitential works were in some cases partially or wholly remitted. Now since Christians form one body among themselves, the communion of saints, they can make satisfaction for one another; hence the martyrs pleaded on behalf of the penitents. St. Thomas Aquinas says that what friends do for us we do in a measure for ourselves, since by reciprocity of affection two are made one.

2. In later times, when public penances were abrogated, the Church permitted the contrite sinner to discharge the debt of temporal punishment due to sin by means of almsdeeds, crusades, or pilgrimages.

Formerly the penitent had to apply for dispensation or mitigation; later on it was offered by the Church to the faithful. In the Middle Ages there were good reasons for remitting penances on the payment of a sum of money, for in those days greed and avarice prevailed, and we know that every vice is best extirpated by its opposite virtue. The money thus collected was expended in the erection of churches and cathedrals for the most part; this is how the funds were raised to build St. Peter's at Rome. At the Council of Clermont in

1095, a total dispensation from works of penance, i.e., a plenary indulgence, was granted to all who took part in the crusades themselves, or in later years provided men or money to carry them on. These indulgences were extended to the near relatives of the crusaders. Crusades were also undertaken on the same conditions against heretics and the adversaries of the Church. In the tenth century we find pilgrimages to Jerusalem, Rome and Compostella mentioned as means of discharging the temporal debt due to sin. When the Holy Land came into the power of the Turks, and pilgrimages could no longer be made to Jerusalem, Pope Boniface VIII. granted full remission of temporal punishment to all who, during the year 1300, should for fifteen successive days visit the basilica of the apostles in Rome. This was the origin of the Jubilee indulgence; it was repeated fifty years later, the condition of a visit to the Lateran Church being added. In that year three million pilgrims are said to have journeyed to the Eternal City. The interval between the granting of these indulgences was reduced by later Pontiffs to thirty-three years, in honor of the period of Our Lord's life on earth; again it was shortened to twenty-five years. Furthermore it was decreed that the same indulgence might be gained by the inhabitants of certain large cities, provided they visited their cathedral church and gave a sum equal to the cost of a journey to Rome, to the preachers of the indulgence, or collectors of alms. This gave rise to great abuses. The collectors who were principally Dominican or Franciscan monks, were sometimes guilty of extravagances, and the Council of Trent had to suppress their office altogether (Council of Trent, 21, 9).

3. In more recent times the Church permitted the substitution of works more easy of accomplishment, such as prayer and the reception of the sacraments, for the more rigorous works of penance, as a means of satisfaction.

In this manner the Church endeavors to incite her children to greater fervor; to induce them to approach the sacraments (this supposes conversion and amendment), to be diligent in prayer, to enrol themselves in confraternities, to recite the Rosary, to increase in devotion to saints and relics, etc. She acts like a mother who mingles sweets with the bitter physic, to induce the child to swallow it. The ancient rule of discipline formerly in force in the Church, is the standard whereby the measure of punishment to be remitted is estimated; thus when it is said that three years' indulgence is granted for the recital of a certain prayer, the meaning is that the penitent by repeating that prayer, does as much in expiation of his sins as would formerly have been done by three years of canonical penance. The object of this is both to testify to the Church's reverence for ancient ordinances, and also by reminding them of the severe requirements of former days, to make the faithful perform cheerfully the easy task they are now called upon to accomplish.

2. The remission of the temporal punishment due to us on account of our sins is called an indulgence, and is obtained by the performance, while in a state of grace, of certain good works enjoined on us by the Church.

An indulgence (pardon or remission) is therefore a kind of absolution from the temporal penalty of sin, after absolution from the guilt and eternal punishment. An indulgence is very similar to an amnesty; if this is granted by a monarch, a free pardon, or mitigation of sentence, is accorded, on account of their good conduct, to some criminals among others, who, though condemned to death, have had their verdict commuted to a term of incarceration. An indulgence is by no means a remission of mortal sin and the eternal punishment due to it; these must already be remitted before an indulgence can be gained. It is not absolution from sin, but the remission, partial or plenary, of satisfaction due to sin. It is not a means of evading the Sacrament of Penance and rendering sin easy; on the contrary it obliges us to a real conversion of life.

Indulgences only remove those temporal sufferings which do not conduce to our eternal salvation.

An indulgence only exempts us from such sufferings as are exclusively primitive; it does not remove those which God sends upon us for our advancement in holiness, or to prevent our relapse into sin; for suffering such as these no satisfaction can be made, as we see in the case of David. When the death of his child was foretold to him, as the punishment of his sin, he besought the Lord for the child and kept a fast (2 Kings xii.), but God would not accept this satisfaction; the child died. Nor do indulgences deliver us from sufferings which are a probation, or are intended to enhance our eternal felicity; in that case they would be prejudicial to salvation, not beneficial. Without suffering no man can be saved; even the immaculate Mother of God, who was free from all sin, had no small measure of suffering as her lot on earth.

It is necessary for gaining an indulgence to be in a state of grace; otherwise good works can only conduce to the conversion of him who performs them, and are valueless for the remission of temporal punishment.

As a member of the human body, if it be dead, can derive no benefit from the action of the other living members, so the living members of the Church are powerless to aid, by the application of the satisfaction they have made, the soul of one who is spiritually dead, i.e., in mortal sin.

The Church grants indulgences for the recital of certain prayers, for visiting certain holy places, for the use of certain sacred things, besides personal indulgences.

The heavenly treasures of the Church are not administered for gain, but godliness (Council of Trent, 21, 8). As instances of indulgenced prayers we may mention the acts of the three theological virtues, the Angelus, the usual prayers of Mass, etc. These prayers must be vocal; it is not necessary to repeat them kneeling, unless this should be definitely specified. They may be recited in any language, provided the translation is approved by the bishop. Not a single word must be omitted or altered, and the prescription as to time, place, etc., must be strictly observed; but the indulgence is not lost on account of some trifling mistake. The indulgence attached to some prayers may be gained each time they are repeated (*toties quoties*); in the case of others, only once a day. As instances of places where indulgences may be gained, we may mention the *Via Crucis* in Jerusalem, and the stations wherever they are canonically erected. The *Scala Santa* in Rome, the stairway, that is, in Pilate's house up and down which Our Lord was dragged. It consists of twenty-eight marble steps, and was brought from Jerusalem to Rome by the Empress Helena in 326. By ascending this staircase on one's knees, meditating meanwhile on Our Lord's Passion, an indulgence of nine years for every step may be gained. Large indulgences are also granted for visiting the tomb of the holy apostles, the stations in Rome (churches where remarkable relics are preserved), the Chapel of the Portiuncula at Assisi, the sepulchre of St. James at Compostella, besides many others. As instances of holy things and sacred objects to which indulgences may be attached, we may mention: Crucifixes, medals, rosaries, pictures, statues, etc., provided they are not made of very fragile material. These objects must be blessed by the Sovereign Pontiff, or some priest possessing the powers. The indulgence is lost if the object to which it is attached is more than half destroyed; if, that is to say, the greater part of the beads of a rosary are worn away, or more than half of the crosses have fallen from a set of stations, also if a blest object is sold, or lent to another person for the sake of gaining the indulgence, but not if it is given away after being blessed. More than one indulgence may be attached to the same rosary; a crucifix can likewise be indulgenced for the hour of death, and for the stations; but one and the same prayer will not avail to gain all the indulgences attached to any one object. Partial indulgences may be gained daily; and plenary very frequently if the usual conditions are fulfilled. All crosses or rosaries brought from Palestine, which have touched the holy places, have the Papal blessing attached to them. The members of confraternities and some secular priests have personal indulgences granted to them.

3. An indulgence is either plenary, when a full and entire remission of all the temporal punishment due to sin is gained, or partial, when only a portion of the temporal punishment is remitted.

Indulgences are ordinarily greater or less in proportion to the prescribed works; for a small work, a small indulgence, for a work of difficulty a large indulgence is granted. Let no one imagine that it is an easy thing to gain a plenary indulgence. For he who retains any undue attachment to earthly things, is not altogether free from the guilt of sin; nor consequently from the penalty of sin, and he yet needs purification by suffering. Only in as far as the offence against God is hateful to the penitent, does God remit the chastisement due to His justice.

Plenary indulgences are granted by the Church, provided that we approach the sacraments and pray for the Holy Father's intention besides performing the prescribed works; sometimes the condition of visiting a church is added.

For instance: For daily acts of the three theological virtues, a plenary indulgence may be gained on any one day in the month on the usual conditions. The same privilege is attached to several other prayers and ejaculations, such as: "Sweetest Heart of Jesus, I implore, that I may ever love Thee more and more." Those who are in the habit of going to confession every week can gain any indulgence in the course of the week without going again to confession, except the Jubilee indulgence. More than one plenary indulgence may be gained at one and the same communion, provided the works prescribed for each severally be accomplished. If a visit to a church or public chapel is enjoined, it must be made on a separate occasion. Infirm persons are only required to go to confession; instead of receiving communion and visiting a church, if these be the conditions, they can gain the indulgence by performing some other work prescribed by their confessor. All who by illness or other unavoidable circumstances are prevented from visiting a church, do not lose the indulgence, if they fulfil all the conditions within their power. Prayers for the intention of the Church are left to every one's discretion. In general, five Our Fathers and five Hail Marys are considered sufficient; they must be repeated audibly, either before or after communion, and offered up for the peace of Christian princes, the extirpation of heresy, and the exaltation of the Church.

The most important plenary indulgences are the Jubilee indulgence, the indulgence of the Portiuncula, and that of the Papal benediction.

The Jubilee indulgence is granted every twenty-five years to the whole Church, and lasts for the whole year. The Jews kept the fiftieth year as a year of jubilee, or rejoicing. We have already explained how this custom was introduced into the Church. The conditions for gaining it are: The reception of the sacraments and the visit to a church, besides at least one day of fasting and an alms. In the Jubilee year all other indulgences for the living are suspended (except that of the Angelus and for the hour of death), but if applied to the dead they continue in force. As a rule, the Jubilee indulgence can only be gained once, and that for one's self; but sometimes it is otherwise. Occasionally an extra Jubilee is proclaimed by the Sovereign Pontiff under special circumstances, such as his accession to the Papal throne, the opening of a council, etc. The indulgence of the Portiuncula can be gained repeatedly on the second of August, and on the evening before; as often, in fact, as any one who has been to confession and communion visits the Portiuncula Chapel, or any other public chapel of the Franciscans or Poor Clares, and prays for the intentions of the Holy Father. The indulgence originated in this wise: While St. Francis was praying in his favorite church near Assisi, Our Lord appeared to him, with His blessed Mother and several saints. Francis entreated Our Lord to grant a plenary indulgence to all who after approaching the sacraments, should visit that church. Our Lord consented, bidding him go to the Pope, who would ratify the privilege. Francis accordingly repaired to Rome; the Holy Father granted the indulgence, fixing it for the second of August. Later Pontiffs extended it to all public chapels of the Franciscan Order, and some others. This indulgence can only be gained once for one's self; if gained more often, it must be applied to some one else. The communion need not necessarily be made in a church of the Order. A plenary indulgence may be gained by all who, after confession and communion, and prayer for the intention of the Church, receive the Papal benediction. Previous to the year 1870 this used to be solemnly given after High Mass on great festivals from the balcony of St. Peter's. Bishops and priests are now and again authorized to give the Papal blessing to their flocks on special occasions, such as the close of a mission.

A plenary indulgence may be gained in the hour of death by those who, having received the sacraments and invoked the holy name, receive the Papal blessing, or keep beside them some object blessed by the Holy Father; also by the members of most confraternities, and by all who have daily recited the three acts of faith, hope and charity, or some other similarly indulgenced prayer.

If a sick man, desirous of gaining a plenary indulgence, should find it impossible to receive the sacraments, he may at least make an act of contrition; if he cannot utter the name of Jesus with his lips, he can at any rate invoke it in his heart. In any case perfect conformity to the will of God is essential. The majority of priests are empowered to give the papal benediction to the dying. Those who have received the necessary faculties can indulgence crosses, medals and the like for the hour of death. It is enough if the faithful keep objects thus blessed in their houses, to enable them to gain the indulgence. Indulgences for the hour of death are also attached to membership of various confraternities. They may also be gained by making acts of faith, hope, and charity daily, in one's own words or otherwise. The same applies to several other short prayers, such as "Angel of God," etc. Indulgences obtained in the hour of death are purely personal; they cannot even be applied to the souls in purgatory. As the dying cannot, with the best of wills, perform works of penance, the Church almost entirely exempts them from the obligation of trying to discharge the temporal debt of punishment due to their sins.

The partial indulgences granted by the Church are generally a quadragena, or forty days; or for a period of a hundred days, a year, five or seven years, very rarely for thirty or a hundred years. Those fixed periods do not mark the number of days or years by which the purgatorial fires are abridged; they do but indicate that as much of the temporal punishment of sin is remitted as would have been remitted by a corresponding period of the canonical penances formerly imposed on penitents.

4. **The Pope alone has power to grant indulgences which are for the whole Church; for in him alone jurisdiction over the whole Church is vested, and he is the steward of the Church's treasures.**

Bishops have the power to grant partial indulgences, but only for those in their own diocese; just as secular magistrates can only judge cases which come within the sphere of their jurisdiction. Bishops are sometimes authorized by the Holy See to grant indulgences of a year, or forty days, on such occasions as the dedication of a church.

5. **Indulgences may also be applied by way of suffrage to the suffering souls in purgatory, if this be expressly stated respecting the indulgence; a plenary indulgence is gained for them every time the holy sacrifice of the Mass is offered on a privileged altar.**

The communion of saints enables us to assist the holy souls in purgatory by applying to them our good works; those good works, that is, to which the remission of temporal punishment is attached. If we desire to gain an indulgence for the faithful departed we must see that we are ourselves in a state of grace. "Let him who would help to deliver the holy souls from purgatory," says St. Francis Xavier, "first see that he delivers his own soul from hell." The application of indulgences to the souls of the departed is by way of suffrage, not of absolution. It is by no means certain that the individual for whom a plenary indulgence is gained will be forthwith released from purgatory; the amount of punishment thereby remitted to him rests entirely with God to determine. The indulgence of the privileged altar consists in this, that whenever Mass is celebrated at that particular altar a plenary indulgence is given from the treasures of the Church to one of the souls in purgatory. In every cathedral there is one such altar, and in many parish churches or churches of an Order; the altars thus privileged are generally indicated by the inscription *altare privilegiatum,* and black vestments must be used when Mass is said at one of them, if the rubrics allow of it on that day. The privilege must be renewed by application to the bishop every seven years. The indulgence can be gained for one individual only, and for that one the Mass must be offered, but the priest may include in his intention other persons deceased. The intention of the priest is not necessary to the gaining of the indulgence; it will be seen that by no other means is a plenary indulgence so surely gained as by this, since it depends entirely upon the offering of the holy sacrifice, not upon the spiritual state of any individual. But whether the Mass celebrated at the privileged altar effects the complete deliverance of the soul from the pains of purgatory cannot be known, as it depends solely on the mercy of God. Priests who have made the heroic act of charity for the holy souls have the same privilege in their own person.

6. **The gaining of indulgences is most salutary (Council of Trent, 25), because we thereby keep far from us temporal evils, and are stimulated to the accomplishment of good works.**

The indulgences we gain avert from us sickness, calamities, temptations, etc., which, if no indulgence be gained, come upon us as the temporal punishment of sin. Thus those who neglect this practice, may be compared to a traveller who although he might reach his destination by a short and easy route, prefers to take a long and toilsome road; he is his own worst enemy. Some people take exception at the doctrine of indulgences, but this is because they do not understand it; others condemn it, because of the abuses in the Middle Ages. Was there ever a good and holy thing which was not misused by the wicked? The abuse of a thing does not diminish its usefulness. Therefore do not despise indulgences, for by despising them many have fallen into error and perdition.

5. EXTREME UNCTION.

Christ is the Good Samaritan, for by the hands of His representative, the priest, He pours into the wounds of the sick oil to effect his spiritual and physical cure.

1. In administering Extreme Unction the priest anoints the Christian who is in danger of death with the holy oils upon the organs of his five senses, and prays over him; by means of which the spiritual and not unfrequently the bodily malady of the sick man is cured.

The priest anoints the sick man with consecrated oil in the form of a cross on his five senses, which have been instrumental to his sins (eyes, ears, nose, mouth, hands and feet); at every unction he repeats the following form of prayer: "Through this holy unction and through His most tender mercy, may the Lord pardon thee whatever sins thou hast committed by seeing, hearing, etc." If the sick man is actually expiring, the priest only anoints his forehead; but he continues to anoint the other parts, so long as life has not departed. Extreme Unction is also called the last sacrament, because it is generally the last which is administered to the dying.

Extreme Unction is mentioned by St. James in his epistle.

We read: "Is any man sick among you? Let him bring in the priests of the Church, and let them pray over him, anointing him with oil in the name of the Lord; and the prayer of faith shall save the sick man, and the Lord shall raise him up: and if he be in sins, they shall be forgiven him" (Jas. v. 14, 15). Pope Innocent I., in the fourth century, expressly declared that these words referred to the Sacrament of Extreme Unction; and in the sixth century St. Cæsarius, Bishop of Arles, exhorts Christians in case of serious illness, to receive the Lord's body and be anointed with oil for their bodily restoration and the forgiveness of their sins. The sacred unction of the sick was instituted by Our Lord as a true sacrament of the New Law (Council of Trent, 14, 4). It confers grace, remits sin, and comforts the sick.

2. Extreme Unction acts spiritually as oil does materially; it strengthens, heals, and aids the soul to attain eternal salvation.

Oil strengthens the body (pugilists or wrestlers are rubbed with oil to give them greater power, and render it difficult for their adversary to grasp them); it possesses a healing power (witness the Good Samaritan, who poured oil on the wounds of the man who had fallen among thieves); and it imparts suppleness and flexibility.

1. Extreme Unction strengthens the sick because it confers on him grace to bear more easily the inconveniences and pains of sickness, and enables him more readily to resist temptation of all kinds.

A complete change is sometimes wrought in the sick by the reception of this sacrament; whereas they were previously impatient and in great dread of death, they become tranquil and patient and resigned to the will of God. At the close of life the adversary of our souls strains all the powers of his craft to ruin us utterly if he can, and make us fall from our trust in the mercy of God (Council of Trent, 14). Extreme Unction banishes the demon. It is recorded of St. Eleazar that on the near approach of death, his countenance became distorted, and he cried out that the devil was tormenting him; but after he had been anointed, peace and joy returned to him.

2. Extreme Unction is for the healing of the soul, and oftentimes of the body; it effects the remission of mortal sins, which through infirmity of mind or body the sick man has not been able to confess, as well as the remission of some temporal punishment. And besides, at times it obtains bodily health, when expedient for the welfare of the soul.

Extreme Unction compensates for all that, through no fault of his own, the sick man left incomplete in the Sacrament of Penance. It is thus the completion of the Sacrament of Penance, or the penance of the sick. By reason of physical and mental weakness the sick are rarely capable of making a good confession or doing penance; therefore the Church deals leniently with them, and by this unction commends them to the mercy of God. This anointing cleanses away sin, if there be any still to be expiated, and cancels a part of the penalty of sin, in proportion to the contrition and devotion wherewith the sacrament is received. Extreme Unction often obtains restoration to health. If God foresees that the sick man, if he recover, will make a good use of the remainder of his days for his spiritual advancement, He restores him to health, granting him a reprieve, as it were, that he may prepare himself better for death. But if He foresees that it will be otherwise, He takes him out of the world. As a rule, the sick experience some alleviation after receiving Extreme Unction; this is not to be explained on natural grounds; the peace of mind produced by confession and reconciliation with God acts beneficially upon the body. And in some cases by the interposition of divine power health is restored when human skill could do nothing. How foolish are those who imagine that if they receive Extreme Unction it will be their death warrant!

3. Extreme Unction facilitates our salvation, by increasing in us sanctifying grace and divine charity.

In common with all the other sacraments Extreme Unction imparts a higher degree of sanctifying grace. This is of more importance to us at our death than at any other moment, for the degree of our future felicity depends on the degree of sanctifying grace we possess. And the greater our love of God, the more capable shall we be of the enjoyment of eternal bliss.   Thus this holy sacrament cleanses away all that is an impediment to our eternal salvation.

3. Extreme Unction can only be administered to persons who are in danger of death; and they ought to receive it without delay for the sake both of their physical and spiritual health.

Only in cases of serious illness, that is, when there is danger of death, can the sick receive Extreme Unction. A soldier cannot receive it before going into action, nor a criminal condemned to death. Exception may be made in regard to very aged persons; their advanced age renders them constantly liable to death. The administration of the holy oils should not be postponed until the last moment, for if the sick man be unconscious, they will profit him little; since, as has been already remarked, the utility of this sacrament to the soul depends upon the contrition and devotion with which it is received. And the body cannot profit by it, if the vital spark be all but extinct.   It is little use calling out the fire engine when the house is almost burnt down. He who enters upon the journey from time to eternity without fortifying himself with the last sacraments, is like a traveller who starts on his way with an empty purse. Nor can there be contempt of so great a sacrament without heinous sin and an injury to the Holy Ghost Himself (Council of Trent, 14, 9).

Those who have not yet received the Sacrament of Penance cannot receive Extreme Unction since it is the completion of penance.

To this class belong idiots, and children who have not yet attained the age of reason. It must not, however, be supposed that this includes all children under seven, for children of five years of age have been known on their death-bed to ask for a priest, because they were conscious of having sinned against their parents.

Extreme Unction can only be administered to the sick once in the same illness; but if the sick person recovers temporarily, and then has a relapse, he may be anointed again.

4. Before being anointed the sick man ought to confess his sins, and receive holy communion; and afterwards the Papal blessing is generally given to him.

Confession should precede Extreme Unction, because the recipient of the sacrament must be in a state of grace. Extreme Unction is a remedy; and as medicine is for the living, not the dead, so this sacrament is of no utility to those who are spiritually dead. Every priest who has been duly authorized by the bishop, may give the Papal benediction, or general absolution, provided he makes use of the prescribed formula. The sick man must call upon the holy name of Jesus (the priest usually repeats some ejaculatory prayer to him, in which the name of Jesus occurs) verbally, if he can still speak, if not, mentally, and the crucifix is offered him to be kissed, otherwise the indulgence is not gained.

It is the duty of relatives, and of those who are in attendance upon the sick, to see that he receives the last sacraments in due time.

This responsibility rests partly with the doctor, who, as a matter of course, ought to apprise the friends of a sick person of his condition when it becomes serious. Catholics ought therefore if possible to secure the services of a Christian physician. Sometimes the attendants on a sick man fear to agitate him by mentioning the last sacraments to him. This is indeed mistaken kindness, for they cannot thereby retard the approach of death. Such false friends resemble people who do not warn a blind man that he is nearing a precipice, lest they should frighten him. Their cowardice will give them much to answer for. The friends of the sick man should set the room in order, and have everything that is needed in readiness for the administration of the last sacraments. A table should be covered with a white linen cloth, with a crucifix and two lighted tapers upon it, besides a vessel containing holy water, because the priest has to sprinkle both the chamber and the bystanders, and also a glass containing a little clean water, for the priest to wash his fingers and give the ablutions to the sick man after communion. Some cotton wool must also be provided to wipe the parts that have been anointed. While the sick man makes his confession let all leave the room, as the priest may have to speak above a whisper.

6. HOLY ORDERS.

At the time of His ascension, Our Lord lifted up His hands, blessed His apostles, and sent them forth into the world to preach the Gospel and dispense the sacraments (Luke xxiv. 50). The bishop does much the same when he ordains priests. (The imposition of hands signifies that something is given, since gifts are distributed with the hand.)

1. At the administration of Holy Orders the bishop lays his hands on the candidates for ordination, calls down upon them the Holy Ghost, anoints their hands, and presents the sacred vessels to them.

They thereby receive, in addition to a plenitude of grace, the sacerdotal powers; more especially the power to offer the holy sacrifice and to forgive sins.

Holy Orders are administered during the celebration of Mass. The candidates for ordination first prostrate themselves upon their faces before the altar; then the bishop lays his hands upon the head of each one severally, the priests present doing the same. He next arrays them in the sacerdotal vestments; the *Veni Sancte Spiritus* is sung, and he anoints the hands of each one in turn with the sacred chrism in the form of a cross. He then gives the chalice and paten into their hands, thereby conferring on them the power to offer the holy sacrifice; after which he addresses to them the words of Our Lord: " Receive ye the Holy Ghost; whose sins you shall forgive, they are forgiven, etc." Finally the newly-ordained are required to promise respect and obedience to the bishop. The ceremony of anointing the hands, and presenting the sacred vessels is only an accessory; it was not in use until the ninth century, and now has no place in the Greek ritual. Not only supernatural powers, but graces are imparted in the Sacrament of Orders. By this sacred ordinance the Holy Ghost is given (Council of Trent, 13, 2).

The Sacrament of Holy Orders was administered in the time of the apostles.

We read that the apostles consecrated Paul and Barnabas with prayer and imposition of hands (Acts xiii. 3), and in like manner St. Paul consecrated Timothy (2 Tim. i. 6). St. Augustine speaks of Orders as a sacrament when he inveighs against the Donatists, who asserted that while Baptism confers what can never be lost, the right of administering Baptism may be lost. " Both," he declares, " are sacraments, and can only be received once." The Sacrament of Orders was unquestionably instituted by Our Lord at the Last Supper.

2. The office of the priesthood, to which a man is raised by Holy Orders, is one of great dignity, but likewise one of no slight difficulty and of vast responsibility.

The priesthood is the highest dignity upon earth. It surpasses that of kings and emperors, nay, even of the angels themselves. " For," as St. John Chrysostom remarks, " the power of kings is only over the bodies of men, whereas that of the priest is over their souls." On the priest are conferred powers not accorded to angels; for to what angel was it ever given to convert bread into the body of the Lord by his word? and not all the angels together could grant pardon for a single sin. By his office a priest is only concerned with heavenly things; he stands between God and man; he lays our petition before the Most High and conveys divine graces to us. He is a mediator between God and man, the angel of the Lord of hosts (Mal. ii. 7), the messenger of God to make known His will to men. He is God's representative, His ambassador, His plenipotentiary; therefore whatsoever honor we show to the priest, we pay to God Himself. Does not Our Lord Himself say: " He that heareth you, heareth Me; and he that despiseth you, despiseth Me" (Luke x. 16)? In fact, St. Peter Damian says, God actually follows the priest, for what he declares on earth is ratified in heaven; and at his word the Second Person of the Holy Trinity becomes flesh beneath his hand as at the Incarnation. Hence we do well to address the priest as " your reverence." St. Francis of Assisi used to say that if he met an angel and a priest at the same time he should salute the priest first. The sacerdotal office is also one of great difficulty; the obligations resting upon the priest are neither few nor light. He has to recite the breviary daily, which cannot be done under an hour and a quarter; he is pledged to lifelong celibacy; he has to visit the sick at any hour of the day or night when he may be called upon; he has to take the last sacraments to the dying, however contagious the disease from which they are suffering; he has often to sit for long hours in the confessional, to fast late, on account of the late Masses; he is bound to renounce all worldly amusements (such as dancing), to be liberal towards the poor, and much more besides. Priests ought to be the salt of the earth (Matt. v. 13). Nor must it be overlooked that zealous priests are in the present day frequently the objects of suspicion and persecution, and their apostolic labors are ill-rewarded. The votaries of the world are inclined to treat their priests like the dog in the fable, who bit the hand that was stretched out to save him from drowning. The priestly office is besides one of immense responsibility. If the wolf comes and rends the sheep, the shepherd is taken to task. So it is with the priests; they have to render an account of the souls committed to their charge (Heb. xiii. 17). "The duties of those who will have to give account for souls," says St. Bernard, "are heavy and onerous." On the day of his ordination St. John Chrysostom said: "I now need your prayers a thousandfold more, lest in the Day of Judgment I should be cast into the exterior darkness."

Since the sacerdotal office is in itself an office of such great dignity, we owe profound respect to the priest on account of his office, even if his life should not correspond to it.

Nothing can take away the dignity attaching to the priestly office, not even an ungodly life; therefore we ought always to entertain great reverence for it. Even pagan monarchs have been known to manifest deep veneration for the priests of the true God. When Alexander the Great was about to make a triumphal entry into Jerusalem, the high priest went out to meet him with all the priests arrayed in festal vestments, in order to ask a favor of him. Alexander dismounted from his horse, and instantly granted all that he asked. And when the general of the army expressed his surprise, Alexander replied: "It is not the high priest to whom I pay homage, but to the true God, Whose servant he is." Attila also, the terrible King of the Huns, when advancing upon Rome to plunder the city, allowed himself to be prevailed upon by Pope Leo the Great, to desist from his purpose. Yet almighty God permits His priests to be encompassed with infirmity, in order that they may have the more compassion on them that are ignorant and that err (Heb. v. 2). St. Francis of Sales said of priests: "I will close my eyes to their faults, and only see in them God's representatives." How blameworthy are those who publish far and wide the misdeeds of a priest! "Are we," asks St. Augustine, "to think slightingly of Christ and the apostles, because there was a Judas among them? Who will show me any body of men upon earth who are without faults?"

Since the office of the priesthood is one of much labor and grave responsibilities, no man ought to take Holy Orders who is not called to the sacerdotal state.

Let no man become a priest who feels no attraction for the sacred ministry; who has no longing to save souls, who leads an irregular life, or who only thinks of the priesthood as a means of gaining a living easily, and enjoying a comfortable competence. Parents are greatly to blame who force their sons to take Orders without a vocation, for those who enter the priesthood without a true vocation are unhappy and discontented all their life long. They neglect the duties of their calling, give scandal, and finally too often lose their souls. For this reason many eminent saints positively refused to receive Holy Orders or to be raised to the episcopate. St. Francis of Assisi remained a deacon to the end of his days. St. Cyprian concealed himself when he was to be appointed Bishop of Carthage; St. John Chrysostom and St. Basil acted in a similar manner. They all considered themselves unworthy of the dignity offered them, and only accepted it when they recognized it to be the will of God that they should do so. Almighty God calls to the priesthood whom He will; witness Our Lord's words to the apostles: " You have not chosen Me, but I have chosen you " (John xv. 16).

3. The Sacrament of Holy Orders only confers the perpetual power, not the right, to exercise the functions of a priest. The newly ordained cannot therefore make use in any place of their sacerdotal powers, until they have received ecclesiastical authorization.

The qualification for the sacred ministry consists in the transmission of the powers appertaining to the sacerdotal office: those of a teacher, a priest and a pastor. In the Old Testament the priestly powers were hereditary in Aaron's family (Exod. xxviii.); in the New Testament they are handed down by spiritual descent by means of Holy Orders. Besides these powers, the priest receives at ordination abundant graces belonging to his state. Outwardly he may appear the same, but inwardly he is a changed man. An indelible character is imprinted upon his soul by that ordinance; the powers he has received can never be lost, into whatever sins he may fall. He who has once been a priest cannot again become a layman (Council of Trent, 23, 4); a priest who has apostatized and been reconciled to the Church is not re-ordained. All the sacerdotal acts of a priest who has seceded from the Church are valid, only he cannot forgive sins (except in the case of the dying, when no other priest can be had). Priests of the schismatic Greek Church are not ordained again, if they return to the allegiance of the Catholic Church; but the Protestant clergy most certainly are. Ecclesiastical jurisdiction is given to the priest by his bishop; the bishops receive it from the Pope. The secular authorities have no power to grant ecclesiastical jurisdiction, for it is not theirs to give. Even in the time of the apostles the deacons were not nominated by the people; the apostles ordained those who had been chosen and appointed them to the work (Acts vi. 3, 6). St. Timothy was consecrated to the episcopate by the imposition of the hands of the priesthood (1 Tim. i. 14). Consequently the apostles called themselves the " ministers of Christ " (1 Cor. iv. 1). Any one who should attempt to exercise sacerdotal functions without the authorization of the bishop, would, as Our Lord says, be a thief and a robber, because "he entereth not by the door into the sheepfold, but climbeth in some other way" (John x. 1). A priest must have faculties for hearing confessions, from the bishop of the diocese where he happens to be. This is separate from the pastoral office. A catechist, or teacher, who imparts religious instruction should also have the episcopal authorization. Any one who should be so daring as to exercise any priestly functions without having been admitted to Holy Orders or without episcopal authorization, would, in Catholic countries, be punished by the secular government; at any rate, terrible chastisements would fall on him from God. King Ozias presumed, in spite of the warning of the priests, to burn incense on the altar of incense; he was immediately struck with leprosy, and was a leper until the day of his death (2 Par. xxvi.). In the time of Moses, Core, with two hundred and fifty of the leading men of the synagogue, rebelled against Moses and presumed to offer incense in the tabernacle; they were destroyed by fire from the Lord, and the earth swallowed up the three ringleaders (Numb. xvi.).

4. No one can be admitted to priest's Orders who has not attained the age of twenty-four years (Council of Trent, 23, 12).

The Holy See has the right of dispensing candidates for the priesthood if they are within twenty months of the required age. Besides the prescribed ages, those who are to be raised to the priesthood must possess the following qualifications: They must have the knowledge suited to, and necessary for, the due discharge of their functions; they must be conspicuous for piety and chastity; they must have been born in wedlock and be free from physical defects which might excite derision in others. Men who have been married twice are disqualified for the priesthood, although those who have been married once may, under certain conditions, be received. All men cannot be priests (Eph. iv. 11; 1 Cor. xii. 29). Yet we frequently find all the faithful spoken of as priests (1 Pet. ii. 9), inasmuch as they ought to accomplish to the glory of God good works which are in a certain measure a spiritual oblation; they are priests inasmuch as they immolate themselves in the service of God as spiritual victims. In the same sense the faithful in general are spoken of as kings, because they ought to rule over their fleshly lusts.

5. Six other órders of ministry precede the priesthood, four lesser and two greater.

By these several and divers Orders, as by certain steps, advance is made unto the priesthood (Council of Trent, 23, 4). This is to emphasize the dignity of the priesthood. For the same reason a fixed period of time must intervene between the reception of the different degrees of higher orders. The first preparation for Orders is the reception of the tonsure, by which a man is taken into the ranks of the clergy, and becomes a cleric, no longer a layman. In giving the tonsure, the bishop cuts off some of the hair from the top of the candidate's head. After this the four minor Orders are given, which impart to him who receives them the right to minister

to the priest by virtue of his office. The first of the three greater
Orders, the subdiaconate, follows. This was formerly reckoned
among the minor Orders, but is classed by the Council of Trent
among the major Orders; it confers the right to arrange everything
in the sanctuary, and serve the priest at the altar, and pledges the
recipient to celibacy and to the recitation of the breviary. The
bishop may empower an ordinary priest to administer the tonsure
and the four minor Orders, but not so the greater.

6. There are three degrees in the Sacrament of Orders: The
consecration of deacons, priests, and bishops. These three constitute but one sacrament.

The second of the greater Orders is the diaconate, which was instituted by the apostles for the relief of the poor. It confers the
power to preach, to baptize, and to dispense holy communion. The
three most celebrated deacons mentioned in the annals of the Church
are St. Stephen, who was stoned by the Jews; St. Lawrence, who
was broiled upon a gridiron in Rome; and St. Francis of Assisi, the
founder of the Franciscan Order, who bore in his body the sacred
stigmata. One year after the acceptance of the diaconate follows
ordination proper, the priesthood, whereby the power is given to
offer the holy sacrifice of the Mass, and to forgive sins. There is
one degree higher than the priesthood, and that is the episcopate.
By this power is conferred to ordain priests, to administer Confirmation and to rule the Church of God. For the consecration of a
bishop three bishops must take part. These three ordinations form
but one sacrament. The consecration of deacons appertains virtually to the Sacrament of Holy Orders, because it confers an inferior
part of the sacerdotal powers, and is administered with imposition
of hands and prayer. St. Paul mentions deacons together with bishops and priests; the Fathers speak of them with the utmost reverence, as the "ministers of God," and the Council of Trent reckons
them of the ecclesiastical hierarchy (Council of Trent, 23, 6). The
consecration of priests appertains to the Sacrament of Orders, because by it the greater part of the sacerdotal powers are conferred.
The consecration of bishops is the completion of the Sacrament of
Orders; by it the plenitude of the sacerdotal power is communicated.
The principal distinction between a bishop and a priest is that the
former can ordain priests and the latter cannot. When at the
Council of Alexandria in 319, the Arians accused St. Athanasius,
who was then bishop of that town, of having treated a priest named
Ischyras with undue severity, the Synod dismissed the charge on
the ground that Ischyras was not a priest, since he had been ordained
by a priest, not a bishop.

7. It is the duty of the faithful to pray God to send them
good priests.

Our Lord says: "Pray ye the Lord of the harvest that He send
forth laborers into His harvest" (Matt. ix. 38). Remember that a
priest is the salvation or the perdition of his flock. In the Old Testament we read that when other scourges were of no avail to turn the

people, hardened in sin, from their evil ways, God sent upon them the heaviest scourge of all, wicked and corrupt priests. Let us therefore make it our continual prayer, that we may have good priests. The Ember days are appointed for this purpose. Special prayer should be offered to the Holy Ghost, for unless a priest is enlightened by the Holy Spirit we may apply to him the words: " If the blind lead the blind, both fall into the pit " (Matt. xv. 14).

7. MATRIMONY.

The Institution and Nature of Matrimony.

What food is to the individual, matrimony is to humanity in general. For as food serves to maintain the life of the individual, so marriage serves to maintain the life of the human race. Since the principal object of marriage, the right training of children, can only be attained when a man and a woman are united together by an indissoluble bond, the wise Creator in the beginning only created two human beings, saying: " They two shall be one in flesh " (Gen. ii. 24).

1. God Himself instituted matrimony in the beginning of the world, for the procreation of the human race, and the mutual assistance of husband and wife.

Matrimony was instituted by God for the propagation of the human race; for He said to our first parents: " Increase and multiply and fill the earth " (Gen. i. 28). St. Francis of Sales calls matrimony the nursery-ground of Christianity, destined to fill the earth with believers, and complete the number of the elect in heaven. It was also instituted for the mutual support of the parties contracting it, for God said before Eve was created: " It is not good for man to be alone, let us make him a help like unto himself " (Gen. ii. 18). The woman being the weaker, needs some one on whom to lean; the man needs some one to care for him. The man is characterized by greater strength and energy; he seeks a sphere of activity in the world. The woman's nature is cast in a softer mould; her sphere of work is beside the domestic hearth. Thus the two complete each other, and each acts beneficially on the other. Matrimony has also a third object, that of preventing the sin of which the Apostle speaks in the first Epistle to the Corinthians (1 Cor. vii. 2). He who would set marriage aside, would give free rein to impurity. Many take a low view of marriage; they consider it as affording a legitimate means of indulging their lusts. Such persons will not be happy or contented, and will neglect the duties of their state. The happiness of matrimony depends to a great extent on taking an exalted view of its object.

Matrimony is a divine and by no means a human institution.

It is because matrimony was ordained of God that the Church calls it a " holy and godly state." The opinion of the Manichees, that marriage was to be rejected, was condemned by the Church.

Even the most uncivilized nations considered matrimony to be a divine institution, for they practised religious ceremonies of some kind on the occasion of a marriage, offering sacrifices or prayers. God Himself appointed the laws of marriage first through Moses and afterwards by Our Lord.

2. Christian marriage is a contract between man and woman, binding them to an undivided and indissoluble partnership, and conferring on them at the same time grace to fulfil all the duties required of them.

Marriage is therefore not merely a contract; it is at the same time an act by which grace is conferred. This contract is not concluded in the presence of a minister of the Church solely for the sake of obtaining the ecclesiastical benediction upon the betrothed couple, but in order that they may be truly united together before God in wedlock. It was this covenant, entered into in presence of a minister of the Church, which Our Lord raised to the dignity of a sacrament. Marriage contracted without the solemnities required by the Church in all countries where the decree of the Council of Trent has been duly promulgated is invalid and null (Council of Trent, 24, 1). A contract which is invalid cannot become a sacrament, any more than wine, if it be not really wine, can be converted in the Mass into the blood of Christ. Matrimony is a type of the union between Christ and the Church (Eph. v. 32). As the Church, the Bride of Christ is one, so the man has but one wife. As Christ and the Church are inseparably united, so the union of the married is perpetual and indissoluble. As the union of Christ and the Church is a covenant of grace, so also is the union of husband and wife. Christ is the Head of the Church, and the man is the head of the woman. The Church is subject to Christ, so the wife is obedient to the husband. Christ and the Church are animated by one spirit, and so it should be with husband and wife. Christ never abandons the Church, and the Church can never be unfaithful to Christ; so married people must never be unfaithful to one another.

Matrimony is declared to be a sacrament by St. Paul, and the early Fathers of the Church.

St. Paul calls matrimony a great sacrament, because it is typical of the union of Christ with the Church (Eph. v. 32), a union by which grace is imparted. St. Augustine says that the superiority of marriage among the people of God consists in the sanctity of the sacrament. "The heathens," says St. John Chrysostom, "estimated the happiness of marriage by the number of children, whereas the Christian considers rather the sanctity of the sacrament." Some of the Fathers are of opinion that Christ raised matrimony to a sacrament at the marriage of Cana. At any rate the Church expressly declares that it is truly and properly one of the seven sacraments of the evangelical law instituted by Christ (Council of Trent, 24, 1).

3. Civil marriage is to be distinguished from Christian marriage, inasmuch as it is no sacrament, and consequently in the sight of God no true and real marriage for Catholics.

Civil marriage may be said to have originated with Luther, for he prepared the way for the State to legislate concerning marriage. What he began, the French revolution completed; for marriage was then declared to be a civil contract, concluded before a government official. Civil marriage is obligatory or compulsory when, as is the case in some countries, the marriage is otherwise not recognized by the State; it is optional, when the parties are free to choose whether the ceremony shall be civil or religious, as in America; finally it is unavoidable, if on account of the priest being debarred from marrying them through political reasons, or on other obvious grounds, the persons desirous of being married cannot be united otherwise than by the secular authorities. Civil marriage is not a sacrament, because it is not contracted in the manner ordained by God and the Church; it is nothing more or less than a legal form, which must be gone through in order that the marriage may be recognized by the State, and Catholics must submit to it, if there is no other means of having their union recognized by the State. They should, however, see that the ecclesiastical ceremony takes place as soon after as possible; for until their marriage has been solemnized by the Church, they are bound to live apart, as in the sight of God they are not really husband and wife. Catholics who contract a civil marriage and are not afterwards married in a church, cannot obtain absolution, and are excluded from the sacraments until they obtain the sanction of God and of the Church upon their union, or give it up altogether. Catholics who prefer civil marriage when it is optional, or content themselves with it when it is unavoidable, are excommunicated. The Holy See condemns civil marriages in no measured terms; Pope Pius IX. declares that the union of man and woman, if not a sacrament, is a shameful concubinage, although perfectly legal according to the civil code.*

Civil marriage has disastrous results for the State, for it undermines faith, authority, and morals.

The Holy Father asserts civil marriage to be a fatal institution. To render it compulsory is to overthrow the law of God, for it is tantamount to asserting that Christian marriage as ordained by God is invalid, that a union blessed by the Church is contrary to law. What would be said if stealing, or any other crime forbidden by the divine command, were enforced by the law of the land? Rebellion such as this against God cannot fail to undermine faith in God and respect for His commandments; and experience proves that the government which undermines the divine authority brings about its own downfall. Civil marriages are also detrimental to morality. Divorce is

---

* What is said in this paragraph respecting the *invalidity* of civil or clandestine marriage is only true in those countries where the decree *Tametsi* of the Council of Trent has been duly promulgated. In England, Scotland, and most of the United States of America marriage contracted between two baptized Catholics without the sanction of the Church is a valid marriage and a sacrament, although an unlawful and sacrilegious act. In all cases where there is any doubt about the validity of a marriage the parish priest or the bishop of the diocese should be consulted.

an easy matter for persons who have been married by the registrar; on a comparatively slight disagreement or offence they are separated, each being free to contract a second marriage. What is the consequence? The flood-gates are opened to admit unbridled license, the so-called free-love advocated by the Socialist. This is proved by the number of divorce cases following on the introduction of civil marriage; nor need we wonder, for in a civil marriage no promise of mutual love, no vow of fidelity is required from the contracting parties.

The Characteristics of Matrimony.

According to the ordinance of Christ, Christian marriage is strictly a union of two persons only, and it is indissoluble.

Matrimony was raised by Our Lord to the dignity of a state of evangelical perfection, to which weightier responsibilities and more laborious duties were attached than in the ages preceding His advent. He therefore granted greater graces to those who should enter into wedlock.

1. Christian marriage consists of the union of one man and one woman only.

By creating only one man and one woman, God manifested it to be His will that marriage should be the union of two persons only. Our Lord pointed out that in the beginning this was so (Matt. xix. 4). The marriage that does not answer to this description cannot possibly be a true and lasting partnership; domestic strife must infallibly ensue. Yet in the earliest times God permitted polygamy, to prevent greater evils. A plurality of wives is forbidden by Our Lord (Luke xvi. 18), consequently it is prohibited most strictly by the law of the Church. Polygamy is unlawful, and a violation of the natural law (Council of Trent, 23, 2). It continues, however, to exist among Mohammedans, and among Jews in the East; but in the West ever since the Middle Ages the Jews have given it up, in deference to the code of morality observed by European nations.

2. Christian marriage is indissoluble; that is to say, neither husband nor wife can contract a second marriage during the lifetime of the other.

The principal object of matrimony is to provide for the proper bringing up of children, an object which could not be attained if the nuptial tie were dissoluble. What would become of the children if the parents were free to separate at their pleasure? Our Lord strictly forbids any one to marry again as long as the partner of his or her first marriage is living (Matt. v. 32; Mark x. 11). Under the law of Moses, the Jews were, it is true, permitted under exceptional circumstances to put away their wives; but this was only by reason of the hardness of their hearts, and to prevent worse evils (Matt. xix. 8). Christ withdrew this permission; He says expressly: " What

God hath joined together, let no man put asunder " (Matt. xix. 4-9). Hence the Popes have never allowed one of two lawfully married persons to contract a second marriage during the lifetime of the other party. Not even for the sake of averting the most serious calamities could they consent to such a thing. It is well known that King Henry VIII. of England could not wring from the Holy See permission to divorce his rightful wife, and marry another. That even in consideration of the services he had rendered to the cause of religion, and of the fearful consequences which would ensue upon the introduction of the Lutheran heresy into England could Clement VII. be prevailed upon to give any other reply than this: "*Non possumus;* I have no authority to set aside the divine law." " Matrimony," says St. Augustine, " is an iron chain." A man can sell a house which he has bought if it does not suit him; but once married, he cannot get rid of his wife. The soul can separate from the body sooner than the husband from the wife. And if either party should contract a second marriage while the other is still alive, he or she commits a mortal sin, and the marriage is invalid. It is, however, possible for a married couple to be separated, provided there are sufficient grounds for separation. If either party is guilty of adultery, the separation may be for life, since by the violation of a contract the rights conferred by that contract are lost; yet neither can enter upon fresh espousals (Matt. v. 32). Dissolute conduct, or cruelty on either side, would afford a reason for a temporary separation, which must be judicial. And if the parties agree to cohabit again they can do so at will.

The Graces Conferred in Matrimony.

The Sacrament of Matrimony confers upon Christians who embrace that state both an increase of sanctifying grace, and in addition the special graces necessary to enable them to discharge the duties required of them.

The special graces annexed to this sacrament are: (1), The mutual affection of those who receive it is confirmed and sanctified; (2), Strength is given them to preserve inviolable fidelity to one another, and bear with patience the ills of life. For as soon as a man is married, he is no longer free as when single; no longer absolute master of his will, his time, his goods, his person, but he is in a measure dependent on the will of his wife; he wears the yoke, " for marriage," as St. Ambrose says, " is a yoke, a double yoke which rests on the neck of both husband and wife, obliging them to pull together." To this is added many trials such as ill health, the faults and failings of the other, which must be borne with; troubles with the children, etc. Finally grace is given to discharge the most important duty of all, that of bringing up their children in the fear and love of God. " Unhappy those," says Pope Gregory XVI., " who enter upon the married state from merely earthly motives, or for sensual gratification, and do not think of the graces and mysteries which this sacrament confers and represents."

Impediments to Matrimony.

A marriage can only be concluded in the absence of all impediments to it. The impediments may be such as nullify marriage, or such as render it unlawful.

1. Those that render marriage null or invalid, are: Coercion, defect of age, consanguinity, and affinity, a previous marriage tie still existing, the greater degrees of Holy Orders, solemn vows, the prohibition concerning the marriage of Catholics with unbaptized persons.

Coercion: If undue stress is brought to bear on a man, if he is forced into marrying some one against his will by threats of personal injury, or fear of being disinherited, his marriage is invalid. Defect of age: Boys under fourteen, girls under twelve cannot enter into wedlock. Consanguinity: A Papal dispensation is required for the marriage of first cousins; in the case of more remote relationship an episcopal dispensation is sufficient. The voice of nature condemns the union of persons nearly related to one another, and their offspring are not unfrequently physically or mentally afflicted. Affinity is the result of a previous marriage; the survivor cannot espouse the blood-relations of the deceased party; that is, a man cannot marry the mother, sister, or daughter (by a former husband) of his deceased wife, and vice versa. But no affinity exists between the blood-relations of the several parties; for instance, a man may marry the sister of his brother's wife. Previous marriage: It has already been explained that one of the parties to a marriage cannot marry again during the lifetime of the other. Should a woman, believing her husband to be dead, have married again, she must immediately leave her second husband, if she discover the first to be still living. Holy Orders and religious vows: Clerics who have received deacon's or subdeacon's orders, and monks and nuns who have taken a vow of celibacy, cannot enter upon the married state. Difference of creed: A Christian cannot, without a dispensation from the Holy See, be married to a Jew, a Mohammedan, or any other unbeliever. There are besides, impediments of a purely ecclesiastical nature, such as spiritual affinity, contracted in Baptism or Confirmation. These are not recognized by the State, and therefore the Church readily grants a dispensation if required.

2. The impediments that render marriage unlawful, are:
The prohibition in regard to certain times, diversity of religious belief, betrothal, simple vows, complete ignorance of religious truth.

The times when marriages cannot be celebrated are from the beginning of Advent until the Epiphany, and from Ash Wednesday until Low Sunday (see the fifth precept of the Church). Diversity of religious belief: Marriages between Catholics and non-Catholics (Protestants, Old Catholics, non-uniate Greeks), can only be permitted under certain conditions. Betrothed: Any one who has pledged his troth to one person cannot marry another until the previous engagement is broken off. Simple vows: Vows which are not solemn, vows of perpetual chastity, of celibacy; the vow to enter a religious Order or become a priest, are a hindrance to marriage. Ignorance of religious truth: Those who are about to marry must, if they are ignorant of the fundamental truths of religion, place themselves under instruction for some time previously, otherwise they will be unable to teach their children the elements of the Christian religion. Hence it is usual for the priest to question those who announce to him their purpose of marrying, about the truths of religion, and if necessary instruct them in the duties and obligations of the married state.

3. Impediments of a purely civil nature, such as minority, military service, recent widowhood.

In some States minors cannot marry without the consent of their father, or if he be dead, of the magistrate. Soldiers, the term of whose military service has not expired, must have the sanction of the government officials; widows and widowers should allow a certain interval to elapse before concluding a second matrimonial alliance. The civil regulations in regard to matrimony must be observed, not from fear of the penalties incurred by violating them, but for God's sake, since the secular powers are ordained of God (Rom. xiii. 1). This rule would not hold good if the decrees of the legislature were opposed to the commandments of God.

4. The ecclesiastical authorities are accustomed to dispense from matrimonial impediments where good reasons exist; the secular authorities do likewise.

The Pope alone can dispense from some impediments, such as near blood-relationship, or affinity by marriage; from others the bishop can grant dispensations, either in virtue of his office, or empowered by the Holy See. There are some natural impediments from which not even the Supreme Pontiff can grant a dispensation; nor is one ever granted to step-fathers and step-daughters, to fathers-in-law and daughters-in-law. Very rarely can a dispensation be obtained from solemn vows, or the greater Orders; nor in the case of one party being unbaptized, of spiritual affinity contracted in Baptism, or in the relations of uncle and niece, aunt and nephew. Purely ecclesiastical impediments allow much more readily of a dispensation.

5. If a marriage to which any impediment rendering it invalid exists, should have been contracted, it must either be dissolved, or the impediment must be removed by means of a dispensation, and the ceremony performed over again.

If the invalidity of the marriage is known publicly, the nuptial contract must be renewed in the church, in presence of the parish priest and two witnesses; if not, it can be renewed privately. If one only of the parties to the marriage is aware of the impediment, and if the other, should it come to his knowledge, would make use of it to dissolve the marriage, or if it would destroy the conjugal happiness of both, the Pope has power to dispense from the renewal of the matrimonial contract, and declare the union valid. It is advisable, in order to bring to light any impediments that may exist to their marriage, that the parties intending to be united in wedlock should be subjected to an interrogation by the clergyman in presence of two witnesses. It is a grievous sin on the part of betrothed persons wilfully to conceal any impediment which would annul their marriage. It is for the sake of ascertaining whether any such hindrances exist that the banns of marriage are published three times in the church.

The Celebration of Matrimony.

1. Marriage must be preceded by betrothal, by the publication of the banns, and by the reception of the Sacraments of Penance and of the Altar.

1. Betrothal consists in this: An unmarried man and an unmarried woman, after due reflection, pledge their troth to one another, promising each to marry the other at the time agreed upon between them.

Rash and hasty engagements always turn out badly, therefore young people should not take this step without mature deliberation. They ought also to ask advice of their parents, or trusted friends. Listen to the exhortations of Holy Scripture: "My son, do thou nothing without counsel, and thou shall not repent what thou hast done" (Ecclus. xxxii. 24). They ought also to make it a subject of prayer, for a prudent wife is properly from the Lord (Prov. xix. 14). A matter so important as the tying of the nuptial knot, which can never be unloosed, must not be done without prayer. In making choice of a partner for life, advantages of wealth, high birth, and the like, ought not to be as much considered as virtue and piety. The fear of God, the love of virtue, are the best marriage portion for Christians; for a man who does not love God will not love his wife. "Let him who desires happiness in the married state," says St. Augustine, "not choose for his bride one who has a large dowry, but one who is proficient in virtue; let him look to the beauty of the heart, to the nobility of a pure life." Personal beauty, if not accompanied by interior loveliness, may captivate for a time, but its power is not lasting. Yet no man is to be blamed who has an eye to such attractions in his wife as beauty, wealth, and rank, for these in no wise interfere with the sanctity of the marriage bond. A virtuous man will surely have a partner worthy of him. A good wife is the portion of those that fear God, and is given to a man for his good deeds (Ecclus. xxvi. 3). During the interval between the betrothal and the conclusion of the marriage, the affianced parties ought seriously to reflect upon the step they are about to take, and make the best possible preparation for wedded life. Let them avoid all association on familiar terms with other suitors, and conduct themselves in

general with great decorum; the holy Synod exhorts the bridegroom
and bride not to live in the same house until they have received the
sacerdotal benediction which is given in the Church (Council of
Trent, 24, 1). "Happy the young men and maidens," says St. John
Chrysostom, "who come to the nuptial altar with a pure heart! How
true will be their mutual love! how sincere their mutual esteem!
how firm their mutual friendship! how tenderly will that man
cherish his wife who has never bestowed his affections on another!"
Those who have formed illicit connections before marriage will
quickly tire of one another, their love will change to hatred. Those
who are betrothed ought to acknowledge frankly to one another, without attempt at concealment or misrepresentation, any circumstances
which it may be advisable or necessary to make known before the
marriage is consummated. Those who resort to deception or falsehood only prepare for themselves annoyance, embitterment, misery in
the future. If after betrothal, the conviction is borne in on either of
the affianced parties that their union will not be productive of happiness, let the engagement be broken off by mutual consent; moreover
one party is warranted in withdrawing from the contract if the other
should be found guilty of any grave delinquency, such as breach of
promise, treachery, theft, or the like; or if his circumstances should
be altered by any unforeseen event of importance, such as the complete loss of property, severe illness, etc.

2. The publication of banns is as follows: The names of
the contracting parties between whom the marriage is to be concluded, shall be announced publicly three times in the parish
church during the solemnization of Mass on three successive
Sundays or festival days (Council of Trent, 24, 1).

The name, calling, birthplace and place of residence of the affianced couple are proclaimed at the publication of their banns. The
purpose of the announcement is to ascertain whether any impediment
exists to their lawful union, and to announce to the parishioners the
intended nuptials, that no scandal may be caused by their cohabita-
tion. The marriage must on no account take place until after the day
of the third announcement, but if it is not celebrated within six
months of that time, the publication of the banns must be repeated.
Only in exceptional cases is the publication of banns to be omitted,
and the omission must be sanctioned by the bishop of the diocese.

3. It is also enjoined on persons intending to marry to approach the Sacraments of Penance and of the Altar, because it
is indispensable that they should be in a state of grace, in order
to participate in the graces conferred in the Sacrament of Matrimony.

All who are about to marry are exhorted, at least three days before
the consummation of their marriage carefully to confess their sins
and receive devoutly the Most Holy Sacrament of the Altar (Council
of Trent, 24, 1). The confession should be general, embracing the
whole life, because it will then have the effect of awakening greater

contrition, and of setting the conscience more fully at rest. Our Lord, Who condescended to be present at the marriage at Cana, must also be invited to come to the bridgroom and bride, to sanctify them, and bestow His grace and blessing on their nuptials. Happy those who prepare a fitting dwelling in their heart for the divine Guest! Without presumption on their part, they may hope that He will remain with them until death, and impart to them the gift of His grace in abundant measure. But those who do not approach the sacraments worthily, and enter upon the matrimonial state in mortal sin, deprive themselves of grace, and call down on themselves the curse of God. They who thus act are like warriors going to the fight without armor and without arms.

2. The Church expressly commands that the marriage be concluded in the presence of the priest of the parish, and two witnesses; or the parish priest may authorize another priest to act in his place.

The decree to this effect was issued by the Council of Trent. The marriage ceremony must therefore be a public and an ecclesiastical ceremony. In early times it took place in presence of the bishop. St. Ignatius, Bishop of Antioch, says: " It is right that affianced persons should conclude their nuptials only with the knowledge and sanction of the bishop, that thus their union may be in accordance with the will of God." " It was God," says St. Francis of Sales, " Who gave Eve to Adam, and He it is Who must bind the marriage bond." Those who shall attempt to contract marriage otherwise than in the presence of their parish priest, and in presence of two or three witnesses, consequently not in accordance with the Tridentine decree, form a contract which is null and void (Council of Trent, 24, 1).*

3. Marriages are, as a rule, celebrated in the forenoon, in the house of God, with solemn ceremonies, and Mass is usually said at the time.

Entrance into the state of matrimony is an event of great moment, one which influences the whole life. St. Paul terms matrimony " a great sacrament." Hence the affianced couple ought to conduct themselves with the utmost reverence, and not hasten out of the church the moment the ceremony is ended, but remain a while kneeling before the altar to make their thanksgiving. Thus Tertullian declares that the early Christians sealed their marriage contract with prayers, and ratified it with the holy sacrifice. In the missal a special Mass *pro sponso et sponsa*, is provided. For the celebration of nuptials in secret, in the presence of trusted witnesses only, the episcopal sanction must be obtained, and also for the celebration of marriage in the afternoon.

The ceremonial for the celebration of matrimony is significant of the duties of the married and of the graces in which they participate.

* See note on page 651.

The bride usually comes to the altar wearing a wreath, which is emblematical of the victory she has won in the preservation of her innocence. The bridegroom stands on the right of the altar, the bride upon the left, the witnesses stand behind them. The priest then asks each separately if with their free will and consent they enter into wedlock, and on their answering in the affirmative with an audible voice, they join hands, each holding the right hand of the other (to confirm their promise as by an oath); they pledge their troth, repeating the formula after the priest, in which they each promise separately to have and to hold the other for better, for worse, for richer, for poorer, in sickness and in health, till death do part them. The priest then placing his stole round their joined hands (to indicate the indissolubility of the nuptial tie), unites them in the name of the Holy Trinity, and sprinkles them with holy water. This done, the bridegroom places upon the book the ring, which the priest blesses and gives back to the bridegroom, who places it on the thumb of the bride, saying: "In the name of the Father;" then on the second finger, saying: "and of the Son;" then on the third, saying: "and of the Holy Ghost;" lastly on the fourth, saying: "Amen." After this, some prayers are recited over the newly married couple, and if the nuptial benediction is to be given, Mass is said, at which it is usual for them to communicate. In conclusion the solemn benediction is given, in which peace, happiness, long life, are besought for them. On their return home, a wedding-feast is prepared. In this there is nothing blameworthy; we know that Our Lord honored such a festivity with His presence. The newly-married should, however, be careful to spend the day in such a manner as not to lose the blessing which they received in the morning, as they would do were they to profane it by dissipation or sinful diversions.

The Duties of the Married.

The following are the duties incumbent on married persons:

1. It is the duty of the wife to obey her husband, as the man is the head of the family, the representative of God.

That the man is superior to the woman is shown by the fact that he was created first, and the woman was only created of his flesh, and as a helper for him (1 Cor. xi. 9). The man being the head of the family, the woman is subservient to him, as the members of the body are to the head. The Apostle says: "As the Church is subject to Christ, so also let the wife be to the husband in all things" (Eph. v. 24). The woman is commanded to cover her head in the church, to indicate that she is under the dominion of the man; whereas the man uncovers his head, because there is no one over him but God (1 Cor. xi. 10). The wife ought to fear her husband (Eph. v. 33), that is show him the deference due to him. After the Fall God ordained that the woman should be under her husband's power, and should yield him obedience (Gen. iii. 16), because Eve lusted after power, and ate the apple first. The husband therefore has every right to rule his wife, but he ought to rule with kindness, gentleness and leniency, for she is in one sense his equal, having been made out of flesh taken from his side. Therefore St. Ambrose bids the husband remember that his wife is not to be treated as a servant, that he must not make his authority felt to be a burden. Besides the woman, being the weaker, can claim to be gently treated (1 Pet. iii. 7). It is more shame for the man than for the woman, if he resorts to blows to enforce his authority. As the representative of God, the husband has the right of controlling the household. The angel did not appear to Mary, but to Joseph, when the flight to Egypt was to be made, because the husband's duty is to rule and govern.

2. The husband and wife owe to each other love, fidelity, and mutual aid in all circumstances of their life.

Husbands ought to love their wives as Christ loves the Church (Eph. v. 25), as their own bodies (v. 28), as themselves (v. 33). The love of husband and wife ought not to be a purely natural love, like that of the lower animals, nor a purely human love, like that of the heathen, but a holy and supernatural affection, like that of Christ for the Church, and of the Church for Christ. Hence they ought each to bear with the infirmities of the other patiently and indulgently, or generously close their eyes to them. An example of this is given by the Greek philosopher Socrates, whose wife was a perfect virago. When she stormed at him, he took no more notice of it than of the rattling of a passing vehicle. One day when he was seated before the house with his scholars, from a window above she rated him soundly, and finally threw a jug of water over him. Socrates rose and changed his place, remarking with a smile: " I might have known that the storm would have ended with a thunder shower." The wife will influence her husband for good far more effectually by silence, meekness and prayer than by reproaches. St. Augustine tells us that his mother did more for the conversion of her husband Patricius by the saintliness of her life, than by her words. Dissensions between husband and wife ruin their happiness; without peace at home nothing pleases, even amid all the luxuries wealth can command. Married people owe fidelity to one another (Heb. xiii. 4). They ought scrupulously to guard against every appearance of unfaithfulness, and avoid familiar intercourse with persons of the other sex. For where jealousy enters, all conjugal happiness is at an end. St. John Chrysostom is of opinion that the direst poverty, the most incurable malady, fire even and sword, are lesser evils than jealousy. The Jews used to stone the unfaithful husband or wife, for they considered adultery a no less heinous crime than murder (Lev. xx. 10). St. Paul declares everlasting damnation to be the portion of adulterers (Eph. v. 5). The married must not defraud one another of their conjugal rights (1 Cor. vii. 1-5), but they must abstain from excesses inconsistent with the sanctity of their state (Tob. vi. 17), and only keep in view the object indicated by the angel to Tobias (v. 22), otherwise the devil will prevail over them (v. 16). To the duty of mutual aid it appertains that husband and wife should live together, and that neither the one nor the other should avail himself or herself, if contrarieties or calamities overtake them, of any pretext to leave the other; they are bound to assist each other in the training of their children, to succor each other in illness, to aid each other to bear more easily the ills of life, and to perform their religious duties with greater facility. Eve was created for the sole purpose of helping Adam; for God said: "It is not good for man to be alone, let us make him a help like unto himself" (Gen. ii. 18). It is, however, a sad misfortune when the wife is not a support but a cross to her husband; when instead of lightening his burdens, she only adds to their weight. Almighty God declares that a really good woman is a treasure of inestimable price (Prov. xxxi. 10), far above the most costly jewels. Jewels serve to adorn their owner, and that which is to him a brilliant ornament in the day of prosperity, is to him in adversity a timely aid. So a good wife is in herself a source of riches, a valuable jewel which retains its worth amid all the vicissitudes of life.

3. It is the duty of both husband and wife to provide for their children, and train them in the fear and love of God.

Children are no more the property of their parents than riches are; they are a gift from God (Ps. cxxvi. 3). They are His creatures, destined to be happy with Him forever; they are the children of their Father in heaven, and are only given in trust by Him to their parents, to be brought up in His service. Thus parents are only servants, bound to carry out the will of God in regard to their offspring.

The duties which parents have to discharge towards their children are these: They have to safeguard them from everything which would be prejudicial to their health; they have to supply them with their daily sustenance; they have also to provide for their future.

It is the duty of parents to deny themselves everything which might prove injurious to the health of their children. They must refrain from giving way to their passions, or indulging in excesses, lest they transmit a heritage of disease or sin to their offspring. Like father, like child, the proverb says. Parents ought not to give themselves up to the pursuit of pleasure and amusements, to the neglect of their young children. Let them remember how distressed Mary and Joseph were when the Child Jesus was lost, how for three days they sought Him, sorrowing (Luke ii. 48). Let them learn a lesson from the birds; they do not leave the nest until their young are fully fledged, they are indefatigable in supplying them with food, they teach them to fly. Parents ought to work for the daily bread of their family; even wild beasts take the utmost care of their young, yet some parents are, as Holy Scripture says, "cruel as the ostrich in the desert" (Lam. iv. 3), which lays her eggs in the sand and heeds them no more. "Children ought not to lay up for the parents, but the parents for the children" (2 Cor. xii. 14). They ought to provide for their children's future by laying by a certain amount of money to bequeath to them; by sending them to school; by fitting them to follow the calling most in accordance with their inclinations and capabilities; above all by training them in the fear of God, which is the surest means of promoting their temporal as well as their spiritual welfare; (David declares: "I have been young and now am old, and I have not seen the just forsaken, nor his seed begging bread," Ps. xxxvi. 25); finally it is the bounden duty of parents to pray for their children, and thus call down on them the blessing of God. Job offered holocausts daily for every one of his children, lest perchance they should have sinned against God (Job i. 5). St. Monica prayed fervently for her son, and with the happiest results. "Parents," says St. Francis of Sales, "ought often to speak of God to their children, but yet more often to speak to God of their children."

In regard to the bringing up of their children it is the duty of parents to have them baptized immediately after their birth, to give them their first religious teaching, to set them a good example in all respects, and to treat them with kindness rather than severity.

St. Charles Borromeo says that training children means bringing them to Christ. Parents ought to have their new-born infant baptized as soon as possible; to defer baptism for more than ten days after the birth of a child, without good reason, is a sin. They ought to instruct their children early in the fundamental truths of religion; to teach them that there is a God in heaven; that He knows and sees everything, that if we obey Him, He will take us to Himself in heaven, etc. They should beware of frightening their children by threats of hell and of the devil, lest they inspire them with a repulsion for religion, also of allowing them to imbibe false ideas, for if later on they find they have been deluded, they will not believe anything. Parents must instruct their children in the law of God, as Tobias did. He taught his son from his infancy to fear God and to abstain from sin (Tob. i. 10), and when he thought his death was near, he gave him godly admonitions (Tob. iv.). They should endeavor to stifle evil propensities in their children, and bring them up in the discipline and correction of the Lord (Eph. vi. 4). They should teach them to pray, beginning with the sign of the cross and the invocation of the holy name, and proceeding to the Our Father, Hail Mary, and the Creed. The children's daily prayers should be very short, so as not to become wearisome to them. Furthermore parents should set their children a good example. We all know how much more influential example is than precept, and that what is seen makes a far more lasting impression than what is heard. The actions of the father and mother are the lesson books of their children; how careful should they therefore be not to let them see them do anything blameworthy, and also to warn the servants not to say or do anything in the presence of the children which they ought not to see or hear. For the imitative faculty is strong in children; they are sure to do what they see their elders do. Let parents remember Our Lord's words: "He that shall scandalize one of these little ones that believe in Me, it were better for him that a millstone should be hanged about his neck and that he should be drowned in the depth of the sea" (Matt. xviii. 6). Those who neglect this warning will have reason to tremble, for if the soul of the child is lost through the parents' fault, they will hear the voice of God saying: "I will require his blood of thy hand " (Ezech. xxxiii. 8). In training their children parents should combine kindness and firmness. Too great severity is a fault; for rebukes and punishments are a medicine, which if administered too frequently or in too strong doses, does harm instead of good. It is not by incessant beating with the hammer that the goldsmith fashions the most elegant ornaments. To be always finding fault is a great mistake, but it is no less a one to let the children's wrong-doing pass unpunished, to pamper and spoil them through ill-regulated affection and false kindness. He that spareth the rod hateth his son (Prov. xiii. 24). " Give thy son his way, and he shall make thee afraid " (Ecclus. xxx. 9). To allow a child to have his own will in all things is highly reprehensible; he should be firmly, not sternly compelled to yield.

Of all parental duties, that of training their children in the fear of God is the most important; for on the manner in which it is discharged the temporal and eternal happiness both of parents and children will depend.

The education of their children ought to be for parents a matter of such moment, that nothing should grieve them so much as to see them turn out badly, or rejoice them so much as to see them walking in truth (2 John i. 4). The religious training of the child devolves principally on the mother, as his earliest years are spent at her knee. The father, engaged in the occupations of his calling, has little time and less inclination for the work of instruction. The father and mother supplement each other. The father, by his position of command and force of character, represents the divine power and justice; the mother, with her gentle kindness and tender love, represents the divine attributes of bounty and compassion. It is the part of the father to confirm with his paternal authority what the mother teaches, and enforce the orders she gives. The future happiness of the child depends upon the early training he receives; for, as a rule, what he is in his youth that he is in his old age. Just as out of a piece of soft wax one may model an angel or a devil, so it is with the character of a young child. The first impressions are always the most lasting; they are never wholly effaced from the soul, any more than marks made in the bark of a young tree ever disappear; they do but widen with its growth. In later years the character cannot be moulded afresh; as the sapling is bent, the tree is inclined. The land, if it is to yield a harvest in autumn, must be tilled in the early spring, not left uncultivated until the summer. The great majority of criminals in houses of correction are those whose training has been neglected in their childhood. Can it be supposed that if the souls of these culprits are lost, their parents are not to blame for it? Consider, O parents, what a responsibility rests upon your shoulders! Those who pay no heed to the bringing up of their children are more culpable than those who put them to death; for the latter only take the life of the body, whereas the former cause the destruction of the soul. Some parents are at great pains to amass wealth to bequeath to their children, but they do not care in the least how they are brought up. The temporal and eternal happiness of the parents also depends in a great measure on the training they give to their children. Those who bring them up badly are generally severely chastised by God in this world, and often it is their own children who are their scourge. By that wherein they have sinned, by that same they are punished. King David, through an exaggerated fondness for his son Absalom, did not correct him for his faults; and in after years he had cause bitterly to regret his weakness, when Absalom rebelled against him (2 Kings xviii.). Heli, the high priest, was too indulgent towards his wicked sons, and the chastisement foretold to him by God through the mouth of Samuel speedily overtook him; his two sons were slain in battle, and the old man, on hearing the sad tidings of Israel's defeat, fell off his seat and died (1 Kings iv. 18). Nor can negligent parents expect to fare better in another world, for the Apostle compares them to unbelievers: " If any man have not care of his own, and especially those of his house, he hath denied the faith and is worse than an infidel " (1 Tim. v. 8). On the other hand, a rich reward is promised hereafter to those who have brought up their children well. The eternal felicity of a mother depends on the manner in which she has trained her offspring (1 Tim. ii. 15). The father of a good son will not be sorrowful at the approach of death, neither will he be confounded before his enemies (Ecclus. xxx. 5). Good parents who have conscientiously fulfilled their duties will, when they appear before God, be able to say: " Behold, those whom Thou gavest me I have kept, and none of them is lost " (John xvii. 12).

Mixed Marriages.

1. **Mixed marriages, by which is understood the marriage of Catholics to non-Catholics, have always been disapproved of by the Church.**

(1), Because in such marriages the proper training of the children is a matter of great difficulty, if not altogether impossible; (2), Because such unions are productive of no concord, no true happiness; (3), Because the Catholic is in great danger of losing his or her faith; (4), And besides, the non-Catholic may at any time obtain a divorce, leave his or her Catholic partner, and contract another marriage.

Even in the Old Testament mixed marriages were prohibited; the Jews were not permitted to make marriages with the Chanaanites (Deut. vii. 3), nor indeed with the Samaritans, although they kept the law of God and had the books of Moses, because of the heathen ceremonies they observed. In like manner in the present day the Church discourages the marriage of Catholics to non-Catholics, who, though they call themselves Christians, hold doctrines which are at variance with the teaching of Christ. The Church warns her children against such alliances, just as a loving father might warn his son against undertaking some journey which he knows will expose him to great perils. In early times parents who gave their daughter in marriage to a heretic were subjected to a five years' penance. The dangers attendant on mixed marriages are these: The non-Catholic party, whether a Protestant or not a Christian, far from assisting in the education of the children, will be an obstacle to it, and will perhaps throw scorn and ridicule on Catholic faith and practice. And even if this is not the case, the example of the unbelieving parent will have the worst consequences for the children. And not unfrequently it happens that the non-Catholic, urged by the ministers of his religion, or by his relatives, who represent that it will be prejudicial to their temporal interests if his children are brought up as Catholics, yields to their persuasions, and departs from his promise that they should be so brought up. And what becomes of the children if their Catholic parent dies, and the other espouses a member of his or her own religion? A Catholic cannot do his children a more cruel wrong than by marrying one who is not of his own religion. Moreover, true happiness can hardly exist in such a marriage, where there is not union on the most important of all matters. Heartfelt affection and confidence between husband and wife are scarcely possible if they differ on a point which is all-important, namely religion. Mixed marriages are, moreover, fraught with no slight danger to the salvation of those who contract them. The wise and enlightened King Solomon took to himself heathen wives in his old age, and they prevailed over him so far, that from a worshipper of the true God he became an idolater, and allowed temples of the false gods to be erected in his kingdom. The influence of heretics who call themselves Christians is often more perilous than that of open unbelievers. If reading heretical books is apt to mislead, how much more is continual and close contact with heretics to be dreaded! Besides, we are far more ready to adopt the opinions of one to whom we are attached, for we are blinded by affection. The Holy Father declares that mixed marriages have the effect of obliterating the distinction between truth and error, and fostering the idea that all religions are equally good. Furthermore mixed marriages are most unfair for the Catholic party. The non-Catholic may at any time obtain a divorce and marry again; whereas the Catholic is bound not to take a second partner as long as the former lives. What an equivocal position is that of a divorced woman! She is married, and yet she has no husband; she has the mortification of seeing her rightful husband with another wife, while she is condemned to live a lonely life, looked down upon perhaps by the world; and worst of all, to be separated from some, if not all, of her children. Well then may the Church exhort Christian people to beware of entering into matrimony with those who are aliens to the faith they hold!

2. The Church tolerates mixed marriages on three conditions:

(1), Both parties must promise that their children shall be brought up as Catholics; (2), The Catholic must promise to endeavor to bring the non-Catholic to the knowledge of the truth; (3), The non-Catholic must promise to allow the Catholic liberty for the free exercise of his or her religion. Without these three conditions the Church will not sanction a mixed marriage.

By tolerating or permitting mixed marriages the Church does not approve them; on the contrary she strongly disapproves of them;

and she insists so forcibly on the children being brought up in the Catholic faith, because this is the main object of matrimony. It has already been shown that the chief end of marriage is to train up children in the knowledge and fear of God; the aim of the Christian parent should rather be to leave behind him inheritors of the kingdom of heaven than heirs of his earthly possessions. Consequently it is the first duty of a Catholic, who has wedded one who does not hold the faith, to insure his child's salvation in as far as he can. How deeply is that parent to be commiserated who destroys the soul of her offspring, by allowing the poison of error to be instilled into its mind! When the first glamour of an ill-regulated affection fades away, and conscience again makes its voice heard, the path of wedded life is beset with thorns. The birth of the first child, which ought to be an occasion of glad rejoicing, is a source of anxiety to the mother, for she fears that it will be taught to regard the true faith with hostility. How her conscience reproaches her! And each successive child, which ought to be welcomed as a blessing from the hand of.God, is a fresh accuser, calling to mind her treachery. The Catholic party is also bound to bring the non-Catholic to the knowledge of the truth, not by coercion or persuasion, for proselytizing only adds to the number of nominal Catholics, not of the loyal children of the Church, and is abhorrent to the Catholic Church, who only desires the erring to be brought to her fold of their own free will, and through full conviction. Let them be won by prayer and good example: " Let the unbelieving husbands be won by the conversation of the wives " (1 Pet. iii. 1). If the Catholic wife is seen to be modest, yielding, patient, faithful, etc., the non-Catholic husband will be led to reflect, anl consider whether he may not judge of the tree by its fruits. At any rate he will gradually divest himself of all his former prejudices against our holy religion. He must not be pressed with arguments and instructions, but rather every word should be carefully avoided that might wound his susceptibilities. For those who are outside the Church are not to blame because they have not had the privilege of being born and brought up in the true faith. Furthermore the Catholic party must fearlessly observe his or her religious duties; the other will respect such observance. A man who is not devoid of good feeling will have no wish to oppose the pious practices of his wife; he will know himself to be a gainer, not a loser by them. Sometimes Protestants assert that they agree with Catholics on the fundamental truths of religion, and only differ in non-essentials; this is utterly false. What the Catholic holds most sacred, the Protestant despises; witness the holy sacrifice of the Mass, which Protestants regard as an act of idolatrous worship. In the face of differences so deep-rooted all idea of unity is a mockery.

3. The Catholic who contracts a mixed marriage without the benediction of the Church commits a mortal sin, and cannot be admitted to the sacraments.

Catholics who act thus are declared to be guilty of mortal sin, because they sin through disobedience, by refusing to conform to the precepts of the Church; they give great scandal, and deny the faith; they turn their back upon the sacraments of the true Church and receive the rites of an heretical sect. Thus they give the preference to a false Church, or at least allow its equality with the true one. They cannot be re-admitted to the sacraments unless they manifest sincere contrition on account of their sinful union, and are ready to comply with the requirements of the Church. Many a one takes a just view of his conduct on his death-bed. Conscience often slumbers, like a volcano, which for long years shows no signs of activity, then suddenly bursts into flame; so conscience awakens at last, and the unhappy soul is consumed by the flames of remorse and despair. No one who firmly believes the Catholic to be the only true and saving faith will be content to see his children brought up in soul-destroying error; and it may safely be affirmed, that in the majority of cases, those who contract mixed marriages sooner or later heartily regret the step they have taken.

The Unmarried State.

1. The unmarried state is better than the married, because those who do not marry have far more opportunity for attending to their spiritual welfare, and can attain a higher degree of glory hereafter.

It is better and more blessed to remain in virginity or in celibacy than to be united in matrimony (Council of Trent, 24, 10). The state of virginity surpasses the married state in excellence as much as angels surpass men. It is as far above matrimony as the heavens are above the earth; it is as much superior to it as the soul is to the body. Marriage is honorable, but virginity is far more honorable. Such is the opinion of the Fathers. The heathen entertained a great respect for those who voluntarily embraced a life of celibacy and chastity; witness the reverence shown by the Romans for the vestal virgins. The richer and nobler the bridegroom, the more a bride is congratulated upon her espousals. How much the more ought those to be deemed happy, who by the practice of chastity have chosen Christ for their Spouse; and for His sake, like St. Agnes of old, despised every earthly suitor, however wealthy and powerful. The unmarried are more free to study the concerns of their soul; St. Paul says: "He that is without a wife is solicitous how he may please God; but he that is with a wife is solicitous how he may please his wife; and he is divided" (1 Cor. vii. 32-34). The unmarried also can attain a higher degree of glory. St. John beheld a multitude "before the throne, who sang a new canticle, that no man could say but those a hundred forty and four thousand; for they were virgins" (Apoc. xiv. 1-5).

2. Our Lord when on earth commended the state of virginity both by precept and example.

Our Lord says that there are some who renounce matrimony for the kingdom of heaven's sake, adding: "He that can take, let him take it" (Matt. xix. 12). St. Paul also says: "He that giveth his daughter in marriage doth well, but he that giveth her not doth better " (1 Cor. vii. 38). And again, speaking of widows, "more blessed shall she be if she so remain" (v. 40). The apostles did not marry, and many of the saints took vows of perpetual virginity; of this the greatest example is given us in the blessed Mother of God, as we learn from her own words to the angel (Luke i. 34); it is also the opinion of the Fathers that St. Joseph did the same. Some of the saints, especially in the early ages of the Church, endured the most agonizing tortures and a cruel death rather than break their vow of virginity. It is related of St. Hilary, Bishop of Poitiers, who before he received Holy Orders had been married and had a daughter, that while he was in exile he received a letter from his daughter, telling him she was grown up, and was about to be married. He wrote in answer to say that he was soon returning home, and would bring the portrait of another suitor; she could compare the two and choose between them. On his arrival he gave her a crucifix, and exhorted her to consecrate herself to Christ by a vow of virginity. This she did, and shortly after died a holy death. Just before she expired her father said to her: " Behold your celestial Spouse; He has come to take you to your eternal nuptials." In the pages of hagiology we read of many saints who, although married, led a life of chastity.

III. THE SACRAMENTALS.

Sacramentals are rites which have some outward resemblance to the sacraments instituted by Christ, but which are not of divine institution. The name is applied both to the blessing or consecration given by the Church, and to the objects blessed or consecrated.

Our Lord gave the apostles power over unclean spirits, to cast them out, and to heal all manner of diseases (Matt. x. 1). The Church makes use of this power; by means of her ministers she blesses or consecrates certain objects, praying that God would render these objects efficacious in banishing evil spirits and healing sicknesses. That is to say, the priest implores the blessing of God the Father, for the averting of evils both corporal and spiritual. At the same time he makes use of visible signs, such as the sign of the cross, the holy water, the sacred oils, etc. A light is kindled, to signify the Saviour, the Light of the world. Incense if often used, to indicate that the sacramentals must be employed with pious dispositions. Sacramentals are called by this name because of their resemblance to a sacrament. In both there is a sign and form of words which possess a supernatural power and represent the invisible grace. But the sacraments have incomparably more power than the sacramentals; the latter are not necessary to salvation, whereas the former are. Sacramentals are means of grace of the second class.

The blessing consists in this, that the minister of the Church invokes the divine benediction upon certain persons or things.

The divine blessing is quite distinct from divine grace. The latter has the effect of beautifying the soul, the former averts earthly ills and promotes temporal welfare. Thus objects are only blessed for the sake of the persons who use them, or on whose behalf they are used.

The following are the benedictions which are customarily conferred on persons: The blessing at the conclusion of the Mass, the blessing given to communicants, the nuptial benediction, the benediction after childbirth, the last blessing, and the blessing of the remains of the departed.

It is usual for women after childbirth to go to the church to implore the blessing of God upon their child, and receive the benediction of the priest. This custom was observed in the Old Testament; every mother had to present herself in the Temple with her infant forty days after its birth if it was a boy, and eighty if it was a girl. The Mother of God herself conformed to this rule.

Exorcism belongs also to the blessings conferred on persons. It consists in commanding the devil to depart, in the name of Christ, from possessed persons or things.

The evil effects of original sin rest upon every creature (Rom. viii. 20), and upon the whole of inanimate nature (Gen. iii. 17). It is this that renders the blessings of the Church and her exorcisms necessary. The power granted by Our Lord to His apostles to cast out unclean spirits is employed in the exorcism at baptism and when holy water is blessed. Cases of possession or obsession rarely occur in the present day; the exorcism can only be performed by a bishop, or by a priest with his permission. Only one who is himself animated by a firm faith and whose life is pure, can exorcise, and even then the exorcism will be of no avail if the person exorcised perseveres in his evil dispositions, or if God wills that His elect should be delivered into the power of the devil for their sanctification. For the sacramentals do not remove afflictions which are for the spiritual welfare of the individual.

1. Consecration by the Church consists in this: That the ecclesiastic empowered for this purpose sets apart some person or some object, and dedicates him or it to the exclusive service of God.

The persons whom it is customary to consecrate in a solemn manner are: The Pope, kings and emperors, abbots, monks, and nuns.

The consecration of priests, be it remembered, is a sacrament.

The things which it is customary to bless are: Holy water, the water to be used in Baptism (this is blessed on Holy Saturday and on the eve of Pentecost); candles (on the Purification, and the Paschal candle at Easter); ashes (on Ash Wednesday); palms (on Palm Sunday); the holy oils (on Maundy Thursday in the cathedrals), besides crosses, images, rosaries, medals, banners; places also are blessed, such as churches, chapels, altars, cemeteries.

The Church blesses everything which appertains to divine service.

2. Our Lord sanctioned the use of sacramentals, but the rites themselves are an institution of the Church.

Our Lord while on earth blessed the loaves and fishes (Matt. xiv. 19); He blessed the young children who were brought to Him (Mark x. 16); He gave His blessing to His apostles before His ascension (Luke xxiv. 50). We read moreover that God blessed our first parents (Gen. i. 28); that Noe blessed his two sons (Gen. ix. 26); Isaac blessed Jacob (Gen. xxvii. 27); Jacob when dying blessed his twelve sons (Gen. xlix. 28); and Moses the tribes of Israel (Deut. xxxiii.). Aaron and the priests that succeeded him gave their benediction every morning and evening to the people in the outer court of the Temple; stretching forth their hands over them, they blessed them, invoking the name of the Lord three times over the children of Israel (Numb. vi. 23).

The ceremony of blessing or consecrating is generally performed by the priests.

Several acts of consecration appertain to the episcopal office, and may only be performed by a priest with the authorization of the bishop, as for instance, the dedication of churches and altars, the blessing of bells, chalices, etc. The laity can bless, but not in the name of the Church; parents frequently bless their children, and the more pious they are, the more effect has their blessing.

3. The use of blessed or consecrated objects is profitable; for if used with pious dispositions, they increase our fear and love of God, remit venial sins, and preserve us from many temptations and from bodily harm; excepting such temptations and ills of the body as are for our spiritual welfare.

The sacramentals remit venial sin, and deliver us from some of the evil consequences of sin. They help us in the hour of temptation; St. Teresa cannot say enough concerning the power of holy water to drive away the devil. They are also of use in bodily ills and infirmities; the apostles anointed with oil many who were sick and healed them (Mark vi. 13). They are thus a remedy and a shield. Is it superstition on the part of the soldier who carries with him a blessed crucifix when he goes to battle, hoping that by God's mercy it may be his protection? By no means. Nor is the sick man to blame if he sprinkles himself frequently with holy water, thinking thus to accelerate his recovery. But we must beware of trusting too much to the efficacy of sacramentals; or imputing to them more power than the prayer of the Church imparts to them; they are not like the sacraments. The sacraments confer upon those who receive them the grace of the Holy Spirit; the sacramentals only purify the soul, and render it more fit for the reception of sanctifying grace. The sacramentals derive all their power from the prayers of the Church; it is in the name of the Church that the priest blesses them. The petitions of the Church have immense power, for they are united to the prayer of Our Lord and to the supplications of the saints.

4. The sacramentals can, however, only be used with profit by persons who are free from mortal sin, and who use them in a spirit of faith and confidence.

The effect of the sacramentals depends upon the worthiness and the pious dispositions of the individual who uses them. Those who live in mortal sin will derive no more benefit from wearing some blessed object, or from the use of holy water, than the Jews did from bringing the Ark of the Covenant on to the field of battle, when they had incurred God's wrath by their sins (1 Kings iv.). Nor will they profit one who places no confidence in them, any more than prayer profits the man who does not ask in faith, nothing wavering (Jas. i. 6). Our Lord abstained from working many miracles in some places, because of the unbelief of the inhabitants (Matt. xiii. 18). Remember what He said to the woman who touched Him: " Thy faith hath made thee whole " (Mark v. 34). We find that devout Christians always reverence sacramentals and use them diligently. They wear blessed objects on their person, they frequently take holy water, they like to say their prayers in consecrated places, knowing that prayer offered in a church is more efficacious than what is offered elsewhere. In times of temptation or of sickness above all, we should have recourse to the assistance afforded by sacramentals.

IV. PRAYER.

1. THE NATURE OF PRAYER.

1. Prayer is the elevation of the heart to God.

When we are engaged in conversation with any one, we forget everything else. This is what we should do when we talk with God, that is, when we pray. In prayer, we must direct all the powers of the soul to God; the understanding, for we must think of Him; the memory, for we must forget the things of earth; the affections, for we must delight in Him. The mere thought of God is no prayer; the devils think of God, but they do not pray to Him. Let Our Lord's ascension be to us a symbol of prayer; so are the clouds of incense that float upwards on the air; the lark that soars aloft as she warbles her song. It is recorded of some saints that the elevation of their souls in prayer was made manifest by external signs; they were raised from the ground, they were surrounded by a supernatural radiance. St. John Chrysostom says that to be permitted to talk with his Creator and hold familiar intercourse with Him, is the greatest honor and privilege mortal man can enjoy. Who can fail to admire and wonder at the gracious condescension of the Most High, that He not only permits, but commands us to converse with Him?

When we pray it is customary to employ external signs of devotion, such as kneeling down, folding the hands, striking the breast, etc.

By kneeling down we acknowledge our own littleness in God's sight; by folding our hands, we signify that we are helpless, bound by the chains of sin; by striking the breast, that we are deserving of stripes. Sometimes we prostrate ourselves upon the ground, to testify our sense of our nothingness before God; this Judith did, before she went into the enemy's camp (Judith x. 1). Our Lord did the same on Mount Olivet (Matt. xxvi. 39). So does the priest at the foot of the altar on Good Friday. When prayer is very fervent and importunate, the hands are lifted up and the arms outstretched; thus Moses prayed during the battle between the Israelites and the Amalekites (Exod. xvii. 12), and Solomon at the dedication of the Temple (2 Par. v. 12). The priest often does the same during the celebration of holy Mass. The Jews of old turned their faces towards the Temple at the time of prayer; we may do likewise. David worshipped towards the holy Temple (Ps. v. 8), and so did Daniel (Dan. vi. 10). God needs not these outward signs, for He reads the heart of man; but we thereby excite ourselves to greater activity and more humility in prayer. These postures are not a necessary adjunct to prayer; they may be dispensed with on account of weariness, sickness, or in the presence of others. One may even pray while walking abroad, as pilgrims do, or if we happen to hear the Angelus rung while we are in the streets of a town.

2. We may pray either in spirit only, or with the lips as well.

One may raise one's heart in prayer to God without those who are around us perceiving it; this is mental prayer. Vocal prayer is both useful and necessary. Man consists of soul and body, and with both he must yield homage to God (Osee xiv. 3). It is, moreover, natural to express in words the thoughts of the heart (Matt. xii. 34). In the absence of vocal prayer the Christian religion would lack its mainstay. Vocal prayer quickens the attention of the mind, and inflames the devotion of the suppliant himself as well as of others. Vocal or common prayer is more efficacious with God; Our Lord says: " Whatsoever they shall ask, it shall be done unto them by My Father Who is in heaven " (Matt. xviii. 19).

Prayer with the lips only, and not with the spirit, is worthless.

Our Lord complains of the Pharisees: " This people honoreth Me with their lips, but their heart is far from Me " (Matt. xv. 8). St. Augustine says many call upon God with the voice of the body, not with the voice of the soul. All attitudes and gestures too, which are merely formal have no value. God is a spirit, and they that adore Him must adore Him in spirit and in truth (John iv. 24).

We can also pray with the voice of song.

Hymns and spiritual canticles are an excellent form of prayer, which the Apostle admonishes the Colossians to practise. It is a powerful factor in raising the heart to God. St. Ambrose and Pope Gregory the Great did much to promote the custom of singing in churches.

In our prayers we may either make use of the authorized forms of prayer, or address God in the words our own heart will suggest.

It is well to recite the usual well-known prayers, such as the Our Father and Hail Mary, but not to keep slavishly to the use of forms. We should speak to God from time to time in our own words; He loves to hear us address Him with filial confidence. The three children in the furnace of Babylon cried to Him in their own language. There is no need to employ well-turned phrases; how much better to speak to God simply and straightforwardly. The plainest language is the language of the heart, and it is not the words which God regards, but the desires of the heart. Nor need one make long prayers (Matt. vi. 7). Our petitions are not valued on account of their length, but of their fervor. How richly was the brief supplication of the good thief rewarded!

We may either pray alone, or in union with others.

Our Lord exhorts us to pray to Our Father in secret (Matt. vi. 5), and also to offer our petitions in common with others.

3. Our prayers have a threefold object: That of praise, of supplication, and of thanksgiving.

We ought to praise God on account of His infinite perfections. The Church gives praise to Him unceasingly; the *Gloria* and the *Sanctus* in the Mass, the *Te Deum* which is sung on great festivals, the *Gloria Patri* which we repeat so often, are all ascriptions of praise. The thrice holy of the seraphim (Is. vi. 3), the song the angels sung at Our Lord's birth (Luke ii. 14), are hymns of praise. We read in the Apocalypse that the principal occupation of the happy denizens of heaven is to give honor and glory to the Lord their God (Apoc. iv.), and by praising Him we may while still on earth join in their ceaseless song. The *Magnificat* uttered by the Blessed Virgin is a canticle of praise. It is God's will that we should implore of Him all that we need. God gives nothing to those who ask nothing of Him (Jas. i. 5). "He who asks not," says St. Teresa, "receives not." Nay more, God desires that our petitions should be fervent and importunate; that we should not merely ask, but compel Him to hear us. The Lacedemonians used to place the bread for their children on a high beam, and force them to fetch it down for themselves; thus God would have us earn what we beseech of Him. He is not, it is true, ignorant of our needs (Matt. vi. 32), and He could supply them without our telling Him of them; but He will have us ask for what we want, that we may not accept His gifts as a matter of course, but may recognize our dependence upon Him, and learn to be humble and thankful. The prayer of Our Lord in the garden and on the cross was a prayer of supplication; as was that of the apostles on the sea of Galilee, that of the Christians for St. Peter when he was in prison. Prayer for the forgiveness of sin is a penitential prayer; witness the *Miserere* (Ps. l.). Furthermore it is God's will that we thank Him for the benefits we receive from His hand (1 Thess. v. 18). Remember what Our Lord said to the leper who was healed (Luke xvii.). Gratitude is the surest means of obtaining fresh favors from God. The holocaust Noe offered was a sacrifice of thanksgiving (Gen. viii. 20). God withdraws many blessings from man because he takes no heed of them and neglects to render thanks to the Giver; He also sends calamities as a chastisement upon the unthankful.

2. THE UTILITY AND NECESSITY OF PRAYER.

1. By means of prayer we can obtain all things from God; but He does not always grant our petitions immediately.

We have Our Lord's promise: Ask and it shall be given you (Matt. vii. 7), and again: "All things whatsoever you shall ask in prayer, believing, you shall receive" (Matt. xxi. 22). St. John Chrysostom declares that by prayer man becomes almost omnipotent. St. Augustine terms prayer the key that unlocks the treasury of the divine riches. As a man can get almost anything from his fellow-men for gold, so he can obtain almost anything from God by means of prayer. Let him therefore who is in affliction call upon God for succor. If he fail to do this, let him blame his own indolence and folly, not complain of his misery. Who would have patience with a beggar, half-starved with cold and hunger, if he would not apply for aid to a rich man who had promised to help him? The apostles prayed when the storm arose on the lake, and it was calmed. God does not always grant our petitions at once. One must knock long and loudly at the gate of this sovereign Lord, before it is opened to us. Monica prayed for her son's conversion for eighteen years. God keeps us waiting for an answer to our prayer, both to try us, whether we are really in earnest, and also to make us value His gifts more when we do obtain them. He who is truly in earnest perseveres with more insistence than ever, the longer the answer to his prayer is delayed. So the blind man by the wayside on the road to Jericho cried out much more when Our Lord appeared to pay no heed to his cry: "Jesus, Son of David, have mercy on me" (Luke xviii. 39). "Thou dost delay, O Lord," says St. Augustine, "to give us what we ask, that we may learn how to pray." Sometimes God does not grant us what we implore, because He knows it would be prejudicial, not beneficial to us.

Our prayers obtain a speedier answer if they are accompanied by fasting, almsdeeds, a promise, or if we invoke the intercession of the saints on our behalf; a petition is sooner granted if it is proffered by several persons at the same time; also if the suppliant is of the number of the just.

Fasting and almsdeeds are said to be the wings of prayer. Remember the prayer of the centurion Cornelius (Acts x.). That prayer receives a speedier answer in which several persons join. Our Lord promises: "If two of you shall consent upon earth concerning anything whatsoever they shall ask, it shall be done to them by My Father Who is in heaven" (Matt. xviii. 19). "When the Christians assemble together in large numbers to pray," says Tertullian, "they are like a great army, which compels almighty God to grant their petition." Wood burns more fiercely if several logs are piled together, for one kindles the other. In the time of the Roman emperor, Marcus Aurelius, a Christian legion was surrounded by the enemy, and the supply of water cut off. In dire distress the Christian soldiers prayed fervently for rain; and before many hours had passed, a storm came up, and there was a heavy downpour. The united prayer of the Church for St. Peter was the cause of his deliverance from prison. How great is the power of united prayer! This is why processions are held in times of calamity. The prayer of the just, moreover, obtains a speedier answer. The continual prayer of a just man availeth much (Jas. v. 16). The prayer of the prophet Elias for rain was quickly granted (3 Kings xvii.).

Oftentimes God turns a deaf ear to our petition and the reason is generally because He will not give us what would be harmful for us; or because we do not deserve that our prayer should be granted.

God acts like a wise physician who for the good of his patient will not allow him to have what would be injurious to him. If God sees that we shall employ His gifts amiss, He of His mercy withholds them from us (St. Augustine). St. Monica earnestly implored almighty God to prevent her son from going to Italy. Her prayer was not granted, because God designed that the preaching of St. Ambrose should be the means of Augustine's conversion. St. Augustine himself at a later period exclaims: "Thou didst then deny my mother's request, O Lord, in order to grant that which had long been her continual prayer." God often does not grant our entreaty because we do not deserve that grace. Those who pray without devotion and without faith (Jas. i. 7), or who are in mortal sin, and will not renounce their evil ways, are unworthy of being heard (John ix. 31). Many persons do not obtain what they ask, because they do not persevere in prayer, their whole heart is not in their petition. Yet no prayer is offered in vain; if God does not give what is asked, He bestows on the suppliant something else, something better; like a parent who gives his child a rosy apple instead of the knife he is clamoring for. Even the sinner does not pray in vain, for by his prayers he earns the graces necessary for his conversion. When you pray, and your petition is not granted, do not ascribe this to unwillingness on God's part, but to the imperfection of your prayer, or to the poor use you would perhaps make of the grace if it were bestowed on you. Act thus, and if you have prayed aright, God will give you some other gift far more worth having than that which you asked for. God is able to do all things more abundantly than we desire or understand (Eph. iii. 20).

2. By means of prayer sinners become just, and the just are enabled to continue in a state of grace.

By prayer sinners obtain forgiveness. The penitent thief said only these few words: "Lord, remember me when Thou shalt come into Thy kingdom" (Luke xxiii. 42), and immediately Our Lord pardoned him. The publican in the Temple did but strike his breast, saying: "O God, be merciful to me a sinner," and he went down to his house justified (Luke xviii. 13). As soon as David heard Nathan's rebuke, he exclaimed: "I have sinned against the Lord," and the prophet immediately assured him that the Lord had taken away his sin (2 Kings xii. 13). "When a man begins to pray," says St. Augustine, "he ceases to sin; when he ceases to pray, he begins to sin." Mortal sin is incompatible with the habit of prayer. Prayer transforms the character; by it the blind become enlightened, the weak become strong, sinners become saints.

By prayer sinners become just, because it earns for them the graces of contrition and amendment.

By prayer we draw down upon us the Holy Spirit, we obtain actual grace. As the nearer the earth approaches the sun, the greater the light and heat she derives from it, so the nearer we draw to Christ, the Sun of justice, the more our soul will be enlightened and strengthened. We have said that the soul is enlightened by prayer; she learns to estimate more justly the majesty and goodness of God, to perceive more clearly the final end of man, the will of God, the worthlessness of earthly things and her own poverty. In the case of some saints this inward illumination manifested itself externally. The countenance of Moses shone, after he had been conversing with God on the Mount. Our Lord, while He prayed, was transfigured (Luke ix. 29). Many saints are known to have been surrounded with an aureola of glory while at prayer. By prayer we gain strength and power to endure the ills of life. Prayer is like a celestial dew; as the earth is refreshed at night by the dew from heaven, so the soul is revived and fortified by prayer. Thus we should have recourse to prayer when our work is ended and before we commence anything of importance. Our Lord when on earth often spent the night in prayer, and before His Passion He prayed long and earnestly. The man who is given to prayer will never be a coward.

Prayer enables the just to continue in a state of grace, because it is a safeguard against temptation and sin.

Prayer is an antidote to the poison of temptation. The assaults of the devil darken the understanding and weaken the will; prayer does the very opposite; it enlightens the understanding and strengthens the will. It acts upon temptation as water does on fire; it is a shield which the fiery darts of the evil one cannot pierce; it is an anchor to the tempest-tossed vessel. It banishes sadness; the Holy Ghost is a comforter, He imparts joy to the heart. Our Lord promises to refresh all who labor and are burdened, if they come to Him (Matt. xi. 28). St. James says: "Is any among you sad? let him pray" (Jas. v. 13). During prayer, sometimes, a foretaste is given us of the joys of heaven. Prayer affords to the troubled heart such solace as a child may find, who pours out his sorrows on the breast of a compassionate father. "O taste and see," says the Psalmist, "that the Lord is sweet" (Ps. xxxiii. 9). One day spent in prayer is better than years devoted to the pleasures and distractions of the world. By prayer the just man acquires many virtues. Pray aright, and you will live aright. Between those who are much together a certain resemblance may be perceived; thus if we are much with God, we shall become like to Him. Prayer is to the soul what the sunshine is to a plant; it makes it grow and bear fruit abundantly.

3. By prayer we obtain the remission of the temporal penalty due to sin, and merit an eternal recompense.

When prayer ascends to heaven, the mercy of God descends; it prevents the outburst of the divine wrath (St. Augustine). By every prayer we repeat some indulgence is gained, even though one is not definitely attached to it by the Holy See. Our Lord says: "When thou shalt pray, enter into thy chamber, and having shut the door, pray to thy Father in secret; and thy Father, Who seeth in secret, will repay thee" (Matt. vi. 6). Prayer is a work which cannot be accomplished without toil and conflict, for the spirits of evil employ all their wiles to distract those who pray, by suggesting irrelevant thoughts to their mind. Hence those who preserve their recollection in spite of the assaults of the devil, and the hindrances he casts in their way, expiate many sins and merit a reward.

4. He who never prays cannot save his soul; for without prayer he will fall into grievous sins.

A servant who never saluted or spoke to his master would not long be retained in his service. Were one to look into hell, we should see that the majority of souls have been lost through neglect of prayer. "If Our Lord," says St. Ambrose, "spent whole nights in prayer, what ought not we poor mortals to do to save our souls?" He who does not pray is powerless to resist in the hour of temptation; he may be compared to a warrior without weapons, a bird without wings, a ship without sails or rudder; he is a reed, driven to and fro by every blast of wind. St. John Chrysostom says one who does not pray has no life in him, he has ceased to breathe. As corn must be stored in barns, not left lying on the damp ground, or it will grow mouldy and decay, so the heart of man must not continually rest upon earthly things; it must be lifted up to God, or it will lose its purity. Hence Our Lord bids us watch and pray (Matt. xxvi. 41). All nations of the world worship some deity or other; the obligation to pray is imprinted upon the human heart.

3. HOW OUGHT WE TO PRAY ?

By praying we learn to pray. In this the proverb holds good: Practice makes perfect. Pray often, and you will find delight in prayer; pray seldom, and it will appear to you irksome and wearisome. God does not regard the length of our supplications but their fervor.

If prayer is to be of utility to us, we must pray:
1. In the name of Jesus; that is, we must ask what is in accordance with Our Lord's desires.

Our Lord desires whatever promotes the glory of God and the salvation of souls. If we pray for what is opposed to our spiritual welfare, we do not pray in the name of Christ; e.g., if we pray for earthly riches or honors, for the acquisition of superfluities. But we pray in the name of Christ, that is, in union with His intention, in His spirit, if we ask for such things as the means of earning our daily bread, for succor in the time of tribulation, for the conversion of a sinner. The Church prays in the name of Christ, for all her petitions conclude with the words: "Through Jesus Christ Our Lord." "If you ask the Father anything in My name, He will give it to you" (John xvi. 23). Such is Our Lord's promise. What monarch could refuse the petition of one who said he was authorized to present it by the king's own royal son?

2. We must pray with devotion; that is, we must fix our thoughts on God when we pray.

In our prayers we hold intercourse with God. When we hold intercourse with our fellow-mortals, we give them our whole attention; how much more when we converse with God, should we fix our mind on Him alone! Some people honor God with their lips, while their heart is far from Him (Matt. xv. 8). Their thoughts wander, they think of their earthly employments, they do not heed what they say. Prayers that are so tepid and distracted avail nothing with God. Who, when pleading before an earthly judge, would turn to those about him and begin to talk to them? He would be put out of court for his disrespectful behavior. How can we expect God to heed our prayers if we do not heed them ourselves? He who prays without devotion and yet looks for an answer to his prayer, is like a man who sows bad grain, and anticipates a crop of first-rate wheat. It is not, however, necessary to have sensible devotion, to experience extraordinary consolation and delight in prayer. That is a supernatural gift, bestowed by God generally as a recompense; it does not add to the value of our prayers. Nor are they necessarily the worse, if we feel distaste and aridity. St. Teresa says that prayer under such circumstances may even be more meritorious because it is painful to nature. That prayer which costs us an effort, which we have to compel ourselves to offer, is perhaps the most acceptable in God's sight. Do not therefore give up prayer on account of aridity and the disinclination for it. The evil enemy seeks by this means to withdraw us from prayer, and God permits this trial to come upon us, in order that we may feel our own weakness and humble ourselves on account of it. And if during the whole time of prayer we do nothing else but resist temptations and distractions, let us not think we have prayed badly; God looks to our good will, in that He takes pleasure.

In order to pray devoutly we must prepare ourselves beforehand, and during the time of prayer we must guard our senses and see that we do not assume an irreverent posture.

"Before prayer prepare thy soul, be not as a man that tempteth God" (Ecclus. xviii. 23). The harper tunes his harp before beginning to play, lest there should be any discord in the melody. How carefully those who are admitted to an audience of some earthly monarch perform their toilet! Before commencing our prayer, we should place ourselves in the presence of God, endeavoring to realize that we stand in His sight, and then banish from our thoughts all worldly cares and interests. Let us imitate the patriarch Abraham, who when about to offer up his son Isaac on Mount Moria, left his servants, his ass, and all that was not wanted for the sacrifice, at the foot of the mountain, saying: "When we have worshipped, we will return unto you." As Our Lord drove those that sold out of the Temple, so we must banish all worldly affairs from our heart, when it is made a temple of prayer. Yet the distractions that are involuntary are not sinful, only they must be repulsed and withstood. At prayer we must close the door, that is keep custody of the eyes, and withdraw into the secret chamber of the soul. The use of a prayer-book often keeps the eyes from wandering. As a rule one prays with more recollection before the statue of a saint, or in a holy place, where all around breathes an atmosphere of devotion. Our attitude during prayer should not be lacking in reverence; as far as possible we should remain upon our knees as an aid to devotion.

3. We must pray with perseverance, that is, we ought not to desist from prayer, if our petition is not immediately granted.

We should take example from children, who will not leave off clamoring until they get what they want. We mortals are apt to grow angry if a suppliant is too persistent, but it is not so with God; He is pleased when we "batter the gates of heaven with storms of prayer." Remember the parable of the importunate friend, who continued knocking (Luke xi. 5). God sometimes puts the endurance of the suppliant to a severe test, as was the case with the woman of Chanaan (Matt. xv.). The Jews in Bethulia prayed all night, desiring help of the God of Israel, when Holofernes besieged their city, but the more they prayed, the more desperate the situation appeared. Yet they held out, and God sent them a deliverer in Judith. We have already said that for eighteen long years St. Monica ceased not to pray for her son's conversion, and how richly her constancy was rewarded! For God loves to come to our aid when our need is greatest. Let us not then be discouraged, as some are, and cease to pray if our prayers are not answered; the wise course would be to pray more earnestly the longer God delays granting our petition. For the longer He keeps us waiting, the more will His succor surpass our expectations. He is able to do abundantly more than we desire or understand (Eph. iii. 20). "We have to wait a whole year," says St. Francis of Sales, "before the seed we sow in the ground bears fruit; and are we more impatient in regard to the fruit of our prayers?"

4. We must pray with a pure heart; that is, our conscience must be free from grievous sin, or at any rate we must be in penitential dispositions.

The man whose heart is not clean has not power to raise his soul to God, for when he begins to pray, thoughts and images of sin crowd in upon his mind, and hold it captive upon earth. He who prays with an impure heart is like a man who enters the presence of royalty with mud-stained garments, to implore a favor. It is only just that he who will not conform to the divine precepts should be excluded from a share in the divine benefactions. Listen to the commands of God, if you would have Him listen to your supplications. But as soon as the sinner is sincerely contrite, he may hope to obtain a hearing; God will receive his petitions as graciously as if he had never offended Him. In this He is unlike men, who are prone to cast former offences in the teeth of those who ask a favor of them. God looks at the present intention, not at the past actions of a man. Remember how the prayer of the penitent publican in the Temple was accepted (Luke xviii. 13).

5. We must pray with humility; that is, we must acknowledge our own weakness and unworthiness.

The prayer of him that humbleth himself shall pierce the clouds (Ecclus. xxxv. 21). How lowly is the obeisance of one who approaches one of the magnates of the earth to present a petition! Prayer is in itself an act of humility, for by it we testify a sense of our dependence upon the Lord of heaven and of earth; we take the position of beggars, knocking at the door of the great Father of mankind.

6. We must pray with confidence, that is, with a firm conviction that of His infinite mercy God will grant what we ask, provided it will tend to His glory and to the true welfare of our souls.

The prayer of him that humbleth himself shall pierce the clouds of what the prayer of faith ought to be (3 Kings xviii.). Our Lord says: "All things whatsoever you shall ask in prayer, believing, you shall receive" (Matt. xxi. 22). Confidence hath a great reward (Heb. x. 35). Let not him that wavereth think that he shall receive anything of the Lord (Jas. i. 1).

7. We must pray with resignation to the will of God; that is, we must leave the granting of our petition entirely to God's good pleasure.

"Not My will, but Thine be done" (Luke xxii. 42), was Our Lord's prayer on the Mount of Olives. God knows best what is for our good; we ought no more to dictate to Him than a sick man, who knows nothing of the healing art, ought to tell the physician what drugs he is to give him. A certain mother once was importunate in prayer for the recovery of her sick child. The priest told her she would do better to ask that God's will might be done. "No," she exclaimed indignantly, "God must grant me my desire." The child was restored to health, took to evil ways, and at last came to the gallows. Happy would it have been for that man had he died in his childhood! How much wiser it is to leave all in the hands of God, for He knows the future.

4. WHEN OUGHT WE TO PRAY ?

1. As a matter of fact we ought to pray continually, for Our Lord requires of us " always to pray and not to faint " (Luke xviii. 1).

The Apostle bids us: "Pray without ceasing" (1 Thess. v. 17). We may approach God at any moment; there is no sentry before His door to turn us back; we have but to call upon Him by His name of Father, and His ear is open to us at once. "He who seeks God," says St. Alphonsus, "will find Him at all times and in every place." If our heart is continually raised to Him in prayer, we shall be like the angels who continually behold His countenance. If we are unceasing in prayer, we shall obtain our requests from God without difficulty, and we shall be preserved from many temptations. Our Lord says: "Watch ye and pray, that ye enter not into temptation," (Matt. xxvi. 41). The habit of constant prayer may be compared to a rampart against the malign foe; to a breastplate from which his arrows rebound; to a harbor, in which the rough waves cannot reach us. We are liable at any moment to the assaults of the devil, wherefore let us ever be ready, armed with prayer, as those who are exposed to the danger of fire always have water at hand in case a conflagration should break out. By continuing in prayer, we shall have a surer hope of maintaining ourselves in the grace of God until our life's end.

It is, however, by no means required of us, nay, it would be impossible for us to remain constantly upon our knees; what we are to do is to pray while we work.

Martha's vocation, that of active work for one's neighbor, ought to be united to Mary's vocation, that of contemplation and prayer. St. Bernard says Martha's employment was good, Mary's was better, but a combination of the two is best of all. Christ, Who is in all things our Model, united a life of activity to a life of prayer. While we are in this world, work must oft-times be our prayer; hereafter, when there is no more occasion for work, the contemplation of the divine majesty will be our only occupation. He who gives up work for the sake of prayer, deserves not, according to the dictum of the Apostle, to have bread to eat (2 Thess. iii. 10).

While engaged in our work we can utter ejaculatory prayers, and we ought on commencing our work to direct our intention so as to do all to the glory of God.

St. Teresa had in her cell a picture of Our Lord at Jacob's well; when her eyes fell upon it she said: "Lord, give me that living water." St. Ignatius frequently exclaimed: "All for the greater glory of God." Let us accustom ourselves to say from time to time: "Lord, remember me in Thy kingdom." He who raises his heart to God ever and anon by ejaculatory prayers, will keep calm and recollected amid the turmoil and distractions of life, for ejaculations are no weak weapons of defence; their brevity, too, enables them to be said with greater fervor than longer prayers. St. Francis of Sales recommends the frequent and fervent repetition of the same ejaculation. Our Lord on the Mount of Olives prayed using the same words. St. Francis of Assisi spent the whole night repeating the words: "My God and my all." St. Paul bids us: "Whether ye eat or drink, or whatsoever else you do, do all to the glory of God" (1 Cor. x. 31). It is well to direct one's intention in the morning, and renew it before every undertaking of any importance.

We should do well to employ our leisure time in prayer.

Blessed Clement Hofbauer answered a man who complained that his time hung heavy on his hands, with the words: "Well, then, you can pray." The saints spent as much time as they could in prayer; it is recorded of St. James that through being constantly on his knees, callosities formed on them. The Christian need not pray in a manner to be observed by others, but he can always pray in spirit, whatever his occupations may be. The saints used to make use of visible things to raise their thoughts to what is unseen; natural objects suggested to them thoughts of the supernatural. St. Gregory Nazianzen, seeing the shells washed up on the seashore and the immovable rocks that resisted the shock of the waves, compared the former to men who had no mastery over themselves, and the latter to those whom no temptation could seduce. The sight of a lamb led St. Francis of Assisi to speak of the meekness of the Redeemer; to other saints the sight of a flower, a picture, a church, was enough to inspire holy thoughts and practical reflections. This is no wonder, for all visible objects should recall to our mind the omnipotence and bounty of the Creator, and invite us to pay Him homage. Our life ought to be one uninterrupted prayer; for our mind ought to be detached from earthly things, and our conversation in heaven.

2. We ought to pray more especially every morning and evening, before and after meals, and when we hear the Angelus.

1. In the morning we ought to give thanks to God for having preserved us during the night, and beseech Him to protect us during the day from misfortune and from sin, and to give us what is needful for our bodily sustenance.

The morning prayer should be said kneeling, and before we take our breakfast. The birds set us an example in this respect; they warble their morning song before they seek to satisfy their hunger. "We ought to prevent the sun to bless Thee, and adore Thee at the dawning of the light" (Wisd. xvi. 28). A particular blessing rests upon our morning prayer. As the Israelites could only gather the manna before the sun was up, so we cannot expect God's blessing on the day if we do not consecrate its earliest hours to Him by prayer. As a well-spent youth influences a man's whole life, so the manner in which the day is begun influences all its later hours. In the morning God is more easily found: "They that in the morning early watch for Me shall find Me" (Prov. viii. 17). The early Christians used to meet together at daybreak for divine worship. He who on rising neglects to pray, and gives his attention at once to temporal concerns, cannot expect God's blessing on his day's work. If the foundation of a house is unsound, the super-structure will soon fall in.

2. At night we ought to give thanks to God for the benefits we have received during the day, and beseech Him to pardon the sins we have committed in its course, and to protect us during the coming night.

At our night prayers we ought to make an examination of conscience. Every merchant at the close of the day reckons up his gain or loss, although only temporal profits are in question; how much more ought the Christian to make a careful scrutiny of the transactions which affect his spiritual interests. Priests and religious have to recite the breviary at seven different times in the day. David says: "Seven times a day have I given praise to Thee" (Ps. cxviii. 164). The early Christians used to pray at midnight (Acts xvi. 26), and at the hours of the Passion: When Our Lord was condemned (nine o'clock), crucified (noon), when He died (three o'clock), and when He was laid in the grave (sunset). These are the fixed hours for reciting the divine office, but priests are not obliged to adhere to them strictly.

3. Before and after meals we ought to give thanks to God for our nourishment, and implore His grace to avoid such sins as are committed at table.

"When thou shalt have eaten and art full, take heed diligently lest thou forget the Lord" (Deut. vi. 12, 13). Daniel when in the lion's den thanked God for the dinner that He sent to him (Dan. xiv. 37). Those who do not give thanks before and after their meals are like the beasts of the field. King Alfonso of Aragon, observing that his courtiers did not give thanks either before or after their repasts, gave them a practical lesson in this respect. He invited a beggar to his royal table, forbidding him most strictly either to make an obeisance on entering the dining hall, or to express his gratitude to the king when departing. The man obeyed his orders, and went away without a word or sign. The courtiers were highly incensed; but the king checked their wrath, saying: "Is not this exactly how you act towards your heavenly King? You neither ask a blessing nor return thanks; has He not as much reason to be indignant with you as you have with this ignorant mendicant?" The courtiers acknowledged the justice of the rebuke and never after omitted to say grace before and after meals. The sins committed at table usually are sins of intemperance, anger (if all is not to our liking), and detraction. And when the appetite is satisfied, there comes the temptation to sloth and self-indulgence.

4. We ought also to pray when the Angelus rings, calling upon us three times a day, morning, noon, and evening, to say the Angelic Salutation; and if we are near a church, when we

hear the bell for the consecration, or for benediction of the Blessed Sacrament.

3. Furthermore we ought to pray in the hour of affliction, distress, or temptation, when entering upon an important undertaking, and when we feel an inspiration and desire to pray.

We ought to pray in times of distress, for God enjoins this upon us: "Call upon Me in the day of trouble; I will deliver thee and thou shalt glorify Me" (Ps. xlix. 15). How did the apostles act when the storm arose on the lake? Too often in their troubles men seek after human aid. In temptation we ought also to have recourse to prayer. "Watch ye and pray, that ye enter not into temptation" (Matt. xxvi. 41). St. Francis of Sales says that when we are assailed by temptation we should do as little children do if they are frightened by the approach of some animal; they run to their father or mother. On commencing any important undertaking we ought to pray. Tobias exhorts his son: "Desire of God to direct thy ways" (Tob. iv. 20). Our Lord passed the whole night in prayer to God before He chose the twelve apostles (Luke vi. 12); He prayed before the raising of Lazarus (John xi. 41), and before He went to His Passion (Luke xxii. 41). The apostles prayed before they chose Matthias by lot (Acts i. 23). St. Peter prayed before he recalled Tabitha to life (Acts ix. 40). St. Jerome admonishes us to arm ourselves by prayer at our outgoing, and on our incoming to let prayer be our first action. We should also make use of those moments when we feel moved to pray. The mariner hastens to put to sea when he finds the wind is favorable; so we, when we perceive the impulse of the Holy Spirit, must follow His gracious inspirations. Unhappily those moments are too often allowed to slip by, or distraction is sought in worldly amusements. Of this the entertainments held after weddings, and on great festivals of the Church, the feasts the poor make after funerals, etc., afford abundant evidence. How much those who thus act will have one day to answer for! Such solemn times should be times of greater devotion.

5. WHERE OUGHT WE TO PRAY?

1. We can and ought to pray in every place, because God is everywhere present.

Our Lord Himself prayed, not only in the Temple at Jerusalem, and in the synagogues, but also in the desert, on the mountains, in the cenacle, in the Garden of Olives, on the cross. Jacob prayed in the open country, Jonas in the belly of the whale, Job on the dunghill, Daniel in the lion's den, Manasses in prison. Paul and Silas lying bound in a dungeon, prayed and praised God, so that the foundations of the prison were shaken. We can only speak with God when He is present, and He is present everywhere (Acts xvii. 24). Remember Our Lord's words to the woman of Samaria (John iv. 23). God does not regard the place in which we pray, but the dispositions with which we pray.

2. The house of God is the place specially set apart for prayer.

The house of God is the house of prayer (Matt. xxi. 13). Some say there is no need to go to church, because the whole earth is the temple of God. This is false; God enjoins upon us by the mouth of the Church to go to His house on Sundays and festivals. Our Lord Himself set us an example in this respect, for He was often to be found in the Temple at Jerusalem. Petitions offered in a church have greater efficacy, because the place is consecrated, and we can also pray with more devotion, because our surroundings are an aid to recollection, and we can put aside our daily cares. Besides, the prayers we offer in church are heard more quickly because Our Lord is present there under the eucharistic veils; He has promised that: " Where there are two or three gathered together in My name, there am I in the midst of them," and He will help us to pray aright. However it must not be thought that true piety consists in spending long hours in the church.

3. A solitary place is also suitable for prayer.

Our Lord was accustomed to withdraw into solitude for prayer. He prayed in the desert (Luke v. 16), on mountains, in the Garden of Olives (Luke xxii. 39). He bids us retire into our chamber and shut the door (Matt. vi. 6), for in solitude one is less likely to be distracted, and one can pray more fervently.

6. *FOR WHAT OUGHT WE TO PRAY ?*

1. We ought to implore of God many things and great things; benefits not appertaining to time so much as to eternity.

Supposing a king said to you: " Ask what you will;" would you not ask a great favor of him ? Well, it is nothing more than what God says to you. We ought to ask great things of God, because we have to do with One Who is infinitely rich and powerful. Let us not be contented with what we have already received, but ever beg for more. God is more ready to give than we to receive. Let us not ask so much for temporal and transitory benefits, but rather for those that are eternal. No one would presume to ask of an emperor what was useless and worthless; much less should we venture to implore the Lord of heaven and earth for the things of time and sense. It is the act of a fool to treasure up worthless shells and cast away precious pearls; to choose glittering tinsel rather than pure gold. Let us therefore pray for the joys of heaven, and for whatsoever will help us to attain them.

2. We ought more especially to beseech almighty God to grant us such things as are conducive to His glory, and to our salvation, and in no wise to ask for what will only serve to gratify our earthly desires.

To those who pray Our Lord says: " Seek ye first the kingdom of God and His justice, and all these things shall be added to you "

(Matt. v. 33). Hence we may conclude that if we ask for the good
things of eternity, those of time will also be bestowed on us. King
Solomon prayed for wisdom to govern his people aright; God gave
him a wise and understanding heart and in addition earthly riches
and glory in abundance (3 Kings iii.). It is not right to ask of God
what is only calculated to gratify our earthly concupiscences; such
prayers are not granted (Jas. iv. 3). "There are many," says St.
Augustine, "who, in what they ask, do not seek God's glory, but their
own sensual pleasures; they would degrade God to be their servant,
the servant of their covetousness, their pride, their avarice, their
luxury." King Jeroboam's hand was withered, because he stretched
it out against the man of God. He prayed that his hand might be
restored, not that his sin might be forgiven (3 Kings xiii. 6). Many
people do likewise; in their prayers they think only of the needs of
the body, not those of the soul. Let us never pray that our will, but
that God's will be done; let us not wish for the accomplishment of
those desires which arise from our fallen nature, but of those with
which the Holy Spirit inspires our soul.

7. MEDITATION.

1. Meditation, i.e., contemplative prayer, consists in dwelling upon the truths of religion, in order to awaken within our
minds good resolutions.

Costly spices give out their aroma most freely when they are
bruised in a mortar; so the truths of religion have most influence
upon the soul that ponders on them. One who meditates upon holy
things is like a man striking fire with flint and steel; he strikes the
stony heart with the keen edge of the understanding until sparks
fly out, that is, good resolutions are elicited from the will. Meditation is only difficult until the Holy Spirit makes His gracious action
felt. Like a vessel that must be propelled by toilsome rowing until a
favorable wind springs up and inflates her sails, then the oar is no
longer needed, for she runs swiftly before the breeze—so in meditation
the powers of the mind must be exercised laboriously, until the Holy
Ghost breathes upon the soul, guiding it and elevating it. If we
strive to elicit a succession of beautiful thoughts and elaborate meanings, this is not prayer, but study. When once we have struck fire,
let us toil no more, but forthwith kindle the torch.

2. Meditation is a most excellent method of prayer, but it
must not be pursued to the exclusion of vocal prayer.

By mental prayer we imitate on earth the occupation of the
angels who constantly contemplate the face of God, and meditate on
His perfections. The saints have bequeathed to us many books of
meditations; if we read these attentively it is equivalent to prayer.
Mental prayer must alternate with vocal prayer; these two methods
of prayer are the two feet that carry us forward on the way to heaven.
Meditation is a necessary preliminary to prayer; without it **prayer**
will be imperfect, the needful devotion will be lacking.

3. By means of meditation we obtain actual graces, and advance rapidly on the path of perfection.

We obtain many actual graces in meditation; for as we receive light and warmth when we stand by a fire, so by meditation upon the truths of religion the mind is enlightened to see the worthlessness of earthly things, the end of man, the rigor of the divine judgments, and the heart is inflamed with the love of justice. It is a furnace wherein the fire of divine charity is kindled, a door whereby divine grace enters into the heart of man. A soul that practises meditation is like a cultivated field which produces abundant fruit, a well-watered garden in which flowers bloom luxuriantly. He who neglects to ponder upon the truths of religion knows nothing of their force; his spiritual sight is dimmed, he is engrossed with the things of earth. With desolation is all the land made desolate, because there is none that considereth in his heart (Jer. xii. 11). The subjects chosen for meditation ought to be those which have most power to attract and influence us, and to these we should frequently recur. Thus bees alight upon the flowers which contain the sweet juice whence they make their honey. Meditation is a means of attaining perfection. St. Ambrose says daily meditation is the antidote for tepidity. It was the foundation of the conversion of St. Ignatius and other saints. St. Teresa declares that mental prayer and mortal sin are incompatible; they exclude one another; one or the other must of necessity be given up.

THE MOST IMPORTANT PRAYERS.

THE OUR FATHER.

The Our Father is also known as the Lord's Prayer, because it was taught us by Christ Our Lord Himself.

1. The Our Father takes precedence of all other prayers; it is especially distinguished by its power, its simplicity and its comprehensiveness.

There is no more holy and excellent prayer than the Our Father. It has greater cogency than any other prayer, because in it we do not merely pray in the name of Jesus, but in His own words. Of this prayer more than of any other Our Lord's promise holds good: "If you ask the Father anything in My name, He will give it you" (John xvi. 23). It is the simplest of all prayers; its words are few, but it is rich in meaning. It is so simple that a child's lips may utter it devoutly; yet the theologian seeks in vain to sound its depths; it is suited to every class and condition of men. In the Lord's Prayer we ask for all things that are needful for our soul and our body; it comprises all for which we ought to pray; nothing that can be found in the most excellent of prayers is lacking in it. It is an epitome of the holy Gospel. Not only does it teach us the things for which we ought to ask, but the right order in which to ask for them.

The Our Father consists of an address, seven petitions, and the word Amen.

2. The address places the soul in the right disposition for prayer; it awakens within us confidence in God and raises our thoughts to Him.

The word " Father " awakens confidence in God, the words " Who art in heaven" raise our thoughts to Him. Thus at the very commencement of this prayer we make acts of faith, hope, and charity.

We call God Father, because He created us to His image (Gen. i. 27), because the Son of God became our Brother by His Incarnation (Eph. i. 5), and because at baptism the Holy Spirit took up His abode within us, and made us the children of God (Rom. viii. 15).

In approaching the great ones of the earth, we are doubtful by what title we ought to address them; it is not so with God. We address Him as Father, and this familiar title pleases Him better than any other. No mortal would have dared to call the almighty Ruler of the universe by the name of Father, had not His only-begotten Son given us permission to do so. God would not have us address Him as our Creator, Lord, or King, because these titles convey an idea of severity, and inspire fear. He would have us call Him Father, because this is a title which bespeaks affection, and love is a far more exalted feeling than fear.

We call God *Our* Father because we, as brethren, ought to pray for one another.

In the Lord's prayer the individual prays for all, and all for the individual, hence it is the common prayer of all Christians. Our own needs compel us to pray for ourselves; fraternal charity urges us to pray for others. Our Lord Himself says: " All you are brethren " (Matt. xxiii. 8), and calls the apostles His brethren (Matt. xxviii. 10). The apostles spoke of the faithful as their brethren (Rom. i. 13; xii. 1). Those may rightly be called brethren, who have but one Father in heaven.

We say: " Who art in heaven," because although God is present everywhere, heaven is His throne, and there only is He beheld face to face (1 Cor. xiii. 12).

3. In the first petition we pray that God may be glorified.

The meaning of the first petition is this: Grant, O God, that we may acknowledge and revere Thy majesty more and more.

To give glory to God is the end of creation, and consequently it is the highest aim of every creature.

4. In the next three petitions we ask for these blessings: Eternal salvation, grace to fulfil the divine will, and the possession of

those things which are indispensable to the maintenance of our earthly existence.

The meaning of the second petition is this: Give unto us eternal life after death.

The meaning of the third petition is this: Give us grace to fulfil Thy will as perfectly on earth as the angels do in heaven.

The meaning of the fourth petition is this: Bestow upon us all that is necessary for the maintenance of life, such as food, clothes, money, health.

5. In the next three petitions we pray that three evils may be averted from us: The evil of sin, the evil of temptation, and those evils which are prejudicial to life.

The meaning of the fifth petition is this: Forgive us our sins, as we forgive those who have sinned against us.

The meaning of the sixth petition is this: Deliver us from those temptations to which we should succumb.

The meaning of the seventh petition is this: Avert from us all things which are injurious to life, such as famine, pestilence, war, etc.

The evils mentioned in the last three petitions are exactly opposed to the blessings enumerated above.

Eternal happiness is opposed to sin, which makes us eternally wretched.

The grace of God is opposed to temptation; for grace enlightens the understanding and fortifies the will, whereas temptation darkens the understanding and weakens the will.

The things which are necessary for the maintenance of our life are opposed to those which are injurious to it.

The seven petitions may therefore be divided into three divisions, of which the first has reference to God, the two others to ourselves.

6. The word Amen is the answer of God to the suppliant; in this place it is equivalent to the words: Be assured that thy prayer is heard.

In other prayers the meaning of the word Amen is " So be it," or: We entreat most earnestly that our prayer may be granted.

As in the Lord's Prayer the word Amen is to be considered as God's answer, whenever it occurs in the Mass the priest says it, speaking in God's name; but at the conclusion of the other prayers and collects of the Church, the server says Amen. Our Lord often employed the word Amen, principally as an asseveration.

The Our Father has from time immemorial been in use in the Church, both in holy Mass and almost all other public acts of worship.

THE AVE MARIA.

The principal prayers to the Mother of God which are in common use are (1), The *Ave Maria* or the Angelical Salutation; (2), The Angelus; (3), The Rosary; (4), The Litany of Loretto and the *Salve Regina*.

Catholics almost invariably add the *Ave Maria* to the *Pater Noster*.

It has always been customary among Christians to imitate the example of the archangel Gabriel, and salute our blessed Lady in his words. The devotion to Mary was not introduced by the decree of a council, nor at the behest of any Pope; at all times the faithful have been wont to pay their devout homage to the Queen of heaven. She herself foresaw that this would be so; that all generations would call her blessed (Luke i. 48).

The *Ave Maria* is also called the Angelical Salutation, because it commences with the words of the archangel.

1. The Ave Maria consists of three parts: The salutation of the archangel Gabriel, the greeting of Elizabeth, and the words of the Church.

The salutation of the archangel runs thus: "Hail, full of grace, the Lord is with thee; blessed art thou among women" (Luke i. 28). The greeting of Elizabeth is this: "Blessed art thou among women, and blessed is the fruit of thy womb" (v. 42). The remaining words were added by the Church. The first and second parts are an ascription of praise, the third part is a supplication. The first and second parts were recited by the faithful in the earliest ages of Christianity in their present form, while the concluding words were varied. St. Athanasius used to add: "Pray for us, Patron and Lady, Queen and Mother of God." From the time of Luther it was customary to end with the words: "Holy Mary, Mother of God, pray for us." The final clause now in use dates from the reign of Pope St. Pius V., who directed it to be printed in all the authorized prayer-books. After the heretic Nestorius denied the right of the Blessed Virgin to the title of Mother of God, the *Ave Maria* was more frequently on the lips of Christians than it was in earlier times. And when, in the thirteenth century, other sects arose who refused to give the saints the veneration due to them, the devotion to Our Lady assumed a more and more prominent place, and from that time forth the *Ave Maria* became an invariable adjunct to the *Pater Noster* in all the public services of the Church.

2. The Ave Maria is a most potent prayer, and one which is full of meaning.

The *Ave Maria* is especially efficacious in time of temptation; many saints recommend the faithful to recite it, when evil thoughts assail them.

By the words: "Hail Mary" we testify our reverence for the Mother of God.

It is the part of the inferior to salute the superior. Mary is the Mother of the King of kings, she is the Queen of angels and saints, and yet our Mother also. The highest adoration of angels and men is due to her, and therefore we ought reverently to salute her. The words *Ave Maria* indicate that Mary is a second, a happier Eve; she is the Mother of mankind. Ave is a play on the name Eva, the order of the letters being reversed. Thus the words of the archangel seem to signify: "Eve was full of sin, thou art full of grace; the devil was with Eve, God is with thee; Eve was cursed among women, thou art blessed among women; Eve gave birth to the accursed Cain, whereas the fruit of thy womb is the blessed Jesus."

The words: "full of grace" have this signification: "Thou hast received the graces of the Holy Spirit in a higher degree than all the saints together."

As the moon gives more light than all the hosts of stars, so the Mother of God possesses the supernatural light of the Holy Spirit to a greater extent than all the saints. The full plenitude of grace was poured out on her, whereas it was bestowed but partially on all the other saints. So richly was Mary endowed with grace that she approaches more nearly than any other being to the Author of all grace. God might have created a greater heaven, a greater earth, but a greater Mother than Mary He could not create. The name Mary means *sea;* she is indeed an ocean of grace. The angel said to her: "Thou hast found grace with God." Only that which was lost can be found: Mary had not lost grace, therefore she found what man had lost. Let those then who have by their sins lost the grace of God, hasten to Mary, that they may recover it at her hands.

The words: "The Lord is with thee," have this signification: "Thou art united, body and soul with God in the closest union."

In the Temple at Jerusalem, which was outwardly of a dazzling whiteness, and inwardly overlaid with gold, God was continually present in a luminous cloud. The Temple was a type of the Mother of God, for in her the incarnate God dwelt, making her the temple of the Deity. In celebrating Holy Mass the priest turns seven times to the people with the words: *Dominus vobiscum;* thus wishing them the closest union with the Godhead, through the sanctifying grace of the Holy Spirit. Of old such forms of greeting were customary; Saul made use of similar words when dismissing David before his contest with Goliath (1 Kings xvii. 37): David when dying, addressed Solomon in the same manner (1 Par. xxii. 11): and Tobias did the same when his son was starting on his journey (Tob. v. 21).

The words: "Blessed art thou among women, and blessed is the fruit of thy womb, Jesus," have this signification: "Thou art the most blessed among women because thy child Jesus was supremely blessed."

As a tree is considered good if it bears good fruit, so Mary is lauded for the sake of her Son. She is the tree of life in paradise, and Christ is the fruit of that tree. All the angels of God adore the Child that was born of her (Heb. i. 6). Mothers who have had good children have always been called blessed; witness the woman, who after listening to Our Lord's discourse, lifted up her voice to extol His Mother (Luke xi. 27). It is not because Mary was blessed that her Child was blessed, but the contrary. He, the Author and Source of all grace, filled her with benediction. Christ is not said to be blessed among men, as Mary is among women, because He is the Creator of all men, and cannot be placed in comparison with His creatures. When Judith appeared before King Ozias after slaying Holofernes, he declared her to be blessed above all women on the earth (Judith xiii. 23). How much more does Mary merit this praise, since she co-operated in the redemption of the whole human race! Both the archangel and St. Elizabeth addressed the same words to her to indicate that she was to receive homage alike from angels and men.

At the close of the *Ave Maria* we entreat the Mother of God to pray for us in the hour of death, for then above all other times we have most need of assistance.

At the hour of death, in addition to physical suffering, we shall perhaps have to sustain violent assaults of temptation. " How vehemently," exclaims St. Bonaventure, " does the devil attack man in his last hour, and for this reason, because so short a time is left for him to accomplish his work." The uncertanty of our salvation also causes us terrible anxiety at the hour of death. In all these tribulations Mary is our surest helper, for she is " the Health of the sick, the Comforter of the afflicted, the Refuge of sinners." When she appears beside the dying, all evil enemies take to flight. Many a one who was devout to the Mother of God, owed it to her that he was reconciled with God on his death-bed, that he had the last sacraments, or received other supernatural aid. She even appeared in person to several saints. " Mary," says St. Jerome, " assists her faithful servants in death; she goes to meet them on their way to heaven, she prevails upon the Judge of all men to give them a merciful sentence."

We speak of ourselves as sinners, to render the Mother of God more inclined to listen to us.

Mary is most ready to interest herself on behalf of sinners; she knows what it cost her divine Son to redeem mankind and restore to our fallen race the graces we had lost. It would seem as if Mary did not estimate at its true value the sacrifice of Christ, if she had no great love for sinners. There is no sinner fallen so low that the Mother of God would not willingly befriend him were he to invoke her aid with a real intention to amend. God has committed judgment to His Son, grace and mercy to His Mother's hands.

THE ANGELUS.

If the Mohammedan three times a day turns his face towards Mecca, and calls upon God and His prophet Mohammed, how much more ought the Christian frequently to look up to heaven during the day, and invoke the divine Redeemer and His blessed Mother.

The Angelus is a prayer which is to be recited morning, noon, and night, when the bell rings, in honor of the Mother of God and in adoration of the mystery of the Incarnation.

The words are as follows: (1), The angel of the Lord (the archangel Gabriel) announced unto Mary (the birth of the Saviour), and she conceived of the Holy Ghost (through the operation of the Holy Ghost she became the Mother of Christ); (2), Behold the handmaid of the Lord, be it done unto me according to thy word (by these words Mary drew down from above the Son of God); (3), And the Word (the Son of God) was made flesh, and dwelt among us (for thirty-three years He lived on earth).

The custom of ringing the Angelus bell three times a day dates from the period of the crusades (1095).

At first the bell was only rung twice a day, half an hour before sunrise and half an hour after sunset, to call upon the faithful to pray God for the successor of the crusaders' arms. The midday bell was added about three centuries and a half later. At first the prayer said consisted only of a *Pater Noster*, afterwards the *Ave Maria* was added. The manner of ringing three separate times at the interval of about a minute, an *Ave Maria* being said each time, was introduced later by order of the Holy See, the object of the prayer being to entreat the Mother of God to exterminate the heresies that had arisen. The Angelus as it is now said is of more recent date.

. In some places after the evening Angelus the bell sounds again to admonish the faithful to pray for the souls in purgatory.

Pope Clement XII. granted an indulgence of one hundred days to all who, hearing the bell, should recite kneeling one Our Father and Hail Mary, with the versicle: "Eternal rest give to them, O Lord, and let perpetual light shine upon them."

THE ROSARY.

The supplicant who prays fervently is wont to repeat over and over again words which come from the depth of the heart. Our Lord did this on Mount Olivet; David in Psalm cxxxv., exclaims no less than twenty-seven times "His mercy endureth forever," and St. Francis of Assisi spent whole nights repeating: "My God and my all." The devout servants of Mary used to address her frequently in the words of the archangel, adding one *Ave Maria* to another, as one places roses in a wreath.

1. **The Rosary is a prayer in which the Our Father, followed by ten Hail Marys, is repeated five or fifteen times, accompanied by meditation on the life, the Passion, and the exaltation of the Redeemer.**

We begin the Rosary with the Creed and three Hail Marys, for the increase within us of the three theological virtues. While reciting the Rosary every one must hold his own rosary in his hand, and touch the beads as he says the prayers; but if several persons join in saying it, it is only necessary for one to hold the rosary, in order thereby to regulate the number of the prayers. The Rosary is divided into the joyful, the sorrowful and the glorious mysteries; in the first we honor God the Father Who sent us the Saviour; in the second, God the Son Who redeemed us; in the third God the Holy Ghost, Who sanctifies us.

2. The Rosary owes its origin to St. Dominic.

The hermits of the first centuries, who could not read the psalter, used to recite one Our Father and one Hail Mary in the place of every psalm; and in order to note the number they had said, they made use of small stones, or of seeds strung on a cord. St. Dominic was the first who made the custom general of substituting one hundred and fifty Hail Marys for the one hundred and fifty psalms; hence the rosary used to be called the Psalter of Mary. When, about the year 1200, the heresies of the Albigenses wrought great mischief in the south of France and the north of Italy, St. Dominic was commissioned by the Pope to preach in refutation of their erroneous tenets. His efforts availed little, and he besought the aid of the Mother of God. She appeared to him, and bade him make use of the rosary as a weapon against her enemies. He accordingly introduced it everywhere, and before long it had effected the conversion of more than a hundred thousand heretics. The use of the Rosary soon spread throughout Christendom, and it became a most popular devotion. It is a method of prayer at once simple and sublime; the prayers are so easy that a child can repeat them, and the mysteries are so profound that they supply a subject for meditation to the most learned theologians. It is a prayer of contemplation as well as a prayer of supplication, for it places before the mind the principal truths of the faith. The Rosary is a compendium of the Gospels; a complete and practical manual of instruction wherein the chief points of Christian doctrine are presented under the guise of prayer. By meditation on the events of Our Lord's life faith and charity are increased; from the example of our divine Redeemer we learn to be humble, gentle, obedient; we are incited to imitate the virtues which the mysteries teach, to strive after what they promise us. Moreover the union of vocal and mental prayer makes the Rosary easy, pleasant, and profitable. As a method of prayer it is unrivalled; the longer and more devoutly it is practised, the more one appreciates its excellence and becomes convinced of its supernatural origin.

3. The Rosary is well pleasing to God, because of its humility, and because it is an imitation of the unceasing song of praise sung by the angels.

The Rosary is the prayer of the humble, for in it well-known truths.are simply stated and constantly repeated. The proud despise it, but God, Who looks down on the low things (Ps. cxii. 6), approves it. It is an imitation of the angel's song: we read in Holy Scripture that the angelic choirs cry to one another: "Holy, holy, holy, Lord God of hosts; all the earth is full of His glory" (Is. vi. 3). And when we recite the Rosary, we praise the Mother of God in a similar manner. It is beyond a doubt that this form of prayer is most acceptable to the Mother of God, for when she appeared at Lourdes she had a rosary in her hand. Pope Pius IX. unhesitatingly asserts that it is her gift to men, and she loves no other prayer as well.

4. The Rosary is a most useful devotion, for by it we obtain great graces and sure help in time of trouble; many indulgences are besides attached to it.

The Rosary is a very treasury of graces. Many sinners owe their conversion to it. It possesses marvellous power to banish sin and restore the transgressor to a state of grace. By it the just grow in virtue. All the saints who have lived subsequently to the institution of the Rosary have been assiduous in its use, and this may have contributed largely to their sanctification. Several holy bishops and servants of God are known to have pledged themselves by vow to recite it daily; St. Charles Borromeo, despite the numerous and pressing duties of his position, recited it every day with the seminarists and the members of his household. Blessed Clement Hofbauer was accustomed to say the Rosary while passing through the streets of Vienna, and rarely did he recite it in vain for the conversion of a sinner. It is recorded of several distinguished officers and victorious commanders that they never engaged in battle without first saying the Rosary, and to this they attributed their military successes. The Rosary has been called "the thermometer of Christianity," for the reason that where it is diligently recited faith is ardent, and good works are manifest; and where it is neglected religion is at a low ebb. In seasons of general calamity, miraculous aid has been granted to Christendom by means of the Rosary; this was especially the case in wars with the Turks, the victory of Lepanto (1571), the deliverance of Vienna (1683), the victory of Belgrade were all owing to the power of the Rosary. It.was said that the beads of the chaplet did more execution than the bullets of the soldiers. It was in thanksgiving for these victories that the Holy See instituted the feast of the Holy Rosary on the first Sunday in October. Pope Sixtus IV. declared that many dangers which threatened the world are averted, and the wrath of God is appeased by the prayers of the Rosary. Our Holy Father Leo XIII. says that, as in St. Dominic's time the Rosary proved a sure remedy for the evils of the age, so it may now effect much towards the amelioration of the ills that afflict society. Every one who recites the Rosary must feel its supernatural power; there is no prayer which affords more consolation in affliction, more tranquillity to the troubled breast. It soothes in sorrow, it imparts the peace spoken of in the Gospel. Another proof of its excellence is the hatred and contempt wherewith unbelievers regard it. The devil incites them to decry what is a fruitful source of grace to the Christian, and by which souls are wrested from his grasp. The Rosary has been richly indulgenced by the Holy See, and the recital of it strongly urged upon the faithful. An indulgence of a hundred days may be gained for every *Pater* and *Ave*, if five consecutive decades be said, on a properly indulgenced rosary. Our Holy Father Leo XIII. has decreed that every day during the month of October, the Rosary, together with the litany of Loretto, be said in church either during the parish Mass, or in the afternoon, with the Blessed Sacrament exposed. For every time of assisting at this devotion seven years and seven quarantines are granted. Pope Pius IX. bequeathed, as a legacy to the faithful, this admonition: "Let the Rosary, this simple, beautiful method of prayer, enriched with many indulgences, be habitually recited of an evening in every household. These are my last words to you; the memorial I leave behind me." Again he said: "In the whole of the Vatican there is no greater treasure than the Rosary."

THE LITANY OF LORETTO AND THE SALVE REGINA.

The Litany of Loretto is a form of prayer in which the most glorious titles are given to the Mother of God, and her intercession is unceasingly implored.

The litany of Loretto takes its origin and its name from the place of pilgrimage in Italy, Loretto, where the holy house of Nazareth now stands. In this litany first of all God is called upon for mercy, as in the *Kyrie Eleison* of the Mass. This is followed by the invocation of the most Holy Trinity. Then the Blessed Mother of God is invoked, and her intercession is besought. These invocations may be divided into six groups: (1), The first three invocations express her special prerogatives: her sanctity, her divine maternity, her immaculate virginity; (2), Then her perfections as a Mother are enumerated: Mother of Christ; (3), She is next extolled in virtue of her virginity: Virgin most prudent, etc.; (4), Her glories are then depicted under a number of figures and types: Mirror of justice, etc.; (5), Mary is next shown in her relation to the Church Militant: Health of the sick, etc.; (6), And finally in her relation to the Church triumphant: Queen of angels, etc. At the conclusion of the litany, confiding in the mediation of our Advocate, we appeal to her divine Son, beseeching Him to spare, to hear, to have mercy upon us. Several of the invocations have been added by the Holy See in the course of centuries; for instance, "Help of Christians" after the victory over the Turks; "Queen conceived without original sin," after the proclamation of the dogma of the Immaculate Conception; and recently, "Queen of the most holy Rosary," on the introduction of the custom of reciting the Rosary in public during the month of October. An indulgence of three hundred days may be gained for each recital of this litany. The *Salve Regina* or "Hail, holy Queen," as it is also called, was composed in 1009 by Blessed Herman, and in 1146 the illustrious St. Bernard added to it the sweet words: "O clement, O pious, O sweet Virgin Mary."

THE PRINCIPAL DEVOTIONAL EXERCISES.

1. There are ordinary and extraordinary practices of devotion.

The former take place at regular, appointed times; the latter only on special occasions.

2. The regular services held in the parish church on Sundays and holydays both in the forenoon and the afternoon, as well as week-day services, belong to the ordinary practices of devotion.

On Sundays and festivals, in all parish churches, one Mass or several Masses, according to the size of the parish and the number of priests, are said one after another, at one of which a short sermon is generally preached. In the afternoon or evening, either the Rosary and a litany are said (the Litany of the Saints, the Litany of the Holy Name, the Litany of Loretto and the Litany of the Sacred Heart are approved by the Holy See for the public services of the Church, no other being allowed without the permission of the bishop); or Vespers are sung, with Benediction of the Blessed Sacrament. On week-days in almost every parish church a parochial Mass is said daily with afternoon or evening services, consisting generally of the Rosary or some other devotion, and Benediction, on one or more days in the week.

3. Processions, pilgrimages, the Way of the Cross, Exposition of the Blessed Sacrament, and Missions, belong to the extraordinary practices of devotion.

Christian burial services come under the class of processions, and the Way of the Cross is in fact nothing more or less than visiting the scenes of Our Lord's Passion at Jerusalem, without leaving our own country.

PROCESSIONS.

1. Processions are a solemn religious ceremony, during which prayers are recited in common by those who take part in them.

Processions were customary under the Old Dispensation. We read of the Ark of the Covenant being carried round about the city of Jericho (Josue vi.); of the ark being brought in solemn procession to Mount Sion by King David (2 Kings vi.), and thence transferred to the Temple built by Solomon (3 Kings viii.); Our Lord also made a solemn entry into Jerusalem on Palm Sunday (Matt. xxi.).

The ceremonial observed in our Christian processions is intended to portray the truth that we have not here a lasting city, but we seek one to come (Heb. xiii. 14).

The procession issues (*proceeds*, hence the name *procession*) from the church and returns thither, to show that we must enter the

Church on earth if we would reach the Church in heaven. The cross is carried first, because in this life we can never be wholly free from crosses and sufferings, if we follow the maxims of Our Lord. The banners are to remind us that we are warriors, because here below we have constantly to contend against the malignant foe and our own evil proclivities. Those who walk in the procession go two and two, to signify the twofold precept of charity, especially that of charity to our neighbor. The children take the lead, because their greater innocence renders them more pleasing to God; the adults follow, first the men, with the priest in their midst, and finally the women. Processions, if possible, are held in the open air. The prayers recited vary according to the object of the procession; on Rogation days the Litany of the Saints is sung. By rights the men ought to walk bareheaded, but not so the clergy and persons in official dress; this is to show the respect due to authorities both ecclesiastical and civil. In the procession of Corpus Christi all heads are uncovered, by reason of the presence of the Blessed Sacrament.

2. The Church holds processions either for the purpose of setting before us more forcibly certain events in the life of Christ, certain doctrines of the faith, or in order to obtain speedy help from God; on these occasions an opportunity is afforded us of testifying in a public manner our faith and our loyalty to the Church.

The object the Church proposes in setting before us more vividly certain events in Our Lord's life, or certain doctrines of the faith, is to confirm our beliefs. Processions are a means of obtaining more speedy assistance from on high, because God inclines His ear more readily to petitions offered in common; and experience proves that processions are most efficacious modes of supplication. The processions on Candlemas Day and on Palm Sunday are in remembrance of events in Our Lord's life; those on Holy Saturday and on the feast of Corpus Christi are illustrative of doctrines of the faith; the processions of St. Mark and of the Rogation days are for the purpose of entreating the divine help.

3. The following processions form part of the ritual of the Church everywhere:
The procession on the feast of the Purification.

At this lighted tapers are carried round the church, because on that day the aged Simeon declared the Child Jesus to be " a light to the revelation of the Gentiles " (Luke ii. 32).

The wax tapers are emblematic of Christ, the Light of the world. The wax betokens His manhood, the flame His Godhead; as the light shines forth from the taper, so the divinity of Christ shines forth from His sacred humanity by His teaching and His miracles; and as the taper is consumed, while illuminating all around, so the human nature of Our Lord was sacrificed for the sake of enlightening mankind. Christ is in very truth the Light of the world, since by His teaching He dispels the darkness of ignorance and error.

The procession on Palm Sunday.

When blessed palms are carried round the church, in memory of the day of Our Lord's triumphal entry into Jerusalem.

The palm branches borne by the Jews were symbols of victory—the victory that Christ was to gain by His death over the devil, the prince of this world. Our procession is significant of the Christian's triumphal entry into heaven. The priest knocks three times at the door of the church with the processional cross, then it is opened, to show that only through trials and tribulation can we enter the gate of heaven, and be admitted to the realms of bliss.

The procession on Holy Saturday.

When the Blessed Sacrament is solemnly taken from the place where it was deposited, and borne by the priest, attended by the clergy, back to the high altar.

This procession is significant of our future resurrection. The ceremony ought by rights to take place at daybreak on Easter Day, but as few could then be present, it is anticipated on the eve of the feast.

The procession on the feast of Corpus Christi.

When the Blessed Sacrament is carried to one or more altars of repose, to testify publicly our faith in the presence of Our Lord in the Adorable Sacrament of the Altar.

The festival of Corpus Christi (the body of Christ) is on the Thursday following Trinity Sunday, consequently in the second week after Pentecost, because soon after the descent of the Holy Ghost the apostles began to dispense holy communion to the faithful. This festival was instituted some six centuries ago. It was first celebrated in Belgium, by order of the Bishop of Liège, in consequence of a revelation made to a nun, Blessed Juliana (1250), and shortly after Pope Urban IV. decreed that it should be kept throughout the whole Church. In this procession the sacred Host is carried in a monstrance beneath a canopy, flowers are strewn on the way, and censers swung; the altars of repose are beautifully decorated with lights and flowers in honor of the Blessed Sacrament. In some places four altars are erected, and a pause is made at each, and one of the accounts of the institution of the Blessed Sacrament given by the four Evangelists is read. The four altars signify the four quarters of the world. After the reading of the Gospel, a prayer is added for protection against lightning and tempest, and for a good harvest. This solemn ceremony, which is generally terminated by the *Te Deum* in the church, cannot fail to impress every beholder, and lead the non-Catholic to inquire what it is towards which such profound reverence and veneration is displayed.

The procession on St. Mark's Day.

When, in Catholic countries, the priest goes out to bless the fields, and prays God to grant the fruits of the earth in due season.

St. Mark is commemorated on the twenty-fifth of April. The procession on this day owes its origin to Pope St. Gregory the Great about the year 600. At the time when the plague raged in Rome, St. Gregory ordered the procession to be held for the purpose of imploring the mercy of God; and immediately after the pestilence was stayed.

The procession on the three Rogation days.

The object of which is to ask of God the blessing of an abundant harvest.

The Rogation days are the three days preceding the ascension of Our Lord. The processions were first introduced by St. Mamertus, Bishop of Vienne in France, about the year 470, at a season when a failure of crops and the damage occasioned by earthquakes had brought about great scarcity and destitution.

In addition to the processions above named, there are local processions held yearly in honor of the patron saint of the place, or to some shrine in the vicinity. Sometimes processions are ordered by the Pope or the bishop of the diocese, as for instance, on occasion of a jubilee, or in seasons of great calamity.

When the bishop visits a church, the clergy go in procession to meet and receive him; processions are also formed at funerals. Prayer is the soul of processions; he who does not go to join in the supplication had better remain at home.

CHRISTIAN BURIAL.

1. Christian burial is a solemn service accompanied by special ceremonies, in which the remains of a departed Catholic are carried in procession to the place of interment.

As is usual in every procession, the cross is carried first, to denote that our prayers are offered in the name of the crucified Redeemer. The bells are tolled, psalms and funeral hymns are sung.

2. The special ceremonies customary at Christian obsequies are all significant of our prayer that God may have mercy on the soul of the deceased.

The lighted tapers express the desire that the departed may be admitted into the realms of perpetual light; the holy water sprinkled on the coffin expresses the desire that his soul may be cleansed from sin; the incense that is burned expresses the desire that our prayers on his behalf may ascend to the throne of the Most High, even as the clouds of smoke roll upward. A requiem Mass is generally celebrated at funerals, and sometimes an oration is delivered, to invite the mourners to pray for the departed. If the body is not present, a catafalque occupies the place of the coffin. The ceremonies observed at the obsequies of a child under seven years of age are such as express joy and gladness; white vestments are worn by the priest. The wreaths placed on the coffin are supposed to represent the victor's crown gained by the departed. The present custom of loading the coffin and covering the grave with costly floral decorations of every size and shape is greatly to be deprecated; it is a waste of money that had far better be given to the poor, or expended on Masses for the repose of the departed. St. Augustine expressly says that unnecessary display should be avoided at funerals. The soul of the departed can surely reap no benefit from what is reprehensible.

3. Christian obsequies are conducted with so much solemnity, because it is well pleasing to God that we should show reverence to the mortal remains of those who have departed this life in the grace of God.

It is becoming to treat the human body with respect after death, for during our lifetime our bodies are sacred, as being the abode and instrument of the soul which is made to God's image. They are also the temple of the Holy Ghost, and to be held in honor for God's sake. Moreover the burial of the dead is a work of mercy which is not without its reward. Remember how Tobias acted. In the early days of Christianity persons of the highest position, even Popes, did not consider it demeaning themselves to carry the remains of the martyrs in their arms to the graves, and bury them with their own hands. In the days of persecution the place of burial was in the Catacombs, where the holy sacrifice was offered. Hence it came to pass that in later times the dead were buried in the crypts of churches, or in the ground surrounding the church, which is called the churchyard. This custom is now abolished, on sanitary grounds. cemeteries being situated on the outskirts of towns for the most part. An exaggerated idea as to the unhealthiness of intramural sepulture has contributed to the introduction of the unnatural and pagan custom of cremation. No danger to the living may be apprehended from the proximity of a burial-ground, provided the graves are of a proper depth, for earth is known to be the best possible disinfectant.

4. Cremation is condemned by the Church as being an abominable abuse.

Originally the custom of interring the dead in the ground was common to all nations, for the most ancient human remains that have been discovered bear no signs of having been subjected to fire. Vaults containing skeletons have also been met with. closed by a slab of stone. We know that the Jews buried their dead; Holy Scripture constantly speaks of the burial of kings and prophets. That his corpse should be left unburied was a chastisement threatened to the transgressor (Deut. xxviii. 26). Only during a time of pestilence were the Jews allowed to burn individual corpses (Amos vi. 10). The Romans in earlier times buried their dead. Cicero tells us that their graves were considered as sacred, and the profanation of a tomb was severely punished, even by the loss of a hand. Bodies were often deposited in sarcophagi, where they were reduced to dust. Pliny records that the Romans only burned their dead when they feared they might be outraged by the enemy. In later times when manners became corrupt, cremation was practised among them. The custom of embalming the dead prevailed among the Egyptians. It is a noteworthy fact that all barbarous nations, who in an uncivilized state burned their dead, substituted the grave for the funeral pyre as soon as civilization shed its light in their land. Christianity did, in fact, abolish cremation. But in these days, when Christian faith is on the decrease, cremation is once more becoming the fashion. St. Augustine denounces the practice as horrible and barbarous. It offends our Christian instincts. For we are taught to regard death as a sleep; the dead sleep in Christ (1 Cor. xv. 18), for they will rise again; they are laid to rest in peace, and the idea of the repose they enjoy is connected with the churchyard, not with the crematorium. When we commit our dead to the kindly earth, we tacitly express our belief that our body is like a seed, which is cast into the ground, to germinate and spring up. " It is sown in corruption, it is raised in incorruption " (1 Cor. xv. 42). As Christians we have a higher esteem for the soul, which partakes of the divine nature, and consequently for the body, which is the servant and tool of the soul. No true Christian can fail to shrink from the horrors of cremation; only those who are lost to all sense of the dignity of human nature, to all belief in the truths of religion, can desire it for themselves. Let us remember that Christ, our great Exemplar, was laid in the tomb and rose again. For pagans such considerations naturally have no weight; they disliked the sight of the sepulchral monument, the mound raised over the dead, because it reminded them of death, which would put an end to their earthly enjoyments. For the same reason unbelievers in our own day advocate cremation. Burial suggests to them too strongly the immortality of the soul, whereas cremation appears to promise the annihilation that they desire as their portion after death. Yet let no one imagine that the Christian dreads the destruction of the body by fire as an impediment to its future resurrection, for God can effect the reintegration of the body after it has been dissolved into gaseous elements. In the interests of justice destruction of the body by fire is highly reprehensible, since, if a body is buried, it can be afterwards exhumed if this is necessary for the detection of a crime, such as murder. By this means many a murderer has been brought to justice: after cremation this is impossible. Those therefore who speak in favor of cremation befriend criminals, inasmuch as they aid in the removal of all traces of their crime.

5. Christian burial is denied to the unbaptized, to non-Catholics, and to Catholics who are known to have died in mortal sin.

Catholics to whom Christian burial is denied are: Suicides (unless they are insane at the time of death and therefore irresponsible); duellists, and any persons who obstinately refuse to receive the last sacraments, or who have not for years past fulfilled the Easter precept. In the two last cases the matter is generally laid before the bishop. The denial of Christian burial to bad Catholics is not intended as a sentence of damnation, but merely as the public expression of abhorrence of their sin, and for the purpose of deterring others from falling into the same sin. An association would be little thought of if one of its members followed to the grave a fellow-member who had been a disgrace to that society; so it would be derogatory to the Church and her ministers if she were to celebrate the obsequies of an unfaithful Catholic. The Church also refuses ecclesiastical burial to non-Catholics, because she holds to the principle expressed by Pope Innocent III. in the words: "It is impossible for us to hold communion after their death with those who have not been in communion with us during their life. To do so would give rise to the idea that all religions were alike. It would destroy the prestige of the Church, and injure the souls of men. The maxim of the Church is that the ground she has consecrated is the last resting-place of her children, and none but members of her family have a right to be interred therein." Yet she permits non-Catholic relatives to be laid in a family vault. For suicides a portion of the cemetery which has not been consecrated is set apart.

PILGRIMAGES.

1. Pilgrimages are journeys made to sacred places, where God oftentimes vouchsafes to give miraculous assistance to the suppliant.

The Jews were accustomed to make pilgrimages; on the three principal solemnities of the year, the Paschal feast, the feast of Weeks, and the feast of Tabernacles, all the men had to go up to the Temple at Jerusalem. Thus we read that Our Lord, when twelve years old, went on a pilgrimage to Jerusalem (Luke ii. 41).

2. The places of pilgrimage are either the holy places in Palestine, spots sacred to the holy apostles, or shrines of the blessed Mother of God.

The principal places of pilgrimage in the Holy Land are: The scene of the crucifixion and the holy sepulchre on Calvary at Jerusalem; the place where Christ was born in Bethlehem, and the place of the annunciation at Nazareth.

The Church of the Holy Sepulchre is situated on Mount Calvary; it consists of three separate churches, called respectively the Church of the Crucifixion, the Church of the Ascension, and that of the Invention of the True Cross; all are under one roof. The early Christians journeyed thither in great numbers; in order to deter them from doing this, the Emperor Hadrian erected a heathen temple in the holy places, about one hundred years after Our Lord's death. About the year 325 the Empress Helena, mother of Constantine the Great, discovered the cross of Christ; this gave a fresh impetus to the pilgrimages. The Emperor Charlemagne erected a hospice close to the Holy Sepulchre for the accommodation of pilgrims to Jerusalem. In the ninth century the Saracens conquered the Holy Land; the crusades undertaken to recover it from them were nothing less than heroic pilgrimages. In the fifteenth century pilgrimages to the Holy Land again became frequent, but in Luther's time the number of those whose piety prompted them to undertake what was then a long and toilsome journey greatly diminished.

The principal places of pilgrimage in honor of the holy apostles are: The tomb of the princes of the apostles in Rome, and the tomb of St. James at Compostella.

The remains of St. Peter rest in the Church of St. Peter in Rome, the largest church in Christendom, of world-wide renown; it was a hundred and ten years in building, and was finished in 1626. The remains of St. Paul are laid in the church dedicated to him outside the walls of the city.

Some of the principal places of pilgrimage sacred to the Mother of God are: Lourdes in France, Loretto in Italy, Maria-Zell in Hungary, Einsiedeln in Switzerland, Altötting in Bavaria, Kevelaer in the Rhineland.

Lourdes is situated in the south of France on the slope of the Pyrenees. It was there that, in 1858, the Mother of God appeared in a grotto to a little peasant girl named Bernadette, and intimated to her her desire that a church should be built on the spot, and that pilgrims should go thither in procession. Our Lady proclaimed herself to be the Immaculate Conception. From that time forward a spring has flowed out of the grotto, the water of which has been the means of healing thousands of sick persons. No less than one hundred and twenty thousand bottles of this water are annually sent out into all parts of the world; and the number of pilgrims who visit the shrine can only be counted by millions. They come from the remotest quarters of the world. Loretto in Ancona has, since 1295, possessed the holy house of Nazareth, where our blessed Lady lived. This lowly house was seen in the year 1252 by St. Louis in Nazareth; forty years later it suddenly appeared at Tersato in Dalmatia; thence it was miraculously transferred to Ancona, and finally found a permanent resting-place at Loretto. There is no doubt that it was carried to these various spots by the angels. An altar which was miraculously conveyed thither at the same time, is supposed to be that upon which St. Peter offered the holy sacrifice. The statue of Our Lady which stands on that altar, carved in cedar-wood, three feet in height, is said to be the work of St. Luke. A spacious church has been erected over the holy house; copies of the latter have been made, and are seen in several places. At Loretto Pope Pius in his youth was cured of apoplexy. The most eminent saints are known to have made pilgrimages thither; and the number of pilgrims who visit it yearly is computed at five hundred thousand. The place of pilgrimage known as Maria-Zell owes its origin to the Benedictine monks. About the commencement of the thirteenth century attention was attracted to it by the miracles wrought there. King Louis I. of Hungary built a large church at Maria-Zell, in thanksgiving for the victory he gained over the Turks in 1363, with an army immensely inferior in numbers, which he attributed to the intercession of Our Lady. Einsiedeln was originally the humble dwelling of the hermit St. Meinrad, a priest and Benedictine, a scion of the house of Hohenzollern. In 861 he was slain in his forest solitude by robbers; later on a church was built on the site of his hermitage, in which an ancient and venerated image of Our Lady was preserved. While the bishop who came to consecrate the church was watching in the sacred edifice during the night preceding the appointed day, he beheld Our Lord Himself perform the ceremony, attended by saints and angels, amid the chanting of celestial choirs. In consequence of this vision, both he, and his successors in the see, with the Papal sanction, desisted from any attempt to consecrate the church. This circumstance, together with the canonization of Meinrad, whose remains were interred at Einsiedeln, and the numerous miracles which were wrought there, brought the spot into great repute as a pilgrimage. During the French revolution the church was burned down, the miraculous image alone escaping injury. The shrine at Altötting dates from a somewhat earlier period, the church having been built by St. Rupert, the Apostle of Bavaria, in 700. A Benedictine monastery was afterwards erected there. Thousands of pilgrims visits the shrine. That of Kevelaer on the Rhine was built in 1642 by a citizen of Geldern, who while at prayer heard a voice commanding him to raise a sanctuary in honor of Our Lady. The number of pilgrims, principally from the adjacent country, who annually visit Kevelaer is also very great.

3. The object for which, as a rule, Christian people visit places of pilgrimage, is to beseech the divine assistance in season of deep affliction, or to fulfil a vow.

When Dom Bosco was cruelly persecuted on account of his efforts to instruct the neglected youth of Turin, and he was at a loss what course to pursue, he made a pilgrimage, and obtained the aid he sought in an unexpected and marvellous manner. God hears our petitions more quickly in places of pilgrimage; they are the audience chamber of the King of kings; there graces are lavishly bestowed. Many sick persons make a vow to undertake a pilgrimage if they are restored to health; the number of *ex votos* on the walls of these sanctuaries afford evidence of the frequency with which suppliants obtain their cure.

4. A visit to some place of pilgrimage leads many to a complete amendment of life.

The pilgrim on his way to a shrine forgets his worldly cares, and is more diligent in prayer; when he arrives at his destination he makes his confession to a strange priest, and under the influence of the Holy Spirit, makes perhaps a better confession. Pilgrimages are works of penance; they are fatiguing and often expensive. They are also public professions of faith, for no one would undertake them without deep religious convictions. Thus many actual graces are

obtained by the devout pilgrim. In former times they were frequently enjoined as penances; sometimes indeed they were abused,
and made occasions of sinning more freely, hence the saying: "The
more of a pilgrim, the less of a saint." But what is in itself good
must not be rejected because it is sometimes abused; who would
condemn the use of wine, because occasionally a man gets drunk?
St. Jerome says: "It is no great praise to have seen Jerusalem, but
it is very great praise to have offered pious and devout prayers within
its walls."

THE WAY OF THE CROSS.

It is said that the Way of the Cross owes its origin to the
Mother of God.

Tradition says that the Blessed Mother of God was wont often to
walk in the steps of her Son to Calvary, pausing at the spots marked
by some special incident. The early Christians flocked in crowds
to the holy places to follow the *Via Crucis.* But when, in the Middle
Ages, the Holy Land fell into the hands of the infidels, and the devout pilgrim could only visit the scenes of Our Lord's sufferings at
the risk of his life, the stations were erected in churches, and enriched by the Popes with large indulgences. St. Francis of Assisi
contributed greatly to spread this devotion.

**1. The Way of the Cross is the name given to the fourteen
stations which depict the way along which Our Redeemer passed,
bearing His cross, from Pilate's palace to Mount Calvary.**

The fourteen stations consist of fourteen wooden crosses, to which
pictures and inscriptions are generally added. They are erected in
churches, sometimes in the open air, on the slope of a hill; occasionally in cemeteries.

**2. The manner of performing the Way of the Cross is to
go from one station to another, making meanwhile a meditation
on Our Lord's Passion.**

It is not necessary to go from station to station in the church if
one stands up and kneels down as every station is being made. It
is enough to meditate on the Passion in general, without making a
special meditation at each station. An Our Father, Hail Mary, and
an act of contrition are generally recited at every one.

**3. By performing the Way of the Cross large indulgences
may be gained; we also obtain contrition for sin and are incited to the practice of virtue.**

Daily meditation on the Passion of Christ is more profitable than
fasting every Friday in the year on bread and water, or taking the
discipline to blood. A single tear shed in compassion for Our Lord's
sufferings is of greater value in God's sight than a pilgrimage to the
Holy Land. We learn how acceptable meditation on His Passion is

to Our Lord, from the revelations of St. Bridget. Our Lord once
appeared to her, with blood streaming from all His wounds. She
asked what had reduced Him to this pitiable condition? He answered: " It is the doing of those who never consider the great love
I manifested towards them by all I suffered upon the cross." It was
as a continual memorial of His Passion that Our Lord instituted
the holy sacrifice of the Mass. The same indulgences are granted
for making the Way of the Cross as for visiting the corresponding
places in the Holy Land. What the indulgences are we do not know
precisely; let us be content to know that they are great and numerous; they can however only be gained once in the day. The wooden
crosses must be blessed by a Franciscan, or some priest who has the
requisite powers, and the stations must be visited without any break.
The Way of the Cross is a means of obtaining the grace of contrition.
As the Israelites who were bitten by the fiery serpents were healed
by looking upon the brazen serpent, so sinners are healed of the deadly
wound of sin by frequent meditation on the Passion of Christ.
The Way of the Cross is also an incentive to the practice of virtue.
The saints often tell us that meditation on Our Lord's Passion imparts strength to suffer not merely with patience, but with joy. Our
arrogance, our avarice, our anger will be cured by the humility, the
poverty, the patience of the Son of God. If, O man, you would
progress from virtue to virtue, contemplate with all possible devotion
the sufferings of your Lord, for this is most conducive to sanctity.

4. If we are prevented from making the Way of the Cross,
we can gain the indulgence by reciting the Our Father, Hail
Mary, and the *Gloria* twenty times, holding meanwhile a crucifix blessed for the stations in our hand.

The hindrances must be of a sufficient nature, such as long distance from a church, sickness, etc. The cross for performing the
stations at home must be of strong material, with the figure of the
Saviour attached to it, and must have been duly blessed for the purpose. The indulgences are not gained if the crucifix is not the
property of the individual using it; but if several persons perform the
devotion together, it is enough for one to hold in his hand the cross.
For the sick it suffices to take the cross in the hand and make an act
of contrition. The Our Father, Hail Mary and Glory be to the
Father are recited fourteen times for the fourteen stations, five times
in honor of the five wounds of Our Lord and once for the Holy
Father. If the cross has been blessed by a Redemptorist the prayers
need only be repeated fourteen times.

EXPOSITION OF THE MOST HOLY SACRAMENT.

1. The solemn exposition of the Most Holy Sacrament consists in placing the sacred Host in a monstrance, unveiled, at
some height above the altar for the adoration of the faithful.

In the early ages of Christianity the Blessed Sacrament was concealed as much as possible from sight, lest the unbaptized might

conceive contempt for the Christian mysteries. Public exposition was not introduced until after the institution of the feast of Corpus Christi. The number of lighted tapers must not be less than twelve. The mere opening of the tabernacle is not a solemn exposition; every parish priest may do that on his own authority.

2. Exposition of the Blessed Sacrament generally takes place on these occasions: After the parochial Mass, at the afternoon services on Sundays and festivals, on Holy Thursday on the altar of repose, on the feast of Corpus Christi. The bishop of the diocese often orders an exposition to be held for some reason of local or general interest; such as a public calamity, the dangerous sickness of the ruler of the land or of the Holy Father, etc.

MISSIONS AND RETREATS.

1. Missions are a course of sermons and other religious exercises conducted by able priests, for the purpose of giving a fresh impetus to the spiritual life of a community or congregation.

The home missions are quite distinct from foreign missions; they are held for the most part by Religious, the Jesuit, Redemptorist, or Lazarist Fathers, who are specially trained for the work, since the constitutions of their Order specify giving missions as part of the duties of their calling. These missions effect an immense amount of good. Being something out of the common, they make more impression on the parishioners, and the sermons coming close upon one another, exercise a potent and gentle influence on the heart, as a soft spring rain does upon the dry soil. The Holy Ghost speaking through the mouth of His servants imparts to their words an unction calculated to soften the hardest heart. Many persons also make their confession more freely to a priest who is a complete stranger to them. Missions are generally seasons of grace to a parish; how many feuds are ended, disputes settled, bad habits eradicated; how often is restitution made of property wrongfully acquired, how many souls are won for God, sinners converted and just persons incited to progress in virtue!

2. Retreats have much the same effect as missions.

Retreats, or the spiritual exercises, consist of a series of discourses and religious services held in convents or any other place, for a certain class of persons, whether priests, teachers, or men and women living in the world. The retreat ends with the reception of the sacraments. The exercises, which require the retreatant to labor with greater fervor at the work of his salvation, conduce signally to quicken faith and inspire morals. A clock, although it is wound up daily, after a time needs to be cleaned and repaired; it is the same with the soul, it must ever and anon be stimulated to increased exertion by the spiritual exercises. The saints were wont to withdraw into solitude for a time; Our Lord Himself spent forty days in the desert. The Holy See has frequently urged upon the faithful to make diligent use of the spiritual exercises.

CATHOLIC CONGRESSES AND PASSION PLAYS.

Catholic congresses and Passion plays contribute largely in the present day to the revival of faith in Christendom.

1. Catholic congresses are public meetings of Catholics for the purpose of taking counsel together and passing resolutions suited to the times and to the present needs of the Church.

These congresses are either general or provincial, according as the Catholics of a whole kingdom or only of a single State take part in them.

Ever since the year 1848 the Catholics of Germany have held annual congresses in one or other of the chief towns of the land. In other countries their example has been followed; general congresses are now a common occurrence both on the continent of Europe and also in England and the United States of America. Provincial meetings of a local interest are also frequently held in various places.

The object of Catholic congresses is not in any wise to control or take part in the government of the Church, but only to support those whose office it is to govern her.

The bishops alone possess authority to rule the Church of God. Hence those who proposed and arranged these assemblies of Catholics, remembering the saying of St. Ignatius of Antioch: "Let nothing be done without the bishop," took no steps without previously obtaining the sanction and blessing of the Holy Father and of the bishops on their scheme. Nor have these congresses ever interfered with the direction of ecclesiastical matters; they have merely been instrumental in carrying out Christian principles; their members are a militia under episcopal command. Consequently the bishops have always highly approved of congresses and attended them in person.

These public meetings of Catholics are of great utility to the Church; they have been instrumental in founding sodalities adapted to meet the needs of the day, in promoting unity and concord among Catholics, in inspiring them with courage and confirming their convictions, in increasing the prestige of the Church, and gaining for her greater liberty of action.

Every one who has been present at a Catholic congress will have perceived what enthusiasm is evoked by the forcible addresses of the different speakers, how faith is kindled inwardly and manifested outwardly. And from the remarks of the anti-Catholic press, it may be seen how these congresses win respect even from the enemies of the Church by their vigorous protests and energetic action. The work of these congresses has been said to be to pull down the edifice of modern paganism stone by stone, and raise in its place a noble basilica.

2. Passion play is the name given to the portrayal of Our Lord's Passion, and other biblical events in a series of tableaux vivants.

In the Middle Ages, before the invention of printing had placed Holy Scripture within the reach of the people, it was customary to present to their view the chief events of Our Lord's life in theatric representations. For instance, St. Francis of Assisi obtained the Papal permission to construct a stable of brushwood and moss in the midst of a pine-wood. In it he placed a real manger in which was laid an image of the divine Infant, while figures representing Mary and Joseph stood beside it. A real ox and an ass were tied up to a stall outside the stable; inside an altar was erected, at which at midnight the Christmas Mass was solemnly celebrated, St. Francis serving as deacon, to the great edification of the crowds who flocked from all parts round to witness the unwonted spectacle. From that time forth the custom of making a crib in churches began to prevail. In the Middle Ages, pains were taken to make representations of this description as picturesque and true to nature as possible; scenes from the life of Our Lord or other scriptural personages were represented on the stage in tableaux. The subject of these religious dramas or miracle-plays as they were called, was generally adapted to the season of the ecclesiastical year in which they were performed. At first they were enacted in the church, the actors speaking in Latin; later on they were given in the open air, and the vernacular was used. In the fourteenth century these sacred dramas were customary in almost every village in France and Germany, but owing to abuses having arisen, they were strictly prohibited by the Holy See. In 1633 they were however revived at Oberammergau, in Bavaria, in consequence of a vow made by the inhabitants to perform a Passion play every ten years if they were delivered from a pestilence which was ravaging the village. This Passion play, as well as two others in the Tyrol, has acquired a world-wide renown. It is performed with wonderful skill by the peasants, and in a spirit of heartfelt piety and recollection. Experience proves that far from being, as some allege, a profanation of holy things, the representation of the solemn scenes of Our Lord's sacred Passion has the effect of impressing and touching the spectators, inspiring feelings of devotion, and elevating the heart so that the actors are forgotten in the entrancing interest of the scenes enacted. Besides, the gracious answer to the petition of the people of Oberammergau ought to silence the objector, for that cannot be reprehensible of which God manifests His approval in so signal a manner.

RELIGIOUS ASSOCIATIONS.

The Church makes use of religious associations as a further means of promoting the salvation of souls.

In the present day, when the enemies of the Church are so numerically strong, it behooves her loyal children to form, as it were, into ranks, and with united forces to withstand the foe. Only in this wise can victory be ensured. "Few men," says Mirabeau, "acting conjointly, can make a hundred thousand isolated individuals tremble." This language may appear somewhat exaggerated, but there is much truth in it. Union is strength. We cannot raise a weight with a single thread; but a twisted cord is not easily broken.

1. Religious associations are voluntary societies formed among the faithful, with the object of furthering their own salvation or the salvation of their fellow-men.

Religious associations have much the same aim as secular associations; the object of the latter is to promote their own earthly advantage or the public weal; that of the former to promote in the first place their own spiritual interests or those of their fellow-men, and for the most part, as a secondary consideration, the temporal welfare of their neighbor.

2. Religious associations may be divided into confraternities or sodalities, and charitable societies.

Confraternities are, as a rule, exclusively for purposes of devotion; charitable societies are for the relief of the spiritual and temporal needs of others.

Thus the members of confraternities make their own spiritual advancement their primary aim, while charitable societies seek the good of their neighbor. Religious societies have nothing to do with politics; but friendly intercourse and innocent amusements are encouraged as a means of promoting the main object of the association, and preventing the members from taking part in undesirable dissipation.

3. Religious associations are in all spiritual matters subject to episcopal authority; in some countries the legislature exercises a certain control over them.

In all that concerns religion, the Church has exclusive right over confraternities and sodalities. Only the bishop, or the general of an Order has power to erect them; and their rules must be submitted to him for approval, unless they have been already approved by the Holy See. To the bishop it belongs to direct the devotional exercises of the confraternity, to prohibit anything peculiar or extraordinary. It is for him to prescribe the manner in which funds are to be raised, and how they are to be expended when collected. He can attend their meetings or send some one to represent him; he can also appoint the parish priest to be director of the confraternity. It is also necessary to obtain ecclesiastical sanction for the forming of charitable societies.

4. The formation of religious associations has always been highly commended by the Holy See, and large indulgences have been granted to them, because they are of great benefit both to the individual members and to the community in general.

Our Holy Father, Leo XIII., in his encyclicals of 1884 and 1891, expressed high approval of religious associations, especially of the Society of St. Vincent of Paul, and the guilds of artisans and workingmen. Pope Pius IX. says they are an army set in battle array, to combat the adversaries of the faith, not with the clash of arms, but with the silent weapons of prayer. Confraternities may be compared to Noe's ark, because persons living in the world seek in them a refuge from the rising tide of crime and corruption. The members of these confraternities, as a rule, lead a more devout and well-ordered life than the rest of the world. They are not as apt to neglect prayer, because their rule prescribes certain prayers to be recited daily; they approach the sacraments more frequently, because days are marked for them on which a plenary indulgence may be gained; they learn obedience because they submit to the decisions of their director. They spend more time in religious exercises than in running after excitement and worldly amusements, and the observance of the regulations cultivates in them a salutary habit of self-restraint. They tend to keep up a high standard of faith and morals in the parish to which they belong, and by their good example lead others to frequent the sacraments. They assist in the diffusion of good and useful books; they all contribute their mite for ecclesiastical purposes; for the most part, they discharge the obligations of their calling with conscientious regularity, and the parish priest often finds them a great help in the duties of this office. And if some members give scandal, the rules of the confraternity are not to blame, but the neglect of them; and it must be remembered that cockle always grows among the wheat. Charitable societies are also most useful. Through combined action with those who are likeminded with themselves, the members are encouraged to profess their faith openly and carry into practice the maxims of the Gospel, and be ready to take part in all good works. It is remarked that in parishes where there are no confraternities or sodalities, religion is generally at a low ebb.

5. There is this advantage in such associations, that the rules enjoining the performance of certain good works are not binding under pain of sin.

St. Francis of Sales was a member of several confraternities; he gave as a reason for this that one might gain much from them, and lose nothing. However, if the rules are not observed, the indulgences and graces are lost; this is often the case if one joins too many confraternities. Let no one think it is a mark of predestination to be inscribed in the books of a number of societies, for by a holy life alone can we hope for heaven.

6. Third Orders are, however, in every way more important than ordinary religious associations.

The Third Order is not to be classed with confraternities, as it is affiliated to one of the great monastic Orders. "The religious state," says St. Alphonsus, "is preferable to all the dignities and riches of the world."

THE THIRD ORDER OF ST. FRANCIS.

1. The Third Order was founded by St. Francis of Assisi for the sake of seculars, in order that, by the observance of certain rules, they might, while still living in the world, attain speedily and easily to sanctity of life.

After St. Francis of Assisi had already founded the Orders of the Friars Minor and of the Poor Clares, he was requested by a wealthy Italian merchant to furnish him with a rule, by following which he would be enabled to lead a holy life, although his calling obliged him to hold constant intercourse with men of the world. The saint gave him a rule, which was soon adopted by other persons. Thus the Third Order of St. Francis originated about the year 1220. Its members lived in the world and wore a gray habit fastened round the waist by a cord. This Third Order was, with some alterations, confirmed by the Holy See, and spread rapidly throughout Christendom. It is intended for those who live in the world and are not of the world.

2. The Third Order is distinguished from ordinary confraternities by the fact that its members are entitled to wear a habit, and are subject to a religious superior.

Tertiaries, i.e., members of the Third Order, wear a small scapular under their upper garment, as a part of the religious dress, and a cord as a girdle, a token of penance. These things are given to the postulant when he is clothed; no one is admitted before the completion of the fourteenth year of his age; he must also be of good morals and a peaceful disposition. After a year of probation, he is professed; that is he takes a solemn promise to keep the law of God and the rule of the Order with all fidelity. The director of the Third Order is a Franciscan monk, appointed to the office by the general of the Franciscan Order. This post, which gives power to receive new members, to give dispensations, to examine aspirants, to exercise supervision over the professed, may also be filled by a secular priest, appointed by the provincial. In every parish there is a Zelator, whose duty it is to see that the members live conformably to the spirit of the rule.

3. The Third Order is distinguished from the First and Second Orders, because it does not impose the obligation of keeping the evangelical counsels, but only the commandments of the Gospel; moreover the rules of the Order are not binding under pain of sin.

The obligations of the rule are very light. They were considerably mitigated in 1883 by Pope Leo XIII. and adapted to the requirements of the times. The rule enjoins upon the tertiaries:

" To obey God's commandments and the precepts of the Church; to avoid faction and quarrelling, to observe moderation in food, drink and clothing; to avoid luxury, to refrain as far as they can from the dangerous seductions of dances and the theatre." They are also required to fast on the eve of the feast of St. Francis and of the Immaculate Conception, to approach the sacraments every month, to recite twelve *Paters*, *Aves* and *Glorias* daily, to hear Mass, if possible, every day, to attend the monthly meetings, to assist those of their fellow-members who are sick or destitute, and to pray for deceased members. Any one who is unable to perform one or more of these obligations can be dispensed. Special privileges are conceded to priests.

4. The members of the Third Order have greater graces within their reach than the members of almost any other existing confraternity.

They can gain a plenary indulgence, on the ordinary conditions, once a month on any day they may choose, on the day of the monthly meeting, besides some other days, and in the hour of death. Once a month, by reciting six *Pater Nosters*, *Ave Marias* and *Glorias*, they may obtain the indulgences of the holy places in Rome, Jerusalem, Compostella and the Portiuncula. These, and many other rich indulgences attached to various prayers and good works, are all applicable to the souls in Purgatory. Every Mass said for a departed member has the indulgence of a privileged altar. The Third Order enjoys the benefit of the intercession of many eminent saints belonging to the Order, especially that of their holy father, St. Francis; the members are all assisted by the prayers of the numerous saints of the Franciscan Order and of the Poor Clares before the throne of God.

5. The Third Order has counted among its members many distinguished personages and eminent saints.

It would be impossible to enumerate in these pages the crowned heads, the saints and servants of God whose names are familiar to all Christians, who have been enrolled in the Third Order of St. Francis. Our Holy Father Leo XIII. is, and his predecessor in the Chair of Peter was, a tertiary of this Order. "If this Order were once more to flourish among us as it did in days of yore," are the words of our Holy Father, "the lawless greed for temporal things would be weakened, men would obey their lawful rulers, they would learn to conquer their natural propensities to evil, they would outrage no one's rights, and the relations between rich and poor would be satisfactorily arranged." By means of the Third Order of St. Francis the kingdom of God would triumph upon earth, and the kingdom of Satan be overthrown.

THE MORE WIDESPREAD CONFRATERNITIES.

No confraternity can be established in a parish without the permission of the bishop; affiliation to an archconfraternity is also necessary.

1. The object of the Society for the Propagation of the Faith is to aid and support the work of missions to the heathen by means of prayer and alms.

The members of this confraternity are required to recite one Our Father and Hail Mary daily with the invocation: "St. Francis Xavier, pray for us!" and to pay a small weekly or monthly sum. Among the indulgences granted to the members of this confraternity, the principal is a plenary indulgence on any two days in the month which they may choose, and one in the hour of death. This work was founded in 1822 in Lyons, where it still has its centre. The contributions amount to nearly two million dollars annually, half of which sum is collected in France, chiefly from the working classes. In the course of forty years no less than one hundred and fifty episcopal sees have been erected in different parts of the world and millions of heathen have been converted to the faith of Christ. Some say: "There are plenty of poor at home." Let these remember that there is no work so meritorious as one which contributes to the salvation of souls, or one to which such abundant blessings are promised.

2. The object of the Confraternity of the Child Jesus is to provide funds to enable missioners to receive and educate in a Christian manner heathen children who are abandoned by their parents.

The members of this association are required to recite a Hail Mary daily, with the prayer: "O Blessed Virgin Mary, pray for us and for the unhappy heathen children." No one is admitted into this association who is not under twenty-one years of age. Oftentimes a mother will enrol her child in this confraternity, and herself perform the obligations attached to it; thus by helping to rescue an unknown child from eternal destruction, she obtains a special blessing for her own offspring. This association was originally founded in China, where sickly children or those of whom their parents would fain be rid, are ruthlessly exposed and left to perish.

3. The object of the Confraternity of St. Michael is to assist the Supreme Pontiff by the prayers and alms of the faithful.

The members of this association are required to recite one Our Father, one Hail Mary and the Creed daily for the intentions of the Holy Father, and to contribute not less than twenty-five cents yearly to the Peter's Pence. This confraternity is under the protection of the archangel St. Michael. A plenary indulgence is granted to the members in the hour of death.

4. The object of the Confraternity of the Blessed Sacrament is the adoration of the Most Holy Sacrament of the Altar.

In the present day the Confraternity of the Perpetual Adoration is being widely propagated. Each member pledges himself to spend an hour every month in adoration of the Blessed Sacrament. The

members watch in turn, generally on Sundays or holydays. The
chief indulgences are a plenary indulgence once a month, the day
being optional; on the first Thursday in the month; on the feast of
Corpus Christi or in the octave; on the five principal feasts of Our
Lady, besides other festivals, and in the hour of death. It is meet
that Our Lord, present under the eucharistic veils, should be perpetually adored. Just as there is no hour of the day or night in
which in some place on earth the holy sacrifice is not offered, and as
in heaven the hosts of angels and the company of the redeemed unceasingly sing the Tersanctus, so it is right that on earth the ascription of praise should incessantly resound: " O Sacrament most holy,
O Sacrament divine! All praise and all thanksgiving be every moment Thine." In addition to the Confraternity of Perpetual Adoration there are besides in every town, tabernacle or altar societies,
the object of which is to honor the Adorable Sacrament of the Altar
by doing the sacristy work, and providing altar linen, vestments, etc.,
for poor churches. Each member of these societies pledges herself
to spend an hour in church every month in watching before the
Blessed Sacrament.

5. The object of the Confraternity of the Sacred Heart of
Jesus is to venerate and adore the Sacred Heart of Our Lord, and
participate in the abundant graces He promises to those who
practise this devotion.

The members of this confraternity are required to recite an Our
Father, Hail Mary, and the Creed daily, with the prayer: " O sweetest Heart of Jesus, I implore that I may ever love thee more and
more; " they are moreover to approach the sacraments every month,
if possible on the first Sunday or Friday of the month; to keep the
feast of the Sacred Heart (on the Friday or Sunday after the octave
of Corpus Christi) with all solemnity, and to pray for the members
of the association both living and dead. Many rich indulgences are
attached to this confraternity; among others, an indulgence of sixty
days is granted for every good work performed during the day. In
order to belong to this confraternity, it is not necessary that it should
be erected in the place where one lives; any one who is once enrolled can gain all the indulgences by complying with the obligations
imposed on the members. When Our Lord appeared to Blessed Mary
Alacoque,. He made known to her the great and abundant graces
vouchsafed to all who honor His Sacred Heart with particular devotion.

6. The object of the Confraternity of the Holy Rosary is
to promote the devotion of the Rosary.

To form the " living rosary " fifteen individuals unite every month
to apportion among themselves (generally by drawing lots) the fifteen
decades of the Rosary; each one recites the decade which falls to his
share daily throughout the month; thus between them they recite the
whole Rosary every day. This confraternity is under the direction
of the Dominicans. A plenary indulgence may be gained by the
members on the third Sunday of every month, on Trinity Sunday,

oς the principal feasts of Our Lord and of His blessed Mother. The recitation of the Rosary is also indulgenced in a special manner. The Confraternity of the Holy Rosary was established in the lifetime of St. Dominic; the members are required to recite all the fifteen decades of the Rosary every week, but not all on one and the self-same day. This confraternity is affiliated to the Dominican Order; its members share in the good works of the whole Order, and are placed under the special protection of Our Lady. A plenary indulgence is granted on the first Sunday of the month, on all feasts of Our Lady, on the three great festivals of the Church, and in the hour of death.

7. The object of the Confraternity of the Holy Scapular is to implore the protection and intercession of the blessed Mother of God in all the perils of this life, in the hour of death, and in the flames of purgatory.

This confraternity was founded in 1250 by St. Simon Stock, then general of the Carmelite Order. The Mother of God appeared to him and gave him a scapular, with the promise that every one who wore it, and lived piously, should escape eternal death, should experience her protection in seasons of danger, and should be speedily released from purgatory. An aspirant will be admitted into the confraternity by a priest who has the necessary faculties from the provincial of the Carmelites; his name will be entered in the register of the confraternity and the scapular hung round his neck. This scapular consists of two small pieces of brown cloth, fastened together by braid, so that one piece hangs on the breast, the other on the back; this must be worn night and day. Members of the Third Order of Mount Carmel are obliged to recite the little office of Our Lady (which may, if necessary, be commuted to a certain number of *Paters* and *Aves*), to fast on every Friday throughout the year, besides other specified days; to make a daily meditation of at least half an hour, and observe certain other rules. Plenary indulgences may be gained by members of the confraternity on all the festivals of Our Lady, and on days when the principal saints of the Order are commemorated, on the usual conditions, with a visit, if possible, to a church or chapel of the Order. There are four other scapulars: that of the Holy Trinity, of the seven dolors, of the Immaculate Conception, and of the Passion. The five are often worn all together. For each of these certain prayers are prescribed to be repeated daily. Our blessed Lady acts towards her children as Rebecca did to her favorite son Jacob; she arrayed him in the garments of his brother Esau, in order that he might obtain the blessing of his father; so Mary clothes us with the scapular, the livery of her divine Son, to render us acceptable in the sight of our heavenly Father and obtain for us His benediction.

8. The object of the Confraternity of the Bona Mors is to obtain for its members who are yet on earth the privilege of a happy death, and for the departed a speedy release from the cleansing fires.

The members of this confraternity are bound to have a Mass said once every year for the intention of their fellow-members, that the one who is the next to die may have a happy death, and those who are already gone before may experience a mitigation of the pains of purgatory. They are also exhorted to approach the sacraments frequently, to entertain a special devotion to the Immaculate Conception, to St. Joseph, the patron of a good death, and often to make acts of the theological virtues and of contrition. This confraternity is very richly indulgenced. For every visit to a sick person, twenty years; for every meditation of half-an-hour's length, sixty years; for every visit to a church, seven years, etc. All these indulgences are applicable to the souls in purgatory.

9. The object of the Confraternity of the Holy Ghost is to beseech the Holy Ghost to multiply the number of priests, and enlighten them with His divine light.

The members of this confraternity are required to repeat daily seven *Glorias* and one *Ave* for this intention, also to make a novena before Pentecost and receive the sacraments frequently. Among other indulgences they may gain one hundred days for every good work they perform, a plenary indulgence at Pentecost and on the Annunciation (or in the octaves of these feasts) and in the hour of death.

THE APOSTLESHIP OF PRAYER.

This is a league of prayers in union with the Sacred Heart of Jesus.

The Apostleship of Prayer is not a confraternity or sodality, but a pious organization, whose object is to give an apostolic character and power to all our prayers, work, and sufferings. This object it attains by the union of its members with the unceasing pleading of the Sacred Heart in the sacrifice of the Mass: and this union is effected by the morning offering, which constitutes the First Degree of the Apostleship of Prayer and the only essential duty of its members. The morning offering is thus worded: "O Jesus, through the immaculate heart of Mary, I offer Thee the prayers, work, and sufferings of this day in union with the intentions of Thy Divine Heart in the holy Mass."

Two things are necessary for membership:

(1), Registration of one's name by a local director in an affiliated centre; (2), A certificate of admission. Centres are affiliated by diplomas from the director general (a father of the Society of Jesus, residing at Toulouse, France) and transmitted to them by the diocesan directors, whom, with the license and in accordance with the nomination of the Ordinary, he has appointed for that purpose. The second degree consists in the daily recital of one Our Father and ten Hail Marys for the monthly intention approved by the Holy Father; and the third degree in offering a communion of atonement to the Sacred Heart, once a week, or at least once a month on a day or days

fixed by arrangement with a promoter of the Apostleship of Prayer.
The organ of the association is called " *The Messenger of the Sacred
Heart*," published by the authorized editors in various countries under
the direction of the director general. There are thirty-seven distinct
editions of the *Messenger*. The members of the Apostleship of Prayer
in the whole world number some twenty to thirty millions.

CHARITABLE SOCIETIES.

1. The Society of St. Vincent of Paul is very widespread;
its object is to seek out the destitute and afford them spiritual
and temporal relief.

The work of the active members of this society is to visit the
poor in their own dwellings, to assist them with money and the
necessaries of life, and to make use of every means to ameliorate
their moral and spiritual condition. They also collect voluntary
donations and subscriptions from those who are interested in the
work. Conferences of the members are held every week, as a rule,
for consultation respecting the most necessitous cases and the most
necessary works of mercy. For visiting the poor, for every alms distributed to them, as well as for everything that is done in their
service, a large indulgence is granted. This society was started in
Paris in 1830 by eight students, after imploring the help and guidance of St. Vincent of Paul, whose remains rest in the Church of
St. Lazare. It has spread with astonishing rapidity throughout all
the countries of Europe, and it is impossible to estimate the amount
of good effected by its means.

2. Mention may also be made of the Society of St. Boniface,
the object of which is to preserve German Catholics living in
Protestant surroundings from losing their faith, by providing
them with priests of their own nation, and establishing schools
for the education of their children.

3. The Society of St. Raphael, instituted for the purpose of
affording counsel and protection to German subjects emigrating
to America.

It is not intended to encourage and promote emigration; on the
contrary, many persons are deterred from it, and the intending
emigrant is warned of the dangers awaiting him in a strange land.
He is exhorted to go to his religious duties before starting on the
voyage, and on his arrival in the United States he is provided with
suitable shelter, and often employment is found for him.

4. The Catholic Society for Friendless Youths.

This proposes as its object to lead young workingmen to follow
a religious and upright life, to encourage a spirit of industry and
brotherly kindness among them. A priest presides over this society;
the youths are assembled of an evening for innocent entertainment,

reading, and religious instruction. They are assisted in sickness or poverty, and every endeavor is made to render them useful members of society.

5. The Workingman's Guild.

This association, as well as the one spoken of above, was originated in Germany by Adolf Kolping, the so-called "apostle of the working-classes," who began life as a shoemaker's apprentice, and through diligent study and pious perseverance, fitted himself for the office of the priesthood. A great number of friendly societies and charitable works for the improvement of the laboring classes, and for the promotion of kindly feeling between employers and employed, owe their establishment to him.

Various societies suited to the needs of the people.

It would be difficult to enumerate the various associations, suited to the exigencies of the day in different countries, and corresponding to the special needs of the different classes of men and women, which the charity of Catholics has instituted. The Catholic Truth Society has for its object to supply instructive and useful literature at a low price; its work is rapidly extending, and is productive of most satisfactory results. "In the present day," as one of our bishops remarks, "the need is strongly felt for combination and centralization in all great undertakings in the field of politics, commerce and finance. Let us then, who are Catholics, unite to form a healthy body, powerful to promote and maintain the spirit of Christianity in our families. The striving after union, now so strongly marked in every department of social life, surely ought to play a no less prominent part in our religious life."